W9-AIZ-500

DAILY LIFE IN

the Colonial City

DAILY LIFE IN

the

Colonial

City

KEITH KRAWCZYNSKI

The Greenwood Press Daily Life Through History Series:

Daily Life in the United States

 GREENWOOD

AN IMPRINT OF ABC-CLIO, LLC

Santa Barbara, California • Denver, Colorado • Oxford, England

Library of Congress Cataloging-in-Publication Data

Krawczynski, Keith.
  Daily life in the colonial city / Keith Krawczynski.
    p. cm. — (The Greenwood Press daily life through history series : daily life in the United States)
  Includes bibliographical references and index.
    ISBN 978–0–313–33419–1 (cloth : alk. paper) — ISBN 978–0–313–04704–6 (ebook)
  1. United States—Social life and customs. 2. United States—Social conditions.
  I. Title.
  E162.K73   2013
  973—dc23   2012040054

ISBN: 978–0–313–33419–1
EISBN: 978–0–313–04704–6

17 16 15 14 13   1 2 3 4 5

This book is also available on the World Wide Web as an eBook.
Visit www.abc-clio.com for details.

Greenwood
An Imprint of ABC-CLIO, LLC

ABC-CLIO, LLC
130 Cremona Drive, P.O. Box 1911
Santa Barbara, California 93116-1911

This book is printed on acid-free paper ∞

Manufactured in the United States of America

To the family I obtained during the course of writing this book:
Margaret, Charlie, and Kenny.
And to the memory of Spike, a "rescue dog"
who rescued me during a difficult time in my life.

Contents

Series Foreword

The books in the *Daily Life in the United States* series form a subset of Greenwood Press's acclaimed, ongoing *Daily Life Through History* series. They fit its basic framework and follow its format. This series focuses on the United States from the colonial period through the present day, with each book in the series devoted to a particular time period, place, or people. Collectively, the books promise the fullest description and analysis of "American" daily life in print. They do so, and will do so, by tracking closely the contours, character, and content of people's daily lives, always with an eye to the sources of people's interests, identities, and institutions. The books in the series assume the perspective and use the approaches of the new social history by looking at people "from the bottom up" as well as the top-down. Indian peoples and European colonists, blacks and whites, immigrants and the native-born, farmers and shopkeepers, factory owners and factory hands, movers and shakers, and those moved and shaken—all get their due. The books emphasize the habits, rhythms, and dynamics of daily life, from work to family matters, to religious practices, to socializing, to civic engagement, and more. The books show that the seemingly mundane—such as the ways any people hunt, gather, or grow food and then prepare and eat it—as much as the more profound reflections on life reveal how and why people ordered their world and gave meaning to their lives. The books treat the external factors shaping people's lives—war, migration, disease, drought, flood, pest infestations, fires, earthquakes, hurricanes, and tornados, and other natural and man-made disasters that disrupted and even shattered daily lives—but they understand that the everyday concerns and routines of life also powerfully define any people. The books therefore go inside homes, workplaces, schools, churches, meeting halls, stores, and other gathering places to find people on their own terms.

Capturing the daily life of Americans poses unique problems. Americans have been, and are, a people in motion, constantly changing as they move across the land, build new communities, invent new products and processes, and experiment with everything from making new recipes to making new governments. A people always in the process of becoming does not stand still for examination of their most private lives. Then, too, discovering the daily life of the diverse American peoples requires expertise in many disciplines, for few people have left full-bodied written accounts of their prosaic but necessary daily activities and habits, and many people have left no written record at all. Thus, the scholars writing the books in the series necessarily borrow from such fields and resources as archaeology, anthropology, art, folklore, language, music, and material culture. Getting hold of the daily life in the United States demands no less.

Each book at once provides a narrative history and analysis of daily life, set in the context of broad historical patterns. Each book includes illustrations, documents, a chronology, and a bibliography. Thereby, each book invites many uses as a resource, a touchstone for discussion, a reference, and an encouragement to further reading and research. The titles in the series also promise a long shelf life because the authors draw on the latest and best scholarship and because the books are included in Greenwood's Daily Life Online, which allows for enhanced searching, updated content, more illustrative material, teacher lesson plans, and other Web features. In sum, the *Daily Life in the United States* series seeks to bring the American people to life.

Randall M. Miller

Acknowledgments

It is with pleasure that I acknowledge the debts I have accrued in the course of writing this book. My greatest debt and appreciation is to my editor, Randall Miller of St. Joseph's University. His encyclopedic knowledge of American history, his keen editorial skills, and his sagacious advice have not only saved me from an embarrassing number of blunders but have significantly influenced both the content and direction of virtually every page of this book. I must add that Randall's enormous editorial skills and historical knowledge are matched by his kindness and patience. Despite giving him numerous 80+ page chapters (several over 100 pages in length), Randall never once complained, at least not to me. Instead, he patiently and carefully edited these lengthy chapters while offering much-needed encouragement during the all too many years it has taken to write this book. In short, I could not have asked for a more skilled, kindly, and supportive editor.

I must also acknowledge the patience and kind understanding of Mariah Gumpert, former editor of the *Daily Life* series at Greenwood Press. My contract with Greenwood required me to deliver the manuscript in a year. Embarrassingly, it has taken seven times that long to complete it. My only excuse is that my own daily life experiences significantly impinged on the time I could devote to researching and writing what my family and friends came to refer to as "The Book": writing lectures and teaching, grading papers and exams, hunting for a house, hunting for a wife, marriage and its many pleasant demands, the birth of two children and their many needs, the death of loved ones, maintaining a 90-year-old home surrounded by giant oaks that crashed down on my wife's car (twice) and our house (just once), a drum set next to my desk always begging to be played, and five hyperactive Boston Terriers frequently demanding my attention. Despite the long delay in delivering the manuscript, Mariah never threatened to end my contract. Instead, she offered patience and understanding that are all too rare in an industry that lives by deadlines. For that I am very grateful.

I am also fortunate to have had wonderful teachers throughout my academic career. Two of the most influential are Drs. Robert M. Weir and Jessica Kross, both now emeriti professors of history at the University of South Carolina. Not only did they teach me the historian's craft, but they have also served as model scholars and teachers. More specific to this project, Dr. Kross's popular course "Daily Life in Colonial America" was not only the most enjoyable class I every took, but it has also served as both a guide and an inspiration to me in writing this book.

Most importantly, I must thank my wife Margaret. Although she did not perform the duties of many other spouses married to writers—researching, typing, and editing—she did something more important by frequently pulling me away from my computer to show me that there are many more important things in life than writing a book. For that, I will always be grateful. For similar reasons I am also grateful for my two sons, Charlie and Kenny, "Irish twins" whose recent arrival added much-needed joy and encouragement during the last leg of a long and tiresome project. Although they do not realize it, my dogs—Spike, Pig, Loverboy, Curly, and Taz—performed a similar function. While writing this book they were literally at my feet (as Pig is right now) and often laying on my desk (as Curly and Loverboy are right now), providing additional companionship. In their own way, they too insisted that I take myself away from my desk and do something they thought was more important—play with us! In doing so, they prove, at least to me, that dogs are indeed man's best friend.

Librarians have also been my best friends while researching this book. I owe much thanks in particular to Karen Williams of the interlibrary loan division at the Auburn Montgomery library. Over the years she has processed hundreds of requests for books and articles, some of which were quite obscure. Never once did she fail to locate and produce a requested item. Without Karen's assistance, and that of numerous other librarians across the country, I could not have written this book.

I also would have been unable to write this book without the published research by hundreds of scholars. Although the notes at the end of each chapter are an inadequate acknowledgment of their contributions to this project, I hope they accept this form of thanks with the sincerity it is given. Carl Simpson, computer technician at Auburn Montgomery, formatted the many illustrations for the book. Finally, I must thank the Auburn Montgomery Research Council for giving me a one-semester sabbatical that allowed me to work full time on a particularly difficult section of the book.

Chronology

1609   Henry Hudson sails up the Hudson River near Manhattan Island.

1612   Dutch send ships to trade with Indians on Hudson River; huts are built (at present site of 45 Broadway).

1617   Smallpox, introduced by English and Dutch fishermen, kills 90 percent of Massachusetts Bay Indians, opening the region for European settlement.

1624   Dutch West India Company establishes town of New Amsterdam.

1626   Peter Minuet and Dutch settlers arrive at Manhattan Island, where they buy the island from Canarsee Indians for 60 guilders worth of beads and trinkets.

1628   First Reformed Dutch Church established at New Amsterdam.

        First primary school created in New Amsterdam.

1629   Dutch West India Company establishes patroon system to encourage immigration to New Netherland.

1630   Massachusetts Bay Company founds town of Trimontaine on the Shawmut peninsula, quickly renamed Boston.

        Boston authorities impose on all nonprofessionals a 72-hour work week and an earnings limit of two shillings per day.

1631   First launching of an American-built ship (30-ton sloop *Blessing of the Bay*) in Boston.

1632   Governor Peter Minuit of New Netherland sets up America's first public beer brewery in New Amsterdam.

1633   The first secondary school in North America, the Boston Latin School, is established.

1634   First public tavern in British North America opened by Samuel Cole in Boston.

1635   Boston establishes Latin Grammar School.

            Boston passes mandatory church attendance law in response to rising absenteeism in church.

            Massachusetts General Court in Boston banishes Roger Williams from the colony for heresy and sedition.

1636   The first college in the New World, Harvard College, is chartered in Cambridge, Massachusetts.

            Roger Williams founds Providence, Rhode Island.

1638   Ancient and Honorable Artillery Company, one of the first military units in colonies, is chartered in Boston.

            Dutch West India Company introduces headright system in New Netherland to attract immigrants.

            First printing press in North America established in Cambridge, Massachusetts.

1639   Massachusetts General Court enacts law against drinking toasts.

            First printing press in America is established in Cambridge, Massachusetts, near Boston.

            First document printed in North America, *The Oath of a Freeman*, is published.

            First almanac in America is published by Harvard.

            Newport founded as a farm colony.

1640   The first book is printed in North America, *Bay Psalm Book*, at Cambridge, Massachusetts.

1641   First patent in colonies, for a salt-making process, is given to Samuel Winslow of Massachusetts.

1642   Massachusetts passes the Old Deluder Act, the first law in North America mandating compulsory primary education.

First college commencement held at Harvard.

Dutch in New Netherland slaughter lower Hudson Valley Indians (Lenape).

1643 First restaurant (or "cook shop") in North America opened by Goody Armitage in Boston.

1644 Shipbuilding guild formed in Massachusetts.

Roger Williams writes pamphlet *The Bloudy Tenent of Persecution*, which defends religious freedom and argues for a "wall of separation" between church and state.

1646 William Kieft ousted as governor of New Netherland.

Dutch patroonships fail in New Netherland.

First antismoking legislation in North America passed by Massachusetts Bay, prohibiting smoking in towns as a fire hazard.

1647 General Court in Boston bans Catholic priests from colony; penalty is banishment, or death for a second offense.

1648 Cambridge Platform adopted in Massachusetts, establishing Congregational religious polity.

Massachusetts General Court charters Boston's shoemakers, the first officially recognized labor organization in North America.

1651 General Court in Boston passes law forbidding poor to adopt excessive dress.

General Court in Boston levies fine for anyone observing Christmas.

1652 Massachusetts establishes a mint in Boston to coin money and contracts blacksmith John Hull to operate it.

1654 Joseph Jencks of Boston commissioned to build first fire engine in America.

First Jews (Sephardic), banished from Brazil, arrive in New Amsterdam.

Boston jurist Edward Johnson publishes *History of New England*.

1655 Dutch West India Company rules that Jews must be allowed to stay in New Netherland.

1656 First Quakers to enter Massachusetts (Boston), Mary Fisher and Ann Austin, are met with strip searches, jail, and banishment.

1658   *Ratelwacht* (rattlewatch) in New Amsterdam is formed, the first police force in North America.

1659   Quakers William Robinson and Marmaduke Stevenson hanged in Boston for resisting banishment.

1660s   John Winthrop II of Boston discovers fifth satellite circling Jupiter.

1660   Quaker Mary Dyer executed in Boston for resisting banishment.

1661   First Quaker annual meeting in North America held in Rhode Island.

         Bakers in New Amsterdam go on strike against price limits on bread.

1662   Halfway Covenant, a form of partial church membership, formed in Massachusetts.

         Reverend Michael Wigglesworth publishes 224-stanza poem *Day of Doom*.

1663   Colony of Carolina established by eight English lords proprietors.

1664   Governor Peter Stuyvesant meekly surrenders New Netherland to England; the colony is renamed New York and the capital renamed New York City.

         Horse racing becomes first organized sport in America, as Governor Nicolls establishes Newmarket course at Hempstead Plains, Long Island.

1665   Statute in Rhode Island offers freemanship with no specifically Christian requirements, thus effectively enfranchising Jews.

         Butchers in New York City go on strike against price limits placed on meat.

         New legal code in New York guarantees religious freedom to all Protestants.

1666   Boston suffers first major smallpox epidemic, killing over 180 residents.

1668   Thomas Gold, William Turner, and John Farnum are the first Baptists exiled from Massachusetts.

         Yellow fever kills many in New York City and prompts a "General Day of Humiliation."

1670   Joseph West founds Charles Town at Albemarle Point.

         The Baptist Rhode Island Yearly Meeting is formed, becoming the first Baptist association in America.

Woodcut of Richard Mather of Boston is first portrait engraving in colonies.

1672 General Court in Boston passes first copyright law in colonies, which establishes exclusive publishing rights for seven years.

Regular mounted mail service between Boston and New York City begins.

1675 Puritans in Boston begin locking church doors to keep congregation inside until end of sermon.

King Philip's War begins in New England between local Native Americans and English colonists and their Indian allies. The three-year war, which costs the lives of more than 600 colonists and 3,000 Indians, opens up much of the region's land to white settlement free of military resistance by the Native Americans.

1676 First coffee house is licensed in Boston to John Sparry.

Increase Mather publishes *A Brief History of the Warr with the Indians*, about King Philip's War.

Fire destroys over 50 homes in Boston.

1678 Smallpox epidemic in Boston kills more than 800 residents.

1679 Boston forms America's first fire company.

Bakers in Boston go on strike against price limits on bread.

1680 Charles Town moved to its present site at junction of the Ashley and Cooper Rivers.

Thomas Brattle of Boston accurately tracks comet with telescope.

1681 English Quaker William Penn founds Pennsylvania, with Philadelphia as its capital.

1682 Mary Rowlandson publishes *A True History of the Captivity and Restoration of Mrs. Mary Rowlandson*, the first American bestseller that details her 11 weeks as a captive to Native Americans during King Philip's War.

1683 Increase Mather leads in forming the Boston Philosophical Society, North America's first scientific society.

1684 New York City cartmen strike against wage restrictions imposed by city officials.

First African slaves arrive in Philadelphia.

Massachusetts Bay charter is revoked; Massachusetts becomes a royal colony.

1686   Sir Edmund Andros arrives in Boston to form Dominion of New England, a royal plan to unite colonies.

1687   King James's Declaration of Indulgences is published in Boston, freeing religious dissenters from penalties for religious nonconformity.

1688   Four Quaker men in Germantown, Pennsylvania, draft the first protest against slavery in the New World in response to neighbors who decided to practice slavery.

1689   Armed uprising in Boston deposes much-hated Governor Edmund Andros.

Boston minister Cotton Mather publishes his *Memorable Providences, Relating to Witch-crafts*.

The William Penn Charter School, free to the needy, is founded, the first school in the colonies to teach such practical subjects as science and invention.

Parliament's Act of Toleration allows religious freedom for Protestant dissenters only.

Smallpox epidemic in Boston kills at least 320 residents.

1690   Benjamin Harris of Boston publishes first newspaper in North America, the *Publick Occurences*, which local officials suppress after one issue for criticizing the government.

Massachusetts legislature in Boston issues first paper money in colonies, originally to pay its soldiers fighting the French.

1691   Jacob Leisler is hung and dismembered for leading a rebellion in New York overthrowing autocratic rule of Governor Francis Nicholson.

Bakers in New York City go on strike against price limits placed on bread.

1692   Witch trials held in Salem, Massachusetts. Nineteen suspected witches are hung, another crushed to death, and five accused die in overcrowded prison awaiting trial.

Increase Mather receives America's first divinity degree, from Harvard.

1693   New York City gets its first printing press.

1696   South Carolina passes oath test prohibiting Catholics from voting or holding office.

Bakers in New York City go on strike against price limits placed on bread.

1697   First paid fireman in America appointed in New York City.

Trinity Church (Anglican) is founded in New York City.

Smallpox epidemic in Charles Town kills more than 300 residents.

1698   Outbreaks of yellow fever and smallpox in Charles Town kill more than 300 residents and halt business in the city.

One-third of Charles Town is destroyed by fire following an earthquake that rumbled through the town.

1699   Yellow fever epidemic in Charles Town kills more than 300 residents.

1699   Yellow fever epidemic in Philadelphia kills one-third of residents.

Brattle Street Church in Boston is first Puritan church to allow communion without public confession of faith.

Captain William Kidd is captured and arrested in Boston on charges of piracy and is extradited to England, where he is hanged on May 23, 1701.

1700   Massachusetts assembly in Boston orders all Catholic priests to leave colony.

First commercial distillery to make rum opened in Boston.

Pennsylvania assembly passes law banning "stage-plays, masks, revels," and "rude and riotous sports."

Judge Samuel Sewall of Boston writes *The Selling of Joseph*, an appeal for the abolition of slavery.

Hurricane strikes Charles Town, causing much property damage.

1701   Pennsylvania creates Charter of Liberties, the colony's first constitution, calling for a unicameral legislature with assembly given consent role only in setting of laws.

Philadelphia authorities ban smoking in the streets as a fire-prevention measure.

1702   Yellow fever epidemic in New York City kills 570 residents.

Outbreaks of yellow fever and scarlet fever in Boston kill over 300 residents.

Cotton Mather forms the Society for Suppression of Disorders to monitor swearing and blasphemy.

Cotton Mather publishes *Magnalia Christi Americana*.

1704   John Campbell founds weekly newspaper, the *Boston News-Letter*.

1705   Massachusetts statute bans marriage between whites and blacks.

1706   Anglicanism becomes established religion in South Carolina.

Cotton Mather publishes *The Good Old Way,* a polemic that rues the "decay of Christianity."

Fire destroys much of Boston.

The earliest known gallstone operation is performed by Dr. Zabdiel Boylston at Boston.

Yellow fever epidemic in Charles Town kills nearly 70 people.

Spanish and French forces unsuccessfully attack Charles Town.

1707   Mechanics in Philadelphia form guild to protest unfair competition from slaves.

1708   *Boston News-Letter* carries first illustration printed in a colonial newspaper.

1709   Quakers in Philadelphia establish first center in the colonies for the treatment of mental illness.

Quakers establish first meetinghouse in Boston.

1711   Fire sweeps through Boston, leaving at least 110 families homeless.

1712   First slave revolt in northern colonies erupts in New York City, leading to the death of at least 9 whites and 18 slaves.

First fines for speeding given to cart drivers in Philadelphia.

1713   Anglican King's Chapel in Boston becomes first church in North America to use organ in religious services.

Outbreak of measles in Boston kills over 150 people.

Hurricane hits Charles Town, destroying much property and drowning about 70 people.

1714   Cotton Mather gives sermon favoring Copernicus's heliocentric model of the universe.

Governor Robert Hunter of New York writes and prints first play in the colonies, *Androborus,* which was never produced.

1716   First lighthouse in colonies built in Boston to guard harbor.

1717   Cotton Mather begins a school for blacks and Indians.

1718   North America's first private fire company established in Boston.

The pirate Major Stede Bonnet, who raided in the Caribbean, the Carolinas, and the coast of New England, is captured and hanged in Charles Town.

England begins sending convicts to labor in the colonies for 7 to 14 years. By 1775 the colonies receive about 50,000 convicts.

1719 Colonists in South Carolina overthrow British proprietors; the province falls under royal control.

Eliakim Hutchinson of Boston presents first streetlight in America, a single lantern.

1721 Dr. Zabdiel Boylston of Boston becomes first physician in North American to use inoculation against smallpox. Still, smallpox epidemic kills about 900 residents. Many survivors flee the city.

John Copson of Philadelphia establishes the first marine insurance company in colonies.

1722 Judah Monis, the first Jew to earn a college degree in America (Harvard), is baptized as Christian and begins teaching Hebrew at Harvard.

1723 The earliest known public concert in British North America is performed in Boston.

1724 Founding of the Carpenter's Company of Philadelphia, a group of builders.

1725 William Bradford founds *New York Gazette*, first paper in New York City.

1727 Christ Church (Anglican) in Philadelphia, a handsome example of Georgian architecture, is completed.

Benjamin Franklin forms the Junto, a philosophy club dedicated to the "sincere enquiry after truth."

Cadwallader Colden of New York City publishes *History of the Five Indian Nations*.

1728 John Bartram of Philadelphia opens first botanical garden in North America.

Officials in Boston ban horses and carriages on town commons, turning the park into a fashionable setting for late-afternoon promenades.

Benjamin Franklin begins printing the *Pennsylvania Gazette*.

Hurricane hits Charles Town, sinking 23 ships in harbor, destroying 2,000 barrels of rice, and drowning several people.

Yellow fever sweeps through Charles Town, killing many people and bringing life to a standstill as many survivors flee into the countryside.

1729   Mob of poor folk in Philadelphia breaks into mayor's garden and destroys plants to protest deteriorating economic conditions.

1730   Smallpox epidemic in Boston kills over 500 residents.

Smallpox epidemic reaches Philadelphia, killing over 100 people.

George Berkeley, an Irish-born philosopher and Anglican bishop recently arrived in Newport, founds Literary and Philosophical Society.

Romeo and Juliet performed in New York City, the first known performance of Shakespeare on the American stage.

1731   Philadelphia Library Company, America's first subscription library, is founded.

1732   Mass celebrated for the first time at St. Joseph's in Philadelphia, the only public Catholic church in colonies.

Philadelphia Zeitung, the first foreign-language newspaper in the British colonies, is published by Benjamin Franklin in Philadelphia.

Quakers in Philadelphia found first known publicly funded alms-house in colonies.

First planetarium in colonies is established when Harvard College imports from England an orrery, a mechanical model that shows the position and movement of stars and planets.

Benjamin Franklin begins publishing *Poor Richard's Almanack* in Philadelphia.

1733   New York City and Philadelphia struck by first major influenza epidemic in colonies.

Charles Town gets its first printing press.

1734   Peter Zenger, publisher of the *New York Weekly Journal*, arrested for seditious libel against Governor William Cosby.

Botanist James Logan of Philadelphia publishes his investigation on the propagation of Indian corn.

Founding of the Library of the Carpenters' Company of Philadelphia, a repository of works on building design.

1735   Charles Town holds the first known opera performance in colonies with *Hob in the Well*.

Gustavus Hesselius of Philadelphia paints pictures of Native American leaders Tishcohan and Lapowinsa.

Scarlet fever sweeps through Boston, killing over 100 people.

Physicians in Boston form the first medical society in colonies.

1736   The Friendly Society of Charles Town is North America's first fire insurance company; it goes bankrupt in 1740 when a major fire destroys much of the city.

Karl Pachelbel gives harpsichord recital at Tod's Tavern in New York City, becoming the first notable European musician to perform in the colonies.

1737   Jews in New York City are denied the right to vote in assembly elections.

The Charitable Irish Society of Boston holds first municipal (as opposed to purely religious) celebration of St. Patrick's Day.

The first greenhouse in the colonies built by Andrew Faneuil at Boston.

1738   Yellow fever epidemic in Charles Town kills 795 residents.

1739   Stono slave rebellion in South Carolina leads to the death of 21 whites and 44 slaves. In response, colonial assembly passes harsh slave code.

Anglican itinerant minister George Whitefield begins tour of colonies spreading the Great Awakening.

1740   Fire destroys nearly half of Charles Town.

John Winthrop IV of Boston publishes report on the transit of Mercury over the sun.

Charity School (University of Pennsylvania) is chartered in Philadelphia.

1741   Alleged slave plot to take control of New York City results in 11 slaves burned at the stake, 18 hung; four white accomplices are also executed by hanging.

Revivalist minister Jonathan Edwards publishes popular sermon "Sinner in the Hands of an Angry God."

American Magazine, founded in Philadelphia by Andrew Bradford, discontinued after two-month run as first magazine in the colonies.

Benjamin Franklin invents his "circulating stove."

Yellow fever outbreak in Philadelphia kills over 200 residents.

1742   Faneuil Hall, designed by the artist John Smibert and built by French Huguenots, is opened in Boston.

1743   Charles Chauncy gives sermon "Seasonable Thoughts on the State of Religion in New England," stressing rationalism over the passions of revivalism.

217 New York City residents die from yellow fever epidemic.

Benjamin Franklin and other Philadelphians found the American Philosophical Society, the colonies' first organization for promoting scientific knowledge.

1747   German Reformed Church organized in Philadelphia.

Jonathan Mayhew of Boston is one of the first New England clergymen to dispute the doctrine of the Trinity and preach Arminianism, a belief in free will and salvation by works.

New York Bar Association is first legal society in colonies, founded to protect against hostility directed towards Lieutenant Governor Cadwallader Colden.

Redwood Library is founded in Newport.

1748   First Lutheran synod in America is formed in Philadelphia.

Charles Town Library Society formed.

1749   City leaders in Philadelphia found University of Pennsylvania.

The first waxworks museum in North America is opened by James Wyatt in New York City.

Benjamin Franklin invents the lightning rod.

1750   The first American acting company, founded by Thomas Keane, gives *Richard III* at New York City as its premier performance.

A group called the Young Junto starts meeting in Philadelphia to discuss scientific questions and other issues.

1751   Smallpox epidemic in Boston kills 569 residents.

John Bartram publishes his *Observations* detailing his travels through the colonies.

Philadelphia establishes a system of public streetlights using whale oil.

Founding of the Society for Encouraging Industry and Employing the Poor, a Boston group that sets up a linen factory to employ poor Boston women and children in spinning.

1752   Hurricane hits Charles Town, killing more than 100 residents and destroying much of city.

Benjamin Franklin publishes *Experiments and Observations on Electricity*, which, among other things, proposes use of lightning rods to protect buildings.

The first general hospital (other than a "pesthouse") is opened in Philadelphia.

1754   King's College (now Columbia University) is chartered in New York City.

New York Society Library founded in New York City.

1758   Quaker annual meeting in Philadelphia bars slave traders.

New York City shipyard owners combine to fix wages for laborers at eight shillings per day.

1759   Michael Hillegas of Philadelphia opens first music store in America.

Presbyterian Ministers Fund, the first recorded life insurance firm in the American colonies, is established in Philadelphia.

1760   Smallpox epidemic in Charles Town kills 730 residents.

The colonial era's most destructive fire destroys 176 warehouses in Boston and 1 out of every 10 homes.

1761   Mrs. E. Smith's *The Colonial Housewife*, containing more than 200 recipes and 300 home remedies for ailments, is published.

John Winthrop IV of Harvard leads expedition to Newfoundland to observe transit of Venus across sun.

1762   The St. Cecilia Society is formed in Charles Town, North America's first music society.

Boston lawyer James Otis publishes *A Vindication of the Conduct of the House of Representatives*, which elaborates colonial rights.

1763   Chimney sweeps in Charles Town form first organization of black workers, refusing to work until city raises the price charged for their labor.

Sephardic Jews in Newport open the Touro Synagogue, the first major center of Jewish culture in America.

Smallpox epidemic in Boston kills over 170 residents.

1764   Merchants in Boston organize boycott of luxury imports from England to protest Parliament's Sugar Act.

Outbreak of smallpox in Boston kills 170 residents.

1765   College of Philadelphia offers first professional medical training in America.

Mob sacks house of Governor Thomas Hutchinson following sermon entitled "Ye Have Been Called unto Liberty," delivered by Jonathan Mayhew.

Stamp Act Congress in New York City convenes in protest to Parliament's Stamp Act.

More than 200 merchants in New York City vow not to buy British goods until Parliament repeals Stamp Act and Sugar Act.

More than 400 merchants in Philadelphia join nonimportation movement.

John Singleton Copley paints "Boy with a Squirrel."

1766   The Gloucester Fox Hunting Club, the first hunting club in America, is founded in Philadelphia.

General Thomas Gage closes New York assembly for refusing to comply with the controversial Quartering Act.

Southwark Theater in Philadelphia opens; the first edifice in the colonies built expressly for the staging of drama.

1767   In Philadelphia, Thomas Godfrey's *Prince of Parthia* is the first professionally performed American play.

Thespian David Douglass builds theater in New York City modeled on his Southwark theater in Philadelphia.

Fire in Boston destroys more than 50 homes and many shops and warehouses.

Parliament imposes the Townshend Duties on the American colonies, a tax on imported British goods used to pay the salaries of royal governors and judges so that they would be independent of colonial rule and thus in a better position to enforce imperial measures.

1768   Chamber of Commerce holds founding meeting in New York City.

Merchants in New York City agree to stop importing British goods until Parliament repeals Townshend Duties.

Wesleyan Chapel, the first Methodist church in colonies, is dedicated in New York City.

John Dickinson of Philadelphia publishes first patriotic song, "In Freedom We're Born."

1769   Benjamin Franklin reorganizes American Philosophical Society in Philadelphia and charts Gulf Stream.

Dysentery outbreak in Boston kills 180 people.

1770   King's College in New York City award's North America's first two doctorates of medicine.

The Boston Massacre, a clash between British soldiers and a hostile crowd, leaves four civilian men and a 17-year-old boy dead. Propaganda of the event heightens tension between Americans and the mother country.

Quakers in Philadelphia establish school for African Americans.

1771   Philadelphia tailors combine to limit wages for workers at four shillings per day.

The first volume of the *Transactions of the American Philosophical Society* is published in Philadelphia. It includes observations of the 1769 transit of Venus.

David Rittenhouse of Philadelphia builds first orrery in North America.

1772   Measles epidemic in Charles Town kills over 900 residents, mostly children.

Mercy Otis Warren's first play, poking fun at the British, is published in the *Massachusetts Spy* (Boston).

1773   Parliament passes Tea Act, which leads to Boston Tea Party.

Smallpox epidemic in Philadelphia kills over 300 residents.

First museum in North America is founded in Charles Town.

1774   Continental Congress passes antitheater act to "discourage every species of extravagance and dissipation, especially horse-racing, and all kinds of gaming."

Parliament passes Coercive Acts, known in America as the Intolerable Acts, as punishment for Boston's Tea Party. This galvanizes Americans throughout the colonies against British imperial measures.

First Jewish elected official in North America, Francis Salvador, elected to South Carolina Provincial Congress in Charles Town (seated in 1775).

1775   Benjamin Franklin and Dr. Benjamin Rush form the Society for the Relief of Free Negroes Unlawfully Held in Bondage, first colonial group formed to combat slavery.

1776   Second Continental Congress meeting in Philadelphia writes the Declaration of Independence.

Introduction

American history is filled with irony. One of the more intriguing ironies in our nation's past—as well as its present—is the American people's love-hate relationship with cities. From the first arrival of Europeans to the North American wilderness, settlers sought to establish towns and cities. And almost from the beginning, urban residents, and some rural ones for that matter, complained about the unhealthy and corrupting elements of city life. One of the earliest and strongest critics of urban life was Thomas Jefferson, who believed that "our governments will remain virtuous for centuries as long as they are chiefly agricultural," but feared that "when they get piled upon one another in large cities, as in Europe, they will become corrupt as in Europe."[1] Although many people since then have echoed Jefferson's concerns about urban life and his praise of rural life, Americans have, for a variety of reasons, increasingly gravitated to cities.

Indeed, the most radical transformation of American life over the past 300 years has been the growth of cities and the accompanying dominance of urban values, models, and styles on the nation. With all due respect to Frederick Jackson Turner and his "frontier thesis," the city, not the frontier, has had the greatest influence on the direction of American civilization. This influence can be traced back to the colonial period when British North America's five major urban centers—Philadelphia, New York, Boston, Charles Town (Charleston), and Newport—dominated their regions' social, cultural, economic, and political scenes and set the tone for the subsequent urbanization of the United States and the development of a national culture. These five cities managed to accomplish this despite containing only about 5 percent of the population in British North America on the eve of the American Revolution.

Several reasons explain their dominance. The major ports, with their distributing, producing, and marketing centers, were the centers of intercolonial and international commerce and communication. As such, they imposed an economic imperialism on their own hinterlands that encouraged the development of new villages and towns. At the same time, the numerous opportunities and amenities offered by these cities attracted some of the most intelligent, educated, and ambitious people from within America and from abroad. This helped enable the cities to become the intellectual and cultural centers of America. Politically, these urban areas were all provincial capitals and centers of colonial authority. Their influence was felt, one way or another, deep into the American hinterland.

Not only did these five cities have an influence that far outweighed their size, they also had unique needs, opportunities, and problems that distinguished them from the countryside: a tremendous demand for a wide variety of skilled and unskilled workers, all of whom labored under conditions particular to major urban centers; a greater racial, religious, and ethnic diversity that fostered both a rich culture and considerable social tension; an especially strained family life due to frequent economic dislocations, early entry of children into the labor market, and the separation of home and workplace; a greater variety of foods and specialty goods available to local residents, at least for those who could afford them; and more opportunities for both entertainment and education for all classes of people. These opportunities in the cities were balanced by the greater occurrence of fires, hurricanes, diseases, disorder, and crime. Finally, urban residents in the eighteenth century had to endure decreasing economic and political opportunities along with mounting filth in the streets and inadequate housing.

Despite the influence and distinctiveness of these five colonial port cities, scholars have largely ignored urbanization in early America. The first histories of colonial American urban life were uncritical and sterile "city biographies" written in the late nineteenth and early twentieth centuries by antiquarians and genealogists who provided interesting anecdotal information about the urban experience but who failed to place it in a larger historical, geographic, and analytical context. Beginning in the 1920s, urban sociologists, determined to better understand the urban condition, called for a rigorous, empirical, and analytical approach to the study of city life. Even Frederick Jackson Turner confessed in 1925 the need for an "urban reinterpretation" of American history. Fifteen years later Arthur Schlesinger published a seminal article arguing that American history could not be adequately understood without taking into account the enormous influence of the city and therefore urged scholars to examine urban life as a topic important in its own right.[2]

One of the first historians to answer these clarion calls for urban studies was Carl Bridenbaugh, whose path-breaking two-volume history of the five major colonial cities published in 1938 and 1955 provides a richly detailed examination of institutional life in early American urban centers.[3] Despite their significant contribution, these books are a product of their time and therefore lack analysis of such issues as race, gender, and class that were not in vogue at the time he wrote them. His work is also blatantly elitist. Bridenbaugh bends over backwards to paint the most favorable image of urban grandees while adopting a patronizing attitude toward blacks, Indians, and the poor, when he discusses them at all. His silence on the considerable suffering of the urban poor, in particular, is deafening to the ears of modern scholars. Also conspicuously absent is a discussion of the tentative encroachments by the urban underclass on the elite's political, social, and cultural hegemony. Instead, in Bridenbaugh's cities, the middle and lower classes "accepted with cheerful awareness their assigned stations in life."[4]

Despite its many shortcomings, Bridenbaugh's pioneering study remains the most exhaustive treatment of early American urban life. The 1960s and 1970s were promising decades for early American urban history as numerous scholars published books examining scores of "little communities" in colonial America. Unfortunately these many studies, which focused on the small interior villages—the boondocks of early America—did little to advance our understanding of life in the major colonial urban centers. By the mid-1980s a few scholars of early American urban history began urging their colleagues to move away from the study of "small places," which they believed had bred "intellectual sterility and mental atrophy" in the field, and towards study of the influential and dynamic urban centers like Boston, New York, and Philadelphia.[5] Since then a few historians have responded by writing cutting-edge works analyzing previously unmined data, thereby illuminating various aspects of colonial urban life from gender, class, ethnicity, and race to religious pluralism, cultural development, economic mobility, and even marriage relations, among other topics.[6] Despite the seminal nature of such works, their topics are narrow and fail to detail the richness and complexity of life in the colonial American urban centers.

My goal in this book is not necessarily to make Bridenbaugh's books obsolete (which is impossible) but instead to fill this gap in the historiography of urban America by using recent scholarship to describe the routine life of city folk during the colonial period, from childhood, marriage, family life, death, recreation, and race relations to clothing, diet, health, poverty, crime, work, and worship. In the process, I hope to provide a larger understanding of early American urban society and answer some inherent questions about it: How did early Americans cope with the many problems of rapid urbanization? How did people of different faiths, cultures, and races interact and assimilate with one another? How did urban life impact the individual, family, and community? How did the urban experience affect such great events as the American Revolution? And, finally, how did urban life and values help shape the American character and culture? At the least, a study of daily life in the major colonial urban centers can help to provide a greater understanding of the genesis and process of American urbanization, its impact on city dwellers, and their various and evolving responses to it. At the most, an insightful analysis of the early American urban experience can help us to better understand modern American society. Like all good historical writing, this book strives to have a contemporary value.

NOTES

1. "Rural and Urban America," *The Annals of America: A Conspectus*, vol. 2 (Chicago: Encyclopedia Britannica), 289.

2. Arthur M. Schlesinger, *Paths to the Present* (New York: Macmillan, 1949), 210–33.

3. *Cities in the Wilderness: The First Century of Urban Life in America, 1625–1742* (New York: Ronald Press, 1938); *Cities in Revolt: Urban Life in America, 1743–1776* (New York: Ronald Press, 1955). An insightful analysis of Bridenbaugh's classic study of the colonial cities is Benjamin Carp's "*Cities* in Review," *Common-Place* 3 (July 2003).

4. Bridenbaugh in Carp, "*Cities* in Review."

5. Michael Frisch, "American Urban History as an Example of Recent Historiography," *History and Theory* 18 (October 1979): 353–54; Michael H. Ebner, "Urban History: Retrospect and Prospect," *Journal of American History* 68 (June 1981): 69–83; Richard R. Beeman, "The New Social History and the Search for 'Community' in Colonial America," *American Quarterly* 29 (Autumn 1977): 423–28; Darrett B. Rutman, "Assessing the Little Communities of Early America," *William and Mary Quarterly* 43 (April 1986): 165–70, 177 (quote); Kathleen Neils Conzen, "Community Studies, Urban History, and American Local History," in *The Past before Us: Contemporary Historical Writing in the United States*, ed. Michael Kammen (Ithaca, NY: Cornell University Press, 1980), 270–81.

6. A sampling of the more important recent works on early American urban life includes Gary Nash, *The Urban Crucible: The Northern Seaports and the Origins of the American Revolution* (Cambridge, MA: Harvard University Press, 1979); Billy G. Smith, *The "Lower Sort": Philadelphia's Laboring People, 1750–1800* (Ithaca, NY: Cornell University Press, 1990); Richard L. Bushman, *The Refinement of America: Persons, Houses, Cities* (New York: Vintage Press, 1992); Richard W. Pointer, *Protestant Pluralism and the New York Experience: A Study of Eighteenth-Century Religious Diversity* (Bloomington: Indiana University Press, 1988); Thelma Wills Foote, *Black and White Manhattan: The History of Racial Formation in Colonial New York City* (New York: Oxford University Press, 2004); Karin Wulf, *Not All Wives: Women of Colonial Philadelphia* (Ithaca, NY: Cornell University Press, 2000); Joyce D. Goodfriend, *Before the Melting Pot: Society and Culture in Colonial New York City, 1664–1730* (Princeton, NJ: Princeton University Press, 1992); Douglas Greenberg, *Crime and Law Enforcement in the Colony of New York, 1691–1776* (Ithaca, NY: Cornell University Press, 1974); Sally Schwartz, *"A Mixed Multitude": The Struggle for Toleration in Colonial Pennsylvania* (New York: New York University Press, 1988); Emma Hart, *Building Charleston: Town and Society in the Eighteenth-Century British Atlantic World* (Charlottesville: University Press of Virginia, 2010); Benjamin Newcomb, *Political Partisanship in the American Middle Colonies, 1700–1776* (Baton Rouge: Louisiana State University Press, 1995).

1

Settlement

INTRODUCTION

The sociologist Leo Schnore has compared cities to a social organism. Cities are founded, or born, if you will. Like an organism, they evolve. Of course, this growth is never steady but experiences periods of rapid development along with periods of stagnation. Like the process of "cellular turnover" in organisms, the individuals who make up cities are replaceable and interchangeable. Cities, like all organisms, need nutrients, which in this case are supplied by the flow of commodities, information, and individual persons. Like an organism, cities compete with one another for these "nutrients." In doing so, they are greatly affected by their own unique circumstances and surroundings. As cities confronted the unique challenges of their environment, they developed a distinctive "urban personality," marked most notably by a collective responsibility. Finally, like an organism, each city evolves at its own pace and develops its own unique character and history.[1]

Although perhaps overdrawn and overly simplistic, these characterizations of cities nevertheless remind us that cities are living entities that are continually evolving and that have a political, economic, and cultural influence far beyond their borders. This is certainly true for the five great port cities of English colonial America: Boston,

Philadelphia, New York, Charles Town, and Newport. The development of these cities was greatly affected by the objectives of their financial backers in the mother country as well as the origins, makeup, motives, educational backgrounds, and religious convictions of their early settlers. Distinctive climates, economies, immigration patterns, social demographics, and settler-Indian relations also contributed to the uniqueness of each city. Cultural geographer Colin Woodard has recently identified five discrete Euro-American cultures established on the eastern rim of North America by the mid-eighteenth century. The principal cities, excepting Newport, played a key role in creating and shaping four of these cultural hearths: New Amsterdam ("New Netherlands"), Boston ("Yankeedom"), Charles Town ("Deep South"), and Philadelphia ("The Midlands"). Many of the distinctive characteristics of these four "nations," as Woodard calls them, have carried on to today and go far toward explaining "who we North Americans are, where we've come from, and where we might be going."[2]

Still, these five cities had common traits. To a certain degree, all five cities were either economic, social, or political experiments. Much of this experimentation in society-building was self-conscious; some of it was not. A couple of these experiments were successful; most were not. Nevertheless, the five colonial cities demonstrate that America, from the beginning, has been an experiment of one kind or another. Many Americans today share this concept of our nation but, like our forefathers, cannot agree on what type of society to build. One thing not in dispute is that the five colonial cities were centers of civilization, at least by English standards. It is no coincidence that political power, capitalist enterprise, intellectual pursuit, and cultural refinement—things that the English associated with civilization—were concentrated in the major urban areas. Similarly, colonial cities were the political, economic, administrative, and cultural capitals of their respective provinces. As such, they had the same kinds of public buildings: town hall, jail, almshouse, warehouses, schools, hospital, customs house, exchange, and markets. Each city also served as a center of trade and commerce in its region, a trade that extended westward or northward into the backcountry and eastward or southward throughout the Atlantic world. In critical ways, they also developed their hinterlands, stretching the urban influence inland. This commerce, in turn, supported a growing number of laborers, artisans, and professionals. Residents of these cities, finally, were forced to confront challenges unique to large urban centers: sanitation and health problems, crime and disorder, fire protection, and poverty relief.

NEW AMSTERDAM/NEW YORK CITY

Present-day New York City, originally named New Amsterdam, was founded in 1625 by the Dutch West India Company as a trading post in its burgeoning colonial commercial empire. This global corporation established New Amsterdam as a company town and settled it for purely economic reasons by investors who wanted a handsome return on their money. As such, New Amsterdam was an experiment, or at the very least a model, in purely capitalist or corporate colony building. Like many Europeans in the sixteenth century, the Dutch had imperial ambitions that included exploiting New World resources. Because of their small population, the Dutch focused on building a commercial empire that did not involve establishing large overseas colonies. Instead, they sought to monopolize the increasingly lucrative trade between the Old and New Worlds. For a time, the Dutch succeeded in this goal. By 1600 they had developed the most formidable fleet of warships in Europe and owned three-fourths of Europe's merchant ships, both of which allowed them to undercut their European rivals and conquer much of the world's markets. Still, the Dutch needed a rich American possession to serve as both a commercial center in the New World and a staging ground for attacks on Spanish American ports and shipping. They found this possession in 1609 when Henry Hudson, an Englishman employed by the Dutch East India Company to find the elusive Northwest Passage to the fabled riches of the Orient, returned to Holland with a shipload of furs following a journey up a broad river that now bears his name to present-day Albany. Excited by the commercial possibilities of furs, the newly created Dutch West India Company in 1614 established a fort and trading post (Fort Nassau) near present-day Albany. Recognizing that their European rivals might try to capture this lucrative commercial outpost, the company decided to establish a settlement to protect the mouth of the Hudson and its fur trade. To that end, the company in 1625 sent three ships to set up a settlement on a tip of an island they called New Amsterdam (Manhattan Island). With the finest harbor on the Atlantic seaboard, New Amsterdam would also serve as the colony's largest town, major seaport, and government headquarters.

Most early settlers of New Amsterdam were young, poor, restless, uneducated, single men who were salaried servants of the company. Their length of service was usually for six years, after which the company would reward them with their own land, tools, livestock, and grain. Until then, the company required its employees to work in either the fur trade or as farmers to feed the colony. On the other hand, emigrants who came as freemen were allowed to farm on their own, but they still had to buy and sell through the company storehouse. This arrangement benefitted the company, which made considerable profits by monopolizing the local commodity trade, but it proved pernicious to settlers, who seldom came out ahead in buying and selling at the company store. Exploiting settlers was standard operating procedure; after all, New Amsterdam was a profit-motivated, company-owned and -operated town that was governed to financially benefit wealthy company shareholders back in Holland. To help ensure that the colony was profitable to its shareholders, the company governed New Amsterdam not unlike a modern corporation; that is, its government, if one can even call it that, was highly authoritarian and tended to view both human beings and natural resources as mere commodities to advance the company's bottom line. To that end, the West India Company appointed the governor/director and a small advisory council who made law without the interfering nuisance of an elected body. With the will of the people out of the way, the company passed laws ensuring that it monopolized all trade with the mother country and the most profitable commodities—furs and alcohol. To maintain discipline among the employees and colonists, company officials favored extreme forms of punishment: branding, pillorying, whipping, garroting, beating with rods, slicing off ears, boring tongues with a red-hot poker, and "riding the horse," the latter of which involved shackling an evildoer to a wooden horse with heavy weights attached to his arms and legs to further intensify the pain in his groin.

This exploitive and dictatorial capitalist/corporate approach toward colony building enticed few Dutch, who enjoyed economic prosperity, a high standard of living, and political rights at home, to settle in New Amsterdam. By 1643 the town had grown to barely 500 inhabitants, most of whom were a rough lot of "down-and-out adventurers, fugitive husbands, runaway servants, and waterfront riffraff" who frequently fought each other in the streets and taverns and who had to be kept at work "by force." Even the relatively few women in New Amsterdam, according to one observer, were bawdy, lewd, and "exceedingly addicted to whoring." Illustrative is one wife who, while her husband was sleeping in a nearby chair, "dishonorably manipulated the male member of an Irishman" while two other men looked on. Even bolder was Griet Reyniers, who enjoyed sauntering along the waterfront raising her petticoats to sailors and strolling into the fort and crying out to the soldiers: "I have long enough been the whore of the nobility. From now on I shall be the whore of the rabble!" True to her word, she serviced the lustful sailors and soldiers while gaining a notorious reputation in town for measuring the penises of her customers on a broomstick.[3]

To promote settlement, the company in 1629 introduced the patroonship system, whereby any company investor who brought 50 families or more to New Amsterdam at his own expense would be entitled to a county-sized parcel of land to rule over like a feudal lord. The would-be manor lords, or "patroons," would serve as judge and jury over all civil and criminal proceedings, including capital crimes, thereby giving them the power of life and death over their tenants. This medieval arrangement failed to bring in large numbers of settlers, but it did contribute to the concentration of political and economic power into fewer hands while limiting opportunities for individual settlers. More successful in enticing emigrants to New Amsterdam, particularly family groups, was the headright system. Borrowed from the English practice in Virginia and introduced by the company in 1638, the headright scheme granted a freehold of 200 acres to each colonist who brought over a family of five. Thereafter, emigrants began trickling in from Germany, Belgium, France, Scandinavia, Ireland, Portugal, Poland, Brazil, and even from New England, which all contributed to an "arrogance of Babel," according to one resident, that "has done much harm to all men."[4]

Further encouraging settlement was the company's policy of religious toleration, which attracted persecuted people of all Christian denominations (and a few Jews) throughout Europe and South America to the Dutch colony. When the colony's autocratic and religiously bigoted director Peter Stuyvesant outlawed the practice of all faiths excepting the Dutch Reformed, company officials in Amsterdam ordered him to "allow every one to have his own belief, as long as he behaves quietly and legally, gives no offense to his neighbors, and does not oppose the government." Religious toleration, as it turned out, was good for business. So was slavery. The Dutch West India Company therefore used its extensive merchant fleet to import hundreds of African slaves into New

Amsterdam. It sold some slaves into private hands but kept many to labor in company enterprises. By 1670, African slaves comprised an estimated 20 percent of the city's population. As a result of this heterogeneous immigration (and forced migration) pattern, New Amsterdam became the most ethnically, racially, and religiously diverse settlement in North America. By the mid-1660s, only about 40 percent of New Amsterdam's 1,500 inhabitants were actually Dutch. Important to the survival and growth of the town, nearly three-quarters of Amsterdam's population belonged to family groups of modest means who wanted to make a life in the colony. Many were farmers, but a significant number were also skilled artisans. Only about one in eight worked as either laborers or servants. These characteristics of New Amsterdam—diversity, tolerance, and an all-consuming emphasis on private enterprise—have come to be strongly identified with present-day New York City and, to a large degree, the United States.[5]

With company officials in Amsterdam fixated on profits, they devoted little effort toward laying out New Amsterdam, which developed with no overall plan. The town was closely settled in variously shaped blocks reminiscent of the meandering medieval patterns of the Old World except for a single broad avenue that led to the fort from the main town gate. New streets were laid out in an irregular fashion, usually following lanes already established by men and animals in their efforts to find the most convenient paths between houses, farms, and the walled fort. As the population grew and land near the fort became more valuable, residents increasingly encroached onto the streets by building houses, pig pens, and even privies on the public roads.[6] Making matters worse, privies overflowed onto roads that were clogged with numerous hogs and other animals. Meanwhile, Fort Amsterdam, manned by a measly 10 soldiers, was in a "ruinous condition," as were many of the windmills and other public buildings. One-fourth of the town's buildings were grog shops where residents spent much of their time in heavy drinking that contributed to "daily mischief and perversity." Even Sundays were filled with rowdy behavior as soldiers performed noisy plays near the church while other residents played ninepins, bowled, danced, sang, and engaged in other "profane exercises." For the most part, company officials looked the other way at the squalor and disorder in New Amsterdam, focusing instead on the profits from liquor sales, which ran second only to those from the fur trade.[7]

After nearly 40 years of settlement, New Amsterdam remained a small, disorderly commercial town with barely 1,500 inhabitants. Further retarding New Amsterdam's growth was the autocratic nature of its company-controlled government, which proved highly unpopular for its practice of imposing arbitrary taxes on residents and inciting wars with those Native Americans who were seen as an obstacle to capitalist expansion. After a particularly brutal massacre of 80 Indians on Staten Island in 1643, some survivors "came to our people in the country," wrote one Dutch settler, "with their hand or legs cut off and some holding their entrails in their arms."[8]

Company director Stuyvesant imposed many positive reforms that helped to bring order to New Amsterdam during the mid-1600s, but it was not enough to either satisfy most residents or save the corporate-controlled colony from a hostile takeover. When three English warships entered the harbor into New Amsterdam in August 1664, few residents were willing to defend the city. To many, English rule was better than rule by the exploitive, dictatorial, and negligent Dutch West India Company. Stuyvesant, with only 1,150 troops and with a citizenry disinclined to fight, had little choice but to surrender New Amsterdam to the English. If the Dutch West India Company colony of New Amsterdam teaches anything, it is that creating a society based upon capitalist and corporate principles of exploitation, greed, autocracy, and individualism is a recipe for failure.

The Duke of York, who received the former Dutch colony from his brother King Charles II, did not learn this lesson. Instead, he continued the policy of Dutch authoritarianism as an experiment in royal absolutism. The Duke of York, who would later serve briefly as king of England (James II) from 1685 to 1688, organized New York, at least in part, to show his brother how to improve English government and society through arbitrary rule. To that end, he imposed on his colony a code known as the Duke's Laws that preserved the power of government in the hands of those whom the Duke appointed to administer the affairs of his province. The code did not provide for either town meetings or a legislative assembly, which made New York the only English colony without a representative body. Royal absolutism did not sit well with residents, some of whom protested by refusing to pay their taxes. With increasing unrest and prospects of colonial bankruptcy, the Duke of York finally yielded in 1683 and allowed the calling of an elected assembly. The first assembly promptly issued a Charter of Liberties, which was essentially a constitution for the colony that

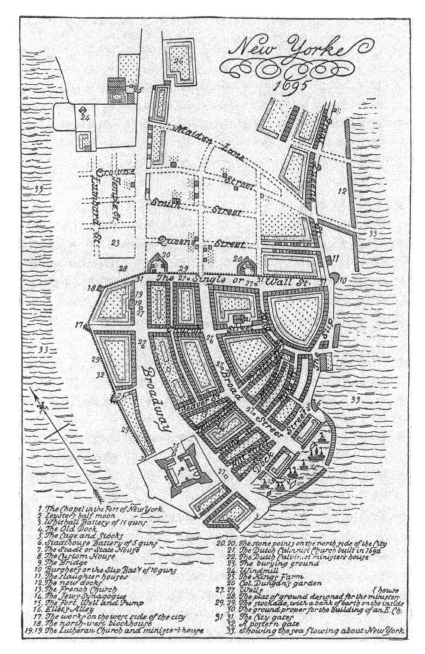

Map of New York in 1695. The map and its legend provide interesting details of early New York City, particularly the location of such things as the fort, slaughtering house, places of worship, water wells, gates, batteries, cemetery, stockade, prison, and other public buildings. (Woodrow Wilson, *History of the American People, vol. 1* [New York: Harper & Bros., 1902])

guaranteed free elections and freedom of worship, among other principles of English law. Representative government in New York lasted only two years before James II, the former duke of York, revoked the Charter of Liberties as part of his larger plan as the king of England to bring all English territory under his personal dominion. People both in England and America rose up in arms against this attempt at royal absolutism in 1688 and overthrew James II and his political minions. Thereafter, New York was established as a royal colony with all the political rights and principles of the English.

BOSTON

The founding of Boston in 1630 centered on the mission of its early settlers to create a new Zion in the American wilderness that would serve as a model for the rest of the Christian world. As it turned out, no other Christian people would imitate their version of religious utopianism, which was so repressive and cruel, even for its time, that the Puritan experiment in social control quickly broke down and the English Crown eventually felt compelled to take over the colony. Part of the problem was the self-righteous and intolerant attitude of the English Puritans, strict Calvinists who believed that they knew best the true intentions of the Christian fathers and who believed that they were God's only chosen people, bound to him in an Old Testament–style covenant to do his work. This work included purifying the Church of England of all its Catholic remnants—vestments, rituals, hierarchy, holy days, the display of religious symbols, and the playing of musical instruments—thereby recovering the original and simple church of Jesus Christ. The Puritans also tried to take England back to a simpler time by purifying English society of its individualism, materialism, defiling of the Sabbath, and behavior that they believed God deemed immoral. These efforts at religious and social reform angered many English people, who increasingly viewed the Puritans as self-righteous kill-joys, and especially angered religious and secular authorities, who equated Puritan goals with both heresy and treason. When the Puritans foolishly challenged the monarch's claim to rule by divine right, their days in England were numbered. In March 1629, King Charles I, glad to rid his realm of the pesky Puritans and eager to establish stronger claims to North America, granted a land patent to Puritan leaders allowing them to take up land in New England. This charter, originally held by the Massachusetts Bay Company, was sold to a group of Puritan settlers, who took it with them to Massachusetts. In doing so, it allowed the colony to operate almost autonomously until it lost the charter in 1692. That autonomy gave leaders considerable latitude in creating laws that deviated from English tradition.

In 1630, 17 ships filled mostly with English Puritans arrived in Massachusetts Bay. John Winthrop, governor of the nascent colony, selected the site of present-day Boston (named for a town of the same name in East Anglia where many Puritan settlers originated) on the southern portion of the Shawmut peninsula as the location for the province's principal city because of its abundance of fresh water and its good harbor. Geography played a large role in Boston's future development. The area was lacking in forest and level farm land, which made Boston unfit as an agricultural settlement, but the harbor facilities were excellent and the narrow neck of land leading to the peninsula could easily be defended, both of which made Boston ideal as a center of commerce and government. After a difficult first winter that killed at least 200 settlers and forced another 100 to return to England, Boston grew rapidly and prospered to an extent that surprised even the most optimistic founders. By 1640, Boston's population had grown to 1,200, and the city dominated the political, social, and economic life of the Massachusetts Bay colony. Dominating wealth and power in the capital itself were a small group of men from leading families. This elitist arrangement, a carryover from old England, was by design as Boston's gentry— some 30 families—received almost one-half of the land initially granted by the town. From the beginning, Boston's upper crust made sure that they had an unfair advantage over their less fortunate neighbors, an advantage intended to perpetuate plutarchy and a socially stratified society.[9]

Unfortunately for Boston and its residents, town leaders failed to create a thoughtful plan for its capital city that would accommodate such rapid urban development. Except for two wide intersecting thoroughfares—State and Washington Streets today—street development followed no systematic order. Instead, cow lanes, footpaths, rocky banks, marshes, and muddy sinks shaped Boston's early street pattern. In the midst of this irregular street pattern was a space reserved for a market and public buildings such as the governor's house, meeting house, town house, church, and jail. Adding to the city's irregular visage were sundry wharves and docks that projected into the harbor. Much of Boston's early construction—particularly shops, warehouses, and homes—clustered at the waterfront where much of the town's economic activity took place. In 1650, a contemporary described Boston as "crowded on the Seabankes, and wharfed out with great industry and cost, the buildings beautiful and large, some fairly set forth with Brick, Tile, Stone and Slate, and orderly placed with comely streets, whose continual enlargement presages some sumptuous City." Just a generation later a visitor to Boston was surprised to find that houses there were "close together on each side of the street as in London" and the many large streets "paved with pebble stone."[10]

Much of Boston's rapid early growth resulted from the tremendous productivity of the thousands of settlers in the New England hinterland who grew a surplus of small crops such as wheat, rye, maize, potatoes, beans, and garden plants. Boston also profited from the harvesting of forest products and animal furs from inland. With its strategic position and first-class harbor, Boston provided an excellent entrepôt for the marketing of farmers' produce as well

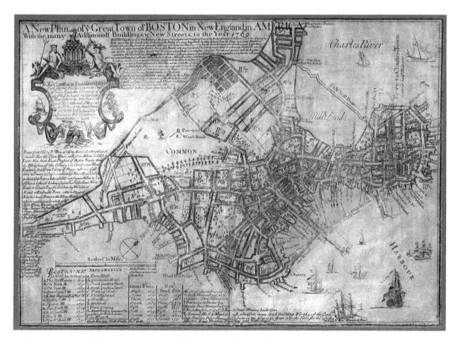

1769 Map of Boston by William Price. The founders of Boston and its early leaders failed to give the Puritan capital a coherent plan for its pathways, leading to crowded and often narrow streets laid out in a haphazard pattern dictated more by geography than preplanned design. (Library of Congress, Geography and Maps Division, Call #G3764.B6 1769 .P7)

as for the distribution of imported goods. A system of roads, rivers, and streams facilitated transportation from the small villages and towns of New England to Boston. One contemporary compared Boston to a giant tree spreading its roots out to all other New England towns so that "all trade and commerce fell her way."[11] By 1700, Boston lagged behind only Bristol and London in the amount of trade it carried throughout the British empire.

The reason for Boston's early tremendous growth cannot be summed up with simple economics. A host of other factors explain why Boston became the most important urban center in New England. First, nearly 20,000 colonists emigrated to Massachusetts Bay in the first dozen years of settlement, thus ensuring the colony's survival and providing ready consumers of colony products. Second, most of the settlers during this "Great Migration" were middle-class families with skills as artisans, farmers, businessmen, merchants, and household producers who planned to stay in the New World. Their stress on work as a primary way of serving God—the famed "Puritan work ethic"—further contributed to the colony's enormous economic success. Third, the colony benefitted from well-educated leaders with extensive experience in government. To help ensure that the following generations would continue the founder's providential mission, officials passed a law in 1647 requiring all towns to establish an elementary school that would promote social conformity and obedience to both church and state. Similarly, leaders established Harvard College in 1636 to provide a ministry trained in Puritan theology. A final factor contributing to Boston's early success is that the first generation of settlers were bound together by a common purpose: to establish a community of pure Christians that would serve as a holy model for England.

The first generation of Puritans did establish their Christian commonwealth in Boston, but it proved to be anything but a religious utopia for many residents. Instead, the Puritan fathers created a repressive Protestant theocracy that stressed strict conformity to Puritan doctrine, which they thought was necessary to ensure the success of their providential mission. Both secular and religious leaders eschewed the idea of a separation of church and state and instead worked assiduously together to make sure that everyone behaved and worshiped in the only one true godly way—the Puritan way. The ministers of the church were to declare God's will, while the magistrates executed it. As the Puritan synod put it in their *Platform of Church Discipline* of 1649: "It is the duty of the magistrate to take care of matters of religion...the end of the magistrates office is...godliness." The "church government," meanwhile, was to "furthereth the people in yielding more hearty...obedience unto civil government." Anyone disobeying the state was therefore both a "rebel and traitor" to God. To help prevent such blasphemy, Puritan officials created two systems of public espionage: "holy watching" and "tithingmen." The first involved encouraging residents to snoop on each other for any misconduct, while the second was more systematic in that local leaders appointed "righteous" men to supervise the private affairs of 10 of their closest neighbors. Similarly, only those who proved themselves committed to the Puritan way, called "saints," were given the right to vote and govern. Granting themselves God-like powers in carrying out God's will, these self-proclaimed saints prescribed death sentences for infractions such as adultery, idolatry, sodomy, blasphemy, bestiality, and witchcraft. In 1644, Boston officials hanged a young married woman and her 18-year-old paramour for adultery. This spirit of authoritarianism also motivated Puritan leaders to impose a form of religious tyranny on residents by requiring everyone to attend Sunday church service so that they could receive regular indoctrination of the Puritan way. "They are very strict observers of the Sabbath Day," noted one foreigner visiting Boston in 1750, "and in service times no persons are allowed [on] the streets but doctors. If the constables meet you they compel you to go either to church or 'meeton' as you choose."[12]

Those who opposed this oppression—and many did—were fined, placed in stocks, and publicly whipped. So, too, were those who had the audacity to sully the sanctity of the Lord's Day by either working or playing on Sunday. For cursing or swearing they bored through the tongue with a hot iron. Suffering most from this theocratic repression were religious dissenters, whom Puritan leaders disfigured, tortured, banished, and exterminated as enemies. Illustrative are the Quakers, whom authorities disfigured for easy identification by slitting their nostrils, slicing off their ears, and branding their faces with the letter "H" for "heretic." For those stubborn Quakers who still refused to leave Boston, the Puritans were happy to hang them. The intolerance and cruelty of Boston's Puritan theocracy even reached England, where a relative of Governor John Winthrop wrote from London: "I had heard divers complaints against the severity of your government."[13]

From the very start, Bostonians rebelled against this theocratic dystopia. Within just a few months after establishing the Puritan capital, Governor John Winthrop complained that "I think here are some persons who never showed so much wickedness in England as they have done here."[14] The most obstreperous rebels were shunted from the holy land into the wilderness. Some departed with no urging, while others—the merchants, in particular— remained to undermine the holy experiment from within. Only a relatively small percentage of residents, moreover, were devoted enough to building the City of God in America to become "saints." After 20 years, Boston had only 625 full church members out of a total population of 3,000. This indifference may partly be because many rank-and-file residents complained that they were "ruled like slaves" by the Puritan-controlled government. In 1692, the English Crown finally emancipated the people of Massachusetts from Puritan rule by granting the colony a new charter giving residents full rights of English citizenship, which included freedom of conscience to all Protestants. By then, the city's providential mission was long forgotten by descendants of the original settlers. Largely responsible for this selective amnesia was the economic prosperity of the city, which encouraged residents to devote more energy towards making money than making a holy community. Encouraging this capitalist behavior were Puritan ministers who provided moral sanction for usury, market pricing, and pursuit of profit by preaching to their congregations that aggressive participation in Britain's transatlantic market system was both a patriotic and religious duty. As it turned out, it was capitalism, with its inherent values of individualism, materialism, and competitiveness, that doomed the Puritan mission of creating a model "city on a hill" for the Christian world, an endeavor that could only succeed if people were willing to subordinate much of their own self-interest for the welfare of the larger community. Guided by capitalist values instead, residents of Boston rather quickly transformed their Christian commonwealth into a capitalist commonwealth that contributed to the development of a much more contentious and atomistic society that the original founders sought to avoid.[15]

In the end, seventeenth-century Boston did serve as a "city upon a hill" for the rest of the Christian world, but not one the Puritan founders had intended. Instead of a type of society to imitate, it proved to be a type of society to avoid. Christians outside of America largely ignored the Puritans' holy experiment. Early Boston therefore demonstrates that applying strict enforcement of a conservative interpretation of Biblical scripture to human relations is counterproductive to creating a free and just society. Rather than champions of freedom and democracy, as the central myth of American history would have us believe, the New England Puritans were cultivators of authoritarianism and theocracy. Still, Puritan culture has had a profound impact on the development of American society, a culture that put great emphasis on education and intellectual achievement, the belief in the potential of government to improve society, and the idea of American exceptionalism and Manifest Destiny.[16]

NEWPORT

Much more conducive toward creating a free and just society were the enlightened and liberal ideas of the founders of Newport. Located in the southwest corner of the island of Rhode Island, Newport was founded in 1639 by men cast out from or fleeing the religious and economic restrictions of the Massachusetts Bay colony. The combination of religious and economic motives for leaving Massachusetts determined the course for Newport's development. The original founders—William Coddington, William Hutchinson, and John Clarke—were persecuted antinomians (those who, justified by faith, had no need for scriptural or moral law) and acquisitive merchants who sought to build a commercial city based on the novel concept of religious liberty and the separation of church and state. These two liberal goals proved to be a positive benefit to political and social stability. As Rhode Island leaders argued, compulsory support of a state church was nothing more than "forced extortion" that opened the door for strife. Religious liberty also proved beneficial as many of the religious dissidents who settled in the city, particularly the Quaker and Jewish merchants, contributed significantly to the town's economic growth and social development. Careful planning and able leadership also played an important role in making the founder's "lively experiment" a success. Newport flourished on shipbuilding and trade with the continental colonies, the West Indies, Europe, and Africa. Wealth from this lucrative, multiangular trade in American farm and forest products, European goods, and African slaves helped turn Newport into a truly cosmopolitan and cultured city complete with a circulating library, music and dancing schools, a philosophical society, and various artists, artisans, and architects plying their trade. By the middle of the eighteenth century, Newport ranked as one of the chief commercial and cultural centers of the eastern seaboard.

The founders of Newport could hardly have selected a better location for their commercial city. The land on Aquidneck Island was fertile and contained forests of oak trees that could provide timber for a shipbuilding industry. The harbor at the southern end, where Newport was located, was protected from the elements, safe for ships to enter and exit, and warm enough that it rarely froze during the winter. The bay and ocean, additionally, teemed with fish.

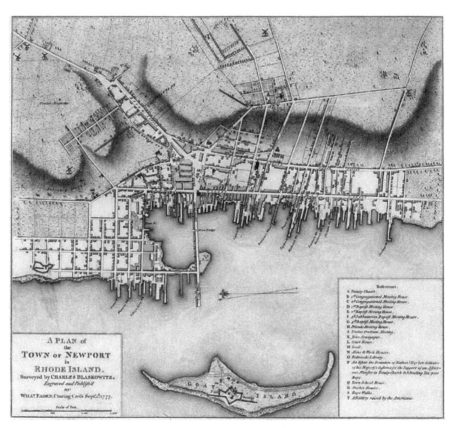

1777 Map of Newport by Charles Blaskowitz. Colonial Newport crowded along the waterfront in a long and lean pattern dominated by Thames Street. Numerous quays jutted out into the harbor, illustrating the importance of trade in the city's economy. The map's legend identifies 19 of the most important buildings in town, including Touro Synagogue, Trinity Church, the courthouse, prison, and almshouse, among others. (Library of Congress, Geography and Maps Division, Call #G3774.N4 1777 .B5)

Although the founders carefully and ably selected the site for their commercial city, they did not put as much thought and effort in laying it out and planning for its long-term development. Instead, geography, more than human design, shaped the growth of Newport. Without a town plan, streets were laid out in a haphazard and irregular manner. Newport's expansion therefore followed the shape of the marshy shore and cove and by common water lots and upland meadows. Most of the early growth occurred along the cove, where the founders set aside choice lots and built wharves and water mills to attract tradesmen. Throughout the colonial period, Newport was dominated by one narrow street, Thames Street, which lay parallel to the harbor with several lanes intersecting it on both sides. Most houses had large lots complete with orchards, gardens, and even stables—all of which gave Newport a rural appearance and the moniker of "the garden of New England." Not until the early eighteenth century did Newport experience rapid urban development and an economic boom that transformed the town from a frontier community into a commercial city. Its population grew from approximately 2,200 in 1708 to over 9,200 by 1774. This tremendous population growth resulted not just from economic prosperity but also from the colony's explicit commitment to religious tolerance. Many Quakers, Baptists, Jews, and other persecuted peoples found sanctuary in Newport, which became one of the most religiously diverse cities in North America.[17]

These original settlers of Newport intended from the beginning to create a commercial town—exporting local commodities in exchange for imported manufactured goods. To pay for these overseas products, settlers took advantage of the high quality of grazing land and protection from wild animals on the island to raise hogs, cattle, sheep, and horses for sale. Shingles, barrel staves, cider, fish, and leather hides also became important export items. For most of the seventeenth century, Newport merchants, who lacked large seagoing vessels and substantial capital, were forced to confine their trade to Boston and New Amsterdam/New York. However, by the early 1700s, circumstances came together that allowed Newport to end its economic subservience to Boston and New York City. The arrival of Quaker and Jewish merchants from Western Europe, the Caribbean, and South America in the mid-to-late 1600s gave a significant boost of energy, intelligence, and commercial associations to Newport's economy. These new arrivals used their connections with fellow Quakers and Jews throughout the Atlantic world to blaze new trade routes to and from

Newport. The development of a large shipbuilding industry further allowed the city to enter the mainstream imperial trade throughout Europe, Africa, the West Indies, and the continental colonies. Perhaps the most lucrative aspect of this complex trading network was the slave trade, which Newport dominated by the mid-1700s. Newport's extensive commercial activities spawned a host of other industries, particularly shipbuilding, the distillation of rum (Newport had 22 distilleries), and candle making (from whale oil). Shipping also encouraged subsidiary production and manufacture needed to sustain commerce—barrel-making, wagon-building, blacksmithing, and rope-making. Nearly everyone in Newport was involved either directly or indirectly in trade. Seamen alone comprised at least one-quarter of the city's able-bodied workforce.[18]

Newport's expanding trade and industry also resulted from a political system dominated by the merchant aristocracy that promoted commerce. Nearly 70 percent of the men who served on Newport's town council in the eighteenth century were merchants or shipmasters. Newport merchants also dominated the colony's government, which they used to pass laws intended to help support commerce. Merchant leaders further consolidated their influence by forming organizations, sponsoring civic projects, and banding together to control the potentially disruptive lower classes. They further reinforced their sense of common class interest, and their ties to other cities, by marrying among other elite families in British North America. Helping to enable them to maintain their dominance were property qualifications for voting that prevented the poorest 40 percent of Newport residents from participating in the political process. With the reins of government firmly in their hands, Newport's merchant elite sought to create an efficient political and financial order that would promote commerce by appointing judges and officials who favored trade, building wharves and bridges, paving roads, and establishing regular communication with the other major port cities. There is little evidence that the common folk, who were accustomed to following the dictates of their social superiors, were dissatisfied with this political arrangement.[19]

This may be because the merchant aristocracy, more so than leaders in the other cities, also used their wealth and political power to improve Newport for the benefit of all. To that end, they paid a growing attention to street lighting, drainage, garbage removal, fire protection, and care for the poor and homeless. Town leaders also set aside land for parks, schools, and a circulating library. A small group of intellectuals formed a literary and philosophical society, which in turn supported an enlightened press. The increasing wealth of the city also encouraged the development of music, art, and architecture. Newport's prosperity, culture, "salubrious climate," and easy accessibility by sea made it a favorite summer vacation spot among many wealthy planters and merchants from South Carolina and the West Indies, who sought to escape the heat and disease of their home environment.[20]

CHARLES TOWN

Charles Town, the capital of Carolina, could not be more different than Boston and Newport in its origins, the motives of its founders and settlers, the makeup of its population, its economy, and its early development. Rather than England, the founding and settlement of Charles Town was closely tied to the island of Barbados. By the mid-1600s, Barbados, like other West Indian sugar islands, was in a crisis. All of its land was either exhausted or claimed. Small planters and younger sons found it increasingly difficult to compete with the large sugar planters who monopolized the land and labor on the small island. As a solution, Sir John Colleton, a Barbadian planter with powerful connections in London, convinced seven other wealthy English noblemen to establish a colony in North America that would provide a place for Barbados's excess population. In turn, the colony would provide the sugar island with much-needed food, lumber, and other raw materials. In 1663, the eight lords proprietors asked King Charles II for a charter granting them the right to establish a colony in North America. The king could hardly refuse the request of these men, all of whom had supported him while he was in exile during the English Civil War. The charter granted to the proprietors all the lands from Virginia to central Florida, which they named Carolina.

To guide the direction of the colony, Sir Anthony Ashley Cooper, the leader of the Carolina venture, along with his personal secretary, the philosopher John Locke, penned a "Grand Model" of government called the Fundamental Constitutions that sought to create a utopian society organized around the constitutional and political principles of a radical English theorist named James Harrington. The organizers of Carolina wanted to show England how a truly decent society conducted its affairs. Consisting of 120 provisions, this carefully crafted constitution was a curious combination of conservative and liberal

elements that reflected the mixed motives of the eight lords proprietors. On the conservative side was the desire to establish a landed
aristocracy based on a manorial system that provided for manors,
manorial courts, and serfs. To that end, the Fundamental Constitutions called for a local nobility of one landgrave, two caciques,
and the eight lords proprietors to own two-fifths of the land in every
county, with the remaining land reserved for the people. Tilted even
more favorably to the rich was a plutocratic government intentionally
designed to avoid the dangers of "erecting a numerous Democracy."
Only the eight lords proprietors and local nobility could serve in
the eight administrative courts and the 42-member Grand Council,
the latter of which prepared legislation for a unicameral parliament whose distribution of membership, writes historian Eugene
Sirmans, "tipped the scales toward the nobility rather than the people's representatives," who had to own at least 500 acres of land to
serve on that body. Much more liberal and attractive to potential settlers were the generous land bounties and the policy of religious toleration to all Christians. Although the Fundamental Constitutions
proved unpopular among most early settlers, who never ratified the
document, it still left a lasting legacy on the colony by attracting
many religious dissenters and accelerating the development of a
landed gentry in South Carolina.[21]

In planning Charles Town, the proprietors created detailed
instructions, a grand model, as they called it. This grand model,
influenced by the street pattern proposed for the city of London following the great fire of 1666, directed that streets be laid out in a
gridiron design with an open square at the center where the two
principal streets were to intersect and where the most important
public buildings and market were to be located. To protect the
town from hostile natives and the nearby French and Spanish
settlements, the proprietors ordered the construction of a moated,
earth-and-stone palisade with regularly placed bastions. Outside
the walled city, the proprietors set aside a common ground of 200
acres to be used for gardens, pasture, and military exercises.[22] By
1682, Charles Town had about 100 houses and public buildings.
Still, it was a small frontier outpost with bobcats and wolves lurking in and around the capital.

Despite its careful planning, Charles Town teetered on the brink of
destruction for the first several decades of its existence. A series of
natural calamities shook the small, struggling town with frightening
regularity, and in the process decimated its inhabitants. Many settlers
did not survive their first months ashore, the so-called "seasoning

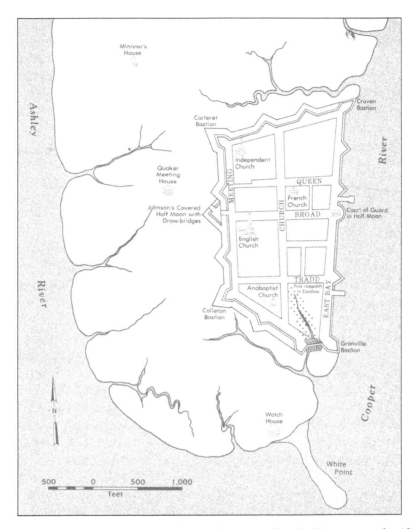

Map of Charles Town in 1702. In its early years, Charles Town was a fortified city, surrounded by a wall with armed bastions at each corner to protect residents from Native Americans and European rivals. In laying out the capital, the lords proprietors sought to avoid the narrow, twisting streets of European cities by following a checkerboard pattern with broad and regular streets. Resembling a narrow trapezoid four squares long by three wide, the town originally covered about 80 acres. By the mid-1750s the geographical center of the city moved to the crossroads of Meeting Street and Broad Street where the presence of distinctive symbols of authority—the State House, the Watch House, St. Michael's Church, and the slave market—characterized the central square. (From George C. Rogers Jr., *Charleston in the Age of the Pinckneys* [Columbia: University of South Carolina Press, 1969]. Reprinted with permission of the University of South Carolina Press.)

time," when their immune system was assaulted by a variety of diseases that flourished in the near-tropical climate. The high mortality rate gave the city a reputation throughout Europe as being the graveyard and "great charnel house" of America.[23] In the summer of 1697, smallpox broke out in the capital, killing nearly 300 people, or 15 percent of the population. People were still dying from smallpox in February when an earthquake shook the capital and started a fire that destroyed a quarter of the town. The following summer, yellow fever ravaged the residents of Charles Town and temporarily halted trade and government business. While survivors were still burying the dead, a hurricane struck Charles Town, flooding much of the capital. As if these calamities were not enough, Charles Town residents also had to contend with raids from Spanish and French soldiers, Indians, and pirates. These series of calamities strongly discouraged settlement of the southern capital for some time.[24]

After surviving these disasters and attacks, Charles Town finally began to flourish. By 1706, about 3,500 people crowded into the town, which had about 250 dwellings. Public inns, taverns, and brothels sprouted along the waterfront, along with prostitution, disorder, and public drunkenness. Most of the inhabitants, according to a local Anglican minister, were the "Vilest race of Men upon the Earth[;] they have neither honour, nor honesty nor Religion enough to entitle them to any tolerable Character, being a perfect Medley or hotch potch made up of Ban[kr]upts, pirates, decayed Libertines, Sectaries and Enthusiasts of all sorts."[25] Other public leaders expressed similar concerns over the low moral standards of the people who "profanely violate" the Sabbath and commit other "grand abuses."[26] With life expectancy so short, Carolinians developed a carefree, reckless, and self-indulgent, hedonistic attitude and behavior toward life that significantly retarded the development of a communal spirit. Social institutions were nearly nonexistent, and unpaved streets were filled with livestock, prostitutes, drunken sailors, pickpocket artists, the dung and entrails of beasts, and the contents of overflowing privies.

Parts of Charles Town's social problems were rooted in its political shortcomings. Simply, the town had no governing body. Instead, the provincial assembly enacted legislation for the capital city and appointed commissioners to carry out its policies. Unfortunately for Charles Town, the legislature in its early years was bitterly divided by ethnic and religious factions that spent most of their energies fighting each other for control of the provincial government. The legislators devoted little attention to the capital, allowing it to develop with virtually no guidance. Additionally, the proprietors, none of whom lived in Carolina, did little to aid the residents of Charles Town in their fight against warring Indians, marauding Spaniards, and plundering pirates. Instead, they issued meddlesome instructions to the colony that only irritated its residents so much that in 1719 they declared themselves free of proprietary rule and elected their own governor. The Crown accepted the coup, purchased the proprietors' interest, and made South Carolina a royal colony. However, South Carolina's change in ownership did not alter control of Charles Town by a small, self-centered, and egotistical planter elite who believed that government and people existed solely to support their own needs and aspirations. This elitist attitude and behavior by South Carolina's planter plutocracy partly explains Charles Town's downturn in the postrevolutionary period.[27]

Well before its eventual decline, Charles Town suffered from social and cultural retardation derived from the materialistic motives of early settlers who sought private fortune through an aggressive trade in furs and Indian slaves, cattle and timber, and especially rice, which thrived in the swampy land of the low country. By the early 1700s, the delicate and shallow-rooted plant became the dominant commodity in the province's production of staples, with exports to Europe surpassing 40 million pounds by 1740. The cultivation of rice proved enormously profitable to low-country rice planters, who became the wealthiest colonial elite on the Atlantic seaboard. They gained their wealth by working their many African slaves long and hard in the killing fields of South Carolina's rice plantations. The inhumanity inherent in this capitalist enterprise finally drove about 80 freedom-loving slaves in September 1739 to strike back in what was colonial America's largest slave revolt. The death of 21 whites in the Stono Rebellion drove the anxious white minority to create a harsh slave code that allowed slave owners to whip, brand, slice off ears, sever Achilles tendons and testicles, and even execute disobedient bondsmen to better terrorize and control them. The slave code almost invited masters to murder recalcitrant slaves by requiring the government to compensate a slave owner who killed his slave while being apprehended, whipped, or castrated. While white masters castrated black men, they raped black women. One German immigrant to Charles Town in 1742 was shocked to discover "many slaves who are only half black, the offspring of those white Sodomites who commit fornication with their black slave women. This is a horrible state of affairs."[28]

This "horrible state of affairs" proved salutary to Charles Town, as nearly all of the rice cultivated by slave labor, and nearly all of the profits from it, flowed through the Carolina capital. By the American Revolution, per capita wealth in Charles Town was nearly six times higher than that of either New York City or Philadelphia. This wealth gave the well-to-do the time and leisure to participate in a whirlwind of social activities that made Charles Town the cultural center of North America. These nouveaux riches sought to stabilize their authority by emulating the English gentry in their housing, clothing, manners, and recreations and by sending their sons back "home" for a proper English education. Despite this gentrification, Charles Town did not lose its rough and deadly edge; residents still displayed a gay, reckless, and carefree attitude toward life. As a reflection of its residents, Charles Town's character remained a curious combination of "old world elegance and frontier boisterousness." The Carolina capital also served as "the bastion of white supremacy, aristocratic privilege, and a version of classical Republicanism modeled on the slave states of the ancient world," according to Colin Woodard, "where democracy was a privilege of the few and enslavement the natural lot of the many." Over the subsequent decades, Charles Town would spread its culture of apartheid and authoritarianism throughout the Deep South, and this culture would eventually clash violently with the culture of Yankeedom over the future direction of the nation.[29]

PHILADELPHIA

The founding of Philadelphia in 1682 was largely the vision and effort of one man, the English Quaker leader William Penn, who dreamed of creating a "holy experiment" and an "example to the nations" by establishing a colony that would serve as a sanctuary for all persecuted peoples throughout Europe but especially for his fellow Quakers in England, who were severely persecuted by officials for their refusal to use any deferential terms of address, even to royalty, for their refusal to swear oaths, and for their pacifist beliefs. But perhaps more irritating was the Quakers' zealous proselytizing. Committed to converting the rest of the world to their beliefs, evangelical Friends invited persecution by disrupting the religious services of other sects, which included strolling into churches covered in excrement in efforts to provide models of humility. Reviled by nearly everyone, Quakers were persecuted, imprisoned, and deported by the thousands. Between 1660 and 1685, approximately 15,000 Quakers were jailed in England for refusing oaths of allegiance, evading church tithes, or publishing their unorthodox ideas.

One Friend who was imprisoned several times for publishing Quaker devotional tracts was William Penn, an Oxford-educated English aristocrat who looked to the New World to realize his dream of establishing an ideal Christian commonwealth for his fellow Quakers and other persecuted peoples. In 1681, Penn asked King Charles II to grant him a charter to establish a colony for his fellow Friends as payment for a £16,000 debt owed to his late father. Anxious to rid his realm of its troublesome Quaker population, pay off the debt, and establish an English presence in the mid-Atlantic, the English monarch readily made Penn proprietor of 45,000 square miles of land north of Maryland. Penn, who viewed his province not only as a holy experiment but also as an income-producing project, energetically promoted the settlement of his colony. He sent agents throughout Europe to drum up immigrants and circulated pamphlets in several languages that advertised the many benefits of Pennsylvania: an abundance of fertile land, freedom of worship, representative institutions, free elections, trial by jury, a liberal voting franchise, and a mild and humane penal code. He also laid the foundation for peaceful relations with local Indians by promising them his friendship and by dealing fairly with them in land transactions. Penn also gave careful attention to the location and planning of the capital of his colony, Philadelphia. He chose a site approximately 100 miles up the Delaware River for its natural advantages as a commercial entrepôt: a varied but not severe climate, a deep and commodious harbor, a fertile hinterland, and a river system that offered excellent transportation into the interior of Pennsylvania.

To plan his capital, Penn commissioned Thomas Holme, a Yorkshire man who had spent much of his life in Ireland and who was familiar with the grid plan used in the creation of the Ulster towns in the early 1600s. Holme's design was largely conditioned by the long, narrow tract of land available to him and Penn's desire to create a widely dispersed, low-density "greene countrie towne" that allowed for maximum flow of traffic and expansion in any direction in a regular and controlled manner. To that end, Holme created a city with broad avenues in a regular grid pattern, four large parks placed in a quadrant, and a large central square for a market and public buildings. Unique in America for the time was the lack of a walled fortification surrounding the town. Penn, who

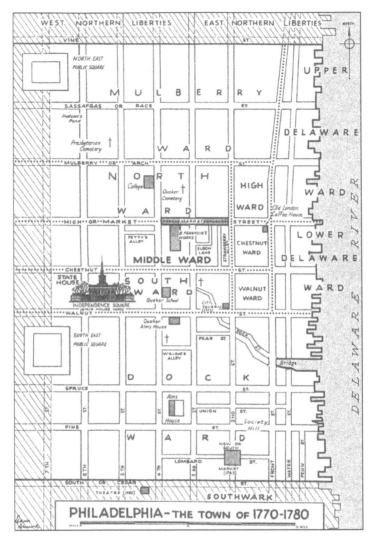

Map of Revolutionary Philadelphia. Thomas Holme, an Englishman who served as the first surveyor general of Pennsylvania, laid out the original plan for the city of Philadelphia with a grid pattern of streets and public squares to promote health and fire safety in reaction to London's numerous disasters. By 1770, Philadelphia was the largest city in North America, with nearly 40,000 residents. The map designates the location of various public buildings, cemeteries, the market, a theater, the almshouse, schools, and taverns. (From Sam B. Warner Jr., *The Private City: Philadelphia in Three Periods of Its Growth.* [Philadelphia: University of Pennsylvania Press, 1968]. Reprinted with permission of the University of Pennsylvania Press)

planned to get along with his neighbors, saw no such need. Thus residents of the city of "brotherly love" were spared the garrison mentality common in other North American port towns.[30]

Penn's careful planning of his colony paid off, and Philadelphia flourished from the beginning. Within two years, over 2,500 people had immigrated to Pennsylvania, fleeing war, persecution, and famine and drawn by the promise of economic opportunity and religious freedom. Most early settlers to Philadelphia came in freedom as families of middling means, though among the first people to remove to Philadelphia were over 180 African slaves brought there to build the town. Only about one-third of first-generation immigrants were indentured. By 1700, nearly 5,000 people lived in Philadelphia, described by one visitor as "a Noble and Beautiful City" containing over 2,000 brick homes generally three stories high, a "Noble Town-House," a "Handsome Market-House," and a "convenient Prison." Unfortunately for Penn, the phenomenal growth of Philadelphia shattered his dream of creating a loosely settled "country town." Nearly everyone crowded within four blocks of the Delaware River, which served as the lifeblood of the city. Pigs and goats roamed freely through the streets, no doubt enticed by the large amounts of garbage. To accommodate the growing number of people residing in this small and congested area, city planners cut up Holme's generous city blocks to create additional streets, most of which became glorified alleys. As the population grew to over 10,000 by 1720, city blocks were further subdivided so that Philadelphia became one of the most congested communities in America, with narrow streets filled with rows of tightly packed tenement houses, alley dwellings, taverns, shops, warehouses, and coffee houses.[31]

Packed within Philadelphia's narrowing and congested streets was a virtual Noah's ark of ethnic and religious groups. The first settlers of the area had been Dutch Calvinists and Swedish and Finnish Lutherans, whose residence dated back to the days when the area had been a Dutch and Swedish colony. With English rule and Penn's promotion came English, Irish, and Welsh Quakers, German Mennonites, English Anglicans and Baptists, Scotch-Irish Presbyterians, Spanish and Portuguese Jews, French Huguenots, and a few Catholics and mystics. African slaves, first introduced into the capital in 1684, quickly became a common sight in Philadelphia. With such a rapid immigration of diverse peoples and faiths, Quakers soon lost their majority position. Nevertheless, they remained the dominant religious group and controlled much of the city's commerce and the colony's government.[32]

Philadelphia's tremendous growth had more to do with its development as a major commercial entrepôt and port for the Delaware Valley than to Penn's careful planning. A number of factors contributed to its commercial success: it was surrounded by rich farmlands and forests and had access to raw materials; the Delaware and Schuykill Rivers offered cheap and easy transportation from the hinterland to the port of Philadelphia; it possessed an excellent waterfront and was located at the crossroads of several trading routes; the colony's generous land policy encouraged immigration and attracted skilled craftsmen and talented merchants; and the province's peaceful relations with the Native Americans allowed Pennsylvanians to avoid costly Indian wars that hindered the development of other English colonies. With all of these advantages, Philadelphia soon joined Boston and New York as a major trading center, exporting lumber, furs, flour, and wheat to the English West Indies in exchange for rum, sugar, and molasses.[33]

The liberal frame of government that Penn created for his colony also explains Pennsylvania's early success. As proprietor, Penn retained certain powers over his colony, such as the right to initiate and reject laws and to appoint the governor, judges, and other leading officials. Still, he believed that a representative government would help allow people of varying faiths and nationalities to live in harmony. To that end, he established an elected council of 72 men of "wisdom and virtue" who were to help the governor prepare legislation, and an elected assembly of 200 freemen whose initial role was limited to approving, rejecting, and amending bills. With the right to vote accorded to any adult male who owned 50 acres of land or who paid the local taxes, the franchise was just as liberal as the frame of government. To maintain harmony in the capital, Penn issued a charter for Philadelphia in 1701 that allowed a mayor, alderman, and councilmen to have full powers of justice within the city along with the right to issue ordinances and regulate markets and fairs. However, the Quaker belief that all people were innately good and could govern themselves through self-discipline and following the Golden Rule prompted them to apply a conservative, laissez-faire approach toward governing society; that is, government would be small and unobtrusive in the daily lives of the people. This small-government approach toward ordering society proved disastrous as the Dutch, Swedes, and Finns of the "lower counties" became so desperate for proper government that they broke away to form their own colony of Delaware. In Philadelphia, most streets went unpaved and uncleaned, the public wharves were left in disrepair, and there was little effort by government authorities to establish public schools and public water facilities, to provide charity to the poor, or to provide adequate defense to western settlers. Philadelphians and western Pennsylvanians would suffer considerably throughout the colonial period for such a conservative, free-market approach toward governing society.

As it turned out, the pluralistic culture of the Quaker capital would eventually spread directly westward to spawn the "culture of Middle America and the Heartland," according to Colin Woodard, "where ethnic and ideological purity have never been a priority, government has been seen as an unwelcome intrusion, and political opinion has been moderate, even apathetic." In this way, Woodard argues, Philadelphia and the Midlands were the most prototypically American of the "nations" within America.[34]

CONCLUSION

The five principal cities illustrate the various means by which Europeans sought to colonize North America. This diversity is a reflection of the different purposes and visions that organizers of these colonial ventures had in establishing settlements in the American wilderness. Together, these experiments in society building reveal much about what factors proved most beneficial towards creating a society acceptable to most and which would pave the future direction of the nation, and what factors did not. Those factors most popular and successful include the liberal policy of religious freedom, an idea that our Founding Fathers thought so important to social harmony that they made it a constitutional right for all citizens; representative government and a broad franchise, both of which Americans would continue to extend, at considerable struggle, over the next 300 years; and a powerful and active government that provided essential defense, economic stimulation, consumer protection, public safety and health, poor relief, and education that colonists increasingly realized was much more effective than a free-market approach to these, and other, concerns. This growing realization among Americans, over time, would eventually lead to the formation of our modern "big government" and its more liberal-leaning policies that have significantly improved both the working and living conditions of Americans.

These liberal policies, especially as they apply to the later colonies, were largely the product of the enlightened political and social thinking of the times. More anachronistic and less successful were the more traditionally conservative policies applied to colonization that have been left on the ash heap of history. Authoritarianism, either in the form of a capitalist/corporate dictatorship as in New Amsterdam, a Puritan theocracy as in Boston, a political autocracy as in early New York City, or a semifeudal plutarchy as in early South Carolina, proved unpopular and counterproductive towards creating a free and civil society. The values upon which those conservative regimes were based proved to be their ultimate downfall. In the case of the capitalist enterprise of New Amsterdam these were greed, exploitation, and authoritarianism, values that are highly destructive to social harmony. Equally destructive was the religious intolerance, self-righteous dogmatism, and spirit of authoritarianism among conservative Puritan leaders that finally compelled the English Crown to restructure the Massachusetts government with more liberal policies that contributed to greater religious and social harmony. Meanwhile, the semifeudal arrangement of South Carolina's Fundamental Constitution was such a conservative throwback to a more authoritarian time that residents in Charles Town did not even implement it. The successes and failures in the early decades of the five colonial cities therefore illustrate the importance of values in guiding both private behavior and public policy.

NOTES

1. Leo Schnore, "The City as a Social Organism," in *American Urban History: An Interpretive Reader with Commentaries*, ed. Alexander Callow Jr. (New York: Oxford University Press, 1969), 53–60.

2. Colin Woodard, *American Nations: A History of the Eleven Rival Regional Cultures of North America* (New York: Viking Press, 2011), 4.

3. Edwin G. Burrows and Mike Wallace, *Gotham: A History of New York City to 1898* (New York: Oxford University Press, 1999), 27, 34; Russell Shorto, *The Island at the Center of the World: The Epic Story of Dutch Manhattan and the Forgotten Colony That Shaped America* (New York: Vintage Books, 2004), 85–86 (quotes).

4. Woodard, *American Nations*, 66 (quote).

5. Oliver A. Rink, "The People of New Netherland: Notes on Non-English Immigration to New York in the Seventeenth Century," *New York History* 62 (1981): 17–25; Burrows and Wallace, *Gotham*, 50; Woodard, *American Nations*, 70 (quote).

6. John W. Reps, *The Making of Urban America: A History of City Planning in the United States* (Princeton, NJ: Princeton University Press, 1965), 148; Woodard, *American Nations*, 66.

7. Burrows and Wallace, *Gotham*, 30–34, 37.

8. Ted Morgan, *Wilderness at Dawn: The Settling of the North American Continent* (New York: Simon & Schuster, 1993), 157 (quote).

9. Darrett B. Rutman, *Winthrop's Boston: Portrait of a Puritan Town, 1630–1649* (Chapel Hill: University of North Carolina Press, 1965), 87.

10. Reps, *Making of Urban America*, 140–41.

11. David R. Goldfield and Blaine Brownell, *Urban America: A History* (Boston: Houghton Mifflin, 1990), 28.

12. Sherwood Eddy, *The Kingdom of God and the American Dream: The Religious and Secular Ideals of American History* (New York: Harper & Bros., 1941), 53 (quote).

13. Morgan, *Wilderness at Dawn*, 170 (quote); George F. Dow, *Everyday Life in the Massachusetts Bay Colony* (Boston: Society for the Preservation of New England Antiquities, 1935), 211. For a book-length discussion that shatters the myth of Puritanism as the source of modern liberty, see Milan Zafirovski, *The Protestant Ethic and the Spirit of Authoritarianism: Puritanism versus Democracy and the Free Civil Society* (New York: Springer, 2007).

14. Morgan, *Wilderness at Dawn*, 170.

15. Jack Greene, *Pursuits of Happiness: The Social Development of Early Modern British Colonies and the Formation of American Culture* (Chapel Hill: University of North Carolina Press, 1988), 55–80; Stephen Innes, *Creating the Commonwealth: The Economic Culture of Puritan New England* (New York: W. W. Norton, 1995), 39–63, 140–49, 192–99, 308–12; Mark Valeri, *Heavenly Merchandize: How Religion Shaped Commerce in Puritan America* (Princeton, NJ: Princeton University Press, 2010), 3–9.

16. Woodard, *American Nations*, 5, 60–63.

17. Lynne Withey, *Urban Growth in Colonial Rhode Island: Newport and Providence in the Eighteenth Century* (Albany: State University of New York Press, 1984), 13, 15; Richard Rudolph, "Eighteenth Century Newport and Its Merchants," *Newport History* 51 (1978): 21; Charles P. Jefferys, *Newport: A Short History* (Newport, RI: Newport Historical Society, 1992), 6, 10; Sheila Skemp, "A Social and Cultural History of Newport, Rhode Island, 1720–1765," Ph. D. dissertation, University of Iowa, 1974, 51–52, 160.

18. William G. McLaughlin, *Rhode Island: A History* (New York: W. W. Norton, 1978), 60–67; Withey, *Urban Growth*, 6–29; Rudolph, "Eighteenth Century Newport," 23–27; Jefferys, *Newport*, 10–13.

19. McLaughlin, *Rhode Island*, 69; Withey, *Urban Growth*, 17–28; Rudolph, "Eighteenth Century Newport," 50–53.

20. Jefferys, *Newport*, 15–25.

21. M. Eugene Sirmans, *Colonial South Carolina: A Political History, 1773–1763* (Chapel Hill: University of North Carolina Press, 1966), 6–16,

quote on p. 13; Robert M. Weir, *Colonial South Carolina: A History* (Millwood, NY: KTO Press, 1983), 54–58.

22. Michael D. Holmes, "Planning Method: The Case of Colonial South Carolina," *Planning Historians' Notebook* 1 (1992): 10.

23. Walter J. Fraser, *Charleston! Charleston!: The History of a Southern City* (Columbia: University of South Carolina Press, 1989), 9.

24. Robert M. Weir, "Charles Town circa 1702: On the Cusp," *El Escribano* 39 (2002): 66–67; Fraser, *Charleston!*, 17, 26–36.

25. Weir, "Charles Town circa 1702," 73.

26. Fraser, *Charleston!*, 4.

27. David A. Smith, "Dependent Urbanization in Colonial America: The Case of Charleston, South Carolina," *Social Forces* 66 (1987): 18–25; Woodard, *American Nations*, 84 (quote).

28. Morgan, *Wilderness at Dawn*, 254–55 (quote); Woodard, *American Nations*, 86–87.

29. Richard S. Dunn, "The English Sugar Islands and the Founding of South Carolina," *South Carolina Historical Magazine* 70 (1971): 93 (quote); Woodard, *American Nations*, 9 (quote), 84.

30. Sylvia D. Fries, *The Urban Idea in Colonial America* (Philadelphia: Temple University Press, 1977), 89, 96–97; Mary Maples Dunn and Richard S. Dunn, "The Founding, 1681–1701," in *Philadelphia: A 300 Year History*, ed. Russell Weigley (W. W. Norton, 1982), 10; Reps, *Making of Urban America*, 160.

31. Reps, *Making of Urban America*, 161; Dunn and Dunn, "The Founding," 15.

32. Dunn and Dunn, "The Founding," 28–30.

33. Dunn and Dunn, "The Founding," 18–21; James T. Lemon, "Urbanization and the Development of Eighteenth-Century Southeastern Pennsylvania and Adjacent Delaware," *William and Mary Quarterly* 24 (1967): 507–10.

34. Woodard, *American Nations*, 6.

2

Government

INTRODUCTION

Government in the colonial cities was not democratic. Urban officials never intended to govern society in a democratic manner. Given that colonists came from countries without a democratic tradition, this is not surprising. John Winthrop, the first governor of Massachusetts, expressed the attitude of many early leaders when he stated, "A democracy is, amongst civil nations, accounted the meanest and worst of all forms of government." The Puritan divine John Cotton gave such antidemocracy sentiment providential approval with his assertion, "Democracy, I do not conceive that ever God did ordain as a fit government either for church or commonwealth." Instead, the well-to-do ruling class felt much more comfortable governing society through a combination of oligarchy and plutocracy; that is, a government controlled by and for a small group of wealthy men more than by and for "the people." To establish and maintain this plutarchy, the ruling elite created laws that placed stiff property requirements for holding public office or made many of them unpaid positions that only the economically independent could fill. Moreover, because many political and judicial positions were appointive, either by the Crown or the governor, only those with wealth and connections had the opportunity to serve in them. For elective offices, the ruling elite ensured that only the "right" type of people could vote in political elections and so passed laws disfranchising women, Catholics, Jews, atheists, blacks, Indians, indentured servants, and poor free men. Together, this accounted for fully 75 percent or more of the urban population. To ensure that even this small voting bloc did not threaten plutocracy, affluent governing officials used a variety of methods to insulate themselves from electoral activism. As historian Alan Tully explains, "They used their monopolies over information to advantage when-ever possible to extend their political hegemony; they used patronage to try to entrench themselves in power; they exploited their experi-ence and their tradition of service; and they frequently tried to force a strengthening of deferential attitudes and patron/client bonds." As a result, the five cities were governed at all levels by a small num-ber of affluent men, who were often linked by ties of blood, marriage, business, and religion.[1]

The structure of plutocratic government differed from city to city, a difference reflected in the distinctive conditions of the eras in which they were founded and the separate social visions of their founders. This included the town-meeting form of govern-ment of Boston and Newport, the corporate oligarchy of New Netherland (already discussed in Chapter 1), the closed corporation of Philadelphia, the open corporation of New York City, and the city-state of Charles Town. Pieced together, the political picture of the five cities was a misshapen mosaic made up of elements and styles that were distinct from each other. Still, the principal cities were all centers of trade and commerce. As such, they required spe-cial governing institutions and offices to promote and regulate the local economy. Urban leaders, businessmen, craftsmen, and con-sumers all rejected the concept of free-market capitalism as a guid-ing principle in the city's economic affairs. They all understood that unfettered capitalism was ineffective in promoting economic growth and counterproductive to social harmony. As a result, they all demanded significant government intrusion in the urban economy and, concomitantly, in their daily lives.

One of the most important duties of municipal government was regulating trade and manufacturing. City folk feared shortages of necessities, unfair competition, and unscrupulous tradesmen and craftsmen. To help protect consumers, city governments established rules of commercial conduct: creating standards of price, weights, and measure; regulating quality control on food and manufac-tures; and enacting market rules and vocational trades. Municipal governments not only regulated the economy, they also stimulated it by operating public markets and constructing and maintaining such vital commercial facilities as docks, wharves, and warehouses. Providing local services such as sewage removal, paved and lighted streets, fire and police protection, and care for the poor also became increasingly important duties of these urban governments during the eighteenth century as the free-market approach failed to adequately address these needs and concerns.[2]

NEW ENGLAND TOWNS: NEWPORT AND BOSTON

At the center of local government in New England was the town meeting, which could be held as frequently as the townspeople felt necessary. Residents in Newport held an average of only five town meetings a year in the early 1700s, a number that increased to about 16 a year by the late colonial period when the city had a much larger population and a more complex economy. The number of people attending the town meetings in Newport also varied, anywhere from eight to over 200, depending on the issues scheduled for discussion. Every resident could attend the meeting and speak his mind, but voting was limited to those who met certain property requirements that classified them as either "inhabitants" or "freemen." In Newport, this amounted to £20 of taxable property, a requirement that barred about 60 percent of adult white males from the polls on the eve of the American Revolution.

Boston's town meeting, at least in its early years, was a more open body that allowed nonfreemen to vote because local officials believed that the useful abilities of these men, "if improved to public use," could go a long way towards advancing the interests of "this commonwealth." A committee of the General Court held in Boston disagreed, complaining in 1655 that everyone, including "scotch servants, Irish negers and persons under one and twenty years," was voting. Nearly a century later, Governor William Shirley arrogantly remarked that the Boston town meetings were spoiled by too many "working Artificers, seafaring Men, and low sort of people" who gave them a "mobbish spirit."[3]

Voting itself was by secret ballot rather than by *viva voce* as practiced most elsewhere. At an annual election held in March, freemen voted for a wide variety of officials: clerk, treasurer, constable, tax assessors, overseers of the poor, and over 40 lesser officials such as highway surveyors, tithingmen, clerks of the market, and numerous inspectors. These lesser offices had no political power and involved considerable work. Local elites in Newport and Boston therefore increasingly eschewed these posts and allowed middle-class tradesmen and craftsmen to perform this civic drudgery. More appealing to local aristocrats was the influential office of selectman, which had executive, ordinance-making, and limited judicial authority. This included administering the city's fiscal affairs, determining taxes, selling and allotting lands, settling land claims, admitting new inhabitants, and dispensing justice for minor offenses.

The funneling of most governing authority into the hands of so few men made government in Newport and Boston a virtual oligarchy, a rule by the few. This does not necessarily mean that it was the same men who monopolized the top offices, although men from leading families tended to dominate town affairs. This practice made city government plutocratic as well, as wealthy lawyers, professionals, merchants, and "gentlemen" maintained a stranglehold on the key administrative offices. Such political circumstances were normal for the times and were not seriously questioned by anyone, at least not too openly. Nor did the oligarchic nature of local government in Newport and Boston necessarily lead to misrule and malfeasance. On the contrary, historian Bruce Daniels argues that officials in Newport kept the town "reasonably well maintained and protected," while Carl Bridenbaugh argues that colonial Boston was "undoubtedly the best governed town in the colonies." The local merchants who dominated political office in Newport used their power in a manner that would benefit their interests while continuing to provide for the basic needs of the larger community. To secure at least the passive acceptance of promerchant policies from the rest of the residents, the merchant class enlisted the active support of ministers, lawyers, and secular pamphleteers who worked assiduously to encourage loyalty to the civil government. This "manipulation of power," as historian Sheila Skemp calls it, allowed Newport merchants to maintain their political hegemony by, at least in part, convincing the larger community that they were serving the "public good."[4]

Less manipulative and self-serving were Boston leaders, who focused attention on preserving safety and order and eliminating annoyances. No more than 10 percent of the town's ordinances, for example, involved trade. This is because Boston "was not a commercial community governed by commercial participants for the service of trade and industry," explains Jon Teaford. The city was founded principally as a social experiment, not as a commercial venture. Its leaders therefore devoted as much attention to promoting the public welfare as to advancing commercial interests. The responsiveness of local leaders to public needs may partly explain why so many residents in the two New England cities failed to attend town meetings and freemen refused to exercise their franchise. Voter turnout in Newport, for example, averaged 10 to 25 percent of eligible voters, while in Boston the percentage was even lower. Even during elections involving issues of taxation and charges of government malfeasance only one-third to one-half of eligible voters bothered going to the polls, a circumstance that demonstrates that political apathy has a long history in our country.[5]

PHILADELPHIA'S CLOSED CORPORATION

Far less democratic and far less responsive to the needs of its citizens was the government of Philadelphia, which was a closed corporation on the English model with a mayor, alderman, and councilors, who co-opted someone as a vacancy arose. Freemen in Philadelphia therefore had no opportunity to elect their governing officials, who were responsible to no one but themselves. Under such circumstances, the corporation became an incestuous association dominated by a relatively few wealthy families, with about 85 percent of members related to one another. This oligarchic and plutocratic political arrangement was significant because the corporation, which consisted of less than 30 men, had extensive powers and responsibilities: organizing and supervising a public market; maintaining standard weights and measures; regulating the admission of applying for status as freemen; maintaining peace and order; supervising garbage removal; constructing and maintaining wharves, bridges, ferries, and jails; and inspecting the streets, water supply, slaughterhouses, chimneys, bread, and flour packed for export. As if these duties were not enough, the corporation also kept a city court four times a year and undertook a number of ceremonial functions. Unlike Boston selectmen, Philadelphia's aristocratic leaders used their political influence to advance their interests while largely ignoring the needs of the larger community. At least 53 percent of the ordinances passed by the city corporation between 1705 and 1724 were devoted to trade, while only 38 percent were devoted to issues like public safety, public works, and annoyances. Public markets, docks, and wharves were all "primary concerns" of Philadelphia's merchant-dominated government, according to historian Jon Teaford, "outweighing secondary questions of safety, comfort, learning, and religion."[6]

Believing the corporation was too aristocratic and self-per-petuating, the provincial assembly during the eighteenth century gave more and more of its functions, like tax collecting and oversee-ing the poor, to overseers, wardens, and commissioners. This politi-cal emasculation proved fatal to the corporation, which lost its autonomy, authority, and identity with the community. With less to do, it distanced itself from the day-to-day interests of the larger community, passing only one new ordinance between 1740 and 1776. During this time the Philadelphia corporation was a "mori-bund oligarchy," in the words of historian Ernest Griffith. Helping to place the corporation on its deathbed was the Quaker belief in very limited government. To best serve God, the interfering influen-ces of government had to be kept to a minimum, explains Alan Tully, allowing Quakers to practice "a family life suffused with charity, and to the mutual forbearance that adherence to the golden rule produced." These circumstances compelled private individ-uals to step forward to provide much-needed public services. Public health, education, fire protection, poor relief, street improve-ments, and other aspects of public welfare were almost entirely handled by voluntary efforts. However, much of these "public" services provided by private groups were largely available only to those who had bought them, primarily the well-to-do who could afford the membership dues. Philadelphia's poor received little pri-vate, or public, assistance when it came to fire protection of their homes, cleaning and lighting of their streets, or even education from so-called "charity schools." Perceiving the poor as an increasingly restless and unruly lot, anxious local officials during the late colonial period increased resources toward the building of poor houses and prisons to better maintain social order.[7]

NEW YORK CITY'S OPEN CORPORATION

Nearly as oligarchic as Philadelphia's closed corporation, and cer-tainly more plutocratic in its policies, was New York City's open corporation. Governor Thomas Dongan's city charter of 1686 di-vided the town into six wards, with freemen (adult white men own-ing a freehold worth £40) in each electing a constable, an alderman, and an assistant, the latter two of whom combined to form a common council that enacted local ordinances and oversaw the city's financial and commercial affairs. This was the extent of the freemen's ability to elect their governing officials as the governor appointed the posts of mayor, sheriff, record (who was responsible for the town's legal business), and a clerk of the market. With the opportunity to elect only a few local officeholders, the freemen's real power in New York City was severely limited. Further limiting their choice was the practice of voice voting, which made it difficult for voters to escape the watchful eye of employers who, at least theoretically, had considerable leverage in coercing their workers to vote for a particular candidate.

According to Dongan's city charter, officeholders were to be "persons of Good Capacity and Understanding," which in seventeenth-century terms meant men of "sound reputation and wealth." Although the reputation of many New York City officials was certainly questionable, their considerable wealth was not. Local merchant princes and large landowners ruled supreme in the capital and brazenly used their political power to advance their economic interests while addressing larger public concerns only as an afterthought, if at all. As historian Thomas Archdeacon explains, the New York City common council regarded itself as "an exclusive and privileged body" that sought to maintain the status quo rather than spend even "meager funds" for public improvements. As a result, nearly half of all city ordinances dealt with trade, while only one-quarter involved public safety and public works.

The behavior of the common council as essentially a chamber of commerce caused considerable grumbling among the common folk. In 1734, local artisans mobilized to win 10 of the 12 seats on the common council. They used their power to pass ordinances advantageous to their own business interests. Later, the artisans combined with politically ambitious lawyers to further limit the power of the merchant princes. This artisan/lawyer combination gave the middling group of society a stronger political voice, which it used to force the corporation into being more responsive to the needs of its residents, at least to those with some wealth and property. This political warfare between middle- and upper-class groups helped to make the internal political life of New York City, in the words of Ernest Griffith, the "most stormy, the most striking, the most cosmopolitan, of any American city." The "stormy and cosmopolitan" nature of urban politics contributed to a politically active citizenry, with sometimes 40 to 55 percent of eligible voters casting ballots at annual elections.[8]

THE CITY-STATE OF CHARLES TOWN

At the opposite political extreme was Charles Town, where harmony prevailed among the aristocratic planter-merchant oligarchy, who shared a strong interest for consensual politics. Growing economic prosperity, waning religious zeal, the sharing of similar economic interests, and fears of attack from the Spanish in Florida, Indians in the west, and a revolt among the numerous slaves—all these compelled South Carolina's ruling elite to avoid bitter factionalism that might jeopardize the colony's security. Charles Town merchant and planter Henry Laurens reflected the sentiment of his peers when he boasted that "I am for no Man nor for any Party." Further contributing to the relative political harmony in Charles Town is that the city had no municipal government during the colonial period. The only meaningful institution of local government was the parish vestry of the Church of England, administered by two churchwardens and six vestrymen. Although these were elective offices, the wealthy planters dominated the parish vestry, which carried out such functions as caring for the poor, managing the town's free schools, assessing the parishioners for a poor tax, and occasionally exercising police and judicial powers. The vestries depended upon annual grants from the assembly for their income, which made the colonial legislature in Charles Town the dominant political body at both the local and provincial level. For this reason, scholars have likened the southern capital to a city-state. Meanwhile, judicial duties rested largely with the county and district justices, who also belonged to local aristocratic families. For most of the colonial period the well-to-do also monopolized the many elected offices of commissioner that performed the more mundane yet necessary functions of city administration. The political harmony that the local ruling elite was so proud of was therefore achieved partly by keeping real power in the hands of a small circle of like-minded ambitious aristocrats and partly by not addressing important but potentially contentious issues of public policy. It is no wonder therefore that voter turnout in Charles Town was generally quite sparse.[9]

However, underneath the façade of political harmony was an undercurrent of discontent among the city's middling artisans and tradesmen, who beginning in the 1750s publicly expressed their dissatisfaction with the poor quality of leadership among the city's ruling elite. Showing little deference to their superiors, this middle-class "civic faction" took advantage of the Charles Town grand jury's thrice-yearly presentments to express their complaints about the underperformance of constables, cartmen (garbage collectors), slave patrols, market regulators, justices, and election monitors, and the need for proper prisons, workhouses, charitable relief, and urban incorporation. These middling men backed their complaints with real action by aggressively campaigning to win election to the more than 20 commission posts that were responsible for regulating various areas of the urban environment—markets, streets, the harbor, the workhouse, and the wharves. Motivated by a strong desire to create a well-ordered and modern urban environment, these middle-class commissioners carried out their duties with a seriousness that not only made Charles Town a better place in which to work and live but also propagated an alternative political culture of civic responsibility to that of South Carolina's self-interested and negligent aristocratic ruling elite.[10]

CORRUPTION, INEFFICIENCY, AND NEGLECT

Despite attempts at urban reform, corruption and inefficiency in city government was all too common. Before unfairly judging early city leaders, however, it is important to emphasize that using public office to advance one's interest was common practice at this time and rarely frowned upon. Political leaders argued that it was only right that they receive some remuneration from their office in return for unpaid service to the city. Rather than a public trust, politicians often saw political office as an opportunity for personal profit. Thus urban officials saw no problem with awarding themselves lucrative government contracts, giving themselves first crack at purchasing much desired water lots, or allowing themselves to rent wharves, docks, and market stalls at reduced rates. One relatively mild, yet bold, example of this practice is found in the following announcement in the *South Carolina Gazette*: "The Firemasters for Charles-Town hereby give notice that on Monday, the 5th of May next they intend to go about and examine the Inhabitants of the said Town, how they are provided with Buckets and Ladders. (N.B. Buckets to be had of John Laurens, Saddler)." This public notice probably would have raised a few eyebrows among some readers had they known that John Laurens was one of the firemasters. But such profiteering from public office paled in comparison to outright peculation that occasionally occurred in city government. With an ineffective system of auditing, local governments almost invited unscrupulous politicians to embezzle city funds. In 1731, officials in Philadelphia found the mayor to be £2,000 short in public funds which he was handling. This was pocket change compared to the £40,000 Alexander Parris, the treasurer of South Carolina, owed the province in 1731 after years of "fiscal irregularities."[11]

Lesser urban officials also used their positions of authority to enrich themselves. For instance, the grand jury of Charles Town in 1772 complained that the local constables, who it described as "Persons of mean low Character," frequently took bribes from "Villains" which allowed them to "often escape justice." The jurors added that the town watchmen regularly "beat and abuse Negroes sent on errands except those who can raise 10 shillings." Such illicit and often harmful practices were all too common in the major urban centers. On the other hand, other city officials, perhaps because they served in an unpaid capacity and had other jobs, were simply negligent in their duties. The enforcement of the sundry city ordinances was "ridiculously ineffective," according to one expert on the subject, and most were "virtually unenforced" after a couple of years of their passage. People still dumped garbage in the streets, firemasters failed to inspect chimneys, clerks neglected to enforce market rules, and watchmen failed to watch.[12]

In the final analysis, one must not judge too harshly the quality of urban government at this time. After all, most city officials carried out their duties with little or no pay. They also had scarce resources available to them and even less knowledge of the science of public administration. A populace that was frequently unwilling to serve in minor posts or even to abide by city by-laws only added to the difficulties faced by urban leaders in governing their towns. Given these circumstances, officials in the five capital cities did an adequate job administering to the needs of their inhabitants. In assessing the quality of urban government at this time, the adage "you get what you pay for" is perhaps fitting.

POLITICAL TRANSFORMATIONS

For much of the colonial period, municipal elections, according to Jon Teaford, "were not forums for expressing competing ideologies, nor did the townspeople view them as a means for ensuring representative government responsible to the governed."[13] Most candidates faced no opposition unless an incumbent had supported an unpopular policy. Contested elections were the exception rather than the rule. However, the pacific nature of city elections began to change in the early 1700s as provincial assemblies, believing they best protected the rights of the people, sought to dominate political affairs by aggressively grabbing power from governors and proprietors. Over time the colonial assemblies won this political warfare, which had the salutary effect of giving politicians in the capital cities considerable confidence and experience in exercising self-government.

To help themselves gain the upper hand in these political contests, politicians on both sides organized themselves into factions and cabals. Before long the main cities, excepting Charles Town, were "run mad with faction & party" that, according to historian Patricia Bonomi, kept local political life "in an almost constant state of turmoil." Contributing to this political turmoil was the increasing involvement of the urban masses, whom the upper-class candidates aggressively courted in their contests for power. Making their task more difficult was the religious and ethnic pluralism and variegated economic structure and social hierarchy of the five cities, which forced political candidates, in order to win election, to mobilize these different identities and interests. In doing so, political factions employed such modern campaign techniques as outdoor political rallies, coalition building, caucuses, incendiary campaign literature, petition campaigns, and occasionally even bribery, vote buying, and behind-the-scenes intrigue—from all of which "a modern American conception of politics would be born," asserts historian Richard Beeman. This modern political transformation occurred first in the major urban centers because it was in the large cities that leaders could influence the greatest number of people. These five provincial capitals, additionally, had printing presses to publish political literature and numerous taverns to organize political clubs, mass meetings, and electioneering tactics. Also, in the port cities, disparities in wealth were growing most rapidly, creating an underclass ripe for politicization.[14]

These political innovations were not intended to democratize urban politics, and they did not. Instead, these efforts at political populism were always top-down affairs initiated by one elite group seeking to gain advantage over another. "The socioeconomic backgrounds of incumbent city officials and their challengers were very similar," explains Alan Tully, "and their profiles indicate little to suggest they shared, or wanted to share, very much with the working men of their neighborhoods."[15] Still, their appeals to "the people" tended to activate a previously quiescent lower-class element, which became far less deferential, increasingly antiauthoritarian, and sometimes violent. With their new power, artisans, tradesmen, and laborers were increasingly able to influence local politics through their various channels of protest. This protest, which upper-class leaders often orchestrated, sometimes involved intimidation and violence through mob action. But the propertied classes intended such action to advance their interests, not that of their inferiors. Insofar as the ruling elite recognized the electorate, they did so only as a means to use it for their own political gain, not to advance the interests and rights of the unwashed masses. Further making it difficult for the urban masses to influence the political process to their advantage is that they were too divided, transient, and lacking a strong sense of class consciousness that would enable them to unite behind a common cause. Urban politics therefore represented more of a contest among the elites for the votes of the masses than a clash of classes. This began to change somewhat during the heated Anglo-American crisis (1763–1783) when the urban masses increasingly realized their political strength and demanded that patriot leaders address their concerns in exchange for their support against imperial policies, and later, for the eventual goal of American independence. In the end, the urban elite, in fighting each other for political dominance, had unwittingly created a political Frankenstein's monster known as "the people" that they could no longer control with confidence. This ironic twist made the American Revolution not just a contest over "home rule" but also one of "who shall rule at home."

EIGHTEENTH-CENTURY URBAN POLITICS

Clubs and Caucuses

Rather than provide a tedious and tiresome description of the various political factions in the cities and their many battles over land, banks, paper money, defense, and taxes, it is perhaps more worthwhile to emphasize the more modern political techniques they used in their attempts to win these political contests. One political innovation was the creation of political clubs, often organized by class, occupation, and ethnicity. Philadelphia, for example, had the silk-stocking Gentleman's Club, the artisan Tiff Club, and ethnic-oriented clubs composed of Germans and Scotch-Irish. Another innovation was the use of political tickets, whereby leaders of a particular faction would "arrange entire tickets well in advance of the balloting," explains historian Robert Dinkin, "place candidates in those contests where they could bring the greatest advantage, provide backers with money to get out the vote, and send letters to friends and relatives to request assistance." To create these political tickets, faction leaders held closed caucuses to nominate a slate of candidates. The Boston caucus, first organized in 1719, was perhaps the best-organized caucus in colonial America. It nominated candidates for the city's four seats in the General Court and proposed selectmen and other town officials at the annual elections. The caucus managed to develop a broad network of political influence by working with numerous local social groups and clubs, which, over time, became heavily politicized. Political leaders in New York City and Newport also utilized the caucus effectively to recruit and mobilize voters during elections. In Philadelphia, especially, it was customary for a "certain company of leading Men to . . . settle the ticket for Assemblymen," observed one resident, "without ever permitting . . . a Mechanic to interfere." Even the Quakers "entered into cabals in their yearly meeting," observed a local lawyer, "which is convened just before Election, and being composed of Deputies from all the monthly meetings in the province, is the finest Scheme that could possible be projected for conducting political intrigues under the Mask of Religion."[16]

Tavern and Street Politics

One of the most important places where political leaders gathered for strategy sessions and to campaign was the tavern, where men of all social classes gathered for both business and pleasure. Here candidates had a ready-made audience to which they could express their views. New York City's merchant-controlled Hum-Drum Club, for example, regularly held its meetings in local taverns to recruit and entertain allies. In Boston, John Adams groused that taverns were the "nurseries of our legislators" for their popularity among "artful men" who undermined the traditional method of choosing the best and most virtuous men for public office by carousing and plotting with "the rabble of the town." William Cosby, governor of New York during the 1730s, went so far as to dine with men of "low rank" on election days. Outside of the tavern, candidates and their supporters (which sometimes included women) employed such time-honored campaign techniques as canvassing the electorate door to door. During Pennsylvania's bitter 1764 election, for example, a faction led by Benjamin Franklin held mass meetings and a door-to-door petition drive throughout Philadelphia in an unsuccessful attempt to convince voters to replace rule by the Penn family with the English Crown. The proprietary party replied by also aggressively courting people in their homes. "Never in Pennsylvania's history," writes historian Gary Nash, "has the few needed the many so much."[17]

Intimidation and Treating

Some aristocratic candidates refused to glad-hand their inferiors in an attempt to get their vote. Instead, they preferred using crass intimidation. As Alan Tully explains, "contemporaries were well aware that the power wielded by trustees of the loan office, supreme court judges, justices of the peace, lawyers, creditors, business partners, employers, and the socially preeminent could be turned to political ends." Such intimidation might be as subtle as offering a vote as payment for "Private Favours," or it could be as blunt as an employer telling his workers to vote for a particular candidate or else risk losing their jobs. With voice voting common in many elections, this was a real threat. One Philadelphian complained that during an election one of the "Great Men" of the city came into his neighborhood pushing a particular ticket and threatened to "sue some of us if he and his neighbors did not fall in line." New York landlords and creditors were notorious for writing letters to their "Tenants or Debtors or Dependants," complained a contemporary, "in order to intimidate them to vote as he wanted them to." Political bullying by the well-to-do was so prevalent in New York City that by the mid-1700s workers began calling their employers *boss*, a term used to describe those grandees who "exploited their various sources of power for political purposes." On occasion governors in New York City and Philadelphia even sent armed troops, sailors, and street gangs to the polls to drive away voters believed hostile to their position. The most notorious example of this is Philadelphia's election riot of 1742 in which the proprietary party hired a group of 70 club-wielding sailors well fortified with rum to storm the city's courthouse to prevent the voting of unnaturalized German immigrants, whom leaders of the opposition Quaker party had directed to the polls in an attempt to maintain its majority in the assembly. In response, the Germans, along with a few Quakers, launched a successful counterattack that resulted in bloodshed and broken bones. Although the proprietary party lost the election, the election riot nevertheless provided it with political ammunition for the remainder of the colonial period.[18]

Most politicians, however, preferred using the "carrot" approach to gaining votes. At times candidates bribed voters with cash. In Newport, voters were sometimes paid to vote for a particular candidate while others, perhaps because they were less trustworthy, were simply "silenced by connexions." However, the carrot most used to bring a reluctant electorate to the polls was alcohol, the primary

To the *Independent Freeholders and Freemen,* of this City and County.

IT having been induftrioufly propagated, that Numbers of the Voters of this City and County, have been long intimidated at Elections, and are therefore defirous of voting for the future in a *fecret Manner,* by *Way of Ballot*; which Report being by many furmifed to be void of a proper Foundation, and only intended to anfwer the particular private Purpofes of certain Perfons ; it is therefore requefted, that the *independent Freeholders and Freemen* of this City, will meet at the Merchant's Coffee Houfe To-morrow, at Eleven o'Clock in the Forenoon, to convey their Sentiments refpecting this Matter to their Reprefentatives, and to convince them that they are not to be diverted by any Motives whatever, from daring and chufing to fpeak their Minds freely and openly; to do which at all Times, is their *Birthright* as *Englifhmen,* and their Glory as *Americans.*

New-York,
Jan. 4, 1770.

Abel Hardenbrook,
Gerard Wm. Beekman,
John Alfop,
William Ludlow,
John Thurman,
George Harrifon,
Theophylact Bache,
Thomas Randle,
Ifaac Low,
Edward Laight,
Jonathan Lawrence,
Charles Nicoll.

Voter Intimidation in New York City. Voter intimidation had a long history in colonial New York City politics, as illustrated in this 1770 political broadside. (Charles Evans, *Early American Imprints,* Series 1, no. 11677, 1770) lubricant of the colonial political machine. Much of this liquid bribery was done in taverns with candidates buying rounds for their followers. During New York City's elections, taverns regularly conducted "vote buying operations" where any freeman "willing to part with his vote," explained a contemporary, "might there meet a purchaser." A similar state of affairs ruled in Philadelphia, where it was a common practice among candidates for sheriff and coroner to "engage persons to vote for them by giving them strong drink," complained one critic, "and using other means inconsistent with the design of voting freely at elections." During one election in Philadelphia, thirsty voters consumed some 4,500 gallons of beer provided by the candidates and their backers, after which they stumbled to the polls to cast their vote. Although such bountiful amounts of liquor consumed on election days often made elections joyous affairs, many people complained of widespread bribery "by the custom of intoxication."[19]

Dirty Tricks and Mudslinging

As urban political contests grew more contentious during the early to mid-1700s, candidates employed more artful and unsavory strategies to help them win political office. One dirty trick was to make temporary freeholds; that is, creating qualified voters out of unqualified ones by giving land to a number of landless males just in time for election and then regaining title of the land shortly thereafter. Other crafty candidates spread the false rumor that their opponent was withdrawing from the race. Overcoming such a charge was difficult given the slow pace of communication at the time. In 1706, Governor John Evans of Pennsylvania spread the false rumor that French brigantines were sailing up the Schuylkill River towards the capital in a hapless attempt to convince the pacifist Quaker leaders of the need for a provincial militia. His efforts backfired as Philadelphia erupted into such pandemonium that even supporters of the governor became convinced that he was an "incompetent and hotheaded youth." During hotly contested elections where every vote counted, faction runners would go into the streets and round up "The Deaf, the Blind, the Young and the Old," complained one Philadelphian, and then dull their emotional and physical aches with alcohol before taking them to the polls to vote for their ticket. Writing of New York City's 1737 election, the physician Cadwallader Colden recounted gross violations of local election laws: "The sick, the lame, and the blind were all carried to vote," he complained. "They were

carried out of prison and out of the poor house to vote." In Boston
and Newport, where voting was done using a written ballot rather
than a voice vote, stuffing ballot boxes was the voting-fraud tactic of
choice. Encouraging such illegal activity was the difficulty of proving
it and a cavalier attitude by local election monitors, who rarely questioned voters even when they "saw two votes drop into the box,
which appeared to come from one hand." Just as brazen were those
unqualified to vote who cast their ballot anyway, some by bribing
the town clerks and others by merely lying under oath. The use of
bribery, treating, intimidation, and dirty tricks in urban elections
was so prevalent that historian Ernest Griffith has concluded that
"the actual results in a time of open ballot could by no stretch of the
imagination be alleged as necessarily representing a 'public opinion'
functioning in an ideal democracy."[20]

   Indeed, political candidates and their supporters increasingly
sought to shape public opinion during elections through the use of
the local press. In doing so, they increasingly resorted to the unso-
phisticated yet effective political tactic of character assassination.
Instead of questioning the legality or wisdom of their opponents'
policies, candidates called each other "little pestilent Creature,"
"dirty miscreant," "stinking Skunk," "wild beast," "drunkard,"
"Pimp," "an indefatigable liar," a "consummate sycophant with a
head full of *flatulent Preachments*," and a "Minister of the Infernal
Prince of Darkness," among other choice epithets. Candidates also
accused each other of questionable behavior, such as sleeping with
slaves, conniving with "tricking judges," engaging in sodomy, and
having an "insatiable Lust of Power." Even founding father
Benjamin Franklin had political mud thrown at him during the
1764 election when his opponent accused the printer-philosopher
of being a sexual letch who fathered an illegitimate child, a squan-
derer of public funds, and a corrupt politician familiar with "every
Zig Zag Machination." Such insulting public attacks made politics
very personal and contributed to less-than-genteel behavior among
legislators. Governor Lewis Morris of Pennsylvania reported that
"there grew so great a rancour among [assembly] members that
they shun'd the conversation of Each other Out of the house, and
could not preserve the rules of common decency in it descending
to downright scolding, giving the lye, threatening to spit in the faces
& were (as I am inform'd) often very nigh getting together by the
Ears." According to some people, this political "contention and
wrangling" threatened the internal harmony of the cities and
undermined respect for its leaders. One New York City aristocrat

lamented that "elections are carried on with great animosity and at a vast expense, as if our alls were at stake." "What," he asked, "is all this for? Is the public good really the point in view?" Many people today ask the same question about the United States' bitterly contentious and divisive political process.[21]

Populist Rhetoric

When not trying to manipulate public opinion with "foul-mouth'd Aspersions" and "shameless Falsehoods," political candidates sought to do the same with popular appeals to political liberties, constitutional rights, and doing the "people's will." These were mostly self-serving pronouncements designed to gain appeal among the people, not legitimate planks of their political platform. Illustrative is Sir William Keith, governor of Pennsylvania in the 1720s, who exploited every means to "ingratiate himself with the Common People," including organizing political clubs, making direct appeals to the electorate through broadsides that denounced the wealthy, and holding outdoor political rallies that welcomed voters and nonvoters alike. By such means Keith was able to manage the elections in Philadelphia into the hands of a small number of his "upper-class friends." New York City residents also received an earful of populist rhetoric from political candidates. During the 1734 election, for example, the "country" faction made a crass appeal to the common man with its assertion in the local press that "the Almighty made us equal all." At the same time, it denounced the rival "court" party for its alleged contempt for "those they call the Vulgar, the mob, the herd of Mechanics." Similarly, James Otis Jr. of Boston was able to garner votes and to even call the mob into action in the mid-1760s by branding Governor Thomas Hutchinson and his clique as unfeeling aristocrats who "disdained the humble folk." The governor and his allies responded in kind in the local press with such popular catchwords as "public good" and "public virtue" to describe their administration. Despite such populist rhetoric, well-to-do politicians had no desire to allow common folk to participate in politics other than as voters.[22]

Pluralism and Politics

The ethnic and religious pluralism of the main cities intensified political factionalism and demagoguery. The large German population in Pennsylvania, for instance, forced both the proprietary and Quaker parties to try to win over the German-speaking vote. They did so mostly by using the tried-and-true "Popular and Plausible Cry of Standing for liberties," but at times candidates charged their opponents with ethnic bigotry. During the election of 1764, for example, the proprietary party gleefully publicized Benjamin Franklin's description of German immigrants as "Palatine Boors" and a "Herd of Hogs," while the Quaker party shot back with accusations against Joseph Galloway of calling them "damn'd Dutchmen." In order to win election in New York City, candidates had to aggressively court the large Dutch minority, which usually held the balance of political power. Rather than play upon opponents' alleged ethnic prejudice, Presbyterian candidates appealed to the Dutch as fellow Calvinists to make common political cause. Religion was therefore an important element shaping urban elections as ministers and lay leaders became parapolitical proponents on one political side or another. Thus, in the election of 1764, Benjamin Franklin found himself dealing with the local German Reformed Church mobilized against him as well as the Presbyterians, whom one Franklin supporter ungenerously described as "Piss-Brute arians—a bigoted, cruel and revengeful sect." In seeking to win elections by specifically courting various ethnic and religious groups, urban candidates were charting the way for all future American politicians.[23]

Popular Politics

One path of American politics blazed by upper-class urban politicians, and one they had not originally intended to chart, was the politicization of the common man. The local ruling elite, in courting the masses, only sought to exploit them as voters. But the ordinary folk, empowered with a growing sense of self-importance from the attention given to them by affluent politicians, increasingly lost their sense of deference in the political arena and refused to be manipulated by their superiors. Although never a unified body, the ordinary people "shared a marked prejudice in favor of popular rights," writes Alan Tully. The poor, in particular, shared a growing awareness that the growing wealth of the urban elite was based on class exploitation. In Boston, where poverty was greatest in the five cities, writers exploited this nascent class consciousness to score political points with the common man. "From your Labour and Industry," proclaimed "Phileleutheros" for the mechanics of Boston during the election off 1751, "arises all that can be called Riches, and by your Hands it must be defended: Gentry, clergy, Lawyers, and military Officers, so all support their Grandeur by your Sweat, and at your Hazard." One

New York City resident writing in 1765 was certainly raising the specter of class warfare when he charged that:

Some individuals, by the smiles of Providence, or some other Means, are enabled to roll in their four wheel'd Carriages, and can support the expense of good Houses, rich Furniture, and Luxurious Living. But it is equitable that 99, rather 999, should suffer for the Extravagance or Grandeur of one? Especially when it is considered that Men frequently owe their Wealth to the impoverishment of their Neighbors?

Advocates of egalitarianism sometimes used colorful colloquialisms to make their point with the common folk. "It is an old saying with us," wrote Roger Plowman, "that we must never grease the fat sow in the Arse, and starve the Pigs." Meanwhile, Timothy Wheelwright of New York City complained about the inequities of the law between rich and poor. "Suppose any great Man should . . . whip you through the lungs . . . or Knock your Brains out, and he should be presented to the Grand Jury, pray what notice would be taken of it? Very little."[24]

CITIES IN REVOLT

Such rhetoric shows that by the mid-1700s the major cities held considerable class tension. As the decades wore on, and as poverty increased amid plenty, this class tension slowly rose closer and closer to the surface. But it was not until the politically charged years of the Anglo-American crisis (1763–1783) that this socioeconomic division brought about a true political awakening on the part of lower- and middle-class urban folk who were influenced by the stentorian cries of patriot leaders against British tyranny and oppression. Such trumpeting rang hollow to many urban poor and laboring classes, who felt that the real oppressors were their own employers and politicians who ignored their needs and interests. Motivated by a growing hostility to these elitist oppressors and the revolutionary rhetoric of the period, the urban laboring class worked in coordinated and purposeful ways to protest both British imperial measures and the hegemony of local oligarchies. Although the lower sort may not have had a unifying ideology, they all experienced the momentous changes and conflicts happening in America in the decade preceding independence. As the Revolution approached, these changes and conflicts contributed to a radical consciousness among many urban folk who exploited America's cries for liberty and equality to make similar claims for themselves.

Stamp Act Riots

This is perhaps most graphically witnessed in the extralegal and sometimes destructive activity among ordinary people in protesting Parliament's stamp tax of 1765. Except in Philadelphia, where the stamp distributor was a former baker turned merchant and a close friend of Benjamin Franklin, resistance to the Stamp Act involved the hanging and burning of effigies of imperial officials, the ransacking of their homes, and the attacking of institutions of elitist authority. Some common folk in Newport staged an orderly funeral for "Liberty," murdered by "Lawless Tyranny and Oppression." Slaves in Charles Town protested tyranny and oppression of another sort by parading through the streets crying "Liberty! Liberty!" They quickly realized that liberty was for whites only as local authorities dispersed the black marchers and arrested the ringleaders.

The most violent protest over the Stamp Act occurred in Boston, where 28-year-old shoemaker Ebenezer Mackintosh organized an autonomous army of unemployed and working poor who stormed through the streets on August 14, 1765, demolishing the house holding the stamps and ransacking the home of Andrew Oliver, a local aristocrat responsible for implementing the Stamp Act. Twelve days later, Mackintosh and his mob of the desperately poor demonstrated their deep hostility toward their elitist oppressors by ransacking the mansion of Governor Thomas Hutchinson while he and his family were having dinner before turning their "War of Plunder" on 15 additional houses belonging to the affluent. By attacking the homes of the rich not even associated with imperial measures, Mackintosh's mob demonstrates that their street justice was more than just an expression of anger against Parliamentary policy. It was an attempt to settle some scores against the wealth and extravagance of the "prerogative faction" who had for years demonized the lower sort as lazy "rabble" who they claimed "live too well." Thus when imperial authorities sent troops to cure the "cancer of sedition" in Boston in 1768, many upper-crust residents breathed a sigh of relief. Thereafter, the presence of armed redcoats pacing the streets of the Puritan capital quieted much of the grumbling among the city's destitute and laboring poor.[25]

Class Warfare

Residents in the other cities had no such muffler to quiet them when the next major imperial controversy hit the colonies— Parliament's 1767 Revenue Act that imposed duties taxing paper,

The repeal, or the funeral of Miss Ame-Stamp. This 1766 print satirizes the repeal of the Stamp Act, with supporters of the act gathered at a dock to carry a small coffin containing the remains of the bill toward an open vault. Leading the procession is a minister, who is followed by George Grenville (carrying the coffin), Lord Bute, and others who were responsible for passing the Act. Quantities of unshipped cargoes destined for America have accumulated on the dock during the time that the act was in force. (Library of Congress, Prints and Photographs Division, Reproduction # LC USZ62-21264)

paint, lead, glass, tea, and other goods imported into America. Merchants and artisans in the main cities protested this indirect tax by organizing a general boycott of British goods to pressure England's merchant princes to convince Parliament to repeal the offensive duties. However, the embargo also hurt American merchants, some of whom began importing English contraband. When merchants in Philadelphia attempted to free themselves of the embargo in early 1770, local artisans warned their economic superiors that violators "will be dealt with by the Mechanicks Committee." Despite this warning, merchants continued to import illicit goods, prompting local mechanics to form a new political party radically opposed to imperial policies and supportive of economic issues beneficial to ordinary people. In the next two elections, these middle-class artisans won numerous local offices and even a seat in the assembly. They used their political power to successfully oppose taxes on liquor and leather goods that would have hit the laboring class hardest, and the "absurd and tyrannical custom of shutting the Assembly doors during debate." This "mechanic revolution" struck fear into more genteel Philadelphians. "It is time the Tradesmen were checked," exclaimed one local aristocrat, "they take too much upon them—they ought not to intermeddle in State Affairs—they will become too powerful." The tradesmen could not be checked, and they continued to meddle in state affairs. By 1770, there was a full-fledged "mechanic revolution" that turned out of office a number of candidates hostile to their interests. This contagion of populism even turned the Philadelphia militia into a "school of political education" for the common folk who served in it. Shedding the habit of obedience to their superiors, the lowly privates in 1775 pressured the assembly to take a stronger stand on independence and to pass some internal reforms: the right to elect their officers, the right to vote for all militiamen regardless of age and wealth, and a fine on every man who refused militia service commensurate with his wealth. More so than elitist patriot leaders, it was common folk like the Philadelphia mechanics and militiamen who were most aggressive in trying to advance political democracy and economic justice.[26]

Demands for greater democracy and economic justice by ordinary men in the other cities were causes for concern among the urban plutocrats. During New York City's vituperative 1768 election, middling men called for "No Lawyer in the Assembly," a populist cry that helped to bring over half of all eligible voters to the polls to oust some of the most conservative assemblymen. Fearful of the declining deference of their inferiors and its potential consequences if left unchecked, aristocratic leaders in New York City sought to slap down the uppity underclass during the 1770 election with economic intimidation. As explained in a political broadside, "many of the poorer People . . . deeply felt the aristocratic Power, or rather the intolerable tyranny of the great and opulent, who . . . have openly threatened them with the loss of their employment, and to arrest them for debt, unless they gave their voices as they were directed." Most voters were not so easily intimidated, however, and continued to vote as they pleased.[27]

Meanwhile, the growing aspirations for political power and influence among common folk in Newport prompted some merchants in that city to form the Newport Junto. This elitist political organization held an utter distaste for the "stupid herd of voters," as they called the common electorate. In published screeds, the Junto countered the middling sort's claims to greater political opportunity by remarking that they should instead exhibit "more Moderation & Civility, more Meekness and better Manners" to their superiors. The Junto also directed its derision on the political aspirations of the lower class by insultingly asserting that "the tyranny of a mob is more hateful than that of [a king]." But with little access to the polls or political office, what other choice did the lower sort have but to engage in the kind of street politics that so offended the Junto?[28]

This class warfare was also waged in Charles Town, where the Stamp Act crisis and nonimportation movement had crystallized awareness among the middling sort that they were a separate entity from the supercilious ruling class, who grew increasingly irritated by demands among the common folk to replace elitist office holders with more civic-minded men who would address their concerns and those of the larger community. Believing that only the wealthy and educated possessed the qualifications necessary to govern, the aristocrat William Henry Drayton expressed the sentiment of his peers by disdainfully telling local artisans in 1769 that the ability to "cut up a beast in the market . . . to cobble an old shoe . . . or to build a necessary house [privy]," did not prepare a person for the difficulties of government. "We are pleased Mr. William Henry Drayton, in his great condescension," has allowed us "a place amongst human beings," the local mechanics sarcastically replied. The mechanics reminded Drayton that not everyone is "so lucky as to have a fortune ready provided to his hand, either by his own or his wife's parents." More seriously, the proud mechanics challenged Drayton's elitist and self-serving conviction that wealth and education were qualities necessary for participation in government and insisted instead that one needed only enough common sense to distinguish between right and wrong in order to serve in political office. Completely casting off any appearance of deference, the middle-class artisans ended their acerbic attack by claiming that Drayton lacked enough common sense to serve even as a packhorseman in the Indian trade and suggested that he required a room in the local asylum to treat his "disorder."[29]

CONCLUSION

These events clearly show that there was a crisis in class relations in the principal cities during the decade prior to independence as the common folk "developed a political awareness of imperial proportions," according to historian Benjamin Carp.[30] This crisis in class relations only intensified during the American Revolution as patriot leaders, in mobilizing the much-needed masses behind their cause, were forced to grant them greater political, military, and religious rights and opportunities that only encouraged the people, already filled with a heightened sense of class consciousness and revolutionary rhetoric about human equality, to make further demands and challenges to traditional authority. With this genie out of the bottle, America could never return to the old system of social and political relations. Ordinary folk would not allow it. In the ensuing years, this contest over who should rule at home quickly spread from the largest cities throughout the American hinterland as conservative elites, desperately wanting to maintain the status quo, fought a bitter and protracted battle with more liberal-minded common folk who sought to advance greater liberty and equality as expressed in the nation's founding documents. Over time, a majority of Americans would come to view the traditional conservative philosophy as both backward and bankrupt, a progressive attitude that would usher in a social and political revolution that the upper-class patriot leaders—who had no intentions of destroying artificial privilege, advancing political democracy, promoting social mobility, or making the way for a natural aristocracy—neither anticipated nor wanted when they declared America's independence in 1776. In this way the American Revolution was truly a revolution. In the end, Americans today have the common man of the past to thank for the liberal social, economic, and political policies that have made our nation more egalitarian and just, not our elitist and conservative Founding Fathers.

NOTES

1. Robert C. Winthrop, *Life and Letters of John Winthrop*, 2 vols. (Boston: 1869), 2: 430; Thomas Hutchinson, *History of the Colony and Province of Massachusetts Bay*, 3 vols. (Boston: 1764), 1: appendix 3; Alan Tully, *Forming American Politics: Ideals, Interests, and Institutions in New York and Pennsylvania* (Baltimore: Johns Hopkins University Press, 1994), 380.

2. Jon C. Teaford, *The Municipal Revolution in America: Origins of Modern Urban Government, 1650–1825* (Chicago: University of Chicago Press, 1975), 3–11; Ernest S. Griffith, *History of American City Government: The Colonial Period* (Oxford, UK: Oxford University Press, 1938), 127–40.

3. Darrett B. Rutman, *Winthrop's Boston: A Portrait of a Puritan Town, 1630–1649* (Chapel Hill: University of North Carolina Press, 1965), 161–62 (quotes); Gary Nash, *The Urban Crucible: The Northern Seaports and the*

Origins of the American Revolution, abridged edition (Cambridge, MA: Harvard University Press, 1986), 171 (quote).

4. Bruce Daniels, "Governing Rhode Island's Metropolitan: The Town Meeting and Its Officers in Colonial Newport, 1700–1776," *Newport History* 52 (1979): 113; Carl Bridenbaugh, *Cities in the Wilderness: Urban Life in America, 1625–1742* (New York: Ronald Press, 1938), 144; Sheila Skemp, "A Social and Cultural History of Newport, Rhode Island, 1720–1765," Ph.D. dissertation, University of Iowa, 1974, 153–93.

5. Teaford, *Municipal Revolution in America*, 37; Robert J. Dinkin, *Voting in Provincial America: A Study of Elections in the Thirteen Colonies, 1689–1776* (Westport, CT: Greenwood Press, 1977), 146–73.

6. Judith Diamondstone, "The Government of Eighteenth-Century Philadelphia," in *Town and Country: Essays on the Structure of Local Government in the American Colonies*, ed. Bruce Daniels (Middletown, CT: Wesleyan University Press, 1978), 245; Teaford, *Municipal Revolution in America*, 18–19 (quotes), 56–57.

7. Griffith, *History of American City Government*, 217 (quote), 255; Tully, *Forming American Politics*, 339 (quote); Bridenbaugh, *Cities in the Wilderness*, 8–9; Diamondstone, "Government of Eighteenth-Century Philadelphia," 248–56.

8. Patricia Bonomi, *A Factious People: Politics and Society in Colonial New York* (New York: Columbia University Press, 1971), 36 (quote); Bruce Wilkenfeld, "The New York City Common Council, 1689–1800," *New York History* 52 (1971): 254–63; Thomas Archdeacon, *New York City, 1664–1710: Conquest and Change* (Ithaca, NY: Cornell University Press, 1976), 153 (quote); Griffith, *History of American City Government*, 367 (quote); Dinkin, *Voting in Provincial America*, 146–51.

9. Robert M. Weir, " 'The Harmony We Were Famous For': An Interpretation of Pre-Revolutionary South Carolina Politics," in *Colonial America: Essays in Politics and Social Development*, 3rd edition, ed. Stanley Katz and John Murrin (New York: Alfred A. Knopf, 1983), 441 (quote); Richard Waterhouse, "The Responsible Gentry of Colonial South Carolina: A Study in Local Government, 1670–1770," in *Town and Country*, 162–80; Griffith, *History of American City Government*, 246–50. For a study that challenges the prevailing interpretation of colonial South Carolina as politically harmonious, see Jonathan Mercantini. *Who Shall Rule at Home?: The Evolution of South Carolina Political Culture, 1748–1776* (Columbia: University of South Carolina Press, 2007).

10. Emma Hart, *Building Charleston: Town and Society in the Eighteenth-Century British Atlantic World* (Charlottesville: University of Virginia Press, 2010), 171–76; Griffith, *History of American City Government*, 218–19.

11. Griffith, *History of American City Government*, 389–91; Marion Eugene Sirmans, *Colonial South Carolina: A Political History, 1663–1763* (Chapel Hill: University of North Carolina Press, 1966), 252–53.

12. Griffith, *History of American City Government*, 392, 402.

13. Teaford, *Municipal Revolution in America*, 31.

14. Bonomi, *A Factious People*, 11–12; Richard R. Beeman, *The Varieties of Political Experience in Eighteenth-Century America* (Philadelphia: University of Pennsylvania Press, 2004), 247; Gary Nash, "The Transformation of Urban Politics, 1700–1765," *Journal of American History* 60 (1973): 606–32.

15. Tully, *Forming American Politics*, 357.

16. Dinkin, *Voting in Provincial America*, 98–99; Tully, *Forming American Politics*, 369 (quote); Beeman, *Varieties of Political Experience*, 216 (quote).

17. Tully, *Forming American Politics*, 355; Beeman, *Varieties of Political Experience*, 77 (quote); Nash, *Urban Crucible*, 179 (quote).

18. Tully, *Forming American Politics*, 326–27 (quote), 376 (quote); Nash, *Urban Crucible*, 95–96; Norman S. Cohen, "The Philadelphia Election Riot of 1742," *Pennsylvania Magazine of History and Biography* 92 (1968): 306–19; William T. Parsons, "The Bloody Election of 1742," *Pennsylvania History* 36 (1969): 290–306.

19. Dinkin, *Voting in Provincial America*, 117; Skemp, "A Social and Cultural History of Newport," 370 (quote); Griffith, *History of American City Government*, 393 (quote).

20. Tully, *Forming American Politics*, 327 (quote); Nash, "Transformation of Urban Politics," 610 (quote); Gary Nash, *Quakers and Politics: Pennsylvania, 1681–1726* (Boston: Northeastern University Press, 1968), 260 (quote); Michael Zuckerman, *Peaceable Kingdoms: New England Towns in the Eighteenth Century* (New York: W. W. Norton & Co., 1970), 181 (quote); Skemp, "A Social and Cultural History of Newport," 440; Griffith, *History of American City Government*, 374 (quote).

21. Nash, "Transformation of Urban Politics," 616–20 (quotes); Beeman, *Varieties of Political Experience*, 244 (quote); Benjamin H. Newcomb, *Political Partisanship in the Middle Colonies, 1700–1776* (Baton Rouge: Louisiana State University Press, 1995), 96–97 (quote); Dinkin, *Voting in Provincial America*, 108 (quote).

22. Tully, *Forming American Politics*, 357 (quote); Beeman, *Varieties of American Politics*, 118 (quote); Nash, *Urban Crucible*, 173 (quote).

23. Newcomb, *Political Partisanship*, 83 (quote), 124; Beeman, *Varieties of Political Experience*, 246 (quote).

24. Tully, *Forming American Politics*, 358 (quote), 355 (quotes); Nash, *Urban Crucible*, 166 (quotes).

25. Nash, *Urban Crucible*, 185–88; Beeman, *Varieties of Politics*, 251–59.

26. Nash, *Urban Crucible*, 241–42 (quotes), 244.

27. Newcomb, *Political Partisanship*, 174 (quote).

28. Skemp, "A Social and Cultural History of Newport," 387–88.

29. Keith Krawczynski, *William Henry Drayton: South Carolina Revolutionary Patriot* (Baton Rouge: Louisiana State University Press, 2001), 51–52 (quotes); Hart, *Building Charleston*, 177–84.

30. Benjamin Carp, *Rebels Rising: Cities and the American Revolution* (New York: Oxford University Press, 2007), 5.

3

Family and Community

INTRODUCTION

The family was the most important social institution as it served several critical functions: as the only legal outlet for sexual behavior, the main purpose of which was procreation; as the center of education for children, including their first letters, the basic tenets of their faith, and important life skills; and as a hierarchical model of the larger society that provided the foundation for social stability. "Well-ordered Families," Boston minister Cotton Mather explained, "naturally produce a Good Order in other Societies. When Families are under an Ill Discipline, all other Societies being therefore Ill Disciplined, will feel that error in the First Concoction."[1] A primary function of families therefore was to promote social order and communal harmony. This was paramount for a people living in a strange and hostile environment far from the stabilizing center of European civilization. To prevent the "Creolean Degeneracy" of society, colonists created patriarchal families headed by the husband/father who, at least theoretically, was the unchallenged master in his household. In addition to wife and children, this household often included people who were not related by either blood or marriage, such as apprentices, servants, slaves, and boarders. Extended families (three generations in the same household), on the other hand, were relatively uncommon. Elderly parents might live with an adult child, but such arrangements affected only one child and his family.[2]

Household stability was too important a responsibility to give only to the head of the household. Local governments also played a key role in trying to maintain domestic harmony by imposing family governance on single people, regulating marriage announcements and ceremonies, intervening in cases of domestic discord, controlling the granting of divorces, overseeing the welfare of widows and orphans, and upholding patriarchal customs. Nearly equally intrusive was the church, which at times regulated religious instruction to the family, intervened in cases of family strife, and among some denominations, tried to prevent people from marrying others of different faiths. Additionally, both church and state officials punished individuals engaged in behavior that they believed undermined both family and community harmony. More so than Americans today, colonial Americans believed that society is made up of families, not individuals, and therefore family and social order should supersede individual rights and private life.

Despite such determined efforts by the church and state to maintain family cohesion, the colonial family was particularly unstable. Least stable of all were slave families, whose members might be sold off to satisfy masters' debts, for profit, or for punishment. White families faced somewhat similar disruption as their members were frequently taken away by diseases, accidents, and death at childbirth. These unfortunate consequences often led to the creation of households that included an array of step-parents, step-siblings, and orphaned children. The inherent cruelties of poverty often ruined family stability among the urban poor, while many women married to sailors had an equally difficult time maintaining family cohesion during their husbands' lengthy sojourns at sea. Many other couples simply could not get along, a failure that often resulted in domestic discord. The unwillingness of authorities to grant divorces in all but the most extreme cases of spousal abuse and neglect forced unhappy and truculent couples to remain together, at least in law. Further contributing to the breakdown of family life were prostitution and adultery—both of which were growing problems in the eighteenth-century cities.

To help combat the uncertainties of family life, some urban folk relied on a complex kinship network that included brothers, sisters, cousins, aunts, uncles, and in-laws and that was sometimes further extended by the death of a spouse and remarriage of the remaining partner. Residents of the major cities could also rely on nearby neighbors for help when needed. However, this neighborliness was a double-edged sword. The relatively densely populated cities put severe constraints on individual privacy. Neighbors were everywhere and knew everything. In sum, family and community were inseparable in the colonial cities. Any discussion of one must include the other.

INCENTIVES TO MARRY

Early Americans emphasized the need of all people to marry. Both carrot and stick incentives encouraged most colonists to take the nuptials. On a practical level, marriage was an act of economic necessity, even one of survival in the remote American environment where economic safety nets were nearly nonexistent. The low wages paid to working women made marriage truly an act of self-preservation for the fairer sex. Perhaps the strongest motive for marriage among the Christian colonists was their belief that marriage between man and woman was an act reflecting God's will and his wisdom. When God presented Eve to Adam, he "solemnized the First Marriage," and in doing so, gave his sanction to marriage itself. With such strong theological support for the institution of marriage, young people who refused to marry were perceived as opposing God's will and therefore as a threat to both the religious and social order. To coax single men into marriage, authorities in parts of seventeenth-century New England and the South required bachelors to either live with families or pay a fine for the "selfish luxury of solitary living." When the Massachusetts authorities discovered John Haverill living "in a house by himself . . . whereby he is subject to much sin and iniquity, which ordinarily are the companions of a solitary life," they ordered him to "settle himself in some orderly family . . . and be subject to the orderly rules of family government" or else the sheriff would find him living accommodations in the local "house of correction." Such penalties were not as persuasive as social pressure, however. A young man was not recognized as a "real man" until he married. In 1749 a group of women calling themselves the "Petticoat Club" published a letter in the *Boston Evening Post* that accused "Old Batchelors" of being "in contempt of the Laws both of God and Nature," of "insufferable Stupidity and Obstinacy," and of forcing women to "remain useless, and even burdensome" to society. For these reasons, this female club called for officials to tax bachelors and force them to wear "some publick *Badge of Disgrace.*" Young, single women also faced community reproach. "Old maid," "spinster," and "thornback" were all scornful terms used to describe husbandless women, whom it was believed had no real purpose in life. Moreover, the law prohibited sex outside of marriage, so that young men and women had a stark choice: either marry or remain celibate. Celibacy was a bad choice for women, however, as early Americans believed that women who remained celibate were subject to hysteria and a malady called "green sickness" in which the face turned greenish, the arms and legs swelled, and the patient experienced heart palpitations. The cure for these afflictions was, of course, marriage. Similarly, early Americans believed that marriage would cure men of the harmful symptoms of masturbation—physical emaciation, a pale and lean "visage," a stomach "depraved," and "depauperated Blood fill'd with acid, and acrid Particles."[3]

Despite such pressures to marry, the large port cities abounded with numerous single people: young adults (many of whom were recent transients from the countryside or immigrants from Europe), widows and widowers, hired and bound servants, sailors, and slaves. In mid-eighteenth-century Philadelphia, for example, nearly 20 percent of the city's adult white men were single at any time while an astonishing one-third of adult free women were unmarried. Widows made up many of these single women, but others bravely ignored social custom and community reproach and refused to marry because, as one single woman from Philadelphia put it, "Everyone is not fitted for the single life—nor was I ever moulded for the wedded one." Many other young women hesitated to marry, daunted by the overwhelming responsibility of managing a household and raising children, and fearful of death resulting from childbirth. The relatively large percentage of single people in the cities forced a growing tolerance of unmarried life that would later become one of the hallmarks of modern American society.[4]

COURTSHIP

Couples desiring marriage had to follow several customary steps: courtship, a contract showing an intent to marry, a public announcement of the contract (publishing the banns), the marriage ceremony, a celebration following the nuptials, and a physical consummation of the marriage. The courtship itself was often a quick, matter-of-fact affair that involved no clear rituals, calling hours, or prescribed activities. Among the well-to-do in Charles Town, young people met at barbecues, dances, and by the early eighteenth century, elaborate balls. Young folk in Boston, on the other hand, participated in hormone-charged and alcohol-fueled "frolicks." "Every Room, kitchen, Chamber was crowded with People," wrote a young John Adams in describing a frolick he attended in 1760. "Negroes with a fiddle. Young Fellows and Girls dancing in the Chamber as if they would kick the floor thro…Fiddling and dancing, in a Chamber full of young fellows and Girls, a wilde rab[b]le of both sexes, and all Ages, in the lower Room, singing and dancing, fiddling, drinking flip and Toddy, and drams."[5] Unmarried men and women also gathered in taverns to drink, engage in flirtatious banter, and if they had consumed enough alcohol, play risqué games like "grading the beef," a sexually charged gropefest where men would place their hands on certain parts of a woman's body to guess her measurements. A woman's breasts received special attention from men as female fashion at the time created an eye-popping décolletage. Still, a single woman had to play the "demure damsel" in attracting a mate. To behave otherwise would tarnish her femininity and her ability to find a respectable husband.

While single women played a safe waiting game in early courtship, courting men were in a no-win situation. To prove their manhood, they had to take the initiative in courtship and win a woman or else face public mockery that included charges of "dronish effeminacy." Even if a man won over a woman, society still viewed him as effeminate and unmanly—a spark, a beau, and a gallant—for devoting too much attention to his dress, comportment, and social etiquette during the courtship. Even more publicly humiliating was rejection, or getting "bagged," as colonials put it. Future president John Adams grew quite worried when he learned that relatives and neighbors were talking about his courtship of Hannah Quincy. "[T]he Story has spread so wide, no, that, if I don't marry her, she will be said to have Jockied me, or I have Jockied her, and says the Girl shall not suffer. A story she [will] spread that she repelled me." Meanwhile, courting Quaker men faced further community reproach if they "go from one Woman to another" because such behavior, explained the 1694 Philadelphia Monthly Meeting, "make more like Sodom than Saints."[6]

Preferred Traits

In courting the opposite sex, seventeenth-century colonial men belonging to the upper and aspiring middle class were warned against pursuing beautiful women and instead to choose for a wife someone who was "virtuous, sensible, good-natured, complaisant, neat, and cheerful in disposition, of good size, well proportioned, free from hereditary disorders, and of the same social rank and religion as he." These priorities began to change during the next century when men began to search for women with beauty, intelligence, and wealth. "Looks Tolerably well," wrote Ebenezer Baldwin in describing one woman he had his eyes on, while another he curtly dismissed as being "tall & gracefully shaped in Body—but not very handsome in the face." Still, men like the Quaker John Smith of Philadelphia recognized that "a fair outside did not Constitute happiness." Almost certain to bring happiness to a groom was a large dowry from the bride-to-be. The *South Carolina Gazette* emphasized in its November 6, 1749, issue that the bride Susannah Seabrook of Charles Town was not only "endowed with all agreeable Accomplishments" but also brought "a fortune of £15,000." Upper-class families were especially noted for pursuing mercenary marriages to both increase and consolidate their wealth and status. Rarely did they condone marriages of their sons and daughters to someone belonging to a lower class. Studies of colonial New York City and Charles Town, for example, reveal that middling artisans and upper-class merchants in these two cities were socially distinct groups with very little intermarriage between them.[7]

Close-Kin Marriages

Some leading urban families engaged in close-kin marriages to augment their wealth and form a tight-knit, homogenous group to better establish a hegemonic upper class. This is especially true among the Bostonian merchant class and the planter/merchant aristocracy of low-country South Carolina. In the Puritan capital, merchant families integrated themselves over time through cousin marriages to consolidate their wealth, thereby enabling them to adjust to the emerging modern corporate economy that required massive infusion of capital. Through such savvy yet incestuous marriages, a relatively few merchant families emerged as the dominant class in nineteenth-century Boston. For similar reasons, elites living in and around Charles Town preferred marrying their relatives, with cousins marrying cousins, uncles wedding nieces, nephews marrying aunts, and step-brothers and step-sisters taking the nuptials together. By doing so, Charles Town elites created an exclusive society virtually impregnable by their social inferiors. Somewhat similarly, wealthy Philadelphians married one another in a dynastic pattern that forged multiple kinship connections among a fairly small coterie of families. Such an interconnected set of family trees helped affluent families to combine their economic assets while defining membership boundaries into the elite rank. Marriage for the upper class was therefore an important part of the larger process of elite formation.[8]

Interethnic Marriages

Still, the ethnic pluralism of the cities contributed to many marriages of people from different ethnicities and faiths. Joyce Goodfriend's study of colonial New York City, for instance, suggests that many interethnic marriages occurred more because of a lack of opportunity to marry within their own group than a desire to marry outside it. This explains why over 60 percent of Englishmen in the New York capital in the late 1600s married women of non-English origins. On the other hand, New York City Quakers, who were subject to considerable harassment for their pacifist beliefs, waged a defensive campaign by marrying almost exclusively within their group to safeguard their marginal position in society. Likewise, historian Thomas Archdeacon found that French New Yorkers married primarily within their own group, as did over three-fourths of Dutch men and women as late as the 1730s. However, as families of English descent gained greater economic and political control of the city during the eighteenth century, some Dutch fathers sought to preserve their families' status by marrying their children to up-and-coming English families. The Dutch baker Jacob DeKey, for example, was particularly fortunate in marrying four of his five children to affluent families of English descent.[9]

Parental Consent

For these reasons, among others, custom required children to receive parental consent to a match. This was especially true among the middle and upper classes, who viewed marriage in pecuniary terms and who had considerable leverage over their children with inheritances and dowries. Nicholas Anthony of New York City found this out the hard way in 1685 when his father willed him only 1 shilling for behaving "disobedient to me, in his marriage with Angie, his now wife." Authorities in seventeenth-century Boston and New Amsterdam added further economic penalties by imposing fines and imprisonment for disregarding this custom. With such strong monetary incentives, a man interested in a girl first had to request permission from her father. Judge Samuel Sewall of Boston noted this custom in a December 7, 1719, journal entry that reads: "Mr. Cooper asks my consent for Judith's Company; which I freely grant him." On the other hand, when a middle-aged fortune-hunting Frenchman paid unauthorized visits to the daughter of Charles Town merchant Henry Laurens, the latter lambasted the foreigner's conduct as a "species of dishonourable fraud."[10]

Seduction

Parents believed that they had good reason to have some say in their children's marriage choices. Popular belief held that children were the possession of their parents. Children who unilaterally gave themselves away therefore committed a "kind of theft." More importantly, parents recognized that love-struck youngsters might not be able to make rational decisions in choosing a mate. Of particular concern to them were predatory men who used "Nonsense gilded with a little humour" and a "Dose of Poisoning flattery" to woo unsuspecting young maidens, often under false pretenses of marriage.[11] A 1774 almanac garnered more than a few chuckles at the expense of abandoned women when it printed the following poem:

> Says Dolly, "Me, Thomas, you promised to wed,
> And I, silly girl, believed all that you said."
> "That I promised to wed you, and love you, 'tis true,
> But I've tried you, my Doll, and I find you won't do."[12]

Authorities took a more serious attitude toward such conduct by criminalizing seduction as a lesser form of rape and a breach of promise. A judge in Philadelphia, for example, fined one young Casanova the hefty sum of £80 for seducing a woman with "fair promises of marriage" so that he could simply have "carnal Knowledge of her body." Yet the "fairer sex" could be just as deceptive in courtship, at least according to the Virginian William Byrd, who argued that women, through skillful use of the "arts of dress and disguise . . . drugged and duped" men looking for an "idealized female body" into "unsatisfactory marriages" that only afterwards encouraged infidelity. Even Benjamin Franklin's *Poor Richard* asserted that "Three things are men most liable to be cheated in: A horse, a wig, and a wife."[13]

Lower Classes

While more well-to-do youngsters had to seek parental approval in choosing a mate, lower-class youth in the main cities pursued the opposite sex with no such restrictions. Many laboring men, with little or no inheritance to give, could not exercise much economic leverage over their children. Moreover, many parents were either dead or lived far away. Many urban youths therefore had considerable freedom in their sexual behavior and selection of marriage partners. When one Philadelphia minister refused to marry a man who lacked his mother's consent, the man replied angrily that "he was his own master and could, if chose, kill himself tomorrow." Parental consent for marriage waned over the course of the eighteenth century for young couples of all classes as more liberal attitudes in rearing children allowed for greater independence in selecting a mate. One father calmly accepted these changes by explaining that "all marriages [ought] to be entirely from the choice of each party." When John Smith of Philadelphia called on the parents of Hannah Logan to declare his feelings for her, they "referr[ed] me entirely to their daughter," he later wrote. In essence, Hannah's parents had reversed the courting custom, as Smith discovered. "[T]he old Gentleman told me that if I was her choice, he would give consent &c." However, this increased freedom in selecting a mate went only so far, especially among the upper crust, who "subtly influenced each other's courtship decisions in ways that kept them marrying within a fairly tight social cohort," explains historian Sarah Fatherly. Wealthy Philadelphians, for example, kept abreast of the courtships in their ranks by maintaining "a constant stream of gossip about what matches were—or might be—in the works and offered social judgments of those matches." In doing so, they put social pressure on courting couples as they made their decisions about whom to marry. A wrong choice in marriage partner could result in social ostracism, as Harriet Hill of Philadelphia found out when, after marrying a man of lower social rank, she did not "receive one line" from her friends.[14]

Courting Customs

Once gaining parental approval, young couples began the official courtship that, like today, was a recreational activity. Single men and women took walks together in the streets, commons, and parks; enjoyed picnics in the countryside; took boat rides in nearby rivers and ponds in summer; ice skated and rode sleighs in winter; and simply enjoyed each other's company at mixed dances, parties, and romantic taverns. Like today, courting couples were chastised by parents for staying out too late. John Cresson of Philadelphia was admonished by his father for sitting up with his "precious Molly" until 1:00 AM, which prompted the young Quaker to complain that there should be greater allowance made for "the Ardour of Youthful Affection." These "youthful affections" often led to racy language and behavior with the opposite sex. One New England woman, for example, told her beau that he made her heart leap, to which he replied that "she made his heart leap in his britches." While visiting New York City in 1744, the straightlaced and single Dr. Alexander Hamilton observed that women there were "extraordinarily forward," telling the young physician that they would "like to be his patient."[15]

Bundling and Premarital Sex

Increasing the temptation for sexual relations between courting couples in New England was the practice of bundling, a quaint custom allowing couples in advanced stages of courtship to bundle underneath the covers together in the same bed, albeit fully clothed, with a bundling board between them and sometimes "bundling stock" tied tightly around the woman's legs. Despite such restrictions, hormone-crazed couples found ways to satisfy their lusts. One foreigner visiting New England observed that "I have entered several bedchambers where I have found bundling couples, who are not disturbed and continue to give each other all the honest tokens of their love."[16]

Such honest tokens of love before marriage were illegal, and transgressors were punished with public humiliation, whippings, and fines. The numerous cases of premarital pregnancies in early America show that young couples were willing to take such risks to satisfy their cravings. By the mid-1700s, as many as one-third of all brides went to the altar pregnant. For those men who tried to "play the rake," social and legal controls compelled them to "play the man" and marry the woman. Still, some men tried to play the rake by contesting bastardy claims by women. Geleyn Verplank of New Amsterdam, for example, denied paternity by denying conception. Geleyn admitted to intercourse with his lover, "but I minded my pullbacks," he claimed. "I sware I did not get it." Despite his denials, the court ordered him to pay the lying-in charges and child support.[17]

Love and Marriage

During much of the colonial period, love was not considered necessary before marriage. Selecting a mate was too important to leave to irrational romantic feelings. Instead, young couples should enter marriage based upon rational considerations of property, religious piety, and family interest. Still, nearly all recognized that mutual love was necessary for marital bliss but that such affection would develop *after* marriage. However, by the 1720s romantic courtship began to replace the emotionless, business-like affair of marriage. Prompting this reassessment of love and marriage were enlightened ideals that emphasized individual happiness and a growing belief that virtuous behavior derived directly from feelings. Most important in bringing happiness to married life was love, for as a 1733 article on marriage in the *New England Weekly Journal* told readers, "Marriage enlarges the Scene of our Happiness and miseries. A Marriage of Love is *pleasant*; a Marriage of interest, *easy*; and a Marriage where both meet, *happy*." Most serious in attaching love to marriage were Quakers, who followed the advice of their leader William Penn to "Never marry but for Love." Jane Hent was not alone among female Friends who backed out of marriage to her fiancé at the last minute because "she could not love him well enough to be her husband."[18]

The Contract

In love or not, a couple desiring marriage had to enter into a contract similar to our engagement. This was considered a legal arrangement that was difficult to break. In 1654, a New Amsterdam woman asked the local court to disallow the engagement to her fiancé because of "certain misbehavior" by him. The judge refused her request, stating that "the promise of marriage having been made and given before the Eyes of God, shall remain in force." The courts also looked askance at men who contracted with two women at the same time, sentencing one Massachusetts polygamist to pay a £5 fine and to receive a severe whipping. Giving the contract such legal importance were the financial arrangements made between the two families. Among the gentry, in particular, the marriage contract took on the tone of a modern corporate merger. Many upper-class parents also required prenuptial "marriage settlements" that placed their daughter's inheritance in the care of third-party trustees to prevent potentially profligate husbands from "intermeddling" with their wives' estates in any way. Once the couple signed the contract, they were considered married, although this did not give them license to have sex until after the wedding ceremony. Dutch couples usually exchanged a ring or two halves of a broken coin after signing the engagement contract, which some did in their own blood.[19]

Publication of the Banns

A final step toward marriage in New England and New Amsterdam was the publication of the bann, an act intended to subvert young couples trying to get married without parental approval. To that end the law required couples to post their announcement on three consecutive church services or leave it on the meetinghouse door for two weeks. Once done, the promise of marriage was legal in the eyes of the courts, which viewed any violation of it as a punishable offense. One New Amsterdam man probably wished he had never reneged on his promise of marriage, a violation that earned him a court-imposed head shaving, a severe flogging, an ear boring, and a two-year sentence of hard labor alongside slaves.[20]

Marriage Ceremony

The actual marriage ceremony differed according to religions and regions, but a few things pertained to all. The high cost of clothing prevented couples from wearing special wedding attire, except in the most well-to-do families. Most others simply wore their best clothing they already owned. Brides did not always wear white, and if they did, it was not a symbol of virginal purity. The marriage ceremony itself was, in the words of historian Dale Taylor, "merely a symbolic rite of passage into a period of acknowledged sexual activity, with a few religious overtones." Just as symbolic was the wife trading her father's surname for her husband's, giving him the right to "govern, direct, protect, and cherish" her.[21]

Among Puritans, who did not recognize marriage as a holy sacrament, the ritual was a simple, sedate, and solemn affair performed by a magistrate. As a secular act, the wedding ceremony usually took place in the house of the bride, at least until 1686 when England established royal government throughout New England, thereby allowing ministers to perform marriage ceremonies in the meetinghouse. The ceremony itself lacked the exchanged vows of today and instead involved informal, spontaneous remarks about marriage made by the guests and a stock sermon by the minister on the duties and obligation of husbands and wives. Puritan couples rarely exchanged rings.

Colonial Wedding. Artist Frederick Dielman's 1898 rendition of the marriage between Dr. Frances LeBaron and Mary Wilder of Plymouth in 1695. (Library of Congress, Prints and Photographs Division, Reproduction # LC USZ62-12716)

Anglican weddings in Charles Town took place almost exclusively in the home, a symbolic testimony to lay control over religious affairs. Their marriages followed a set pattern outlined in the Book of Common Prayer whereby the priest began by instructing the bride and groom to raise their children "in fear and nurture of the Lord," to "avoid fornication," and to promise to "have of the other, both in prosperity and adversity." This was followed by stock vows by the man to love, comfort, and honor his wife, while the woman vowed to obey, serve, love, and honor her husband. The exchange of rings solemnized the vows, followed by the priest's prayerful request for God to bless the marriage. Some couples took holy communion before exiting the church.

The Dutch wedding was a church ceremony that began with the reading of parts of the epistles of Saint Paul, with psalm singing between the lessons. The bridal party entered the church with the bride and groom escorted by their parents, if living. The minister then read the formulas of marriage, took the oath, and ordered the singing of a psalm. After taking up a collection for the poor, the newlyweds led a procession to the bride's home, the pathway sometimes covered with flowers or palms.[22]

The Quaker marriage ceremony took place in the meeting house and differed little from the Quaker worship with the exception of the couple breaking the traditional silence by standing up and exchanging egalitarian "promises" to "be faithful and loving" towards each other "until death should separate them." No clergy presided to marry the bride and groom as the Quakers believed that they were married directly by God. Following this brief, matter-of-fact ceremony, the bride and groom signed the wedding certificate.[23]

Wedding Celebration

Newlyweds of all faiths often topped their wedding day with a boisterous and lavish public reception filled with merriment sometimes lasting all weekend. The reception usually began innocently enough with a bountiful feast followed by the giving of presents. The drinking of numerous toasts to the couple's health and happiness undoubtedly relaxed tensions between the two families and intensified the dancing, music, singing, foot races, and the firing of arrows and guns that were a common part of the festivities. "Wooing the widow," a game similar to "spin the bottle," was popular among young single folk, who found wedding receptions a grand opportunity to meet potential mates. Less ribald were the customary pranks of cutting the reins to the groom's horse or bobbing his horse's tail. A stock joke of nearly all receptions involved the groom pretending to run away, only to be caught and "dragged back to duty" by the other men. Sometimes these same men would "steal the bride" in the middle of the reception and take her to a nearby tavern for a second party. All of this drunken revelry was too much for some newlyweds, who would surreptitiously seek sanctuary in the home of a friend or relative. If caught, guests would surround the house holding shovels, tongs, and other metal items they used to clang together until the couple appeared. Unlike today, colonial newlyweds did not enjoy the tradition of a formal honeymoon.[24]

MARRIED LIFE

Patriarchy

Early Americans believed a stable family was critical towards creating a stable society. The foundation for this stability was the patriarch, the father-husband-master who legally, if not in reality, held absolute authority in his home. Cotton Mather even insisted that his wife address him as "My Lord." Like a king and his subjects, the patriarch and his family had reciprocal obligations. The patriarch was responsible for the physical, moral, and spiritual needs of those in his household, who in exchange were expected to subject themselves to his will. This relationship made practical sense, at least to men who believed that they held greater capacity for reason and self-control than overly emotional and irrational women. An even more powerful justification for patriarchy was the Biblical injunction found in Ephesians 5:22 that commanded, "Wives, submit yourselves unto your own husbands, as unto the Lord." Women who did not follow this providential directive might be written out of their husband's will, like the wife of a Philadelphia laborer who received from her deceased husband the insulting sum of "one English Half Crown" because of her "Loose & Scandalous behavior."[25]

Harmony

Responsibility for marital harmony fell heavy on the "fair sex," who were instructed by books on the "Rules for the Advancement of Matrimonial Felicity" to never dispute with their husband "whatever be the Occasion . . . and if any Altercations or Jars happen, don't separate the bed, whereby the Animosity will cease . . . by no Means disclose his imperfections, or let the most intimate Friend know your Grievances . . . Read often the Matrimonial Service, and over look not the important word OBEY." To what extent colonial women followed such advice is unknown. What is known is that early Americans like Samuel Sewall recognized that both sexes had to "take care to govern their Passion" in order to maintain the "tranquility and Good Order of Families." This included, among other things, that husbands and wives not "needlessly expose each others failings," wrote the Bostonian Benjamin Wadsworth in his 1712 book *The Well Ordered Family,* but instead to "cover them with a mantle of love." Among Puritans, at least, this "mantle of love" between husband and wife was not to become too passionate, "lest it overshadow a person's love for God and disorder his or her mental balance," explains historian Anne Lombard.[26]

Evidence from letters and wills shows that many couples were madly in love with each other. One Massachusetts husband serving in the Continental Army wrote his wife that "these cold Nights I am Sensible of the want of a Bed fellow, I know not how long it will be before I enjoy the satisfaction of having you by my side." John Winthrop began letters to his wife with "My Love, my Joy, My

Faithful One," and labeled her "dear heart," "my Most Sweet Heart," and "My Sweet Wife" who was "more dear to me than all earthly things." Much of this love was based on friendship and respect. The Connecticut jurist Tapping Reeve wrote to his "lovely Sally" about his "Pleasure of reflecting that I have one friend in you that will be ever an unshaken friend," while Selleck Silliman, also of Connecticut, frequently consulted his "best friend" about decisions great and small. "What shall I do My Dearest?" he asked his wife about possibly leaving public office, "I wish I had your Advice,—I am at a great loss how to conduct." The love and respect husbands had for their wives is reflected in wills in which the testator made careful provision for his "beloved wife." John Rutledge of Charles Town explained that because of his wife's "good under-standing" and tenderness to his seven young children, he was leav-ing her his entire estate with the right to use or dispose of it according to her discretion. When wives died first, their husbands often felt a deep and irreplaceable loss. The Charles Town merchant Henry Laurens was overwhelmed at the death of his "bosom friend," whom he praised as "ever loving, cherishing and ready to obey—who never once, no, not once, during the course of twenty years' most intimate connection threw the stumbling block of opposition."[27]

Discord

But as long as men and women have lived together, there have been unhappy, loveless, and strife-torn marriages. The colonial period was anything but a golden age of family relations, and both religious and secular leaders disciplined husbands and wives for behavior destructive to the family and therefore disruptive to society. The First Church of Boston, for instance, excommunicated Mary Wharton for "reviling her husband and striking him and other vile and wicked Courses." Church leaders also showed no mercy on Mercy Verin by excommunicating her for "uncivil Carriage with Samuel Smith and bad Language to her husband." Meanwhile, judges punished men like John McElwee of Philadelphia for pushing and threatening his wife for her purchase of an expensive shawl sim-ply because "a neighbor had one." Other men married to prodigal and nagging women also felt that their wives provoked them towards violence. Jacob Eliot of Connecticut used his fists in defend-ing himself against his wife Ann, whom he said would fly into "pro-digious Rages" over such trifling things as being teased for "letting

[out] a rousing Fart." The courts sometimes sided with men who struck their spouses, as in the case of a Boston man who received a fine for hitting and kicking his wife but had his sentence reduced when the judge learned that his wife was a woman "of great provocation."[28]

As today, low wages and the constant struggle to make ends meet provoked considerable marital strife among the laboring poor, whose marriages suffered from wide-scale violence, adultery, desertion, and divorce. Contributing to domestic discord among the lower sort was a financial power struggle between husband and wife, both of whom contributed to the family economy in order to survive. Spirited arguments over how money would be budgeted and spent all too often led to domestic violence. Philadelphia shoemakers Joseph Cressman and John Young, tailor John Cline, and laborer Charles Curry were all charged with "wife beating." Michael Digney, also from the Quaker capital, "beat his wife and young child insomuch that the Neighbors were apprehensive that murder might ensue," while John Clendenin treated his wife Elizabeth "with the most inhuman violence" that included strangling her, punching and kicking her, hitting her with a hammer, and horse whipping her back and face, among other "barbarous and brutal usage." The notorious abuse of alcohol by despondent poor and laboring men also contributed to domestic violence. Jane Houston of Philadelphia, for example, complained to the court that her husband frequented "tavern & Lewd houses, & frequently returns home intoxicated with strong liquor & beats and abuses your libellant." Court records reveal that women often times did not passively accept such abuse but instead fought their violent husbands by hitting them with rocks, hammers, knives, bottles, pots, oven mops, and flaming pine torches and scratching, hitting, and kicking them while slashing them with their "cutting tongues."[29]

Sexual infidelity was the cause of much marital discord among both rich and poor. Two Boston wives certainly caused some domestic fireworks when their husbands found them in a tavern "sitting in other men's laps with their arms about their necks." Women married to sailors had a notorious reputation for infidelity while their husbands were at sea. Mariner John Groggin of Philadelphia, for example, unsuccessfully petitioned for divorce from his wife who, while her husband was away, ran him into debt, developed an "extravagant fondness for strong liquors," and became a "Prostitute for Negroes" that resulted in the birth of a mulatto child. While her husband was at sea, Mary Banes of Philadelphia openly lived with merchant Richard Duffield. Neighbors testified that they had often seen the two lovers together in bed where they "acted towards each other as man and wife." Many married men were also caught in sexually illicit acts with neighbors, servants, slaves, prostitutes, and sometimes with their own children. An enraged New Amsterdam wife stormed into her husband's favorite watering hole to find him "with another man's wife," she later told the court. When Adam Air of Massachusetts was caught by neighbors having sex with another woman while "he had a Wife at home," he unashamedly responded by telling them that "one woman was as good to him as another." Even more disturbing is the case of a New England mother of 10 who filed for divorce because her husband was "courting" their eldest daughter. Another wife took her husband to court on charges that he sexually violated their 14-year-old daughter. On occasion, mothers encouraged the sexual molestation of their children, as when a New England woman forced her daughter to go to bed with her stepfather who "had his will of me," the young girl told the court, "whilst my mother held me by the hand."[30]

Perhaps most exploitive in their sexual pursuits were well-to-do planters like William Byrd of Virginia, who used sex to demonstrate his entitlement to and power over all women, including his wife, whom he regularly and "powerfully flourished" not just in bed but also on the couch, in the library, and on the pool table. Even when his wife was "much indisposed" from pregnancy, Byrd felt entitled to have his way with her, an act in which he admitted "she took but little pleasure." The lusty planter also sexually molested female servants and slaves, sometimes taking them by force. Byrd blamed his extramarital affairs on the institution of marriage, which he described as a "galling yoke" and a "troublesome sea." Undoubtedly Byrd's sexual misconduct contributed to the "troublesome" nature of his marriage.[31]

Sexual Intercourse

Early Americans considered sexual intercourse, as long as it was between husband and wife, as critical for domestic harmony. Sex was a duty a married couple owed each other not just for procreation but also for pleasure. Even Puritans believed that sex was part of human nature and that denial of sexual intercourse by either husband or wife "Denies all relief in Wedlocke unto Human necessity," wrote Cotton Mather. Additionally, both scientific and popular belief held that the female womb needed "refreshment" by regular orgasms in order to be healthy enough to carry a baby. Too much sex, on the other hand, would satiate the womb and render it "unfit for its office." For men, "semen discharged too lavishly," warned a physician writing in the *Boston Evening Post* in 1770, would cause "weariness, indisposition to motion, convulsions, leanness, dryness, heats and pains in the membranes of the brain, with a dullness of the senses, especially of the sight . . . foolishness, and disorders of the like kind." Sexual pleasure and procreation were considered so important to the institution of marriage that failure to perform one's "conjugal fellowship" was grounds for divorce and excommunication. Women were also thought to need regular sex or risk "going a little crazy." In 1744, a Boston wife petitioned for divorce from her husband because of his impotency, a condition that she claimed left her "in a very infirm low state of health." Similarly, a New England woman successfully gained a divorce when a local physician examined her husband's "Parts of Generation" and testified in court that they were "utterly incapable of procreation." Less successful was Mary Holten of Boston, who sought the impotency route for divorce by giving her husband something she hoped would make his penis "shrinke up."[32]

More seriously, the inability to father a child could be devastating to a man as it was a sign of sexual failure and thus a failure in manliness. Some men were so desperate to increase their virility that they consumed nauseating "remedies" that included the testicles of various animals, the eggs of game birds, boiled turnips and parsnips, all mixed with various herbs and spices. One Massachusetts husband was so distraught at his failure to become a father that he beat his wife to death and then hanged himself. Some husbands simply avoided sex with their wives and instead satisfied their sexual cravings with other women, behavior that carried numerous risks. One philandering Philadelphia husband had a justifiable reason for not performing his conjugal duties when he discovered that he had contracted a venereal disease. "Must keep away from my Wife," he admitted.[33]

PREGNANCY AND CHILDBIRTH

Fecundity

Besides the inherent enjoyment involved, the primary objective of sexual intercourse was procreation, which most early Americans believed to be a scriptural command to replenish the Earth. In fulfilling this command, pregnant women gained considerable importance and were met with smiles by relatives, friends, and neighbors. Barren women, on the other hand, faced silent scorn and pity from those around her and suspicion that she had either "unmanned" her husband or that God was punishing her for some secret sin. Children, therefore, were the key to a woman's happiness as they both justified and sanctified her existence. For men, having children demonstrated their virility and masculinity. On a more practical level, couples "multiplied" to fill a labor need and to provide insurance against old age. With nearly 50 percent of children dying before reaching adulthood, couples doubtless applied the adage "safety in numbers" in their family planning. Financial security, too, played a part in family size. In Philadelphia, at least, the gentry class averaged 7.5 children, compared to 6.0 children among merchants and artisans and 5.0 children for mechanics and laborers. Such relatively high birth rates prompted one southern man to observe in 1772, "I do believe women have nothing in the general view but the breeding contests of home. It began with poor Eve and ever since then has been so much of the devil in woman."[34]

Contraceptives and Abortions

To determine if a woman was afflicted with "Eve's curse," colonists had "pregnancy tests" that were based more on folklore than on science. One test required a woman to urinate on seed corn or some other seeds, and if the seeds sprouted, she was pregnant. Another test involved leaving a woman's urine to sit in a bottle for a few days. If the woman was pregnant, contemporaries believed that tiny animals would spontaneously grow from her urine. In the end, the only way to confirm a pregnancy definitely was the presence of fetal movement. To lessen the frequency of "Eve's curse," colonial women turned to a number of contraceptive methods. The city's many apothecary shops allowed urban women access to contraceptive concoctions like Hooper's Female Pills, juniper, pennyroyal, madder, and Seneca snakeroot that were often made into a tea to ensure the onset of the menstrual cycle. Other contraceptive practices included douching, inserting into the vagina a sponge soaked in spermicidal fluid, having sex on an inclined plane, and practicing coitus interruptus. One child-craving wife took her husband to court for practicing the "abominable sin of Onan" [withdrawal] because "he feared the charge of children."

"Gut condoms," known as "armor," were not a well-known option for men at the time.[35]

The failure rate of these contraceptive methods was high, leading to unwanted pregnancies and desperate measures by women to abort their unborn babies. England's antiabortion law of 1623, rarely enforced in the colonies, discouraged few women from practicing the few abortive methods available to them—taking hot baths, delivering sharp blows to the abdomen, engaging in violent exercise, and ingesting "Potions of Physic" that included the herb savin, a well-known supposed abortifacient. A measure of last resort was poking sharp instruments into the uterus. Only when a pregnant woman's life was in danger would a physician perform an abortion. Such was the case in 1750 when a Philadelphia woman in her first trimester complained of "violent pain in my Back and Bowells." A physician determined that only a rapid delivery would save her life. Not long after receiving the enema that induced the abortion, "the Child came from in the After Birth," the mother later wrote, "all together and with very Little Pain."[36]

Dangers of Child Birth

Fear of dying in childbirth undoubtedly prompted some women to abort their pregnancies. With approximately one birth in 30 resulting in the death of the mother, such fears were warranted and largely explain why many were less than enthusiastic about becoming pregnant. Husbands also feared childbirth as they faced widowhood every time their wives gave birth. Even if a woman survived childbirth, she might still suffer a lifetime of miseries resulting from torn bladders, vaginas, and rectums, all conditions that were irreparable until the mid-nineteenth century. Molly Drinker of Philadelphia, for example, suffered a rectovaginal tear while giving birth, an injury that left her incontinent of feces and "not fit to be around other people." Her mother Elizabeth was left an invalid following the difficult delivery of her ninth child. Many other women who survived numerous pregnancies and births complained of being physically drained by the end of their reproductive years. Despite their fears of death and dangers surrounding the "dreaded aberration" of childbirth, women generally accepted their "natural calling" as childbearers.[37]

Infant and Child Mortality

Sadly, many mothers gave their lives during childbirth only for those children to die soon. Between 10 and 30 percent of colonial children died before their first birthday, depending on time, place, and epidemics. At least 40 percent of children did not reach the age of six. Hannah and Samuel Sewall of Boston had 14 children, half of whom died before the age of two. All too common was the experience of William Allison and his wife, who "brought me a fine Boy," he wrote, "but poor fellow he stayed only 26 days with us, and made an Exchange much for the better." Measles, diphtheria, whooping cough, mumps, chicken pox, and dysentery took the lives of many children. The Reverend Cotton Mather of Boston observed in 1659 that a diphtheria epidemic "removed many children" from the city. Colonists also listed teething as a cause of death in some infants, which explains why many children wore necklaces of red coral beads that parents believed aided in teething and warding off disease. Accidents both inside and outside the home also killed many youngsters. Tragically, unattended children stumbled into open fires, fell into privy holes and open wells, tumbled into kettles of hot water, ingested poisons and pins, or were crushed by heavy grindstones, trampled and kicked by horses, or bitten by snakes and rabid dogs. From such evidence, colonial parents evidently did not regard rearing and watching children as a top priority. Instead, they delegated such responsibilities to older children, servants, and slaves while they engaged in more pressing domestic and occupational concerns.[38]

This casual child rearing did not mean that parents suffered any less when an infant or child died. Indeed, the high infant mortality rate only increased anxiety among parents over the fragility of their young ones. Samuel Sewall had nightmares in which all of his surviving offspring had died but one. Cotton Mather lived in "Continual Apprehension" that his son Samuel "will dy in its Infancy," which is what eventually happened. Colonial parents devoted enormous time, energy, and emotion in caring for sick infants and children, often praying to God to save their little ones. In her diary, Elizabeth Drinker of Philadelphia described her vigilance over her youngest child Charles, who became "oppres'd with phlegm," prompting the doctor to administer a purgative. This "did not work," she sadly wrote, "and in little more than 20 minits from the time he took it, he expired aged 2 years 7 months and one day ... thus I was suddenly deprived of my dear little Companion over whome, I had almost constantly watch'd from the time of his birth, and his late thriving state seem'd to promise a [reward] to all my pains." Clergymen did their best to console the grieving parents by telling them that their child was in heaven and that in the end, "We are to Bless God even when he takes away." Despite such consolations, the loss of a child ran deep and long in a family. Parents often named newborn children after those who preceded it in death, while surviving children named their offspring after their deceased siblings.[39]

Longings

A more positive consequence of pregnancy was the superstitious belief that a pregnant woman might miscarry if denied what she longed for. At the very least, such longings left ungratified would scar the unborn child's body in the shape and color of the figure the mother longed for. Most common longings were for special foods, often out-of-season fruits. Dirt, clay, and chalk were less common cravings but popular enough that medical manuals proposed beans boiled with sugar as a more healthy and palatable substitute. Some materialistic women took advantage of the superstition of longing to obtain new furniture and clothes. Husbands often gave in to these cravings in the hopes that doing so would ameliorate the "hysterick fits" and "sad apprehensions" that afflicted their wives while "breeding."[40]

Pregnancy

The term "breeding" that early Americans applied to pregnant women implies an animalistic condition that, at the very least, suggests that pregnancy lacked much special consideration. For example, no specially designed maternity clothing was available to pregnant women, who were also expected to perform their normal work routine until shortly before delivery. For a safe pregnancy, midwives and doctors simply advised women to avoid horseback riding, riding in shaky coaches, lifting great weights, wearing a corset, consuming "strong drink," and sex in the first two trimesters. Many couples ignored the last bit of advice, although some women "with child" cautioned their husbands to "use them gently." Remaining calm and sober during pregnancy was also important to those who believed that a mother can impress her child through sudden frights and strong passions. A hare jumping quickly in front of a woman would cause a harelip, it was feared, while lascivious feelings might cause depravity in the child. Superstition also drove some pregnant women to wear minerals and gems in the belief that they would hold a child in the womb, while removing the stones late in pregnancy would hurry labor. In the last days of pregnancy, desperate women seeking a quick and easy birth rubbed their abdomens with oil of lilies or capon's grease; some even drank a nauseating concoction that included a pint of milk mixed with beaver testicles, basil, dittany, powdered hair from a virgin, and dried ant eggs.[41]

Labor and Birth

The first stage of labor incited a rush of activity for both mother and husband who behaved anything but like rugged individualists in delivering their child. While an expecting mother set out refreshments like "groaning beer" and "groaning cakes" for her attendants, her husband summoned the midwife, attendants, and gathered supplies. Thereafter, men stayed out of the way—usually in the kitchen, hallway, or a separate bedroom. While husbands anxiously waited nearby, numerous female friends and relatives crowded the birthing room, where they tried to ease the anxiety of the mother-to-be with reassurances and bawdy jokes. Meanwhile, a few attendants performed much of the necessary drudgery: brewing tea, bringing cakes, emptying chamber pots, and changing the linen. When the time came for delivery, the expectant mother downed a sweet and spicy alcoholic beverage called "caudle." Sufficiently fortified, she leaned against some of her attendants as she squatted on the low, open-seated midwife's stool or knelt on a pallet. Few colonial women delivered children while lying in bed. As the woman pushed, the midwife applied lubricants such as butter or hog's fat to her hands and the mother's vagina and perineum to facilitate stretching during labor. If labor progressed slowly, the midwife might administer herbal medicines that could stimulate uterine contractions or employ less effective folk remedies such as applying a magnet or horseshoe to the genitals to draw out the child. Breech births were most dangerous and required the midwife to reach into the womb and turn the baby before pulling it out. In one breech case, the baby "sucked my fingers" wrote the midwife, which "concern'd me, fearing it impossible for the poor Infant to be born alive." If circumstances deteriorated, the husband was ordered to bring the minister to pray with the mother. Midwife manuals discouraged "that cruelty and barbarousness of the *Caesarean* Section" as it was always fatal to the mother. Once the midwife had delivered the child, she tied and cut the navel string, washed the child, and swaddled it before handing it to the mother. Old wives' tales warned against letting the cord touch the ground lest the child grow up incontinent of urine. Nor should the midwife cut the cord too short for boys lest he prove "insufficient in encounters with Venus," nor too long for a girl lest she become immodest.[42]

Lying-In

A mother's "travail" did not necessarily end with the birth of her child. Her "lying-in" time, usually a one- to three-week-long period when new mothers were confined to bed and granted a much-deserved respite from work, was sometimes filled with complications. Elizabeth Manigault of Charles Town endured over 12 hours of childbirth that left her so sick that she could not see company for almost a month. Many other postpartum women suffered from abscesses in the breasts. "Dr. Hemingway came in the morning and opened my Wife's Breast," noted Ebenezer Parkman of Massachusetts in 1758. "Its issue was corrupt Matter and blood." One Charles Town mother who could not nurse suffered "violent pain" in her engorged breasts from milk within them that had turned "as hard as cakes." More of a nuisance were postpartum and menstrual discharges, which women treated with pads made of dried grass, fuzzed bark, linen, and rags. Once fully recovered, the mother was expected to provide a dinner in appreciation of those who attended her during the labor and delivery.[43]

Breastfeeding

During this time of convalescence, some mothers avoided breastfeeding their newborn children as it was believed that colostrum was an "unclean purgation" that would harm the child. Instead, the mother employed a neighbor or relative to wet-nurse the child the first few days of its life. To stimulate the flow of milk, midwives would massage their patient's breasts and nipples or employ nursing puppies or kittens to perform this task. Still, some women had to hire a wet-nurse for want of sufficient milk. Since early Americans believed that babies would acquire the characteristics of the woman who nursed them, it was important to hire a wet-nurse virtuous in character and with no physical defects. Some wealthy women continued to employ wet-nurses for years after the birth of their child in an attempt to preserve their figures and avoid a tedious task that usually resulted in chapped nipples. One

New England husband noted, "My wife distress'd with her Nipples. She got up, but she grows weaker by Reason of the Childs sucking her when her Nipples are so Sore." To treat cracked and sore nipples women used salves of herbs, beeswax, and honey. Some women avoided this painful condition by using "sucking bottles" with pewter or silver nursing nipples that were sold in urban shops. Although more convenient for mothers, bottle feeding had its dangers. Cotton Mather noted with shock on March 6, 1700, that his eight-month-old son "received almost a miraculous Deliverance from Choaking, by a Pin, which he suck'd out of the silver nipple of his Bottel, tho' we know not how it came there."[44]

RAISING CHILDREN

If a baby was fortunate enough to survive birth and infancy, its daily life growing up depended more on the accident of birth than on anything else. Children lived different lives according to the class to which they were born, the geographic location of their birth, the century in which they were born, the religion of their parents, their sex, and their race. The daily experiences of a seventeenth-century boy born to a Puritan merchant in Boston differed considerably from that of an eighteenth-century girl born to an Anglican physician in Charles Town, the child of an immigrant laborer in Philadelphia, or a black child born to a New York City slave.

Still, some commonalities existed among all children regardless of class, gender, religion, or race. Most apparent was children's placement at the bottom of the family hierarchy. Symbolic of this are the words *child*, *boy*, and *girl*, all of which derive from Old English derogatory terms for servants. More concrete was the casual way in which colonial parents raised children—at least by modern standards. Caring for and nurturing children was a relatively low priority for parents consumed in an economic struggle for daily life. This was particularly true for lower-class families who had little time or resources to devote to their children. Yet even affluent parents often ignored their young children because they were not yet old enough to be trained in culture and the social graces. When parents deigned to spend time with their little ones, they tended to treat them as "amusing little pets." Otherwise, genteel parents cast off their offspring to servants and slaves who tended to the child's daily needs. Among the less affluent, young children were looked after by older siblings, if available. This left younger children among the least-attended members of the household, expected to fend for themselves as best they could. Sadly, this negligence led to the numerous needless childhood accidents and deaths described earlier. If a child survived such dangers, he or she, no matter the social class or gender, was often fostered out for a long period of time in order to learn a trade, to work as a servant, or to attend a boarding school. Thereafter, these urban children were under the care and discipline of other adults who all too often mistreated their new charges. Typical is the case of Jan Bout of New Amsterdam, who was hauled to court for hitting a foster girl in the head with iron tongs.[45]

In raising children, historian Philip Greven has distinguished three themes: evangelical (New England), moderate (Middle Colonies), and genteel (Southern Colonies). Evangelical parents, who viewed children as tainted with original sin and therefore inherently naughty, employed harsh psychological and physical measures to break the child's will and instill a sense of obedience, responsibility, self-control, and surrender to God. Samuel Sewall's favorite method for disciplining his children was to provoke their fear of death, sin, and the "torments inflicted in Hell." Other Puritan parents suppressed their children's will and developed within them a strong sense of self-denial in all aspects of their lives by using shame and guilt. Too much affection, they believed, interfered with thoughts of God. The result was anxiety-ridden, insecure, and unhappy children. Meanwhile, moderate parents sought to bend the will of their child, not break it, by stressing self-control rather than self-repression. More so than any other group, the Quakers employed the "benevolent art" of shaming when correcting their children's behavior. One Quaker son recalled that his mother conquered his stubborn nature by simply "looking at me in *her* way. I could stand anything but that." Genteel parents, on the other hand, sought to cultivate love and reverence in their children by engaging in "unbounded indulgence" of and "intense affection" for their children that encouraged self-assertion rather than self-control. Discipline was lax. Instead, parents often placed their children under the guidance of nurses, slaves, and tutors. Such indulgence and indifference often produced spoiled, undisciplined, and ungrateful children who gave their parents a lifetime of maddening frustration.[46]

Parents frustrated with their children did not hesitate to inflict the sting of corporal punishment on them for any perceived disobedience. Parental advice manuals of the seventeenth century all emphasized the use of physical punishment in correcting children's

19 Spit not, Cough not, nor blow thy Nofe at the Table, if it may be avoided : but if there be neceffity do it afide ; and without much noife.

20 Lean not thy Elbow on the Table, or on the back of thy Chair.

21 Stuff not thy Mouth fo as to fill thy Cheeks, be content with fmaller mouthfuls.

22 Blow not thy Meat, but with patience wait until it be cool.

23 Sup not Broth at the Table ; but eat it with a Spoon.

24 Smell not of thy Meat, nor put it to thy Nofe : turn it not the other fide upward to view it upon thy Plate or Trencher.

25 Throw not any thing under the Table.

26 Hold not thy Knife upright in thy hand, but floping, and lay it down at thy right Hand, with the Blade upon thy Plate.

Proper Behavior for Children. As today, children in colonial America were expected to behave a certain way. To help instruct children in proper behavior, many eighteenth-century schoolmasters and parents turned to *The School of Good Manners*, first published in 1715 by Boston schoolmaster Eleazar Moody, who borrowed heavily from sixteenth-century French courtesy books in writing his children's etiquette manual. Above is a page from his book on proper behavior of children at the dining table. Other parts of the book provide rules of conduct for youngsters in church, school, the home, and in company. Moody's *School of Good Manners* was popular for well over a century, going through at least 34 editions between 1715 and 1846. (Charles Evans, *Early American Imprints*, Series 1, no. 40702) recalcitrant behavior. Even more influential among Christian parents was the Bible, which served as the primary guide to child rearing and discipline. The book of Proverbs, in particular, provides parents with plenty of moral justification for physically abusing their children: "He that spareth the rod hateth his sons, but he that loveth him chasteneth him betimes" (13:24); "Foolishness is bound in the heart of a child; but the rod of correction shall drive it far from him" (22:15); "Withhold not correction from the child; for if thou beatest him with the rod, he shall not die. Thou shalt beat him with the rod, and shalt deliver his soul from Hell." (23:13–14). Encouraged by such providential approval, parents whipped their children with hickory switches and horsewhips, either one of which could leave lasting physical scars on tiny bodies and deep emotional scars in undeveloped minds. Here, too, the Bible eased the minds of colonial parents by telling them that such injuries resulting from physical punishment were perfectly normal, for as Proverbs 20:30 explains, "The blueness of a wound cleanseth away evil."[47]

Youth Culture

No amount of discipline could prevent the development of a distinctive adolescent subculture among urban youth that transcended class, religious affiliation, and regional distinctions. Urban residents recognized a noticeable "revolt of the young" seeking individual autonomy, which they often expressed in illicit and antisocial behavior. Most threatening were the gangs of youth who started riots, lit large bonfires, vandalized and stole property, and discharged guns. Night watchmen brave enough to confront such gangs were sometimes met with a fusillade of stones. Other teenagers were on the "high road to ruin" by haunting taverns and drinking themselves sick, joining "vile company," "rabbl[ing] up and down [the streets] in the evening," where they "are let alone to take other sinful courses without check or restraint." Pious instruction often failed to curb such "sinful courses" in teenagers. Even Cotton Mather's own "miserable son" Increase "brought himself under public trouble and infamy," the Puritan minister lamented, by participating in a "night-riot" with some "detestable rakes in town."[48]

DIVORCE

With early Americans placing a high value on the institution of marriage and family, it is not surprising that colonial authorities rarely granted divorces. Ironically, it was New England that had the most divorce proceedings in the colonial period. This is because Puritans considered marriage a civil contract, not a sacrament, and therefore allowed couples to divorce if one of the parties egregiously violated the terms of the contract by engaging in adultery, cruelty, bigamy, or desertion or was proven impotent. Still, divorces were relatively rare. Massachusetts, for example, saw only 151 divorce petitions between 1620 and 1764, most of which authorities granted, especially those cases involving desertion and infidelity. In one extreme case, Bostonian Tabetha Hearsey successfully petitioned for divorce after accusing her husband of "inflicting the most grievous pains" because of her "refusal to comply" with his attempts to use her for "things too shocking to utter." On the other hand, the southern colonies, where divorce was covered by English law, did not allow absolute divorce but did permit judicial separation from bed and board on grounds of adultery and extreme cruelty. Here, as well as in New York, a marriage could only be dissolved by the governor and council, while Pennsylvania used legislative proceedings to hear divorce petitions. Consequently, divorce in these colonies was nearly nonexistent because persons seeking a divorce had to go through a complicated and expensive legal procedure that involved the governor and assembly, neither of which were eager to become involved in legislative divorces. Illustrative of this is Pennsylvania, which had no divorce petitions between 1728 and 1766. In the decade thereafter, five men petitioned for divorce, only two of which the authorities granted.[49]

With legal divorces so difficult to obtain, unhappily married folk found other ways to escape matrimonial hell. Legal separation was an option, a process that involved both parties agreeing to and signing legal papers detailing the provisions of separation. A wife either deserted by her husband or evicted from her home could apply to the courts to have her husband's goods seized or him ordered to pay alimony. Husbands married to nagging wives or overwhelmed with the responsibilities of family life simply fled to the frontier or boarded a merchant ship. Wives married to unsupportive and abusive husbands frequently sought sanctuary at a relative's or friend's house. Many runaway wives simply sought a temporary respite from the monotony of child rearing and domestic drudgery while trying to instill some sympathy and appreciation in their husbands for their work by forcing them to temporarily play the housewife and mother. After a little rest, many wives returned home to haggard husbands who were

WHEREAS James Dunlap, of Piles Grove, in the county of Salem, in the province of New - Jerfey, by an advertifement lately inferted in the *American Weekly Mercury*, and in the *Pennfylvania Gazette*, did publifh the elopement of Elizabeth Dunlap his wife, and forwarned all perfons to truft her for any goods or other things, &c.

Thefe are therefore to certify all perfons whom it may concern, that the contents of the faid advertifement, as to the elopement of the faid Elizabeth is utterly falfe, for the faid Elizabeth, never eloped from the faid James Dunlap her hufband, but was obliged in fafety of her life to leave her faid hufband becaufe of his threats and cruel abufes for feveral Years paft repeatedly offered and done to her, and that fhe went no farther than to her father's houfe in faid county, where fhe has refided ever fince her departure from her faid hufband, and ftill continues to refide. And the faid James Dunlap having a confiderable eftate in lands in faid county, which the faid Elizabeth is informed he intends to fell as foon as he can, fhe therefore thought proper to give this notice to any perfon or perfons that may offer to buy, that fhe will not join in the fale of any part of faid lands, but that fhe intends to claim her thirds (or right of dower) of and in all the lands the faid James Dunlap has been feized and pofleffed of fince their intermarriage, whofoever may purchafe the fame. ☉ Elizabeth Dunlap.

Runaway Wives. Colonial newspapers contain thousands of advertisements such as the one above by husbands and wives publicly airing their marital problems. With little recourse for divorce, unhappy wives often fled to the homes of family and friends, prompting some husbands to place notices in newspapers telling the public that their wives had eloped with another man and warning merchants that they would not honor any charges by their wives made in their name. The above newspaper ad from a June 17, 1767, issue of the *Pennsylvania Gazette* is a fiery response from one wife against her husband for publicly slandering her reputation.

undoubtedly grateful for their return. Not all men were so fortunate. When a Philadelphia cordwainer begged his wife to return home, she replied that she "would be damned to Hell, if ever she lived with him again."[50]

WIDOWHOOD

The most permanent form of marital separation, of course, was the death of a spouse. Disease, accidents, intemperance, childbirth, and the harshness of pioneer life prematurely took the lives of many. A study of 271 Quaker marriages reveals that 20 percent were dissolved by the death of one partner before their 15th wedding anniversary, and another 20 percent after a quarter century. Marriages in one New England town lasted an average of 24 years before the death of a spouse. Such cold statistics say nothing of the emotional devastation resulting from the death of a spouse. The Reverend Ezra Stiles of Newport was so consumed with depression following the death of his wife that it prevented him from preaching. He could only ambulate desultorily throughout his home overwhelmed by its "great Emptiness." "Everything reminds me of my dear departed absent Wife," he wrote sorrowfully.[51]

The five seaport cities, with their regular epidemics and numerous seamen who often ended up in Davy Jones's locker, had more than their share of widows. Typical was the city of Boston, which in 1742 had 1,200 widows in a total population of 16,300. All but 200 of these widows were designated as "poor" despite the fact that the law entitled widows to at least one-third of their deceased husband's estate. Widowhood was therefore a "state of Affliction" for many who were left destitute and constantly harassed by creditors. This was especially true for lower-class women whose husbands had little wealth and property to begin with. Even middle-class widows with children faced "New Encumbrances coming upon her; Debts to be paid, and Mouths to be fed." The more fortunate widows found employment as live-in domestics, which provided food, clothing, and shelter. Younger widows sometimes turned to prostitution while older ones opened brothels. Others depended on poor relief and occasional odd jobs to sustain themselves. The most destitute widows were forced to apprentice their children to other families, while those widows ending up in the local almshouse had their children bound out by the overseers of the poor to reduce the financial burden to the city. Rather than raise taxes slightly to keep children with their mothers, pinch-penny local officials instead sent them to live with strangers, often many miles away. In short, the death of a husband and father was a disaster for many urban families.[52]

In addition to financial distress, widows also had to deal with the social stigma of being labeled a "relic." Thereafter she was known and referred to as "widow Jones" or "widow Smith" and expected to focus her remaining years on behaving in a pious manner as an example for younger women and longing for the day "when the Lord Jesus will send his Angels to fetch her unto the regions of ever-lasting Light and Life." Many younger widows, however, refused to pine so piously for death. One young Boston widow was charged with "lewd Carriage towards diverse men at Sundry Times" and "having an unlawful offspring in the Time of Widowhood." Similarly, the "widow Stickney" habitually frequented taverns shortly after the death of her husband, where she was found "sitting in the laps" of sailors. Clearly, some widows were not sorry to see their husbands dead.[53]

Remarriage

A quick remarriage following the death of a husband or wife was not uncommon. Both John Laurens and Benjamin d'Harriette of Charles Town, for example, remarried only three months following the death of their wives. By contrast, Quaker widows and widowers waited years before remarrying, an average of 6.2 years for widows and 3.6 years for widowers. In fact, widowers were more likely to remarry than widows because the benefits of remarriage far out-weighed the liabilities: he gained the new wife's property and her services as housekeeper, caretaker of children (if any), and sexual partner. In exchange he gave up one-third of his real estate (the dower) unless otherwise stipulated in a prenuptial contract. Only about one-fourth of widows, on the other hand, ever found new spouses. These odds are explained partly by circumstance and partly by choice. Most widows entered widowhood at an advanced age where few men found them desirable, no matter their wealth. Younger widows with children were also unappealing to most mar-riageable men. These cruel realities were somewhat softened by the fact that for the first time a widow found herself in sole control of her finances and her life. By remarrying, she would lose most of her financial and personal independence. For those widows with wealth, remarriage held considerable risks. This explains why the well-to-do widow Dorothy Denison rejected Samuel Sewall's gener-ous financial offer in exchange for her hand in marriage. As he explained in his diary, "She answer'd she had better keep as she was, than give a certainty for an uncertainty." Most affluent widows played it safe by remaining single.[54]

KINSHIP

Many other early Americans played it safe by clinging closely to members of their intergenerational kin. This was particularly true among lowcountry South Carolinians, who had perhaps the lowest life expectancies of any group in British North America. Charlestonians often turned to siblings, kin, and friends to help raise children, educate and socialize younger relatives, aid and advise in marital choices, and provide emotional support throughout their lives. In short, extended kin served as a sort of safety net in a highly unsafe environment. When Henry Laurens's wife died in 1770, the Charles Town merchant sent his five children to live with a varied cast of aunts, uncles, godparents, schoolmasters, and family friends that spanned both sides of the Atlantic. Thereafter, he exercised his parental authority in an epistolary manner. Meanwhile, Laurens assumed a similar authority for a niece, a nephew by marriage, and sons of friends and business acquaintances. This extensive form of parenting network created a modicum of security for South Carolina children, 60 percent of whom lost at least one parent by the age of 16. Such extensive parenting and social networking also allowed the Carolina gentry to lay the foundation for an elite consensus that was social, economic, and political and that was difficult for outsiders to penetrate.[55]

SLAVE MARRIAGES

Courting

The family life of urban blacks differed significantly from that of their white counterparts. Uncertainty, instability, struggle, suffering, and survival were the daily experiences of the urban black family. Their suffering and struggle began in Africa where men, women, and children were forcibly and traumatically ripped from their families by African slave traders and eventually brought to America where, over time, they combined ancestral mating rituals and kinship customs with those of the dominant white majority to create mixed marriages. Courtship was itself a struggle as slaves had to gain permission from masters, who were disinclined to allow their chattel to neglect their tasks. Often, love-struck couples met clandestinely after hours in the garret of the master's house, in lower-class taverns, and at slave funerals and festivals. With a three-to-two male-female ratio among blacks in the cities, many urban males never married, forcing them to satisfy their sexual desires through illicit affairs, sometimes with white women. In

Philadelphia, for example, the overseer of the poor appealed to the legislature in 1774 to make provision for the increasing "maintenance of children born of white women begotten by Negroes or Mulattoes, who are Slaves." Even more common was illicit intercourse, often rape, between masters and their female slaves. This practice was most common in Charles Town, where the numerous mulattos who walked its streets presented a conspicuous display of these illicit unions. But even in Newport mulattos comprised one-eighth of the city's black population, a testament to the numerous progeny resulting from interracial affairs.[56]

For a male slave fortunate enough to win the affection of his lady of choice, he still had to gain the consent of both masters and, in Boston, submit the obligatory wedding banns. Similarly, the records in the Lutheran and Anglican churches of Philadelphia contain numerous references to the marriages of slaves and free blacks. Certainly, some slaves had Christian marriages only to please their masters. Some urban masters put racist beliefs over religious concerns by allowing their slaves to simply cohabit freely without a formal marriage ceremony, which had no legal authority anyway.[57]

Marriage and Family Life

The status of slavery put added strain, struggle, and instability on the relationship between husbands and wives. Most slave spouses were forced to live in different households. Husbands and wives could visit only at the pleasure of their masters, forcing slave couples to meet clandestinely in the dark of night. Often living apart and lacking their own private space made it equally difficult for slave couples and their children to enjoy much valuable family time with one another. One visitor to Charles Town observed that black "husbands and wives most commonly belong to different families. Laboring apart, and having their meals apart, the domestic bonds of domestic life are weak." Thus "a slave, his wife, and their children, around that charmed centre, a family table, with its influences of love, instruction, discipline . . . are too seldom seen."[58]

Family Dissolution

Further undermining the slave family was the legal right of masters to sell their slaves, whom the law defined as personal property. Slave owners disposed of their human property with as little compassion or restraint as they would a pig or a goat, an attitude reflected in thousands of notices for the sale of men, women, and

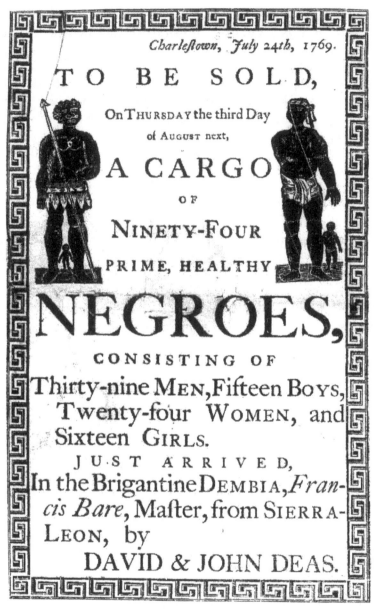

Charles Town Slave Sale. This advertisement for the sale of "a Cargo of Ninety-Four Prime, Healthy Negroes," one-third of whom are children, reveals the instability of the slave family and the inherent inhumanity of the capitalist nature of slavery. Note the crude illustrations of two half-naked Africans that depict their primitiveness, at least from the perspective of white Euro-Americans. (From Charles Evans, Early American Imprints, Series 1, no. 41926)

children placed in city newspapers. Illustrative is the following advertisement from the May 7, 1757, issue of the *Boston Gazette*:

To be Sold at the public Vendue on Thursday the 23d Instant, at the House where the late Mr. *Henry Darrell*, deceas'd, dwelt, the Household Furniture and Goods of said Deceased, consisting of Feather Beds, Bedsteads, Chairs, Tables, Desks, Brass and Copper Ware, 2 Turkey Carpets, a parcel of Ironmongery and Tin Ware, sundry Pieces of Plate, Men's Apparel, and Collection of Books; also a Negro Man and Woman, and a Horse and Chaise.

The actual public sale was a humiliating and heartbreaking experience for slaves, who were carefully examined for permanent injuries and defects like livestock at auction. Particularly humiliating were examinations for gonorrhea, hernias, and potential fertility in women whereby prospective buyers palpated breasts and massaged abdomens into revealing their reproductive history and capacity. More traumatic was the separation of husbands from wives, brothers from sisters, and especially children from parents. Urban masters had little use for slave children, an economic liability in their ledger books, and so would give them away like puppies and kittens. A "fine Negro child of a good healthy breed to be given away of the printer," reads one ad in a Boston newspaper. Another Boston master was so eager to relieve himself of a "Negro child" that he actually offered a sum of money to anyone who would take "it" off his hands.[59]

The fragility of the slave family necessitated the creation of an extended kinship in which aunts, uncles, nephews, nieces, cousins, in-laws, and even friends served as substitute parents in cases of family dissolution. Black parents encouraged their children to refer to their nonrelated elders as "aunts" or "uncles" and their age peers as "brothers" and "sisters." This extended kin group helped black children sustain themselves in the travails of slavery.[60]

OLD AGE

Old age also had its travails—declining mental and physical health, the loss of age peers, increasing loneliness, and often destitution. For those fewer than 20 percent of early Americans who lived to the age of 70, their golden years were usually anything but golden. Retirement was something foreign to colonists, who did not view old age as a time for rest and leisure. Men worked until physically worn out; women, too, dutifully carried their domestic burdens to the end. If one did retire, it was usually the result of physical infirmity. This was especially true for urban laborers and sailors, who were frequently injured on the job. Unable to work and often lacking relatives with the financial resources to care for them, these men often faced a hard and shortened life of severe privation in the local almshouse or on the streets. Nor were the golden years much better for those employed in white-collar work. A study of elderly ministers in colonial New England reveals that congregations showed little Christian charity to the men of the cloth who had given their lives to serving them. In fact, the main reason why ministers worked until death was because few congregations were willing to provide them with adequate pensions. The widow of a minister usually received similar neglect, forcing her either into a hasty remarriage—if she was still young—or destitution if she was old. Even those ministers who were able to retire comfortably complained about a loss of identity and uselessness. Upon retiring from his ministry at the ripe old age of 82, Increase Mather of Boston lamented that "it is a very undesirable thing for a man to outlive his work."[61]

Like everything else about colonial society, class largely defined and determined one's experience in old age. Surviving to 60 did not automatically earn an individual special veneration, for as historian David Hacket Fischer explains, "age operated as a system of social inequality" in early America. This explains why powerful and prosperous white men received the greatest respect and veneration among the elderly. On the other hand, respect was nonexistent among the elderly poor, who were "treated very badly" and whose "sufferings were great." Cities sometimes cast out the elderly poor who arrived by ship and "warned out" poor widows as a means to reduce pauperism. Despite such measures, the seaport towns had their contingent of old and decrepit men who scavenged and begged during the day and slept in deserted cellars or in narrow alleys at night. Their pitiful existence elicited little Christian compassion from residents, sometimes even among family, who fed these elderly poor men with more contempt and scorn than food and drink. "In some strange and paradoxical way," Fischer explains, "old age seems actually to have intensified the contempt visited upon a poor man." The numerous widows in the cities, most of whom were miserably poor, fared little better. Their second-class status as women only deepened the contempt society held toward them. Despite frequent injunctions by ministers to aid one's elderly parents, Increase Mather complained that there were still too many children who were apt to "despise an *Aged Mother.*" Despised and destitute, many aged poor welcomed death.[62]

Further encouraging the elderly to embrace death were the physical and emotional pains that were constant companions for the aged in early America, a time when few palliatives were available to ease their suffering. A long life, wrote one minister, "is not so properly called living, as dying a lingering death." Part of this lingering death included losing one's ability to see, hear, walk, eat solid food, or control urine and bowel movements. These indignities of old age were only intensified by terrible physical pain as one's body succumbed to decades of abuse. Benjamin Franklin, for example, suffered horribly from "the stone" and gout in his last years. He made his life somewhat tolerable by taking massive quantities of opium. When Franklin lay on his death bed, his daughter tried to console him with the hope that he would live many more years, to which he replied, "I hope not." But perhaps the worst suffering experienced by the few elderly was emotional. Often their only companions were extreme emptiness, loneliness, and isolation. They had few if any age peers with whom to commiserate, leaving them to feel as if they had lived to become "strangers in their own society," writes Fischer, "aliens in their own time." As if this emotional suffering was not enough, many old folk, particularly Puritans, were wracked with psychic anxiety over the uncertainty of their salvation. More than a few lay on their deathbeds wondering if they would soon find either eternal peace in heaven or eternal suffering in hell.[63]

DEATH AND FUNERALS

Death was a daily experience for urban residents, who experienced a higher death rate per thousand population in the eighteenth century (30–40 per 1,000) than their rural counterparts (15–25 per 1,000).[64] This high mortality rate encouraged a morbid fascination with death among urban residents, who read with relish the latest accidental deaths, murders, hangings, Indian massacres, deadly fires, and funerals printed in city newspapers. Even young children were reminded of their eventual death in learning the alphabet with the following rhymed verse from the *New England Primer*: "Xerxes the Great did die, and so must you and I." The colonists' infatuation with death is also reflected in numerous superstitions surrounding the dead. The following is a small sampling:

1. If a dead person's eyes are left open, he will find a companion to take with him.

2. Cover mirrors in a house where there is a corpse. The person who sees himself may be Death's next victim.

3. Do not attend a funeral if you are pregnant.

4. A corpse must be taken from the house feet first. If his head faces backward, he may beckon another member of the family to follow him.

5. If the deceased has lived a good life, flowers will bloom on his grave; if he has been evil, weeds will grow.

6. It is bad luck to meet a funeral procession head on. If you see one approaching, turn around.

7. If you hear a clap of thunder following a burial, it indicates that the soul of the dead person has reached heaven.[65]

Such superstitions arose in part because death in early America was an intimate and social event that belied any sense of rugged individualism. With no hospitals or institutions for the aged, colonists died mainly in their homes. When the end approached, family, friends, and close neighbors knelt down in the "death room" while the pastor read the prayers for the dying and spoke some consoling words. At this point Quakers sometimes wrote down the advice and pious expressions of the dying and kept them as family memorials as they believed the dying were in closest relationship with God. The moment of death could be a highly emotional scene both for the living and the dying. One New England woman on her deathbed pleaded over and over to her husband "don't leave me my dear." When lucid, she refused to acknowledge that her death was close at hand. Her husband resorted to shaking his wife to bring her back to reality. With her senses regained, she asked her husband if she was dying, "I told her she was." Her last moments were filled with the "most shocking pain" until she finally fell "into a gentle sleep."[66]

To confirm death, a mirror was placed before the mouth or smoke blown into the nostrils. If necessary, the eyes of the deceased were closed. Thereafter neighbors laid out the body; undressed the corpse and washed, shaved, and combed or braided the hair; and dressed the body. At least in the cities, this morbid task increasingly fell to lower-class women, called "Layers out of the Dead," who advertised their services in local newspapers. Besides some basic cleaning, combing, and dressing, nothing was done to cosmetically improve the corpse. Unlike today, no fake smile sewn on the face of the deceased greeted the bereaved in early America, who looked at death with a grim and unadorned reality. Nearly as rare was embalming, a crude process that involved disemboweling and filling the cavity with charcoal or immersing the body in alcohol or wrapping it in alum. The lack of embalming necessitated a quick burial, often performed the day after death. Close friends usually watched the body overnight, passing their time drinking, smoking, and eating while reminiscing on the life of the deceased.[67]

Funerals were distinct from burials. Many funerals were held in private homes, especially among the Dutch, but others preferred having them in churches. In the Anglican service, the Order for the Burial of the Dead was read that included the reading of penitential psalms, various "Lessons" from either 1 Corinthians or Revelation, and the recitations of prayers. Puritans, on the other hand, sought to avoid the "popish error" of saying prayers over the dead. Their funerals therefore were usually brief, simple affairs, especially in the earliest period. Instead, they followed the 1645 *Directory for the Publick Worship of God* that instructed the public to bury the dead "without any ceremony." As one critic observed in disgust, "the dead [are] thrown into the ground like dogs, and not a word said." However, the increasing urbanization of and wealth in Boston slowly broke down traditional Puritan control. Within a few decades the simple and secular nature of Puritan funerals was replaced by more ostentatious and religious ceremonies that included short prayers, communal recitations of psalms, and short eulogies. Ministers increasingly exploited the terrors of death to persuade the living toward greater piety before they, too, met their maker.[68]

As a social and public event, funerals became another means by which the urban gentry sought to distinguish themselves from their social inferiors—even in death. Some advertised their funerals with engraved obituary notices. The well-to-do also buried their dead in coffins crafted in fine polished and stained hardwoods. The less fortunate were laid in a pine coffin painted with lamp black. While the gentry rode to their final resting ground in a stately hearse pulled by a team of well-groomed horses, their social inferiors were carried in a well-used open wagon pulled by an overworked nag. The urban gentry further displayed their wealth (and alleged superiority) by giving expensive gifts of gloves, rings, scarves, and other "funerary finery" to participants of all social classes at funerals. By doing so, the urban elite hoped to create "visible signs of connection for people who feared they were out of touch with their local communities," explain Steven Bullock and Sheila McIntyre. The extraordinary expense of funerals eventually prompted the General Court of Massachusetts in 1721, 1724, and again in 1742 to limit the number of scarves, gloves, and rings given at funerals. Such laws failed to curb the urban gentry from having large and expensive funerals, which they saw not as heedless waste but "an investment in relationships, an attempt to move beyond cold calculations of interest to create what social scientists call social capital."[69]

No matter the expense and conduct of the funeral, all required a procession from the home to the cemetery. In the earliest days, young men called underbearers, often the poor, carried the coffin on the bier to the churchyard while older men called pallbearers held the corners of the pall, which was the cloth laid over the coffin. This could be an exhausting trip for underbearers, who took regular breaks to rest the heavy coffin on "mort stones" conveniently placed throughout the cities. Later, underbearers were replaced by horses that pulled an open wagon (for the poor) or a hearse (for the rich) that carried the deceased to their final resting place. As the cortege proceeded to the cemetery, people lined the streets, doffing their hats and standing with bowed heads in respect. Children, on the other hand, often showed less respect for the dead by following the coffin through the streets and making "such noise as to profane the sacred day." More respectful was the act of burying the dead, whereby funeral attendants solemnly prayed over the recently deceased before placing the body in the ground close to deceased family, friends, and neighbors. Thus even in death, early Americans could not stand to be rugged individualists.[70]

The obligatory postfuneral dinner at the home of the deceased was often just as expensive and ostentatious as the funeral itself. All too many families spent beyond their means in sending off the dead into the next world and feeding and entertaining friends and relatives of the deceased. Arguing against the "needless and exorbitant Expense of Funerals," one New York City resident opined in 1753 that the cost of carrying a deceased loved one "with fashionable Apparatus" and "buried Alamode" often led to financial calamity among many families who followed this "ruinous custom."[71] Typical of this "ruinous custom" is the funeral charges of Peter Marius of New York City:

From the amount of liquor listed it is safe to say that friends and relatives of the deceased enjoyed considerable merrymaking following the funeral.

Table 3.1. Funeral Charges

	£	s
29 gallons of wine	9	15
19 pairs of gloves	2	4
4 bottles and glasses broke	0	3
2 female attendees	0	15
mourning suit	3	4
800 cookies and 1.5 gross of pipes	6	7
spice for wine and sugar	0	1
grave digger and bell ringer	2	2
coffin	4	0
14 mourning rings	2	16
3 yards of beaver for mourning suit	1	14
1/2 vat of beer	0	7

Source: Singleton, *Dutch New York*, 262.

Slave Funerals

While white folk made great efforts to bury their dead with respect and dignity, callous slave owners sometimes treated their bondsmen in death as they had in life. "Less care was taken of their [the slaves'] bodies than if they were dumb beasts," remarked one slave in disgust. Still, slaves persisted in conducting meaningful and proper funerals for their dead by following West African burial customs that included washing and shrouding the body, singing, chanting, praying, and clapping to send off the deceased into the next world, and often embracing the corpse as mourners passed it. The music, singing, and clapping at slave funerals often provoked disgust from many urban whites, not just because it made a racket resembling a carnival but also because they thought it was simply an excuse to hold a "jubilee for every slave in the city," remarked one Charles Town resident. This largely explains why New York City officials forbade night funerals for slaves and, fearing the bondsmen might use such events to organize a rebellion, allowed only 10 of them to assemble for a burial. When buried, the deceased slaves were segregated in death as they were in life. The common burying ground in Newport, for example, reserved a small section of the graveyard for burials of both free and enslaved blacks. Officials in Boston simply tried to hide their deceased slaves within the shadows of the city by ordering their interment in a locale designated as the place to "bury strangers and negroes."[72]

COMMUNITY

Obviously, families in the colonial cities did not exist in a vacuum but were part of a larger community that allowed for greater social interaction than could be found elsewhere in the colonies. Large enough to have numerous networks of associations yet small enough for residents to recognize each other as individuals, eighteenth-century colonial towns were "walking cities" that contributed to a face-to-face and highly personalized society. Unlike the modern metropolis where close proximity breeds a fear of intimacy, early Americans saw the intimacy of their neighborhoods as one of the more pleasant and necessary aspects of their daily lives. Life in the cities gave residents meaningful personal relationships outside of the family, a sense of participation, and feelings of collective responsibility for one another. Still, isolation existed for many of the city's laboring poor, many of whom were either immigrants or peripatetic natives who lived in neighborhoods that were in a continuous flux with residents who moved in and out in a "perpetual cycle of subsistence migration." As strangers in a strange land, many urban laboring poor did not affiliate with a church, and few could rely on kin or friends for aid. This alienation only encouraged internal bonding within many lower-class families, who were looked upon with disdain and contempt by their social superiors. For most others, urban neighborhoods contained numerous networks of association based on familial, religious, economic, educational, and recreational circumstances. Churches, schools, fraternal organizations, taverns, markets, fairs, militia training, births, deaths, and work of all kind brought residents together on a regular basis. Proving that early Americans were anything but rugged individualists, urban neighbors relied on each other for a variety of services, especially during times of crisis. This was especially true for women, who assisted each other in childbirth, death, and heavy domestic tasks like making soap, rag carpets, and annual housecleaning. Men also relied on each other in sharing tools, gathering firewood, and repairing homes.[73]

Class and Community

Of course, this social interaction had limitations, much of it by design. Members of the upper class, for example, seldom deigned to rub elbows with their social inferiors. To maintain a social segregation and symbolic superiority, they sat in walled pews in churches, created exclusive clubs, conducted business in gentlemen's coffee houses, rode around in enclosed carriages, moved to exclusive neighborhoods in the suburbs, and sent their children to private academies. Hypocritically, this disdain for the common folk did not prevent rich residents from purchasing and exploiting servants and slaves to serve them in their homes and places of work. By doing so, the urban upper class intentionally created an authoritarian-servile relationship with their social inferiors. Most of the interaction the lower sort had with the upper crust involved being ordered around and physically punished.

Contributing to the compartmentalization of urban communities were churches, which obviously catered to specific religious affiliations. The many urban taverns also catered to specific clientele based largely on class. The various ethnic groups in the cities created their own exclusive organizations, as did urban tradesmen, sea captains, servants, and even slaves. For all their pluralism, the main cities were anything but a melting pot of religions, cultures, and ethnicities. Much as today, people preferred to associate with their own kind. An extreme example is found among Philadelphia Quakers, who rarely strayed far beyond their circle of fellow Friends. Still, residents formed important and lasting relations with their neighbors. A sampling of eighteenth-century New York City wills reveals that 40 percent of men and 42 percent of women appointed friends as executors of their wills, a strong indication of the ties and trust between neighbors. However, these figures drop precipitously when applied to Philadelphia's working poor, who hardly mentioned friends in their wills. This suggests that "close and dependable" friendships were difficult to establish among the many poor immigrants who formed a significant portion of the city's population.[74]

Visiting

Like today, living next door to someone did not guarantee a neighborly friendship. One authority on New England households claims that except for relatives and women visiting the wife during the day, common folk rarely had visitors in their homes. Working-class people struggling to make ends meet had little leisure time necessary for casual visiting. The city's leisured "better sort," on the other hand, turned formal visiting into a systematic ritual that consumed much of their energy and time. One genteel Englishwoman visiting Philadelphia felt oppressed and haggard by incessant visiting. "I have now a great heap of work that decreases very slowly through gossiping about," she complained, "which is unavoidable without giving my kind friends offense ... It is the custom to visit here more than with us, and they destroy the social freedom of it by too much dressing." One Boston merchant actually boasted that it was "quite common" for his wife to have "from six to ten visitors of a forenoon." Such extensive visiting patterns among the urban gentry exemplified the considerable wealth that allowed them to engage in such a time-consuming custom.[75]

"Tyranny of Neighbors"

Perhaps one reason why formal visiting did not extend far beyond the upper class is because there was no escaping neighbors in the cities. "They seemed to be always there, to go everywhere and to know everything," explains historian Helena Wall. "What a neighbor did not see for herself she could easily surmise or hear from someone else." Doors were often unlocked, allowing visitors to enter without knocking. In 1771, Sarah Powell and Leonard Miller of Boston entered the home of a neighbor and quietly crept to the bed chamber and peeped into a large crack in the door to catch their hosts in an act of adultery. The cities also had their complement of eavesdroppers and voyeurs who in the dark of night peeped into neighbors' windows or cracks in the walls.[76]

It is no surprise therefore that at times neighbors in the cities simply got on each other's nerves. Court records are filled with cases involving residents slandering each other with "bad words" leading to "discord among neighbors." Puritan ministers like Cotton Mather contributed to the "tyranny of neighbors" by recommending that "if any in the neighborhood are taking to bad courses, lovingly and faithfully admonish them." Likewise, the Reverend Andrew Eliot of Boston admonished his flock to be "faithful monitors" of their neighbors "when they have done amiss." One Bostonian fed up with the "claustrophobia of city life" threatened to "set his house on fire and run away by the light" because "he would no longer live among such a company of hell hounds."[77]

Pets

Residents of the five cities were surrounded by hounds of another kind as numerous dogs roamed the streets, terrorizing livestock and small children and barking incessantly both day and night. Many of these canines were strays, but families of all social classes kept dogs for companionship and protection. Many dog owners today can relate to the experience of Elizabeth Drinker of Philadelphia, whose lap dog Tartar woke her with his barking one night. The next morning she commented that "something there was to set him agoing, as he is too fat and lazy to exert himself for nothing." The value of dogs and the attachment that owners had for them is revealed in lost-dog ads like the following: "Lost or stolen on Sunday morning last . . . a small Lap Dog, called Juliet. She is all white, except about her eyes which are brown—she was very round by the great care taken by her owner—who will be much obliged to any person that will give information where she may be got, or will deliver her at No. 101 Church street. A reasonable reward will be given if required."[78]

Cats were also a favorite pet among urban folk. Not only did they make great companions, but they also kept the rodent population under control. Elizabeth Drinker's cat, Puss, had such a reputation as a "mouser" that her progeny were "much in demand." Perhaps the most common pure pet—one that served no useful function— were caged songbirds like mockingbirds, cardinals, and goldfinches. Domesticated squirrels were also popular pets, as were rabbits. Many Americans also grew attached to working animals and had favorites among their livestock. The Drinkers of Philadelphia had a white cock they called Chanticleer that was "a favorite of our sons," wrote Elizabeth. By the mid-eighteenth century, the guinea pig and white mouse entered the category of pet. Some families even kept a fish globe and experimented with the more complex "balanced" aquarium. In short, early Americans kept pets of all kinds as part of their extended families.[79]

CONCLUSION

Daily life in the colonial cities was difficult and uncertain. Deadly epidemics, economic depressions, and frequent fires, along with the hazards of work and childbirth, brought considerable instability to the lives of city folk. Against this onslaught of uncertainty was the family, which provided people with security and guidance, if not always love and affection. To that end, the colonial family was first and foremost an economic unit, with all members participating in a family economy—with the exception of the urban gentry. Yet the unique peculiarities of the urban economy and society also allowed for the emergence of a more modern family, one which diminishes the necessity of the family economy for survival. The urban economy required vast amounts of labor, and employers rarely cared whether or not workers were married or single. Consequently, colonial cities abounded with single folk—men and women, young and old, native and immigrant, free and enslaved—who often lived on their own outside a family environment. By the early eighteenth century, single folk were a significant and permanent fixture of urban life, so much so that political and religious leaders rarely devoted any special attention to them. In this way, the colonial cities can be considered more modern than premodern, illuminating the future direction of American society.

NOTES

1. Edmund S. Morgan, *The Puritan Family: Religion and Domestic Relations in Seventeenth Century New England* (New York: Harper & Row, 1966), 143.

2. Helena M. Wall, *Fierce Communion: Family and Community in Early America* (Cambridge, MA: Harvard University Press, 1990), 1.

3. Morgan, *Puritan Family*, 29 (quote); Irene Ktorides, "Marriage Customs in Colonial New England," *Historical Journal of Western Massachusetts* 2 (1973): 6 (quote); Kai T. Erikson, *Wayward Puritans: A Study in the Sociology of Deviance* (New York: Macmillan, 1966), 169 (quote); Thomas A. Foster, *Sex and the Eighteenth-Century Man: Massachusetts and the History of Sexuality in America* (Boston, MA: Beacon Press, 2006), 103 (quote), 124 (quote); Rebecca Tannenbaum, *Health and Wellness in Colonial America* (Westport, CT: Greenwood Press, 2012), 55; Anne S. Lombard, *Making Manhood: Growing Up Male in Colonial New England* (Cambridge, MA: Harvard University Press, 2003), 59; Karin Wulf, *Not All Wives: Women of Colonial Philadelphia* (Ithaca, NY: Cornell University Press, 2000), 17.

4. Wulf, *Not All Wives*, 12–17, quote, p. 16; Billy G. Smith, *The "Lower Sort": Philadelphia's Laboring People, 1750–1800* (Ithaca, NY: Cornell University Press, 1990), 177–78.

5. Adams quoted in Lisa Wilson, *Ye Heart of a Man: The Domestic Life of Men in Colonial New England* (New Haven, CT: Yale University Press), 43.

6. Lombard, *Making Manhood*, 66–67, 91 (quote); Wilson, *Ye Heart of a Man*, 37, 57, 65 (quote); J. William Frost, *The Quaker Family in Colonial America: A Portrait of the Society of Friends* (New York: St. Martin's Press, 1973), 154 (quote).

7. Julia Cherry Spruill, *Women's Life & Work in the Southern Colonies* (Chapel Hill: University of North Carolina Press, 1938), 154 (quotes); Wilson, *Ye Heart of a Man*, 55, 49 (quote); Frost, *Quaker Family*, 179 (quote); Joyce D. Goodfriend, *Before the Melting Pot: Society and Culture in Colonial New York City, 1664–1730* (Princeton, NJ: Princeton University Press, 1992), 177; Emma Hart, *Building Charleston: Town and Society in the Eighteenth-Century British Atlantic World* (Charlottesville: University of Virginia Press, 2010), 126.

8. Robert J. Gough, "Close-Kin Marriage and Upper Class Formation in Late Eighteenth-Century Philadelphia," *Journal of Family History* 14 (1989):

119–21; Lorri Glover, *All Our Relations: Blood Ties and Emotional Bonds among the Early South Carolina Gentry* (Baltimore: Johns Hopkins University Press, 2000), 9–10, 48–49; Sarah Fatherly, *Gentlewomen and Learned Ladies: Women and Elite Formation in Eighteenth-Century Philadelphia* (Bethlehem, PA: Lehigh University Press, 2008), 38–41.

9. Goodfriend, *Before the Melting Pot*, 93–98, 179, 185; Thomas Archdeacon, *New York City, 1664–1710: Conquest and Change* (Ithaca, NY: Cornell University Press, 1976), 47–48.

10. Goodfriend, *Before the Melting Pot*, 34 (quote); Esther Singleton, *Dutch New York* (New York: Dodd, Mead & Co., 1909), 212; Ktorides, "Marriage Customs in Colonial New England," 6 (quote); Spruill, *Women's Life and Work*, 144 (quote).

11. Spruill, *Women's Life and Work*, 143; Wilson, *Ye Heart of a Man*, 41 (quote); Richard Godbeer, *Sexual Revolution in Early America* (Baltimore: Johns Hopkins University Press, 2002), 265, 279–80; Lombard, *Making Manhood*, 92.

12. Godbeer, *Sexual Revolution*, 278.

13. Ruth H. Bloch, *Gender and Morality in Anglo-American Culture, 1650–1800* (Berkeley: University of California Press, 2003), 94 (quote); Richard Godbeer, "William Byrd's 'Flourish': The Sexual Cosmos of a Southern Planter," in *Sex and Sexuality in Early America*, ed. Merril D. Smith (New York: New York University Press, 1998), 151 (quote); Godbeer, *Sexual Revolution*, 272 (quote).

14. Billy Smith, *Lower Sort*, 177–78, 179 (quote); Bloch, *Gender and Morality*, 89; Estelle B. Freedman and John D'Emilio, *Intimate Matters: A History of Sexuality in America* (New York: Harper & Row, 1988), 43 (quote); Fatherly, *Gentlewomen and Learned Ladies*, quotes from pp. 44, 47, and 49.

15. Ktorides, "Marriage Customs in Colonial New England," 7–8; Frost, *Quaker Family*, 165 (quote); Bruce C. Daniels, *Puritans at Play: Leisure and Recreation in Colonial New England* (New York: St. Martin's Press, 1995), 128, 134 (quotes).

16. Godbeer, *Sexual Revolution*, 247.

17. Freedman and D'Emilio, *Intimate Matters*, 33 (quote); Ktorides, "Marriage and Customs in Colonial New England," 9; Wall, *Fierce Communion*, 65; Bloch, *Gender and Morality*, 85–86; Lombard, *Making Manhood*, 84–88; Wilson, *Ye Heart of a Man*, 40.

18. Frost, *Quaker Family*, 162 (quote); Barry Levy, " 'Tender Plants': Quaker Farmers and Children in the Delaware Valley, 1681–1735," in *Colonial America: Essays in Politics and Social Development*, ed. Stanley Katz and John Murrin (New York: Alfred A. Knopf, 1983), 183 (quote); Foster, *Sex and the Eighteenth-Century Man*, 14 (quote); Lombard, *Making Manhood*, 63–64, 89; Morgan, *Puritan Family*, 54; Freeman and D'Emilio, *Intimate Matters*, 42.

19. Wall, *Fierce Communion*, 61–62 (quotes); Singleton, *Dutch New York*, 217; Daniels, *Puritans at Play*, 118; Marylynn Salmon, "Women and

Property in South Carolina: The Evidence from Marriage Settlements, 1730–1830," *William and Mary Quarterly* 39 (1982): 239, 250–51.

20. Wall, *Fierce Communion*, 63–64; Singleton, *Dutch New York*, 210; Nicholas Beasley, "Domestic Ritual: Marriage and Baptism in the British Plantation Colonies, 1650–1780," *Anglican and Episcopal History* 76 (2007): 334–36.

21. Dale Taylor, *The Writer's Guide to Everyday Life in Colonial America: 1607–1783* (Cincinnati: Writer's Digest Books, 1997), 121–22.

22. Singleton, *Dutch New York*, 218–27.

23. Levy, "Tender Plants," 182–84; Frost, *Quaker Family*, 174.

24. Singleton, *Dutch New York*, 222–34; Daniels, *Puritans at Play*, 119; Ktorides, "Marriage Customs in Colonial New England," 13–14.

25. Lombard, *Making Manhood*, 115; Richard P. Giljie, *The Profane, the Civil, & the Godly: The Reformation of Manners in Orthodox New England, 1679–1749* (University Park: Pennsylvania State University Press, 1994), 87 (quote), 94 (quote); James M. Volo and Dorothy D. Volo, *Family Life in 17th and 18th Century America* (Westport, CT: Greenwood Press, 2006), 176; Ronald D. Cohen, "The Family in Colonial America," *Forum Series* (1976): 184–85; Billy Smith, *Lower Sort*, 186 (quote).

26. Spruill, *Women's Life & Work*, 164 (quote); Gilje, *The Profane*, 94 (quote), 87 (quote); Lombard, *Making Manhood*, 111 (quote).

27. Wilson, *Ye Heart of a Man*, quotes from pp. 76, 77, and 79; Spruill, *Women's Life & Work*, 165 (quote), 166 (quote).

28. Gilje, *The Profane*, 94 (quote); Elizabeth Pleck, *Domestic Tyranny: The Making of Social Policy against Family Violence from Colonial Times to the Present* (New York: Oxford University Press, 1987), 21, 18 (quote); Morgan, *Puritan Family*, 141 (quote); Merril D. Smith, *Breaking the Bonds: Marital Discord in Pennsylvania, 1730–1830* (New York: New York University Press, 1991), 111 (quote); Wilson, *Ye Heart of a Man*, 95; Edmund S. Morgan, "The Puritans and Sex," *New England Quarterly* 15 (1942): 605 (quote).

29. Billy Smith, *Lower Sort*, 190 (quote); Merril Smith, *Breaking the Bonds*, 108 (quote).

30. Elaine F. Crane, *Ebb Tide in New England: Women, Seaports, and Social Change, 1630–1800* (Boston: Northeastern University Press, 1998), 189 (quote); Merril Smith, *Breaking the Bonds*, 18 (quote); Billy Smith, *Lower Sort*, 191 (quote); Lombard, *Making Manhood*, 118; Freedman and D'Emilio, *Intimate Matters*, 25; Russell Shorto, *The Island at the Center of the World: The Epic Story of Dutch Manhattan and the Forgotten Colony That Shaped America* (New York: Vintage, 2004), 83–84 (quote); Foster, *Sex and the Eighteenth-Century Man*, 41 (quote); David H. Flaherty, *Privacy in Colonial New England* (Charlottesville: University Press of Virginia, 1972), 80 (quote).

31. Godbeer, "William Byrd's 'Flourish,' " 140–49.

32. Morgan, "Puritans and Sex," 592–93 (quote); Lombard, *Making Manhood*, 5, 113 (quote); Gloria L. Main, *Peoples of a Spacious Land: Families*

and Cultures in Colonial New England (Cambridge, MA: Harvard University Press, 2001), 96 (quote); Foster, *Sex and the Eighteenth-Century Man*, 12 (quote), 27 (quote); Martha Saxton, *Women's Moral Values in Early America* (New York: Hill and Wang, 2003), 72 (quote).

33. Lombard, *Making Manhood*, 112–14; Susan E. Klepp, "Lost, Hidden, Obstructed, and Repressed: Contraceptive and Abortive Technology in the Early Delaware Valley," in *Early American Technology: Making and Doing Things from the Colonial Era to 1850*, ed. Judith McGaw (Chapel Hill: University of North Carolina Press, 1994), 72 (quote).

34. Spruill, *Women's Life and Work*, 44–45; Main, *Peoples of a Spacious Land*, 96–97; Klepp, "Lost, Hidden, Obstructed," 94; Catherine Scholten, *Childbearing in American Society, 1650–1850* (New York: New York University Press, 1985), 13 (quote); Tannenbaum, *Health and Wellness*, 66; Foster, *Sex and the Eighteenth-Century Man*, 9.

35. Tannenbaum, *Health and Wellness*, 56–57; Klepp, "Lost, Hidden, Obstructed," 70–71, 83–84; Freeman and D'Emilio, *Intimate Matters*, 26 (quote).

36. Klepp, "Lost, Hidden, Obstructed," 90–91.

37. Scholten, *Childbearing in American Society*, 22.

38. Cohen, "The Family in Colonial World," 4 (quote); Tannenbaum, *Health and Wellness*, 78 (quote), 74; Keith Krawczynski, "A Note on Accidental Death in Colonial New Jersey, 1730–1770," *New Jersey History* 110 (1992): 63–70; Volo and Volo, *Family Life*, 38–39.

39. Peter G. Slater, " 'From the *Cradle* to the *Coffin*': Parental Bereavement and the Shadow of Infant Damnation in Puritan Society," in *Growing Up in America: Children in Historical Perspective*, ed. Joseph Hawes and N. Ray Hiner (Urbana: University of Illinois Press, 1985), 27, 29, 34 (quotes); Helena M. Wall, " 'My Constant Attension on my Sick Child': The Fragility of Family Life in the World of Elizabeth Drinker," in *Children in Colonial America*, ed. James Marten (New York: New York University Press, 2007), 160 (quote), 161.

40. Ulrich, *Good Wives*, 136; Scholten, *Childbearing in American Society*, 21, 15.

41. Scholten, *Childbearing in American Society*, 15–16, 18–20; Harry M. Ward, *Colonial America, 1607–1763* (Englewood Cliffs, NJ: Prentice Hall, 1991), 159.

42. Wilson, *Ye Heart of a Man*, 83–85; Main, *Peoples of a Spacious Land*, 99 (quote), 101; Joseph E. Illick, "Child-Rearing in Seventeenth-Century England and America," in *The History of Childhood*, ed. Lloyd de Mause (New York: Psychohistory Press, 1974), 304 (quote); Ulrich, *Good Wives*, 129 (quote); Tannenbaum, *Health and Wellness*, 59.

43. Ross W. Beales Jr., "Nursing and Weaning in Eighteenth-Century New England Household," in *Families and Children*, ed. Peter Benes (Boston: Boston University Press, 1985), 54 (quote); Glover, *All Our Relations*, 26 (quote); Wilson, *Ye Heart of a Man*, 85–86.

44. Ulrich, *Good Wives*, 129; Main, *Peoples of a Spacious Land*, 99; Beales, "Nursing and Weaning," 53 (quote); Ernest Caulfield, "Infant Feeding in Colonial America," *Journal of Pediatrics* 41 (1952): 684 (quote); Tannenbaum, *Health and Wellness*, 62–64.

45. Stephanie Grauman Wolf, *As Various as Their Land: The Everyday Lives of Eighteenth-Century Americans* (New York: Harper Perennial, 1994), 108; John F. Walzer, "A Period of Ambivalence: Eighteenth-Century American Childhood," in *The History of Childhood*, 358; Cohen, "The Family in Colonial America," 9; Steven Mintz and Susan Kellog, *Domestic Revolutions: A Social History of American Family Life* (New York: Free Press, 1988), 15; Mariah Adin, " 'I Shall Beat You, So That the Devil Shall Laugh at It': Children, Violence, and the Courts in New Amsterdam," in *Children in Colonial America*, 93.

46. Philip Greven, *Protestant Temperament: Patterns of Child-Rearing, Religious Experience, and the Self in Early America* (New York: Alfred A. Knopf, 1977), 21–150, 265–334; Frost, *Quaker Family*, 77 (quote); John F. Walzer, "Ambivalent Infant Care in Eighteenth-Century America," in *Loving, Parenting and Dying: The Family Cycle in England and America*, ed. Vivian C. Fox and Martin H. Quitt (New York: Psychohistory Press, 1980), 269–70; Michael Zuckerman, "Penmanship for Saucy Sons: Some Thoughts on the Colonial Southern Family," *South Carolina Historical Magazine* 84 (1983): 156–59.

47. Philip Greven, *Spare the Child: The Religious Roots of Punishment and the Psychological Impact of Physical Abuse* (New York: Vintage Books, 1992), 46–49.

48. Gerald F. Moran, "Colonial America, Adolescence In," in *Encyclopedia of Adolescence*, vol. 1, ed. Richard Lerner, Anne Petersen, and Jeanne Brooks-Gunn (New York: Garland Pub., 1991), 160–63; N. Ray Hiner, "Adolescence in Eighteenth-Century America," in *Loving, Parenting and Dying*, 361 and 363 (quotes); Roger Thompson, "Adolescent Culture in Colonial Massachusetts," *Journal of Family History* 8 (1984): 128–40.

49. Freedman and D'Emilio, *Intimate Matters*, 29; Giljie, *The Profane*, 90; Crane, *Ebb Tide in New England*, 192–93; Foster, *Sex and the Eighteenth-Century Man*, 33 (quote); Nancy F. Cott, "Divorce and the Changing Status of Women in Eighteenth-Century Massachusetts," *William and Mary Quarterly* 33 (1976): 597.

50. Billy Smith, *Lower Sort*, 191 (quote); Wall, *Fierce Communion*, 68; Clare Lyons, *Sex among the Rabble: An Intimate History of Gender and Power in the Age of Revolution, 1730–1830* (Chapel Hill: University of North Carolina Press, 2006), 22–32; Spruill, *Women's Life and Work*, 182; Herman Lantz, *Marital Incompatibility and Social Change in Early America* (Beverly Hills, CA: Sage Publications, 1976), 10–11, 18; Merril Smith, *Breaking the Bonds*, 17–19.

51. Robert V. Wells, "Quaker Marriage Patterns in a Colonial Perspective," *William and Mary Quarterly* 8 (1974): 24–26; Alexander Keyssar, "Widowhood in Eighteenth-Century Massachusetts: A Problem in the History of the Family," *Perspectives in American History* 8 (1974): 88–89; Wilson, *Ye Heart of a Man*, 147–48 (quote).

52. Keyssar, "Widowhood in Eighteenth-Century Massachusetts," 99 (quote); Giljie, *The Profane*, 101–3; Vivian Conger, " 'Being Weak of Body but Firm of Mind and Memory': Widowhood in Colonial America, 1630–1750," Ph.D. dissertation, Cornell University, 1994, 20–21, 111–14; Volo and Volo, *Family Life*, 183–85; Carole Shammas, "The Female Social Structure of Philadelphia in 1775," *Pennsylvania Magazine of History and Biography* 107–8 (1983): 75; Wulf, *As Various as Their Land*, 96–99.

53. Ulrich, *Good Wives*, 7 (quote); Conger, "Being Weak of Body," 131–33; Saxton, *Being Good*, 92; Giljie, *The Profane*, 102 (quote).

54. Frost, *Quaker Family*, 152; Spruill, *Women's Life and Work*, 156–61; Wilson, *Ye Heart of a Man*, 144; Main, *Peoples of a Spacious Land*, 85; Keyssar, "Widowhood in Eighteenth-Century Massachusetts," 94; Volo and Volo, *Family Life*, 184 (quote).

55. Glover, *All Our Relations*, 6–21; Darcy Fryer, " 'Improved' and 'Very Promising Children': Growing Up Rich in Eighteenth-Century South Carolina," in *Children in Colonial America*, 109–10.

56. Lorenzo J. Greene, *The Negro in Colonial New England* (New York: Columbia University Press, 1942), 193, 204; William D. Piersen, *Black Yankees: The Development of an Afro-American Subculture in Eighteenth-Century New England* (Amherst: University of Massachusetts Press, 1988), 93, 196–98, 200–201, 208–10; Merle Brouwer, "Marriage and Family Life among Blacks in Colonial Pennsylvania," *Pennsylvania Magazine of History and Biography* 99 (1975), 370; Lyons, *Sex among the Rabble*, 89 (quote).

57. Greene, *Negro in Colonial New England*, 195; Piersen, *Black Yankees*, 90–92.

58. Richard C. Wade, *Slavery in the Cities: The South, 1820–1860* (New York: Oxford University Press, 1964), 118 (quote); Piersen, *Black Yankees*, 94.

59. Greene, *Negro in Colonial New England*, 176, (quote), 213 (quotes), 42–43; Piersen, *Black Yankees*, 87–95.

60. Loren Schweninger, "A Slave Family in the Antebellum South," *Journal of Negro History* 60 (1975): 40–44.

61. David Hacket Fischer, *Growing Old in America* (New York: Oxford University Press, 1977), 3, 46; Gerald F. Moran and Maris A. Vinovskis, *Religion, Family and the Life Course: Explorations in the Social History of Early America* (Ann Arbor: University of Michigan Press, 1992), 199, 191, 192 (quote).

62. Fischer, *Growing Old*, 60, 63.

63. Paula Scott, *Growing Old in the Early Republic: Spiritual, Social, and Economic Issues, 1790–1830* (New York: Garland Press, 1997), 23–38; Fischer, *Growing Old*, 36, 67, 72.

64. Moran and Vinovskis, *Religion, Family and the Life Course*, 212.

65. Margaret M. Coffin, *Death in Early America* (New York: Thomas Nelson, 1976), 97–98.

66. Moran and Vinovskis, *Religion, Family and the Life Course*, 218–19; Wilson, *Ye Heart of a Man*, 145 (quote); Frost, *Quaker Family*, 42.

67. Singleton, *Dutch New York*, 252–53; Wulf, *Not All Wives*, 140–41; James Naglack, "Death in Colonial New England," *Historical Journal of Western Massachusetts* 4 (1975): 25–26; Coffin, *Death in Early America*, 73, 81; Alice M. Earle, "Death Ritual in Colonial New York," in *Passing: The Vision of Death in America*, ed. Charles O. Jackson (Westport, CT: Greenwood Press, 1977), 32.

68. Wilfred Talman, "Death Customs among the Colonial Dutch" *De Halve Maen* 43 (1968): 13–14; Robert W. Habenstein and William M. Lamers, *The History of American Funeral Directing* (Milwaukee: Bulfin Printers, 1955), 197; Daniels, *Puritans at Play*, 86; Moran and Vinovskis, *Religion, Family, and the Life Course*, 225.

69. Moran and Vinovskis, *Religion, Family and the Life Course*, 222; Peggy Robbins, "A Look at Death in Early America," *Early American Life* 10 (1979): 81; Habenstein and Lamers, *History of American Funeral Directing*, 204–6; Martha Fales, "The Early American Way of Death," *Essex Institute Historical Collection* 100 (1964): 75–79; Steven Bullock and Sheila McIntyre, "The Handsome Tokens of a Funeral: Glove-Giving and the Large Funeral in Eighteenth-Century New England," *William and Mary Quarterly* 69 (April 2012): 331, 334.

70. Coffin, *Death in Early America*, 104; Habenstein and Lamers, *History of American Funeral Directing*, 206–9; Robbins, "A Look at Death," 77 (quote).

71. William Livingston, "Of the Extravagance of Our Funerals," in *Passing: The Vision of Death in America*, 45–46.

72. Edgar McManus, *Black Bondage in the North* (Syracuse, NY: Syracuse University Press, 1973), 82; David Roediger, "And Die in Dixie: Funerals, Death & Heaven in the Slave Community, 1700–1865," *The Massachusetts Review* 22 (1981): 166 (quote), 169–71; Albert J. Raboteau, *Slave Religion: The "Invisible Institution" in the Antebellum South* (New York: Oxford University Press, 1978), 13; Wade, *Slavery in the Cities*, 170 (quote); Ann and Dickran Tashjian, "The Afro-American Section of Newport, Rhode Island's Common Burying Ground," in *Cemeteries & Gravemarkers: Voice of American Culture*, ed. Richard E. Myer (Logan, UT: Utah State University Press, 1992), 163; Greene, *Negro in Colonial New England*, 284 (quote).

73. Wulfe, *Not All Wives*, 121; Flaherty, *Privacy in Colonial New England*, 97, 110 (quote), 112; Billy Smith, *Lower Sort*, 188–89, 200 (quote).

74. Nancy Tomes, "The Quaker Connection: Visiting Patterns among Women in the Philadelphia Society of Friends, 1750–1800," in *Friends and Neighbors: Group Life in America's First Plural Society*, ed. Michael

Zuckerman (Philadelphia: Temple University Press, 1982), 186; David Narrett, *Inheritance and Family Life in Colonial New York City* (Ithaca, NY: Cornell University Press, 1992), 183–84; Billy Smith, *Lower Sort*, 183.

75. Flaherty, *Privacy in Colonial New England*, 90–91; Tomes, "The Quaker Connection," 177 (quote).

76. Wall, *Fierce Communion*, 13; Flaherty, *Privacy in Colonial New England*, 92, 89.

77. Wall, *Fierce Communion*, 18 (quotes); Flaherty, *Privacy in Colonial New England*, 94 (quote).

78. Katherine Grier, *Pets in America: A History* (Chapel Hill: University of North Carolina Press, 2006), 23, 21.

79. Ibid., 24.

4

Religion

INTRODUCTION

Religion was the most important guiding principle in the daily lives of most early Americans. It served as the basis of how they understood the world and their place in it, as well as how they identified themselves and viewed others. It provided important rites of passages along with daily, weekly, and seasonal rituals. It guided their views on morality and, concomitantly, their behavior. To that end, religion played a critical role in fostering educational institutions (both secondary and university level) and in providing much of the school curriculum. Educated colonists devoted most of their thoughts and writings to religious subjects. Some of this religious writing, along with certain religious practices, was used to justify and maintain a strict class, gender, and racial hierarchy throughout society. More specific to this study, those living in colonial cities had, in varying degrees, the difficult and unique task of working out the problems of living in a religiously plural environment. In such places there was considerable religious bigotry, persecution, and spiritual confusion, especially when new religious movements came up against the established church.

The religious experience of those living in the colonial cities is a complex story. Part of the complexity lies in the fact that each city

had its own unique religious experience. Three of the principal cities
—Boston, Philadelphia, and Newport—were founded on strong religious motives that contradicted each another. Early Puritan leaders
in Boston imposed a strict religious conformity on residents with the
purpose of establishing the ideal Christian commonwealth, while
William Penn and Roger Williams granted religious freedom to
Protestant settlers in Pennsylvania and Rhode Island, respectively.
This largely explains why Boston was religiously homogenous, at
least in its early years, while the remaining four large urban centers
were more religiously plural. No other areas in British North
America, in fact, had a greater diversity of faiths than the major cities.
Adding to the religious complexity of urban life is that the Anglican
Church in New York City and Charles Town and the Congregational
Church in Boston had official and financial support from the local
government, a privilege that angered residents in those towns belonging to the various dissenting faiths. Believers in Newport, on the other
hand, were more united by the established practice there of separat-
ing church from state. As if all this is not perplexing enough, religious
services among the many religious denominations varied, sometimes
considerably, and superstition, magic, and witchcraft still had a hold
on many colonists.

Despite these many distinctions, religion among Protestants in the
colonial cities shared important elements. Most Protestant churches
held to the Five Points of Calvinism as defined by the Synod of Dort
in 1619: the depravity of humans, unconditional election, limited
atonement, irrevocable grace, and the perseverance of the saints. The
Congregational, Presbyterian, Baptist, Dutch Reformed, German
Reformed, and French Reformed Protestants broadly agreed upon
the fundamentals of theology. Quakers, Lutherans, and Anglicans
were the only sizable exceptions among Protestants. More specifically,
all these denominations derived their idea of God from the infallibility
of the Bible. God was "an intimate personal deity," explains historian
Arthur Schlesinger, "not an aloof observer. He judged the daily
actions of men and sought ceaselessly to save their souls from the
blandishments of Satan." Believers were therefore "less concerned
with doctrine or with introspection than with tangible results in character and conduct."[1] To that end, churches sought to promote social
order and hierarchy by imposing certain standards of behavior on
members (often codified into law). However, such practices, together
with considerable religious intolerance between members of different
faiths, tended more to promote division and hostility than peace and
order. It was this intolerance and its negative consequences that

eventually compelled people of various faiths reluctantly and hesitantly to practice greater freedom of conscience. In addition to practical necessity, the influence and interference of England furthered religious liberty in early America, together with a large number of colonists who took no part at all in religion and the introduction of a rationalist movement in the eighteenth century. As religious historian Perry Miller further explains:

Protestants did not contribute to religious liberty, they stumbled into it, they were compelled into it, they accepted it at last because they had to, or because they saw its strategic value. In their original intention, Protestants were intolerant; because of the sheer impossibility of unifying colonies made up of a hodge-podge diversity, because of the example of toleration set and enforced by England, and because of a complete shift in the intellectual situation in the eighteenth century, whereby religious liberty became a perfect solution for new issues—for these reasons, the Protestant churches did not so much achieve religious liberty as have liberty thrust upon them.[2]

Thus the origins of religious freedom in the United States, one of the most cherished principles of the nation, have a long and turbulent history. Residents of the colonial cities played the leading role in this religious drama.

RELIGIOUS TYRANNY

It is a common misconception among Americans today that our ancestors came in search of religious toleration. As historian Louis Wright explains, toleration was a concept that "few of them recognized or approved. What they wanted was freedom from interference by opposing religious sects or unfriendly official authorities. Once firmly in the saddle themselves, sects that had been persecuted in England became equally zealous to root out heretics from their own order."[3] Efforts to impose conformity and suppress dissent therefore marked much of the religious scene in early America. Such an understanding should come as no surprise given the background from which European settlers came, a background that included near-constant religious warfare for two centuries between militant Catholics and Protestants that left hundreds of thousands of people dead. Religious persecution of minority faiths became the norm throughout Europe, a fact that contributed to the flow and character of the settlement of British America. With few exceptions, Christian colonists firmly planted their deep-rooted religious prejudices in the early American cultural landscape that contributed to the flowering of a familiar form of religious tyranny.

Sabbath Laws

Illustrative of religious tyranny in early America were Sabbath laws prohibiting both work and play on Sundays. All colonial legislatures, following English law dating back to the mid-fifteenth century, required everyone to attend church on Sunday and to rest from doing business. The collective nature of worship in early America was intended to promote a spiritual community of Christians united "in a complete, perfect, and glorious body in a state of eternal union and oneness with the head of the Lord Christ and all his members." Both religious and secular leaders considered the creation of a united Christian community so important that they made collective worship mandatory for all people. Penalties for skipping mandatory church service or working on the Sabbath ranged from fines for a first offense to jail sentences, public whippings, brandings, and mutilations for multiple violations. In one exceptional case, a Boston man in 1656 was forced to sit in the stocks for two hours for "lewd and unseemly behavior" on the Sabbath. His crime: kissing his wife upon returning home from three years at sea. More typical was a Philadelphia barber who in 1712 was arrested for cutting hair on Sunday and a New Amsterdam baker who was fined 12 guilders for rolling a barrel of maize along the street on the Sabbath.[4]

Such examples, out of many, illustrate that numerous people considered Sabbath laws a form of religious tyranny and social control that violated their perceived natural right not to attend church and instead to work and play on Sunday. Consequently, authorities in the five cities fought a tireless yet losing battle to prevent Sabbath breaking. As early as the 1640s, Boston judges complained of young people profaning the Sabbath by hunting, stealing, drinking, playing cards, abusing Indians "for sport," and participating in "filthy dalliances" that included indecent exposure outside the meeting-houses during services. By the end of the century, "many persons of riper years do too often profane the said day," opined the governor, "by frequenting Taverns and Ale-houses for Tipling and Drinking, Walking abroad in the streets and fields for diversion and recreation, and otherwise misspend the said Holy Time." A £100 fine for failing to show proper "Observation of the Lord's Day" failed to curtail violations. Nor did threats of larger fines discourage many Philadelphians from violating the law against "game, play, sport or diversion" on Sunday. Meanwhile, Sabbath violations were so numerous in Newport by the mid-1700s that the town council ordered local constables to round up all people in taverns, disperse all "disorderly gatherings," and prevent "all unnecessary walking in the streets and fields upon the said day."[5] Nevertheless, residents of Newport tended increasingly to treat Sunday as a day to work and play. Sabbath breaking was also "deplorably common" in New Amsterdam, where officials complained in 1667 that:

many of the inhabitants almost make it a custom, in place of observing the Sabbath ... to frequent the taverns more than on other days and to take their delight in illegal exercises ... trade and traffic, gaming, boat-racing or running with carts and wagons fishing, fowling, running and picking nuts, strawberries, etc., all riotous racing, calling and shouting of children in the streets, together with all unlawful exercises and games, drunkenness, frequenting taverns or taphouses, dancing, card playing, ball playing, rolling nine-pins or bowls, etc., which is more in vogue on this than on any other day.[6]

Many residents of Charles Town, both rich and poor and black and white, behaved in a similarly contemptuous manner on the Lord's Day, at least according to Boston's Josiah Quincy, who described the Sabbath there in 1773 as a time of "visiting and mirth with the rich, and of license, pastime and frolic for the negroes." At times this contempt for oppressive Sabbath laws manifested itself in some rather crude behavior, as when Alexander Colman of Boston showed up for mandatory religious service wearing "only a dirty frock of canvice all bloody & no other cloaths," or when Samuel Terry was caught one Sunday "standing with his face to the meeting house wall ... chafing his yard [masturbating] to provoak lust."[7]

Blasphemy Laws

Religious tyranny in the colonies extended beyond forced church attendance to include criminalizing speech deemed blasphemous to the Christian faith. All colonies passed blasphemy laws that imposed fines, floggings, and jail sentences to anyone "Denying, Cursing or reproaching the true God, his Creation or Government of the World ... or the Holy Word of God ... contained in the Books of the Old and New Testament." Authorities in early Boston and New Amsterdam even criminalized speech considered contemptuous against a minister or in disagreement with the "subject of religion." Violators in the Dutch colony were placed on bread and water for three days in the ship's galley, while those in the Puritan capital had to stand in public with a paper inscribed with "A Wanton Gospeller" fixed on his or her chest. In colonies with an established church where creed and government were interfused, any questioning of the essentials of Christianity was also considered an attack against the state. This may explain why Massachusetts imposed particularly harsh penalties for those who persisted in "maintaining his wicked opinion" that included banishment, dismemberment, having one's tongue bored with a "red hot Iron," or execution. Officials never carried out the latter penalty, although they sometimes forced convicted blasphemers to stand on the gallows with a noose around their necks as a reminder to onlookers that the crime was punishable by death. Other blasphemers suffered the punishment experienced by Robert Shorthouse, who had his tongue put into a cleft stick in 1636 for calling the church of Boston "a whoare [and] a strumpet." More unfortunate were Philip Ratcliff, a Boston servant who had his ears chopped off in 1631 for "most foul, scandalous invectives" against the church, and Joseph Gatchell, who in 1684 had his tongue bored through with a hot poker for publicly asserting that "there was no God, Devil, or Hell" and that Jesus was an "imperfect Savior & a foole."[8]

RELIGIOUS PLURALISM

A second dominant feature of religion in the colonial cities was its heterogeneous nature. By the early eighteenth century, the British North American cities were arguably the most religiously plural in the Western world as a result of immigration from many European countries and principalities and the importation of slaves from Africa and the Caribbean. Virtually every Christian domination and sect was represented in the cities, along with a smattering of Jews, atheists, and worshipers of African gods. While visiting a Philadelphia tavern in 1744, the Scottish physician Alexander Hamilton observed men of many faiths: "Roman Catholicks, Church men, Presbyterians, Quakers, Newlightmen, Methodists, Seventh day men, Moravians, Anabaptists, and one Jew."[9] This religious diversity created unique and sometimes contradictory experiences for urban residents that included intolerance and persecution, spiritual competition and confusion, and eventually a degree of cooperation and harmony.

Intolerance and Persecution

The religious prejudices brought to America by Christian settlers contributed to considerable religious dissension and intolerance in the first generations of settlement. This discord was particularly virulent in the major port cities, where the multitude of diverse churches and sects "mingled like prickly porcupines," in the words of historian Susan Mackiewicz. At one time or another, people of all faiths felt the prick of religious persecution. In New Amsterdam, for example, Dutch authorities temporarily outlawed all dissenting faiths and fined, imprisoned, and sometimes banished from the province Lutherans, Baptists, Presbyterians, and especially Quakers, whom they described as "instruments of Satan" for their annoying practice of disturbing the religious services of others and preaching in the streets. When two young Quaker women "began to quake and go into a frenzy, and cry out loudly in the middle of the street that men should repent for the day of judgment was at hand," two constables "seized them both by the head" and led them to the rat-infested prison where they "continued to cry out and pray." In justifying such religious intolerance, a Dutch Reformed minister explained, "If the Lutherans should be indulged in the exercise of public worship, the Papist, Mennonites and others, would soon make similar claims. Thus we would soon become a Babel of confusion, instead of remaining a united and peaceful people." To further deter this religious Babel, Dutch leaders directed much of their intolerance toward the small community of Jews in the capital, whom they demonized as "Christ-killers," "godless rascals," and a "deceitful race" who "have no other God than the unrighteous Mammon." Such anti-Semitism had the desired effect of driving most of New Amsterdam's Jews from the city.[10]

Even after the English took control of the city in 1664 and later imposed a Toleration Act in 1689, residents in New York City only reluctantly tolerated those of differing faiths. Anglicans and Presbyterians, for instance, eyed each other with suspicion and bickered over the creation of a Presbyterian college, the validity of Presbyterian ordinations, and proselytizing by the Anglican Society for the Propagation of the Gospel (SPG). Meanwhile, Quakers there criticized Calvinist doctrines, while Congregationalists denounced the preaching of Moravians. Lutherans in the city bitterly complained that the numerous Dutch Reformed insisted on having "everything their own way." Finally, all the dissenting faiths in New York City denounced the ecclesiastical privileges of the established Anglican church, an attitude that may explain why in 1714 some "wicked and Sacrilegious" persons broke into Trinity Church and destroyed the sanctuary and smeared dung on the surplices, the Book of Common Prayer, and psalm books. Lutheran minister John Hartwick was not alone in being "very much griev'd" over the "bad Affects w[h]ich the many Divisions in religious Sentiments and Worship have [here] with Respect to the General Cause of Christianity."[11]

Religious divisions in Boston also proved detrimental to peace and harmony in the Puritan capital. Desecrating the Christian concept of brotherly love, Puritan leaders there had a simple message to those following an alternative orthodoxy: "all Familists, Anabaptists and other enthusiasts shall have free liberty to keep away from us." Four Quaker martyrs who refused to "keep away" in the mid-1600s met their fate at the end of a hangman's noose. Dozens of other Friends were publicly whipped, were branded with the letter H, and had their ears cropped for disrupting Puritan services in Boston by running through the meetinghouse partially nude and covered in ashes as a sign to the Puritans of their dark and naked sins. The jurist Samuel Sewall recorded one such spectacle in 1677: "In Sermon time there came in a female Quaker, in a canvas Frock, her hair disshevelled and loose like a Periwigg, her face as black as ink, led by two other Quakers, and two other followed. It occasioned the greatest and most amazing uproar that I ever saw." The persecution of Baptists in Boston provoked an uproar of another kind, as when local Puritans in 1651 cheered the public flogging of Obadiah Holmes for practicing his dissenting faith. Nor did Puritans want Anglicans in their midst. When Anglicans opened their first church in Boston in 1689, a Puritan mob christened it by smashing its windows and making "Crosses of Mans dung on the Doors" and "filling the Key-holes with the same."[12]

Religious bigotry never had such deadly, sadistic, and crude consequences in Charles Town, but intolerance between Anglicans and dissenters there intensified political discord in the colonial legislature during its early years. Anglicans and their Huguenot allies, in particular, used religion as a weapon in their quest for political hegemony. By 1704, officials in Charles Town were complaining that "the admitting of persons of different religious persuasions hath often caused great contentions and animosities in this province and hath very much obstructed the public business." Two years later, Anglicans obstructed public business even more by passing an act restricting membership in the assembly to those who attended Church of England worship, a blatant act of religious intolerance that even the Queen in council would not allow. Equally intolerant Anglicans in Philadelphia caused similar political turmoil at about this same time by unsuccessfully trying to convince the English Crown to repeal local laws accommodating dissenters. Meanwhile, the Quakers' pacifism contributed to a bitter and protracted political contest among officials in Philadelphia over military funding. Similarly, the egalitarianism among Friends in Charles Town earned them considerable persecution for not observing the prevailing "etiquette of power" that put a heavy emphasis on hierarchy and deference to the established order. One Quaker certainly showed little respect to a neighbor on his recent baptism by remarking: "Why didn't thee desire the Minister rather to piss upon [your] Head; that would have been of more effect."[13]

This religious intolerance and self-righteousness among Christians infected and corroded single denominations and even individual churches in the cities. Newport's sectarian rivalry, for example, produced so many narrow-minded religious zealots who were bent on proving the righteousness of their own causes that it destroyed much of the spirit of religious toleration upon which Rhode Island was founded and led to numerous splits within churches of various denominations. Petty internal rivalries also tore churches apart. The Congregational Church, for example, split apart in the 1720s over a dispute between its parishioners and pastor, who refused to administer communion to his own congregation because he said its members were "not of sufficient holy conversation." The religious divisions and subdivisions over minor points of doctrinal purity among Newport churches convinced the Irish philosopher George Berkeley that the city would not be a good place to realize his dream of founding a college in North America that would reform manners, propagate the gospel, and in general be "an instrument of doing good to mankind."[14]

Religious infighting within churches in the other cities also hindered them from "doing good to mankind." Puritan leaders in early Boston famously expelled from Massachusetts Roger Williams and Anne Hutchinson for preaching a message different from the traditional orthodoxy. Quaker leaders in Charles Town did not go so far as to expel members from the colony, but factionalism within the small group was so intense that they asked Friends from Philadelphia to intervene. Bitter doctrinal differences also tore apart the First Baptist Church in the southern capital as one frustrated faction broke off to form an independent "gospel Church." Other dissenting ministers in Charles Town heaped abuse on each other over differences regarding the Westminster confession of faith, while the quarrel and strife within and between Swiss and German Reformed churches "knew no bounds." Meanwhile, the bitter and protracted schism among Philadelphia Friends in the

1690s over a proposal to shore up the theological and ecclesiastical foundations of Quakerism (the Keithian schism) also knew no bounds. At one point the heated debate erupted into an all-out brawl in their house of worship. The synagogue in Philadelphia was nearly as divided as the more established Jews who had assimilated into the mainstream society mocked newly arrived Jews who still wore long beards, always kept their heads covered, dressed in long shawls, and spoke broken English. The persecution from their fellow Hebrews became so intense that it drove the "new parcel of Jews" to form their own separate congregation in the late 1760s. Jews in New York City could also not get along as Sephardic and Ashkenazic factions frequently slandered, sued, and even exchanged blows in the synagogue. Finally, disputes over doctrine divided New York City Baptists so severely that they eventually formed separate churches. This religious prejudice "functioned in the colonial era much like racial prejudice does in modern America," explains historian Susan Juster, "as an ever-present if not always publicly acknowledged force shaping the everyday life and civic culture of its residents."[15]

Competition and Confusion

This religious discord in the cities was exacerbated by considerable competition for souls among ministers of various faiths that contributed to spiritual confusion among lay people. Anglican leaders in Newport, for example, blamed the "Baptist and Quaker influence" for stealing their members, while the Baptist minister John Gano of New York City frustrated other ministers by "draw[ing] almost all the religious Sort of People from every denomination in [the] City after him." In Charles Town, Anglican laypersons bluntly threatened their clergymen with "going over to the dissenters" if they did not abandon certain ceremonies and liturgical practices of the state church. Some Protestants surreptitiously cultivated friendships with people of other faiths with the intention of converting them to the "true Church of Christ." Much more open and aggressive in stealing souls was the Anglican SPG, which sent scores of missionaries to the cities to wage battle with other denominations for religious converts. Unbelievers and deists, too, competed to pull people away from church with their "loose and atheistical principles." Even without aggressive proselytizing, the Chinese menu of religious denominations in the cities enticed residents to sample the many spiritual offerings that compelled some to switch faiths.[16]

This competition for souls even extended to the building of larger, taller, and more ornate churches, meetinghouses, and synagogues in the cities as a conspicuous symbol of God's alleged favor. In Philadelphia, for example, Quakers, Presbyterians, and Baptists all built spacious meetinghouses, some "in the very face" of the Anglican Church. "By these means," complained a local Anglican priest, "the interest of our church here seems to be more than ever in hazard of greater decay." Similar circumstances in the other cities finally prompted the Anglican SPG to launch a systematic campaign in the early eighteenth century to build superior churches as a means to recover the colonies for the episcopacy. The result was a battle of meetinghouses between the various denominations that radically altered the urban skyline with ever-taller brick churches topped with bell towers and steeples that almost seemed to pierce the clouds. Even Jews in New York City built their grand Mill Street synagogue not "merely to honor God," explains historian William Pencak, "but to establish a symbolic architectural superiority over the Christian churches in town." Likewise, Jews in Newport built Touro synagogue atop a hill so that it dominated the city's skyline.[17]

This aggressive marketing for souls caused confusion among some city folk who grew increasingly bewildered by the array of faiths. One confused Presbyterian in New York City asked: "Among which of these Systems shall a candid Inquirer after Truth look for Christianity? Where shall he find the religion of Christ amidst all this priestly Fustian and ecclesiastical Trumpery?" They all "claim to be orthodox, and yet all differ from one another, and each is ready to Damn all the Rest." Bombarded by this babble of creeds, some people developed "such an Indifferent Temper," explained one New Yorker, "that scarce themselves know what profession they are of." Other perplexed people, feeling misled by ministers of various faiths, "neglected or scoff[ed] at the divine service." Some "nothingarians" simply gave up their spiritual search and belonged to no church at all.[18]

Cooperation and Harmony

Despite all the doctrinal differences and competition for souls among the various faiths, degrees of religious cooperation and harmony eventually emerged in the five cities. A lack of church buildings for all denominations in the first years of settlement fostered much of this cooperation among people of different faiths. During the early years of Philadelphia, for example, Presbyterians and Baptists met together in a storehouse for religious services, while others attended the Quaker meeting for lack of a church in which to worship. For similar reasons, Presbyterians and Congregationalists in Charles Town met together for religious services until the early 1730s. This cooperation among people of different faiths sometimes extended outside the church. In Newport, for instance, Quakers, Jews, Huguenots, Anglicans, Catholics, Moravians, Congregationalists, and Baptists cooperated with one another to establish the Redwood Library, the Freemasons' Lodge, and the Hand-in-Fire Club. Gentiles and Jews alike attended the dedication of the Jewish synagogue there in 1763. Likewise, ministers of different faiths in Philadelphia often reached out to each other to foster mutually beneficial relations. This religious cooperation prompted one Philadelphia Quaker to remark that "good Concord & benevolent Disposition amongst People of all Denominations," prevailed in the capital, "each delighting to be Reciprocally helpful & kind in Acts of friendship for one another."[19]

This growing religious tolerance in the cities resulted from a number of factors. In this regard, Newport and Philadelphia benefitted from being located in provinces founded on the idea of liberty of conscience, a policy that encouraged people to respect the spiritual needs and rights of others. In Newport, for example, the Seventh Day Baptists, who preferred to worship on Saturday rather than on Sunday, were provided with a special Wednesday market day so that they would not be forced to engage in trade on the Sabbath. In Boston, New York City, and Charles Town, where an established church prevailed, residents required more compelling forces to recognize the religious rights of others. One of these forces came in 1689 when Parliament, in an attempt to promote national unity in an age of imperial rivalry, passed a Toleration Act that granted religious freedom to all Protestant dissenters in the empire. Perhaps more effective in promoting religious toleration in the cities was economic self-interest. As historian Richard Hofstadter astutely observed, "In an age of commercial expansion the profit motive quietly undermined the desire to impose a creed." Merchants and other business people in the cities therefore tended to overlook religious differences for the sake of trade. A less pecuniary explanation is offered by historian Thomas Carney, who argues that at least in New York City the initial religious pluralism gave rise to an "expectancy of religious freedom" fostered by a "hands off" policy towards religion by authorities during the eighteenth century. By the 1740s, New Yorkers believed that they had the right to "choose their own religion."[20]

MEETINGHOUSES AND CHURCHES

Houses of worship in the colonial cities varied considerably over time and between denominations. The first religious meetings in New Amsterdam were held either in the upper floor of the horse mill or the fort until residents eventually built a 70-foot by 52-foot stone church complete with a tower topped with a weathercock. Early residents of Boston held religious service in log buildings with earthen floors and unpainted benches that served as pews. Serving a dual purpose as both a house of worship and a place for town meetings, nothing on either the outside or inside of an early Puritan meetinghouse distinguished itself as a church. The Puritans built their meetinghouses square or rectangular, never cruciform. They omitted statues and stained-glass windows and virtually every other form of adornment, unless one counts the numerous public notices of town meetings, sales of cattle, and intended marriages and the wolves' heads nailed to the exterior walls. Over time the exteriors of Puritan meetinghouses were finished with clapboards and the interiors either plastered or lined with cedar board. As congregations grew in size, galleries were built on three sides and a heavy sounding board placed above the pulpit so all could better hear the minister. Seating eventually grew more comfortable, at least for upper-class worshipers, who added pew walls with padded shelf-like seats hanging on hinges that allowed them to turn up their seats and lean against the pew walls during long psalm songs and prayers. To help keep warm during cold New England winters, churchgoers brought foot stoves filled with hot coals, fur bags made of wolfskins, and even dogs to lie on their cold feet.[21]

Anglican churches in the five cities differed in both purpose and structure from their Congregational counterparts. As the established Church of England, the overriding purpose of the Anglican Church was to instill allegiance to both the Lord and the Crown. Visual elements within the church—the Book of Common Prayer, the Ten Commandments, the Decalogue, the Lord's Prayer, the Apostle's Creed, and the Royal Arms—reminded parishioners of both their spiritual and temporal loyalties. On a more secular level, the Anglican gentry, who considered themselves lords in the House of the Lord, sought to use the church as a means to promote social hierarchy and deference. To that end, Anglican churches in the cities

Photo of St. Michael's Church, Charles Town. Built in the 1750s by order of the South Carolina assembly, St. Michael's Church (Anglican) is a conspicuous testimony to the power of state-supported religion in the southern colonies. Indeed, its location opposite to the equally imposing State House reminded the people of the powerful connection between church and state. St. Michael's is also one of the great Georgian churches in the American colonies and graphically reflected the growing wealth and sophistication of eighteenth-century Charles Town. (Library of Congress, Prints and Photographs Division, Historic American Buildings Survey [HABS] SC, 10-CHAR, 8-15)

were built much like a gentleman's house. Lower-class worshipers had to be awed by the genteel environment: the lathed wood walls, plastered and whitewashed; mural decorations and paintings of winged cherubs; colored glass windows; and communion silver and organ all conspicuously displayed. The intent of this rich display was to instill deference in the lower classes toward the gentry, for as in any gentleman's house, visitors must show respect for its owners.[22]

Christianity and Class

In many ways, Christian churches and Jewish synagogues reflected the aristocratic nature of worship in the colonial cities. Churches "belonged to the genteel," explains historian Richard Bushman, and "joined the assemblage of urban places suitable for genteel performances." One eighteenth-century Bostonian observed that the church is the "grand theatre" where the rich attend to "display their extravagance and finery." This religious theater was most pronounced in Anglican services, where custom allowed the upper-class parishioners to enter last and leave first so that their social inferiors had to watch them parade in and out of the house of God in grand fashion. This elitist privilege had the purpose of encouraging deference among the lower sort to better maintain upper-class hegemony. Similarly, most denominations contributed to social order and hierarchy with a carefully assigned seating arrangement determined by a church committee composed of well-to-do members empowered to "dignify the seats." The cost of pew rents further reinforced the hierarchical order. Not surprisingly, individuals of high status, determined by wealth, age, learning, and public service, received the prized "foreseats" nearest the pulpit. Some affluent men built U-shaped family pews with high partitioned walls and decorated them with columns and windows to further distinguish and separate themselves and their families from the common believers. Suffering behind these high pews sat shopkeepers and artisans, while further back and on the sides sat the poor and servants. Blacks and Indians were placed under the galleries, on the stairs, or high up under the beams in a loft. Alongside them sat the children, who were often segregated so that church leaders could keep a closer eye on them. As a reflection of their status, women were placed on one side of the church in the same position as their husbands. Anyone sitting in a seat not allocated to him or her was subject to a heavy fine.[23]

This elitist seating arrangement made the mandatory Sabbath worship a tool for the upper class to assist them in maintaining control over the lower sort by emphasizing to them that some believers were superior to others. That this class distinction and privilege occurred in a house of God gave it the appearance of approval from the highest authority. Therefore, any questioning of this elitist arrangement was tantamount to blasphemy. John Winthrop of Boston echoed the sentiment of other elite leaders when he remarked in a 1629 sermon that "God has so disposed of the condition of mankind as in all times some must be rich, some poor, some high and eminent in power and dignity, others mean and in subjection." More than a century later the Reverend John Callender of Newport was quick to urge his lower-class parishioners to be satisfied with their inferior status and not to question the social arrangement. He assured them that they could be important in their own sphere even if they did not hold public office. "All men," he claimed, "could be truly Benefactors to Society in a Private Station" merely by leading "quiet, peaceful Godly lives." Parishioners of lower rank sometimes took affront to this religious elitism that strove to maintain the traditional social structure. By the 1760s, 75 middling- and lower-rank members of Philadelphia's Christ Church (Anglican) could no longer suffer the supercilious and obnoxious behavior of their more affluent brethren and so split off from them to form their own church. In short, elitism and deference, not equality and democracy, were some of the more important hallmarks of Christianity in early America.[24]

CHURCH MEMBERSHIP

Religious elitism was also reflected in church membership. This is especially true in the Congregational, Baptist, and other churches where only those who had demonstrated that they had been "wounded in the hearts for their original sin and actual transgressions" could be declared "saints" and allowed into the church as full members. Only these "visible saints" could receive the Lord's Supper and vote on civil and ecclesiastical matters. To prove that one was actually reborn, the potential member had to give a relation of conversion to the members of the congregation. This was a two-part ritual that involved giving a written statement to the pastor, who then read it to the congregation. Afterwards the candidate had to give an oral "relation" before church members of his past sins, the first stirring of religious faith, the conversion experience itself, and finally a formal profession of faith. Throughout this "oral exam," church elders commonly asked the applicant probing questions of his past behavior and conversion experience.[25] Not surprisingly, those who had a reputation for drunkenness, adultery, fornication, and habitual gambling rarely applied for church membership. Even many with a clean record refused to put themselves through this personally intrusive interrogation.

To solve the problem of declining church membership, New England ministers meeting in Cambridge, Massachusetts, in 1648 established a "Platform" calling for greater privacy, moderation, and compassion in the admission process. This leniency failed to encourage the most reticent to reach the exclusive summit of church membership by making a relation. In Boston, a greater attraction to rising commercial values contributed to this religious declension, a moving away from the ideals of the Bay Colony's founding fathers. To keep the younger generations on the spiritual path, clergymen made a compromise in 1662 with the "Half-Way Covenant" that allowed the children and grandchildren of professing saints to become "half-way members" with the right to receive baptism but not the Lord's Supper. Still, perhaps no more than one in seven Congregationalists were church members by the early 1700s.

Far from serving as a unifying institution promoting peace on Earth, these conservative Christian denominations divided families and fragmented local communities. As Puritan Thomas Lechford explained in 1642, "sometimes the Master is admitted" to membership "and not the servant, *and e contra*; the husband is received, and not the wife; . . . the child and not the parent." One can only imagine the tension and strife such religious arrangements caused within families, especially with women comprising upwards of two-thirds of church membership in many denominations. Moreover, by excluding men and women from communion, families from the baptismal font, and even whole segments of the population from the government, religious and secular leaders also "drove a wedge into the community," writes historian Darret Rutman about early Boston. It certainly gave church members a feeling of superiority and inclusiveness while treating nonmembers as virtual outsiders. "If the church had merely separated the good from the bad, the moral from the immoral," Rutman adds, "the division would not have been painful."[26]

CONGREGATIONALISM

Although Congregationalists had established churches in all of the five largest colonial cities, their greatest numbers and influence were in Boston, the spiritual center of the denomination.

Its members, better known as Puritans, were zealous religious pro-
testors and reformers who believed they had a covenant with God
to create the ideal Christian commonwealth that would be a model
for the rest of mankind. To that end, Puritan leaders imposed an
unceasing, invasive, and authoritative doctrine on both the public
and private lives of residents. Compulsory church attendance,
Sabbath laws, and the divine service itself were all "measures of
community control," explains Michael Zuckerman, intended to
"bring men to civil obedience & allegiance unto magistracy as much
as to faith." Obedience and allegiance to both state and church were
further advanced in a real fear of hell. This real fear of hell and the
belief in their own innate depravity burdened Puritans with guilt
for the "most ordinary desires and frailties," writes historian
Claudia Johnson, and led them to "discipline themselves and their
children with psychologically crippling severity."[27]

Indoctrination of Children

This psychological conditioning of Puritan children started at an
early age during their religious indoctrination, an indoctrination
that dwelt more on fear than on reason. Parents and preachers
intentionally selected frightening verses from the Bible of God's
judgment on the sinful, of horrifying suffering and agony, and of
destruction and desolation. Selections from the book of Revelation
and the book of Samuel, according to one seventeenth-century
Puritan, filled him with such unspeakable terror that he called the
enforced reading of them "a piece of gratuitous and unprofitable
cruelty." Boston divine Cotton Mather regularly impressed upon
his children the sinful condition of their nature and the possibility
they would burn in hell for eternity. It is no wonder that Cotton
Mather's son Nathaniel, who died prematurely at 19, prayed constantly, even in his sleep, fasted often, and strictly adhered to the
religious duties imposed by his father. Such indoctrination filled
young Nathaniel's short life with "self-loathing, horrible conceptions of God, unbounded dread of death, and all the horrors of a
morbid soul." Likewise, the seventeenth-century Boston jurist
Samuel Sewall frequently brought his children to tears when reading to them passages from the Bible graphically describing God's
destructive wrath against sinners. Religious books specifically targeting children, like Thomas White's *Little Book for Children*, used
similar fear tactics by including the following warning: "yet mistake
me not, I say not all little Children shall be saved; for little Children

that Swear or Lie, or break the Sabbath, playing upon the Lord's Day, or live in any other sin, shall go to Hell, you shall not go to Heaven." Therefore hell, Satan, and eternal torments were branded on the psyche of Puritan children, whose childhoods were filled as much with fear as with fun.[28]

Religious Practices

The importance of religious devotion to Congregationalists was reflected in their intensive and extensive religious practices that included both individual and group activities. Dedicated Puritans maintained a daily regimen of reading the Bible and devotional books and engaging in private meditation, self-examination, and prayer upon rising and before retiring. Many of them sought out a favorite secret spot to pray—a closet or garret in the home, or outside underneath hedges, or a hideaway in the woods. Cotton Mather, for instance, prayed most fervently in his study, often while groveling on the floor. Still, Puritans emphasized the family aspect of their church and so encouraged regular family spiritual exercises that included scripture reading and psalm singing. As if this were not enough spiritual devotion, many laymen and women held biweekly or weekly private pious readings segregated by age, sex, or occupation. Puritans even spent their Saturday evenings and Sunday mornings in intensive meditation and prayer in preparation for the Sabbath worship itself.[29]

Sunday worship was an all-day affair that included morning and afternoon services, each lasting about three hours. The order was basically the same in both services: opening prayer, scripture reading, exposition of scripture, psalm singing, sermons, main prayer, psalm singing, sacrament (monthly or bimonthly that included the Lord's Supper in the morning and baptism in the afternoon services), admission of new members, and blessing. The Congregational service was therefore formulaic despite the Puritans' rejection of traditional liturgy and ritual. At about 2:00 PM, the worshipers repeated the processes at their second service of the day. Dividing the two services was the noon break, which churchgoers turned into a pleasant opportunity to meet with friends and acquaintances, to court the opposite sex, to spread news and gossip, to drink and eat in nearby taverns, and to discuss and sometimes lampoon 'the minister's morning sermon. One Boston minister opined that even those who "pretend high to religion" talk about their "Corn and Hay, and the prices of Commodities, or almost anything they discourse of on Working

Days. They are mute about what they hear [in sermons]." Apparently many Puritans did not listen to their minister, at least according to Boston divine Increase Mather, who lamented that in the post-Sabbath revelry "there is more wickedness committed usually on that night than in all the week besides."[30]

The main event of the Puritan church service was the sermon, a carefully crafted performance filled with tension and emotion in which the pastor sought to bring the souls of his parishioners towards Christ and to promote harmony among Christians. To that end, the minister preached in a plain yet passionate style that often included metaphors related to household chores, trades, farm work, sports, and even sex so that even the "simplest hearer" could understand his fear-inspiring jeremiads against sinful behavior and God's wrath against sinners. The imagery and passion with which Puritan divines sometimes delivered their sermons convinced more than one listener to believe that their minister not only "certainly knew what a sinner I had been" but who also "thought that I was as good as in hell already."[31]

Sacraments

The Puritans recognized only two sacraments—baptism and holy communion. Participation in both was restricted to saints, or full church members—at least before the creation of the Half-Way Covenant. Receiving the Lord's Supper instilled severe anxiety in many who went through the public ritual. The anxiety began before the actual event when the pious were to prepare themselves for receiving the sacrament by peering into their souls. Many did not like what they saw as they engaged in this act of introspective self-flagellation. Others, however, found preparing for the sacrament a powerfully uplifting experience and could not wait for the possibility of union with Christ. William Cooper of Boston regarded the partaking of "his Body and Blood" as increasing "my Spiritual nourishment and growth in Grace." Some women, like Sarah Pierpont, had a more sexual view of Christ and the Lord's Supper, as Pierpont described her desire "that my soul may be ravisht with love to thee." A "pious woman" from Boston apparently felt no such love upon receiving the sacrament and so hung herself in her bedroom closet later that Sunday evening. However, not all parishioners took communion so seriously. A member of Boston's North Church who had a penchant for strong drink was suspended from partaking of the Lord's Supper after a "particularly inebriated incident."[32]

Unscheduled Worship

In addition to scheduled worship every Sunday, Puritans, more so than any other Christian group, enjoyed extraordinary, unscheduled worship. This included lecture days, which Puritan ministers announced whenever they felt moved by the Holy Spirit, and fast days and days of thanksgiving given during colony-wide elections, war, times of internal discord, perceived moral declension among the people, epidemics of diseases, extreme weather, and other providential events. Attendance at these special services was mandatory for all citizens, who had to endure eight or nine hours of preaching and scriptural explication by the minister elaborating on the sins that had caused the calamity at hand and predicting further troubles if the community and its members refused to repent and change their behavior. In this way Puritan worship "reacted most enthusiastically to the present and constant activity of a living God," explains historian James Walsh, "who was to be always and everywhere adored."[33]

ANGLICANISM

Alongside Congregationalism as one of the two "power churches" in the American colonies was Anglicanism, the official Church of England. Among the five principal cities, it had its greatest strength in Charles Town and New York City, where Anglicans constituted a significant minority and where the Church of England was the established church and was supported by public taxes. Anglicanism in the other cities received a hefty boost from the indefatigable efforts of the SPG missionaries and Parliament's passage of the Toleration Act in 1689 granting religious freedom to all Protestants in the empire. Many wealthy and well-educated residents were attracted to Anglicanism's "broad and liberal rationalism," its "dignified worship," and its lack of "strict conceptions of church discipline," while the less affluent were turned off by its "aristocratic outlook," apparent lack of interest in the common people, and absence of emotional appeal. For these reasons, Anglicanism had far less appeal among the urban masses than among the aristocracy, who controlled every facet of the church and used it to help maintain their power and privilege in society.[34]

The dominant purpose of the Anglican Church, like many others, was to help promote a disciplined and orderly society. For the Anglican elite who controlled church government, this meant maintaining social hierarchy, privilege, and deference. Each Anglican church played a critical role in this process through its parish vestry, a 12-member board consisting of the church's wealthiest members (including the minister), who monopolized the important powers and business affairs of the parish. The institutional structure of the Anglican Church therefore served to "reinforce claims to authority from above," explains historian Rhys Isaac, "and its acceptance from below." In addition to overseeing construction of the church, levying an annual parish tax (a head tax, not a property tax), selecting a minister, and paying his salary, the vestry also assigned seats in church based on wealth and heard applications for poor relief. The latter two functions, in particular, gave upper-class vestrymen an opportunity to publicly demonstrate their power and privilege to the lower sort. In return for serving the needs of their "guests," this elitist "gentleman's club" expected a "silent gratitude" from church members and "obedience to their orders as masters of a parish." Part of these orders included instructing the church-wardens, men of respectable middle-class standing, to carry out the day-to-day business of the parish such as collecting the minister's salary, certifying the accuracy of tithables, ridding the parish of beggars and nonresident poor, overseeing the education of orphans, and undertaking repairs to the church, among many other tedious but necessary tasks.[35]

Anglican Service

Furthering elitism in the Anglican Church were doctrines and practices with a heavy class bias. Anglican theology and worship was "pitched to a sophisticated and well-educated audience," explains historian Charles Bolton. The Anglican service also utilized an elaborate set of rituals that created "an atmosphere of richness and formality that complemented the clothing and manners of the well-to-do planters and merchants." Even before the service started, for example, the gentry collectively entered the church after everyone else was seated and paraded in grand fashion to their great oak-walled pews at the front. Lower-class worshipers had no choice but to watch this public display of manufactured superiority. By "visibly conforming to the doctrines of the established church," historian Robert Olwell explains, "parishioners demonstrated their acceptance of the existing social order and in turn secured public recognition of their rightful place with the social hierarchy." The priest, too, supported this social hierarchy with providential approval by preaching to the lower classes their duty to respect and obey their economic superiors. Charles Town Anglican minister Gideon Johnston, for one, conspicuously reinforced this elitism by allowing his rich communicants to take the Lord's Supper first.[36]

Such elitism aside, the Anglican worship consisted of, in the words of one Puritan eyewitness, "prayers read over in haste, a Sermon seldom under & never over twenty minutes, but always made up of sound morality, or deep studied Metaphysics." The Anglican liturgy itself is largely Catholic in nature and, as such, has a strong ritual element to it that includes weekly repetition of prescribed phrases throughout the service and set readings from the Book of Common Prayer. One Anglican bishop defended the repetitive nature of the liturgy by explaining that if we hear "good things" only now and then, "they may swim for a while in our brains, yet they seldom sink down into our hearts so as to move and sway the affections." If these "same words and expressions" are "continually put into mind," on the other hand, they "will imprint the things themselves so firmly in our minds that ... they will still occur upon all occasions, which cannot be but very much for our Christian edification." The Anglican liturgy, according to historian Rhys Isaac, therefore offered a "powerful representation of a structured, hierarchical community."[37]

QUAKERISM

In sharp contrast to the extravagance and elitism of the Anglican Church and its ritualistic liturgy was the Quaker plain-style meetinghouse and egalitarian service. Eschewing what they considered the meaningless formalities and extravagances of the times, Quakers adopted plain dress, plain speech, and a plain worship service bereft of ministerial leadership, formal ceremonies, and sacred symbols. Their houses of worship, like everything else about the Quakers, were plain both inside and out. No pulpit, altar, or deacon's bench greeted worshipers, who sat on plain benches. The Quaker service reflected the austerity of the meetinghouse in which it was held. Quakers were expected to enter quietly and sit down, filling the seats at the front first. Tired of theological arguments and pedantic sermons, Friends instead sat in silence until God "prepared a mouthpiece for his Word." A Quaker meeting could therefore be entirely silent. This corporate silence was key to the Quaker worship as followers believed one must be "hushed and attuned" in order to achieve spiritual correspondence. Not surprisingly, such silence induced drowsiness among worshipers. Some

Friends stuck themselves with pins during service in order to stay awake. For others, the "hushing" created a palpable tension that sometimes manifested itself in crying and quaking that earned Friends the sobriquet "Quaker" among non-Friends.[38] When the speaking came, it, too, was emotional and often rhythmical. In one example, an elderly man in the front pew suddenly stood up and removed his hat, and according to one eyewitness:

He spoke quietly and so haltingly that several minutes elapsed between sentences. He half-sang the words, ending each cadence of a few syllables with a kind of sob: "My friends" (pause), "put in your mind" (pause), "we" (pause), "do nothing" (pause), "good of our selves" (pause), "without God's" (pause), "help and assistance." The friend used no text; instead, he appeared to wait for inward direction as he spoke. Eventually, he began to talk louder and faster, his words flowing more easily. Then he abruptly stopped in mid-sentence, as if all inspiration had ceased. He sat down and replaced his hat.[39]

The content of sermons varied and might include defenses of distinctive Quaker tenets, ethical exhortation, advice to children, personal narratives, scriptural exegesis, and preparation for death.

Although in theory any member who felt moved by the spirit of God could speak during the meeting, each locality produced its "little school of prophets" who were self-anointed to utter the "Word" for the group. Quaker authorities even instructed those not "rightfully called" to remain silent in meetings. Anyone whose testimony was "lifeless, dry, dead, and burdened" and who was "eager to speak" was considered a "false minister." On the other hand, those who appeared to have an inward struggle before speaking and who spoke plainly, simply, and "nakedly" were considered legitimate "channels" of God's message. Even women and children were considered legitimate "channels." In the early 1740s, Philadelphia Quakers were ministered to by a young girl who, according to one Friend, "speaks very notably and very much to their Satisfaction."[40]

BAPTISTS

Like the Quakers, Baptists faced considerable persecution in seventeenth-century British North America. Also like the Quakers, the Baptists eventually found refuge in the religiously tolerant colonies of Rhode Island and Pennsylvania, where they predominated. By the eighteenth century, Philadelphia had become the strongest Baptist center in the colonies. South Carolina also provided fertile soil for Baptists with its wide toleration and sparsely settled backcountry.

Quaker Meetinghouse, Philadelphia. Although built in the last year of the American Revolution and therefore outside of the colonial period, the Free Quaker Meetinghouse in Philadelphia nevertheless typifies all Quaker houses of worship in its extreme simplicity and the absence of any liturgical symbols. (Library of Congress, Prints and Photographs Division, HABS, PA, 51-PHILA, 158-11)

Least represented by Baptists among the five cities was New York, where bitter doctrinal division between Arminian (General) and Calvinist Baptists in the city stifled growth for most of the colonial period. Even Boston boasted two Baptist churches by the mid-1700s, just one less than in Newport.[41]

In both their creed and their worship service, the Baptists were much influenced by the stern Calvinism of the Puritans. Like the Puritans, the Baptists tried their members in church conferences and admonished them for dancing, drinking, and card-playing. Baptist preachers, like their Congregational counterparts, opted to wear the Genevan gown and bands for preaching. Both Puritan and Baptist churches lacked kneeling benches because they believed there was no scriptural basis for bowing or kneeling during the administration of the Lord's Supper. Worship services were therefore simplified and eschewed any extraneous movement and any pomp and ritual. Equally simple was the order of worship among colonial Baptists, which was similar to that of the Puritans. More catholic in purpose was the centerpiece of Baptist worship, the sermon, which was intended to present salvation through Christ to the hearers by preaching doctrine, scripture, and godly living. The theme of Evan Pugh's sermon at the meeting of the Charles Town Baptist Association in 1767 is one familiar to colonial Christians of all denominations:

A word to sinners, and then I shall have done. O, my poor unconverted hearers; what are you doing? Are you working with Christ? No, no; but against him; and with the Prince of darkness . . . [W]hy will you reject the Savior? Why will you murder your souls, and sink yourselves into eternal burnings?

O stop in time, and consult your best interest. There is mercy yet for the vilest sinner who returns. Turn ye, turn ye, for why will ye die! As workers with Christ, we pray, and beseech you to be reconciled to God.[42]

Helping Baptists feel closer to God was their liberal use of singing during worship. Although Baptists practiced an extensive repertoire of rituals made up of the "nine Christian rites" (adult baptism, communion, the laying on of hands, the right of hand fellowship, the love feast, washing the saints' feet, the kiss of charity, the fellowship of children, and anointing the sick with oil), the most distinguishing mark of the denomination was the practice of adult baptism by immersion. This ritual involved the candidate publicly professing his or her faith and answering stock questions from the 1693 *Baptism Catechism* before the actual immersion in a nearby pond or river. After the baptism, full church members performed the laying on of hands on the initiate, who then received the Lord's Supper.[43]

PRESBYTERIANS

Like the Baptists, the Presbyterians were Calvinists, and the two shared many theological principles. Each subscribed to similar confessions of faith, believed that membership followed from a conversion experience, deemphasized creed and dogma, practiced congregational autonomy, stressed personal piety, and considered the sacraments as not essential for obtaining grace. Differences emerged over baptism—Presbyterians practiced infant baptism—and church organization—Presbyterians believed that churches should be in the hands of church federations called presbyteries.

In 1729, the church formally adopted the Westminster Confession of Faith and Catechism (1646) that set forth a purely Calvinistic theology that included a declaration of the Roman Catholic Mass as idolatry and the Pope as the Antichrist.

Although the method of conducting services varied in Presbyterian churches depending on the minister in charge, prayer, singing of psalms, reading of the Word, preaching, catechizing, administration of the sacraments, and the collection for the poor were among the more important exercises of religious services. The sermon could vary in character from a passionate message of regeneration preached by a revivalist to the cold and methodical approach of a dogmatician like Jedidiah Andrews of Philadelphia, whose sermons, according to Benjamin Franklin, were "chiefly either polemic arguments, or explications of the peculiar doctrine of our sect, and were all to me very dry, uninteresting, and unedifying, since not a single moral principle was inculcated or enforced; their aim seeming to be rather to make us Presbyterians than good citizens."[44]

REFORMED CHURCHES

The Reformed Churches, like the Congregational, Baptist, and Presbyterian churches, followed the doctrines and polity of John Calvin. An example is the Dutch Reformed, which predominated in New York City, originally a Dutch settlement. The Dutch Reformed service as practiced in New Amsterdam was simple. The clerk, standing at a desk beneath the pulpit, began the service by uttering the command: "Hear with reverence the Word of the Lord," followed by reading the Ten Commandments and announcing the psalm. While the congregation sang, the minister entered the church, stood for a few minutes at the foot of the pulpit stairs, and, after a silent prayer, ascended the pulpit. He preached with an hour glass before him. At the end of the sermon the clerk inserted in the end of his staff the public notices to be read and handed them to the minister. This duty ended, the minister delivered a short homily on charity, and the deacons walked through the church to take up a collection, each having a long pole, at the end of which was a black velvet bag for the offerings.[45]

GERMAN PIETISTS

The many Germans who immigrated to America during the eighteenth century brought with them a new religious strain. German churches like the Moravians, Mennonites, and Dunkards were pietists who stressed Christianity as a life rather than a creed. Their worship therefore contained no formal liturgy, although services typically consisted of scripture reading, prayer, sermons, and particularly among the Moravians, a heavy emphasis on congregational singing. Their worship services included a "love feast," washing of feet before partaking the Lord's Supper, and a concluding "holy kiss," an ancient Christian form of greeting. The love feasts were held on notable dates like Watch Night, Good Friday, and Christmas Eve. In colonial times the feast often consisted of bread and water accompanied by singing of hymns that describe love and harmony. Their belief in social equality and salvation through pure living further distinguished these radical faiths from most other Christians. Their egalitarian streak and belief in the separation of church and state prevented them from paying taxes to support established churches, and, like the Quakers, they opposed military service, denounced slavery, refused to take oaths before testifying in court, and held their members to high ethical standards of conduct. Like most Protestant sects, they rejected infant baptism and instead practiced baptism upon profession of faith that included the laying on of hands while the candidate was still in the water. Their belief in the priesthood of all believers, along with no denominational schools or colleges, encouraged them to draw their ministry from among the people. These German pietists were well recognized for their "plainness of speech" and their plain dress. Although these Anabaptist exiles could be found in several cities (especially Philadelphia), they were attracted mostly to Pennsylvania with its policy of religious freedom for Protestants.[46]

LUTHERANISM

More numerous among the German immigrants were Lutherans, who settled primarily in Pennsylvania, South Carolina, and Georgia. Lutherans were in the colonies as early as the 1630s but lacked organization and pastors. The arrival of the German pastor Henry Muhlenberg (1711–1787) to Pennsylvania in 1741 proved a watershed in the history of Lutheranism in America. The indefatigable Muhlenberg preached extensively to scattered congregations along the eastern seaboard, recruited new pastors from Germany, encouraged the building of Lutheran schools and churches, and helped organize the first Lutheran synod in America in 1748, held in Philadelphia. Lutherans church services consisted of a sermon, free prayer, scripture reading, a benediction, and congregational singing.[47]

Love Feast among the Dunkers. This 1883 rendition of a love feast by Howard Pyle show Pennsylvania Dunkards partaking of the agape meal, which usually consisted of lamb or beef and a bowl of soup. A service of foot washing often preceded the meal, followed by communion. (Library of Congress, Prints and Photographs Division, Reproduction # LC USZ62-47222)

METHODISM

Methodism, founded by John Wesley, an Anglican priest, was the last Protestant denomination to appear in the colonies. In 1769, Wesley sent his first missionaries in North America to New York City and Philadelphia, where local laborers and artisans joined the new sect. From there, Methodism spread to Virginia and North Carolina, which held two-thirds of the approximately 7,000 Methodists in America in 1777. Whether in the city or countryside, early Methodist ecclesiastical experience centered on promoting a community of love that was nourished by a fraternity of the Gospel. This fraternity involved small classes consisting of about a dozen believers who used their meetings to deepen their spiritual life and commitment. With that goal in mind, members engaged in emotionally charged and communal acts—singing, praying, praising God, emotional embracing, and other expressions of affection. Methodists called this intense communal experience "melting."

This spiritual melting was perhaps most intensely expressed in the love feast, where Methodists bonded themselves to one another by relating their religious experiences. "Never did I hear such experiences before," wrote one attendee of a love feast. "Our eyes overflowed with tears, and our hearts with love to God and each other. The holy fire, the heavenly flame, spread wider and wider, and rose higher and higher. O! happy people whose God is the Lord, may none of you ever weary in well doing." Unlike many other Christian denominations at the time, the Methodists practiced a "radical spiritual egalitarianism" with members referring to one another as "brother" and "sister" that crossed lines of both class and race.[48]

JUDAISM

Perhaps more than any other group to settle in colonial America, Jews were an urban people. Of the approximately 1,000 to 1,500 Jews residing in North America in 1775, the vast majority resided in six cities—New York, Newport, Philadelphia, Charles Town, Savannah, and Montreal. Of the five principal cities, only Boston lacked a quorum of praying Jews because the Puritans demonized them as "Christ-killers," "convicts of Jerusalem," and the "outcasts of the Holy Land." Generally elsewhere, Jews were welcomed, or at least tolerated, and experienced little overt anti-Semitism, except for a brief period in New Amsterdam during Peter Stuyvesant's tyrannical rule. Such a relatively hospitable climate attracted harried Jews from all over Europe, Latin America, and the West Indies to the North American cities to resurrect their broken lives.[49]

Integration

Urban Jews resurrected their lives while demonstrating their value to the community by working industriously as merchants, shopkeepers, and assorted craftsmen. Jews also helped their integration into the larger colonial society by keeping a low profile: Anglicizing their names, dressing like their Gentile neighbors, and quickly adopting English as their primary language. Jews also facilitated their integration and acceptance with their benevolence and communal spirit as witnessed by their generous donations toward constructing wharves, colleges, libraries, hospitals, theaters, and even Christian churches. Jews in all the cities, additionally, conducted business with Gentiles and sometimes even married them.

They were also prominent members of local Masonic orders, philosophical clubs, and dancing assemblies. Gentiles accepted Jews into these exclusive clubs as long as they could afford the expensive dues. At least among the urban elite, class trumped religion. This may partly explain why the South Carolina legislature in 1775 allowed the wealthy Jew Francis Salvador to take his seat in the assembly following his election despite the statutory requirement that all officeholders be of the Protestant faith.[50]

Religious Life

Although the New World often compelled settlers to modify certain aspects of their Old World culture, Jewish colonial immigrants maintained a strict adherence to the practices of their ancient faith. Daily prayer services were not always possible, but colonial Jews did keep kosher, intoned their Sephardic-rite prayers on the Sabbath, and observed their life-cycle ceremonies: circumcisions, bar mitzvahs, marriages, funerals, and the recital of the kaddish, the Aramaic prayer for the dead. Many of these ceremonies were occasions for sociability that included food, drink, and sometimes the exchange of gifts. More serious was the ritualistic requirements for food preparation, such as the baking of Passover matzos and the certification of kosher meat. Jonas Phillips, the official slaughterer for New York City, almost lost his job when he carelessly allowed his certifying pincers to fall into the hands of a Gentile butcher.[51]

The Jewish Sabbath falls on Saturday, and urban Jews considered the day sacrosanct. Jacob Barsimson of New Amsterdam, for example, refused to honor a court summons issued on Saturday. The court respected his religious scruples and did not reprimand him as "he was summoned on his Sabbath." Some Christians found this practice a nuisance, but most respected the Jewish observance as long as a worker made up for his absence on holy days. On the other hand, Christians who attended Jewish worship found it more than odd. "Their mode of worship has nothing solemn in it," observed Hannah Sanson of New York City in 1756, "nor their behavior neither . . . [T]his people once the chosen people, [had become] the scum of the earth." Besides its inherent anti-Semitism, this harsh judgment was typical of Christians at the time who simply did not understand that a Jewish worship service was not comparable to a Christian one. Its central element was the reading and explanation of texts, not the preaching of sermons and singing of hymns.

Interior Views of Touro Synagogue. Touro Synagogue, designed by Newport architect Peter Harrison and completed in 1763, is the oldest surviving Jewish synagogue building in North America. The plain brick exterior hides an extraordinarily elegant, sprightly, and cheerful interior that, in the words of architectural historian Hugh Morrison, expresses "nothing of the sombre and tragic intensities of the service it was designed to house." The ornate pulpit for reading the Law stands in the center of the floor surrounded by a heavy balustrade. Supporting the gallery designated for female worshipers are 12 columns representing the 12 tribes of Israel (Hugh Morrison, *Early American Architecture*, 457). (Courtesy Library of Congress, Prints and Photographs Division, HABS RI, 3-NEWP, 29-10)

The service could last several hours, during which time people often held private conversations and came and went as they pleased. This lack of decorum in Jewish worship partly explains why one New York Gentile characterized the local synagogue as a "lunatic asylum."[52]

One similarity between Jewish and Christian worship in the colonial cities was an elitism and class consciousness among the well-to-do. Naphtali Phillips of New York noticed that the city's leading Jews "were surrounded with all sorts of affluence and wealth" and when they attended synagogue "had their slaves walking behind them through the streets carrying their prayer books and shawls." As historian William Pencak explains, attending synagogue for the Jewish elite was "primarily a matter of maintaining ethnic and elite solidarity rather than either moral instruction or theological enlightenment." Seating arrangements by class also helped to maintain this elite solidarity in the Jewish community, with wealthier members sitting at the front of the synagogue. This did not sit well (pun intended) with some lower-class Jews who attempted to sit in seats designated for their superiors. Such insolence earned them a fine and physical removal to another seat in the back more befitting their lowly status.[53]

CHURCH DISCIPLINE

One of the most important functions of all colonial churches, including Jewish synagogues, was maintaining social order both inside and outside the church. As today, behavioral problems in church mostly originated with children, who found it impossible to keep still in uncomfortable seats or quiet during long services. To help maintain order, Congregationalists employed tithingmen to walk the aisles watching over the congregation for inappropriate behavior. Still, bored youngsters in church frequently tickled and pinched each other to make them cry out or laugh. One Puritan boy, for example, was brought before a local judge for pulling the hair of his neighbor during religious service and "Smiling and Larfing and Inticing other to the Same Evil." Girls could be just as disruptive by slamming down pew seats and profaning the Lord's Day with "rude and indecent behavior in laughing and playing in ye time of service."[54]

Less disruptive to the service but still annoying to the minister was sleeping by adults. The protracted sermons of Congregational services caused drowsiness among many pious Puritans in Boston, much to the chagrin of preachers like Cotton Mather, who complained in 1713 that sleeping during the "Publick Worship of God is a thing too frequently and easily practiced by very many People," some of whom he added, "have been so wicked as to profess they have gone to hear Sermons on purpose, that so they might sleep." Watchful tithingmen stalking the church aisles eagerly corrected such disrespect by tickling the faces of sleeping parishioners with a foxtail attached to a long stick. Some parishioners in Newport's Seventh Day Baptist church fought boredom during service by carving their initials into the pews.[55]

Most denominations also had rules for the guidance of members outside of the church, which, alongside government, had a responsibility toward promoting virtuous behavior and social stability throughout the larger community. Perhaps the greatest weapon ministers had in advancing morality and order was the threat of eternal damnation. Anglican priest James Honeyman of Newport, for example, brazenly urged his fellow spiritual leaders to "earnestly dissuade" their congregations "from all Advances to Impiety" by using "the Terrors of the Lord, the torment of the Damned." When fearmongering failed to program proper behavior into the people, church officials did not hesitate to discipline members. Much of the disciplining involved enforcing the provincial "blue laws" intended to preserve the sanctity of the Lord's Day. To that end, churches punished members for drunkenness, sexual immorality, bastardy, disorderly behavior, doctrinal differences, and among some sects like the Quakers, marrying outside of the faith, military service, gambling, and attending plays and horse races. Presbyterian churches even intervened on such matters as domestic discord, fighting, swearing, and questionable business dealings. To catch people in these transgressions, church officials encouraged members to engage in mutual surveillance, sometimes referred to as either "holy watching" or "brotherly watching." If caught violating church rules, a person might receive a monetary fine. This form of punishment was popular among the quarrelsome Jews in New York City. Baptists in Newport, however, preferred giving written admonitions to first and second offenders, explaining their offense and exhorting them to repent before the church. If repeated admonitions failed to bring repentance in the offender, church leaders reluctantly expelled him or her from church. In other denominations like the Presbyterians, Quakers, and Congregationalists, violators had to make contrite confessions before the church of their wrongdoing in order to get back into the good graces of the church. Such public confessions of scandalous behavior could provide voyeuristic entertainment for listeners, especially in cases involving sexual transgressions. The Presbyterian Isabel Wilson certainly piqued the ears of her congregation by humbly confessing her "aggravated sin" of fornication before the church "for three several Sabbath days."[56]

CATHOLICS AND ANTI-CATHOLICISM

The dominant experience among the few Catholics residing in the colonial cities was anti-Catholicism. No other religious group suffered as much from intolerance and persecution as Roman Catholics. Even in Maryland, originally founded as a sanctuary for persecuted Catholics in England, conditions became so intolerable for Catholics by the late 1600s that many fled across the border to Pennsylvania. Nor did Parliament's ill-phrased Toleration Act of 1689 provide relief for Catholics as it granted freedom of conscience to all Christians—except Catholics. Nowhere in America were Catholics allowed to vote or hold public office (except for brief periods in Maryland and New York). Some colonies even prevented Catholics from opening their own schools or openly practicing their faith. Only two colleges admitted Roman Catholics—the College of Pennsylvania and Rhode Island College. In its founding charter, the Anglican SPG declared war on "Divers Romish priests and Jesuits" who, it claimed, were trying to "pervert and draw Our said Loving Subjects to Popish Superstitions and Idolatry." To counteract this "papist" influence, the SPG sent to the colonies thousands of books and pamphlets exposing the "errors and absurdities of Popery." Indeed, all forms of colonial literature, from newspapers, pamphlets, and poetry to sermons, almanacs, and histories, were replete with antipapist sentiments that, in the words of one scholar, would make the modern gangster a "paragon of virtue" compared with the Catholic clergy. In addition, virtually every calamity, including plagues, fires, slave revolts, and Indian attacks, were blamed on some "hellish papist plot." The annual celebration of Guy Fawkes Day, moreover, was essentially an anti-Catholic orgy of intolerance. Protestant parents even passed down this anti-Catholic prejudice to their children, who played a game called "Break the Pope's Neck."[57] Similarly, the *New England Primer*, the children's school text used throughout the colonies, included the following verse:

Abhor that arrant Whore of Rome,
And all her Blasphemies;

And Drink not of her cursed cup
Obey not her decrees.[58]

What made such prejudice so absurd is that the Catholic presence in the colonial cities was minuscule. Philadelphia, which had more Catholics than any other city outside of Maryland, had only 139 Catholics according to the 1757 census. No matter its absurdity, this pervasive and pernicious antipapist paranoia was part of the daily experience for Catholics residing in the colonial cities and consumed considerable thought and action among Protestants.[59]

As much as the various Protestant sects differed on theology, they were all united in their fear of the Pope, whom they believed to be conspiring with Satan to take control of the world. Part of this fear developed from England's numerous wars with Catholic Spain and France during the seventeenth and eighteenth centuries. With French settlers in Canada and Spanish colonists in Florida posing an ever-present threat, anti-Catholicism in the colonial cities spiked sharply during these conflicts. Protestants also attacked the Catholic church for being idolatrous, tyrannical, and representative of the antichrist while at the same time demonizing priests as sadistic and avaricious leches who used their positions to torture Protestants, seduce unsuspecting female parishioners, and trick people into giving them money for "the Whoredoms, Murthers and Incests of the many Popes, Cardinals and Prelates of the Roman Church." Protestants also believed that Catholics gave their loyalty first and foremost to a scheming Pope; therefore, they could not be trusted with any civil power. Believing the worst of Catholics, Protestants in the colonial cities savagely persecuted their religious foes with the intent of driving them from the colonies. During the colonial period, America came with a warning label: Catholics Not Wanted![60]

This anti-Catholic warning was most pronounced in Boston, where Puritan leaders passed an "anti-priest" law in 1647 requiring all Catholic clergymen to either leave the colony or face execution. In addition to being unable to conduct religious services, Catholics in Boston were not allowed to vote or hold public office because, according to the city's freeholders, "their recognizing the Pope in so absolute a manner" will "subver[t] the Government leading directly to the worst anarchy and confusion, civil discord, war, and bloodshed." Fueling this anti-Catholic sentiment were local newspapers that printed numerous stories demonizing the Pope and Catholic priests as buffoons, beasts, rapists, and mass murders. Even Harvard College, the bastion of New England Puritanism,

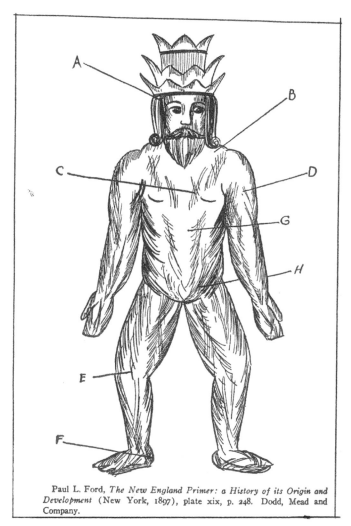

Paul L. Ford, *The New England Primer: a History of its Origin and Development* (New York, 1897), plate xix, p. 248. Dodd, Mead and Company.

The Pope, or "The Man of Sin." This illustration of the Pope, or "The Man of Sin," is found in some editions of the *New England Primer* school text. Its purpose was to instill within Protestant children an intense hatred of Catholics and of Catholicism. Lines designated by capital letters radiate from various parts of the Pope's body. The key that accompanied the illustration explained the diagram with the following "advice to children": "Thou shall find in his Head, (A) Heresy. In his Shoulders, (B) The Supporters of Disorder. In his Heart, (C) Malice, Murder, and Treachery. In his Arms, (D) Cruelty. In his Knees, (E) False Worship and Idolatry. In his Feet, (F) Swiftness to shed Blood. In his Stomach, (G) Insatiable Covetousness. In his Loins, (H) The Worst of Lusts." (Paul L. Ford, *The New England Primer: A History of Its Origin and Development*. New York: Dodd, Mead & Co., 1897, p. 248) did its part to inflame anti-Catholic passions in its annual "Dudley Lectures," given by prominent alumni who were instructed by its endower Paul Dudley to "expos[e] the idolatry of the Romish church, their tyranny, usurpations and other crying wickedness." Faced with such hostility and persecution, few Catholics settled in Boston, where one Anglican missionary reported that the city was "happily free from papists."[61]

For similar reasons the Anglican missionary Francis Lejau happily reported in 1709 from Charles Town that there were no "professed Papists" in his parish and "few thank God that I hear of in the Province." Still, the provincial assembly felt compelled in 1716 to pass a law preventing Roman Catholic servants from entering the capital. Nor did Protestants in New York City want Catholics in their midst, especially after 1693 when the legislature established the Church of England as the official state religion and prohibited religious liberty "for any persons of the Romish religion." A few years later, New York officials disarmed local papists, required them to give bond with surety for their good behavior, and forced all priests and Jesuit missionaries to leave the province or face "perpetual imprisonment." By 1748 an Anglican minister gleefully wrote that New York City was free of "the least face of Popery."[62]

Only in Philadelphia could Catholics worship freely, though not too publicly. Still, the Protestant majority denied Catholics the right to serve in public office or purchase land. By 1729 local Catholics had a regular priest and 37 congregants with enough money to build an official church (St. Joseph's) tucked in an alley adjacent to the Quaker almshouse. Fifteen years later, Philadelphia's Catholic population had risen to 140, a frightening figure to one local Anglican minister, who complained that the city "is much infested with Popery." When Britain and its colonies went to war against France in 1754 (the French and Indian War), paranoid Protestant mobs attacked the Catholic church in Philadelphia. Meanwhile, the provincial legislature enacted laws prohibiting Catholics from carrying arms and forcing them to pay double taxes and register their movements with local authorities.[63]

GUY FAWKES DAY

Protestants in all five cities released their anti-Catholic bigotry every year in the public ritual known as Guy Fawkes Day. Named for the Catholic who tried, but failed, to blow up Parliament on November 5, 1605, the annual celebration soon turned into an anti-Catholic holiday in which mechanics, laborers, servants, and slaves with clubs paraded through the streets on floats carrying the effigies of the Devil and the Pope, the latter frequently displayed as a servant of Satan. Crowds of bystanders hurled insults and refuse at the effigies as they made their way through the streets. When the floats had completed their circuit through town, Protestant celebrants cheerfully torched the effigies. This anti-Papal ritual served two important purposes: it helped to unify a socially disparate Protestant people behind a message of bigotry while encouraging colonists to support an imperial authority that they believed would defend them from Popish enemies.[64]

THE GREAT CHRISTIAN CIVIL WAR

Whereas anti-Catholicism never waned among Protestants during the colonial period, the same could not be said for their religious devotion. By the 1720s, more unchurched people were living in North America than any country of the Western world. In the five principal cities, no more than 15 percent of eligible adults were church members. A peeved minister in Charles Town complained that on the Sabbath, "the Taverns have more Visitants than the Churches." Some New England pastors even hoped for a smallpox or diphtheria epidemic or perhaps an earthquake to prod the people to greater spirituality. The percentage of the unchurched was perhaps even greater in the frontier where there was a dearth of ministers. In both regions too many churches were catering to the upper classes and failing to meet the spiritual needs of the common folk, who were increasingly demanding a more emotional and personal type of preaching. That the pulpits were left more and more to "second-rate talents" who droned out dry, legalistic, and unedifying sermons that scolded rather than inspired their parishioners only fueled popular contempt against the ministry. As revivalist minister Jonathan Edwards explained, "Our people do not so much need to have their heads stored as to have their hearts touched."[65]

This strong desire for an emotional religion, coupled with the dissatisfaction toward ministers among a religiously frustrated laity, provided much of the raw material for a religious revival that earlier scholars have mislabeled the "Great Awakening." Far from "great," this religious awakening, although intense, quickly flamed out in the five cities.[66] Beginning in the 1720s, ministers like Theodore Frelinghuysen (Dutch Reformed) and Gilbert Tennent (Presbyterian) tossed away stale sermons and instead preached an evangelical and often extemporaneous message from the heart that "bleached out" most doctrinal distinctions and instead emphasized the need for individuals to accept their absolute dependence on God, their innate sinfulness in God's eye, the inevitability of divine punishment, the joy of joining with God through an emotional "new birth" (born-again religious conversion), partaking of his pardon, and praying for the "blinding light" of grace.

The highly emotional and simplified sermons of evangelical preachers caused a wave of local revivals throughout rural and urban America during the 1730s that eventually turned into a tsunami in late 1740 with the arrival from England of George Whitefield, a 26-year-old, cross-eyed, and portly Anglican priest with a talent for oratory and controversy. For two years the indefatigable "boy preacher" electrified audiences from New Hampshire to Georgia with theatrical performances that would make a modern televangelist green with envy. His greatest performances were in the five main cities, where he preached to spellbound crowds that sometimes exceeded 20,000 people. Not much of a learned man nor much of a deep thinker, Whitefeld was unconcerned with fine points of doctrine. Instead, his main concern, according to historian Richard Hofstadter, was to "produce the orgiastic conversions and the repentant tears that he knew so well how to evoke, then to move on and leave others to cope with the social or institutional consequences." Like a tornado tearing through a trailer park, Whitefield's visits to the main cities left behind a destructive trail of intolerance, division, controversy, spiritual anarchy, and religious warfare.[67]

Church of England

Ironically, Whitefield inflicted his greatest devastation on his own Protestant denomination, the Church of England, which had an openly hostile reaction to the Great Awakening. Anglican clergy in Philadelphia, New York City, and Charles Town viewed Whitefield as a youthful and vainglorious disturber of the peace who was undermining clerical status and authority by ignoring doctrinal differences, downplaying the sacraments and church liturgy, and adopting extemporaneous preaching and "irrational enthusiasm." Whitefield's enthusiasm was contagious in Philadelphia, where he preached outdoors to vast multitudes of all sects. His sermons left many in his audience emotionally exhausted: "Some were struck pale as Death," wrote one eyewitness, "others wringing their hands, others lying on the ground, others sinking into the arms of their friends, and most lifting up their eyes toward heaven, and crying out to God." Local Anglican clergy were less impressed with the "Grand Itenerant's" "antick tricks." Nor did they appreciate the boy preacher calling them "rotten pillars" of the church who preached "false doctrines."[68]

Word of Whitefield's inflammatory performance in Philadelphia preceded his arrival in New York City, where he received an angry reception from local Anglican clergy who made every effort to sabotage his visit. The Reverend Jonathan Arnold even wrote a letter to the local newspaper accusing Whitefield of being "Remarkable for Ignorance and Confidence" and encouraging readers to shun the preacher "as an open Enemy to Religion." So demonized, Whitefield preached in the fields to only moderate crowds and to the small Presbyterian congregation. The grand itinerant met a similarly icy reception in Charles Town, especially after unwisely denouncing residents for their balls and assemblies, "that Bane of all that is serious and religious," and chastising the clergy for preaching "false doctrines" and ignoring the spiritual needs of slaves. The Reverend Alexander Garden, the local Anglican commissary, responded to this "most virulent, flaming, foul mouthed Persecutor of the Church of God" by accusing Whitefield of being the two worst things imaginable to a Protestant slaveholding community: a "Romish Emmissary [sent] to distract and confound weak Minds" and an abolitionist trying to incite a violent slave rebellion. When Whitfield refused to tone down his ascetic and acerbic message, Garden temporarily jailed the "Pedlar in Divinity" for preaching without a license.[69]

New England

When Whitefield arrived in Newport, he was met with more religious indifference than hostility. A century of religious toleration, the practice among religious leaders of promoting Christian unity, and a growing devotion to the affairs of the world all encouraged religious indifference among residents of Newport. John Callender opined in 1742 that the "anxious Desire and eager Pursuit of earthly things, the Hurry and Multiplicity of Affairs, so engross the Man as to leave little room and less inclination for our spiritual and eternal Concerns." Another resident admitted that all too many residents preferred to "tarry at home" on Sunday rather than to attend church services. Meanwhile, Quakers frequently expressed fears that they were losing their "Antient Discipline." The Reverend Ezra Stiles admitted that there were "many of no religion in Newport." Those

Anti-Whitefield Print. This antirevivalist print titled "Enthusiasm Display'd" satirizes the evangelical preaching of George Whitefield, who is supported by two women, one holding a mask labeled "Hypocrisy," the other a Janus-faced "Deceit." On the left are three woodcocks, one with a worm and one apparently dead, which are labeled "Trap'd." On the right is a woman labeled "Folly" reclining on the ground holding a jester's staff. (Library of Congress, Prints and Photographs Division, Reproduction # LC USZ62-137507)

who did attend church services preferred ministers to deliver sermons that were mild and nonjudgmental. Even the city's Jewish population, which perhaps had the greatest tendency to identify with its religious faith, was "infected with a spirit of indifference." Thus when Whitefield arrived in Newport, relatively small crowds came to hear him preach. The evangelist later explained that the city's inhabitants placed "the Kingdom of God too much in Meats and Drinks," and that any rivalry among churches there was more the result of pride than conviction.[70]

Whitefield met with much greater success in Boston, although local Anglican clergy still denounced him as a clever religious chameleon whose revivals promoted "madness and enthusiasm." His enthusiasm was quite contagious, at least according to Congregational minister Charles Chauncy, who claimed that when Whitefield preached "he generally moved the passions, especially of the younger people, and the females among them; the effect whereof was a great talk about religion, together with a disposition to be perpetually hearing sermons to neglect of all other business." His farewell sermon in October 1740 on the Common drew an estimated 20,000. However, Boston had little chance of returning to order with the arrival in the winter of 1741 of the confrontational evangelist Gilbert Tennent, "a burly, salty, downright man" who preached protracted, fiery sermons on sin and repentance that took people "off from their callings," wrote one astonished observer, "and the introducing a neglect of all business but that of hearing him preach." In his "beastly brayings" Tennent targeted rationalist ministers whom he claimed were doomed to hell because they lacked the evangelical experience with Christ and because they preached a dull and unemotional religion. "They have not the Courage, or Honesty, to thrust the Nail of Terror into sleeping Souls," Tennent brayed.[71]

Evangelical Terrorism

To awaken sleeping souls, evangelical ministers employed psychological terror intended to convince listeners that they were evil in God's eyes and therefore deserved the death and punishment the Bible promised—unless they completely surrendered themselves to God. In terrorizing their congregations, revivalist ministers painted vivid pictures of hell and the likelihood that their listeners would end up there. Most notorious in exploiting terror to provoke conviction was Jonathan Edwards, who in his famous sermon *Sinners in the Hands of an Angry God* bombarded his congregation with at least 20 horrifying metaphors of God's vengeful wrath against sinners damned to hell. The Congregational minister even directed his fire toward children, terrorizing youngsters with the horrifying question: "And you children that are unconverted, don't you know that you are going down to hell, to bear the dreadful wrath of that God that is now angry with you every day, and every night? Will you be content to be the children of the devil, when so many other children in the land are converted, and are become the holy and happy children of the King of Kings?" Edwards concluded his exercise in psychological terror by telling his listeners that "There is reason to think that there are many in this congregation . . . that will actually be the subject of this very misery to all eternity . . . before tomorrow morning." While delivering his hellfire-and-brimstone sermon, "there was a great moaning & crying out through ye whole House," wrote one eyewitness. "What shall I do to be Saved—OH I am going to Hell—Oh what shall I do for Christ. So yet ye minister

was obliged to desist—ye shrieks & crys were piercing and amazing."[72] Not to be outdone in terrorizing his audience, Whitefield, in
his famous sermon "The Eternity of Hell's Torment," recreated in
gripping drama the scene of a sinner's arrival at the gates of hell:

O wretched man that I am, who shall deliver me from this body of death! O
foolish mortal that I was, thus to bring myself into these never-ceasing tor-
tures, for the transitory enjoyment of a few short-lived pleasures, which
scarcely afforded me any satisfaction . . . O damned apostate! . . . O that I
had never hearkened to his beguiling insinuations! O that I had rejected
his very first suggestions with the utmost detestation and abhorrence! O
that I had taken up my cross and followed Christ! O that I had never ridi-
culed serious godliness . . . But, alas! These reflections come now too late
. . . But must I live for ever tormented in these flames? O eternity! That
thought fills me with despair. I must be miserable for ever.

The objective of such hellish portrayals by Edwards, Whitefield,
and other evangelicals was to "literally scare the hell out of their
people," explains historian David Lovejoy, and the shouts and cries
of some listeners indicated that they succeeded. One eyewitness to a
Whitefield revival wrote that "the bitter cries and groans were
enough to pierce the hardest heart. Some of the people were as pale
as death; others were wringing their hands; others lying on the
ground; others sinking into the arms of their friends; and most lifting their eyes to heaven, and crying to God for mercy." One clergymen described behavior in a Massachusetts revivalist church as
"shocking": their "groans, cries, screams, & agonies . . . excite both
laughter and contempt . . . They tell you they saw the joys of
Heaven, can describe its situations, inhabitants, employments, &
have seen their names entered into the Book of Life & can point
out the writer, character & pen." Even days after a revival men,
women, and even children could be seen in their homes, and at
times walking the streets of Boston, in a cataleptic trance during
which they later claimed to have participated in celestial spirit jour-
neys to heaven and hell. Such bizarre conduct prompted considerable criticism from more rationalist ministers like the Reverend
Ezra Stiles of Newport, who described the religious revivals in
New England as a time when "multitudes were seriously, soberly
and solemnly out of their wits." One Anglican priest placed full
blame on evangelical ministers for this madness: "Instead of
instructing the people to serve the Lord in *gladness* and to have joy
in the holy host," he said, "these miserable teachers advance a
gloomy and dreadful religion which has . . . made many [listeners]

fitter objects for a *Hospital* than a *Church*." Even worse, some revivalist ministers like Jonathan Edwards made listeners fitter objects for the cemetery as some people, including an uncle of Edwards, committed suicide after hearing one of the evangelist's gloom-and-doom sermons.[73]

Consequences

The emotionalism of these "exhorting enthusiasts" had devastating consequences on religion in early America, the lives of their followers, and the well-being of society generally. In the long run, the religious awakening did little to increase the size of congregations because most conversions occurred in "one-to-one sessions" between pastor and individual, nearly all of whom already had existing ties to the congregation. After the revivalists left town, the pressures of everyday life squelched much of the original enthusiasm among many converts. Nor did the revivals reform people's behavior, at least not in Boston, according to Charles Chauncy, who professed: "I deny not but there might be here and there a person stopped from going on in a course of sin," he admitted as a consequence of the revivals, "[b]ut so far as I could judge upon the nicest observation, the town, in general, was not much mended in those things wherein a reformation was greatly needed ... but that there was the same pride and vanity, the same luxury and intemperance, the same lying and tricking and cheating as before this gentleman [George Whitefield] came among us."[74]

In the end, the evangelical revivals did more harm than good. This is largely because, as historian Richard Hofstadter put it, the evangelical ministers "came not with peace but a sword." Like holy crusaders, these warriors for Christ wrought destruction, division, and terror through the American religious landscape in their attempt to lure people away from "unregenerate false prophets" of God. In New England alone, the revivals of the 1740s produced more than 200 schismatic congregations that split away from old churches. "[T]he glorious work appears to me now as changed into a ruinous war," wrote one disgusted Congregational minister. Additionally, Old Lights in Massachusetts, those leaders of the original churches, punished followers of the new churches, called New Lights, by forcing them to pay taxes to the original churches and by banishing many from political office. In the Middle Colonies, Presbyterian revivalists split from the old guard in 1745 to form the synod of New York, while the Dutch Reformed churches split into conservative and radical factions. When people finally "returned to soberness," historian Max Savelle writes in his conclusion on the revivals, "institutionalized religion was, perhaps, weaker in the colonies than ever before."[75]

This Christian civil war also created division in the larger society by arousing "latent feelings of class antagonism," according to historian Clinton Rossiter, for its "egalitarian message" that any man could reach salvation and any man could preach. As a result, the revivals appealed primarily to the poor and despised while angering the well-born and well-educated who, writes historian Alan Taylor, "felt that their authority depended upon the power to constrain the religious choices of their dependents." As it turned out, the religious revivals were hardly a threat to the status quo. Even Whitefield believed that "Christianity taught people to accept their situation in life." Nor did the religious awakening weaken racism in colonial society, even within the ranks of white evangelicals, who generally did not challenge slavery or the subjugation of Native Americans. The evangelicals' supercilious and intolerant attitude toward other people and their religious beliefs is reflected in the aggressive attempts made by revivalist ministers to replace the traditional "heathen" faiths among African Americans and Native Americans with the one "True" faith of Christianity. Rather than a "message of liberation and equality," as historian Thomas Kidd has recently claimed, evangelical Christianity promoted religious intolerance and inequality while attempting to psychologically shackle everyone it could into believing only one "true meaning" of Christ's message and one cosmic view of the universe and the world. Even more pernicious, evangelical ministers, by masterfully employing emotional terrorism, instilled within their individual congregants an intense fear of eternal damnation in hell and deep feelings of personal depravity and worthlessness that they could only absolve by completely surrendering themselves to a deity that was graphically described in the most psychopathic and misanthropic terms. In short, the evangelical message, more than anything else, promoted dependency, division, terror, and intolerance that significantly retarded any efforts to create "Heaven on Earth."[76]

"ENLIGHTENED" OR "RATIONAL" CHRISTIANITY

Much more beneficial towards creating the "Kingdom of God" on Earth was the emergence in the eighteenth century of a more rational Christianity based upon the ideas of Enlightenment scientists and philosophers like Galileo (1563–1642), Sir Isaac Newton

(1642–1727), Rene Descartes (1590–1650), and John Locke (1632–1704) who suggested that the universe operated "like a great perpetual motion machine whose workings were governed by knowable, divinely-inspired 'natural laws.' " The new science suggested that individuals had the power, through reason, to unlock the laws of the universe and to apply them to create a kind of heaven on earth. Many college-educated colonial clergy, particularly more liberal-minded Anglicans and Congregationalists in the cosmopolitan cities, wholeheartedly embraced Enlightenment ideas because these appeared to them to buttress rather than attack religious orthodoxy. Sometimes known as Arminians, after the liberal beliefs of the Dutch theologian Jacobus Arminius (1560–1609), these rationalist Christians believed that God's greatest gift to humankind was reason, which enabled all human beings to follow the moral teachings of Jesus and achieve salvation through goodness. An even smaller group of "freethinkers" who sought to align religion with the new scientific advances were deists like Benjamin Franklin, Thomas Jefferson, and James Madison who believed in an impersonal God who created a well-ordered universe endowed with immutable laws but since has left it alone. Institutionalized religion was not important to them, but only that man live by the laws of nature and practice virtue. Perhaps the deists' greatest contributions were their espousal of religious toleration, their concern for ethical standards, and their efforts to harmonize religion with science.

UNORTHODOX BELIEFS

Alongside Christianity in the daily lives of early Americans were unorthodox beliefs such as superstition, astrology, magic, the occult, and witchcraft. Like Christianity, these folk beliefs and practices were a way of perceiving the world and explaining the mysterious and inexplicable occurrences of life. They derived from the Middle Ages and even earlier; many people, both educated and uneducated, considered them complementary to, not in conflict with, Christian doctrine. America, with its strange animals, mysterious forests, lurking natives, and "eerie happenings," only strengthened such supernatural beliefs. Widening the door for belief in superstition and the occult among early Americans was their ignorance of "elemental Christian beliefs and practices," explains historian Jon Butler, and their "indifference to formal religious institutions."[77]

Superstition

Every ethnic group brought its own set of superstitions from the old country that were part and parcel of their everyday life. The Swedes, for example, believed that with the sale of a healthy cow the owner must remove some of its hair to keep good luck on the farm; that saying the Lord's Prayer backward could prevent rain during a harvest; and that cattle on Christmas Eve briefly acquired the power of speech. Some Germans believed that a newly purchased pig must be backed into a pen to assure it of a healthy life, and that if New Year's Day fell on a Sunday, a mild winter and pleasant spring lay ahead. African Americans wore numerous charms for protection against illness or evil spirits or for wish fulfillment. Other superstitions crossed ethnic and racial lines, like the belief that a black cat crossing one's path was an omen of bad luck. Many a sailor believed that a woman brings bad luck to a ship, while many landlubbers refused to unfasten a pin on New Year's Day, fearing doing so would bring bad luck throughout the year. Many early Americans took these superstitions seriously, for to contravene them risked inviting ill fortune upon oneself or others.[78]

Magic and the Occult

Less popular and less accepted both by ministerial and government authorities were magical practice and the occult. The former usually dealt with employing some formula or talisman while the latter centered on the alleged powers of prophecy and the various arts of divination such as necromancy, astrology, geomancy, palmistry, and numerology. Colonial governments outlawed such practices, making anyone who practiced magic and the occult—primarily the poor, women, blacks, and the elderly—a criminal. Such was the opinion of Ezra Stiles of Newport, who wrote in 1773 that magic was a thing of the past except for "some old Women (Midwives) [who] affect it." He cited as one example 70-year-old "Granny Morgan" who practiced "hocus pocus & making cakes of flour and her own Urine and sticking them full of pins and divining in them."[79]

Despite its sometimes disgusting nature, the practice of magic, the occult, and fortune-telling was popular enough in the cities to keep a number of such practitioners employed. Most of this lay magical practice was "white magic," which aimed to discover lost articles (including cattle and children) or tell the future rather than injure an enemy. One New England man, for example, made a nice income telling fortunes using a lobster claw as a talisman. The low estimation of doctors, as well as their expense, also prompted many common folk in the cities to pursue alternative methods of healing that involved "blasphemous attempts to manipulate supernatural power." Its popularity in Boston was large enough to prompt Cotton Mather to complain: "How frequently is *Bleeding* Stanched by writing something with Ceremonies on the Forehead! How frequently is a *Toothache* Eas'd, and an *Ulcer* Stop'd, and an *Ague* Check'd, by papers, with some Terms and Scrawls in them, sealed up and worn about the Neck." Promoting the popularity of occult concepts and practices were the numerous almanacs published and sold in the cities that included numbers, letters, and days thought to have magical significance of the coming year. It was the astrological content of almanacs that made them more popular than the Bible among American colonists, who, according to one Philadelphia almanac publisher, frequently rejected the Bible and prayer in favor of the occult to resolve personal crises: "Billy and Dicky, Peggy and Molly must see the man on the Moon, and where the little child cries the great one runs for the Almanack, to bless the House with Peace."[80]

Witchcraft

Whereas many colonists turned to astrology and other occult beliefs to resolve personal crises, none openly admitted to using witchcraft—unless under severe duress. The Biblical exhortation "Thou shalt not suffer a witch to live" (Exodus 22:18) gave authorities the ultimate justification to execute alleged witches, who were believed to have supernatural powers bestowed upon them by Satan to do his evil bidding. This included causing physical harm to humans and livestock, causing crops to fail, and causing storms and fires, among other calamities. Witches could also turn themselves into an animal, or recruit an animal like a dog or cat, in order to surreptitiously carry out their maleficence. Because of their alleged powers and cunning methods, witches were greatly feared by early Americans. This fear at times turned into hysterical witch hunts, most of which occurred in religiously repressive New England, where at least 344 persons were accused of witchcraft between 1620 and 1725. Apparently some people did practice witchcraft in New England, especially poorer folk who believed they were already damned because of their poverty and therefore "had nothing to lose in giving their allegiance to Satan," explains

Painting of a Salem Witch Trial. Thompkins H. Matteson's 1855 rendition of the trial of George Jacobs of Salem for wizardry show the accusatory and emotional aspect of this deadly witch hunt. One of Jacobs's accusers was his granddaughter, 17-year-old Margaret Jacobs, an accused witch herself, who testified against her 72-year-old grandfather in hopes of saving her own life. In the painting she is the girl in front of the judge's bench pointing to a kneeling Jacobs. Margaret Jacobs later retracted her accusations, a recantation that put her in jail awaiting death for refusing to stand by her initial accusations and confession. Another accuser was Jacobs's daughter-in-law, thought to be mentally ill, who is the woman standing with raised arms being held back. In the foreground are a boy and a girl who are having fits allegedly caused by Jacobs's wizardry. Despite the mendacious nature of the accusations against him, George Jacobs was found guilty of practicing wizardry and hanged on August 19, 1692, along with three other men and one woman. (Library of Congress, Prints and Photographs Division, Reproduction # LC USZ62-94432)

historian Richard Gildrie. "They could have had little regard for the God who had condemned them and no qualms about serving the devil instead."[81]

It is no coincidence that a class element played a role in early America's most hysterical witch hunt, the 1692 Salem witch trials. Although scholars have offered numerous theories for the causes of this controversial and deadly event, they are all in agreement that highly gullible religious and secular authorities accepted at face value specious evidence to justify the arrest of over 150 men, women, and even children for allegedly practicing witchcraft. Despite the mendacious nature of the evidence, provided mostly by teenaged girls, officials executed 14 women and five men by hanging and an 81-year-old man by slowly and sadistically crushing him to death with heavy stones over a two-day period in an unsuccessful attempt to force a confession. Only when those accused of witchcraft reached the highest levels of society did Massachusetts governor William Phips call a halt to the witch hunt and the execution of accused witches. The accusation of witchcraft against his own wife, along with prominent Boston ministers and members of some of the province's wealthiest families, certainly motivated the governor to intercede in the trials on behalf of his spouse and others of his class. Authorities thereafter conveniently denounced the possessed as "Daemoniacks" and mouthpieces for the "Father of Lyes" whose testimony could no longer be trusted.[82]

AFRICAN AMERICAN "SPIRITUAL HOLOCAUST"

The Salem witchcraft hysteria is a singular example of the pernicious consequences of Christianity on the lives of some colonists. Much more pervasive was its destructive effect on both the bodies and souls of thousands of Africans forcibly brought to America by Christians who twisted the infamous Biblical "Curse on Canaan" (Genesis 9:25–28) to justify and promote the enslavement of black-skinned people.[83] The paganism of Africans, at least in the eyes of Christians, made them ripe for enslavement because the Bible offered no opposition to holding non-Christians in bondage. When some early slaves sought freedom through conversion to Christianity, colonial officials closed this loophole with legal statutes allowing the enslavement of Christians. Puritan minister Cotton Mather eliminated moral doubts over slavery by claiming that "neither the Bible" nor the "canons of the Church . . . give Christian slaves a title to liberty." With this religious bar to slave conversion removed, some Christian leaders saw it as their duty and that of slaveowners to convert the Africans to Christianity. Some even argued that slavery was part of God's plan for bringing heathens out of Africa so that they could be brought to Christ. This attempt to Christianize American slaves while suppressing their traditional faiths resulted in an "African spiritual holocaust" that, in the words of scholar Jon Butler, "forever destroyed traditional

African religious systems" and replaced them with select Biblical texts designed to instill within them acceptance of their servile status and absolute obedience to their Christian masters. Illustrative is Mather's 1693 *Rules for the Society of Negroes*, which taught the slaves that they were the "miserable children of Adam and Noah" who were enslaved because they had sinned against God and that God, not their masters, had enslaved them. In the Ten Commandments he prepared for them, Mather replaced the Fifth Commandment ("Honor they Father and Mother") with "I must show all due respect unto everyone and if I have a master or mistress, I must be very dutiful unto them." Meanwhile, clergymen in Charles Town preached to slaves the Pauline doctrine that made it a religious duty for "servants to be obedient to their own masters." Anglican missionaries, along with Lutheran, Baptist, and Presbyterian evangelical ministers in the major cities, instructed blacks in the basic tenets of the Christian religion but emphasized to them that spiritual equality did not equate to temporal equality.[84]

In the end, few slaves would convert to Christianity until the nineteenth century. Before then, most masters simply did not allow ministers to preach to their slaves, either because they believed blacks had no souls or feared that the Christian idea of the equality of all men under God would inspire within their bondsmen behavior threatening to the institution of slavery. Additionally, most slaves recognized Christianity, as it was applied towards blacks, for what it was—a self-serving tool for racial subjugation. Part of this subjugation is reflected in the treatment of blacks as second-class worshipers. When walking to church, for example, blacks were required to follow their masters at a respectful distance. Once in church they were placed in a segregated section away from other parishioners, often in a remote corner of the gallery or under the belfry, commonly referred to by white worshipers as "Nigger Heaven." Whites in the Old South Church in Boston went so far as to board up the seats occupied by blacks so that "the negroes could see no one and be seen by none." Such seclusion only encouraged black worshipers to spend their time in church "playing, eating nuts, and enjoying other diversions." It is no surprise therefore that the "more closely blacks worshiped with whites," explains historian Donald Wright, "the less they wanted to become Christians." The Reverend Samuel Hopkins of Newport noticed that the brutality inflicted upon slaves by their Christian masters instilled the bondsmen with "the deepest prejudice against the Christian religion."[85]

Holding such a deep prejudice toward Christianity, most slaves remained tenaciously addicted to their ancient religious customs that included the use of talismans, conjuring, voodoo, fortune-telling, and divination. One New England slave, for example, always carried a frog's leg in his pocket to ward off the "colic demon" and wore a rattlesnake necklace against the spirit that caused consumption. Other slaves sought the assistance of a conjure doctor who they believed had the power to either place or remove a "fix" on somebody. The central element of the fix involved a charm that might be a drink made of powdered roots, toads' heads, and various herbs or a bag filled with graveyard dirt, hair from the victim, bottles, pins, pieces of clothing, roots, and herbs. Some conjurers worked revenge on an enemy by creating a "voodoo doll" in their image and sticking it with pins to inflict injury on their victim. To protect themselves from such evil spirits, some slaves wore their clothes inside out and hung a bag of eggshells around their necks. Other slaves, particularly women, practiced divination that included telling fortunes, dispensing charms, and locating lost articles. One clever master turned the slaves' belief in divination to his advantage by telling his chattel that by using arithmetic as a kind of white man's magic he could determine if they had misbehaved. When one of his slaves was suspected of stealing a cart chain, for example, he sat down with his chalk and board and began to cipher. After a few moments he mused, "Links three inches long, links three inches long, what does that mean?" He then turned to the suspected slave and confidently said, "you have been stealing sausages." Astonished at such white man's magic, the slave replied frighteningly, "No Massa, me no steal sausage, me steal cart chain."[86]

CONCLUSION

Religious belief and practice among Americans during the long colonial period evolved from a traditional medieval worldview to a more modern rational approach that eventually included adopting and implementing the liberal concept of religious toleration. Pushing colonists in the cities toward spiritual equality was the introduction of Enlightenment philosophy and its emphasis on dignity and reason, and decades-long experience with religious tyranny and oppression. This religious oppression, according to Clinton Rossiter, "did as much as toleration to lead the colonies to more humane and liberal religion."[87] The religiously plural cities played the leading role in this transition from religious tyranny to tolerance. Attempts to impose religious uniformity in the urban centers proved impractical and counterproductive to a commercial people interested in doing business with people of many different faiths. Over time, this religious diversity and desire for material success inspired a spirit of cooperation among people of different religions and denominations. It also created a competitive spirit among clergymen in the cities, who battled each other for members. This free market of faiths forced urban ministers to take a more active and evangelical approach in their preaching style and to accept greater lay control of church government.

However, this democratization of colonial churches only went so far. Colonial leaders still used religion as a weapon to maintain their hegemony against the poor, women, and slaves. Christian doctrine and religious services were tools to advance elitism, sexism, and racism. Most slaves at this time resisted this religiously based racism by rejecting the creed of their oppressors, who used their faith to justify the enslavement and exploitation of Africans. White men and women in the cities, on the other hand, did not have the option of not attending religious services or openly criticizing prevailing doctrine—at least not without suffering fines, public humiliation, and corporal punishment inflicted by upper-class government officials. The objective of such laws was to force people to listen to and observe the indoctrination within Christian churches that served to preserve both plutocracy and patriarchy. In this way, among many others, Christianity in early America served to maintain the status quo through the use of government-supported religious tyranny. Further undermining social harmony was the intolerance and self-righteousness among members of the various Christian denominations who attacked and persecuted each other for spiritual and political dominance. At times this religious warfare led Christians to murder one another. Not until late in the colonial period did a more liberal and rational Christian theology emerge among the better-educated colonists, who sought to end the acrimonious and destructive religious strife in early America by promoting religious toleration. To that end, the Founding Fathers wisely incorporated the liberal concept of religious freedom into the national charter, an act that has done much to advance social harmony in the United States.

NOTES

1. Arthur M. Schlesinger, *The Birth of the Nation: A Portrait of the American People on the Eve of Independence* (New York: Alfred A. Knopf, 1969), 81–82.

2. Perry Miller, "The Contribution of the Protestant Churches to Religious Liberty in Colonial America," in *Essays on American Colonial History* (2nd ed.), ed. Paul Goodman (New York: Holt, Rhinehart and Winston, 1972), 440.

3. Louis B. Wright, *The Cultural Life of the American Colonies, 1607–1763* (New York: Harper & Row, 1957), 73.

4. Lawrence Friedman, *Crime and Punishment in American History* (New York: Basic Books, 1993), 33 (quote); Esther Singleton, *Dutch New York* (New York: Dodd, Mead and Co., 1909), 201; Janet M. Lindman, *Bodies of Belief: Baptist Community in Early America* (Philadelphia: University of Pennsylvania Press, 2008), 53 (quote).

5. Alice M. Earle, *Child Life in Colonial Days* (New York: Macmillan, 1899), 244–45; Robert P. Gildrie, *The Profane, the Civil, & the Godly: The Reformation of Manners in Orthodox New England, 1679–1749* (University Park: Pennsylvania State University Press, 1994), 119–21; David H. Flaherty, *Privacy in Colonial New England* (Charlottesville: University Press of Virginia, 1972), 132–33 (quotes); Bruce C. Daniels, *Puritans at Play: Leisure and Recreation in Colonial New England* (New York: St. Martin's Press, 1995), 79–80 (quote).

6. Singleton, *Dutch New York*, 202.

7. Schlesinger, *The Birth of the Nation*, 96 (quote); Susan Juster, "Heretics, Blasphemers, and Sabbath Breakers: The Prosecution of Religious Crime in Early America," in *The First Prejudice: Religious Tolerance and Intolerance in Early America*, ed. Chris Beneke and Christopher S. Grenda (Philadelphia: University of Pennsylvania Press, 2011), 139–40 (quotes); Gustavus Myers, *History of Bigotry in the United States* (New York: Random House, 1943), 18–19; Singleton, *Dutch New York*, 185–86, 200.

8. Friedman, *Crime and Punishment*, 32 (quote); Juster, "Heretics, Blasphemers, and Sabbath Breakers," 132 (quote); Gildrie, *The Profane*, 55 (quote); Ted Morgan, *Wilderness at Dawn: The Settling of the North American Continent* (New York: Simon & Schuster, 1993), 170 (quote).

9. Milton Powell, *The Voluntary Church: American Religious Life (1740–1865) Seen through the Eyes of European Visitors* (New York: Macmillan Co., 1967), 13.

10. Susan Mackiewicz, "Philadelphia Flourishing: The Material World of Philadelphia, 1682–1760," Ph.D. dissertation, University of Pennsylvania, 1988, 333 (quote); Joyce Goodfriend, "Practicing Toleration in Dutch New Netherland," in *The First Prejudice*, quotes from pp. 113, 101, and 105; Singleton, *Dutch New York*, 189–92.

11. Richard Pointer, *Protestant Pluralism and the New York Experience: A Study of Eighteenth-Century Religious Diversity* (Bloomington: Indiana University Press, 1988), 35 (quotes); Juster, "Heretics, Blasphemers, and Sabbath Breakers," 138 (quote).

12. William W. Sweet, *Religion in Colonial America* (New York: Cooper Square, 1965), 90, 149 (quote); Alan Heimert and Andrew Delbanco, eds.,

The Puritans in America: A Narrative Anthology (Cambridge, MA: Harvard University Press, 1985), 279 (quote); Juster, "Heretics, Blasphemers, and Sabbath Breakers," 130, 139 (quote).

13. Myers, *History of Bigotry*, 60 (quote); Charles Lippy, "Chastized by Scorpions: Christianity and Culture in Colonial South Carolina, 1669–1740," *Church History* 79 (2010): 266 (quote); Martin Lodge, "The Crisis of the Churches in the Middle Colonies, 1720–1750," *Pennsylvania Magazine of History and Biography* 95 (1971): 213 (quote).

14. Sheila Skemp, "A Social and Cultural History of Newport, Rhode Island, 1720–1765," Ph.D. dissertation, University of Iowa, 1974, 156 (quote); Sheila Skemp, "George Berkeley's Newport Experience," *Rhode Island History* 37 (1978): 54 (quote), 59–62; Raymond Irwin, "A Study in Schism: Sabbatarian Baptists in England and America, 1665–1672," *American Baptist Quarterly* 13 (1994): 237–39.

15. Jo Anne McCormick, "The Quakers of Colonial South Carolina," Ph.D. dissertation, University of South Carolina, 1984, 87–88; Thomas Little, "The Origins of Southern Evangelicalism: Revivalism in South Carolina, 1700–1740," *Church History* 75 (2006): 774–88; Andrew Murphy, "Persecuting Quakers?: Liberty and Toleration in Early Pennsylvania," in *The First Prejudice*, 150–54; William Pencak, "Anti-Semitism, Toleration, and Appreciation: The Changing Relations of Jews and Gentiles in Early America," ibid., 248–49; Juster, "Heretics, Blasphemers, and Sabbath Breakers," 142 (quote).

16. Joyce Godfriend, "The Baptist Church in Pre-Revolutionary New York," *American Baptist Quarterly* 16 (1997): 221 (quote); Little, "The Origins of Southern Evangelicalism," 5; Pointer, *Protestant Pluralism*, 34.

17. Richard L. Bushman, *The Refinement of America: Persons, Houses, Cities* (New York: Vintage Books, 1992), 169–80; Mackiewics, "Philadelphia Flourishing," 383 (quote); Hugh Morison, *Early American Architecture: From the First Colonial Settlements to the National Period* (Oxford, UK: Oxford University Press, 1952), 408–9, 431–32, 442–57; William Pencak, *Jews and Gentiles in Early America, 1654–1800* (Ann Arbor: University of Michigan Press, 2005), 94 (quote).

18. Pointer, *Protestant Pluralism*, 37, 39 (quotes).

19. Sally Schwartz, *"A Mixed Multitude": The Struggle for Toleration in Colonial Pennsylvania* (New York: New York University Press, 1988), 64 (quote); Benjamin Carp, *Rebels Rising: Cities and the American Revolution* (New York: Oxford University Press, 2007), 117–18; Elaine Crane, "Uneasy Coexistence: Religious Tensions in Eighteenth Century Newport," *Newport History* 53 (1984): 101–2.

20. Richard Hofstadter, *America at 1750: A Social Portrait* (New York: Alfred A. Knopf, 1971), 188–89 (quote); Thomas Carney, "A Tradition to Live By: New York Religious History, 1624–1740," *New York History* 85 (2004): 302 (quote); Skemp, "A Social and Cultural History of Newport," 161.

21. Singleton, *Dutch New York*, 182–83; Edmund Sinnott, *Meetinghouse and Church in Early New England* (New York: McGraw Hill, 1963), 5; Alice M. Earle, *Home Life in Colonial Days* (New York: Grosset & Dunlap, 1898), 364–76; Claudia Durst Johnson, *Daily Life in Colonial New England* (Westport, CT: Greenwood Press, 2002), 20; Charles Place, "From Meetinghouse to Church in New England," *Old Time New England* 13 (1922): 69–70.

22. Bettina Norton, "Anglican Embellishments: The Contributions of John Gibbs, Junior, and William Price to the Church of England in Eighteenth-Century Boston," in *New England Meeting House and Church: 1630–1850*, ed. Peter Benes (Boston: Boston University Press, 1979), 73; Dell Upton, *Holy Things and Profane: Anglican Parish Churches in Colonial Virginia* (Cambridge: Massachusetts Institute of Technology Press, 1986), 164; S. Charles Bolton, *Southern Anglicanism: The Church of England in Colonial South Carolina* (Westport, CT: Greenwood Press, 1982), 122.

23. Bushman, *The Refinement of America*, 180 (quotes); Joyce Goodfriend, "The Social Dimensions of Congregational Life in Colonial New York City," *William and Mary Quarterly* 46 (April 1989): 261; Robert Dinkin, "Seating the Meetinghouse in Early Massachusetts," in *Material Life in America, 1600–1860*, ed. Robert St. George (Boston: Northeastern University Press, 1988), 407–12; Johnson, *Daily Life in Colonial New England*, 21–22; Sinnott, *Meetinghouse and Church*, 79–80; Upton, *Holy Things and Profane*, 175–80.

24. Larry D. Eldridge, *A Distant Heritage: The Growth of Free Speech in Early America* (New York: New York University Press, 1994), 7 (quote); Skemp, "A Social and Cultural History of Newport," 426 (quote); Sarah Fatherly, *Gentlewomen and Learned Ladies: Women and Elite Formation in Eighteenth-Century Philadelphia* (Bethlehem, PA: Lehigh University Press, 2008), 113.

25. David Hawke, *The Colonial Experience* (Indianapolis: Bobbs-Merrill, 1966), 135 (quote); Erik R. Seeman, *Pious Persuasions: Laity and Clergy in Eighteenth-Century New England* (Baltimore, MD: Johns Hopkins University Press, 1999), 85.

26. Darret Rutman, *Winthrop's Boston: A Portrait of a Puritan Town, 1630–1649* (Chapel Hill: University of North Carolina Press, 1965), 256–57; Patricia Bonomi, *Under the Cope of Heaven: Religion, Society, and Politics in Colonial America* (New York: Oxford University Press, 1986), 111–15.

27. Michael Zuckerman, *Peaceable Kingdoms: New England Towns in the Eighteenth Century* (New York: W. W. Norton & Co., 1970), 60 (quote); Johnson, *Daily Life in Colonial New England*, 13 (quote).

28. Earle, *Child Life*, 228 (quote); 238–39 (quotes); Thomas White, *A Little Book for Little Children* (Boston, 1702), 11 (quote).

29. Charles Hambrick-Stowe, "Spiritual Dynamics of Puritan Worship," *New England Meetinghouse and Church*, 112–16, 119; Daniels, *Puritans at Play,*

88; James P. Walsh, "Holy Time and Sacred Space in Puritan New England," *American Quarterly* 32 (1980): 89.

30. Gildrie, *The Profane*, 121–23 (quotes).

31. Hambrick-Stowe, "Spiritual Dynamics of Puritan Service," 122; Heimert and Delbanco, *The Puritans in America*, 373–77; Francis J. Bremer, *Shaping New Englands: Puritan Clergymen in Seventeenth-Century England and New England* (New York: Twayne Publishers, 1994), 29, 32 (quote).

32. Seeman, *Pious Persuasions*, quotes on pp. 103–5.

33. James P. Walsh, "Holy Time and Sacred Space," 84 (quote); Johnson, *Daily Life in Colonial New England*, 25.

34. Oscar Barck Jr. and Hugh Lefler, *Colonial America*, 2nd edition (New York: Macmillan, 1968), 392 (quotes).

35. Rhys Isaac, *The Transformation of Virginia, 1740–1790* (Chapel Hill: University of North Carolina Press, 1982), 65 (quote); Upton, *Holy Things and Profane*, 7, 169 (quotes).

36. Bolton, *Southern Anglicanism*, 139 (quote); Robert Olwell, *Masters, Slaves, and Subjects: The Culture of Power in the South Carolina Low Country, 1740–1790* (Ithaca, NY: Cornell University Press, 1998), 115 (quote); Upton, *Holy Things and Profane*, 172–73.

37. Isaac, *The Transformation of Virginia*, 60 (quote), 64 (quotes).

38. Antoinette Downing, "History of the Friends Meetinghouse in Newport, Rhode Island," *Newport History* 41 (1968), 157; Sweet, *Religion in Colonial America*, 163 (quote); J. William Frost, *The Quaker Family in Colonial America: A Portrait of the Society of Friends* (New York: St. Martin's Press, 1973), 36–37.

39. Rebecca Larson, *Daughters of Light: Quaker Women Preaching and Prophesying in the Colonies and Abroad, 1700–1775* (Chapel Hill: University of North Carolina Press, 1999), 44.

40. Rufus Jones, *The Quakers in the American Colonies* (New York: W. W. Norton & Co., 1966), 137–38, 242–43; Larson, *Daughters of Light*, 19, 59–60 (quotes); Frost, *The Quaker Family*, 40 (quote), 79.

41. Sweet, *Religion in Colonial America*, 120–41.

42. Amy Lee Mears, "Worship in Selected Churches of the Charleston Baptist Association, 1682–1795," Ph.D. dissertation, Southern Baptist Theological Seminary, 1995, 91.

43. Tripp Hudgins, "Baptismal Rites in Colonial Era Baptist Churches in America," *American Baptist Quarterly* 22 (2003): 460–63; Mears, "Worship in Selected Churches," 71–79, 133–46; Lindman, *Bodies of Belief*, 73

44. Guy S. Klett, *Presbyterians in Colonial Pennsylvania* (Philadelphia: University of Pennsylvania Press, 1937), 107.

45. Singleton, *Dutch New York*, 192–93.

46. Sweet, *Religion in Colonial America*, 210–30.

47. Ibid., 236–44.

48. Jon Butler, *New World Faiths: Religion in Colonial America* (New York: Oxford University Press, 2008), 79–80; Sweet, *Religion in Colonial America*, 306–10; Russell E. Richey, *Early American Methodism* (Bloomington: Indiana University Press, 1991), 3–6, quote from p. 4.

49. Jacob Marcus, *The American Jew, 1585–1990: A History* (Brooklyn, NY: Carlson, 1995), 17–19; Abraham Karp, *A History of the Jews in America* (Northvale, NJ: Jason Aronson, 1997), 12.

50. Marcus, *The American Jew*, 20–26, 37; Pencak, *Jews and Gentiles*, 40; Karp, *History of Jews in America*, 12.

51. Marcus, *The American Jew*, 27–28.

52. Karp, *History of Jews in America*, 8 (quote); Pencak, *Jews and Gentiles*, 190 (quote); Marcus, *The American Jew*, 28 (quote); Martin Aron, "Religious Practices of Newport Jewry Prior to the American Revolution," *Rhode Island Jewish Historical Notes* 11 (1991): 71–75.

53. Pencak, *Jews and Gentiles*, 40–41 (quotes).

54. Earle, *Home Life*, 373.

55. G. E. Bolhouse, "The Moravian Church in Newport," *Newport History* 52 (1979), 11; Gildrie, *The Profane*, 117–18 (quote); Don Sanford, "Entering into Coventry: The History of the Seventh-Day Baptists in Newport," *Newport History* 66 (1994): 33.

56. Skemp, "A Social and Cultural History of Newport," 170 (quote); "The Seventh-Day Baptist Church at Newport, R.I.," *Seventh-Day Baptist Memorial* 2 (1853), 30; Valerie Gladfelter, "Power Challenged: Rising Individualism in the Burlington, New Jersey, Friends Meeting, 1678–1720," in *Friends and Neighbors: Group Life in America's First Plural Society*, ed. Michael Zuckerman (Philadelphia: Temple University Press, 1982), 120, 126–36; Zuckerman, *Peaceable Kingdoms*, 62; Flaherty, *Privacy in Colonial New England*, 154–62; Frost, *Quaker Family*, 60; Klett, *Presbyterians in Colonial Pennsylvania*, 119, 122 (quote).

57. Sister Mary Augustina Ray, *American Opinion of Roman Catholicism in the Eighteenth Century* (New York: Columbia University Press, 1936), 113, 64, 76, 180 (quotes), 165–211.

58. Ibid., 122.

59. Myers, *History of Bigotry*, 98.

60. Joseph Casino, "Anti-Popery in Colonial Pennsylvania," *Pennsylvania Magazine of History and Biography* 105 (1981): 279; Francis Cogliano, *No King, No Popery: Anti-Catholicism in Revolutionary New England* (Westport, CT: Greenwood Press, 1995), 11 (quote), 8–14; Peter Lake, "The Significance of the Elizabethan Identification of the Pope as Antichrist," *Journal of Ecclesiastical History* 31 (1980): 161–67, 174–77.

61. Cogliano, *No King, No Popery*, 8 (quote), 13–14 (quote); Thomas Kidd, " 'Let Hell and Rome Do Their Worst': World News, Anti-Catholicism, and International Protestantism in Early Eighteenth-Century Boston," *New England Quarterly* 76 (2003): 265–71; Douglas Stange, "The

Third Lecture: One Hundred and Fifty Years of Anti-Popery at Harvard," *Harvard Library Bulletin* 16 (1968): 355–57; Ray, *American Opinion of Roman Catholicism*, 132–36, 69 (quote).

62. Richard C. Madden, *Catholics in South Carolina: A Record* (New York: University Press of America, 1985), 8–9 (quotes); John T. Ellis, *Catholics in Colonial America* (Baltimore, MD: Helicon, 1965), 369–79; Jason K. Duncan, *Citizens or Papists?: The Politics of Anti-Catholicism in New York, 1685–1821* (New York: Fordham University Press, 2005), 2 (quote), 20–29; Ray, *American Opinion of Roman Catholicism*, 234–35; Randall Balmer, "Traitors and Papists: The Religious Dimension of Leisler's Rebellion," *New York History* 70 (1989): 344–53; Myers, *History of Bigotry*, 94.

63. Paul Newman, " 'Good Will to All Men . . . from the King on the Throne to the Beggar on the Dunghill': William Penn, the Roman Catholics, and Religious Toleration," *Pennsylvania History* 61 (1994): 470–75; Casino, "Anti-Popery in Colonial Pennsylvania," 288–93; Ray, *American Opinion of Roman Catholicism*, 70, 244–45; Schwartz, *"A Mixed Multitude,"* 104, 152 (quote); Myers, *History of Bigotry*, 98–99.

64. Cogliano, *No King, No Popery*, 23–29; Ray, *American Opinion of Roman Catholicism*, 257–58; Duncan, *Citizens or Papists?* 24–25; Owen Stanwood, "Catholics, Protestants, and the Clash of Civilizations in Early America," in *The First Prejudice*, 233–37.

65. Hofstadter, *America at 1750*, 221.

66. Historians are still debating the "greatness" of the eighteenth-century religious revivals. Those who argue it was a short-lived event invented both by revivalist ministers and historians of the event include Jon Butler, "Enthusiasm Described and Decried: The Great Awakening as Interpretive Fiction," *Journal of American History* 69 (1982): 305–25; Joseph A. Conforti, *Jonathan Edwards: Religious Tradition and the American Culture* (Chapel Hill: University of North Carolina Press, 1995); and Frank Lambert, *Inventing the Great Awakening* (Princeton, NJ: Princeton University Press, 1999). For a defense of the religious revivals as extensive both in time and space, see Patricia Bonomi, *Under the Cope of Heaven: Religion, Society, and Politics in Colonial America* (New York: Oxford University Press, 1986); and Thomas Kidd, *The Great Awakening: The Roots of Evangelical Christianity in Colonial America* (New Haven, CT: Yale University Press, 2007).

67. Hofstadter, *America at 1750*, 253 (quote); Thomas Kidd, " 'A Faithful Watchman on the Walls of Charlestown': Josiah Smith and Moderate Revivalism in Colonial South Carolina," *South Carolina Historical Magazine* 105 (2004): 82–106, provides an excellent example of local evangelicals having to pick up the pieces following Whitefield's visit to a city.

68. Gerald Goodwin, "The Anglican Reaction to the Great Awakening," *Historical Magazine of the Protestant Episcopal Church* 35 (1966): 358–63; Hawke, *The Colonial Experience*, 424 (quote); Schwartz, *"A Mixed Multitude,"* 123.

69. Goodwin, "The Anglican Reaction," 359 (quote); Thomas Kidd, *The Great Awakening: The Roots of Evangelical Christianity in Colonial America* (New Haven, CT: Yale University Press, 2007), 94 (quote); William Kenney, "Alexander Garden and George Whitefield: The Significance of Revivalism in South Carolina," *South Carolina Historical Magazine* 71 (1970): 1–2; Daniel T. Morgan, "The Great Awakening in South Carolina, 1740–1775," *South Atlantic Quarterly* 70 (1971): 596–99; John P. Barrington, "Suppressing the Great Awakening: Alexander Garden's Use of Anti-Popery against George Whitefield," South Carolina Historical Society *Proceedings* (2003): 1–7, 10 (quote).

70. Skemp, "A Social and Cultural History of Newport," 416–18.

71. Charles Chauncy, "Revivalism and True Religion," in *The Annals of America*, vol. 1 (Chicago: Encyclopedia Britannica, 1968), 437 (quote); Gary B. Nash, *The Urban Crucible: The Northern Seaports and the Origins of the American Revolution*, abridged ed. (Cambridge, MA: Harvard University Press, 1986), 129 (quote); Richard C. Simmons, *The American Colonies: From Settlement to Independence* (New York: W. W. Norton & Co., 1976), 219 (quote); Alan Taylor, *American Colonies: The Settling of North America* (New York: Penguin Books, 2001), 350 (quote).

72. Max Savelle, *Seeds of Liberty: The Genesis of the American Mind* (Seattle: University of Washington Press, 1948), 65 (quote).

73. David S. Lovejoy, *Religious Enthusiasm in the New World: Heresy to Revolution* (Cambridge, MA: Harvard University Press, 1985), 181 (quote); Hofstadter, *America at 1750*, 246 (quote); Douglas Winiarski, "Souls Filled with Ravishing Transport: Heavenly Visions and the Radical Awakening in New England," *William and Mary Quarterly* 61 (2004): 12–13, 17 (quote); Schlesinger, *The Birth of the Nation*, 88 (quote); Jon Butler, *Awash in a Sea of Faith: Christianizing the American People* (Cambridge, MA: Harvard University Press, 1990), 167 (quote).

74. J. Richard Olivas, "Partial Revival: The Limits of the Great Awakening in Boston, Massachusetts, 1740–1742," in *Inequality in Early America*, ed. Carla Pestana and Sharon Salinger (Hanover, NH: University Press of New England, 1999), 68–81; Chauncy, "Revivalism and True Religion," 435–36 (quote).

75. Hofstadter, *America at 1750*, 273 (quote); Taylor, *American Colonies*, 352 (quote); Savelle, *Seeds of Liberty*, 69 (quote).

76. Taylor, *American Colonies*, 354 (quote); Kidd, *The Great Awakening*, 217 (quote), 214 (quote).

77. Schlesinger, *The Birth of the Nation*, 74; Jon Butler, "Magic, Astrology, and the Early American Religious Heritage, 1600–1760," *American Historical Review* 84 (1979): 317–18 (quotes).

78. David Hawke, *Everyday Life in Early America* (New York: Harper & Row, 1989), 158–59; M. Drake Patten, "African-American Spiritual Beliefs: An Archaeological Testimony from the Slave Quarter," in *Wonders of the Invisible World: 1600–1900*, ed. Peter Benes (Boston: Boston University

Press, 1992), 48–50; William Pierson, "Black Arts and Black Magic: Yankee Accommodations to African Religion," in *Wonders of the Invisible World*, 38.

79. Seeman, *Pious Persuasions*, 124 (quote); Butler, "Magic, Astrology," 341; Jon Butler, *Awash in a Sea of Faith*, 68–96; John L. Brooke, " 'The True Spiritual Seed': Sectarian Religion and the Persistence of the Occult in Eighteenth-Century New England," in *Wonders of the Invisible World: 1600–1900*, 107.

80. Seeman, *Pious Persuasions*, 117–18, 122 (quote); Butler, *Awash in a Sea of Faith*, 82 (quote); Peter Benes, " 'Pedlars in Divinity': Street Religion in Massachusetts and Rhode Island before 1830," *Dublin Seminar for New England Folklife* 30 (2005): 34; Butler, "Magic, Astrology," 321–30.

81. Gildrie, *The Profane*, 147 (quote); Carol F. Karlson, *The Devil in the Shape of a Woman: Witchcraft in Colonial New England* (New York: W. W. Norton & Co., 1987), 6–8, 19–35.

82. Karlsen, *The Devil in the Shape of a Woman*, 41 (quote); Richard Godbeer, "Chaste and Unchaste Covenants: Witchcraft and Sex in Early Modern Culture," in *Wonders of the Invisible World*, 63.

83. The Curse of Canaan (or Ham) refers to the curse that Ham's father Noah placed upon Ham's son Canaan after Ham saw his father Noah naked and inebriated in his tent. When Noah sobered up and learned what his youngest son (Ham) had done to him, he said:

> A curse on Canaan!
> He will be a slave to his brothers.
> Give praise to the Lord, the God of Shem.
> May God cause Japheth to increase!
> May his descendants live with the people of Shem!
> Canaan will be the slave of Japheth.
> (Genesis 9:25–28. Good News Bible: Catholic Study Edition
> [Nashville, TN: Thomas Nelson, 1979]).

84. Lester B. Scherer, *Slavery and the Churches in Early America, 1619–1819* (Grand Rapids, MI: William Eerdmans, 1975), 90–91 (quote); Butler, *Awash in a Sea of Faith*, 130 (quote), 140–41; Lorenzo J. Greene, *The Negro in Colonial New England* (New York: Columbia University Press, 1942), 286 (quote); Olwell, *Masters, Slaves, and Subjects*, 112 (quote).

85. Greene, *The Negro in Colonial New England*, 283–84 (quotes); William D. Pierson, *Black Yankees: The Development of an Afro-American Subculture in Eighteenth-Century New England* (Amherst: University of Massachusetts Press, 1988), 59–66; Donald R. Wright, *African Americans in the Colonial Era: From African Origins through the American Revolution* (Wheeling, IL: Harlan Davidson, 1990), 96 (quote); Edgar McManus, *Black Bondage in the North* (Syracuse, NY: Syracuse University Press, 1973), 106 (quote).

86. Piersen, *Black Yankees*, 74–78, 80–83, 85 (quote).

87. Clinton Rossiter, *The First American Revolution: The American Colonies on the Eve of Independence* (New York: Harcourt, Brace & Co., 1956), 71–72.

5

Labor and Economy

INTRODUCTION

Work was the quintessential element of the daily life experience for residents of towns and cities. Virtually everyone worked, including the young and the old. Their very survival depended on it. To help ensure their survival, most people worked in a family-oriented economic enterprise in which the breadwinner, spouses, children, the elderly, and in many cases apprentices, servants, and slaves worked cooperatively in a commercial enterprise of the house. Such a work environment narrowed the range of occupations of young people, at least by modern standards, as most children simply followed in the footsteps of their parents in seeking a livelihood. Rising above the economic station one was born into was not an aspiration for most youngsters, who expected the future to replicate the past. Further constricting the lower classes' upward economic mobility, especially among Puritans, was their belief in a "secular calling." This religious tenet proposed that God called men and women to perform particular tasks or work in life. Not surprisingly, women were called to be housewives and mothers, while men were called to be merchants, craftsmen, ministers, chimney sweeps, and so on. Although everyone was responsible for identifying the work God intended for them, Puritan clergy emphasized to the lower classes in particular that it was blasphemy to assume a calling or work above the social level to which one was born, though one should also use the talents God gave so that movement to new kinds of work was possible and acceptable. For those aspiring to rise above their station in life, the moneyed elite built a variety of barriers preventing all but the most fortunate and ambitious from entering their exclusive society.[1]

As a result, most men and women in the colonial cities were confined to a life of hard and dangerous labor. This was particularly true for the numerous indentured servants and slaves who comprised a significant portion of workers in the principal cities. Many people today are surprised to learn that nearly three-fourths of all immigrants to British North America arrived in some condition of servitude, making early America more the "land of the unfree" than the "land of the free."[2] Many of these servants and slaves settled in the major port cities where they disembarked following a long, difficult, and dangerous transatlantic voyage. Nearly all were rewarded with a life of poverty, backbreaking labor, and hopelessness. For them, America was not the "land of opportunity" but the "land of exploitation." Indeed, there was an "ordinariness in the brutality and exploitive nature" of the early American labor system, writes historian Richard Dunn, who explains that the colonial elite believed that "most people needed to be forced into underpaid labor" to support a "few sufficiently free and leisured people" necessary to create the "glories of civilized culture." In short, "society had to be blatantly hierarchical: many drones at the bottom and a few swells at the top."[3] The labor of these many unfree and underpaid "drones" allowed the five colonial ports to become major centers of commerce and the few members of the upper class who governed them to attain their remarkable riches.

GOVERNMENT AND ECONOMIC GROWTH

In addition to human labor provided by the urban masses, government at various levels played the key role in promoting economic growth in the cities and elsewhere. The urban elites who controlled the five ports rejected the concept of free-market capitalism in favor of considerable government intervention into the colonial economy. For example, they used their political influence in directing public funds toward building wharves and docks that merchants and ship captains depended on to conduct their business, constructing roads and bridges both in the city and the interior necessary for transporting goods overland, establishing local courts to resolve business disputes, hiring constables to protect private property, creating provincial militias to displace Native Americans from their land, and hiring inspectors to check the quality of meat, bread, barrels, shoes, and other products sold in the cities. Urban leaders also adopted British laws regarding fire protection and housing codes, building-lease titles, mortgage laws, and formal building contracts that encouraged new money-making enterprises in urban real estate and construction. Of course, money was the life-blood of the colonial economy; and while currency was scarce at times, colonists preferred doing business with government-created money, whether it be the British pound, the Dutch guilder, Spanish doubloons, or American printed currency. American merchants in the cities were even more dependent on the British navy, the largest in the world at the time, for protecting their commercial vessels on the high seas from pirates and foreign enemies. Meanwhile, American planters and manufacturers benefitted enormously from the English Navigation Acts that either protected or subsidized American production of tobacco, molasses, copper, rice, sugar, silk, hemp, hides, whale fins, potash, indigo, and naval stores—all of which passed through the major ports for export. Other provisions of the Navigation Acts stimulated the American shipbuilding industry, important to urban economies, and their ancillary services such as making rope, bolts, anchor chains, lumber, staves, and many other items. Rather than free-market capitalism, it was government at the local, provincial, and imperial levels that served as the engine of economic growth in the major ports and elsewhere. This largely explains why the urban elites sought to control government, so that they could use it to promote and protect their economic interests.[4]

DEPENDANT COLLECTIVISM

As the above narrative details, early Americans were heavily dependant on the government both for their physical survival and their economic success. They were also helped along by a strong collective spirit in which neighbors assisted one another in their daily life struggles. The idea that early Americans were "rugged individualists" and "self-made men" who achieved success with little outside assistance is entirely false. These are concepts that the colonists would have found both odd, and if actually practiced, detrimental to their survival and success. They recognized that their mutual prosperity was deeply intertwined. Rather than rugged individualists and self-made men, early Americans were dependant collectivists who demanded assistance from the government and who embraced a collective spirit in meeting their daily needs. This was true for both rural and urban colonists.

Frontiersmen, in particular, insisted that the government displace the Native Americans from their land, protect them from back-country bandits, build roads and dredge rivers so they could transport their produce to market, create schools to educate their children, and establish courts and jails to help maintain the peace. Farmers were also heavily dependant on their neighbors for many of their basic needs because they simply lacked all the skills and tools necessary to be rugged individualists and self-made men. Early Americans were no more "jack-of-all-trades" than are Americans today. It is ludicrous to think that any one man possessed the skills, resources, and time necessary to build his home and barn, and to make his own gun, plow, wagon, tools, shoes, ropes, barrels, buckets, horseshoes, furniture, plates, cutlery, and cooking pots while also felling trees, building fences, tilling the soil, planting seed, harvesting crops, tanning hides, and tending livestock; or that a housewife possessed all the skills and tools necessary to make clothing, beer, candles, soap, butter, and cheese for her family while also raising children, preparing meals, tending a garden, preserving food, washing clothes, and performing an endless array of other domestic duties. In her study of self-sufficiency in early America, historian Carole Shammas discovered that as late as 1774 less than one half of households in Massachusetts contained a spinning wheel and that two-thirds of households lacked equipment to manufacture butter or cheese. The costs necessary to achieve self-sufficiency simply exceeded the resources and skills available to households. What farmers could not make themselves they either purchased from itinerant craftsmen, bartered with their neighbors, or imported from outside the colony. Self-sufficiency, writes historian John Mack Faragher, was neither an individual nor a family quality, but "a community experience ... Sharing work with neighbors at cabin raisings, log rollings, haying, husking, butchering, harvesting or threshing were all traditionally communal affairs." This collective spirit is also reflected in a borrowing system practiced by frontier folk that allowed scarce tools, labor, and products to circulate for the benefit of all. As one western pioneer told prospective settlers: "Your wheelbarrows, your shovels, your utensils of all sorts, belong not to yourself, but to the public who do not think it necessary even to ask a loan, but take it for granted."[5]

A "BUILT-TOGETHER REALITY"

Residents of the five cities were even more dependant than frontier folk on government and others for their basic needs and individual achievements. The nature of the urban economy forced residents to rely heavily on farmers, hunters, craftsmen, and manufacturers for most everything they wore, ate, drank, and used. Merchants, craftsmen, shopkeepers, and other urban businessmen were just as dependant on others for their economic success. These entrepreneurs did not build their business enterprises on their own; they had considerable assistance from other people and from the government. Businessmen were not self-made men as certain mythmakers would have us believe. They were the beneficiaries of what Mike Lapham and Brian Miller call the "built-together reality." Merchants, artisans, shopkeepers, and even lawyers and physicians would not have been able to establish a business or practice without a master craftsman or professional first teaching them their trade and often teaching them how to read, write, and do simple math. Urban businessmen and professionals also relied on carpenters to build their homes, shops, and warehouses, and blacksmiths to craft their tools. Once established in their enterprise, urban businessmen met their labor needs by exploiting slaves, indentured servants, apprentices, and poorly paid day laborers. Many urban craftsmen and professionals also received assistance from their wives and children, if any. The urban upper-class, in particular, promoted a strong kinship network to support and promote individual members in their professions. Those who lacked a supportive network of family and friends did not fare so well in the five cities. Meanwhile, government often behaved like a chamber of commerce in supporting the economic endeavors of local businessmen by protecting private property, by building an infrastructure necessary to conduct trade, by peacefully resolving business disputes through the courts, by creating laws and contracts important to business transactions, and by subsidizing the manufacture of important commodities, among many other services. In essence, economic life in the colonial city was a community experience, not an individual endeavor.[6]

Even more critical toward individual success than help from either the government or other people was one's class, race, and gender. Individual achievement in colonial America had less to do with a strong work ethic and personal character, although both were important, than with the circumstances in which one was born. Despite the pervasive belief among Americans today that our nation from the beginning has been a land of opportunity, early America was not a land of opportunity for all; it was not even a land of equal opportunity for all. As the following narrative details, those individuals who were born white, male, and with wealth had a significant advantage over those born in different circumstances. Many colonists worked hard, led sober and frugal lives, and in the end had little to show for it. Paramount in determining individual achievement in early America was one's class, race, sex, and birthright.

ECONOMY

The economy of the port cities centered around three functions: commerce (both land and sea), industrial production, and internal services. During the mid-eighteenth century, the service sector provided the largest form of employment with 50 percent of the adult male labor force. Both the industrial and maritime industries employed slightly less than 25 percent of workers each. The remaining 2 percent of workers labored in the government sector. Yet these figures are deceiving because most workers, either directly or indirectly, depended on commerce for their livelihood: sailors manned the commercial vessels, bakers and butchers supplied biscuits and beef to sailors on their transatlantic voyages; coopers made barrels to hold items bound for the sea; distillers relied on West Indian molasses to make rum; laborers, draymen, and porters stowed and unloaded the ships' cargo; assorted smiths and craftsmen cared for the horses, carts, and ships used in transporting goods while others built the ships used in trade; innkeepers and tavern keepers catered to the men involved in moving merchandise by land and by sea; and various retailers from hucksters to wholesalers sold imported goods to residents.[7]

Urban residents were not the only ones who benefitted from the thriving oceanic trade of the port cities. Hundreds of thousands of people living in the hinterland grew a variety of agricultural products, raised an assortment of livestock, and exploited natural resources for export to the outside world via the major ports. Merchants would then exchange these domestic products for finished goods from Europe and slaves from Africa and the Caribbean. Once imported into America, merchants distributed many of these goods to storekeepers in towns and villages throughout the interior. In this symbiotic economic relationship, the port cities served as the major distribution center between the American hinterland and the Atlantic world. They were the hinges of the empire.

TRADERS AND MERCHANTS

The central players in this domestic and international commercial exchange were the traders and merchants, two occupational groups with a distinct hierarchy. The lowest level of traders included peddlers and hucksters who could be seen and heard hawking their cheap goods either on street corners or from door to door. Just above them were petty retailers, often single women struggling to make a living by selling specialty items out of their homes. Closer to the waterfront were larger retail stores owned by middle- and upper-class traders who kept a line of merchandise similar in variety to a modern-day department store. Connecting the economies of the city with the countryside were "primary traders" who operated a country store, usually along the main trading routes.[8]

Merchants proper, who comprised 15 to 20 percent of urban workers, also had their hierarchy. In the top bracket were a handful of merchant princes who dominated all major areas of international and domestic trade, leaving middle- and lower-rank merchants with the occasional cargoes, odd lots, and less significant importations. By monopolizing trade, these merchants also monopolized earnings, bringing in between £15,000 and £35,000 a year during the late colonial period. By comparison, master shoemakers and tailors earned between £45 to £60 a year. Nor did these merchant princes have to labor hard for their fortunes. A busy day for even the most important merchant house was a desultory three trades a day. The merchant never broke a sweat, developed callouses on his hands, or risked personal injury on the job. Apprenticed clerks and bookkeepers tended to the more mundane tasks of overseeing the loading and unloading of cargo and checking inventories. This slow pace of business and the assistance of apprentices allowed merchants the leisure to pursue political careers, participate in civic affairs, and engage in additional money-making ventures such as operating as bankers; investing in land, slaves, shipbuilding, and among Newport merchants, rum distilleries; establishing branch outlet stores in the interior; and building wharves, inns, and taverns. Still, the life of a merchant was not without its headaches. Collecting foreign debts and dealing with confusions over orders, delays in delivery, and damaged goods gave merchants much aggravation, as did the frequent bad weather that hindered trade.[9]

A View of Boston in the Mid-eighteenth Century. This view of a crowded Boston harbor in the mid-eighteenth century depicts the importance of shipping to the Puritan capital and the other main port cities. (Library of Congress, Prints and Photographs Division, Reproduction # LC USZ62-46312)

The occasional war also made overseas trade a risky and frustrating business for merchants. Those daring enough sought to profit from war by either investing or engaging in privateering voyages. Some Charles Town merchants, for example, profited handsomely during King George's War (1744–1748) with France by capturing 21 enemy vessels. Meanwhile, merchants in Newport suffered from a "privateer fever," according to one contemporary, and did not hesitate to trade illegally with pirates who made Newport their base of operations during wartime. Inadequate customs officers also allowed merchants in all the major ports to engage in illicit and highly profitable trade with the enemy during war, behavior demonstrating that some well-to-do merchants put profits before patriotism. Many people, especially British authorities, publicly questioned the loyalty of these capitalists. Merchants in Newport were so stung by such attacks during the French and Indian War (1754–1763) that they felt compelled to draw up a "Defense of Illegal Trade" in order to prove that their indirect commerce with the French was neither illegal nor unpatriotic and actually benefitted the British empire. In the end, this self-serving piece of propaganda only further outraged the public against the arrogant and avaricious merchant-capitalists who jeopardized the welfare of the larger community for their own self-aggrandizement.[10]

PROFESSIONS

Even more exclusive and elitist than the merchant profession were what we might call white-collar jobs: careers in government, the ministry, medicine, law, and teaching. All had built-in barriers that made it difficult for members of the lower sort to rise up into these more lucrative and lofty professions, which may partially explain why these professional trades comprised less than 3 percent of the urban workforce.[11] Intelligence and personal ability had less to do in determining entrance into these professions than wealth and contacts.

Government Offices

Many political and judicial posts like customs collector, postmaster, general surveyor, attorney general, judicial clerk, and judge were Crown-appointed offices. Naturally, only men possessing substantial wealth or political connections received such royal benefaction. Similarly, men seeking elective office had to meet stiff property requirements. Further excluding all but the well-to-do from the policy-making process is that few elective posts paid a salary. In short, government office in the colonial cities was the purview of rich men.

Ministry

Likewise, entrance into the ministry, the one profession with the greatest social prestige and in the established Anglican and Puritan churches a reasonably high income, required professional training and therefore some wealth. This was particularly true among most Protestants, who insisted on a highly educated clergy who could interpret scripture for them. Therefore an expensive degree from Harvard, Yale, King's College (present-day Columbia) or some other denominational college was necessary for consideration to a prestigious position in one of the large urban churches. Some exceptions to this general rule were the Baptist and Presbyterian denominations, which placed much less emphasis on religious training for their clergy.

Doctors

Even more than the ministry, the well-to-do had a lock on the medical profession. By the early eighteenth century, the practice of medicine was a relatively competitive enterprise in the big cities as the best-trained doctors gravitated to the growing concentrations of wealth and potential clients in the major urban centers. The best means of attracting clients was with a costly medical degree from a prestigious medical school in Great Britain. Not until 1752, with the opening of a medical school at the University of Pennsylvania, could Americans avoid a trip to Europe to receive formal medical training. Further putting the practicing of medicine out of the reach of commoners was the requisite multiyear apprenticeship to a practicing physician, who charged a hefty price for training aspiring doctors. Still, much "medicine" was practiced by apothecaries, barbers, quacks, and others who dispensed drugs, remedies, and emoluments to the poor and those unable or unwilling to engage a formally trained, expensive physician.

Lawyers

The inherent complexities of law prevented all but the well-educated and well-to-do from practicing it as a profession. Moreover, most colonies by the early 1700s required lawyers to have been admitted to the bar in order to act in their clients' interest before the courts, a requirement that necessitated some formal legal training either at the venerable Inns of Court, the London legal training ground, or through an expensive apprenticeship with an established lawyer. The result of all this is that the legal profession in the port cities, as elsewhere, was an exclusive and tight-knit club. Unfortunately for the lawyers, the exclusivity of their profession did not necessarily translate into respect. As today, lawyers in the colonial period were regarded with a combination of suspicion and distrust by ordinary Americans, who often equated attorneys with the devil.[12]

Teachers

At the bottom of the professional ladder in both pay and prestige were teachers, who were normally young men with some college education. The few "dames" who provided an elementary and "pretty" education to upper-class city girls were held in even lower regard by colonists. The relatively low salaries given to teachers—approximately half that made by a typical clergymen—discouraged all but the most dedicated from eventually pursuing other, more lucrative lines of work. However, many exceptions could be found in the large cities where the concentration of people and wealth contributed to the establishment of well-funded and well-respected private schools. These urban educational institutions attracted some of the country's best and brightest teachers, nearly all of whom could claim a college degree, and sometimes two.[13]

CRAFTSMEN

Much more inclusive and important to the urban economy than white-collar workers were the more than 100 different specialized craftsmen (masters, journeymen, and apprentices) who comprised over 50 percent of urban workers. No matter if an artisan worked as a silversmith or a sailmaker, he had to first learn his trade by serving a lengthy apprenticeship to a master craftsman. Demand for apprentices was great in the cities, where parents eagerly handed over their teenaged sons to a master craftsman who, in exchange for the child's labor, would teach him his trade and provide for a rudimentary education, room, board, and clothing, and upon completion of the apprenticeship two sets of clothes and perhaps a set of basic tools. Many a boy had little say in selecting the trade he was to pursue for his entire life. That decision was made by his parents. Still, young apprentices dissatisfied with their line of work often labored desultorily and behaved incorrigibly towards their master until the latter, out of maddening frustration, broke the arrangement. Many others, like young Benjamin Franklin, simply ran away from their apprenticeships until their fathers placed them in a trade more to their liking. Meanwhile, girls had even less opportunity to enter a trade, as they were destined for a life of domesticity. Those 16 percent of city girls who received an apprenticeship therefore were taught the less lucrative "female trades" of mantua makers, corset makers, and milliners that gave them little chance of achieving economic independence. Even for women with a skill, marriage and dependency on a man was their destiny.[14]

Professional Apprentices

As a form of occupational training, the apprenticeship system had an inherent hierarchy mirroring the larger economy and society. At the top stood the mercantile and professional apprentices, those boys destined to become merchants, doctors, and lawyers. These were the sons of gentlemen who were given training in a profitable and respectable line of work that would later assure them entrance into colonial high society. As would-be gentlemen, these upper-crust apprentices managed to avoid the menial tasks and severe punishment so common among their less affluent counterparts. The high fee paid by their parents, explains one scholar, put them in a position "to expect treatment that was more considerate and respectful."[15]

Craft Apprentices

Far less enviable were the experiences of craft apprentices, who came from the lower and middle ranks of society. Although the conditions of these child apprentices varied greatly according to the character of their masters, "it was the rare apprentice who was not ill treated," according to historian Claudia Johnson. Apprentices were often housed abominably, inadequately fed, and overworked. Meanwhile, their contracts usually required them to serve their masters "well and faithfully" and prohibited them from playing "unlawful games" or "haunting taverns." At work, masters gave their bound charges the most menial tasks—opening the shop; lighting fires; fetching wood, water, and tools; running errands, and the like. During slow times a master might even hire out his apprentice to sweep chimneys or clean outhouses.[16]

The master also had the legal right to discipline his apprentice, at least within the bounds of custom. Unruliness, laziness, disrespect, or any perceived misconduct by an apprentice often earned him a severe scolding, deprivation, whipping, or a combination of all three. Boys being boys, these teenaged apprentices sometimes gave their masters ample justification for disciplining them. Among their favorite pastimes were wenching, gambling, and drinking. Many urban masters could relate to the frustration of Peter Timothy, editor of the *South Carolina Gazette*, who in 1754 wrote to his friend Benjamin Franklin: "I discharged my villanous Apprentice . . . A Lad very capable of the Business and might have been of vast Service but for 3 years has always pulled the contrary way; owing to an unhappy affection for Drink, Play and Scandalous Company." Such misbehavior drove more than one frustrated master or mistress to severely abuse his or her apprentice. Thomas Smith of Boston, for example, lost his apprentice after beating him until he was "black as a shoe all over his back and shoulders." Likewise, a New Amsterdam magistrate released a girl from servitude in 1656 after her mistress kicked her in the crotch so hard that she "discharged much blood contrary to nature." In 1718 the New York City court discharged James Jamison from his apprenticeship after his master so badly disfigured his face that he was in "Danger of losing his Eyes." In 1762 the same court discharged four apprentices in one day because their masters had beaten them "in a most Cruel and Immoderate manner Without any just reason for the same." One wonders what one master did to terrorize his young apprentice so badly that it caused him to "constantly wett his bedd and his cloathes." Sometimes the abuse led to murder, as in the case of William Smith of Boston, who in 1644 was hanged for killing his servant boy Nathaniel Sewall by exposing him to wet and wintry weather and "divers acts of rigors [used] towards him as hanging him in the chimney, etc . . ." Such abuse was not just physical but also left emotional scars that sometimes lasted a lifetime. Benjamin Franklin, for one, never forgave his half-brother, who was "passionate and had often beaten me, which I took extremely amiss . . . [H]is harsh and tyrannical treatment of me," Franklin admitted, "has stuck to me through my whole life."[17]

No matter the temperament and character of the master, he was to teach his young apprentice a trade. For the first few years this entailed performing simple but labor-intensive tasks. As his familiarity with the trade grew, along with his strength and manual dexterity, the apprentice began to learn the craft, which usually took two to four years. For the remainder of his service the apprentice refined his skill and improved his speed to commercial levels that allowed him to repay his master through his production for the time, materials, and maintenance he had cost. At the end of the apprentice he had to demonstrate his competence by producing a "proof piece" to the satisfaction of his master, who would then award him with the title of journeyman, allowing him to journey in search of work for wages.[18]

Pauper Apprentices

Not all apprenticeships entailed learning a trade. This was the case for the so-called pauper apprentices—poor orphans or children of parents considered incapable of supporting them. In these cases local overseers of the poor bound the pauper children to more affluent families or to private enterprises. As inhumane as it may seem to modern readers, this was a common practice in the colonial cities, where poverty was a growing problem. To prevent the destitute from becoming a public burden, city officials adopted Elizabethan poor laws requiring that poor children be taken from their parents and sold to the highest bidder at "pauper auctions." This "market in children" was extensive. Boston's overseers of the poor, for example, put out for service 1,134 poor children between 1734 and 1806, most of them to families looking for cheap labor. Teaching the child a skill or providing him or her with a rudimentary education was optional in many cases. In Rhode Island, for example, only one-third of pauper children were owed some education, a figure not much higher than that in Charles Town, where only one-fourth of pauper apprentices received some schooling. One exception to this rule were orphans of wealthy backgrounds, who typically received more favorable indenture placements than did those of poor background. This usually included being taught a white-collar trade and exemptions from "common labor" about the house. Thus, wealthy town officers used the indenture system to perpetuate the class structure by giving orphaned children of the well-to-do certain advantages to maintain their elite status while ensuring that orphaned children from impoverished backgrounds remained in their lowly station. In doing so, the urban aristocracy waged a destructive class war against even helpless and impoverished children.[19]

One might think that families with pauper apprentices might grow emotionally attached to these children and adopt them, but city records show that only about 10 percent of orphaned children apprenticed out were adopted by their masters. This is probably because well-to-do masters frequently sold their pauper apprentices to third parties as their labor requirements changed over time. To the rich, the buying and selling of poor and orphaned children was a cold-hearted and calculated business transaction no different than that involving other goods, as illustrated by the following ad in the April 3, 1760, issue of the *Pennsylvania Gazette*: "To be sold by Thomas Overrend, at the Drawbridge, Two white Boys and a Negro lad; all about fourteen Years of Age. Also very good Lime juice, by the Hogshead or Gallon." Many of these children therefore lived with several different families by the time they were emancipated. Upon completing their apprenticeship, many received neither land, tools, nor cash with which to start their new life. As a result, most of these youngsters had a childhood filled with toil and abuse but empty of love and nurturing. Their future was equally bleak as it was limited to even more life-shortening labor for the well-to-do.[20]

WORK ENVIRONMENT

For those who successfully completed an apprenticeship with a master craftsman, the future was much brighter. The successful master craftsman was an independent, self-employed worker who owned his own tools and furnished his own materials. He performed his craft at home, usually on the first floor of his house, or on the job. He worked with a small group of 5 to 10 assistants—journeymen, apprentices, and sometimes slaves—which added sociability to the work environment. Relations between masters and journeymen were relatively harmonious, and an informal atmosphere prevailed in the workplace. Shops never kept regular working hours because the amount of work varied from time to time. Fewer jobs meant shorter workdays. Moreover, customers rarely requested immediate service as they were more interested in the quality of the final product. The result is that craftsmen worked at a leisurely pace and took frequent breaks to eat meals and snacks, to drink rum or cider, to converse, or simply to rest. To help pass the time at work, the master, journeymen, and apprentices talked about politics, religion, or local affairs. While some craftsmen talked, others sang and whistled popular tunes. Adding to the conviviality were the customers and friends who dropped by to join in the drinking, singing, joking, and card playing. Still, these were proud craftsmen who took their craft seriously. They performed every stage of creating a finished product from the simplest procedures to the more advanced technique. Just as importantly, they created goods for neighbors who knew them by name. A poorly made product was therefore damaging to both their reputation and their business.[21]

A master craftsman with an excellent reputation was able to avoid much of the actual labor involved in hand manufacturing. He might oversee quality control or put the finishing touches to a special piece for a prized customer, but that was the extent of his craftsmanship. Instead, he spent more and more time managing the work schedule of his assistants, keeping his own account books, selling and merchandising his products, and exploring investment opportunities. In Charles Town, for example, approximately three-fourths of craftsmen purchased slaves to use either in their shops or to hire out. Clockmaker Joshua Lockwood diversified his business by entering the retail trade, importing and selling British goods directly from the manufacturer. Some Charles Town artisans invested in town land and rental property, while others purchased land outside the city to

Ropemaker. Rope, so essential to ship's gear, was manufactured in all the major seaports. "Ropewalks" were sometimes a quarter of a mile long, with the workman weaving the strands together while he slowly walked along. The finished rope was wound on a wheel at the end. (Edward Hazen, *Popular Technology; or, Professions and Trade* [New York: Harper & Bros., 1843])

produce food and raw materials for the urban market. Such aggressive business behavior earned some master craftsmen the wealth and leisure to join philanthropic clubs for the benefit of their fellow artisans and even to participate in local politics.[22]

Currency and Credit

In transacting business, little cash exchanged hands between the craftsmen or retailers and their customers. Hard currency was sometimes scarce, and credit therefore was the rule everywhere, from the London magnates to the colonial urban merchants, and from them through the craftsmen and retailers to consumers. Such

Saddler. Because horseback riding was the most common form of transportation in colonial America, the urban saddler had plenty of business.
He worked seated on a "horse," with the material in front of him clamped
into a wooden vise, held taut by a leather strip fastened to a stirrup, or simply kept in place by the pressure of his knees. A wooden tree or frame,
made by another craftsmen, was padded and covered to produce the saddle. The saddler made a wide variety of saddles that included hunt
(English) saddles, military saddles, pack saddles, and for ladies, side saddles. For their upscale customers, the saddler sometimes embroidered silver wire into the saddle. (Edward Hazen, *Popular Technology; or, Professions
and Trade* [New York: Harper & Bros., 1843])

circumstances forced businessmen to accept goods or services, or
"Country Pay," in exchange of cash payments. A Boston hat maker,
for example, was willing to sell his beaver hats for 27 shillings in
cash or 30 shillings "Country Produce in Hand." One Newport
retailer had his female customers pay him by knitting stockings
and spinning chocolate, while the barber Benjamin Duncan
received a cupboard from a cabinet maker in exchange for "a year's
shaven, a Cutt Wig, a foretop to the Wigg, and 24 feet of Mahogany."
As might be expected, collections could be frustratingly slow, with
retailers sometimes waiting years before receiving payment. Many
debts also "proved bad," prompting Thomas Gates of Charles

Town to inform potential customers that he would not sell anything but for "real money, without which the game is up, etc. I play no more. I am weary."[23]

LABORERS

Undoubtedly weary were the numerous unskilled laborers who comprised the second largest occupational group next to mariners. In Boston laborers constituted between 10 and 20 percent of the town's working population over the course of the eighteenth century. Unlike craftsmen who relied on their skill to earn a living, unskilled workers counted on their muscles to gain themselves work by the day along the docks or at one of the many construction sites. Work for these day laborers was always tenuous and irregular— a day here and a few days there. The type of work was equally as irregular. A laborer might spend a day sawing wood for a carpenter, another unloading a ship, another packing hides at dockside, and so on. More fortunate laborers acquired permanent posts with the city government to work as garbage collectors, grave diggers, public porters, ferrymen, messengers, and livery keepers. Others worked for the city governments constructing and maintaining the almshouse, workhouse, market, granary, wharfs, prison, gun batteries, wall fortifications, bridges, and streets.[24]

Not only was this work exhausting but much of it also was inherently hazardous, resulting in an assortment of injuries and illnesses for the lower-class men who performed it. By middle age, many unskilled workers had their bodies worn out simply from being "worked hard at Labour" their entire lives. Other laborers lost their ability to make a living from various worksite accidents. Some men were crushed by falling timbers and masts at shipyards; others fell to their deaths from water wheels and ships rigging; some suffered broken bones by overturned wagons, wheelbarrows, and runaway casks; many men suffered hernias and injured backs from heavy lifting; some were severely burned and cut; and still others were crippled by frostbite and rheumatism. One unfortunate brewer's servant from Philadelphia missed his footing while loading beer casks on board a ship and fell into the river; the cask fell in after him, hitting him in the head and causing him to drown. The dangerous and labor-intensive nature of work among poor urban laborers took a heavy toll on their health and life expectancies, which were considerably shorter compared with those of their more affluent neighbors.[25]

For doing this backbreaking and hazardous work, urban laborers received wages that failed to meet the annual basic food, fuel, clothing, and housing expenses for the worker himself, a wife, and two young children. To make ends meet, all members of the family had to work. Women washed clothes, cooked, cleaned, sewed, baked, spun wool, and made soap for the well-to-do, among other drudgery. Children helped out by gathering twigs for fuel, tending cattle, sweeping chimneys, and carrying dairy produce from the countryside, among other odd jobs. At times even the additional income from such work was insufficient to keep laborers and their families out of the almshouse. "Life was hard during the best of times," explains one authority on Philadelphia's "lower sort," and "disastrous during the worst." The upshot of this capitalist labor system is that unskilled workers had little hope of lifting themselves out of poverty. Even more tragically, they could not afford to educate their children or arrange vocational training for them. Their children, like themselves, were destined for an unrewarding life as menial laborers serving the affluent. Such were the rewards for the numerous unskilled urban laborers in the "land of opportunity."[26]

SAILORS

As bad as life and labor was for unskilled urban workers, it was worse for the thousands of sailors who comprised a significant portion of workers in the five cities. In Boston, for example, common sailors made up 18 percent of the local workforce. Between 1720 and 1760, some 600 "tars," as seamen were called, worked on Boston-based vessels at any given time, and as many as 200 of these men would be ashore, between sailings, for up to several months at a time looking for work. Thus sailors had their economic feet both on land and at sea. At sea, the life of a sailor was rough, to put it mildly. They ate a monotonous diet of insect-infested hard tack, salt-pork, and oat porridge, with little or no fresh food. Sailors ate out of a common pot and employed table manners consisting of "hacking here and there, not unlike savages," according to one ships' officer. The absence of fresh fruit and vegetables on long voyages contributed to scurvy, a vitamin deficiency disease that causes bleeding at the gums, loose teeth, swelling of the arms and legs, and joint pain. These tars ate their meager meals in the cramped forecastle, a 12-foot by 12-foot, ill-ventilated, dirty, and often rat-infested room that served as the sailors' dining and dressing room, bedchamber, and "parlor." Beds were little more than "planked bunks" with a moldy mattress, a threadbare blanket for cover, and a canvas bag stuffed with dunnage as a pillow.[27]

When not eating or sleeping in the forecastle, tars performed an endless array of tasks to keep the vessel in "ship-shape" condition. Even before leaving port, the sailors had to rig the head-pump and scrub the decks and sides of the ship. Once at sea the labor continued: repairing and replacing ropes, sewing and tarring sails, maintaining yardarms, sharpening knives, plugging leaks, slushing the masts with tar, swabbing the deck, coiling rope, loosening and furling the sails, securing ever-shifting cargo, and, if there was no other work to do, picking oakum. While at work above deck, the tar faced a nearly constant barrage of seawater and sun that, over time, gave his skin a wrinkled and leathery look. A more serious concern was a watery grave. Storms swept men overboard and sometimes sank vessels. Even in calm seas experienced seamen fell from yardarms and splashed into the sea. Such was the case of a young Boston tar. His mates made every effort to save him to but no avail. "The poor soul," wrote a witness, "Swam after the Ship a large time." Realizing his efforts were in vain, he lifted his hat and "twirled it over his head and threw it from him and gave up the ghost." Many other sailors fell victim to cruising pirates preying on commercial vessels. Newport mariner Nicholas Simmons, for example, found himself "under the necessity to leave off his Employment of a Mariner for fear of the Sd. Pirates" even though this action left him unemployed and in "but low circumstances."[28]

If unremitting toil and a good chance at death were not bad enough, sailors were also subject to harsh discipline from short-tempered captains that included anything from being assigned disagreeable tasks to a painful flogging. One Newport captain even abandoned his crew on an isolated island to rid himself of their harassment. If seamen considered the punishment or conditions on board too severe, they might engage in work slow-downs or throw tools overboard; a few even lashed back at their captain, like the sailor who called his captain "a damned old son of a bitch & whore pimp." More often, sailors simply numbed their dismal life on board ship with ample amounts of rum. Ritualistic hazing of greenhorn crew members and an occasional frolic to music added some merriment to their monotonous routine. Still, the difficulties and dangers on board ship took its toll on tars. Only about 3 percent continued in that occupation past the age of 45.[29]

A CONTROLLED ECONOMY

It is important to note that the economic circumstances of wealthy professionals, middle-class artisans, and lower-class laborers were not the result of a free-market economy. This is a postcolonial concept that, even today, is a fiction. Instead, well-to-do American administrators imitated centuries-old European economic policies that included imposing price controls on the manufacturing of certain goods and wage restrictions on certain types of labor that were considered too important to the general good to be left to the whims of the market or the discretion of profit-minded individuals. Conveniently, these restrictions did not apply to the services provided by wealthy professionals such as lawyers, physicians, and merchants, who were allowed to make as much profit as possible. On the other hand, such policies had a detrimental impact on the ability of some urban manufacturers and laborers to rise up the economic ladder. It is therefore no surprise that business folk of all kinds frequently ignored those regulations, which they felt significantly interfered with their business activities.

Despite the inequality of such regulatory legislation, its purpose was to serve the community interests at all levels and to protect everyone from the inherent chaos and destructiveness resulting from a free-market capitalist economy. This also explains why colonial governments passed acts to force millers to compensate landowners for the inundation of their fields caused by damming up water supplies, to preserve oysters by preventing them from being burned for lime, to prevent the complete damming of waterways so that fish could pass freely downstream, or to prohibit urban merchants from hoarding grain to extort higher prices from consumers and fishermen from using seines and nets in some public ponds as a means of conserving fish. "Under no circumstances," explains Sheila Skemp, "were the rich or rapacious openly to aggrandize themselves at the expense of the poor, the innocent or the foolish."[30]

Wage and Price Controls

At times throughout the colonial period, town officials set the wages of craftsmen and laborers, from shoemakers, millers, coopers, blacksmiths, glovers, saddlers, and hatters to porters, servants, cartmen, carpenters, masons, chimney sweeps, and gravediggers.

They also fixed the prices of some necessities like bread, meat, leather, bricks, firewood, and others, much to the chagrin of bakers, butchers, tanners, brickmakers, and wood corders. City govern- ments also regulated the prices tavern- and innkeepers could charge for liquor, food, and lodging. In all instances the regulations limited the potential wages of workers and profits for owners in those occupations and industries.[31]

At times tradesmen and laborers in the five cities found these government-imposed wage and price restrictions so oppressive that they fought back. Bakers, in particular, chafed under the assizes and did not hesitate to go on strike by refusing to bake any bread. This was the case in Boston in 1679; New Amsterdam in 1661; New York City in 1691, 1696, and 1741; and Charles Town in 1786. At times butchers also openly violated set prices on meat, as was the case in New York City in 1665 when local authorities refused their request for a downward revision of their assize. Other examples of organized resistance include the actions of 22 coopers in New York City who in 1680 combined to protest government price fixing on their products by agreeing not to sell casks except at rates they established. Local officials responded by arresting and prosecuting the barrel makers for combining to raise prices. Even licensed New York City cartmen, who removed garbage from the city's streets, went on strike to protest wage restrictions. Unsympathetic town officers quickly dismissed them for not "Doing their Dutyes."[32]

Freedom Rights

It is important to emphasize that these craftsmen and laborers were not protesting the right of government to regulate prices, only that the fixed prices be in accordance with their cost of production to ensure them a living wage. In fact, craftsmen in all five cities demanded government regulation of the trades to protect them against competition from immigrants and itinerant tradesmen. To that end officials passed "freedom rights," or laws prohibiting non- residents from practicing a trade in the city limits. For example, the Newport town meeting in 1734 decreed that no one could open a shop or practice a trade unless he gained permission from the majority of freemen, had been born in Newport, had lived there all his life, or had a freehold in another town where residents could vouch for his character. Officials in New York City, Philadelphia, and Charles Town extended the right to practice a trade to anyone who could pay a moderate "licensing fee" for this "freedom." Because local authorities often failed to enforce such laws, local retailers in Charles Town formed an association to enforce laws against unlicensed hawkers and peddlars.[33]

Inspection of Goods

To further restrict competition, urban artisans petitioned authorities to grant them the power to regulate their trade within the town. However, this did not lead to the formation of English-style guilds because master craftsmen in America were both retailers and employers of labor and any person could set himself up as a master craftsmen. Instead, ordinances passed by cities like those of Philadelphia in 1718 granted craftsmen the privilege of regulating their crafts "to better serve the Publick in their respective capacities." More specifically, this usually meant allowing self-appointed inspectors in each trade to check the quality of work performed by their fellow artisans. As a result, the five cities had a cadre of official viewers, surveyors, measurers, and inspectors to reduce cheating and misrepresentation by retailers and tradesmen. One observer of Newport, for example, noted that "I am sorry that the People in their dealings with one another, and even with strangers, in matters of truck or bargain have as bad a character for chicane and disingenuity as any of our American colonies." Significantly, the inspectors themselves were also regulated, with fines imposed on them if caught neglecting their duty or taking a bribe. Although city craftsmen pushed for inspection laws ostensibly to protect consumers from "bad wares," their main purpose was to eliminate competition from "inferior workmen."[34]

In addition to combating government-imposed wage restrictions and inspection laws, journeymen craftsmen had to deal with greedy master craftsmen who at times combined to limit wages of their workers. Thus ship carpenters looking for work in New York City in 1758 were unable to bargain for wages because shipyard owners had all agreed to fix wages at eight shillings a day. Likewise, Philadelphia tailors combined to form the "Taylor's Company" in 1771 to increase their profits, and at the same time take advantage of local consumers and journeymen tailors, by agreeing not to sell under prices set by the company nor to pay workers more than four shillings a day.

Competition with Slave Labor

Even more damaging to the wages of white urban workers—both skilled and unskilled—was competition from slaves who served their masters in every conceivable occupation, from chimney sweep to silversmith and everything in between. One visitor to Charles Town observed: "I have seen tradesmen go through the city followed by a Negro carrying their tools—barbers who are supported in idleness and ease by their Negroes who do the business, and in fact many of the mechanics bear nothing more of their trade than the name." In 1744 a number of shipwrights in the southern capital petitioned the legislature unsuccessfully for relief on the ground that they were reduced to poverty owing to the competition from blacks in the shipbuilding industry. Similarly, New York City coopers petitioned the assembly in 1737 for protection against the "pernicious custom of breeding slaves to trades whereby the honest and industrious tradesmen are reduced to poverty for want of employ," while workers in Philadelphia asked an unsympathetic assembly for assistance in 1707 against "the want of employment and lowness of wages occasioned by the number of Negroes ... who being hired out to work by day, take away the employment of the petitioners." Slaves in New York City were also taking away employment from white cartmen, and in Charles Town they combined to corner the chimney-sweeping industry. Competition with slave labor contributed to the economic hardship of many white laborers and even some craftsmen who sometimes had to seek public relief to ameliorate their impoverished circumstances.[35]

Welfare for the Rich

While urban officials placed restrictions on the wages of some white middle- and lower-class residents and refused to protect them against competition from cheap slave labor, they used their control of local and provincial governments to give themselves an economic advantage over others by awarding themselves millions of acres of land (largely for speculative purposes) and monopolies on iron production, the fur trade, and the Indian trade. In 1643, members of the court of assistants in Boston granted Governor John Winthrop's son and his business partners 3,000 acres to develop an ironworks. Merchants in all five cities, moreover, benefitted from public funds used to build the wharves and warehouses that allowed them to conduct their business. No such government subsidies went to shoemakers, coopers, or even cartmen, who had to buy their own carts. On the other hand, the South Carolina legislature appropriated public finds to compensate rich slave owners who murdered their bondsmen while disciplining them. These examples, out of many, show that the urban aristocracy who controlled government waged a destructive class war by using their power to further enrich themselves at taxpayers' expense while placing restrictions on the lower classes in their struggle to provide for themselves and their families.

FEMALE LABOR

Because Anglo-Americans considered women to be morally and physically inferior to men, a belief reflected in English and European tradition, women's "natural" role consisted mainly of domestic drudgery and motherhood. This included cooking and sewing; manufacturing various goods needed by the family; growing, gathering, preserving, preparing, and serving food; tending to family illnesses; bearing, rearing, and training young children; and cleaning and laundering. Her domain was the home and surrounding yard, which is where she spent most of her time. An occasional trip to the market broke the monotony of her routine, a routine that included countless callous-causing chores. Nevertheless, the work of urban women was slightly less onerous than that of her country counterparts, who lacked access to many manufactured items such as candles, soap, butter, cloth, beer, and cider that were available to city folk—at least those who could afford to purchase them. Additionally, the city's diversified economy allowed local women to work outside the home in a variety of trades and crafts. Despite these conveniences and advantages, the daily life for most urban women was one of unrelenting toil. To accomplish everything needed to maintain her home, the busy housewife had to be a master of both organization and multitasking.

Upper Class

One exception to this generalization was the circumstances of upper-class women who hired poorer females to do their domestic drudgery so that they could indulge in more pleasant pursuits. If complaints from husbands are any guide, many genteel women devoted considerable time, and their spouses' money, towards home decorating. One frustrated husband opined to the *New York Mercury* in 1758 that "We have twice as many fire-screens as chimneys and three flourished quilts for every bed. Half the rooms are adorned with a kind of futile pictures which imitate tapestry . . . [S]he has boxes filled with knit garters and braided shoes. She has twenty coverns for side-saddles embroidered with silver flowers, and has curtain wrought with gold in various figures, which she resolves some time or other to hang up . . ." Despite such misogynist stereotyping, genteel women were still kept busy teaching and caring for children, training and supervising servants, polishing silver, dusting furniture, cutting material for sewing, tending a garden, preserving food, hosting teas and dinners, and doing the family shopping. At times, women assisted their spouses in the family business. Wives married to merchants, for example, commonly helped their husbands collect and add up bonds, gather financial papers, answer correspondences, pay bills, and negotiate shipments.[36]

Child Care

One of the primary duties of women of all classes was attending to the everyday care of children, a duty that grew increasingly burdensome as the size of the family grew. Families with 10 and 12 children were common, even in the cities, as women generally married in their early twenties and continued to bear children into middle age. Thus a woman fortunate enough to survive multiple childbirths—about 20 percent did not—could expect to have small children pulling on her skirt for more than two decades. Such extensive child care often left mothers physically exhausted and emotionally frazzled. "Sometimes I never sit down a whole day unless to vittles," lamented one mother, while another wrote, "I snatch a moment from a crying infant, and the noise of two or three ungoverned children, which is as distracting to the brain as a confused din of arms to a timid soldier." One housewife at her wits' end wrote her absentee husband that "I am tired of living a widow and being at the same time a nurse." She added that if she could "still a squalling infant and settle a matter of great contention among a company of unruly boys, I feel myself as happy and as great as an Empress." In hearing of a mother expecting her 15th child, one woman replied: "I should think that she would commit suicide." Of course, few women took this option and instead treasured the joys and dealt with the frustration inherent in motherhood. The attitude of many colonial mothers is perhaps best reflected in the following tribute made by a New England husband to his deceased wife: "Indeed she would sometimes say to me that bearing, tending and burying children was hard work, and that she had done a great deal of it for one of her age, (she had six children, whereof she buried four, and died in the 24th year of her age) yet she would say it was the work she was made for, and what God in his Providence had called her, and she could freely do it all for Him."[37]

Domestic Drudgery

Early Americans also believed that God had called women to do all the cooking, cleaning, sewing, and laundry necessary to maintain a well-kept home. Having none of today's labor-saving household devices or access to processed food, these domestic chores were labor intensive, time consuming, and sometimes disgusting. To feed her hungry family, the housewife had first to get the food, which meant picking some of it from her own backyard garden and obtaining the rest from the local market. Upon returning she toted water from a well and proceeded to prepare the ingredients. If fowl was on the menu, she often had to pluck the feathers and butcher the bird; if fish, she scaled and gutted the aquatic creature before baking, frying, or boiling it. The whole process left women feeling anything but lady-like. After preparing a meal for her family and several guests, one New England woman lamented: "O' I am dirty and tired almost to death cooking for so many people." When not cooking food, the urban housewife devoted considerable time preserving it.[38]

While food was simmering in pot, housewives might take a load off their feet and sit down to spin wool or mend clothing. When not mending clothing, housewives were laundering and ironing them. The first chore required her to first make her own soap by boiling together lye, grease, and ashes and then letting the mixture cool until it formed into a jelly-like substance. The housewife then pretreated the clothes by scrubbing them with soap on a washboard and rinsing them. To help remove tough stains, she might use human urine. Next, the haggard housewife placed the pretreated clothing in a tub filled with boiling water and soap. She then agitated the clothing by manually stirring the heavy load with a long, wooden "washing stick." This toilsome task was made even more unpleasant by having to stand near a fire that sometimes ignited skirts and a large pot of boiling water that occasionally splashed

Kitchen Scene. The never-ending multitude of tasks demanded of colonial women forced them to be masters of multi-tasking. This quaint nineteenth-century illustration shows a colonial housewife working at her loom and cooking the family dinner while tending to a toddler. (A. S. Barnes, *A Brief History of the United States* [New York: American Book Co., 1885])

scalding water on the laundress. A cold rinse in a bucket, a wrist-aching wringing, and the clothes were hung to dry. Of course, this process left clothes wrinkled, which required housewives to use heavy irons heated on a trivet over coals to press out the wrinkles. An experienced woman knew the appropriate heat required for each type of fiber and could accurately gauge the heat of the iron by either holding it near her face or spitting on it. No matter how experienced a woman was at ironing, she still collected many small burn marks on her hands and arms over the years that served as conspicuous badges of womanhood.[39]

At times these numerous tasks became overwhelming. To keep from drowning in a sea of responsibilities, women relied on other women—friends, neighbors, and relatives—to assist each other in their daily tasks. They borrowed tools and kitchen items from one another, traded their products and skills, watched each other's children, helped in the delivery of a child, and swapped food, among many other things. In short, urban women were anything but rugged individualists. Instead, they banded together in a sort of sisterhood to help each other in a variety of common causes.[40]

Employment

In addition to domestic drudgery, many women—especially those single, widowed, and poor—had to work outside the home. Fortunately for them, the urban economy gave them greater opportunities for producing income than the countryside. This was perhaps little consolation because "working for wages," according to historian Mary Ferrari, "was a path that eighteenth-century women followed more out of necessity than desire." This may be because most toiled in "women's work" where low wages forced them into a never-ending struggle for survival. This was true even for women skilled in a trade. Some Charles Town women who did millinery work and staymaking earned so little that they were forced into prostitution to supplement their income. Likewise, tailoresses in Philadelphia sometimes had to sell their flesh to wealthy men to survive. One merchant even bragged about his exploitive dalliances with "a young Quakeress, tailoress by trade, with whom I amuse myself at very little expense." More self-respecting lower-class women eked out a scant existence by going door to door in remote neighborhoods selling cast-off and second-quality goods (eggs, cheese, butter, produce, fish, and cloth) obtained from market vendors. An even greater number worked as servants in the homes of the affluent cleaning, washing, sewing, and ironing. Other women stayed home doing either piecework or spinning and weaving for local entrepreneurs. Widows with spare bedrooms often took in boarders to augment their income. Despite their best efforts, single women at times had to face the indignity of seeking public relief, either in the form of fuel and food supplements or meager wages obtained through work in the local workhouse.[41]

Business Work

More fortunate were married women who contributed to the family economy by helping their husbands in their trade. Women in the cities could be found working as blacksmiths, silversmiths, gunsmiths, shoemakers, shipwrights, tanners, butchers, tailors, and barbers, among many other occupations. The wife of a cobbler, for example, might stitch the uppers of a shoe, a merchant's wife might keep shop, an innkeeper's wife might cook and serve hungry and thirsty patrons, and a printer's wife might set type. Colonial society did not frown upon women who stepped outside of their domestic sphere as long as it assisted in the family economy. Nor did colonists look askance at those women who operated their own businesses, most of which they inherited from a deceased husband. Of these independent businesswomen, nearly two-thirds were shopkeepers catering mostly to other women, tempting them with such alluring objects as "fashionable fans," "fancy hair pins," "laced satin cloaks and bonnets," "tortoise shell combs," "French pearl necklaces," "scented wash balls," "gold and silver laced handkerchiefs," and "neat powder boxes." More unusual was Hannah Breintnall of Philadelphia, who operated an optician's shop where she sold spectacles "of the finest Crystal ... set in Temple, Steel, Leather or other Frames."[42]

The domestic nature of innkeeping steered about one-fourth of urban businesswomen toward operating inns, often out of their homes. Typical was Anne Imer of Charles Town, who advertised "room for a few lodgers, who may be accompanied with breakfast."[43] Other women used their domestic skills making wine, candles, soap, and pastries for sale from their home. The following advertisement of confections and sweet meats offered by Margaret Nelson of Charles Town is revealing:

Rich plum cake at 10s per pound, biscuit and seed ditto, syllybubs and jelleys, 20s per dozen, white custards in glasses at 15 s per dozen, lemon and orange creame blomage, 20s per plate, rice cups at 12 s. 6d per plate, lemon, orange, citron and almond pudding, 20 s. a piece, orange pye, 30s, snow cheese, 30s, apple tarts, curd, and apple cheese cakes, 24 s. per dozen, almond and lemon ditto, 30s. Per dozen, minced pies, 3s 9d a piece, preserved oranges, and orange and apple marmalades, collard and potted beef, and many other articles too tedious to enumerate.[44]

A far less tasty form of employment for urban women was midwifery. Other women entered the health care profession, such as it was, by selling home-made remedies. "Mrs Hughes" of Charles Town offered to cure "Ringworms, Scald Head, Sore Eyes, the Piles, Worms in Children, and several other Disorders," promising *"No Cure, No Pay."* Some women struggled to make ends meet by taking care of the sick and disabled, preparing the dead for burial, playing the organ in churches, painting portraits, running boarding schools for young ladies, and even operating printing presses.[45]

CHILDREN

Economic circumstances also required many colonial children to perform numerous mindless and monotonous chores in support of the family economy. It also helped to keep them from the "sin of idleness," that "handmaiden of mischief" exemplified in the following popular children's poem: "In works of labour, or of skill, I would be busy too; For Satan finds some Mischief still for idle hands to do."[46] To keep children's hands busy, urban parents put children to work spinning yarn, milking the family cow, collecting chicken eggs, churning butter, weeding the garden, and assisting their mother in her many tasks. As they grew older, though, they took on more sexually segregated chores. Boys might chop firewood, tote heavy buckets of water, hunt vermin, and run errands for their parents. This policy continued so that by about the age of 10 or 12 boys spent more time with their fathers in their shops while girls stayed at home learning housewifery skills from their mothers. The daily work experience for girls is perhaps best summarized in the following 1775 diary entry from young Abigail Foote:

Fix'd gown for Prude—Mend Mother's Riding-hood—Spun short thread—Fix'd two gowns for Welsh's girls—Carded tow—Spun linen—Worked on Cheesebasket—Hatchel'd flax with Hannah—Read a Sermon of Dodridge's—Spooled a piece—Milked the cows—Spun linen, did 50 knots—Made a Broom of Guinea wheat straw—Spun thread to whiten—Set a Red due—Had two Scholars form Mrs. Taylor's—I carded two pounds of whole wool and felt Nationly—Spun harness twine—Scoured pewter.[47]

From this long list of chores one can safely surmise that young Abigail had little time for mischief—or fun. Children belonging to poor parents who hired them out to other families and businessmen also had little fun spinning yarn, knitting, cooking, washing, cutting wood, unloading vessels, and carting goods.[48]

INDENTURED SERVITUDE

Indentured servants, immigrants from Europe (mostly Ireland, Scotland, Germany, and Holland) who sold themselves into servitude for four to seven years in exchange for passage to North America, comprised about 10 percent of the urban work force, at least in the mid-1700s. Miserable and hopeless circumstances in their home country coupled with seductive advertisements describing America as the "Land of Promise" enticed many desperate Europeans to bind themselves to a ship's captain and risk a long and dangerous ocean voyage to the New World. However, not all came willingly. To quickly fill a hold, many unscrupulous captains sent their crews out to scour the streets of London, Bristol, and Belfast to kidnap drunkards asleep in the gutter or children wandering the streets, enticing the latter with sweets. An additional 10 percent of these transatlantic servants were British felons who were given a choice: either languish in jail or serve a 7-to-14-year indenture in America. Between 1718 and 1775, about 30,000 took option number two. For most, this turned out to be the wrong decision.[49]

Passage Over

Many indentured servants never even made it to North America, dying under miserable circumstances during the six-to-eight-week transatlantic journey. Contributing to their demise were profit-minded ship captains who crammed onto their vessels as many passengers as possible with a callous disregard for life. To further increase profits, captains also cut corners on provisions for the passengers, often consisting of insect-infested sea biscuits, spoiled beef, sour butter, and rancid water "often very black, thick with dirt, and full of worms," according to one passenger. With such meager portions of unpalatable food and overcrowded, unsanitary conditions, disease flourished as smallpox, yellow fever, typhus, dysentery, constipation, scurvy, and mouth-rot swept through servant ships without discrimination. Lice were also a problem. At times the little vermin were so thick on the bodies of sick passengers that they had to be scraped off. "[N]o other care was taken of those poor Protestant Christians from Ireland," wrote one Philadelphia merchant in 1768, "but to deliver as many as possible alive on shore upon the cheapest terms, no matter how they fared upon the voyage nor in what condition they were landed." On some particularly long voyages only 50 percent landed at their destination, with the remaining ending their journey at the bottom of the sea, where they became food for hungry fish. Children were especially vulnerable; those under the age of seven rarely survived the difficult trip. Some unattended children simply tumbled off the ships and into the sea, never to be seen again.[50]

Work

The exploitation of indentured servants continued after their purchase. The sole purpose of servants was to work hard for their masters, who sought to gain added leisure and money from their labor. For six days a week servants had nothing to look forward to but a 10- to 12-hour work day. Their day began before dawn with heating the kitchen stove so that the family would not have the discomfort of dressing in a cold house or waiting for a hot beverage. After a cold breakfast of leftovers, servants performed whatever chores their masters demanded of them—usually the most tedious and laborious tasks the master wanted to avoid himself. Still, many worked side-by-side with their masters, especially the 65 to 85 percent of servants who arrived during the eighteenth century possessing a skill. Skilled or unskilled, a servant work day did not end with sundown, as owners expected them to be on call 24 hours a day. Household servants, in particular, often slept at the foot of their owners' bed and were called in the middle of the night to fetch a glass of water, to tend the sick, or even to investigate a scary noise or barking dog.[51]

Living Conditions

While exacting as much work as possible form their servants, masters also sought to reduce expenses brought on by their charges by providing them with as little food, clothing, and shelter as possible. Some servants slept in their masters' homes, either in the same room or in unventilated attics, cellars, or basements, while others reposed in backyard huts near the livestock. For clothing, servants received from their masters old, ill-fitting hand-me-downs. Medical care, as with all family members, was for emergencies only. Even less available to the servant was an education, which masters were not required to provide. Thus most servants left the world as unlettered as they entered it. In the end, servants had little control over their daily lives. Masters made all the important decisions for them: what clothes they were to wear; when they were to awaken; what chores they were to perform; when, what, and how much they were to eat; when they would go to a doctor in case of illness; when they were to quit work for the day; and where they were to sleep.

Leisure

Masters had far less success in regulating their servants' leisure time. As much as they might try, masters could not account for every waking or sleeping moment of their man or woman. Many a Sunday in the cities was disturbed by "servants, apprentice boys and numbers of Negroes" causing "great disorders." Even on work days servants managed to steal an hour or two from their masters while on an errand or if their master left the home or shop. Many servants absconded at night to let loose in taverns, brothels, a friend's house, or in the city streets, where they sometimes joined with sailors and slaves to rampage through neighborhoods armed with clubs and staves "to the great Terror and disturbance of Divers subjects." By such means and others, servants were able to craft a personal life for themselves that made their servile circumstances more tolerable.[52]

Punishment and Abuse

Still, the exploitive nature of servitude inevitably led to conflicts between master and servant. Working and living together in close quarters for up to seven years only increased the underlying tension that sometimes erupted into violence. The incorrigible behavior of some servants certainly drove some masters to abuse and even sell their charges. One master sought to sell the remaining time on his servant's indenture because "the said Boy for his Neglect of his Business, unruliness of his Conduct, running away & other breeches of his Indentures has to the great loss of your petitioner layen out at nights, [and] broke into other people's cellars at unseasonable hours." Meanwhile, female servants could greatly upset their mistresses by getting pregnant. Mary Drinker, wife of a wealthy Philadelphia merchant, was so angry with her maid Sally for having a child that she required her to leave the baby behind with a hired nurse and prohibited Sally from seeing her little girl. When the child died a few months later, Drinker callously surmised in her diary that all had probably "worked out for the best." On top of all this, Sally had to serve additional time for the Drinkers. However, no amount of disobedience explains or justifies why one Philadelphia master forced his young servant to "stand in market in the Cold and Wet Days of Winter without sufficient Cloaths to keep him warm or Food to satisfy his hunger" and "repeatedly beat him without cause." One certainly wonders what a New York City servant girl did to be put in chains for several weeks "upon bread and water only" and "Cruelly beat[en]." Such physical punishment was often accompanied by verbal abuse in which masters called their charges "stupid," "wicked," "useless," "lazy," "unmannerly," "liar," "whore," a "stout fat woman," a "chunky fat lump," and worse.[53]

Servant Protests

Given that the well-to-do made all the rules of society and government, it is no surprise that indentured servants had limited means by which to protect themselves against such abuse. Many abused servants avoided the courts because failing to convince the judge of his or her case resulted in either a public whipping or extra time added to his or her indenture. In the end, only about 50 percent

GLOUCESTER COUNTY *Jan. 20th,* 1772.

SIXTEEN DOLLARS REWARD.

RUN AWAY from the Subscriber, on the 16th of this instant, an indented servant man, named PETER WOODFORD, about five feet seven or eight inches high, appears to be about 21 or 22 years of age, of a darkish complexion, strait hair and thin visage : He is very much addicted to liquor, a great boaster, very quarrelsome, and chews tobacco to a great excess. Had on when he went away, an old felt hat, black silk neckcloth, a brown waistcoat, almost new, old blue woollen trowsers, an old oznabrig shirt, old stockings, with half boots. It is very likely he may change his dress and name, and call himself *Benjamin Davis*; also he may probably produce a pass. Whoever takes up said servant, and brings him home, or secures him in any of his Majesty's goals, so that his master may have him again, shall receive the above reward paid by
URIAH PAUL.

Advertisement for a Runaway Servant. Colonial newspapers are filled with advertisements for runaway servants like the one above from the February 10, 1772, issue of the *Pennsylvania Packet*. In helping to secure the capture and return of their servants, masters often included in their ads detailed physical and behavioral traits of their human property, along with a description of the clothing they were wearing at the time of their escape.

of servants who brought complaints before local courts received some semblance of justice. Other mistreated servants mistakenly believed they had better odds running away, but less than 10 percent of runaways made a permanent getaway as city officials pressed men, horses, and boats at public expense to "pursue such Persons both by Sea and Land and bring them back by force of arms." Braver servants confronted their abusive masters face to face by disobeying orders, talking back with a "saucy tongue," and occasionally murdering them with pitchforks, knives, iron bars, and even their fists. Other servants were more surreptitious in their protests, like the mischievous maid who put a toad into the family's milk kettle after being scolded. More frequently, servants vented their anger against their master's property by breaking tools, dishes, kitchen utensils, wash tubs, and even setting homes on fire. Sadly, some servants saw suicide as the best way out of their intolerable situation. One Boston maid killed herself by cutting open her stomach, another servant cut his throat, and still others hanged themselves and jumped into wells where they drowned.[54]

Postservitude

Obviously, many indentured servants who came to America for a better life did not realize their dream. The vast majority suffered a shortened life filled with mindless drudgery, backbreaking labor, a constant struggle to survive, and spirit-crushing hopelessness. This was particularly true for those servants settling in the five major cities during the eighteenth century. Even in Philadelphia, the most prosperous colonial city on the continent next to Charles Town, less than one-fourth of servants who arrived there in the 1740s appeared on the tax rolls 20 years after gaining their freedom, and 80 percent of those well-off enough to pay taxes owned less than £20 worth of property. At least 40 percent of ex-servants required public assistance of some sort during their lifetime—compared with 6 percent for the general urban population. Their already miserable circumstances only worsened by the late colonial period when over 80 percent of ex-servants in Philadelphia were forced at some time in their lives to depend on the public dole. These statistics show that early America, at least in the major cities, offered no real upward mobility for those starting at the bottom of society. For them, serving an indenture "provided a passage to the New World," explains historian Sharon Salinger, "and a ticket into the Poor House." Because most eighteenth century servants were educated, skilled, and ambitious, their inability to succeed in America rests less on any alleged character flaws and more on an exploitive economic system designed and controlled by the upper class primarily to benefit themselves at the expense of the most desperate and vulnerable.[55]

NATIVE AMERICANS

Another dependent and exploited class of people in the five cities was Native Americans, a small and vulnerable group who were at the mercy of the white community. Illustrative is the circumstances of Native Americans in Newport, who according to one visitor in the 1720s were "nearly all servants or laborers for the English, who have contributed more to destroy their bodies by the use of strong liquors than by any means to improve their minds or save their souls." In addition to encouraging alcohol dependency among the local Indians, white Newporters sought to trap them into economic dependency by selling goods (often alcohol) to the natives at extravagant rates, thereby forcing them into debt, and then binding them as servants until such time as the debt was paid to the satisfaction of the creditor. Not surprisingly, creditors frequently extended the length of time indefinitely, making a virtual slave of the entrapped Indian. Further curtailing the freedom of local Indians were laws prohibiting them from being out after nine o'clock at night without a special certificate or from being served alcohol. A belief among whites that Indians were natural-born thieves also encouraged the local government to regulate their ability to buy or sell goods lest they steal from their masters and sell the merchandise on the black market. Violation of any of these laws could result in a public whipping or a branding on the cheek or forehead. With little legal recourse to rectify their exploitive circumstances, Indians in Newport responded by running away, and on a few occasions violently lashing out against their white oppressors. One Indian servant, for example, murdered his master's two young sons by hitting one in the head with a boat paddle and drowning the other.[56]

SLAVES

The most vulnerable and exploited of all city workers were slaves, who worked for their masters in nearly every phase and category of the city's economy, from unskilled domestics and laborers to skilled carpenters and silversmiths. Nearly half of all urban slaves were women, who labored mainly in the homes of the gentry as cooks, laundresses, maids, nurses, and general household workers helping with other domestic crafts such as sewing, spinning, knitting, and weaving. Work for the black domestic was much like that for white indentured servants. They performed all the arduous, distasteful, and tedious tasks the mistress wanted to avoid. As one Boston woman wrote to another in recommending a prospective black serving maid, "she doth all the worst work in her mothers howes and is very servisable." Black house maids also had no regular hours, were at the beck and call of the master and mistress day and night, and were frequent targets of verbal, physical, and sexual abuse. The urban gentry also exploited male slaves to serve them as attendants, butlers, valets, and coachmen. In fact, owning a black coachmen or valet was a status symbol for the urban gentry, who were commonly seen riding about town and country in lordly fashion with a black attendant to help them from their carriages, to open and close gates for them, or to remove impediments from their pathway.[57]

Male slaves were also exploited in nearly every other form of economic enterprise, from skilled artisan to unskilled laborer. But no matter what a male slave did, "it is safe to assume," writes historian Lawrence Towner, "that the dirty repetitious, simple, boring, tedious, and distasteful tasks were regularly assigned to him." As a result, masters had their slaves perform the tedious and sometimes backbreaking and disgusting tasks of hauling tools, loading and unloading ships, carrying and hauling cargo, shoveling dung, draining swamps, building wharves, gutting fish, and slaughtering livestock, among countless other chores. During slow times masters hired out their slaves to artisans, city governments, or anybody looking for cheap, temporary labor. Sometimes this was a contractual arrangement, but masters with no work for their slaves sometimes simply sent them out to hunt for their own employment and lodging with directions to return a set amount of money per day, week, or month. Any money the slave earned above the requested amount was his to keep. With such incentives, urban slaves became very good at driving a hard bargain for their wages. In 1746 the Charles Town grand jury complained of local porters "who refuse to work for a reasonable hire, when they are frequently found Idle, & often insist on as much for an hour or two as pays their masters for a whole day." This "twilight zone" between slavery and freedom also weakened deference among slaves and empowered them with a stronger sense of self-respect and equality. This is perhaps best illustrated among female marketeers in Charles Town, whom whites characterized as "loose," "idle," "disorderly," "insolent," "abusive," "notorious," and "impudent." Even the clerk of the market complained in 1741 that the "insolent abusive Manner" of the slave marketeers rendered him "afraid to say or do Anything in the market" and left him to be made "A Game of." As a result, local whites believed, and rightly so, that black female marketeers were both "free from the government" and "contemptuous" of it.[58]

CONCLUSION

The five port cities served as the center of their region's economy, receiving and distributing goods from and throughout the American interior, the Caribbean, West Africa, and much of Western Europe. This widespread commercial activity encouraged the development of a diversified economy that supported scores of highly specialized skilled craftsmen and many unskilled laborers. As trade expanded in the cities over the course of the colonial period, so did economic growth and wealth. Those residents already at the top of the economic ladder benefitted most from this economic expansion and saw their control and ownership of the city's wealth and property significantly increase. In the 80 years prior to the Revolution, the top 5 percent of residents in Boston, Philadelphia, and New York City saw their share of the taxable wealth increase from approximately one-third to one-half of all wealth in these cities. Meanwhile, the bottom half of urban folk were left with a mere 3 to 5 percent of taxable wealth. Of course, such economic opportunities never existed for the many black slaves who performed the most dangerous and difficult jobs in the cities. And relatively few white indentured servants realized their dream of a better life in America upon completing their indentures. Urban laborers, too, struggled to survive by scrounging daily for a poorly paid temporary job here and there. Even some journeyman craftsmen lived a marginal existence and sometimes had to seek public relief to keep from either starving or freezing. In the end, only a relatively small percentage of successful merchants, professionals, and master craftsmen benefitted from the tremendous economic growth in the colonial cities during the eighteenth century.[59]

To a large degree this gross maldistribution of wealth and opportunity was by design. Much of the wealth gained by the well-to-do was made by exploiting the most exploitable: slaves, indentured servants, apprentices, and journeyman craftsmen. These economic elites also created a number of internal and external barriers, often with the force of law, that limited the ability of lower-class folk to climb up the economic ladder. Meanwhile, those in government used their political offices to grant themselves vast tracts of land and trade monopolies and to pilfer public resources and treasuries to their advantage. By doing so, they made the eighteenth-century colonial city the "land of opportunity" for the established elites and the "land of exploitation" for many of the rest. Or, in the words of Charles Dickens, it was "a tale of two cities."

NOTES

1. Claudia D. Johnson, *Daily Life in Colonial New England* (Westport, CT: Greenwood Press, 2002), 55–56.

2. Seth Rockman, "Work in the Cities of Colonial British North America," *Journal of Urban History* 33 (2007): 1024; Seth Rockman, "The Unfree Origins of American Capitalism," in *The Economy of Early America: Historical Perspectives and New Directions*, ed. Cathy Matson (Philadelphia: University of Pennsylvania Press, 2006), 335–62; Marcus Rediker, " 'Good Hands, Stout Heart, and Fast Feet': The History and Culture of Working People in Early America," *Labour/Le Travailleur* 10 (1982): 129.

3. Richard Dunn, quoted in Barry Levy, "Girls and Boys: Poor Children and the Labor Market in Colonial Massachusetts," *Pennsylvania History* 64 (1997): 287.

4. Jonathan R. Hughes, *Social Control in the Colonial Economy* (Charlottesville: University Press of Virginia, 1976), 89–162; Emma Hart, *Building Charleston: Town and Society in the Eighteenth-Century British Atlantic World* (Charlottesville: University Press of Virginia, 2010), 65–87.

5. Carole Shammas, "How Self-Sufficient Was Early America," *Journal of Interdisciplinary History* 13 (1982): 247–72; John Mack Farragher in Stephanie Coontz, *The Way We Never Were* (New York: Harper Collins, 1992), 75 (quote).

6. Brian Miller and Mike Lapham, *The Self-Made Myth and the Truth about How Government Helps Individuals and Businesses Succeed* (San Francisco, CA: Berrett-Koehler, 2012), 2–24, 40–53. For an historical analysis of the self-made man myth, see Irvin Whyllie, *The Self-Made Man in America: The Myth of Rags to Riches* (New Brunswick, NJ: Rutgers University Press, 1954).

7. Jacob M. Price, "Economic Function and the Growth of American Port Towns in the Eighteenth Century," *Perspectives in American History* 8 (1974): 130–37; Billy G. Smith, *The "Lower Sort:" Philadelphia's Laboring People, 1750–1800* (Ithaca, NY: Cornell University Press, 1990), 64–66.

8. Leila Sellers, *Charleston Business on the Eve of the Revolution* (Chapel Hill: University of North Carolina Press, 1934), 80–81; Price, "Economic Function . . . of American Port Towns," 138–39.

9. Thomas Purvis, *Colonial America to 1763* (New York: Facts on File, 1999), 112–13; Eric G. Nellis, "The Working Poor of Pre-Revolutionary Boston," *Historical Journal of Massachusetts* 17 (1989): 139; Thomas Archdeacon, *New York City, 1664–1710: Conquest and Change* (Ithaca, NY: Cornell University Press, 1976), 64–65; Stuart Stumpf, "The Merchants of Colonial Charleston, 1680–1756," Ph.D. dissertation, Michigan State University, 1971), 161–69; Edwin J. Perkins, *The Economy of Colonial America*, 2nd ed. (New York: Columbia University Press, 1988), 116–38; Sellers, *Charleston Business*, 51–58, 85–86, 178–81; Ian Quimby, *Apprenticeship in Colonial Philadelphia* (New York: Garland Press, 1985), 120–21; Smith, *Lower Sort*, 111; Stuart Stumpf, "Implications of King George's War for the Charleston Mercantile Community," *South Carolina Historical Magazine* 77 (1976): 164–67; Jean P. Jordan, "Women Merchants in Colonial New York," *New York History* 58 (1977): 427.

10. Sheila Skemp, "A Social and Cultural History of Newport, Rhode Island, 1720–1765," Ph.D. dissertation, University of Iowa, 1974, 274–80.

11. Purvis, *Colonial America to 1763*, 113.

12. Perkins, *Economy of Colonial America*, 54–55; Johnson, *Daily Life in Colonial New England*, 60; Quimby, *Apprenticeship in Colonial Philadelphia*, 122; Stephanie G. Wolf, *As Various as Their Land: The Everyday Lives of Eighteenth-Century Americans* (New York: Harper Perennial, 1993), 199–203.

13. Johnson, *Daily Life in Colonial New England*, 60; Wolf, *As Various as Their Land*, 199.

14. Purvis, *Colonial America to 1763*, 113; Carl Bridenbaugh, *The Colonial Craftsman* (Chicago: University of Chicago Press, 1950), 66, 132; Perkins, *Economy of Colonial America*, 66, 115; Samuel McKee, *Labor in Colonial New York, 1664–1776* (New York: Columbia University Press, 1935), 74–75; Sharon B. Sundue, "Industrious in Their Stations: Young People at Work in Boston, Philadelphia and Charleston, 1735–1785," Ph.D. dissertation, Harvard University, 2001), 71–72; James M. Volo and Dorothy D. Volo, *Family Life in 17th-and 18th-Century America* (Westport, CT: Greenwood Press, 2006), 266.

15. Quimby, *Apprenticeship in Colonial Philadelphia*, 118–19.

16. Johnson, *Daily Life in Colonial New England*, 68–69 (quote); Quimby, *Apprenticeship in Colonial Philadelphia*, 51–52 (quotes).

17. Bridenbaugh, *Colonial Craftsman*, 137 (quote); J. William Frost, *The Quaker Family in Colonial America: A Portrait of the Society of Friends* (New York: St. Martin's Press, 1973), 142 (quote); Lawrence W. Towner, *A Good Master Well Served: Masters and Servants in Colonial Massachusetts, 1720–1750* (New York: Garland Press, 1998), 164–65, 169 (quote); Adriana Van Zwieten, "Preparing Children for Adulthood in New Netherland,"

in *Children Bound to Labor: The Pauper Apprentice System in Early America*, ed. Ruth W. Herndon and John E. Murray (Ithaca, NY: Cornell University Press, 2009), 99 (quote); McKee, *Labor in Colonial New York*, 75, 77–78 (quote); Quimby, *Apprenticeship in Colonial Philadelphia*, 77 (quote); Geraldine Youcha, *Minding the Children* (New York: Scribner, 1995), 36 (quotes).

18. Quimby, *Apprenticeship in Colonial Philadelphia*, 80.

19. Edith Abbott, "A Study of the Early History of Child Labor in America," *American Journal of Sociology* 14 (1908): 18–19; Levy, "Girls and Boys," 291–300; John E. Murray and Ruth W. Herndon, "Markets for Children in Early America: A Political Economy of Pauper Apprenticeship," *Journal of Economic History* 62 (2002): 375; Thurston in LeRoy Ashby, *Endangered Children: Dependency, Neglect, and Abuse in America* (New York: Twayne, 1997), 10–11.

20. Levy, "Girls and Boys," 292; Perkins, *Economy of Colonial America*, 97; Murray and Herndon, "Markets for Children," 357; Youcha, *Minding the Children*, 20 (quote).

21. Volo and Volo, *Family Life*, 128; Rediker, "Good Hands, Stout Heart, and Fast Feet," 131; Perkins, *Economy of Colonial America*, 51, 116, 121; Wolf, *As Various as Their Land*, 183.

22. Emma Hart, *Building Charleston*, 98–129; Wolf, *As Various as Their Land*, 184; Perkins, *Economy of Colonial America*, 116, 121–22.

23. Bridenbaugh, *Colonial Craftsman*, 153–54 (quote), 172; Ellen Hartigan-O'Connor, "The Measure of the Market: Women's Economic Lives in Charleston, SC and Newport RI, 1750–1820," Ph.D. dissertation, University of Michigan, 2003, 108; Skemp, "A Social and Cultural History of Newport," 363 (quote).

24. Nellis, "Working Poor," 148–50, 153; Wolf, *As Various as Their Land*, 182; Smith, *Lower Sort*, 81.

25. Smith, *Lower Sort*, 55. For a more exhaustive view of accidents in early America, at least in New Jersey, see Keith Krawczynski, "A Note on Accidental Death in Colonial New Jersey, 1730–1770," *New Jersey History* 110 (1992): 63–70.

26. Smith, *Lower Sort*, 108–11, 112 (quote); Nellis, "Working Poor," 147–48.

27. Purvis, *Colonial America to 1763*, 113; Nellis, "Working Poor," 141; Paul A. Gilje, *Liberty on the Waterfront: American Maritime Culture in the Age of Revolution* (Philadelphia: University of Pennsylvania Press, 2004), 76–77, 78 (quote).

28. Gilje, *Liberty on the Waterfront*, 67–68, 78–79 (quote); Billy Smith, "The Vicissitudes of Fortune: The Careers of Laboring Men in Philadelphia, 1750–1800," in *Work and Labor in Early America*, ed. Stephen Innes (Chapel Hill: University of North Carolina Press, 1988), 237–38; Skemp, "A Social and Cultural History of Newport," 123 (quote).

29. Gilje, *Liberty on the Waterfront*, 88 (quote), 27, 93–94; Smith, *Lower Sort*, 55; Richard B. Morris, *Government and Labor in Early America* (New York: Harper & Row, 1946), 257–65; Skemp, "A Social and Cultural History of Newport," 359.

30. Simon Middleton, " 'How It Came that the Bakers Bake No Bread': A Struggle for Trade Privileges in Seventeenth-Century New Amsterdam," *William and Mary Quarterly* 58 (2001): 347; Skemp, "A Social and Cultural History of Newport," 193–94 (quote).

31. Morris, *Government and Labor*, 20–21, 56–58; John R. Commons and David J. Saposs, *History of Labour in the United States* (New York: Macmillan Co., 1918), 50–52; Bridenbaugh, *Colonial Craftsman*, 145–46.

32. Morris, *Government and Labor*, 158–61; Commons and Saposs, *History of Labour*, 52–56.

33. Ernest S. Griffith, *History of American City Government: The Colonial Period* (New York: Oxford University Press, 1938), 133–35; Bridenbaugh, *Colonial Craftsman*, 144.

34. Morris, *Government and Labor*, 46–49, 139–41, 142 (quote); Bridenbaugh, *Colonial Craftsman*, 146; Commons and Saposs, *History of Labour*, 46–49; Skemp, "A Social and Cultural History of Newport," 131.

35. Walsh, "Charleston Mechanics," 136 (quote); Morris, *Government and Labor*, 183–85; Edgar McManus, *Black Bondage in the North* (Syracuse, NY: Syracuse University Press, 1973), 45 (quotes); Smith, *Lower Sort*, 116–19; Hartigan-O'Connor, "The Measure of the Market," 100; Thelma W. Foote, *Black and White Manhattan: The History of Racial Formation in Colonial New York City* (New York: Oxford University Press, 2004), 77; Sharon Salinger, "Artisans, Journeymen, and the Transformation of Labor in Late Eighteenth-Century Philadelphia," *William and Mary Quarterly* 40 (1983): 63.

36. Jeanne Boydston, *Home and Work: Housework, Wages, and the Ideology of Labor in the Early Republic* (New York: Oxford University Press, 1990), 10 (quote), 78–79; Karin Wulf, *Not All Wives: Women of Colonial Philadelphia* (Ithaca, NY: Cornell University Press, 2000), 138; Sarah Fatherly, *Gentlewomen and Learned Ladies: Women and Elite Formation in Eighteenth-Century Philadelphia* (Bethlehem, PA: Lehigh University Press, 2008), 55–58.

37. Boydston, *Home and Work*, 78 (quote); John Walzer, "A Period of Ambivalence: Eighteenth-Century American Childhood," in *The History of Childhood*, ed. Lloyd deMause (New York: Psychohistory Press, 1974), 367 (quote); Volo and Volo, *Family Life*, 200 (quote).

38. Jane C. Nylander, *Our Own Snug Fireside: Images of the New England Home, 1760–1860* (New York: Alfred A. Knopf, 1993), 147.

39. Nylander, *Our Own Snug Fireside*, 130–35, 140–41; Laurel T. Ulrich, *Good Wives: Image and Reality in the Lives of Women in Northern New England, 1650–1750* (New York: Alfred A. Knopf, 1982), 28; Volo and Volo, *Family Life*, 215.

40. Wulf, *Not All Wives*, 96–99; Nellis, "Working Poor," 156–57; Perkins, *Economy of Colonial America*, 155.

41. Mary Ferrari, " 'Obliged to Earn Subsistence for Themselves': Women Artisans in Charleston, South Carolina, 1763–1808," *South Carolina Historical Magazine* 106 (2005): 239 (quote), 240; Wolf, *As Various as Their Land*, 186 (quote); Boydston, *Home and Work*, 14, 84; Julia C. Spruill, *Women's Life & Work in the Southern Colonies* (Chapel Hill: University of North Carolina Press, 1938), 286–87; Nellis, "Working Poor," 156–57; Gary Nash, "The Failure of Female Factory Labor in Colonial Boston," *Labor History* 42 (2001): 169–71.

42. Ulrich, *Good Wives*, 37–38; Boydston, *Home and Work*, 15; Spruill, 263–64 (quotes); Jordan, "Women Merchants in Colonial New York," 418–19; Wulf, *Not All Wives*, 132 (quote).

43. Spruill, *Women's Life and Work*, 293–95 (quote).

44. Ibid., 287–88.

45. Spruill, *Women's Life and Work*, 257–70, 269 (quote), 280–82, 283 (quote); Patricia Cleary, " 'She Will Be in the Shop': Women's Sphere of Trade in Eighteenth-Century Philadelphia and New York," *Pennsylvania Magazine of History and Biography* 119 (1995): 182–88; Wulf, *Not All Wives*, 132, 135, 142.

46. Sundue, "Industrious in Their Station," 22.

47. Alice M. Earle, *Home Life in Colonial Days* (New York: Grosset & Dunlap, 1898), 253.

48. Alice M. Earle, *Child Life in Colonial Days* (New York: MacMillan, 1899), 316; Darcy Fryer, " 'Improved' and 'Very Promising' Children: Growing Up Rich in Eighteenth-Century South Carolina," in *Children in Colonial America*, ed. James Marten (New York: New York University Press, 2007), 104–6.

49. Abbot E. Smith, *Colonists in Bondage: White Servitude and Convict Labor in America, 1607–1776* (Chapel Hill: University of North Carolina Press, 1947), 68–69, 303–4.

50. Gottfried Mittelberger, "The Crossing to Pennsylvania," in *The Colonial Image: Origins of American Culture*, ed. John C. Miller (New York: George Braziller, 1962), 88 (quote); A. Smith, *Colonists in Bondage*, 215–16 (quote); Salinger, *"To Serve Well and Faithfully,"* 94; Sellers, *Charleston Business*, 118; Johnson, *Daily Life in Colonial New England*, 163; Salinger, *"To Serve Well and Faithfully,"* 91–93.

51. Towner, *A Good Master Well Served*, 105; Salinger, *"To Serve Well and Faithfully,"* 100.

52. Salinger, *"To Serve Well and Faithfully,"* 101 (quote); Perkins, *Economy of Colonial America*, 153–54; Towner, *A Good Master Well Served*, 124–45; Quimby, *Apprenticeship in Colonial Philadelphian*, 90; McKee, *Labor in Colonial New York*, 66 (quote); Johnson, *Everyday Life in Colonial New England*, 166.

53. Quimby, *Apprenticeship in Colonial Philadelphia*, 88–89 (quote), 76 (quote); Sharon Salinger, " 'Send No More Women:' Female Servants in Eighteenth-Century Philadelphia," *Pennsylvania Magazine of History and Biography* 107 (1983): 41 (quote); McKee, *Labor in Colonial New York*, 99–100 (quote), 108; Towner, *A Good Master Well Served*, 169 (quotes), 173; A. Smith, *Colonists in Bondage*, 288–89; Salinger, *"To Serve Well and Faithfully,"* 108–9; Wulf, *Not All Wives*, 104.

54. McKee, *Labor in Colonial New York*, 66, 100 (quote); A. Smith, *Colonists in Bondage*, 245–46; Morris, *Government and Labor*, 502–7; Towner, *A Good Master Well Served*, 172, 179–81, 195; Walsh, "Charleston's Mechanics," 135; Salinger, *"To Serve Well and Faithfully,"* 104–8; Johnson, *Daily Life in Colonial New England*, 166.

55. Salinger, *"To Serve Well and Faithfully,"* 120–28; Salinger, "Send No More Women," 48 (quote).

56. Skemp, "A Social and Cultural History of Newport," 107–11.

57. Towner, *A Good Master Well Served*, 112–13, 115 (quote); Wulf, *Not All Wives*, 103; Foote, *Black and White Manhattan*, 71, 75; Greene, *Negro in Colonial New England*, 110–11; McManus, *Black Bondage*, 42; Sundue, "Industrious in Their Station," 98.

58. Towner, *A Good Master Well Served*, 115 (quote); Robert Olwell, *Masters, Slaves, and Subjects: The Culture of Power in the South Carolina Low Country, 1740–1790* (Ithaca, NY: Cornell University Press, 1998), 163, 170–79 (quotes); Foote, *Black and White Manhattan*, 72; McManus, *Black Bondage*, 44–48; Greene, *Negro in Colonial New England*, 115–21; Hartigan-O'Connor, "The Measure of the Market," 76.

59. Gary Nash, "Urban Wealth and Poverty in Pre-Revolutionary America," *Journal of Interdisciplinary History* 6 (1976): 549–56, 572.

6

Education

INTRODUCTION

As pioneers trying to survive in a new world, early colonists faced an uphill battle in their attempts to establish and maintain schools. The difficulties of taming a wilderness, a divisive class structure, political oligarchy, the slow progress of pedagogy, and the high economic value placed on children—all contributed to a form of education in early America that was informal, discontinuous, and inefficient. Despite these obstacles and their deleterious consequences, most early colonists placed a high value on formal education. This is partly because the colonies were settled by one of the most literate societies of the West during a peak period in its cultural development. To Protestant settlers, who equated illiteracy with degeneracy, the ability to read the Bible and understand the Commandments was the key to understanding God's will and man's dependence on God for salvation. Schooling was also a means by which to perpetuate the culture and values of the community. Along those same lines, education served as an important bulwark against a possible reversion to savagery among a people desperately trying to plant and cultivate "civilization" in a distant wilderness. On a more individualistic level, education also helped each person to lead a more productive life so that, in the words of William Penn, "none may be idle."[1]

Although schooling was supposed to increase individual productivity and improve the material prosperity of society, education in the colonial cities had a strong authoritarian nature designed to maintain religious conformity and the power of established leadership. Far from creating a democratically minded citizenry encouraged to express independent ideas on the nature of society, religion, and government, early American education instead indoctrinated children to obey and to submit to the authority of church and government. As historian Joel Spring explains, "[p]eople were taught to read and write so that they could obey the laws of God and the state." This antidemocratic, proauthoritarian instruction was especially intended to help make the "restless, wretched, and often well-nigh unmanageable" underclass, in the words of Merle Curti, "more temperate, more industrious, more virtuous, in short, more content with their station."[2]

Education in early America therefore had significant gender, race, and class elements intended to perpetuate the existing social order and class structure so that everyone knew his or her proper place in society and did not step too far outside of it. This explains why girls, blacks, and poor boys in the cities received little, if any, formal education. Girls, who were destined for a life of domesticity, were taught to read (at least in New England), and if belonging to the ruling class, perhaps were given an ornamental and genteel education intended only to make them better hostesses and housewives. Only a select few African American children in the cities received a rudimentary education that did nothing to lift them out of their subservient status. Likewise, the urban poor were largely denied an education, both by design and by circumstances of a largely free-market capitalist economy that left them ignorant, dependent, and more easily exploitable by the well-to-do seeking cheap labor. Even most middle-class children received only a rudimentary education that severely limited their opportunities, especially in the first century of colony building. In short, education in the colonial cities was not intended to promote equality, nor even equality of opportunity. Instead, it was designed by the well-to-do to perpetuate their political, economic, and social hegemony. Those few Americans at either the middle or bottom social groups who managed to climb up the economic ladder did so not because of their limited education but despite it.

This should come as no surprise as wealthy officials in the cities, in educating their citizens, essentially reproduced the main types of schools existing in socially stratified Europe. At the most primary level were dame or petty schools, where children learned basic literacy before progressing to the writing schools, which offered instruction in basic writing, composition, and sometimes arithmetic. Generally, only girls belonging to the upper class went beyond the dame schools to learn some of the more "polite" branches of education considered by contemporaries to be useful for young ladies. Likewise, boys from wealthy families attended either Latin grammar schools and private schools or received private instruction by a tutor that prepared them for entrance into either the professional world or college. For the less fortunate, the cities provided a few charity primary schools along with apprenticeship training for orphans and the children of pauper parents. Some schoolmasters even offered night classes for apprentices and adults. With such a variety of schools, inhabitants of the largest cities had greater educational opportunities than the generality of country dwellers.

BOSTON

The Puritans who settled Boston had an eagerness for education equal to their zealousness for religion. Indeed, the two institutions were inseparable in their minds because they believed that firsthand knowledge of the scriptures was essential in preparing for salvation and living "right" with the world. Education was also important to the Puritans because they believed that children were born both ignorant and wicked; proper instruction that strove to suppress and remake children would therefore not only help save youngsters from the corrupting influences of Satan but in case of an early death—a sad but frequent occurrence at that time—prevent them from being denied entrance into heaven due to ignorance. For these reasons, Puritan leaders placed a heavy emphasis on education, so much so that in 1642 the Massachusetts General Court, in response to a perceived "great neglect in many parents and masters in training up their children in learning," passed a resolution allowing courts to fine family heads who failed to ensure that their children and apprentices could "read and understand the principles of religion and the capital laws of the country." To better enable parents to comply with this law, the provincial legislature mandated that all towns of at least 50 families must hire a schoolmaster and establish a grammar school to instruct their children for entrance into Harvard College. In 1635, Boston established a grammar school for boys seeking to attend Harvard but failed to provide an elementary-level public school until 1684. Demands by parents for more public schools increased the number to five by 1720. Even then, attendance in the "public" schools was neither mandatory nor free.[3] Many poor families could not afford either the tuition or school supplies. Still, this did not absolve them of their responsibility to educate their children. Parents who failed to teach their children the alphabet by the age of six risked having local officials take their children and bind them out to a family that would educate them. The affluent, on the other hand, had the option of sending their children to one of the eight private schools operating in the city by 1690. A generation later there were more than 20 masters in the Puritan capital offering private instruction to both boys and girls in a wide variety of practical and ornamental subjects. The city's numerous private schools, coupled with its public education system, gave the residents of Boston the best education available in North America, at least for middle- and upper-class families. Wealthy families from across the continent and as far away as the West Indies sent their children to the famous Boston schools.[4]

NEWPORT

Newport, with its more independent spirit, never instituted a universal system of education like that in Boston. Instead, parents wanted greater control over the education of their children and so placed them in a variety of private schools that dominated the education system during the colonial period. These private institutions included grammar schools that prepared boys for college, trade schools that offered everything from bookkeeping to navigation, girls' schools that provided instruction in "polite accomplishments," and special schools for free blacks and Indians. For those who could not afford a private education, Newport had a public school as early as 1640 and three of them by 1720. As in Boston, though, parents had to pay tuition for their children to attend the public schools as well as purchase school supplies, expenses that prevented many poor from attending school. So-called charity schools conducted under church auspices educated few of the city's poor. Rather than educate the poor, authorities in Newport followed Boston's practice of binding out uneducated poor children who threatened to become a charge on the town. Unlike Boston, Newport officials made no regular inspection of its public schools, which may explain in part why some residents believed the town schools taught children "the corrupt ways, manners, fashions and Tongues of the World." For this reason, among others, many Newport parents sent their children to parochial schools established by the Quakers, Congregationalists, Baptists, Anglicans, and Moravians.[5]

NEW AMSTERDAM/NEW YORK

Of all the major cities, New Amsterdam/New York City had the least concern for educating its children. Under both the Dutch and English regimes, schooling was haphazard and obtained in a patchwork fashion. In New Amsterdam education fell under the control of both the state and the church. The schoolmaster was an officer of the church and devoted most of his time to training his pupils in the catechism. Authorities did a poor job selecting the town's first schoolmasters, men of low character and morals who were convicted of habitual drunkenness, selling liquor to the Indians, slander, and rape. Not surprisingly, parents complained that the schoolmasters "did not keep strict discipline over the boys ... who fight among themselves and tear the clothes from each other's bodies." Circumstances had not improved by 1647 when Governor Peter Stuyvesant wrote the directors to know what provisions were to be made for a school, "as there is none in New Amsterdam," he complained, "and the youth are running wild."[6]

As poor as educational opportunities were in New Amsterdam under the Dutch, they sunk to even lower levels with the English takeover of the city in 1664. Thirty years later the city still had no provision for public schooling and there existed only one public schoolmaster for the entire province. Not until 1702 did the mayor and council of New York City finally pass a bill for a "Free School" in the capital, but it lasted only eight years. It took another 22 years before the assembly passed an act establishing a grammar school in the provincial capital. The government's neglect of education encouraged the growth of numerous private and parochial schools that mainly catered to the rising commercial class who sought special skills such as navigation, bookkeeping, and modern languages. However, the city lacked a proper grammar school, which prompted wealthy New Yorkers to send their boys abroad to prepare them for college. New York City also provided few facilities for the education of its poor children. Cadwallader Colden, a local physician and politician, believed fault for the city's inadequate educational system lay with the residents' insatiable lust for money. "Tho' the Province of New York abounds certainly more in riches than any of the Norther Colonies," he remarked, "yet there has been less care to propagate Knowledge or Learning in it than anywhere else. The only principle of Life propagated among the young people is to get Money, and men are only esteemd according to what they are worth—that is, the money they are possessed of."[7]

PHILADELPHIA

Like New York City, Philadelphia never developed a system of free public education. This was largely due to the early Quakers' anti-intellectualism, which stemmed from their belief that education, particularly in its higher forms, was "apt to clog the Spirit." The Quakers, who largely controlled affairs in the capital, also lacked a trained ministry and therefore saw no need to create higher institutions of learning for ministerial training. Still, the Friends understood the value of literacy and established parochial schools to educate their own children, particularly in practical subjects and the fundamentals of their faith. For all other children, the city provided few educational opportunities except for several elementary schools and a grammar school. Without strong government support for education, various religious denominations and charity schools stepped up to fill the public deficiency. The Anglicans, Lutherans, Dutch Reformed, and Moravians all established their own elementary schools, partly in an attempt to preserve their cultural and religious heritage. Philadelphia's expanding wealth and population also encouraged the development of private schools that stressed utilitarian subjects such as mathematics, surveying, navigation, and especially foreign languages that were essential to those engaged in commerce. So, despite the lack of public support for education in Philadelphia, the city still provided some of the best educational opportunities in the colonies—at least for those who could afford it. Philadelphia's excellent private schools attracted children from throughout the Middle Colonies.[8]

CHARLES TOWN

For the first 40 years of its existence, the government of Charles Town provided few schools for its children. The city's school system suffered partly because many of its leading citizens were planters who resided in the capital only part time, and partly because these same men already employed private tutors for their own children and did not want to endanger their predominant position by promoting a system of popular schooling. Thus when Anglican missionaries from the Society for the Propagation of the Gospel (SPG) came to the city in the early 1700s, they were so appalled by the ignorance of the people that they immediately set up a grammar school. With the help of the SPG, the city of Charles Town in 1712 established a Free School to provide religious instruction along with writing, Latin, Greek, accounting, astronomy, mechanics, classical history, natural philosophy, navigation, surveying, and the "practical Parts of Mathematics." Like public schools in other cities, the Charles Town Free School was only free to a small number of children from the poorest families, and as late as 1725 the school had an enrollment of only 54 students. To fill the void in education left by the local government, some wealthy and civic-minded residents established nearly a dozen schools to educate poor and orphaned children. Additionally, St. Philip's vestry provided elementary education to those children who did not benefit from the above educational opportunities. Of course, these "charity schools" were not good enough for upper-class children, whose parents sent them to the many private schools in the city that offered both classical and practical programs of study for those who could afford it. Even with many private schools, some upper-class parents were still displeased with educational opportunities in the capital. As late as 1763 the wealthy slave trader and planter Henry Laurens opined that schools in Charles Town were a disgrace and that it was outrageous that its children had to go abroad "even for A B C and a little Latin."[9]

FAMILY EDUCATION

No matter where they lived, colonial children received their first education in the home, where the family imparted literacy (if the parents could read and write), inculcated religious morals, and oversaw vocational training. In doing so, a family might use Edmund Coote's *The English Schoole-Maister* (1596), or a simple hornbook that contained the alphabet, a few syllables combining a consonant with a vowel, and the Lord's Prayer or the Apostle's Creed. However, family education in the five major seacoast towns eroded significantly over time due to the growing number of local schools and a thriving industry in trades and crafts. High mortality rates, which often created instability in the home, further undermined the family's ability to instruct its children. Parents were all too aware of the precarious-ness of life and therefore wrote wills providing for the education of their children. Interestingly, these wills reveal that few parents saw education as a means towards upward mobility for their offspring. Josiah Bagley, a ship joiner from New York City, willed that his chil-dren should be educated "in a manner suitable to my condition in life." Educational goals were also modest among Jewish parents, who were satisfied if their children learned Hebrew, the tenets of Judaism, and secular subjects like reading, writing, and arithmetic taught by Jewish teachers in Hebrew schools. Education as the "great equalizer" of society had not yet taken firm root in America.[10]

APPRENTICESHIP SYSTEM

This is also reflected in the apprenticeship system, a form of edu-cational and skill training brought to American from Europe. The purpose was to provide children, mostly lower-class boys between 14 and 17 years of age, with enough learning necessary for them to become productive and successful citizens. This was not always the case, especially for the thousands of pauper and orphaned chil-dren who were apprenticed out by local "overseers of the poor" as a means to reduce the number of poor dependent on public relief. These pauper apprentices generally were sold to people, both in the city and countryside, looking for cheap labor. Many were apprenticed out to less remunerative trades like cordwaining, coopering, and bricklaying. Bonnet making, dress making, and "plain-sewing" were popular skills taught to girls placed in appren-ticeship, along with basic housewifery. However, many pauper apprentices were not taught a trade or given an education, a circum-stance that destined them to a life of destitution and hard labor. Many were also grossly mistreated by their masters. Those who did receive an education were taught basic reading, writing, and the tenets of the Christian faith for the purpose of maintaining reli-gious conformity and the power of the existing authority. In the words of historian Merle Curti, apprentices were "taught to respect their superiors and the sons of their superiors who were conning Latin Verbs and acquiring the other requisites of the culture and polish that characterized the class to which they belonged." Meanwhile, boys belonging to affluent families received expensive and elitist professional apprenticeships from merchants, lawyers, and physicians, who charged a significant fee for their services and who generally treated their young charges in a manner fitting their upper-class status. In short, the apprenticeship system perpetuated the hierarchical nature of colonial society.[11]

PRIVATE SCHOOLS

Although the main educational task of apprenticeship was job training, masters were obligated by law to teach their charges rudimentary reading, writing, and ciphering. To comply with these conditions, masters frequently paid for their indentures to attend one of the private evening schools in the five towns established by entrepreneurial teachers specifically for apprentices and others who worked during the day. The first evening school in North America opened in 1661 in New Amsterdam, largely because evening instruction had a longstanding tradition in Holland. Elsewhere, evening schools did not emerge until much later—Boston in the late 1600s, Philadelphia in the 1730s, Charles Town in the 1740s, and Newport by 1760—as people became increasingly interested in business growth. Generally, apprentices and ambitious men who could afford the tuition attended evening school for a three-month term every year until they mastered rudimentary reading, writing, and some ciphering. Private schoolmasters also offered instruction in practical subjects of higher grades such as algebra, geometry, bookkeeping, surveying, navigation, astronomy, mechanics, gunnery, architecture, and modern languages to young men aspiring to become merchants, engineers, or ships' captains. Evening and private schools therefore offered the ambitious and well-to-do an opportunity for advancement or preparation for a change in employment.[12]

DAME SCHOOLS

Many urban children obtained their basic literacy in a dame school, a private and domestic venture in which a local woman, often a widow who had obtained the rudiments of education in her youth, taught neighborhood children in her narrow and often untidy kitchen or living room. In this homey environment, the dames followed a dead and dull curriculum that focused on the alphabet, simple spelling, reading, and religious training. As if the curriculum was not dull enough, these female teachers frequently performed their domestic chores such as knitting, sewing, and spinning while listening to the younger pupils recite their letters and the older ones read and spell from the primers. Writing was generally not part of the curriculum in dame schools because paper tablets were expensive and the young children could not yet manage pen and ink. Girls, whose education more reflected a future of domesticity, received instruction in knitting, sewing, and sometimes cooking. To motivate the young children to learn and to behave properly, the dames applied both the carrot and stick approaches by offering gingerbread and other treats to good students while thumping troublemakers on the head with a heavy thimble. To deter chatting, some dames went so far as to insert into the child's mouth a "whispering stick"—a wooden gag made with a stick and string that was tied around the poor offender's head much like a bit is placed in a horse's mouth.[13]

ELEMENTARY SCHOOLS

Once a child had learned to read a little, he or she advanced to one of the public or private schools to learn basic writing, composition, and perhaps some arithmetic. When it came to the sexes, teachers usually taught girls and boys separately, with girls receiving their instruction before or after the boys' regular sessions or at noontime. Generally, girls received about the same instruction as boys, but they did not pursue their studies as extensively, often no more than two or three years and often just a few months. But the same could be said for many boys as city ordinances did not mandate when children had to begin attending school, how much schooling they must receive, or when they might quit. School hours, moreover, varied according to season. In the fall and spring masters taught for about six hours a day; during the winter a four-hour teaching day was common, which was made up with eight hours a day in the classroom during the summer. Pupils of both sexes therefore attended school irregularly, depending on family circumstances. Those from impoverished backgrounds often left school in mid-term to add to the family's income and might not return for a year or more—if at all. Such an irregular and abbreviated acquisition of knowledge only perpetuated the cycle of poverty among the underclass.

LATIN GRAMMAR SCHOOL

Boys belonging to more affluent families, on the other hand, usually attended either the public grammar school (sometimes referred to as a Latin school) or a private school for many years. Unlike the elementary schools, the purpose of the grammar school was to educate the leaders of society. The upper class needed educated and cultured leaders if it was to maintain its values and continue its hegemony. To that end, instruction in these elitist schools, which was both rigorous and classical, was intended to prepare boys for entrance into college or the professions. For the first year or two students spent up to nine hours a day, six days a week, mastering basic literacy and numeracy. Thereafter the boys began their precollegiate studies, a curriculum that emphasized the study of Latin and the classical Greek and Roman works considered by the upper class as prerequisites for the development of civic character, wisdom, and leadership. Schoolmasters, who were selected and licensed by the church, also devoted considerable time to religion. Each day began with religious exercises that included reading a verse from the Bible, singing psalms, and reciting prayers. The master devoted much of one day a week to catechizing the boys.

For approximately nine hours a day, six days a week, for seven years, boys sat on hard benches translating Latin; read a challenging succession of texts written by Cicero, Erasmus, Livy, and Ovid, among many others; and studied rhetoric, religion, logic, and ancient history. Instructors gave little attention to utilitarian subjects like mathematics, science, or modern languages, largely because knowledge of these subjects was not a prerequisite for entrance into the colonial colleges. Consequently, by the time a boy finished his course of study at the age of 15 or so, he was usually ignorant in numbers and often unable to write English with any degree of fluency. Nor did masters encourage critical thinking and class discussions, instead using the *memoriter* method of drill and rote learning. More important for a gentleman's training was the development of grace, manners, and bearing, accomplishments considered necessary for polite society and leadership. To that end, boys took private lessons in dancing, fencing, music, and drawing. In doing so, the elites further distanced themselves from the common people who could not afford private instruction. The overall purpose of this elitist education was to demonstrate superiority, a superiority the upper class believed granted them the exclusive right to lead society. Education in colonial America was therefore designed to perpetuate elitism and plutocracy.[14]

FEMALE EDUCATION

Education in the colonial cities, and elsewhere in America, was also designed to perpetuate patriarchy, or male domination of society. Colonists cited numerous Biblical passages they believed provided providential expression of patriarchy. A school curriculum that severely limited educational opportunities for girls further reinforced female subordination and helped to ensure that women both understood and stayed in their "proper place." For lower-class girls whose parents could not afford private schooling, an advanced education was not possible. Endowed free schools and most private schools that offered advanced instruction were not open to girls. For parents with money, there were opportunities for their daughters to learn all sorts of work fit for young ladies. Because contemporaries believed that women were intellectually unfit to comprehend the arts and sciences or to participate in world affairs, the private schooling given to young ladies was of an ornamental nature and primarily aimed at making them good wives and hostesses to their well-to-do future husbands. To that end, the female mistress instructed the "fairer sex" in fancy embroidery, dancing, music, drawing, French, and many "instructing amusements" such as painting on glass, ornamental penmanship, and the art of making artificial flowers.

Although such a polite education helped the upper class to set themselves off from their middling and poorer neighbors, not everyone believed it was sufficient for young ladies. One resident of Charles Town claimed that the education of girls who attended these expensive boarding schools "is scandalously neglected." Another critic agreed, charging that as the young ladies of the town were trained in "no professions except Music and Dancing," they made "very agreeable Companions, but expensive wives." A Philadelphian calling himself or herself "Clio" pointed out the larger social consequences of neglecting female education by asking the pregnant question: "[H]ow many female minds, rich with native genius and noble sentiment, have been lost to the world, and all their mental treasures buried into oblivion?" This partly explains why during the course of the eighteenth century the ornamental nature of female education among the elite gave way to a more substantive curriculum that included studying literature, history, moral philosophy, foreign languages, and science. Studying such subjects, it was believed, would promote reason, rationality, and taste, qualities that would further enable the upper class to distinguish themselves from the middling sort who were gaining wealth and leisure. In this way, at least, the purpose of elite women's education paralleled that of their male counterparts.[15]

Some critics considered this time-consuming and expensive form of female education superfluous considering that a woman's ultimate destiny was marriage and domestic pursuits. "What can be more displeasing to a man of taste," exclaimed a gentleman, "than *female pedantry.*" This female pedantry is exemplified by some affluent urban women who attended public lectures, wrote poetry, organized literary salons, and dabbled in scientific experiments. For example, Mary Pemberton of Philadelphia conducted medical experiments on the effects of ingesting salt water, while her neighbor Elizabeth Norris pursued astronomical studies with her own telescope. Elizabeth Sandwich, also of Philadelphia, owned her own microscope, with which she used to observe "divers objects." Some fearless and inquisitive women even experimented with electricity. Such extracurricular pursuits convinced some men that education would make a woman into a lazy, spoiled, and insubordinate snob who would wreak havoc in both her home and community. Instead of aspiring to be "doctors in petticoats," a young lady should be taught the "polite branches" of education and learn proper deportment, elegance, and carriage. The latter form of learning required girls to wear packthread stays, stiffened coats, harnesses, and backboards. Such torture devices illustrate that learning to be a lady during the colonial period could be a very uncomfortable experience.[16]

SCHOOL BUILDINGS

School buildings often added to the discomfort of learning. A lack of funds early in the colonial period prevented the construction of schoolhouses and therefore forced local authorities to hold classes in meetinghouses, customs houses, basements of public buildings, and even sail lofts. Even when pinch-penny local authorities raised money for a school building, usually through the sale of public lands, it was cheaply built and deteriorated rapidly into a ruinous condition. Even when newly built, the typical school house was a dark, dreary, and damp single-room building roughly 18 feet by 20 feet in size with oppressively low ceilings, only one or two windows (often broken), a sieve-like roof that often leaked, and floors made of either dirt or rough puncheon boards. A chimney furnished a fireplace that left children farthest away from it shivering. When the schoolhouse grew dark the schoolmaster lit tallow candles, which filled the single room with a pungent odor. The teacher usually had the best accommodations, sitting on a raised platform where he could keep a close eye on the students as they recited their lessons. Older students sat at coarse-board shelves lining the interior of the walls, while younger pupils sat on equally uncomfortable blocks or benches of logs full of splinters. Blackboards, maps, and slates were unknown at the time, although in some schools mathematical exercises, examples of fine penmanship, the Ten Commandments, the Lord's Prayer, and other samples of the schoolmaster's calligraphy hung on the walls.[17]

SCHOOLMASTERS

Teachers in the cities were a motley and peripatetic lot. Many were knowledgeable, conscientious, and kind, while others were ill equipped, careless, and cruel. Most teachers, however, fell somewhere between these two extremes. As mentioned above, older women, many of whom were barely literate themselves, dominated the dame schools. At the secondary level, men monopolized teaching. Most schoolmasters were young, single men (averaging 23 years of age) because they demanded a lower salary than a man with a family to support. In hiring a schoolmaster, town officials also focused on the candidate's religious background, general character, and ability to control students rather than his knowledge or teaching ability. Still, many masters during the eighteenth century were university graduates. The best teachers were found in the Latin grammar schools of Boston and Newport. However, they generally taught for only a few years to earn money for ministerial studies or to use the experience as a stepping stone to a more respectable and remunerative position such as one in medicine, business, or public service. Only about 3 percent of college graduates had lifelong careers in education, usually as masters at the better urban grammar schools.[18]

The poorest teachers, on the other hand, were located in the private schools. Many of these were itinerants who taught for a year or two before either taking a teaching position elsewhere or falling out of the profession altogether. Many self-appointed masters who advertised in the urban newspapers turned out to be ill-equipped frauds who had failed in other occupations and turned to teaching as a final resort. New York City had 22 writing masters in 1751, but only 6 of these "pretending teachers," according to one local critic, were "tolerably qualified."[19] Part of the reason parents and city officials were willing to allow men of such questionable character and ability to teach their children was due to a drastic shortage of teachers in the port cities. In Philadelphia and New York City, for example, the number of school-aged children per teacher between 1700 and 1744 averaged 308 and 357, respectively. Most men were reluctant to enter teaching because of the character of the work, the poor compensation, and the low regard for the profession. Masters had to teach a variety of subjects to students with a wide range of ages and learning levels. They also spent a considerable amount of time performing a myriad of tasks: making and mending quill pens, setting copies, supervising time-consuming writing exercises, and most frustratingly, trying to control recalcitrant students. For this difficult and frustrating work, schoolmasters in the mid-1700s received an average salary of between £25 and £50 sterling per year, a sum slightly more than that earned by common laborers. To supplement their meager salary, many masters moonlighted as ministers, town criers, court messengers, bell ringers, translators, copyists, janitors, and even gravediggers. For most schoolmasters, teaching was not a career but a poorly paid temporary job.[20]

INSTRUCTION

As frustrating, unsatisfying, and unrewarding as teaching was for most dames and masters, schoolchildren found their instruction equally dull, monotonous, and tedious. Each day began with singing a psalm or morning hymn and reciting the Lord's Prayer. Following these devotional exercises, students worked on their individual assignments, which usually revolved around rote memorization, oral recitation, and dull repetition. In learning the alphabet, students often used a hornbook, a paddle-shaped instrument about 3 inches wide and 4 inches long holding a printed page covered by a translucent sheet of horn to protect it from children's grimy fingers. It devoted separate pages to the alphabet, capital and small letters, vowels, and Roman numerals and concluded with the Lord's Prayer. Later the *New England Primer*, which first appeared in the late 1600s, superseded the hornbook as the primary school text throughout the colonies. The contents of this slim book, with its 24 religious rhymes, the Lord's Prayer, the Ten Commandments, names of the books of the Old and New Testaments, and a section called "Duty of Children towards Parents," reflects the strong religious and authoritarian nature of colonial education. In learning the alphabet, for example, pupils were required to recite somber rhymes like "In Adams fall, we sinned all," "Job feels the rod, yet blesses God," "Youth forward slips death soonest nips" and "the idle Fool is whipt at school." The authoritarian nature of the text is presented in the first lines of the following verse, which the student was required to memorize:

> I will fear God, and honour the KING.
> I will honour my Father & Mother.
> I will obey my Superiors.
> I will Submit to my Elder.

Far from advancing a democratic society or opening paths to social and economic opportunities, the curriculum of colonial schools was formulated to develop in children a passive acceptance of the existing elitist authoritarianism in government, the church, the family, the workplace, and society. To ensure this, students were expected to memorize and master the contents of this authoritarian primer. After 1662 New England children were also required to memorize Michael Wigglesworth's terrifying poem *The Day of Doom*, which described in vivid terms the Last Judgment and the horrors awaiting unrepentant sinners. One stanza graphically describing sinners cast into the fiery lake of hell instilled lasting terror into the impressionable minds of young children:

> With Iron bands they bind their hands,
> and cursed feet together,
> And cast them all, both great and small,
> into that Lake for ever.
> Where day and night, without respite,
> they wail, and cry, and howl
> For tort'ring pain, which they sustain
> in Body and in Soul.

Because instructors lacked teaching equipment, paper, and often books, they were forced to use an individual method of oral recitation that was quite wasteful of time. The alphabet, spelling, reading, and grammar were all learned through oral recitation. At the beginning of the day the master gave each student his lesson and sent the students to their desks to memorize them. This classroom pedagogy therefore placed the burden of learning almost entirely on the student. Masters often paid little attention to the proper sound of letters when students recited the alphabet or to the meaning of passages and new words when reading aloud. Once a student had memorized his lesson, he came forward to the teacher's desk and recited it to the master. The sound produced by 20 or more children reading or spelling at the same time was often so loud that nearby residents complained. Although boring, this method did at least allow each child to progress according to his or her individual ability and application. However, the process was so wasteful that children might attend school for years and barely learn the basics of

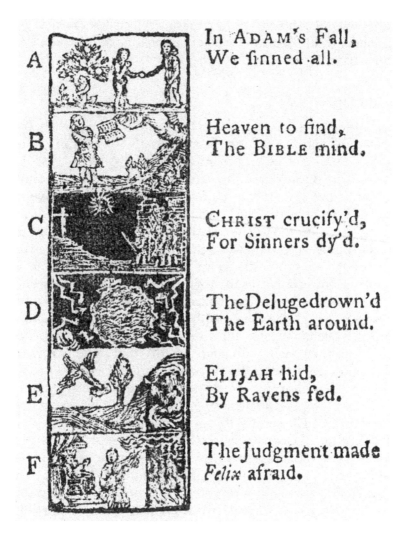

In ADAM's Fall,
We finned all.

Heaven to find,
The BIBLE mind.

CHRIST crucify'd,
For Sinners dy'd.

TheDelugedrown'd
The Earth around.

ELIJAH hid,
By Ravens fed.

TheJudgment made
Felix afraid.

Page from the New England Primer (1762). First published in the late 1680s in Boston by printer Benjamin Harris, the *New England Primer* was the first reading primer designed for the American colonies. The above illustration taken from the 1762 edition of the *New England Primer* show the inseparable connection between education and religion in early America. The language of the primer is generally stern and morbid, at least by modern sensibilities, frequently focusing on death and the need for children to know Christ before their demise. The *New England Primer* served as the leading instructional text for children for at least a century, selling a reported 2 million copies during the eighteenth century.

reading, writing, and ciphering. As for subjects like history, geography, science, and literature, masters almost never introduced them to their students.[21]

DISCIPLINE

As if sitting long hours on a hard log bench in a dreary schoolhouse mindlessly memorizing the fundamentals of reading and the Christian religion was not painful enough, students also had to endure severe discipline at the hands of masters who liberally used a variety of punishments to motivate them both to behave and to learn. Students chafed at the harsh discipline and often made a game of trying to run off the teacher or disrupt the classroom. Recognizing that classrooms were often battlegrounds for control between teacher and students, town officials gave schoolmasters "full power" to use the "rod of correction" on their students and forbade parents and other adults from hindering the teacher in administering discipline unless they thought he did so with "too much severity." One barbarous Boston schoolmaster, for example, struck his students on the head with a thick stick with such severity that parents complained to the school directors, who responded by forbidding the teacher from using that harmful form of punishment. Undeterred, the cruel master then whipped the soles of his scholars' feet and roared out in ecstasy: "Oh! The caitiffs! It is good for them."[22]

Most masters, however, sought to avoid disciplining recalcitrant students with "too much severity" by first using a variety of noncorporal punishments, particularly public shaming. A traditional form of humiliation included sitting on a dunce stool while wearing a dunce cap or a yoke. Students in one Philadelphia school who failed three times in their assignment were called "lazy" by the entire class, while disobedient ones had to stand before a class with a whipping stick protruding up through the back of their shirt or dress. If shaming methods failed to deter students from misbehaving, masters did not hesitate to use more painful forms of punishment. Of these, whipping with a rod, paddle, or switch, which the master usually placed in plain view of his students, was the most common. Hardly a day went by when a colonial school failed to resound with the strokes of hickory switches and the resulting cries of children. Some Boston and Rhode Island schoolmasters added insult to injury by forcing their students to kiss the rod that punished them. Equally painful was the practice of sadistic New Amsterdam schoolmasters who tore the flesh from children's hands

Print of a Scene in a Dutch School. Maintaining discipline among unruly students in the colonial period often involved corporal punishment. The illustration above, depicting a familiar scene in a Dutch school, shows the schoolmaster paddling the hand of a student. Some sadistic teachers attached wire to the paddle that would tear flesh from the child's hand. (Esther Singleton, *Dutch New York* [New York: Dodd, Mead & Co., 1909])

by striking their palms with a wooden paddle that had twisted copper wires and sharp pins attached to it. Some masters made unruly girls sit on leather cushions with tacks pointed upwards. More exhausting than painful was the one-legged stool, a simple yet clever device that some masters discovered could make the most incorrigible student behave. Similarly, other masters made insubordinate boys stand on a table and hold heavy boards over their heads during the lesson. Both exhausting and humiliating was the practice among masters in Dutch New Amsterdam of making unruly pupils walk home from school with a large and heavy wooden block fastened to one of their legs.[23]

Fortunately, such arbitrary and cruel punishment among masters was the exception and not the rule. Most preferred to bring the children to do things from "a love of doing than to force them by the rod." The Quakers, for example, rejected the harsh forms of corporal punishment prevalent at the time and instead gave greater attention to the individual nature of the child. Officials of the SPG instructed its schoolmasters to use "kind and gentle methods" in teaching their students. When punishment was necessary, teachers were to explain that it was administered out of kindness and reason rather than vindictiveness and cruelty. Some savvy schoolmasters, in an attempt to attract more pupils, advertised in urban newspapers that they used a light hand in punishing disobedient children. Others employed a system of rewards that included presents, money, and praise for academic excellence and proper deportment. One Philadelphia master traced the letter "O" on the hand of students who performed well, a mark of excellence that children could show to their parents. In the end, most masters treated their students in a way that they hoped would instill both love and fear of them.[24]

EVOLUTION OF SCHOOLING

Over the course of the colonial period, education evolved correspondingly with the evolution of the cities. During much of the colonial period, the main ports had few schools to educate their many children. The difficult decades of colony building, coupled with an immature economy, discouraged efforts to provide much formal education for children. Additionally, the so-called free schools in the cities required some form of tuition from all but the most destitute. Few parents in the early decades could afford either the tuition or the loss of their children's labor. In Philadelphia, for example, only 3.2 percent of children under the age of 16 were enrolled in school as late as 1741.

A Practical Education

As the urban economies became increasingly sophisticated during the eighteenth century, they necessitated the creation of an equally sophisticated form of education for residents of the five cities. A growing global trade demanded a workforce highly skilled in bookkeeping, accounting, marine engineering, navigation, mathematics, and foreign languages. Wider contact with other peoples and cultures also led to a need for greater knowledge of the history, geography, and literature of the European world. Domestically, America's westward expansion created a demand for skills in surveying and building roads and bridges. Even the many colonial wars brought demands for personnel trained in military engineering.[25]

This demand for a more utilitarian education was greatest in the port cities with their dominant business and commercial classes, who considered Latin and Greek as in "no way necessary for the general education of Youth."[26] Instead, parents who could afford it kept their sons in schools for longer periods so that they might learn the academic and practical skills necessary to succeed in the increasingly complex and commercialized economy. The number of teachers advertising schools in the cities after 1730 increased tremendously to meet this demand. Typical is Charles Town, where the number of schoolmasters' advertisements in the *South Carolina Gazette* increased from 5 to 31 between 1730 and 1765. This educational trend partly explains why the percentage of children attending school doubled in cities like Boston, from 8.4 percent to 16.5 percent, and tripled in places like Philadelphia, from 3.2 percent to 10.3 percent.[27] By the 1760s the quest for useful knowledge was in full swing in all the cities, reflected in the establishment of numerous evening schools that taught practical subjects (described earlier) and the creation of subscription libraries intended to advance self-improvement.

"Confining the Poor to Ignorance"

The urban poor had few opportunities to attend these "people's colleges," or any school for that matter. Traditionally, scholars on the history of American education like to highlight that beginning in the early1700s the primary cities established charity schools for the poor that were either funded and administered privately by wealthy citizens, as in Philadelphia, or publicly funded by the local poor-relief system, as in Charles Town. Except for Charles Town, however, charity schools in the cities educated few poor children. For example, leaders in Boston and Newport made little effort to establish charity schools; instead, pinch-penny leaders in these two New England towns preferred to put poor white children to work so that they would not be a public poor-relief burden. In New York City the responsibility of educating the poor fell to denominational schools, which by the mid-1700s were providing virtually the only education in the capital. Unfortunately, these schools were instructing no more than 130 poor children in any given year during the late colonial period, despite the fact that the city contained more than 6,000 white school-aged youths, many of them living in destitution. Meanwhile, the local aristocracy in Philadelphia created a number of religious and secular-based charity schools in the mid-eighteenth century that provided few educational opportunities for the poor. Instead, most children admitted to local free schools came from middle-class families who could not afford the tuition. By the American Revolution, Philadelphia's charity schools became a token symbol of charity. In Charles Town, economics and fear, more than equality and altruism, encouraged the local elites to provide the poor with a rudimentary education at public expense. As historian Sharon Sundue explains, local elites "stood more to gain by facilitating some social mobility among poor young Whites, whose unskilled labor was not required, and whose close social contact with Blacks was feared." Outside of Charles Town, the urban poor were intentionally confined to ignorance and poverty by the ruling elite, who sought to continue to exploit the uneducated underclass as cheap and dependent labor. "We would not breed them [the poor] too high for that station in life for which their birth has designed them," explained one proponent of charity schools, "nor raise them above the labors of the plough."[28]

COLLEGE

While the urban aristocracy were confining the poor to ignorance and perpetual exploitation, they sent their own children to colleges both at home and abroad to preserve family wealth and influence. Higher education in early America, like primary education, had a strong religious impulse. Of the nine colleges established during the colonial period—Harvard (1636); William and Mary (1693); Yale (1701); New Jersey, now Princeton (1747); Philadelphia, now Pennsylvania (1749); King's, now Columbia (1754); Rhode Island, now Brown (1764); Queens, now Rutgers (1766); and Dartmouth (1769)—all but Philadelphia were created to produce ministers for their respective religious denominations. Three of the above colleges were located in or near one of the five major cities: Harvard (in Cambridge near Boston), King's in New York City, and Philadelphia, of course, in the Quaker city. With Harvard and the College of Rhode Island nearby, residents of Newport did not see the need to establish a college during the colonial period. Neither did leaders in Charles Town, who preferred sending their sons "home" to England for college instruction.

Overall, a college education in the eighteenth century was largely irrelevant to real life, although New England Puritans considered it requisite for a truly civilized society. Except for those students studying to be ministers, college attendance promised very limited educational opportunities. The classical curriculum offered by colonial colleges offered little practical application to those with aspirations in business, commerce, or the law. Only King's College and the College of Philadelphia offered medical programs, and those were not established until the 1760s. Instead, the young men who attended college did so more for purposes of general social leadership—to learn how to think, to communicate, and to lead— than for specific occupational roles. In fact, the degree itself was apparently not important. More important for the upper class was learning how to behave and carry oneself like a "gentleman," which would give them an air of superiority and conspicuously distinguish them from their social inferiors. To that end, a college education in colonial America was intended to maintain elitism and the status quo. Of the 155 students who entered King's College between 1758 and 1775, only 99 graduated. Some students dropped out to go into business, law, and medicine, while others left to go into commerce, privateering, or simply to "do nothing."[29]

Young boys aspiring to enter college had to pass a perfunctory oral and written exam administered by the college president and tutors. In these exams a candidate, who averaged about 15 years of age, had to demonstrate an ability to speak and write Latin, along with some familiarity with Greek grammar. However, colleges at the time were desperate for pupils (most had fewer than 100 pupils) and rarely denied admission to an applicant. Entering freshmen who were deficient in Latin and Greek received remedial work.[30]

Freshmen quickly discovered that college life reflected the hierarchical nature of colonial society. Authorities placed all pupils in a system of seniority that was based mostly on wealth and social ranking. No matter their ranking, few freshmen escaped the ancient custom of hazing by upperclassmen against first-year students. This included requiring freshmen to serve as unpaid errand boys to sophomores, procuring bread and beer at the buttery hatch, taking wigs to be curled and ironed and clothes to be washed and pressed, fetching food and drink from taverns, and carrying notes from one building to another. Students of all ranks enjoyed playing pranks on their tutors by hiding their wigs, cropping their mares, putting snakes in their chambers, and breaking their chamber windows. In 1671 some Harvard students played a truly dirty trick on the college president by smearing dung on the staircase rails and then calling him to the top. When the fuming president thundered "who did this foul deed," one smart-aleck student replied: "Whoever did it, it seems you had a hand in it!"[31]

Harvard College in 1726. William Burgis's *A Prospect of the Colledges in Cambridge* shows Harvard College as it appeared in 1726. On the left is Harvard Hall, in the center is Stoughton Hall, and on the right is Massachusetts Hall. The four-story Harvard Hall, constructed in 1677, is thoroughly medieval in appearance. On the first floor was the dining hall, kitchen, buttery, and student chambers. The college library dominated the second floor while the remaining two floors were devoted to student and tutor chambers. Harvard Hall was destroyed by fire in 1764. The Georgian-style Stoughton Hall, built in 1699, was devoted entirely to dormitory purposes. The building was badly damaged during the American Revolution and torn down in 1781. Massachusetts Hall, built in 1720, is the oldest surviving building at Harvard College. It originally served as a dormitory containing 32 chambers and 64 private studies. Founding Fathers John Adams, John Hancock, Samuel Adams, and James Otis resided in Massachusetts Hall while attending Harvard. (Library of Congress, Prints and Photographs Division, Reproduction # LC USZ62-86631)

These sophomoric pranks were a lighthearted break from the rigors of academic life for college students, who devoted the majority of their time to the study of a medieval curriculum similar to that offered in English universities. Freshmen were required to study the trivium (grammar, logic, and rhetoric), along with more Latin and Greek, while upperclassmen focused on the quadrivium (arithmetic, geometry, astronomy, and music). No matter the subject, the program of study revolved around three academic exercises: the lecture, declamation, and disputation. Lectures served as oral textbooks, with faculty delineating a great author's ideas while students took notes. Students used these lectures for their own declamations, or oral presentations on an assigned topic. Beginning in their second year, pupils engaged in disputations, which pitted two or more scholars in a debate over a philosophical question introduced by a moderator. The disputation gave undergraduates an opportunity to hone the skills of rhetoric, oratory, logic, nimbleness of intellect, and sharpness of wit, all of which were invaluable to men of affairs. By the mid-eighteenth century, colleges began to modernize their curriculum by introducing modern languages, English history, law, and political philosophy into the classroom. The College of Philadelphia, whose aim from the beginning was to increase knowledge as an end in itself, offered the most progressive program of study of any college in North America. Although the school did not neglect the classics, its founders placed a heavy emphasis on what was useful: arithmetic, accounts, physics, chemistry, geometry, astronomy, history, botany, and mechanics. The school also opened the first department of medicine in a colonial college in 1765.

Overall, academic standards at colleges were not particularly high. One seventeenth-century Harvard graduate reported that his instructors required him to only "construe poorly" five or six orations of Cicero, five or six books of Virgil, and most of the Greek testament and to gain "a very superficial knowledge of part of the Hebrew Psalter." As a result, requirements for graduating were not difficult. A student could well expect to receive a degree if he attended classes, paid his fees, and behaved.[32]

College authorities still kept their young charges on a busy and regimented schedule. At Harvard students rose at dawn for morning prayers and a breakfast of bread and beer. Afterwards students studied for an hour before attending lectures from 8:00 AM until 11:00 when students broke for a lunch consisting of boiled or roasted beef or mutton, topped off with a pudding that was washed down with beer. At times, the quality of food served to students was wretched. One Harvard undergraduate was undoubtedly exaggerating when he accused the college chef of feeding students moldy bread, sour beer, "ungutted mackerel," and hasty pudding with "goats dung" in it. Some undergraduates at King's College showed their distaste for the poor quality of food by spitting in the cook's face, while in 1721 students at Yale declared a food strike that included pillaging nearby New Haven for tastier fare. Whether or not they ate their lunch, students afterwards had an hour of recreation followed by several hours of recitations in their tutor's chamber, where they were quizzed on the morning lecture or practiced their disputations. About 4:30 the college bell tolled for an afternoon snack of beer and bread. Evening prayer came at 5:00, followed by more studying until dinner at 7:30, which usually consisted of leftovers from lunch turned into a pie or goulash. After filling their stomachs, students relaxed with one another, talking and smoking, before retiring by 9:00 PM.[33]

No matter how hard college administrators tried to regulate the daily lives of their charges, teenaged boys could not be cooped up in classrooms and dorm rooms at all times studying their lessons. The colleges, which had no bowling greens, tennis courts, swimming pools, or organized sports of any kind, did not make it easy for students to find diversions from their studies. Some scholars stayed in their dorm rooms performing popular English plays, playing musical instruments, gambling, and drinking. On occasion daring students snuck girl friends and women of "ill-fame" into their chambers. Equally daring students broke college rules by skipping classes and slipping into town to attend plays, dances, and horse races; watch public whippings and hangings; visit their girl friends; or simply drink and carouse in public taverns, where they sometimes got into drunken brawls with local toughs. If caught violating school rules, students faced a variety of punishments that included having their ears "boxed" by the college president, being demoted to a lower class, losing certain privileges, and for the most egregious offenses, being expelled from the college. Authorities at King's College added a strong element of shame to this process by bringing in family, neighbors, and potential employers to watch with disappointment as the humiliated student was stripped of his robes and forced to walk out of college with head hung low. Oftentimes, however, the college readmitted students after they made a "suitable confession" and promised to reform their ways.[34]

Despite the small student enrollment in the nine colleges in colonial America, these schools served as important training grounds for leaders of American society, government, and business. The American colleges, because they attracted students from all the colonies, also served an equally important role by helping to unite Americans from all geographic regions. A curriculum that emphasized English political philosophy, law, and history during the late colonial period provided an important basis for an understanding of Americans' rights as Englishmen. In fact, King George III predicted soon after succeeding the English throne in 1760 that American colleges would prepare their students for the "just use of rational Liberty." His prediction proved to be hauntingly correct. At least 80 percent of the approximately 3,000 living graduates of colonial colleges supported and led the American cause; nearly half of the signers of the Declaration of Independence had graduated from American colleges. David Ramsay, a participant of the Revolution and later historian of that epochal event, believed that "without the advantages derived from these lights of this New World [colleges], the United States would probably have fallen in their unequal contest with Great Britain."[35]

CONCLUSION

In making an overall assessment of education in the cities, one must understand its primary purposes: to maintain social uniformity and control and to perpetuate political, economic, and social hegemony for the elites. This is reflected in the primacy of religion in education and the numerous sectarian schools established in the cities by parents to ensure that their children received the proper understanding of Christianity. Nor was education in early America intended to promote independent or critical thinking, particularly of the dominant political, economic, cultural, and religious institutions. Instead, the curriculum in schools had a strong authoritarianism designed to instill obedience to authority and prevailing traditions. Perhaps the most important of these traditions, at least among the elites, was the class structure of society. Schooling in early America therefore reaffirmed that everyone remain in their proper place in society, especially the underclass, who should not gain a superior education that would allow them to upset the status quo. No one at this time advanced the idea of educational democracy, and relatively few people considered education as a means of upward social and economic mobility. Thus educational opportunities in the cities mirrored early America's class-oriented society, with the well-to-do receiving the best education available and the middling group learning rudimentary skills in reading, writing, ciphering, and perhaps a trade, while the urban poor, for a variety of reasons out of their control, were largely confined to ignorance that made them vulnerable to lifelong exploitation by the well-to-do.

These circumstances were the product of a largely laissez-faire approach toward education and the economy. Local governments provided meager funds for the maintenance of schools, forcing most parents to pay for the education of their children. Some middling families in the cities could not even afford school tuition and supplies. And even if a school did offer to educate a limited number of poor children, the capitalist economy that forced the destitute to practice a family economy prevented poor parents from giving up the valuable labor of their children by sending them to school. In essence, the largely laissez-faire educational and capitalist economic systems in colonial America perpetuated poverty among the less fortunate and hegemony among the rich. This was the intended purpose of education by the ruling elite. Not until well into the twentieth century would greater government involvement in promoting public education and the development of a "people's capitalism" allow most American children of all social classes to receive an education intended to promote democracy, equality, and opportunity for all.

NOTES

1. Penn quoted in Clinton Rossiter, *The First American Revolution: The American Colonies on the Eve of Independence* (New York: Harcourt, Brace and Co., 1953), 194.

2. Joel Spring, *The American School, 1642–1993* (New York: McGraw-Hill, 1994), 4; Merle Curti, *The Social Ideas of American Educators* (Paterson, NJ: Pageant Books, 1959), 7.

3. John C. Miller, *The First Frontier: Life in Colonial America* (New York: Dell, 1966), 221–22; Sheldon S. Cohen, *A History of Colonial Education, 1607–1776* (New York: John Wiley & Sons, 1974), 40; Daniel Calhoun, ed., *The Educating of Americans: A Documentary History* (Boston: Houghton, Mifflin & Co., 1969), 21–22.

4. Robert Middlekauff, *Ancients and Axioms: Secondary Education in Eighteenth-Century New England* (New Haven, CT: Yale University Press, 1963), 53–54; Carl Bridenbaugh, *Cities in the Wilderness: Urban Life in America, 1625–1742* (New York: Ronald Press, 1938), 122, 281–82; Miller, *First Frontier,* 224–25; Cohen, *History of Colonial Education,* 44–47, 54.

5. Gilbert Y. Taverner, "A Portfolio of Newport Education: 1640–1840," *Newport History* 61 (1988): 98–99; Middlekauff, *Ancients and Axioms,* 60–61 (quote from p. 60); Bridenbaugh, *Cities in the Wilderness,* 123, 445.

6. Carl Kaestle, *The Evolution of an Urban School System: New York City, 1750–1850* (Cambridge, MA: Harvard University Press, 1973), 5;

Bridenbaugh, *Cities in the Wilderness*, 125 (quote); Esther Singleton, *Dutch New York* (New York: Dodd, Mead, & Co., 1909), 161 (quote).

7. Esther Singleton, *Social New York Under the Georges, 1714–1776* (New York: D. Appleton & Co., 1902), 314–15.

8. Harry G. Good and James D. Teller, *A History of American Education* (New York: Macmillan & Co., 1973), 52–53; Bridenbaugh, *Cities in the Wilderness*, 284, 446–47; Miller, *First Frontier*, 228–30; Cohen, *A History of Colonial Education*, 180–84.

9. Frederick P. Bowes, *The Culture of Early Charleston* (Chapel Hill: University of North Carolina Press, 1942), 34–53; Judith Joyner, *Beginnings: Education in Colonial South Carolina* (Columbia: McKissick Museum, 1985), 14–50; Cohen, *History of Colonial Education*, 118–19, 146–48; Carl Bridenbaugh, *Cities in Revolt: Urban Life in America, 1743–1776* (New York: Ronald Press, 1955), 374 (quote).

10. B. Edward McClellan, *Moral Education in America: Schools and the Shaping of Character from Colonial Times to the Present* (New York: Teachers College Press, 1999), 2–3; Kaestle, *Evolution of an Urban School System*, 12 (quote).

11. Curti, in Spring, *The American School, 1642–1993*, 8 (quote); Ruth Wallis Herndon and John E. Murray, "'A Proper and Instructive Education': Raising Children in Pauper Apprenticeship," in *Children Bound to Labor: The Pauper Apprentice System in Early America*, ed. Ruth Wallis Herndon and John E. Murray (Ithaca, NY: Cornell University Press, 2009), 3–17.

12. Robert F. Seybolt, *The Evening School in Colonial America* (Urbana: University of Illinois Press, 1925), 10–58.

13. Shirley Glubock, ed., *Home and Child Life in Colonial Days*, abridged from *Home Life in Colonial Days* and *Child Life in Colonial Days* by Alice Morse Earle (New York: MacMillan & Co., 1969; reprint from 1898 and 1899 editions), 132–33.

14. Gerald Gutek, *An Historical Introduction to American Education* (Prospect Heights, IL: Waveland Press, 1991), 6–7; H. Warren Button and Eugene Provenzo Jr., *A History of Education and Culture in America* (Boston: Allyn and Bacon, 1983), 25; Good and Teller, *History of American Education*, 46–53; Middlekauff, *Ancients and Axioms*, 76–84, 104–5.

15. Joyner, *Education in Colonial South Carolina*, 56 (quote); Walter J. Fraser Jr., *Patriots, Pistols and Petticoats: "Poor Sinful CharlesTown" during the American Revolution* (Columbia: University of South Carolina Press, 1993), 27 (quote); Keith Pacholl, "'Let Both Sexes Be Carefully Instructed': Educating Youth in Colonial Philadelphia," in *Children in Colonial America*, ed. James Marten (New York: New York University Press, 2007), 197 (quote); Sarah Fatherly, *Gentlewomen and Learned Ladies: Women and Elite Formation in Eighteenth-Century Philadelphia* (Bethlehem, PA: Lehigh University Press, 2008), 68–78.

16. Pacholl, "'Let Both Sexes Be Carefully Instructed,'" 200 (quote); Fatherly, *Gentlewomen and Learned Ladies*, 79–91.

17. Joyner, *Education in Colonial South Carolina*, 21–22; Singleton, *Dutch New York*, 167–68; Glubok, *Home and Child Life in Colonial Days*, 119–20; Middlekauff, *Ancients and Axioms*, 13–14.

18. Lawrence Cremin, *American Education: The Colonial Experience, 1607–1783* (New York: Harper & Row, 1970), 188–89.

19. Cohen, *History of Colonial Education*, 140; Bridenbaugh, *Cities in Revolt*, 175 (quote); Ruth B. Franklin, "Some Early Schools and Schoolmasters of Newport," *Bulletin of the Newport Historical Society* 96 (1936): 20–21.

20. Cremin, *American Education*, 539, 506 (note 26); Good and Teller, *History of American Education*, 30; Button and Provenzo, *History of Education*, 29; Seybolt, *The Evening School*, 46–53; Joyner, *Education in Colonial South Carolina*, 19–20; Kaestle, *Evolution of an Urban School System*, 6; Taverner, "A Portfolio of Newport Education," 100.

21. E. Jennifer Monaghan, "Literacy Instruction and Gender in Colonial New England," *American Quarterly* 40 (1988): 19–26; Good and Teller, *History of American Education*, 31; Singleton, *Dutch New York*, 171; Cohen, *History of Colonial Education*, 61–63.

22. Glubock, *Home and Child Life in Colonial Days*, 132.

23. Good and Teller, *History of American Education*, 65; Calhoun, *The Educating of Americans*, 30; Singleton, *Dutch New York*, 169.

24. Calhoun, *The Educating of Americans*, 29–30, 37 (quote); Good and Teller, *History of American Education*, 65.

25. R. Freeman Butts and Lawrence Cremin, *A History of Education in American Culture* (New York: Holt, Rhinehart & Winston, 1953), 124.

26. Meyer Reinhold, "The Quest for 'Useful Knowledge' in Eighteenth-Century America," *Proceedings of the American Philosophical Society* 119 (1975): 116.

27. Sharon B. Sundue, "Industrious in Their Stations: Young People at Work in Boston, Philadelphia and Charleston, 1735–1785," Ph.D. dissertation, Harvard University, 2001), 131–39.

28. Sundue, "Industrious in Their Stations," 10; Sharon B. Sundue, "Confining the Poor to Ignorance?: Eighteenth-Century American Experiments with Charity," *History of Education Quarterly* 47 (2007): 130–47 (quotes on pp. 137, 146–47, 127); Cohen, *History of Colonial Education*, 164–65; Kaestle, *Evolution of an Urban School System*, 3.

29. Kaestle, *Evolution of an Urban School System*, 14–16.

30. Samuel E. Morison, *Harvard College in the Seventeenth Century* (Cambridge, MA: Harvard University Press, 1936), 447–52; Samuel E. Morison, *Three Centuries of Harvard, 1636–1936* (Cambridge, MA: Harvard University Press, 1936), 103.

31. Morison, *Three Centuries of Harvard*, 106–7; Morison, *Harvard College in the Seventeenth Century*, 463, 109, 29 (quote); Edward P. Cheney, *History of the University of Pennsylvania, 1740–1940* (Philadelphia: University of Pennsylvania Press, 1940), 95.

32. Richard Warch, *School of the Prophets: Yale College, 1701–1740* (New Haven, CT: Yale University Press), 192–94; Cremin, *American Education*, 214; Good and Teller, *History of American Education*, 59 (quote); Cheney, *History of the University of Pennsylvania*, 82–83.

33. Cremin, *American Education*, 214; Morison, *Three Centuries of Harvard*, 28, 117 (quote); Cohen, *History of Colonial Education*, 64 (quote); Warch, *School of the Prophets*, 259.

34. Cohen, *A History of Colonial Education*, 100; Morison, *Three Centuries of Harvard*, 29, 107, 61–63, 114–16; Morison, *Harvard College in the Seventeenth Century*, 452–65; Warch, *School of the Prophets*, 263.

35. Cremin, *American Education*, 468.

7

Crime and Punishment

INTRODUCTION

An unfortunate yet inescapable part of the daily experience for residents of cities was crime and civil disturbance. Criminal activity such as murder, rape, arson, theft, prostitution, assault, public intoxication, and civil disturbances such as Sabbath-breaking were more prevalent in the relatively densely populated and commercial urban centers where wealth was more conspicuous and unevenly distributed, where social structures were more complex and heterogeneous, where populations were more fluid, and where English authorities sent thousands of criminals to relieve their overcrowded jails. A weak law enforcement system in all the colonies made up of either unsalaried or low-paid amateurs further contributed to breakdowns in law and order in the cities.

By the early eighteenth century, the major urban centers were rife with criminal activity—or so lamented preachers and public servants. Thugs and thieves lurked in unlit streets at night waiting to rob an unsuspecting passerby, pickpockets worked their nimble fingers in the crowded public markets, scandalously dressed "streetwalkers" enticed men into illicit carnal behavior, burglars broke into homes of the wealthy to rob them of their valuables, sailors and local toughs fought each other in drunken brawls in waterfront taverns, rapists accosted women in back alleys, arsonists tossed torches onto houses, husbands beat and killed their wives, young mothers murdered their bastard children, and riotous mobs sprung up to attack houses of ill repute, British press gangs, and other perceived threats to the community.

Contributing to the brutal element of urban life were the public forms of corporal punishment administered to many convicted criminals: bloody whippings, bodily mutilation, and gruesome executions. However, an elitist judicial system ensured that only lower-class criminals received corporal punishment. The upper class also created and administered laws against women and slaves that reflected their inferior and subordinate status. As much as to deter criminal activity, early American law was a weapon designed and used by the upper class to maintain social control, protect their property, affirm their hegemony, and reinforce the traditional social structure.

VIOLENT CRIME

Physical violence was an everyday part of life for most colonists. It was impossible, in fact, for residents of the five major cities to escape the violence that surrounded them. Through the thin walls of their homes they could hear slaveowners whipping their bondsmen, masters abusing their servants and apprentices, husbands hitting their wives, and mothers beating their children. While shopping for groceries in the public market, urban residents could watch criminals being executed, whipped, mutilated, or assaulted with rocks, rotten vegetables, and animal excrement. Much of this physical violence was sanctioned by law. People holding positions of authority, whether they were masters, husbands, mothers, or state officials, had the right, even the legal obligation, to correct those under their control, even with the use of corporal punishment if necessary. Much of this socially accepted abuse was inflicted on the dependent and lower groups in society: slaves, servants, apprentices, women, and children. As long as this punishment did not go beyond accepted norms and thus devolve into what contemporaries determined was physical abuse, few people complained to the local authorities. Early Americans were therefore quite callous and tolerant toward the enormous amount of physical abuse and violence that surrounded them.

Homicide

The most heinous crime of all, although the least frequently committed, was homicide. Less than 5 percent of all cases that came before the city courts during the 1700s involved murder. Still, homicide rates were relatively high in the colonial American seaports in comparison with English urban centers. Philadelphia, for example, had a murder rate (about 7 per 100,000) that was 2.5 times higher than that in congested and crime-ridden London between 1720 and 1780. Holding the ignoble distinction as the murder capital of North America was Charles Town, which had a homicide rate in the late colonial period more than twice that of Philadelphia (or approximately 15 per 100,000). Murder rates in colonial Boston and New York City fell somewhere between these two extremes. Murder rates aside, few murderers lurked in the streets preying on unsuspecting victims. Murder was more often an act of passion between family members, relatives, and neighbors than an act of opportunity among strangers. Most murder victims knew their assailants; approximately half of them were killed by a relative.[1]

Domestic violence accounted for a large number of these familial homicides, with the home being the most common location for murders. Jeremiah Meacham of Newport butchered his wife and sister with an axe before setting his house on fire. One Philadelphia man systematically tortured his young daughter on a daily basis by smashing her with his fists and burning her with hot objects, sadistic behavior that eventually led to the girl's death. While in an uncontrollable rage, another Philadelphia man killed his wife, and then murdered his two children by smashing their heads with a rock. One enraged Boston husband slit his wife's throat. Another man beat his wife for refusing his demands to give him the money she had made recaning chairs. After shattering her skull with a hammer, he stripped her naked and placed her in bed with their two young children, one of whom was later found by neighbors eating a piece of bread sopped in his mother's blood. Mental illness caused some men to go berserk, as in the case of a Boston banker who gouged out his wife's eyes with a stick and left her in a forest several miles from town. Spiritual insanity provoked a German Reformed minister from Pennsylvania to stab to death a parishioner during a church service while exclaiming, "My savior did it . . . I will die free now and go to my Jesus." One husband from Charles Town, maddened by jealousy, shot his wife as she slept. One Boston man murdered his 27-year-old son for simply "taunting him."[2]

Other homicides were the result of everyday-life encounters outside the home. Robbery was a common motive in some of these murders. A Philadelphia man, for example, was robbed and shot to death by a footpad as he was leaving the city. In a more comedic anecdote, one Boston girl managed to turn the tables on her would-be robber, a handicapped man, by snatching his cane from him and then using it to beat him to death. A dispute between two men in Boston over ownership of a pig led one of the men to kill the other with a hoe. A depressed businessman from Philadelphia vowed to kill the first person he met on August 30, 1765. Encountering a 12-year-old boy, the businessmen cut his throat and watched impassively as the boy bled to death. Alcohol contributed to some murders, particularly between sailors and local thugs, who all too often killed each other in drunken brawls. Occasionally alcohol even contributed to deadly fights between friends, as when one drunken man killed his best friend over a game of cribbage. Just as ridiculous, at least to modern sensibilities, were men who killed each other in "affairs of honor." Incidents of duels abound, but illustrative is the 1715 case of an Anglican minister from Philadelphia who killed a local man in a duel for having "basely slandered a gentlewoman."[3]

As the above anecdotes suggest, men committed nearly 90 percent of all murders, and most of their victims were other adults. On the rare occasion women murdered, they almost always took the life of their newborn child. In Boston, 84 percent of women accused of murder were tried for infanticide. Nearly all of these cases involved young mothers trying to conceal an illegitimate birth. Because the church condemned bastardy as a sin and English law declared extramarital sex a criminal act, mothers murdered their bastard children for fear of bringing both shame and physical punishment to themselves or to avoid losing their "good character," which for a lower-class woman meant financial ruin and poverty. Such fear motivated these women to kill their newborn children by drowning them, slitting their throats, breaking their necks, crushing their skulls, and then unceremoniously dumping their small, lifeless bodies into wells, privies, dung heaps, trunks, coalbins, haystacks, and nearby ponds and rivers. In 1768 the *Pennsylvania Gazette* carried the news that a dead infant "was taken out of the Brickkiln Pond, in the Northern Liberties of this City [Philadelphia], tied up in a bag."[4]

> A moſt unhappy murder was committed in this Town on Friday the 3d Inſtant, by a Mother upon her own Child, an Infant Son of about Eight Months old, we are told, ſhe firſt cut its Wine-pipe, and afterwards its Head almoſt off. The Mother has been for ſome Time Diſtracted, and is committed to Goal, but inſenſible of the barbarous Action.

Newspaper Report of Infanticide. This notice from the November 8, 1732, issue of the *Rhode Island Gazette* gruesomely describes an incident of infanticide in Newport.

Assault

The colonists' callous and cavalier attitude toward physical violence partly explains why assaults comprised 33 percent, 40 percent, and nearly 50 percent of all criminal charges in New York City, Philadelphia, and Charles Town, respectively. Such figures can be misleading as the vast majority of reported assaults occurred in a small part of each city—poor neighborhoods and the waterfront district—and to a specific group of people—law enforcement officials and poor folk. In Philadelphia, for example, approximately 65 percent of all assault cases involved attacks upon local officials: sheriffs, tax collectors, and especially lower-class constables charged with policing the streets. Evidently there was a considerable amount of contempt held toward government officials, particularly among the poor, single men who were charged with 90 percent of such assaults. Perhaps not so coincidentally, poor, single men comprised the other significant group of assault victims. Testosterone and alcohol likely drove much of this violence among unruly or drunken soldiers, sailors, and local rowdies who beat up each other on a daily basis. Women, on the other hand, were targets of assault in only 15 percent of all cases, at least in Philadelphia. Like today, many assaults against women went unreported. When women did report assaults against them, they usually charged husbands and live-in lovers with beating them. Typical is one New Amsterdam husband who was hauled into court for hitting his wife with an iron crowbar "so that she lay three days bedridden from the pain."[5]

Although men were most often the abusers in assault cases, women who were adequately provoked could be just as violent. Their victims were those closest at hand—husbands, children, servants, and slaves. In part to preserve patriarchy, male authorities aggressively prosecuted violent women, who in Philadelphia faced the unusually high conviction rate of over 70 percent. This did not deter one woman from "beating and reviling her husband" and encouraging her children to help by "knocking him in the head." Perhaps the husband made an uncomplimentary comment about his wife's cooking because during the assault she expressed hope that he would choke to death on his food. Infidelity compelled a New York City woman, with the help of several of her slaves, to viciously beat her husband's mistress with a broomstick and sexually violate her with the handle of a saucepan. Other women sought to end their husbands' philandering by simply castrating them.[6]

Rape

Arguably the most heinous assaults involved rape, which occurred both in the home and in the streets and sometimes ended with murder. The extent of rape during the colonial period, as today, is impossible to determine as many sexual assault victims never publicly accused their attackers. Doing so proved to be risky business if a judge or jury concluded that sexual intercourse had not been forced, a decision that implied that the woman had consented to fornication and therefore was sexually immoral. Lack of corroborative evidence and lack of agreement on what constituted rape also encouraged silence among sexual assault victims who, in the case of a trial, faced male lawyers, judges, and jurors. It is therefore no surprise that court records reveal a low number of rape cases and convictions, especially in the Southern colonies. One study of North Carolina found only nine reported cases of rape in the entire colony before 1776, none of which resulted in conviction of the accused. By searching beyond court records, however, historian Sharon Block recently has uncovered nearly a thousand acts of sexual coercion in early America, evidence suggesting to her at least that most early Americans had "heard about, read about or had some experience with sexual assault in their lives." Her findings reveal that although servants, slaves, and women of "loose morals" were the most likely victims of rape, women of distinction, the mentally retarded, and even young girls were targets of sexual attacks. In one Pennsylvania county, for example, one in five rape cases before 1800 involved the rape of a child under the age of 13. Young rape victims suffered severe physical injuries from sexual assaults. One five-year-old victim bled internally for three weeks after the attack, while a rape so injured a three-year-old girl that a newspaper reported that "her life is despaired of." The emotional toll of rape was just as harmful as it carried such a heavy social stigma in early America that some women, while being sexually assaulted, begged their assailants to kill them.[7]

Despite the physical and emotional trauma of rape, authorities did not consider it a particularly offensive crime, especially if committed against African Americans, servants, Native Americans, and "loose women." The most likely victims of rape were powerless women because "no one would come to their aid," explain historians Jack Marietta and G. S. Rowe, "and because no one would come to their aid, they were apt victims." Most rapes of black women, for example, did not even make it to the courts, and those that did were ignored. Female servants were also raped with impunity, often by their well-to-do masters, with the rapist often being punished with a slap on the wrist. When authorities brought a Pennsylvania man before the court for sexually assaulting his maidservant on several occasions, the judge "had his laugh over the affair" and let the man go after he promised "to do better in the future." The Superior Court of Massachusetts, additionally, never tried men for raping their own servants despite the notoriously widespread practice of masters sexually exploiting their female servants. Men also had little fear of legal repercussions when raping Native American women. James Brown of Pennsylvania evidently had no fear of prosecution when in 1722 he violently beat and raped a "Squaw" in a field as several other Indian women watched in horror. For placing a woman of "loose morals" in the stocks against her will, one Boston night in 1648, and proceeding to "take her in a violent manner," John Robinson received a measly fine of 10 shillings—less than it would have cost him if he had visited a prostitute! Nor did men have much to fear from the courts for raping children, at least not a Philadelphia Quaker who received a month's imprisonment, a fine of £10, and a day in the pillory for raping a four-year-old girl in 1750. The courts showed leniency toward rapists because colonial society did not view females, even young girls, as entirely blameless in sexual matters as they were instilled from a young age with a responsibility for controlling both their own and men's sexuality. Early American society also viewed women as sexual temptresses whose alleged lustful nature only added to their culpability in sexual relations. Victims of rape who went to the authorities were therefore just as likely to be implicated in criminal proceedings as their attackers. When authorities prosecuted alleged rapists, they overwhelmingly targeted defendants of low social standing while overlooking sexual exploitation by wealthy masters against their lower class female servants. In taking a class approach toward the prosecution of rape, well-to-do officials sought to "protect their women against harm by servants, transients, and laborers," explains Thomas Foster, because rape committed by "such men was an attack on the authority of patriarchs as a whole."[8]

Theft

Theft was even more prevalent than assault in the five major seaports, from 30 percent of cases in Charles Town to nearly 50 percent in New York City. The five cities, with their conspicuous wealth, equally conspicuous poor and servant/slave classes, and numerous criminals sent over by the mother country, created a breeding ground for thieves, approximately three-fourths of them men. The urban economy, which contributed to rising poverty rates in the eighteenth century, also contributed significantly to theft in the cities. An overwhelming majority of people charged with theft were desperately poor folk who purloined goods for survival. Dishonest people and kleptomaniacs simply looking for an easier way to make a living constituted the remaining source of urban thefts. At times thieves organized themselves loosely into gangs to better coordinate their illegal activities, with each member having a specific task according to his or her ability. One female gang member served an important role through her ability "to go up and down a Chimney very dextrously." When a sudden rise in thefts occurred in a city, local newspapers were quick to warn the public. The Charles Town *City Gazette* solemnly advised its readers in 1788 to arm themselves against robbers: "Be on your guard, and carry with you a heavy loaded whip, and a well charged faithful pistol." Peter Sanders failed to heed this advice and was therefore unable to defend himself from two highwaymen who "knocked him off his horse and turn'd his pockets out, but finding no Booty there, beat him unmercifully."[9]

Encouraging larceny were country peddlers and city tavern owners who acted as middlemen in the disposal of stolen goods. In procuring such valuables, thieves often targeted the homes of the wealthy, along with warehouses, retail shops, and on occasion even houses of worship. In 1714 a gang of gallows birds broke into New York City's Trinity Church and walked out with the silver communion service and several other articles of value. Less sacrilegious robbers rustled the sheep, pigs, and goats that roamed freely in the streets. Some diabolical thieves committed two crimes at once by deliberately starting fires to cause a public distraction while they stole goods from their neighbors. The crowds at urban fires, as well as those at the local markets and executions, also attracted pickpockets. Often these were impoverished children with nimble fingers and quick feet who worked for cheats who taught them this artful form of theft. Pickpocketing was also a popular form of theft among some clever yet disreputable women who used sex to steal. Illustrative is Gillian Knight of Boston, who was convicted of "Enticing Daniel Herring to her house & there Embracing him pick'ed his pocket." Even more subtle and clever than pickpockets were the confidence men who, through wit, charm, and forged letters of introduction, often succeeded in getting the local aristocracy to "donate" to them money for some nonexistent humanitarian scheme they were allegedly operating. Equally naïve were those taken by fortune tellers, palm readers, and card sharks that operat ed on the streets.[10]

Indebtedness

A form of theft was failure to pay one's financial debts, a circumstance common during economic slowdowns. Some debtors sought to avoid jail by bargaining with their creditors. Samuel Ward of Rhode Island, for example, often allowed those in his debt to either work them off by performing various services for him or required them to bind out their children, break up housekeeping, and work for him by the year until they paid off the debt with interest. Less generous creditors simply allowed those in their debt to go to jail, where their chances of paying their arrears became almost nonexistent and where they became an additional financial burden to the local government. To lessen such an expense, Rhode Island officials required plaintiffs to pay a jailer four shillings six pence a week toward the support of an imprisoned debtor. Many colonies also granted debtors "liberty of the yard" so that they could work in town to compensate their creditors. Still, debtors could languish in jail for years, as did Joseph Fox of Newport, who was confined for two years before he was finally granted a lottery to help finance his release. A letter written by one debtor from a Newport jail to his creditor reveals the bleak position of many debtors:

If you will resolve in your mind my unhappy circumstances of being confined absent from business, from my Wife who lys in, in the midst of winter, & who has no assistance, but on the contrary surrounded with four small children altogether will suffer for whant of my presence, surely from the principals off compassion which I never thought you destitute of, you will give some orders for my relief as to the money or givieing you any Security for it at present is impossible for me to do.[11]

MORAL/SEXUAL OFFENSES

Prostitution

Much more than rural areas, the major seaports were also lusty and seamy places with numerous opportunities to engage in various kinds of activities contemporaries deemed immoral. Prostitution, fornication (sex before marriage), drunkenness, gambling, and profanity/slander were some of the most frequent violations of criminal laws. The scores of brothels and taverns (which often doubled as houses of ill repute) throughout the cities provided ample opportunities for both men and women to engage in drunken debauchery. The prevalence of sailors and foreign merchants and tradesmen in the seaports accounts for much but not all of the steady demand for "ladies of pleasure." Even respectable men consorted with harlots, usually women of low and desperate means, who advertised their services in homes, taverns, brothels, and streets, where they sometimes brazenly flashed their bare breasts to men walking by. One "Little Prude of Pleasure" in Boston kept a house frequented by lawyers, merchants, military officers, and other "gentlemen." Some "pleasure girls" even attracted teenaged sons of the gentry class. One young scion of a Philadelphia merchant gave a woman the astronomical sum of £50 to just "strip Stark naked before him." So many boys in Boston were visiting prostitutes by 1713 that town leaders compiled a "catalogue of young men" who frequented "wicked houses" and presented the information to the local "Society of the Suppression of Disorders" with instructions to admonish the erring youth.[12]

On occasion town moralists strongly protested commercialized vice and made efforts to stem its growth, even publicly whipping and banishing known prostitutes. But as the five towns grew more populous and commercialized and attracted numerous seamen, tradesmen, and foreign merchants, city leaders had greater difficulty controlling the sexual behavior of their inhabitants. Cotton Mather complained in 1713 that there were so many brothels in Boston frequented by "extremely Impudent" men and women of "debauched Character" that he sadly concluded that this "social evil [prostitution] had come to stay." By the mid-eighteenth century, if not sooner, authorities in the cities essentially gave up attempts to curb prostitution. Philadelphia's Mayor's Court, for example, records only three women prosecuted for prostitution between 1759 and 1776. At times private citizens took matters into their own hands to enforce vice laws, as in New York City when a mob of boys in 1754 chased a "pocky whore" through the streets, throwing sticks and stones at the terrified woman while a crowd of spectators cried "Mob the Whore." Except for such rare cases of "street justice," prostitution during the eighteenth century became a common and accepted part of daily life in the seaport communities.[13]

Fornication and Bastardy

Crimes similar to that of prostitution included fornication and adultery. Fornication generally involved premarital sex between committed couples. This illicit behavior was most often discovered when a child was born to a married couple prior to the expiration of the expected number of weeks from the date of marriage. Other cases of fornication were simply discovered by nosy neighbors engaging in "holy watching," like Clement Coldham of Boston, who "hearing that John Pearce was accustomed to take widow Stanard to his house at night and she was seen to go away in the morning, [he] went to Pearce's house and looked in at the window." No matter how such acts were discovered, sex between unmarried couples was a common occurrence in early America. Much of this activity occurred among curious teenagers and servants. One male servant from Boston was caught and punished for behaving "lasciviously" with several servant girls, while another even managed to seduce his master's daughter. Sometimes this illicit sexual conduct crossed over into the incestuous, as in the case of a Boston woman who was convicted of repeatedly fornicating with her 76- year-old father.[14]

Town officials early in the colonial period made a determined effort to curtail fornication and bastardy, particularly in Puritan Boston, where 14 percent of all criminal cases before 1700 involved fornication. Most fornicators received either a fine, a public whipping, or both. As a rule, the court punished both offending parties, but in the case of women, justices justified corporal punishment because contemporaries generally believed it was up to women to exercise self-control and restrain men from going beyond acceptable sexual boundaries. This explains why Hannah Bumpas of

Boston also received a bloody lashing in 1662 "for yielding to him [Thomas Bird] and not making such resistance against him as shee ought." In doling out such harsh punishment, local authorities were equally concerned with the financial expense to the city arising from unwed mothers requiring public assistance to care for their bastard children. By the 1750s the public expense of bastardy was so great in Boston that selectmen there began binding out for five years any woman bearing a bastard, specifically targeting poor women who could not financially support themselves and their child. Over time, bastardy and fornication became less of a concern to law enforcement officials, even in Boston, where authorities increasingly realized that prosecuting vice was a losing battle.[15]

Drunkenness

One vice that law enforcement officials never successfully battled was that against public drunkenness. Not only did alcohol abuse contribute to violence and debauchery, it also added to the public debt. There were many men who "spend much of their time and Money at Taverns," Rhode Island officials explained in 1721, "which tends to the utter Ruin of themselves, but also exposes their Families to Penury and Misery, and brings considerable Charges upon the Towns to which they respectively belong." To discourage such scenarios, local governments passed numerous laws against public intoxication and punished offenders with either a fine, public whipping, or public humiliation. Still, drunks stumbling through city streets, urinating in them or passing out on them, were an all-too common scene in the colonial seaports. Boston officials went so far as to post lists of drunkards in taverns and instructed tavern owners not to serve those on the list. Sailors, who followed the universal practice of heading to the nearest tavern after disembarking from their ships, were particularly prone to heavy drinking and all too often committed "many & great miscarriages" in their inebriated condition. Nearly as abusive of alcohol were teenagers, who easily managed to obtain strong liquor from either their own households or from tavern keepers by "pretending to come in the name of [a] sick person." With alcohol in hand, young people would, in the words of one Boston court, "take liberty to walke & sporte themselves in the streets or fields . . . to the dishonor of God and the disturbance of others in their religious exercises." Yet adults were just as prone to alcohol abuse. One minister in New Amsterdam complained in 1648 that all 170 members of his congregation were more concerned with getting drunk than learning and practicing the word of God. Excessive alcohol consumption was just as common in Philadelphia, where the local grand jury complained in 1748 that the large number of taverns in the city was the main culprit for the "profane oaths and imprecations grown of so late common in our streets."[16]

PROFANITY AND SLANDER

Indeed, residents of the five seaports were daily bombarded with the din of profanity and slander—both crimes in early America. Many sailors lived up to their reputations as notorious swearers by speaking "vile and opprobrious" epithets in public. Nearly as notorious were slaves whose proclivity for profanity greatly offended the sensitive ears of the local gentry. Some swearers were simply insane and stood on street corners shouting "offensive and scandalous speeches" at pedestrians as they walked by. Even houses of God could ring with profanity, as when some young Lutherans in Philadelphia "poured out English curses" upon the deacons who were seeking to curb disorders during religious services.[17]

Nearly as common as profanity in the cities was slander. Because personal reputation was important to one's standing in the community and even to one's livelihood, people did not hesitate to file suits against those who disparaged their name. "A good name is better than precious ointment," stated a 1647 Rhode Island statute, "and slanderers are worse than dead flies to corrupt and alter the savour thereof." To protect their good name, colonists took slanderers to court over such name-calling as "a filthy old Baud," "old filthy baggage," "privateer dogs," "witch," "whore," "cheating rogue," "beastly rascal," "base lying carrion," "one-eyed dog," "that one-eyed son of a bitch," and "a plague to the town," just to cite a few choice examples.

Slander and malicious gossip were particularly identified with women. Because women had little official authority, their use of slander was "perhaps the most valuable and reliable means of advancing or protecting their own interests," argues historian Mary Beth Norton. Profanity and slander among women was so great in Philadelphia that the local grand jury beseeched authorities to build a ducking stool and prison to punish "scolding drunken women" who it said had become a "public nuisance." Massachusetts officials in 1636 quieted one Elizabeth Applegate by requiring her to "stand with her tongue in a Cleft stick for swearing, railing and reviling."[18]

THE following Affidavit, is intended to fhew with how little Truth it hath been reported, in order to injure my Reputation, that I have wronged *Robert Atkins* out of Seventeen Half Crowns, that were due to him for Wages.

JOHN MORIN SCOTT.

City of } fs. ROBERT ATKINS, of the City of New-
NEW-YORK, York, Labourer, being duly fworn, depofeth and faith, That he hath frequently been employed by Mr. Scott, and that his Wages have been always duly paid him, without any Deduction whatfoever; and that every Report, that Mr. Scott hath detained from this Deponent any Sum, that was juftly due to him, is fcandaloufly Falfe. And further this Deponent faith not.   ROBERT ATKINS.

Sworn this 9th January, 1769,
    Before me, ANDREW GAUTIER.

Antislander Notice. The above notice in the January, 1769, issue of the *New York Gazette* illustrates the importance urban businessmen attached to their reputation in the community. In an attempt to preserve his reputation and his business, Robert Atkins of New York City publicly denounced the rumor that he shortchanged a worker of his rightful wages.

Authorities in all the colonies also silenced critics of the government with laws that punished anyone speaking "slightlingly or carry themselves abusively against any magistrate or person in office." Officials in Boston were so upset with Philip Ratliff's libelous "speeches against the government" in 1631 that they ordered him "to be whipped, have his ears cut off, fined forty pounds, and banished out of the limits of this jurisdiction." Nor did leaders in the Puritan capital tolerate criticism of ministers. Jonathan Sprague, for example, received 30 lashes in 1674 for simply "reproaching" the minister. "You believe the scriptures to be God's word," the Boston court told the defendant, "how dare you then revile Magistrates and ministers[?]" Officials in Newport jailed John Martin because he had "grossly and scandalously slandered and abused [the] Honorable assembly." Equally intolerant of free speech were officials in Philadelphia, who in 1699 fined Henry Barnes 30 shillings for saying he "cared no more for constables nor justices than the dirt under his feet" and assemblymen William Biles the astronomical sum of £300 in 1706 for urging his legislative colleagues to "kick out" 28-year-old Governor John Evans who he claimed was "but a boy" and "not fit to Govern us." Officials in New Amsterdam went so far as to banish from the colony the worst critics of government.[19]

As governments became more stable, however, prosecutions for seditious speech that did not immediately threaten the government declined. Further allowing Americans to experience a broader liberty to criticize their government and its officials was the landmark trial of New York City printer John Peter Zenger, who in 1735 received an acquittal from the jury for publishing defamatory, yet truthful, editorials against the policies of New York governor William Cosby. This case established the precedent that a statement, even if defamatory, is not libelous if it can be proved. By doing so, it emboldened editors to criticize officials more freely.

JUVENILE DELINQUENCY

More of a nuisance than a threat to social order were the numerous unsupervised teenagers who loitered the city streets. Many of these youths were runaways from the countryside while others were unattached immigrants from Europe. Most lacked marketable skills and were often underemployed. With time on their hands and little adult supervision, many youths succumbed to the corrupting influences of urban society. During the day these adolescents loitered on street corners cursing and frightening respectable citizens; at night they hung out at taverns, where they consumed "liquid courage" that only encouraged them to engage in illicit and uncivil behavior. Some of these youths stole to survive; others robbed for fun. Some girls gave themselves freely to their male peers while more desperate ones sold their bodies. Other adolescents enjoyed playing pranks on unsuspecting residents. Placing greasy feathers at the doorsteps of homes and then knocking on the front door before running away was fun for those fleet of foot. Others enjoyed throwing sundry objects and shooting fireworks at pedestrians and animals, or tying burning straw to a horse's tail in hopes of making it bolt with its rider still on. Some pranksters evolved into vandals, destroying water pumps, ruining wells, stealing fire buckets, defacing church property, and throwing rocks and sea shells through windows and at street lamps. If caught, the courts might indenture delinquents to responsible families or, for those older than 14, administer fines, whippings, and imprisonment.[20]

MOBS AND RIOTS

Juvenile delinquency was a minor nuisance compared with the violence and disorder caused by the mobs and riots that occasionally erupted in the seaport communities. Much more than rural towns, the five major cities included rowdy elements such as sailors on shore leave, unsupervised teenagers, unemployed and disgruntled workmen, hoodlums, and numerous poor with no real political voice. Although these groups were sometimes quick to rise up and disturb the peace, most mobs did not engage in mindless mayhem. They had specific and limited purposes—to either right perceived wrongs or to enforce laws not otherwise enforceable. This was the case in Boston and Newport when moral crusaders there occasionally tore down local brothels and ran the prostitutes from town. Fear drove some residents of Newport to organize in 1775 to prevent patients with smallpox from leaving the offshore hospital and entering the town. Hunger drove the poor of Boston to organize and prevent merchants from exporting grain from the city during bread shortages in 1710, 1713, and 1729. The poor in Philadelphia also rioted through the streets in 1738 when local officials passed a law forbidding people from placing fish weirs in the Schyulkill River, a common means by which the poor obtained their fish. Many common folk were just as violently protective of their right to cheap alcohol. When customs officials in Newport sought to enforce the trade laws against the importation of cheap foreign rum, local rabble, undoubtedly lubricated with liquor, mobbed the customs officers and beat informers and naval personnel. Outraged mobs also viciously attacked British press gangs that occasionally sailed into colonial ports to impress local men into the royal navy, violent confrontations that sometimes left men dead. During the politically charged years preceding the American Revolution, trained mobs in the five cities looted homes of governing officials, chased stamp officers from town, hung effigies of British political leaders, and harassed shopkeepers suspecting of violating the embargo of British goods by coating their shops with animal dung.[21]

TRIALS

Trials for the prosecution of alleged criminal activity in early America were far from the calm, formal halls of justice of today. Colonial courtrooms were often noisy, bustling places with people in the back talking, others arriving late or stumbling in drunk, and judges even leaving the bench in the middle of arguments to either get drinks or relieve themselves. The fact that justices often held court in local taverns, partly because of their large space for spectators and easy access to liquid refreshments, undoubtedly contributed to the lack of decorum in colonial trials. The consumption of alcohol may have contributed to those instances when the convicted showed displeasure with their sentence by cursing judges, throwing liquor in their faces, and even drawing knives on them. It also makes one wonder how many people's fates were sealed in the cloudy judgment of inebriation.[22]

The informal nature of colonial trials aside, early Americans charged with a crime had a number of procedural rights under English common law that were intended to promote justice: the right to reasonable bail, the right to know the charges, the right to challenge jurors, the right to compel the appearance of witnesses for the defense, the right to confront accusers, the right to appeal, the right to equal protection of the law, and the right to a trial by jury. Despite these rights, receiving a fair trial, at least by modern standards, was nearly impossible, especially for those lacking considerable wealth. Inquisitorial justices of the peace, for example, acted as anything but an impartial moderator by assembling the evidence against the accused, prosecuting the case by interrogating both the defendant and all witnesses, rendering a judgment, and passing sentence. Until the early 1700s, English law additionally prevented the accused from having a lawyer, who, in any event, charged such high fees that only the richest men could afford their services. Most did not even have a jury to plead their case to because colonial judges often had an impossible time rounding up enough men willing to serve as jurors. One New Yorker told a sheriff summoning him to serve as a juror that the judge "might Kiss His Ass." Further discouraging jury trials is that defendants in criminal cases paid the allowances for jurors, along with filing papers, having summonses issued, getting the verdict officially recorded, and reimbursing witnesses. Rhode Island officials in 1698 furthered judicial elitism throughout the colony by doubling the court fees in all cases dealing with settlements under 40 shillings. Such a system clearly worked against the poor, who could not afford to be a party in civil suits on either side. "That alone must have made them subject to considerable intimidation from more well-to-do colonists in many aspects of everyday life," explains historian Larry Eldridge.[23]

This was certainly the case concerning the inquisitorial and intimidating nature of colonial trials that were designed to be just that, a "trial" for the accused. To be a defendant drawn into the colonial criminal justice system was, in the words of one New Hampshire official, to be "ground as copper between two mill-stones." The millstones in the courtroom were upper-class justices who, lacking recourse to modern forensic evidence to prove a case, focused intently upon securing a confession of the accused by aggressively badgering a defendant with either fear of damnation or promise of leniency. Forcing a conviction was crucial to the legal system, which placed a high premium on deference and submission to authority, an authority monopolized by the well-to-do. The dramatic elements of the sentencing process itself were intended to impress upon the community that it was upper-class officials who were in charge, thereby reinforcing the social hierarchy. The judicial system was therefore another tool local elites used to both establish and confirm their hegemony.[24]

LAW ENFORCEMENT OFFICIALS

While upper-class justices used the courts to maintain their hegemony, it was poorly paid, part-time constables and night watch-men conscripted by raffle who did the difficult and dangerous job of pursuing and apprehending murderers, burglars, and peace-breakers, suppressing fights and brawls, and removing from the streets drunkards, vagrants, and prostitutes. For these reasons, well-to-do men dodged this draft by either paying the fine for not answer-ing the call to serve the public or hiring a substitute to serve in his place, usually someone desperately poor. As a result, the dangers and burdens of protecting urban residents from crime fell on lower-class men who generally garnered little respect from local residents. One Newport man told a constable who was issuing him a warrant that he cared "not a fart [or] turd for all their warrants." When a constable guarding an entrance to New Amsterdam asked an approach-ing merchant what he wanted, the tradesmen crudely replied, "lick my Ass." Local hoodlums and sailors, in particular, made a sport out of beating up the night watchmen. Making the office of constable and night watchmen even less desirable were the fines and punish-ments imposed on these officers if they exceeded their authority or failed to exercise it. Caught in an almost no-win situation and con-fronted with almost constant violence, it is no wonder that these ama-teur peace officers sometimes slept on the job or found sanctuary in a favorite tavern, brothel, or friend's house. It also explains why crimi-nal activity was relatively rampant in the five cities.[25]

PUNISHMENT

Once the magistrate or jury convicted an offender, the court decided, within limits prescribed by statute or common law, what sort of punishment was appropriate. The court, for example, might punish the convicted with a whipping, branding, fine, servitude, banishment, exposure to public scorn, or execution. City officials turned much of this punishment into a public affair, sometimes even encouraging collective action in punishing criminals. Unlike today's criminal justice system, the punishment of criminals in early America was often a community event. At the same time, the court might decide to reprieve, suspend, or pardon the convicted, especially if he had made a humble and sincere confession of sin or error. One Boston man in 1643 successfully begged forgiveness from his minister for publicly pronouncing that he would rather "hear a dog bark as to hear master Cobbett Preach."[26] Such leniency was rare, however, especially if one belonged to the lower class. Far from being either blind or balanced, "justice" differed in colonial America depending on one's class, race, and gender. Ultimately, the upper class, who controlled the judicial system, used it as an effective weapon to keep the underclass and dependents in their place while protecting their own economic wealth and authority.

INCARCERATION

Jails in the five cities were little used for either punishing or correcting criminals; instead, most of the prisoners were there to await trial. Rarely did the courts hand down lengthy jail sentences to criminals because colonists were loath to pay the cost of feeding and guarding them, and few people believed that a jail term would have a deterrent effect. In Boston, for example, the courts imposed imprisonment in only 4.3 percent of the total number of criminal cases. As it turned out, severely limiting the incarceration of criminals proved to be a humanitarian act by the courts, albeit an unintentional one. Conditions in the urban jails, many of which were crude make-shifts, were anything but humane by modern standards. Upon entering jail, inmates received a whipping to ensure that they obeyed prison rules. As prisons were often used as workhouses, inmates were put to work processing hemp and flax or performing other useful tasks to help make the facility self-supporting. In return for their work, prisoners received meager rations of bread and poor cuts of meat (sometimes rotten) from pinch-penny guards that left them in a constant state of hunger. Corrections officers claimed this starvation diet would motivate the inmates to work hard and mend their ways. Instead, it only forced prisoners with an opening to the street to beg for food from those passing by the prison. Accompanying the pangs of hunger was an overpowering stench from unwashed bodies "devour'd with all kinds of Vermin" crammed into small cells. An Anglican minister described Charles Town's jail in the 1750s as a "stinking gaol" where 16 prisoners were crammed in a room no bigger than 12 feet by 12 feet. "Hell upon Earth," the "suburbs of Hell," and "a house of meager looks and ill smells" were terms contemporaries used to describe jails in the other port cities. At times conditions in prisons became so abominable that local churches conducted "charity sermons" for the relief of "distressed" prisoners.[27]

It is no wonder that inmates were so eager to escape such inhumane conditions. Enabling them to do so were the actual jails, which in the early period were often poorly secured basements of public buildings, taverns, or as in the case of Charles Town, rented rooms of private homes. Later buildings constructed for the sole purpose of incarcerating criminals were often in disrepair and notoriously insecure. Adding to the insecurity of city jails were poorly paid jail keepers who were often less than diligent in watching over their charges. In 1713 the Pennsylvania common council declared the Philadelphia jail a "public nuisance" because it was "too notorious that criminals frequently escape." Boston's new jail built in 1732 did no better job in containing prisoners within its walls. Neither did the one in Newport, where in 1737 the prison guard received a humiliating note from escaped convicts who wrote in chalk on the prison floor: "Fare you well Davis, your prisoners are fled, Your Prison's broke open while you were in Bed." Conditions were worse in Charles Town, where in 1744 the "want of a sufficient prison" allowed every prisoner confined in private homes and taverns to escape.[28]

FINES

Rather than incarcerate criminals at a significant cost to the community, urban courts actually raised considerable money for the city by imposing fines on lawbreakers. In Boston, the courts utilized this form of punishment in 45 percent of all offenses, particularly for misdemeanors such as breach of the peace, public drunkenness, profaning the Sabbath, gambling, and minor moral crimes like fornication. For thieves and vandals, the courts often ordered such offenders to pay a fine treble the restitution for goods stolen or damaged. If the convicted could not pay the fine—and many could not—the court would sell the malefactor into servitude. One way or another, the court and the victims were going to get their money.[29]

SHAMING

If a petty criminal continued to break the law, the court might punish the chronic wrongdoer with some form of public humiliation. This could include standing in the stocks, sitting in the pillory, or standing in the market while wearing a sign describing one's offense. One sexually immoral Philadelphia woman, for example, was required to stand at the city's whipping post while wearing a sign describing her offense: "I heare stand for an example to all others for committing the most wicked and notorious sin of Fornication." Blasphemy brought one Philadelphia man to stand in the local commons while holding a sign stating, "I stand here for speaking contemptuously of my Sovereign Lord King George." Puritans in early Boston took this form of punishment to even greater extremes by forcing drunkards to wear a red letter D on their clothing for a year and those convicted of incest to wear a large letter I for the rest of their lives.[30]

More physically uncomfortable were those men and women sentenced by the courts to stand in the pillory with head and hands firmly clamped between boards. Not only did these individuals have to suffer the ridicule from friends, neighbors, and kin seeing them in their helpless and humiliating position, they also had to endure, in the words of one eyewitness to this form of punishment, "gross and cruel insults from the multitude who pelted them incessantly with rotten eggs and every repulsive kind of garbage that could be collected." Ants, wasps, and other stinging insects, attracted by the rotten garbage and animal waste, soon swarmed the victim and added to his suffering. To keep from smothering from this distasteful onslaught, victims had someone to regularly wipe the refuse from their face. Thus, in early America one person's punishment was another's entertainment.[31]

CORPORAL PUNISHMENTS

Drawing even larger crowds were various forms of public corporal punishments: whipping, branding, and bodily mutilation. Of

In the Stocks. The punishment of criminals in colonial America was at times a communal act that provided both entertainment and an emotional release for participants. Illustrative is the stocks, a form of punishment that included both public humiliation and some physical discomfort for the convicted, who was exposed to ridicule and mockery from passers-by who threw mud, rotten eggs, moldy fruit and vegetables, offal, and excrement at those constrained in the stocks. (Mara L. Pratt, *America's Story for America's Children: The Early Colonies* [Boston: D. C. Heath & Co., 1901])

these, whipping was the most common form of corporal punishment for those convicted of sexual offenses, assault, theft, and fraud. Local law enforcement officials sometimes maximized the deterrent quality of this bloody public theater by chaining the convicted to the tail of an oxcart driven through the streets of the city and administering a certain number of lashes at every busy corner. Throughout the humiliating journey a crowd followed behind, hurling insults, rocks, and refuse at the prisoner. At other times the sheriff sidestepped the city tour and instead took the convict straight to the whipping post, where he forcefully whipped him or her "amid the screams of the culprits and the uproar of the mob."

The whipping of females, whose breasts were often exposed during the painful ordeal, added to both the humiliating and entertaining aspect of this public spectacle. In some cases the whipping was just a warm-up for the sadistic climax when the sheriff, after flogging a prisoner, would nail his ear to the whipping post and then slice it off with a knife. Other culprits who kept their ears might receive an equally painful branding on the face or on the base of their right thumb, from which comes the custom of raising one's right hand when sworn in so the court could see whether or not the person had a criminal record. Much less frequent were those convicted of blasphemy and slander who had their tongue either sliced down the middle with a knife or bored through with a red-hot poker. Because these punishments left permanent and conspicuous scars, they turned the victim into a life-long social pariah, which made it extremely difficult for him or her to resume a normal role in the community.[32]

EXECUTIONS

The ultimate punishment sanctioned by the courts, and the one that drew the largest crowds, was public execution. When Samuel Parcks and Benjamin Hawkins were hanged in Newport in 1759, for example, nearly 10,000 people gathered to witness their demise. Because hangings brought in so many spectators, local businessmen were especially happy to see someone hang as it brought in many customers into their shops. One Boston shopkeeper boasted that after an execution many spectators came to fill his shop. "When it was over Till Candle Light," he later wrote in his diary, "I had the shop full as it could Hold and Took £160." Part of the popularity of executions is that they were relatively rare in the major urban centers. Philadelphia and Charles Town averaged about two executions a year during the latter half of the eighteenth century, while Boston stood out with only 0.5 executions per year. Courts in the five cities at this time administered the death penalty only for truly serious crimes against people and property: murder, repeated burglary, piracy, counterfeiting, and arson. Additionally, juries in murder cases frequently returned verdicts of not guilty of the murder but guilty of the lesser offense of manslaughter. Many others with a death sentence hanging over them received a reprieve from the court, which sometimes showed mercy if the crime was not too heinous or if it was a first offense. In special cases persons sentenced to death could plead benefit of clergy, a practice carried over from England that allowed first-time offenders to receive a more lenient sentence for some lesser crimes. Officials sometimes pardoned convicts to demonstrate to the people that they could also be merciful. In doing so, they usually announced pardons at the last minute under the gallows amid several simultaneous executions. As a result of such leniency, felons sentenced to death had a better than 50/50 chance of escaping the hangman's noose, at least until the latter half of the eighteenth century, when increasing crime rates in the cities compelled authorities to execute nearly 80 percent of those convicted of a capital crime.[33]

For those unfortunate felons sentenced to the gallows, their executions were a formal and widely advertised public ritual that drew hundreds, sometimes thousands, of curious spectators from the city and the surrounding countryside. The ghoulish nature of colonial executions began before the fateful day when local doctors would bargain the condemned for their bodies to later use for dissection. One black man agreed to sell his body for £10, believing "it might afford me a comfortable subsistence while here and my Bones be of service to mankind after the separation of soul and body." On the day of the execution the shackled prisoner rode on a cart through the crowded streets in a procession that included friends, relatives, ministers, judges, and other prominent officials. Once at the gallows prisoners were expected to make a moral confession of their criminal activity as a warning to others. While standing on the gallows with a noose around his neck for executing his master in 1674, a Boston servant, with encouragement from the attending minister, confessed that his misguided ideals of social equality contributed to his demise: "I am Flesh and Blood, as well my Master, and therefore I know no reason why my Master should not obey me, as well as I obey him," he told the crowd of spectators. "See what my Pride has brought me to![34]

Diabolical in its conception, the gallows confession was a clever means by which political and religious leaders got the condemned, virtually all lower-class men, to publicly legitimize an elitist judicial system used to maintain upper-class hegemony. That it was conducted by a man of the cloth gave it the powerful appearance of being part of God's plan. It was certainly part of a larger process of capital punishment designed and executed by the ruling elites "to maintain and strengthen the power and authority of their class," according to historian Gabrielle Gottlieb. Of the more than 200 people who were executed in Boston, Philadelphia, and Charles Town during the second half of the eighteenth century, nearly all were young, male, and poor—sailors, servants, soldiers, and laborers—who supported themselves and their families, according to one account, "chiefly by Pilfering and stealing." With two-thirds of those executed for offenses against property, the ruling urban elite aggressively used the judicial system they controlled to protect their property against theft and arson. The propertied elites who defined the laws made capital statutes to "assuage the fears of the ruling classes with a 'pragmatic blend of terror,'" adds Gottlieb, "that enforced the vertical hierarchy of society." Yet some lower-class victims challenged the upper classes' claim of legitimacy and justice in weighing human life "on the scales of wealth and status" by refusing to make a gallows confession. One woman hanged for murder in 1795, for example, "boldly persisted to the last" in declaring herself to be innocent and forgave those who she said had been the cause of her "unjust condemnation."[35]

After the leading players in this ghoulish theater had spoken their parts, the magistrate or other public official gave the signal to the hangman, who unceremoniously slapped the horse driving the cart from which the condemned stood. Unfortunately for some victims, the drop was not far enough to break their necks. Some evidence suggests this was intentional on the part of law enforcement officials who wanted to add to the suffering of the condemned while giving the crowd a better show as the victim slowly strangled while kicking and dancing at the end of the rope. Sometimes the hangings were simply bungled. One young Boston woman convicted of infanticide was left dangling by a rope around her neck, kicking and twisting. Between gasps for air she asked the law officers "what did they mean to do," whereupon some men stepped forward and finally ended the girl's suffering by quickly turning the knot of the rope backward and thus breaking her neck.[36]

Those suffering most were the few convicted criminals burned at the stake, an especially cruel sentence reserved almost exclusively for poor white women and slaves. One woman who killed her husband in 1765, for example, was covered with tar and set on fire. "Nothing could be more shocking than to behold," reported a horrified eyewitness," after her Bowels fell out, the Fire flaming between her Ribs, and issueing out at her Ears, Mouth, Eye-holes, etc. In short, it was so terrible a Sight that great Numbers turned their backs and screamed, not being able to look at it." A Philadelphia woman convicted of poisoning her parents in 1730 had the added punishment of being pinched with red-hot tongs all over her body before the executioner lit the pile of kindling below her. To add a

bloody and explosive element to the horrific production, the executioner tied a bag of gunpowder around the woman's neck that
exploded when sparks finally reached it, blowing her head sky
high. One Boston woman sentenced to hang before being set ablaze
received no such merciful ending when the rope around her neck
broke so that she "fell alive into the flames," wrote an eyewitness,
"and was seen to struggle."[37]

JUDICIAL RACISM

Slavery in the cities posed a special problem to authorities, who created special "slave codes" and ad hoc "slave courts" of two magistrates and several freeholders to better control the human chattel
who, in countless ways, exploited the unique circumstances of the
urban environment to aggressively contest all restrictions to their freedom. Some of the many unique restrictions imposed on urban slaves
include those against gambling, cursing, running away, carrying
a weapon, buying liquor, riding disorderly through the streets,
assembling in groups of more than three except during church
services, dressing in a manner "above the condition of slaves," "gadding abroad" without a ticket "from their Mr. Or Mrs," and even
training a dog. Although draconian on paper, these codes withered
under the onslaught of the urban environment and determined resistance by slaves and a local government already overwhelmed by so
many other problems.

Perhaps most damaging to efforts at controlling slave behavior
was a belief among local whites that town life somehow encouraged
an aggressiveness among blacks that belied their servile status. One
Frenchman visiting Charles Town in 1777 observed that local slaves
"have a peculiar kind of pride and bearing" and "did not act like
slaves." All too many bondsmen, he added, talked to whites "in a
surly and insolent tone" and refused to remove their hats to those
appearing "below affluence." Similarly, when Governor Lord
Cornbury arrived in New York City in 1701, he noticed a "great
insolency" displayed by local slaves. One proud slave aptly named
Prince even punched the mayor in the face when the latter tried to
disperse a group of "noisy Negroes."[38]

Such rebellious behavior among urban slaves drove local authorities to maddening frustration, and no amount of bills for the "better
regulating of Negroes" seemed to curb their disobedience. In 1723
Boston officials complained that slaves there were "addicted" to
behaving in "a most audacious manner" that included breaking

street lamps, building bonfires, holding pageants in the streets, and "insulting and abusing pedestrians" with "horrid profanity, impiety and gross immoralities." Despite employing special slave patrols to prevent curfew violators, Philadelphia and New York City regularly were witness to slaves holding nightly gatherings in the streets where they played pranks on unsuspecting residents and fought in drunken brawls with soldiers, sailors, and other rabble. In Charles Town, where blacks outnumbered whites, local slaves essentially owned the streets, where they went "at all times in the night," opined a local grand jury in the early 1760s, rioting, playing dice and other games, and "talking obscenely in the most public manner." Local whites blamed much of this unruliness on taverns that sold alcohol to slaves. New Yorkers looked upon these taverns as "black centers of mischief and revolution." Although rebellions were rare among slaves, they did frequently strike out individually against their owners by setting their homes, warehouses, and ships on fire, physically assaulting them, poisoning them with ratsbane, and even raping and castrating their children.[39]

Slaves accused of such criminal behavior, at least in New York City, had a 70 percent chance of being convicted—a figure 20 percent higher than that for the group with the next highest rate of conviction, Native Americans. This is not surprising considering that the judicial deck was stacked heavily against slave defendants, who had no means for an adequate defense, and who faced racist freeholders filled with fears of an unruly servile class and unsympathetic magistrates who aggressively cajoled slaves into a confession. Most slaves were best off simply cooperating with the court, confessing guilt, and begging the justices for mercy. This mercy was rarely forthcoming, especially as the court administered some form of corporal punishment on slaves no matter the seriousness of the crime. Whipping was the most common form of punishment for minor infractions, followed by branding, castration (later deemed inhumane), and banishment for more serious offenses. Officials in New York City punished drunk and disorderly slaves by dunking them in the harbor and forcing them to swallow a heavy dose of saltwater and lamp oil, which in one case proved fatal. Almost always fatal for slaves were punishments for those who committed murder, arson, rape, and rebellion. White authorities devised unusually cruel forms of execution for condemned black men and women: either being broken on the wheel, drawn and quartered, burned at the stake, roasted alive for hours, or hung in a cage and allowed to slowly starve to death. One Frenchmen visiting

Charles Town in the early 1780s described this latter form of punishment after coming across a slave suspended in a cage and left to die:

I shudder when I recollect that the birds had already picked out his eyes, his cheek bones were bare, his arms had been attacked in several places, and his body seemed covered with a multitude of wounds. From the edges of the hollow sockets and from the lacerations with which he was disfigured, the blood slowly dropped, and tinged the ground beneath ... The living spectre, though deprived of his eyes, could still distinctively hear, and begged me to give him some water to allay his thirst.[40]

As with whites convicted of a capital offense, condemned slaves were expected to make a gallows confession to their fellow bondsmen. Some did, but others defiantly gave their last breath publicly avowing white people as their "declared enemy."[41]

JUDICIAL ELITISM

The colonial judicial system not only had a strong racial caste to it but an equally strong class element. Early America was a hierarchical society with an abundance of inequalities manufactured by elites, one of them being unequal protection of the law. "People stood with the law as they stood in relation to one another in society," explains lawyer and historian Edgar McManus. Contributing to this judicial inequality were judges and jurors, who came exclusively from the upper classes. Justices in Philadelphia, for example, ranked among the wealthiest 10 percent of resident wealth-holders while jurors came from the top 20 percent of wealth-holders and who generally had three times as much wealth as those men and women they tried. In carrying out "justice," these well-to-do and powerful men sought, in the words of scholar Patrick Calloway, "to defend against the fears of the upper classes of society in whatever form that fear appeared." The greatest fear among the urban elites was threats against their property. City records reveal that magistrates in the five cities devoted most of their energies resolving debt litigation on behalf of wealthy merchants and businessmen and aggressively prosecuting thieves, who stole primarily from the rich. Conviction rates involving property cases reached nearly 80 percent in New York City and Boston, compared with only 46 percent in cases involving a personal crime. When criminal activity threatened the interests of the moneyed class, legal authorities responded swiftly and effectively; when it did not, they often turned a blind eye.[42]

Slave Execution. White residents in the five cities were at times thrown into paroxysms of fear over the rumor of a slave revolt. This was especially true for cities with large slave populations like Charles Town and New York City. To quickly quell any slave revolt, either real or rumored, urban officials publicly executed the alleged ringleaders, sometimes burning them at the stake. This illustration horrifically depicts the execution of a slave convicted of participating in New York City's slave conspiracy of 1741. Other convicted slaves were executed by hanging, as depicted in the top right portion of the illustration. (Marshall Bright, *True Stories of American History for Our Young People* [1889])

In deciding the form of punishment, the courts also considered the convicted person's social position. Rarely did upper-class criminals have to suffer the indignity and discomfort of standing in the pillory or experience the pain and physical and emotional scarring of a public whipping. To do so would put them on a level with the lower sort, thereby rubbing away the veneer of their self-ascribed superiority that the elites used to justify their hegemony. At the same time, publicly flogging the underclass for their crimes was a conspicuous and bloody reminder of their inferior and unequal status. As legal scholar Lawrence Friedman explains, the criminal justice system "maintains the status quo," it "protects power and property; it safeguards wealth; and, by the same token, it perpetuates the subordinate status of the people on the bottom." Because "powerful people make the law," he adds, the "lash of the criminal justice . . . tends to fall on the poor." This was literally the case in colonial America, as well-to-do magistrates simply allowed their economic equals convicted of crimes to walk out of the courtroom with a little less money in their pocket. Massachusetts law even prohibited the whipping of "any true gentlemen" unless his crime "be very shamefull" and his lifestyle "vitious and profligate." Court records for Massachusetts during the late colonial period reveal that "gentlemen professionals" convicted of a crime paid a fine in 86 percent of cases. Only 5 percent received a shaming punishment, and less than half a percent received a public whipping. Executions of the wealthy for capital crimes were even rarer. Moreover, colonial courts frequently remitted punishments on the well-to-do. One study of New England shows that defendants of high social standing were five times more likely to receive an acquittal than their low-status counterparts. Such judicial elitism gave cause for complaint among some common folk who were cognizant of the inequality of punishment administered by elitist-dominated courts between the rich and poor.[43] One angry New Yorker opined that:

if a poor fellow not worth a goat, gets drunk, rambles about Town, and meeting with a man's daughter, should offer any violence to her; upon a complaint made, he is immediately taken up, and put in the Sticks till he is sober [and then] whipt, and sent out of Town. . . . On the other hand, if a rich man happens to be guilty of the same Offense, occasioned by drinking too much, upon Complaint being made, the magistrate advises the party complaining, to make it up.[44]

JUDICIAL SEXISM

Men may have had legitimate cause for complaint concerning discrepancies in court-ordered punishment between the sexes. Some capital offenses like idolatry, perjury, and sodomy did not apply to women in colonies like Massachusetts. The courts also generally showed leniency toward women in criminal activity. Proportionately, more females than males received pardons and reprieves, at least in New York City, where the courts acquitted 21.6 percent of female defendants compared with 14.3 percent of male defendants. Women were also much more likely than men to receive a reprieve from the gallows. In Massachusetts during the last half of the eighteenth century, only one woman received a capital sentence for a property crime while the courts condemned to death 36 men for committing the same offense. Similarly, the courts in Philadelphia during the late colonial period never indicted women for killing their husbands although 20 percent of men's homicide cases involved husbands killing their wives. Judges and juries also increasingly acquitted women accused of infanticide, an overwhelmingly female crime. This is especially true if the woman shed tears or had prepared for the coming of the child ("benefit of linen," it was called). One woman convinced a jury that she had accidentally cut the throat of her newborn baby instead of its umbilical cord, while another woman escaped the gallows with her convincing claim that her infant accidentally fell into a pan of water and drowned during a secret delivery. Other newborns drowned in privies filled with feces and urine when their mothers testified in court that they believed they were having a bowel movement instead of delivering a child.[45]

Still, a great deal of sexism against women existed in the criminal judicial system. Women in Massachusetts, for example, suffered a double standard in punishment for property crimes as they were more likely than men to receive corporal punishment for theft. This judicial sexism also extended to prostitutes, whom the courts treated more harshly than their male clients because they sinned for gain while the men sinned out of human weakness. Similarly, the courts punished married women who had an extramarital affair for adultery while charging men who committed the same crime with the lesser crime of fornication, at least as long as his mistress was single. In short, the law treated women "approximately the way male-dominated society perceived them," explains Edgar McManus, as "mindless prattlers, given to railing and scolding," as "temptresses who entice men into sin," and as "breeders and housekeepers whose purpose in life was to assist and make things easier for men."[46]

CONCLUSION

Whether rich or poor or man or woman, urban folk during the 1700s were greatly concerned with increasing criminal activity, particularly theft and assault. Near the end of the century a "Taxable Citizen" of Charles Town summed up the fear of many seaport residents with the following ironic observation: "It is too well known that a herd of the most flagitious banditti upon earth do live among us— that a man's house where property is supposed to be deposited is not safe. Is it not extremely hard that a lady or gentleman who would not choose to walk in the heat of the day, should be debarred of an evening retreat, merely from an apprehension of not returning safe home? We may talk what we please of liberty, but tell me what kind of liberty is that?" As one modern legal scholar similarly noticed, "where order thrived in colonial America, so too did oppression; where liberty prospered, so too did crime." In fighting crime, upper-class city officials were much more concerned with order than with liberty. They used the judicial system they created and controlled to impose a type of order that best protected their interests. Paramount to their concern was the protection of their property and the legitimation of the elitist, racist, and patriarchal social and governing structure. To that end, they formed laws and enforced them in a way that was anything but equitable or humane. This was especially true in reserving cruel forms of corporal punishment exclusively to lower-class criminals, an act that was deliberately intended to rob them of their humanity. City officials also deliberately publicized these brutal, bloody, and sometimes deadly forms of punishment to terrorize the people into docilely submitting to their rule. Far from being fair and balanced, "justice" administered by the urban upper-class was elitist, racist, sexist, and sadistic.[47]

NOTES

1. Jack D. Marietta, "Violent Crime, Victims, and Society in Pennsylvania, 1682–1800," *Pennsylvania History* 66 (1999): 26–28; Michael Hindus, *Prison and Plantation: Crime, Justice, and Authority in Massachusetts and South*

Carolina, 1767–1878 (Chapel Hill: University of North Carolina Press, 1980), 64. By comparison, murder rates in Boston for 2002 were 10.6 per 100,000 while in New York City for 2004 the murder rate was 4.5 per 100,000. Thus residents of the four largest colonial seaports had as much if not a greater chance of dying violently than many modern residents of the nation's large urban centers.

2. Sheila Skemp, "A Social and Cultural History of Newport, Rhode Island, 1720–1765," Ph.D. dissertation, University of Iowa, 1974, 138–39; Marietta, "Violent Crime," 32; Jack D. Marietta and G. S. Rowe, *Troubled Experiment: Crime and Justice in Pennsylvania, 1682–1800* (Philadelphia: University of Pennsylvania Press, 2006), 112 (quote); Julia C. Spruill, *Women's Life and Work in the Southern Colonies* (Chapel Hill: University of North Carolina Press, 1938), 184; David A. Copeland, *Colonial American Newspapers: Character and Content* (Newark: University of Delaware Press, 1997), 105, 76–77; Thomas Purvis, *Colonial America to 1763* (New York: Facts on File, 1999), 308; Negley Teeters, "Public Executions in Pennsylvania: 1682–1834," *Journal of the Lancaster Historical Society* 64 (1960): 762; Bradley Chapin, *Criminal Justice in Colonial America, 1606–1660* (Athens: University of Georgia Press, 1983), 114.

3. John A. Hall, " 'Nefarious Wretches, Insidious Villains, and Evil–Minded Persons': Urban Crime Reported in Charleston's *City Gazette*, in 1788," *South Carolina Historical Magazine* 88 (1987): 166–67; Copeland, *Colonial American Newspapers*, 110, 106; Douglas Greenberg, *Crime and Law Enforcement in the Colony of New York, 1691–1776* (Ithaca, NY: Cornell University Press, 1974), 118–23; Marietta and Rowe, *Troubled Experiment*, 112; Carl Bridenbaugh, *Cities in the Wilderness: Urban Life in America, 1625–1742* (New York: Ronald Press, 1938), 223, 417.

4. Marietta, "Violent Crime," 32; N. E. H. Hull, *Female Felons: Women and Serious Crime in Colonial Massachusetts* (Urbana: University of Illinois Press, 1987), 44–51; Sharon A. Burnston, "Babies in the Well: An Underground Insight into Deviant Behavior in Eighteenth-Century Philadelphia," *Pennsylvania Magazine of History and Biography* 106 (1982): 65–71, 85–86, 109–10; George F. Dow, *Everyday Life in the Massachusetts Bay Colony* (Boston: Society for the Preservation of New England Antiquities, 1935), 202; Chapin, *Criminal Justice*, 114; Clare Lyons, *Sex among the Rabble: An Intimate History of Gender and Power in the Age of Revolution, Philadelphia, 1730–1830* (Chapel Hill: University of North Carolina Press, 2006), 95 (quote).

5. Purvis, *Colonial America to 1763*, 307; Marietta, "Violent Crime," 40–47; Greenberg, *Crime and Law Enforcement*, 50; Linda Biemer, "Criminal Law and Women in New Amsterdam and Early New York," in *A Beautiful and Fruitful Place: Selected Rensselaerswijck Seminar Papers*, ed. Nancy Zeller (New York: New Netherland, 1991), 80 (quote).

6. Greenberg, *Crime and Law Enforcement*, 108; G. S. Rowe, "Women's Crime and Criminal Administration in Pennsylvania, 1763–1790," *Pennsylvania*

Magazine of History and Biography 109 (1985): 625–33, 649; Edwin Powers, *Crime and Punishment in Early Massachusetts, 1620–1692: A Documentary History* (Boston: Beacon Press, 1966), 213 (quote), 177; Steven J. Stewart, "Skimmington in the Middle and New England Colonies," in *Riot and Revelry in Early America*, ed. William Pencak, Matthew Dennis, and Simon P. Newman (University Park: Pennsylvania State University Press, 2002), 62–63 (quotes), 47; Copeland, *Early American Newspapers*, 105, 116; Carl Bridenbaugh, *Cities in Revolt: Urban Life in America, 1743–1776* (New York: Capricorn Books, 1955), 318.

7. Sharon Block, *Rape and Sexual Power in Early America* (Chapel Hill: University of North Carolina Press, 2006), 38; Donna Spindell, *Crime and Society in North Carolina, 1663–1776* (Baton Rouge: Louisiana State University Press, 1989), 108–9; Sharon Block, "How Should We Look at Rape in Early America," *History Compass* 4 (2006): 610 (quote), 606 (quote), 607; Marietta and Rowe, *Troubled Experiment*, 145.

8. Marietta and Rowe, *Troubled Experiment*, 137 (quote), 141–42 (quotes); Block, *Rape and Sexual Power*, 36–38, 83 (quote), 92; Eli Faber, "Puritan Criminals: The Economic, Social, and Intellectual Background to Crime in Seventeenth-Century Massachusetts," *Perspectives in American History* 11 (1977–1978): 101–2; Copeland, *Colonial American Newspapers*, 118, 138, 103; Greenberg, *Crime and Law Enforcement*, 111; Powers, *Crime and Punishment*, 174; Dow, *Everyday Life*, 216 (quote); Greenberg, *Crime and Law Enforcement*, 111 (quote); Thomas Foster, *Sex and the Eighteenth-Century Man: Massachusetts and the History of Sexuality in America* (Boston, MA: Beacon Press, 2006), 33, 58 (quote); Martha Saxton, *Being Good: Women's Moral Values in Early America* (New York: Hill and Wang, 2003), 35.

9. Gabriele Gottlieb, "Theater of Death: Capital Punishment in Early America, 1750–1800," Ph.D. dissertation, University of Pittsburgh, 2005, 139 (quote), 137 (quote); Purvis, *Colonial America to 1763*, 310; Hindus, *Prison and Plantation*, 64; Greenberg, *Crime and Law Enforcement*, 50; Linda Kealey, "Patterns of Punishment: Massachusetts in the Eighteenth Century," *American Journal of Legal History* 30 (1986): 350–51; Hall, "Nefarious Wretches," 167 (quote).

10. Greenberg, *Crime and Law Enforcement*, 115; Bridenbaugh, *Cities in the Wilderness*, 221–22, 70 (quote), 111–12; Rowe, "Women's Crime," 634; Hull, *Female Felons*, 44–46.

11. Skemp, "A Social and Cultural History of Newport," 382–86, quote on page 385.

12. Bridenbaugh, *Cities in the Wilderness*, 72 (quote), 226, 388; Bridenbaugh, *Cities in Revolt*, 121, 318 (quote); Lyons, *Sex among the Rabble*, 101.

13. Bridenbaugh, *Cities in Revolt*, 122, 317–18; Bridenbaugh, *Cities in the Wilderness*, 226–27 (quotes); Stewart, "Skimmington," 46–50; Lyons, *Sex among the Rabble*, 107.

14. Powers, *Crime and Punishment*, 173 (quote); Faber, "Puritan Criminals," 101–2; Dow, *Everyday Life*, 214, note.

15. Powers, *Crime and Punishment*, 404, 174 (quote); Bridenbaugh, *Cities in the Wilderness*, 388; Bridenbaugh, *Cities in Revolt*, 121; Kathryn Preyer, "Penal Measures in the American Colonies: An Overview," *American Journal of Legal History* 26 (1982): 341, 345.

16. Skemp, "A Social and Cultural History of Newport," 140 (quote); Powers, *Crime and Punishment*, 372, 380–81 (quotes); Bridenbaugh, *Cities in the Wilderness*, 77; Sharon Salinger, *Taverns and Drinking in Early America* (Baltimore, MD: Johns Hopkins University Press, 2002), 146 (quote).

17. Dow, *Everyday Life*, 206–16; Bridenbaugh, *Cities in the Wilderness*, 228–29.

18. Larry D. Eldridge, *A Distant Heritage: The Growth of Free Speech in Early America* (New York: New York University Press, 1994), 8 (quote); Mary Beth Norton, "Gender and Defamation in Seventeenth-Century Maryland," *William and Mary Quarterly* 44 (1987): 6 (quote), 19 (quote), 9–11; Helena Wall, *Fierce Communion: Family and Community in Early America* (Cambridge, MA: Harvard University Press, 1990), 47 (quote); Roger Thompson, "'Holy Watchfulness' and Communal Conformism: The Functions of Defamation in Early New England Communities," *New England Quarterly* 56 (1983): 506–8.

19. Edridge, *A Distant Heritage*, quotes from pages 27, 95, 13, 14, and 44; Gary Nash, *Quakers and Politics: Pennsylvania, 1681–1726* (Boston: Northeastern University Press, 1968), 258 (quote); Dow, *Everyday Life*, 209–16; Wall, *Fierce Communion*, 32; Bridenbaugh, *Cities in the Wilderness*, 228; Powers, *Crime and Punishment*, 176; Skemp, "A Social and Cultural History of Newport," 430; Scott Christianson, "Criminal Punishment in New Netherland," in *A Beautiful and Fruitful Place*, 87; Bridenbaugh, *Cities in Revolt*, 119, 319; Norton, "Gender and Defamation," 18.

20. Stephanie Grauman Wolf, *As Various as Their Land: The Everyday Lives of Eighteenth-Century Americans* (New York: Harper, 1993), 131–34; Bridenbaugh, *Cities in Revolt*, 318; Bridenbaugh, *Cities in the Wilderness*, 229; Christianson, "Criminal Punishment," 87.

21. Michael S. Hindus, "A City of Mobocrats and Tyrants: Mob Violence in Boston, 1747–1863," *Issues in Criminology* 6 (1971): 62–63; Paul A. Gilje, *The Road to Mobocracy: Popular Disorder in New York City, 1763–1834* (Chapel Hill: University of North Carolina Press, 1987), 16–17; Pauline Maier, "Popular Uprisings and Civil Authority in Eighteenth-Century America," *William and Mary Quarterly* 27 (1970): 5–6; Bridenbaugh, *Cities in the Wilderness*, 70.

22. Eldridge, *A Distant Heritage*, 74.

23. Douglas Greenberg, "The Effectiveness of Law Enforcement in Eighteenth-Century New York," *American Journal of Legal History* 19 (1975): 274 (quote); Skemp, "A Social and Cultural History of Newport," 184; Eldridge, *A Distant Heritage*, 83 (quote).

24. Lawrence M. Friedman, *Crime and Punishment in American History* (New York: Basic Books, 1993), 25–27; Lawrence M. Friedman, *A History of American Law* (New York: Simon & Schuster, 1973), 81–82; Robert Olwell, *Masters, Slaves, and Subjects: The Culture of Power in the South Carolina Low Country, 1740–1790* (Ithaca, NY: Cornell University Press, 1998), 88–89; Eldridge, *A Distant Heritage*, 67 (quote); Chapin, *Criminal Justice*, 6, 40–41; Douglas Greenberg, "Crime, Law Enforcement, and Social Control in Colonial America," *American Journal of Legal History* 26 (1982): 235–37; Marietta and Rowe, *Troubled Experiment*, 133–34; Greenberg, "The Effectiveness of Law Enforcement," 274–78.

25. Bridenbaugh, *Cities in the Wilderness*, 64 (quote), 216, 375; Russell Shorto, *The Island at the Center of the World: The Epic Story of Dutch Manhattan and the Forgotten Colony That Shaped America* (New York: Vintage Books, 2004), 85 (quote); Hall, "Nefarious Wretches," 158; Greenberg, "The Effectiveness of Law Enforcement," 270–71; Bridenbaugh, *Cities in Revolt*, 107–110; Chapin, *Criminal Justice*, 96; Friedman, *Crime and Punishment*, 26–27.

26. Powers, *Crime and Punishment*, 203.

27. Kealey, "Patterns of Punishment," 357; Greenberg, *Crime and Law Enforcement*, 125–26 (quote); Edgar J. McManus, *Law and Liberty in Early New England: Criminal Justice and Due Process, 1620–1692* (Amherst: University of Massachusetts Press, 1993), 178–79 (quote); Bridenbaugh, *Cities in Revolt*, 118 (quotes).

28. Kealey, "Patterns of Punishment," 357; Greenberg, *Crime and Law Enforcement*, 170–71; Bridenbaugh, *Cities in the Wilderness*, 225 (quotes), 386 (quote).

29. Kealey, "Patterns of Punishment," 353, 356; Herbert Fitzroy, "The Punishment of Crime in Provincial Pennsylvania," *Pennsylvania Magazine of History and Biography* 60 (1936): 247–49.

30. Fitzroy, "The Punishment of Crime," 265, notes 96 and 97 (quotes); Dow, *Everyday Life*, 214 (text and footnotes).

31. Preyer, "Penal Measures," 350; Fitzroy, "The Punishment of Crime," 264–67; Dow, *Everyday Life*, 214; Kealey, "Patterns of Punishment," 353 (quote).

32. Preyer, "Penal Measures," 334; Powers, *Crime and Punishment*, 173; Kealey, "Patterns of Punishment," 353 (quote); Purvis, *Colonial America to 1763*, 305.

33. Foster, *Sex and the Eighteenth-Century Man*, 147 (quote); Gottlieb, "Theater of Death," 95, 32; Gabriele Gottlieb, "Class and Capital Punishment in Early Urban North America," in *Class Matters: Early North America and the Atlantic World*, ed. Simon Middleton and Billy G. Smith (Philadelphia: University of Pennsylvania Press, 2008), 192; Teeters, "Public Executions," 779; Christianson, "Criminal Punishment," 87; Fitzroy, "Punishment of Crime," 255; Preyer, "Penal Measures," 345.

34. Gottlieb, "Theater of Death," 21, 27 (quote); Karen Halttunen, *Murder Most Foul: The Killer and the American Gothic Imagination* (Cambridge, MA:

Harvard University Press, 1998), 24; Daniel E. Williams, *Pillars of Salt: An Anthology of Early American Criminal Narratives* (Madison, WI: Madison House, 1993), 70 (quote).

35. Michael Meranze, *Laboratories of Virtue: Punishment, Revolution, and Authority in Philadelphia, 1760–1835* (Chapel Hill: University of North Carolina Press, 1996), 37, 54 (quote); Gottlieb, "Class and Capital Punishment," 185, 186 (quote), 194 (quote); Gottlieb, "Theater of Death," 9 (quote).

36. Dow, *Everyday Life*, 223, 202 (quote).

37. Gottlieb, "Theater of Death," 29 (quote); Copeland, *Colonial American Newspapers*, 83 (quote); Teeters, "Public Executions," 770 (quote).

38. Greenberg, *Crime and Law Enforcement*, 44–45 (quote); Thomas J. Davis, "Slavery in Colonial New York City," Ph.D. dissertation, Columbia University, 1974, 150; Oscar R. Williams, "The Regimentation of Blacks in the Urban Frontier in Colonial Albany, New York City and Philadelphia," *Journal of Negro History* 63 (1978): 329; Philip D. Morgan, "Black Life in Eighteenth-Century Charleston," *Perspectives in American History* (1984): 187, 226 (quote); Leslie Harris, *In the Shadow of Slavery: African Americans in New York City, 1626–1863* (Chicago: University of Chicago Press, 2003), 37 (quote).

39. Lorenzo Greene, *The Negro in Colonial New England* (New York: Columbia University Press, 1942), 133–34, 155–57 (quote); Morgan, "Black Life," 207–8 (quote); Williams, "Regimentation of Blacks," 331 (quote).

40. Gottlieb, "Theater of Death," 124.

41. Greenberg, *Crime and Law Enforcement*, 72; Olwell, *Masters, Slaves, and Subjects*, 92, 98 (quote); Edgar J. McManus, *Black Bondage in the North* (Syracuse, NY: Syracuse University Press, 1973), 85–86.

42. McManus, *Law and Liberty*, 115 (quote); Marietta and Rowe, *Troubled Experiment*, 53–56; Patrick Calloway, "Fear, Capital Punishment, and Order: The Construction and Use of Capital Punishment Statutes in Early Modern England and Seventeenth-Century New England," in *Invitation to an Execution: A History of the Death Penalty in the United States*, ed. Gordon Bakken (Albuquerque: University of New Mexico Press, 2010), 58 (quote); Deborah Rosen, "Courts and Commerce in Colonial New York," *American Journal of Legal History* 36 (1992): 151–54; Gottlieb, "Class and Capital Punishment," 192; Gottlieb, "Theater of Death," 103.

43. Friedman, *Crime and Punishment in American History*, 83 (quote), 101 (quote); McManus, *Law and Liberty*, 120–21 (quotes); Marietta and Rowe, *Troubled Experiment*, 105; Powers, *Crime and Punishment*, 168; Kealey, "Patterns of Punishment," 359.

44. Copeland, *Early American Newspapers*, 114.

45. Greenberg, *Crime and Law Enforcement*, 77–83; Kealey, "Patterns of Punishment," 360–61; Peter Hoffer and N. E. H. Hull, *Murdering Mothers:*

Infanticide in England and New England, 1558–1803 (New York: New York University Press, 1981), 65–71; Hull, *Female Felons*, 44–51; Burnston, "Babies in the Well," 65–110.

46. McManus, *Law and Liberty*, 119.

47. Hall, "Nefarious Wretches," 168 (quote); Greenberg, "The Effectiveness of Law Enforcement," 263 (quote).

8

Poverty and Poor Relief

INTRODUCTION

Poverty was a constant problem in colonial cities. Indeed, approximately one out of three white residents during the mid-eighteenth century were considered poor by contemporary standards.[1] This "poor" included not just widows, orphans, the sick, the disabled, and the aged but also many able-bodied men and women unable to find work, or at least steady work. The vagaries of a capitalist economy, rapid population increase, maldistribution of wealth, frequent wars, catastrophic fires, epidemic diseases, and increasing immigration all contributed to poverty and strained public and private aid directed to the rising number of indigents. By the mid-1700s the major seaports were littered with numerous poor men, women, and children, some of whom were forced to live and beg in the streets to survive.

The more fortunate poor lived in small, overcrowded, cheaply built, vermin-infested "huts" located in disease-ridden neighborhoods filled with putrefying dead animals, ponds of stagnating water, and piles of trash that created a nauseating stench. Ill-fitting, unwashed, and coarse rag-like clothing clad their filthy bodies, which were often physically broken by labor-intensive and dangerous work. Just as meager and crude was the diet of the poor, which consisted of bland one-pot stews and gruels sopped up with "spoon bread." During particularly tough times dogs, cats, and rats made it into the dinner pots of the urban poor. One New York City resident described "scenes of distress" in the homes of the poor in which huddled "Numbers of Wretches hungry and naked, shivering with Cold, and perhaps languishing with disease."[2] Similarly heart-wrenching scenes of distress could be found in the other major cities.

In confronting this mounting human crisis, urban officials took a hardened approach toward the poor, whom they increasingly equated with criminal elements of society. Instead of increasing relief necessary to meet the needs of the growing indigent population, municipal governments concocted many clever means to reduce the number of people eligible for relief. To further cut expenditures on the poor, urban leaders beginning in the early eighteenth century shifted the focus of poor relief from private homes to more cost-efficient yet less humane established charitable institutions. Realizing that public relief was inadequate, some middle- and upper-class residents established benevolent organizations and employment schemes to assist the needy. In doing so, early Americans rejected the concept of rugged individualism, and instead approached the problem of poverty with collective action. In the end, however, all these efforts failed to reverse rising poverty levels, and the growing number of urban poor continued to suffer horribly from inadequate food, clothing, shelter, and medical care that resulted in poor health and shortened and less fulfilling lives.

In assessing this social failure it is important to remember that the colonial period was an era of limited government and largely unfettered capitalism. There were few government safety nets for those falling on hard times and certainly no unemployment insurance; workman's compensation; food stamps; aid to women, infants, and children; social security for the elderly; or public health care for the aged and the indigent. Neither did colonial governments institute safety requirements in the workplace that would have prevented many injuries that disabled workers and sent them and their families into poverty. Instead, early Americans were left to the unforgiving vagaries of the capitalist economy and the sporadic whims of private charity, both of which failed either to address the root causes of poverty or to significantly alleviate the suffering experienced by the growing urban poor. Poverty therefore turned out to be a daily experience for many early Americans living in the "land of plenty."

ATTITUDES TOWARD THE POOR AND POOR RELIEF

Generally, the poor were looked upon with contempt by early Americans, nearly all of whom called themselves Christians. Even those struggling to make ends meet who were once at the pinnacle of society were viewed with disdain by their former peers. When Richard and Deborah Hill of Philadelphia lost their mercantile fortune, for example, they were met with such "insults & affronts" from Philadelphia's finest that they nearly left the "city of brotherly love." More than a decade later, Deborah reflected on the way other prominent families had mistreated them. "We were shund and neglected on every side when needy," she recalled. "But it's no new thing," she astutely observed, "for Poverty and contempt to go hand in hand."[3] Still, all poor people were not equal in the eyes of early Americans, who categorized the indigent into separate categories: the "deserving poor" and the "undeserving poor." The deserving poor were those people who because of circumstances beyond their control could not support themselves—widows, orphans, the aged, the infirm, and the mentally ill. Thus early Americans did not necessarily see poverty as a sign of sin. Still, many viewed poverty in moral terms. To them, intemperance, immorality, irreligion, and voluntary idleness explained poverty. The undeserving poor who engaged in such self-destructive behavior, according to Boston officials, included a colorful cast of characters:

Persons going about in any town or county begging, or persons using any subtle craft, juggling or unlawful games or plays, or feigning themselves to have knowledge in physiognomy, palmestry, or pretending that they can tell destinies, fortunes, or discover where lost or stol'n goods may be found, common pipers, fidlers, runaways, stubborn servants or children, common drunkards, common nightwalkers, pilferers, wanton and lascivious persons, either in speech or behaviour, common railers or brawlers, such as neglect their callings, mispend what they earn, and do not provide for themselves or the support of their families.[4]

Colonial views about the virtue of hard work and the sin of idleness contributed to a hardened attitude toward these social outcasts and "sturdy beggars." As Boston divine Cotton Mather explained in the early 1700s, "For those who indulge themselves in idleness, the express command of God unto us is, that we should let them starve."[5]

The deserving poor, on the other hand, were eligible for public relief. In providing aid to the deserving poor, colonists were motivated by Christian duty and a belief that moral progress could be furthered by contributing to benevolent causes. Perhaps more importantly, early Americans recognized the connection between poverty and social disorder. Enabling the indigent to get back on their economic feet through public and private relief promoted good order and social harmony. Aid to the indigent also helped to maintain a well-ordered and hierarchical society because each class of people had special privileges and obligations: "the poor to work hard and to respect and show deference to those above them," explains scholar Walter Trattner, "the well-to-do to be humble and to aid and care for those below them."[6] Economic dependence among the indigent therefore helped to promote the deferential society so desired by the upper class.

EARLY RELIEF EFFORTS

Colonial poor relief followed England's Elizabethan Poor Law of 1601 and the Settlement Act of 1662, which charged the unit of local government with care of the poor. Local taxation supported care for the poor, and local officials defined legal residency status as eligibility requirements for assistance. In Boston and Newport responsibility for poor relief fell on the town selectmen and elected overseers of the poor. In the other cities vestrymen and church wardens had charge of aid to the indigent. These overseers of the poor determined methods of relief, investigated applicants for assistance, distributed aid to the needy, and enforced the settlement clauses. They also imposed certain moral standards on those petitioning for assistance. When Frances James of Charles Town applied for relief, overseers of the poor promised her 30 pence per month but only as long as "she remains sober." The poor also had to show at least pretended respect and deference to their social superiors if they wanted aid. Private charities and overseers of the poor typically investigated to see if a person was "worthy" unless that person produced a "proper Recommendation from respectable Inhabitants." Many silk-stocking charity-dispensing groups and upper-crust public officials therefore expected and received "a becoming deference" from the poor.[7]

While local officials always limited aid to those following a certain moral and behavioral code, they did not always have well-thought-out plans for poor relief. Instead, early municipal assistance tended to be a noninstitutional, haphazard patchwork. Much of the aid consisted of outdoor relief—direct grants of money, firewood, food, clothing, and medical care—to the indigent and needy within their homes. Hence in 1664 Boston's selectmen paid Dr. Thomas Oliver

£5 "for seven months attendance upon … Thomas Hawkins," a needy person. When Charles Town commissioners of the market discovered local bakers using weighted scales, they confiscated 900 loaves of bread and distributed them to the poor. A more common form of relief was abatement of taxes. In 1656 the Boston town meeting agreed that a "Mr. Wales hath six shillings abated of his [tax] rate for this year in regard to his poverty." Officials in New York City sometimes provided the indigent with tools, fish nets, flax wheels, wool cards, and other items to assist them in "getting a livelyhood." For those destitute who were unable to care for themselves and with no family or relatives to care for them, local officials usually auctioned them off to the lowest bidder. One New Englander recalled the auctioneer's description of a pauper subject to epileptic fits: "Here is Mr._____; he is a strong, hearty, sound man who can eat anything, and a good deal of it; how much do you bid?" Sometimes the successful bidder was on the verge of poverty himself and was simply looking for either cheap labor or additional income to help him get by. At times the indigent were treated like unwanted dogs, bandied about from one family to another by councilmen seeking the cheapest terms or by caretakers tiring of their charges. One poor Rhode Island widow was moved 12 times during the last six years of her life.[8]

POVERTY LEVELS

However, the poor were not just those who received public relief but also those who lived from hand to mouth and were therefore continually at risk of becoming dependent on charity. This included a relatively large percentage of the urban population. For example, bound laborers, who lived in very circumscribed material conditions, comprised approximately 15 percent of the urban working class during the mid-1700s. Lesser skilled workers and journeymen artisans, who made up nearly one-half of all free men in the cities, often had difficulty providing for their families' basic needs. Many, if not most, lived on the edge of poverty. According to one historian, these unfortunate folk "dined like prisoners, dressed in the same fashion as almshouse inmates, and crowded into cramped quarters." A reduction in income, an injury or illness to the breadwinner, or an increase in expenses forced many honest and industrious tradesmen to slip into poverty. Between one-fourth and one-sixth of mariners, laborers, sawyers, cordwainers, tailors, weavers, and breech-makers in Philadelphia received poor relief in the early 1770s. As one Philadelphia tradesmen

Distribution of Wealth in the Northern Cities

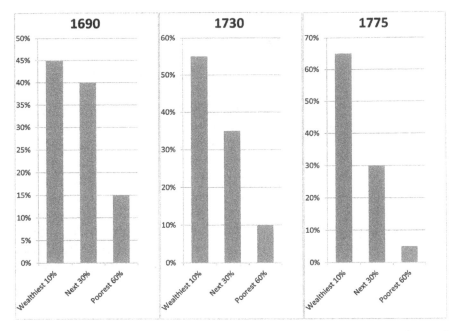

This series of line graphs illustrates the urban elite's expanding share of wealth and the decreasing shares of those belonging to the middling and poorer sections. By 1775, the poorest 60 percent of urban residents owned less than 5 percent of taxable wealth.

complained, "I have a wife and six children, most of them sick. I have strove all in my power and find that I cannot support them; the different taxes, together with the unavoidable necessary expenses of a family, altho' strictly parsimonious, had reduced me ... I could point out a great number in similar circumstances with myself, and I am sure some of them in a more deplorable condition, if possible." Thus even during the best of times life was precarious for many urban working-class people. Taken together, the poor and the near poor comprised fully one-third of all residents of the five seaports by the late colonial period.[9]

CAUSES OF POVERTY

A variety of factors came together in the early to mid-eighteenth century to cause this dramatic rise in poverty levels. Perhaps the most significant of these was skyrocketing population in the five seaport communities between 1700 and 1760: Boston, 6,700 to

15,631; Charles Town, 2,000 to 8,000; Newport, 2,600 to 7,500; New York, 5,000 to 18,000; and Philadelphia, 5,000 to 23,750. Much of this population growth resulted from a significant increase in both foreign and domestic immigration into the seaports. Beginning in the 1760s numerous veterans of the Seven Years War, along with many young ex-servants from the countryside, streamed into the seaports looking for work. The proportion of single men and women in Boston, for example, rose from only 7 percent in the 1720s to 43 percent by 1771. Further inflating the population of the seaports, and adding to the local relief rolls, was the arrival of thousands of German, Irish, and French Canadians looking for better opportunities in British North America. Some of these new arrivals moved on to the frontier, but many made their homes in the seaports. This was particularly true for those foreigners who arrived destitute and "in a bad state of health" and therefore did not have the physical or financial means to establish themselves on a farm. A typical group of 300 Irish immigrants who arrived in Charles Town in the late 1760s were temporarily lodged in the "Old Barracks" because nearly every one of them suffered from a "cruel Flux and Fever." A churchman who visited them found a "dismal and melancholy scene ... Corpses ... many dying ... young children lying entirely naked ... reduced to sickness ... whose parents had expired." Many of these indigent immigrants became expensive wards of the community. Similarly, Indian wars augmented poverty rates and drained local charitable resources as thousands of frightened refugees fled into seaport communities seeking safety and aid.[10]

A growing concentration of wealth in the major cities also contributed to a rise in poverty. Except for Boston, the five seaports witnessed a significant increase in trade during the eighteenth century. Unfortunately for the lower classes, the enormous wealth brought in from this trade did not much trickle down to them. In the 80 years prior to the American Revolution, the top 5 percent of residents in Boston, Philadelphia, and New York City saw their share of taxable wealth increase from approximately one-third to over one-half of all wealth in these cities. In Charles Town, the top 10 percent of residents owned more than half of the town's assets by the late 1760s. Meanwhile, the bottom half of residents in the cities were left with a mere 3 to 5 percent of taxable wealth. These figures suggest that the lower sort after about 1750 had a greater chance of falling further down the economic ladder than climbing up it. Further exacerbating the plight of the working class was rampant inflation. Any financial gains made by most people were wiped out by the approximately 50 percent rise in the price of goods in the major urban centers between 1745 and 1775.[11]

The numerous European wars for empire fought in America during the eighteenth century also disrupted local economies that depended on trade. One New Yorker lamented during the economic depression following King George's War (1744–1748) that "[w]e already begin to experience the Effects of idle Hands; some of the inhabitants have been robbed, others knocked down; many Beggars troubling our doors, and our Poor-House full; our Taxes high, our Provisions dear, and all Trade at a Stand at present..." These wars also diverted numerous men into the military, many of whom were either killed or severely injured, thus leaving families either temporarily or permanently without able-bodied men to provide for them. Further killing off many providers were deadly epidemics that frequently plagued the five cities. Less terrifying but more common was work-related deaths and injuries. Some men simply abandoned their families and fled west to the frontier or to another city. Such circumstances left many women without husbands and therefore often with little means of support. The Boston census of 1742 listed 1,200 widows, nearly all of whom were described as in "low circumstances." Not surprisingly, women comprised a majority of those on public relief. The irregularity of work, caused by dull seasons, vacillating consumer demand, and erratic delivery of raw materials, placed additional economic hardship on workers. With no unions to protect them and little or no property to fall back on when the economy contracted, many urban workers sank swiftly into the ranks of the unemployed and onto the list of public relief rolls. White workers in the cities, especially those in Charles Town, faced the added difficulty of having to compete with slave labor.[12]

PUBLIC CHARITY

The dramatic increase in poverty in the seaports during the eighteenth century naturally witnessed a corresponding rise in poor-relief expenditures for city governments. During the first half of the eighteenth century, poor relief constituted one-third to one-half of Boston's yearly assessments, which rose more than 10 times from £1,200 in 1714 to £15,000 in 1745. Circumstances did not improve much between 1740 and 1770 when poor-relief payments in Boston and Philadelphia tripled, while in New York City and Charles Town they soared over 600 percent. To pay for this aid,

urban officials were forced to raise taxes. However, raising sufficient funds for the indigent became increasingly difficult because
the increase in poor residents brought a corresponding decrease in the
number of taxpayers. The number of taxable residents in Philadelphia
relieved of taxes due to poverty increased from 2.5 percent in 1720
to nearly 11 percent by 1770. In Boston nearly one-third of taxpayers
did not possess any taxable property on the eve of the Revolution
and another 30 percent had to pinch pennies to pay their taxes. The
other cities saw a similar draining of their tax base during the
late colonial period. Thus financing poor relief increasingly fell on
the more well-to-do, who sometimes voiced their complaint against
this financial burden. Tax collectors in New York City, for example,
were regularly "abused" and treated with "harsh Censure and loud
Complaints of Niggardly, selfish and inconsiderate persons" who
claimed that they were "rated too high and beyond all Proportion."
Authorities there became so desperate for funds for poor relief
that they even taxed ownership of dogs! Residents of Newport went
further than most disgruntled taxpayers by regularly staging "tax
revolts" to protest higher taxes for poor relief.[13]

PRIVATE CHARITY

To supplement public relief, more well-to-do citizens, motivated
both by a sense of noblesse oblige and Christian duty, established
a host of charitable and mutual aid organizations associated along
ethnic, occupational, and religious lines. The English, Dutch, Irish,
Scots, French, German, and Jewish residents established their own
mutual aid societies that donated money and basic necessities for
needy members of their community. Likewise, artisans such as tailors, mariners, carpenters, and coopers formed their own occupational benevolent organizations to assist their fellow tradesmen
during hard times. More generally, a growing number of middling
people who did not wish to be "nest pheasants" like the leisured
gentry also established their own charitable organizations that
reflected their middle-class values of piety, charity, and prudence.
The Fellowship Society of Charles Town, founded by an upholsterer
in 1766, devoted its meetings to listening to sermons, gave its
leftover food to the poor, and used its membership dues to build a
charity school and low-rent tenements for needy families. This
benevolence was in sharp contrast to that provided by more gentri-
fied "charitable" organizations whose members devoted more of
their time and money to attending concerts and eating sumptuous

dinners than aiding the less fortunate. Similarly, the middle-class Sons of King Tammany of Philadelphia, in a deliberate rejection of the self-indulgent hedonism of upper-class clubs, declared its purpose as a society "of great Utility to the Distressed; as this Meeting [is] more for the purpose of promoting charity and benevolence than for Mirth and frivolity."[14]

Churches, too, regularly raised and donated significant relief funds through "charity sermons." Some affluent residents willed money and land to local churches and synagogues for the express purpose of assisting the city's poor. In the late colonial period, Boston's 15 churches constituted the town's single largest private source for charity. Although most recipients of church charity had to be members in good standing and had to suffer unusual circumstances, benevolence sometimes extended beyond the parish walls. When a particularly harsh winter hit Boston in 1740–1741, the city's churches transcended their denominational differences and donated their collections to help all of the city's poor. In 1767 ministers of St. Philip's Church in Charles Town raised £200 sterling in two days, as well as food, clothing, and blankets, for a group of newly arrived Belfast immigrants in great distress.

Outside of churches and synagogues, citizens also formed ad hoc charitable organizations during the winter months when work, fuel, and food were in short supply in the cities. Devastation caused by fires, hurricanes, and other natural calamities also brought citizens together to assist the needy. Some well-to-do Bostonians in 1751 hit upon a novel idea to reduce poverty rolls in the capital city by employing destitute women and children in a linen factory created from private subscription. Exploitation disguised as charity, the private enterprise failed as both a charitable effort and a business venture. Full-time spinners received a paltry seven shillings a week, wages not even close to meeting a person's basic needs, and subscribers saw little, if any, return from their investment before the business went belly-up in 1759. This failure aside, scholars estimate that, altogether, private charities provided approximately 25 percent of all money spent on poor relief.[15]

RESPONSES TO RISING POVERTY LEVELS

Reducing Expenses

In dealing with rising poverty levels, urban governments adopted a largely punitive approach, emphasizing reduction of public expenses rather than attacking the causes of poverty. In all of the

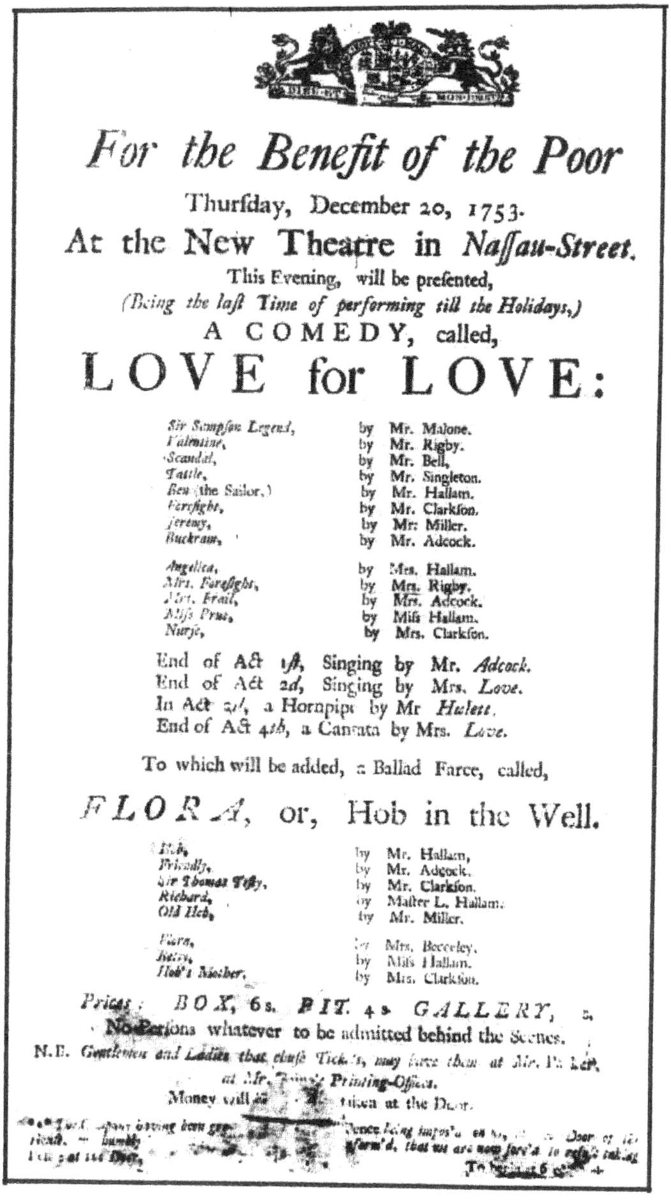

For the Benefit of the Poor

Thursday, December 20, 1753.

At the New Theatre in *Nassau-Street.*

This Evening, will be presented,

(*Being the last Time of performing till the Holidays,*)

A COMEDY, called,

LOVE for LOVE:

Sir Sampson Legend,	by Mr. Malone.
Valentine,	by Mr. Rigby.
Scandal,	by Mr. Bell,
Tattle,	by Mr. Singleton.
Ben (the Sailor,)	by Mr. Hallam.
Foresight,	by Mr. Clarkson.
Jeremy,	by Mr. Miller.
Buckram,	by Mr. Adcock.
Angelica,	by Mrs. Hallam.
Mrs. Foresight,	by Mrs. Rigby.
Mrs. Frail,	by Mrs. Adcock.
Miss Prue,	by Miss Hallam.
Nurse,	by Mrs. Clarkson.

End of Act 1st, Singing by Mr. *Adcock.*
End of Act 2d, Singing by Mrs. *Love.*
In Act 3d, a Hornpipe by Mr *Hulett.*
End of Act 4th, a Cantata by Mrs. *Love.*

To which will be added, a Ballad Farce, called,

FLORA, or, Hob in the Well.

Hob,	by Mr. Hallam,
Friendly,	by Mr. Adcock.
Sir Thomas Testy,	by Mr. Clarkson.
Richard,	by Master L. Hallam.
Old Hob,	by Mr. Miller.
Flora,	by Mrs. Beccely.
Betty,	by Miss Hallam.
Hob's Mother,	by Mrs. Clarkson.

Prices: *BOX,* 6s. *PIT,* 4s. *GALLERY,* 2s.

No Persons whatever to be admitted behind the Scenes.

N.B. *Gentlemen and Ladies that chuse Tickets, may have them at Mr. Parker's Printing-Office.*

Money will not be taken at the Door.

Advertisement for a Theatrical Performance to Benefit the Poor. Urban residents devised a variety of clever means by which to raise money for their less fortunate neighbors. This advertisement for a theatrical performance in New York City "For the Benefit of the Poor" illustrates a common method of poor relief among well-to-do residents who combined their genteel amusements with charity. (Charles Evans, *Early American Imprints*, Series 1, no. 40660) cities, for example, overseers of the poor became more vigilant against alleged "welfare cheats." Pressured to reduce poor-relief expenses, the churchwardens (oftentimes with the assistance of local physicians) judged an increasing number of poor and infirm as "unworthy objects of charity." Officials in Newport forced financially able residents to support their relatives instead of keeping them at taxpayers' expense. Churchwardens also hunted down delinquent fathers and forced them to support their wives and children. When overseers of the poor in Charles Town learned that Henry Beckham had "turned his wife out of doors with a young Infant at her Breast and refused her support," they ordered Beckham to "allow his wife and child a maintenance of Eight pounds per month." Likewise, after Elizabeth Vassals informed the Charles Town churchmen that she was unable to provide for Edward McGrady's "bastard child," the poor-relief officials provided her with relief funds and promptly sent the bill to McGrady.[16]

Urban officials were just as vigilant against paupers entering their city. To keep indigents from disembarking in their communities, city leaders required ships captains to reveal all names and occupations of their passengers and to transport back all those without either a vocation or property. In November 1719 Boston's "sea watcher" prevented 49 Irish paupers from disembarking from the ship *Elizabeth*. Any strangers entering the cities, furthermore, had to register with the city recorder; those householders entertaining strangers had to put up security in order "to save the town from charge." To enforce these measures, municipal governments employed constables to hunt down strangers and bring them before the mayor for questioning and possible expulsion. Ordinary citizens also took it upon themselves to enforce regulations against strangers. In 1744, Dr. Alexander Hamilton of Maryland arrived in Newport at night, was mistaken for a peddler, and was quickly surrounded by townspeople who inquired about his intentions. Such behavior not only helped to limit expenses for poor relief, according to historian Sheila Skemp, it also helped to develop community spirit and cooperation by directing the hostility of the lower classes away from well-to-do town leaders and toward "strangers" and foreigners.[17]

To further slow the skyrocketing cost of poor relief, city governments tightened the rules of eligibility for assistance. The South Carolina legislature, for example, increased residency requirements in Charles Town from 3 to 12 months for anyone seeking welfare. In addition to tightening residency requirements for aid, New York

City officials rounded up people of questionable character (i.e., vagrants) and transported them out of the city. Vestrymen in Charles Town reduced welfare rolls by simply paying the poor to leave town, like George Audrey, who received a blanket and £5 "provided he and his family do go into the country." To protect their cities against "foreign Invasions of Beggary and Idleness," officials in Boston and Newport warned out indigent persons entering their cities. Failure to leave could result in a public whipping before being physically hauled out of town. By the early 1770s Boston officials were warning out of their city over 450 people a year. Selectmen in Newport even ordered out of their town the mentally retarded and women "big with a bastard child" if it appeared they would become a burden to the community. And because sailors and their families comprised a significant portion of the urban poor, officials in Newport went so far as to deduct six pence per month from the salary of every sailor departing from the city. The ship captain was responsible for collecting the money, which authorities placed in a special fund for the sailor's relief.[18]

Urban officials treated children of poor parents in a similar manner by binding them out as apprentices to other families, who frequently exploited them as cheap labor. Some parents, unable to care for their children, reluctantly committed them to terms of "apprenticeship" for up to 15 years. In doing so, they forfeited parental contact and influence. One Philadelphia woman, for instance, gave up her young son because she had no other means to live but by hiring herself out as a maid, "which she could not do," she explained, "with the child." Parents receiving alms or living in the poorhouse often had their children forcibly taken away from them by city officials and bound out as apprentices.

Not surprisingly, this practice deterred many impoverished parents from seeking public aid. It also encouraged pregnant women who resided in the poorhouse to escape before giving birth because authorities would more than likely confiscate the child, especially if the father of the child was unknown. Over time, overseers of the poor had the added authority to bind out to "orderly families" children of persons who "neglect the due care and improvement of their estate... mispend their time and money, and live idle, vagrant and dissolute lives." For example, eight-year-old William Thomas of Philadelphia was taken from his parents and apprenticed out after authorities apprehended him for begging in the streets. The boy explained that his mariner father was "gone to sea" and his mother "goes out washing cloaths for a livelihood," leaving him home to care for his younger brother. As it turned out, these pauper apprentices were rarely given the education and skills necessary to rise out of poverty and become financially successful. Most did manage to avoid seeking public relief after completing their indenture, but they rarely managed to become independent workers or farmers.[19]

Not all cities apprenticed orphans and children belonging to poor and indigent parents. Overseers of the poor in Charles Town preferred placing such children with either foster parents or in church-supported institutions. Of the 618 children assisted by St. Philip's Church in the two decades preceding the American Revolution, churchwardens bound out only 22 as apprentices. Instead, their first choice was to place children in foster homes, but only after carefully investigating the character of the prospective foster parents, who received financial compensation from the government for taking in the children. For example, the city gave Ann Walker 40 shillings per month to rear Samuel Smith, "a soldier's orphan"; Elizabeth Murphy was reimbursed annually to maintain care for Michael, "a child found in the streets"; and Margaret Miller received £6 per month to care for two immigrant children from Germany "whose parents died on the passage." If overseers of the poor could not find foster parents for orphaned or neglected children, they placed them in the city's Free School to be both boarded and schooled. To ensure that children housed there received proper educational and moral development, church officials frequently interviewed the students to "inspect their progress in learning and behavior." In doing so, their intention was to ensure that these young wards of the state became literate, law-abiding, and productive members of society.[20]

Institutionalizing the Poor

The desire to reform the indigent into becoming independent and productive citizens was also behind the movement among urban leaders to institutionalize the poor during the early eighteenth century. To that end, the five major seaports constructed poorhouses or workhouses (often referred to by contemporaries as almshouses) to house their growing number of poor residents. Boston built the first almshouse in North America in 1664, followed by New York City in 1700, Newport in 1723, Philadelphia in 1732, and finally Charles Town in 1736. Further motivating advocates to institutionalize the poor was a desire to cut relief expenditures. In authorizing the construction of New York City's new poorhouse in 1735, for example, officials there referred to the "Necessity, Number and Continual Increase of the poor within this City [as] very great and Exceeding burthensome to the Inhabitants thereof." The government hoped that taking the indigent out of their homes and placing them under one roof would significantly reduce city expenditures for poor relief. Officials also intended the almshouses to operate as work-houses for the able-bodied poor, who would produce marketable goods, the proceeds of which the city would use to defray costs for maintaining the institution. This emphasis on putting the poor to work was the result of a growing belief in Europe and America that labor, not benevolence, best remedied the sin of sloth.[21]

The traditional forms of charity such as out-relief were now thought to encourage idleness and dependency. Instead, labor now became the key toward transforming the poor—who were generally characterized as indolent drunkards—into industrious and independent citizens. For example, the only direct aid and shelter provided for the poor by Newport was the workhouse, where inmates were either set to work making oakum or were bound out as apprentices as a means of minimizing the burden on the town treasury while providing cheap labor for employers. The city's overseers of the poor even had the authority to commit to the work-house any person whom they felt *might* become a charge to the town. Such power left the urban poor extremely vulnerable to exploitation by the well-to-do.[22]

There were other reasons besides cost in placing the poor indoors. Perhaps most importantly, well-to-do residents did not like to see the city streets crowded with beggars, whom they considered an irritating nuisance. William Lawrence, an impoverished New Yorker who suffered from a "cancer in his face," was in such a "miserable condition to behold" that city officials granted him four shillings a week on the condition that he "forebear showing himself in the streets and asking for charity."[23] Residents of New York City praised their government for building the poorhouse because it "in a great Measure delivered [the city] from the scandal of street beggars." But the almshouses did more than keep beggars off the streets. They also served as orphanages where abandoned and neglected children could receive care and supervision, as "old age homes" where the elderly could receive some care and companionship, and as hospitals where the sick, who comprised a large percentage of the poor, could receive attention. In short, the poorhouse met a variety of community needs.[24]

GENDER AND POOR RELIEF

For the most part, the almshouses did not live up to these grand expectations. Before poverty rates skyrocketed, the poorhouses were mainly used as a place of last resort for the most destitute and infirm. Until the 1730s, for example, New York City's almshouse was essentially a boarding house for the seriously ill to "either recover or die in peace." At least 40 percent of those who went there died within a few months of their arrival. But as the number of poor in the cities soared, overseers of the poor used their ideas of gender to determine, at least in part, who received relief and entrance into the almshouse. For a variety of reasons, the vast majority of people admitted into poorhouses during the late colonial period were women. On average, adult women outnumbered adult men on relief by a ratio of more than six to four. Women also received the majority of poor-relief pensions. In Philadelphia, for example, women comprised more than three-fourths of all recipients of poor relief. Overseers of the poor also provided more out-relief to women, thus allowing them to live in their homes, while requiring men to live and labor in the municipal workhouse in return for aid. Most women who received aid either in the poorhouse or at home were able-bodied, although nearly one-third of those admitted into Philadelphia's "Bettering House" were either pregnant or afflicted with venereal disease. Many more had children and no husband. On the other hand, officials admitted few able-bodied men to the almshouses. Nearly all those men who were admitted were either sick, aged, or injured. Wardens of the almshouses also applied a much stricter definition of "fitness" toward male inmates than their female counterparts with the result that the former were more quickly and frequently released from the poorhouse than the latter. For example, the warden at Philadelphia's poorhouse described his inmate Thomas Tanten as "an old infirm Butcher" but released him anyway on the belief that he "yet might perhaps do something" for his own keep. Considering the physical condition of this old man, this "something" was probably to beg on the streets for aid.[25]

These differences between male and female recipients of poor relief reflect the differing causes of poverty between men and women. In general, women were more susceptible to poverty because their employment opportunities were limited, their marketable skills few, and their wages low. Their financial circumstances became even more precarious if they lost a husband and had young children to care for. Women with children seeking public relief in New York City, for example, outnumbered poor men with children 19 to 1. On the other hand, contemporaries assumed that only debilitating illness, injury, or old age prevented a man from providing for himself and his family. For this reason, overseers of the poor frequently rejected young men for public assistance—no matter their physical condition. Thus institutional care for men was primarily designed to get them quickly back on their feet. So while poor women received money, food, blankets, wood, and extended stays in the almshouse, most indigent men received only medical care in the poorhouses until the warden determined them "fit" to fend for themselves.[26]

DESCRIBING THE POOR

No matter their sex, poorhouse inmates were a pitiful lot. Many arrived nearly naked and physically broken. "Lame and worthless," "invalid," "cripple," "blind," "deaf," "broken limb," "missing limb," "scalded," "beaten," and "emaciated with Poverty and Disease" are typical descriptions made by poorhouse wardens of these most destitute people. Thomas Peters was one of many who arrived in the Philadelphia poorhouse "in a naked, starved and ragged condition, and running away with vermin." Likewise, John Brown came in as "a sick man wrap'd in filthy rags & Swarming with Vermin," while Isabella Wallington arrived in "almost naked & every way wretched & abandoned." Lydia Landrum arrived at the same almshouse "in a state of starvation and nakedness, and brought in a cart . . . being so extremely numb with cold that she was entirely helpless." She died a few days later. Elizabeth Deford, a Philadelphia woman suffering from syphilis, also died a few days after entering the municipal almshouse nearly deprived of the use of her limbs "by being exposed to a Street lodging in the night, not having the wherewith to lay her head." In fact, about 10 percent of women entering almshouses suffered from venereal disease, most of them prostitutes. Because these "ladies of the night" were independent of male authority and were sources of bodily and moral corruption, poorhouse employees treated them with scorn rather than compassion. Descriptions by almshouse wardens of these licentious and diseased women as "worn-out Venereal Ladies," "a vile young Hussey severely Pox'd," and "a frequent Pocky Customer of the most worthless kind" typify the general attitude toward prostitutes. Sadly, many harlots died horrible deaths in the almshouses, like Sarah Simpson of Philadelphia, whom the director described as "so very soft and tender as to be nearly or quite Rotten with the Venereal Disease."[27]

Some poor people were so physically weak that they were unable to walk to the poorhouse. Such was the case with John Griffin, a laborer from Philadelphia, who was carried into the almshouse in a cart by the night watchman because he "had no nourishment for the past week, slept at night in any hole or corner he could creep into . . . not being able to walk, and being very dirty and swarming with bodily vermin." Nearly 10 percent of those hauled into almshouses, at least the one in Philadelphia, were simply drunk. Mary Lane, "a very noted Drunken disorderly woman," was brought into the poorhouse one evening "in a Cart & Very Drunk." Likewise, an unknown woman found "beastly drunk in the streets & in danger of perishing" was also carted into the Philadelphia almshouse. Others entered the poorhouse as victims of drunken and abusive behavior by others. One elderly female inmate, for example, was described by its director as "much beat and Bruised in a drunken fight with her husband, in which it appears, she was only second best." Another woman entered the Philadelphia almshouse after a failed attempt to drown herself because her husband had "severely beaten her." Similarly, one woman with two children went to the almshouse to escape the abuse of a "Worthless Drunken Husband." Heartless and pinch-penny authorities further dismembered the family by indenturing the older child as an apprentice rather than spend a few pence to keep the child with his mother.[28]

YOUNG AND ELDERLY POOR

The circumstances surrounding children admitted into municipal poorhouses are the most pitiful and heart-wrenching of all. Some poor children, apprenticed out by churchwardens, were brought back to the almshouses because they were "greatly misused" by their masters. Many others were found abandoned in the streets, such as John Yard, an eight-year-old boy from Philadelphia whose parents "Neglect to provide for him & who was taken up in the Streets Begging." Isaac Potter, a three-year-old black boy whose mother had eloped and whose father was a "lunatic" in the Philadelphia hospital, was also found begging in the streets. Another child was found in the street beside the "drunk and insensible body of his mother," while authorities picked up a young girl begging in the streets with her blind father. Nearly as depressing were the numerous elderly poor and infirm who spent their final days in the overcrowded, noisy, and stinking municipal poorhouses. Of the 102 people 60 years of age or older who entered the Boston almshouse between 1759 and 1771, 99 of them ultimately died there.[29]

THE INSANE POOR

Nearly 10 percent of poorhouse inmates were the "deranged," "insane," or "lunatic." Not much is known about the extent and circumstances of mental illness in early America, but the scant evidence suggests that colonists gave little attention to the insane. This was partly because contemporaries thought insanity to be the result of supernatural and natural phenomena and therefore immune to successful human intervention. The insane were also a common sight in the port cities. Residents therefore gave little thought or attention to mentally distracted persons, as long as they behaved in a nonviolent manner. For example, parishioners in one Boston church tolerated the antics of a crazy congregant who took particular delight in attaching a fishing hook to a pin and lifting the wigs off the heads of fellow worshipers during Sunday service. Less humorous was the behavior of an insane Bostonian who enjoyed walking the city streets making "insulting speeches" in "high flown language" to everyone he met. More titillating was Susannah Hall of Pennsylvania, a woman "so disordered in her reason and understanding" that she strolled from town to town "naked without any regard for the laws and rules of decency." Just plain odd was Joseph Moody, a Boston minister who constantly wore a handkerchief over his face, behavior that earned him the sobriquet "Handkerchief" by parishioners.[30]

Some insane paupers survived through begging and were well known by residents. Occasionally authorities rounded up these "street fixtures" and took them to the local workhouse to earn their food. But for the most part officials left the insane alone. Care for the mentally ill was a family responsibility; if family members sought help for their distracted loved one—and they rarely did—they often called in the local minister to offer the traditional remedies of prayer and fasting. Only when the deranged became a financial burden to the community or when they had a proclivity toward violence did authorities intervene and place them in poorhouses. Those who were not a physical threat were forced to labor in the workhouse section of the almshouse alongside the mentally sound, while those with violent tendencies were chained to walls in unheated basements away from the other inmates. Adding to the cruel mistreatment of the insane inmates were the sadistic forms of treatment inflicted on them by local physicians. Believing that mental illness derived in part from hyperactivity, Dr. Benjamin Rush of Philadelphia constrained the insane in "restraining chairs" and placed a wooden box stuffed with cloth over their head to dull light and sound. Another cruel "cure" for insanity involved placing the patient in a "gyrator," a horizontal board that spun in circles to produce dizziness and redirect circulation. For extreme cases, the Philadelphia physician poured buckets of cold water on overwrought patients to literally "cool" their passions. Not surprisingly, the "outcries and antics" of the mentally ill resulting from such cruel mistreatment oftentimes made life unbearable for the other inmates. To sum up, city almshouses contained a motley cross section of those down and out in colonial urban society: the destitute young and aged, the infirm, the insane, the sick, the alcoholic, and even the criminal.[31]

CRIMINALIZING THE POOR

Colonial officials often housed the indigent and criminals together and generally treated them in a similar manner. Doing so made perfect sense for all but the most enlightened eighteenth-century Americans. Both the pauper and the criminal "blurred in the public mind," explains historian Barbara Bellows, because both groups were viewed as having faulty characters. Indolence, drunkenness, licentiousness, and materialism were all viewed by contemporaries as explanations for the impoverished position of the destitute. And because some poor people resorted to theft in order to survive, being impoverished was therefore considered just one step away from being a true criminal. Authorities in New York City, Philadelphia, and Newport required all people who received public assistance to wear badges of the letter P on their clothing, a humiliating form of punishment similar to that given to common criminals. Moreover, the term early Americans often used to describe the poor—"objects of charity"—connotes an attitude that a relief recipient was seen more as a thing than as a person. In short, city officials came to regard the poor as "flawed members of society" who needed to be "reformed rather than relieved."[32]

These attitudes toward the poor suggest that colonists increasingly viewed crime and poverty as related phenomena demanding "similar correction methods." Directors of city poorhouses therefore treated their inmates much like dangerous criminals in need of reform. In doing so, they had the complete support of town leaders. Charles Town officials bluntly explained their reason for building a poorhouse: "to punish idle and disorderly people" (i.e., poor beggars) and to "prevent the great Increase of poor in Charleston." When the poorhouse opened in 1736, the city's vestrymen ordered all poor people in the parish immediately removed from their homes and placed in the "Work House." This workhouse also functioned as a house of correction for criminals because the provincial assembly refused to build a separate jail, a circumstance that forced the poor who resided there to live side by side with "criminals, vagrants, sailors, and Negroes." Likewise, New York City's institution was given the all-embracing name of "House of Correction, Workhouse and Poor House." As the name implies, poor inmates lived side by side with recalcitrant servants, rogues, vagabonds, and other "disorderly persons." Like its criminal population, Charles Town's and New York City's workhouse poor might face shackles and even "moderate whipping." Tellingly, New York City officials elected the "public whipper" as the first director of the town's almshouse.[33]

This use of physical punishment, along with the rules and regulations governing all almshouses, were intended to educate the poor about the "improprieties of their conduct" and to instill within them the values and skills necessary for them to live without public assistance. To that end, the poorhouse directors, who had virtual dictatorial powers over their charges, created a highly regimented daily routine and draconian rules for the inmates that any modern prisoner or soldier would find familiar. Indeed, officials deliberately made conditions in poorhouses uncomfortable in an effort to discourage the poor from relying on state aid. Like a prison, all poorhouses were surrounded by gates, which the director kept well secured. The warden allowed no one to enter or to leave the premises without his permission. If allowed to travel, an inmate had to return "in good Order at the time appointed" or lose his or her rights to mobility for one month for the first offense and three months for every subsequent offense. Inside, the inmates lived in a very structured environment. Bells awakened the residents at dawn and summoned them to bed at 9:00 (8:00 in the winter). Even the eating process was well regulated. Inmates in Philadelphia's almshouse, for instance, were seated according to the "order or classes settled by the Manager" and were required to wait in silence until the "pious and devout among them" had the opportunity to say grace. During their meals the residents were to "behave with decency & good manners toward each other." Remaining civil towards one another had to be difficult given the appallingly overcrowded rooms in which they resided. The Philadelphia "Bettering House," for example, had six beds crammed into rooms only 10 feet by 10 feet in size. By 1756 Boston's 33-room almshouse was crammed with 148 inmates. Nearly 430 people jostled for space in New York City's overcrowded poorhouse in 1772. Along with cramped conditions, residents there also had to deal with a faulty sewage system that frequently backed up and flooded the building.[34]

In return for their food, clothing, and lodging, those inmates able to work were forced to labor eight hours a day in the winter and perhaps as many as 14 hours in the summer producing something that could be sold to defray the city's relief expenditures. Such labor was also designed to provide residents with the training and discipline they allegedly needed to become independent citizens. Women and the aged generally spent their time picking oakum (a hemp fiber used to caulk seams in ships) while craftsmen labored at their trades. Wayward youth were reformed through learning and labor. Poorhouse rules required boys to receive instruction in the Bible and the "three Rs," while girls learned spinning and sewing. This monotony was broken up every Wednesday and Friday mornings by mandatory prayer services. Those who skipped the religious service were denied dinner that evening. At all times almshouse inmates were required to behave "submissively to their superiors & Governors," a clear indication of their inferior status. Further reminding all inmates of their demeaning position was the physical punishment that awaited them if they refused to work or broke any of the house rules. This might include whippings of up to 15 lashes, being held in shackles, or being placed in solitary confinement in a dark room on a diet of bread and water. Rather than submit to such demeaning and dehumanizing rules and punishments, many urban poor simply stopped applying for municipal relief. Philadelphia's churchwardens noticed that the city's poor would rather "rob & steal" than be coerced into the local workhouse, while Charles Town's vestrymen reprimanded the warden of the city almshouse because his ill treatment of the poor made them "choose rather to beg about the Street than take relief there [in the poorhouse]." Consequently, only "absolute desperate" indigents endured the stigma and degradation of seeking assistance in the public almshouses. Once in, they usually tried to leave as quickly as possible.

Approximately half of all inmates left the poorhouse within three months. Changes in climate explain why others left and returned. Paupers in New York City "made a practice of absenting themselves from the said poorhouse and selling or making away with their clothing in the summertime," complained local officials, "and returning to the said poorhouse on the approaching winter almost naked to the great expense and charge of the parish."[35]

CONCLUSION

The five major seaports witnessed a tremendous increase in their poor populations during the eighteenth century, a development that compelled people to look at the poor in new ways and forced urban leaders to devise alternative methods toward diminishing this social and economic crisis. Motivated more by a desire to relieve the relief rolls than to relieve the destitute, overseers of the poor adopted a generally heartless and patronizing attitude toward the indigent by purging many from the city poor lists for their supposed vices. The tendency of city officials to moralize about the destitute prevented them from devising and implementing programs to attack the true cause of poverty, which had much more to do with the vicissitudes of an unforgiving capitalist economy than any alleged personal character flaws. Churches and private charities, although providing a considerable portion of poor relief, proved ineffective in reducing the numbers of urban poor. That these efforts at poor relief "did nothing to alleviate poverty itself, that aid was at best merely a holding action," argues historian Sheila Skemp, "are, in a sense, irrelevant considerations." They do not refute the fact that "these ameliorative measures did soften the harshest conditions of the urban poor and simultaneously softened the attitude of even the poorest of the poorer sort toward their superiors." Poor relief, in other words, had as much to do with social control as with public charity; indeed, the two were inseparable in the minds of the ruling elite, who sought to dispense just enough crumbs to the suffering poor to ensure that they did not revolt against them.[36]

Public charity also served as an important social force in eroding barriers of localism and facilitating the growth of an American nationalism. During times of considerable privation, residents throughout a city, a region, and even the colonies came together to provide assistance. This is especially seen in Boston, which suffered a number of natural and man-made crises between 1740 and 1775.

The harsh winter of 1740–1741 encouraged all churches to set aside their bitter religious factionalism arising from the Great Awakening to extend their charity to all the city's poor, not just to members of their church. When smallpox swept through the city nearly 12 years later, people throughout rural Massachusetts, who generally had an antagonistic relationship with their urban counterparts, sent considerable aid to those suffering in the capital. Again, when fire destroyed much of Boston in 1760 and when the British closed down the city's port in 1774 as punishment for its infamous "tea party," Americans throughout the colonies sent food, fuel, and funds to the beleaguered Bostonians. In this way, argues historian Peter Virgadarmo, "charity grew from a local concern to a national spirit."[37]

NOTES

1. Jackson Turner Main, *The Social Structure of Revolutionary America* (Princeton, NJ: Princeton University Press, 1965), 37–43, 59, 72–81, 130, 230, 271–72; Stephen E. Wiberly Jr., "Four Cities: Public Poor Relief in Urban America, 1700–1775," Ph.D. dissertation, Yale University, 1975, 56–65.

2. Billy G. Smith, "Poverty and Marginality in Eighteenth-Century America," *Proceedings of the American Philosophical Society* 132 (1988): 90–91.

3. Sarah Fatherly, *Gentlewomen and Learned Ladies: Women and Elite Formation in Eighteenth Century Philadelphia* (Bethlehem, PA: Lehigh University Press, 2008), 30.

4. Wiberly, "Four Cities," 11–12.

5. Walter Trattner, *From Poor Law to Welfare State: A Social History of Social Welfare in America* (New York: The Free Press, 1994), 22 (quote); J. Richard Olivas, " 'God Helps Those Who Help Themselves': Religious Explanations of Poverty in Colonial Massachusetts, 1630–1776," in *Down and Out in Early America*, ed. Billy G. Smith (University Park: Pennsylvania State University Press, 2004), 262–67, 277–82.

6. Trattner, *From Poor Law to Welfare State*, 17.

7. Walter J. Fraser Jr., "Controlling the Poor in Colonial Charles Town," *Proceedings of the South Carolina Historical Association* (1980): 22; John K. Alexander, *Render Them Submissive: Responses to Poverty in Philadelphia, 1760–1800* (Amherst: University of Massachusetts Press, 1980), 23 (quote).

8. Trattner, *From Poor Law to Welfare State*, 18–19 (quotes); Barbara Ulmer, "Benevolence in Colonial Charleston," *Proceedings of the South Carolina Historical Association* (1980): 3; David Schneider, "The Patchwork of Relief in Provincial New York, 1664–1775," *Social Service Review* 12 (1938): 487 (quote); Benjamin Klebaner, "Pauper Auctions: The 'New England Method' of Public Poor Relief," *Historical Collections of the Essex*

Institute 91 (1955): 1 (quote); Charles Lee, "Public Poor Relief and the Massachusetts Community, 1620–1715," *New England Quarterly* 55 (1982): 572; Ruth Wallis Herndon, " 'Who Died an Expence to This Town': Poor Relief in Eighteenth-Century Rhode Island," in *Down and Out in Early America*, ed. Billy G. Smith (University Park,: Pennsylvania State University Press, 2004), 140, 143.

9. Billy G. Smith, *The 'Lower Sort': Philadelphia's Laboring People, 1750–1800* (Ithaca, NY: Cornell University Press, 1990), 125 (quote); Smith, "Poverty and Economic Marginality," 99, 105 (quote); Walter J. Fraser Jr., "The City Elite, 'Disorder,' and the Poor Children of Pre-Revolutionary Charleston," *South Carolina Historical Magazine* 84 (1983): 170–72; Bruce C. Daniels, "Poor Relief, Local Finance, and Town Government in Eighteenth-Century Rhode Island," *Rhode Island History* 40 (1981):86–87.

10. Smith, "Poverty and Economic Marginality," 91–92; Fraser, "The City Elite," 169 (quote); Trattner, *From Poor Law to Welfare State*, 21.

11. Gary Nash, "Urban Wealth and Poverty in Pre-Revolutionary America," *Journal of Interdisciplinary History* 6 (1976): 549–56, 572; Barbara Bellows, *Benevolence among Slaveholders: Assisting the Poor in Charleston, 1670–1860* (Baton Rouge: Louisiana State University Press, 1993), 14.

12. Raymond A. Mohl, "Poverty in Early America, A Reappraisal: The Case of Eighteenth-Century New York City," *New York History* 50 (1969): 13–14 (quote); Eric Nellis, "The Working Poor of Pre-Revolutionary Boston," *Historical Journal of Massachusetts* 17 (1989): 156; Ulmer, "Benevolence in Colonial Charleston," 5; Smith, "Poverty and Economic Marginality," 104; Eric Nellis, "Misreading the Signs: Industrial Imitation, Poverty, and the Social Order in Colonial Boston," *New England Quarterly* 59 (1986): 498.

13. Nian Shang Huang, "Financing Poor Relief in Colonial Boston," *Massachusetts Historical Review* 8 (2006): 79; Nash, "Urban Wealth and Poverty," 566; Fraser, "The City Elite," 168; Smith, "Poverty and Economic Marginality," 91–92; Steven J. Ross, " 'Objects of Charity': Poor Relief, Poverty, and the Rise of the Almshouse in Early Eighteenth-Century New York City," in *Authority and Resistance in Early New York*, ed. William Pencak and Conrad E. Wright (New York: New York Historical Society, 1988), 148 (quote); Mohl, "Poverty in Early America," 15; Daniels, "Poor Relief . . . in Rhode Island," 86.

14. Ulmer, "Benevolence in Colonial Charleston," 9–10; Emma Hart, *Building Charleston: Town and Society in the Eighteenth-Century British Atlantic World* (Charlottesville: University of Virginia Press, 2010), 142–45, quote on p. 143.

15. Bellows, *Benevolence among Slaveholders*, 9–10; Gary Nash, "Up from the Bottom in Franklin's Philadelphia," *Past and Present* 77 (1978): 75; Gary Nash, "Poverty and Poor Relief in Pre-Revolutionary Philadelphia," *William and Mary Quarterly* 33 (1976): 23–26; Alexander, *Render Them Submissive*, 87; Daniels, "Poor Relief . . . in Rhode Island," 82; Herndon,

"Who Died an Expence to This Town," 145–47; Peter Virgadarmo, "Charity for a City in Crisis: Boston, 1740–1775," *Historical Journal of Massachusetts* 10 (1982): 23; Nian Shang Huang presents a more positive interpretation of Boston's linen factory as an experiment in private charity in "Financing Poor Relief in Colonial Boston," 73–76, 81–93.

16. Wiberly, "Four Cities," 24; Daniels, "Poor Relief . . . in Rhode Island," 79–82; Fraser, "The City Elite," 172–73 (quote).

17. Trattner, *From Poor Law to Welfare State*, 21, 19 (quote); Sheila Skemp, "A Social and Cultural History of Newport, Rhode Island, 1720–1765," Ph.D. dissertation, University of Iowa, 1974), 113, 174–75.

18. Fraser, "The City Elite," 174; Fraser, "Controlling the Poor," 22; Smith, "Poverty and Economic Marginality," 94–95; Mohl, "Poverty in Early America," 15–16; Nash, "Urban Wealth and Poverty," 562–63; Ruth Wallis Herndon, *Unwelcome Americans: Living on the Margin in Early New England* (Philadelphia: University of Pennsylvania Press, 2001), 17 (quote); Daniels, "Poor Relief . . . in Rhode Island," 79–82; Skemp, "A Social and Cultural History of Newport," 117.

19. Smith, "Poverty and Economic Marginality," 106 (quotes); Simon P. Newman, *Embodied History: The Lives of the Poor in Early Philadelphia* (Philadelphia: University of Pennsylvania Press, 2003), 29–31; Wiberly, "Four Cities," 15–16; Nellis, "Working Poor," 154–55; Lawrence W. Towner, "The Indentures of Boston's Poor Apprentices," (Boston: Publications of the Colonial Society of Massachusetts *Transactions*, 1962): 423–28.

20. Fraser, "The City Elite," 177–79.

21. Wiberly, "Four Cities," 66 (quote); Ross, "Objects of Charity," 152–55.

22. Skemp, "A Social and Cultural History of Newport," 349–50.

23. Ross, "Objects of Charity,"153.

24. Wiberly, "Four Cities," 68–71, quote p. 68.

25. Ross, "Objects of Charity," 147 (quote); Wiberly, "Four Cities," 25–26; Karin Wulf, "Gender and the Political Economy of Poor Relief in Colonial Philadelphia," in *Down and Out in Early America*, ed. Billy G. Smith (University Park: Pennsylvania State University Press, 2004), 174–75 (quotes); Smith, "Poverty and Economic Marginality," 101; Fraser, "The City Elite," 178.

26. Wiberly, "Four Cities," 27–31; Wulf, "Gender and the Political Economy of Poor Relief," 168.

27. Smith, "Poverty and Economic Marginality," 101; Newman, *Embodied History*, 22–23, 27–34; Billy G. Smith, "The Best Poor Man's Country?" in *Down and Out in Early America*, ed. Billy G. Smith (University Park: Pennsylvania State University Press, 2004), xvi.

28. Smith, "Poverty and Economic Marginality," 101 (quote); Newman, *Embodied History*, 27–30 (quotes).

29. Newman, *Embodied History*, 27–31 (quotes); Wiberly, "Four Cities," 39–40.

30. Mary Ann Jimenez, *Changing Faces of Madness: Early American Attitudes and Treatment of the Insane* (Hanover, NH: University Press of New England, 1987), 33–56 (quote on p. 47); Albert Deutch, "Public Provision for the Mentally Ill in Colonial America," *Social Service Review* 10 (1936): 612 (quote).

31. Rebecca Tannenbaum, *Health and Wellness in Colonial America* (Westport, CT: Greenwood Press, 2012), 147–48; *Deutch*, "Public Provision for the Mentally Ill," 619.

32. Bellows, *Benevolence among Slaveholders*, 5; Ross, "Objects of Charity," 152–59 (quote).

33. Robert E. Cray Jr., "Poverty and Poor Relief: New York City and Its Rural Environs, 1700–1790," in *Authority and Resistance in Early New York*, ed. William Pencak and Conrad E. Wright (New York: New York Historical Society, 1988), 179 (quote); Wiberly, "Four Cities," 78 (quote); Fraser, "Controlling the Poor," 15 (quote); Ross, "Objects of Charity," 156–59; Bellows, *Benevolence among Slaveholders*, 5, 17; Schneider, "The Patchwork of Relief," 477.

34. Wulf, "Gender and the Political Economy of Poor Relief," 176 (quote); Alexander, *Render Them Submissive*, 87, 94 (quote); Sherene Baugher, "Visible Charity: The Archaeology, Material Culture, and Landscape Design of New York City's Municipal Almshouse Complex," *International Journal of Historical Archaeology* 5 (2001): 184–88; Wiberly, "Four Cities," 37–38, 93 (quote), 148–54: Ross, "Objects of Charity," 152–59; Nash, "Urban Wealth and Poverty," 559–60.

35. Towner, "The Indentures of Boston's Poor Apprentices," 428–29; Cray, "Paupers and Poor Relief," 174–79; Wiberly, "Four Cities," 30–34, 68, 91; Alexander, *Render Them Submissive*, 94–95 (quote on p. 95); Ross, "Objects of Charity," 155–59; Mohl, "Poverty in Early America," 11–13; Wulf, "Gender and the Political Economy of Poor Relief," 176; Robert E. Cray Jr., *Paupers and Poor Relief in New York City and Its Rural Environs, 1700–1830* (Philadelphia: Temple University Press, 1988), 48 (quote).

36. Skemp, "A Social and Cultural History of Newport," 188 (quote), 347.

37. Virgadarmo, "Charity for a City in Crisis," 30.

9

Housing and Street Life

INTRODUCTION

During the eighteenth century the five seaports rapidly grew from provincial villages to cosmopolitan metropolises. This was partly due to enormous population growth as the towns, with their great demand for labor, ethnic and religious pluralism, and engaging social life, attracted people from both near and far. Collectively, the five cities saw their populations increase by 500 percent between 1700 and 1775. Some cities, like Philadelphia and New York, saw greater growth than others, as illustrated by Table 9.1.

This growth in population put enormous strains on both the private and public sectors to provide adequate housing, fire protection, and urban infrastructure to the rapidly expanding citizenry. These growing pains reflected an evolution in urban life from that of medieval villages to modern metropolises. Like a medieval village, the crude huts and makeshift, one-room timber framed houses of the earliest settlers were not that different from homes lived in by their ancestors 500 years earlier. The numerous animals that roamed the dirt roads—goats, hogs, dogs, and cattle—further gave the early towns a medieval feel. However, as the population and wealth of the cities dramatically increased during the eighteenth century, along with their development as major centers of domestic and international commerce, these

Table 9.1. Population of Colonial Cities, 1700–1775

	1700	1775
Boston	6,700	16,000
New York	5,000	25,000
Philadelphia	5,000	40,000
Newport	2,600	11,000
Charles Town	2,000	12,000
Total	21,300	104,000

Source: Carl Bridenbaugh, *Cities in the Wilderness: The First Century of Urban Life in America, 1625–1742* (New York: Ronald Press, 1938), 143; Carl Bridenbaugh, *Cities in Revolt: Urban Life in America, 1743–1776* (New York: Capricorn Books, 1955), 216.

medieval villages were transformed into modern cities that rivaled their European counterparts in public services, crime, overcrowding, disease, poverty, and sharp class divisions.

This Europeanization of eighteenth-century American cities is seen in housing, where the poor lived in cramped, overcrowded, filthy, vermin-infested hovels that by modern standards would be condemned as unfit for human habitation. Meanwhile, the increasing wealth of the urban gentry, often made by exploiting the underclass, allowed them to build and live in magnificent, finely furnished palatial mansions that mirrored both their supercilious egos and their economic and social dominance. These same elites who controlled city government used their influence to ensure that the neighborhoods where they lived and worked had relatively well-paved, lighted, and clean streets. The poor, on the other hand, were forced to live and walk on unpaved roads and back alleys filled with garbage, dung, and dead animals. Housing and street life, like everything else about colonial America, was the product of a social, economic, and political system manufactured by the upper class to maintain sharp class distinctions—distinctions that, at least to them, affirmed their hegemony.

HOUSING

Caves and Dugouts

The first concern of seventeenth-century settlers upon arriving in America was finding or making shelter. Lacking sawmills or ovens to make bricks, some of the earliest and poorest pioneers of New Amsterdam, Boston, and Philadelphia were forced to temporarily live in caves and dugouts. The former was the early shelter of choice in

Philadelphia, where newcomers dug holes approximately 4 feet deep into the banks or low cliffs near the Delaware River front. Only half of the chamber was really underground, with the remaining walls made of sod. The roof consisted of layers of tree limbs covered over with sod or bark, while the chimney was often made of either cobblestone or sticks of wood mortared with clay and grass, materials that often turned these hovels into "smoaky homes."[1] Equally crude, cramped, and smoky were dugouts built by the first settlers in New Amsterdam and Boston. Cornelius Van Tienhoven, secretary of New Netherland, described the dugouts used by the first families:

Those in New Netherland and especially in New England who have no means to build farmhouses at first according to their wishes, dig a square pit in the ground, cellar fashion, six or seven feet deep, as long as and as broad as they think proper; case the earth all around the wall with timber, which they line with the bark of trees or something else to prevent the caving-in of the earth; floor the cellar with plank, and wainscot it overhead for a ceiling; raise a roof of spars clear up, and cover the spars with bark or green sods so that they can live dry and warm in these houses with their entire families for two, three or four years, it being understood that partitions are run through these cellars, which are adapted to the size of the family.[2]

Some pioneers from Canada to Carolina avoided the labor involved in building dugouts simply by moving into deserted Indian wigwams and other native structures. Those without this option threw up wigwams based on English shepherds' huts.[3]

EARLY FRAME HOUSES

Boston and Newport

As soon as possible, early settlers abandoned their flimsy and temporary caves, dugouts, and wigwams to build substantial and well-finished timber-frame houses like those they had lived in back in the mother country. Within a generation of settlement, however, housing evolved into regional uniformity. As historian Richard Bushman explains, the adoption of "a certain vernacular style represented a commitment to one's neighbors and to the norms that the local community valued."[4] The similar origins of settlers in Boston and Newport, and their close geographical proximity to one another, gave them a similar architectural style. Of course, each house was shaped by the family's needs and means, but there were three standard plan types in these two New England towns: the

1680s Pennsylvania Cave Dwelling. The first European settlers to North America often had to live in crude and makeshift structures in the first years of colonization. In this illustration, artist Howard Pyle provides a re-creation of a 1680s Pennsylvania cave dwelling that provided housing for some of Philadelphia's earliest settlers. (Woodrow Wilson, *History of the American People*, Vol. 1 [New York: Harper & Bros., 1902])

one-room plan, used by the poorest people throughout the seventeenth century; the two-room plan, which simply involved the addition of a parlor; and the added lean-to plan, which included an addition to the back of the house such as a kitchen, pantry, or another bedroom and loft.

No matter the floor plan, these homes were simple, unadorned structures framed by crudely hewn oak posts and beams that supported walls filled with either wattle-and-daub or brick nogging and a thatched roof, which owners replaced with more permanent wood shingles as circumstances allowed. Many residents of Newport painted their homes in various shades of red, blue, green, and yellow, bright colors that gave the town a pleasing, almost festive air. Some even painted their homes to resemble stone or marble. Ample yards and beautiful gardens graced many of the finer homes. Entering the home, one walked through a heavy front door that immediately opened into the main room, or hall. In single-plan homes this served as living room, dining room, kitchen, work-room, and often bedroom. At only about 16 feet by 18 feet, the hall was a claustrophobe's nightmare, which was made even more oppressive by exposed beam ceilings that barely cleared a man's head. Diminishing the size of the hall even further were miscellaneous necessaries strewn around the room: a dining table, a chair, a backless bench, barrels and chests for storage, a rough bedstead, fireplace tools piled at one edge of the hearth, cooking items hanging above the fireplace, and work tools either hanging from the walls or standing in a corner. There were no closets. Instead, the few clothes were packed in chests or hung on pegs against the wall.

Maneuvering around the clutter became second nature for family members, who still must have occasionally banged their knees and stubbed their toes on the various items that always seemed to be in their way. Amid this crowded and cluttered environment, they engaged in their daily activities—everything from eating, cooking, spinning, and sewing to reading, playing, courting, and sleeping. Privacy was virtually nonexistent, although parents often partitioned the main room with blankets to provide a semblance of seclusion during their more intimate moments. Of course, living in such close quarters could at times fray the nerves of even the most passive person. If one wanted to sulk, to vent one's frustrations, or to simply have some solitude, there was no place to go but outside.[5]

The outdoors may have been preferable at times considering that the interiors of these early homes were not only cluttered and cramped but also dirty and smelly. Dirt floors prevailed in the homes of the poorest settlers, but even plank floors were impossible to keep clean as family members constantly dragged in dirt, mud, and snow. The fire that burned almost constantly in the cavernous chimney billowed smoke that sometimes choked the inhabitants and always left an ashy grime on everything inside. Mixed with the smoke in these close confines were the odors of cooking food and of bodies, clothes, and bedding left unwashed for sometimes months at a time. One visitor to a particularly unkempt household noted with disgust that the odor from the bedding was so strong that it "reminded me of the description I have had of the middle passage of a slave ship." Such a foul environment attracted irritating and parasitic bedbugs that could ruin a night's sleep. The Reverend William Tennent found this out one night when the "fury of the little Inhabitants" of his bed kept him scratching throughout the night. When daylight broke the wearisome minister was shocked by the "blood & slaughter" throughout his calico sheets.[6]

When not being bitten by bedbugs, many colonists suffered from oppressive heat in the summer months and bitter cold during the

winter in homes that were poorly insulated and lacked much ventilation. In fact, so much heat escaped through chimneys that pitch at
the end of logs often froze and ink in wells congealed. A common
complaint in winter was that "one side roasted while the other
froze." Meanwhile, the flickering glow of the indoor fire often provided the only light, making homes dark and gloomy places.
Windows at this time were small and made of oiled paper that
admitted little light and lacked transparency. More well-to-do families might mitigate some of this gloom with small grease lamps
and sputtering candles made from home-rendered tallow or bay-
berry wax. Still, cabin fever and depression were common companions of early New England settlers, especially during winter months
when the weather prevented them from leaving their homes for
extended periods. Despite the depression, early colonists did not
desire to bring the outdoors inside. To them, nature was not synony-
mous with beauty and peace but with dangers that they wanted to
keep out—chilling cold, ice, snow, brutal winds, predatory animals,
and hostile Indians. To early settlers, their homes were fortresses
against the outside world.[7]

As cities grew in size and wealth, the more affluent refined their
homes to better reflect their wealth and social standing. Practical but
simple furniture gave way to finer pieces crafted by local artisans,
many of whom were trained in Europe. Embracing the finely crafted,
polished furniture were plastered walls that were often painted in
bright blues, yellows, and greens and wainscoted to the height of the
chair rails. Meanwhile, tongue-and-groove heart-of-pine floors prevented dirt from making its way through the floor. Trimming the
walls were baseboards along the floor line and molding on the ceilings. Carpets were still too expensive for most middle-class folk,
who improvised with "floor clothes," which were canvasses covered
with built-up layers of paint done in a decorative pattern. To better
display these furnishings, owners lit their homes with whale-oil
lamps made of pewter or glass. To help heat a room in winter, they
added box iron stoves. After 1742 Benjamin Franklin's cast-iron stove
could be found in many homes whose owners could afford it.
Although the stove rarely warmed a room above 56 degrees in winter,
it was an improvement over more primitive heating units.

By the end of the colonial period, the average home in Boston and
Newport had six rooms, twice the rooms from a century earlier. But
even with this extra space, privacy was rare as already large families often shared their homes with an aged parent, a widowed
relative, or one or more boarders, apprentices, servants, or slaves.

Family Living Room in Paul Revere's House, Boston. The Paul Revere House, located in the historic North End of Boston, was originally built around 1680. At first the house was of the familiar one-room plan, but by the time the famed silversmith lived in it from 1770 to 1780, it had expanded to three stories in height. The above photograph of the family living room shows typical Massachusetts Bay timber construction with heavy framing posts and exposed overhead beams supporting a low ceiling, at least by modern standards of home construction. (Library of Congress, Prints and Photographs Division, Reproduction # LC-D4-71180)

Further encroaching on the privacy of families is that the homes of many urban folk, particularly artisans and shopkeepers, included front rooms used to serve customers. Interestingly, contemporaries did not complain much about being crowded in their houses because the main purpose of the home was for the family to enjoy intimacy when alone together. This intimacy was not always private as the low quality of early wooden homes made it easy to hear and see through the floors and walls. Elizabeth Cresy of Massachusetts admitted that while staying in the home of Elisha Engerson and Dorothy Satarly she "looked into a Crack" and saw Dorothy "upon her back and her coats up and She saw her thighs and His Breeches down and Laying upon her and her hands about his neck."[8]

New Amsterdam/New York

More unique in architectural style were the homes in Dutch New Amsterdam, where the curving streets were lined with quaint, two- and three-story homes made of brick of various sizes, shapes, and colors ranging from red, pink, and purple to yellow, orange, and black. Further enlivening the colorful walls were curious patterns of brick mixed with inset glazed tiles. Equally unique to Dutch homes were the crow-stepped gables that faced the street and that allowed chimney sweeps to climb up to the steep, tile-covered roofs. The decorative coloring and distinct design of Dutch homes gave New Amsterdam some of the most unique architecture in British North America. When Madam Knight visited New York City in 1707, the city was still characteristically Dutch:

The Buildings are Brick generally very stately and high, though not altogether like ours in Boston. The bricks in some of the Houses are of divers Coullers and laid in Checkers, being glazed, look very agreeable. The inside of them are neat to admiration, the wooden work, for only the walls are plaster'd and Sumers and Gist are plained and kept very white scour'd, as so is all the partitions if made of Bords ... [T]he hearths were laid with the finest tile that I ever see and the stair cases laid all with white tile, which is ever clean, and so are the walls of the Kitchen which had a Brick floor.[9]

New York City remained largely Dutch in appearance until the great fire of 1776 destroyed most of the old city.

Charles Town

The oppressively hot and humid environment of Charles Town, along with its strong English, French, West Indian, and African heritage, contributed to a unique architectural style in the southern capital known as the single-house plan. Not found elsewhere in colonial North America, the single-house plan refers to its width, that of a single room, as rooms both upstairs and downstairs were strung out in a line so as to allow cross ventilation. The heat of Charles Town summers also dictated that ceilings be high, up to 14 feet, and windows large. A piazza, usually on the south or west side and sometimes double or triple decked, provided shading for the long side that overlooked a small, well-manicured garden. A Frenchmen visiting Charles Town noticed that "everything peculiar to the buildings of this place is formed to moderate the excessive heat. The windows are open and the doors pass through both sides of the houses. Every endeavour is used to refresh within with fresh air." Residents "vie with one another, not who shall have the finest [home]," the Frenchman added, "but who [shall have] the coolest house." Upper-class Charlestonians were not only obsessed with making their homes cooler but also with turning their urban palaces into virtual compounds by surrounding them with high walls of brick to shield them from the turmoil of the nearby streets. Although the city's well-to-do symbolically turned their backs on their less fortunate neighbors in the design of their homes, they certainly brought public attention to them by painting the stuccoed exteriors in many tints of yellow, pink, blue, and purple and covering the roofs with red and purple tiles. This distinctive architectural style gave Charles Town a strong "foreign" feel to it unmatched elsewhere in the colonies.[10]

Philadelphia

Homes in early Philadelphia, on the other hand, closely resembled the three-story brick row houses of London. A visitor to the city around 1700 described Philadelphia's houses as "most of them stately, and of brick, generally three stories high, after the mode in London, and as many as several families in each." This last observation shows that even in its earliest decades Philadelphia suffered from inadequate housing. The housing shortage only increased over the course of the eighteenth century as successful retailers, innkeepers, and sea captains lived in homes averaging only 900 square feet, while the families of many craftsmen crowded into homes averaging less than 650 square feet. Making such already tight living arrangements even more cramped is that the homes of Philadelphia shopkeepers and artisans, like those in other cities, also doubled as places of work. In the end, perhaps only two-thirds of a middle-class home was actual living space, which the inhabitants often had to share with other cash-strapped individuals and families. This was the case with Christian Fight, who with a wife and four children shared his small Philadelphia home and lease with fellow shoemaker Christian Nail and his family.[11]

The furnishings of middle-class urban homes in Philadelphia were just as modest as their size. Most middling folk walked on unadorned, sand-scrubbed floors. Few if any paintings adorned the whitewashed walls to offer a pleasant distraction. In the best room, the parlor, the inhabitants sat on hard chairs in front of tables and desks often described as "plain and cheap." When eating, they

Charles Town Single House. The single house is the architectural style most associated with Charles Town. Its unique design is well suited to the city's tropical climate. The one-room-wide houses offered cross ventilation, and the piazzas, which stretched down the long side, offered a shady place to sit and view the side garden. The above single house is located at 321 Tradd Street. (Library of Congress, Prints and Photographs Division, HABS SC, 10-CHAR, 321-1)

dined on ordinary pewter plates and cutlery. Less than a third owned table knives. At night the middle class slept on poorly made and uncomfortable beds. Typical was the home of brickmaker James Stoops, which contained only a few inexpensive beds, tables, chairs, and desks, some bedding and pewter, "sundry old books," and a clock worth £4. In sum, the home of the average urban middle-class family was cramped, modestly and inexpensively furnished, with little separation between work space and living space—a reflection of the simple and humble position of the middling rank of urban dwellers.[12]

Georgian Homes

To reflect their pretentious position in society, the urban elite during the eighteenth century built stately and ostentatious brick palatial mansions similar to those of the English upper class. The urban elite's identification with the English gentry and their concern with status and hierarchy were a way of establishing claims to their legitimacy as a ruling class. Believing that a home reflected the character of the owner, the urban grandees associated their elegant brick mansions with such traits as sobriety, honesty, good morals, and financial responsibility—all characteristics important for leadership. By contrast, the mean and much-decayed wooden homes occupied by the poor reflected the antithesis of these positive traits and thereby disqualified them from any claims to power. Thus, in building their pretentious mansions, the urban aristocracy was converting economic capital into political, social, cultural, and symbolic capital to bolster their status as rightful leaders of the community.[13]

As a symbol of their self-proclaimed superiority, the well-to-do often built their expansive Georgian-style homes (named after the monarchs who ruled during the 1700s) on a high basement that elevated them above homes belonging to their social inferiors. The typical plan consisted of a large central hall that ran through the house from front to back flanked by two rooms on each side. A grand stairway with exquisitely turned balusters and polished mahogany handrails carried guests upstairs to sitting rooms and grand ballrooms with decoratively framed fireplaces, windows, and doors; high-ceilinged interior walls covered with elegant floor-to-ceiling paneling or wallpaper and finished with decorative crown molding; and polished hardwood floors laid with rich Turkish carpets. Carefully placed throughout rooms were well-padded and ornately carved

Elfreth's Alley, Philadlephia. This view of Elfreth's Alley takes one back in time to Philadelphia during the mid-eighteenth century. Named for Jeremiah Elfreth, a blacksmith, it is considered the oldest inhabited residential street in America with dwellings on both sides. The alley was the home of various craftsmen and a printer by the name of Benjamin Franklin. By the American Revolution, one-third of the households on the alley were headed by women. (Library of Congress, Prints and Photographs Division, HABS PA, 51-PHILA, 272-3)

wing chairs, sofas, love seats, and graceful side chairs for residents and guests to comfortably repose on. Queen Anne, or later Chippendale, style mahogany and black walnut side tables, card tables, and tea tables displayed silver punch bowls, tankards, urns, and expensive porcelain dishes. Further accenting the rooms were gilded mirrors, paintings, sculptures, and other pieces of fine art that owners collected during their trips to the other colonies, the Caribbean, and Europe. Charles Town grandees were particularly fond of decorating their homes with Chinese luxuries like porcelain dining sets, black-and-gold lacquered hardwood furniture, scenic wallpaper, hand-painted textiles, and reverse paintings on glass. The well-to-do in Newport, on the other hand, preferred to accent their rooms with such special items as telescopes, maps, terrestrial globes, coats of arms, and delicately carved cherubs.[14]

These grand homes and their expensive household furnishings were visible attempts by the ruling elite to display their cosmopolitan sophistication while demonstrating their alleged superiority over their economic inferiors, a superiority that, at least to them, proved their right to lead society. Typical is the supercilious attitude of Philadelphia's leading families, whose "pride, haughtiness, and ostentation are conspicuous," observed an Englishman visiting the city. "It seems as if nothing could make them happier than that an order of nobility should be established," he added, "by which they might be exalted above their fellow citizens as much as they are in their own conceit." The urban aristocracy perpetuated this conceit among themselves by using the spaciousness and elegance of their homes to entertain lavishly with sumptuous dinners and elegant balls complete with formal dances and live music. A Frenchmen visiting the Quaker city observed that "at the tables of the wealthy, in their equipages, and in the dresses of their wives and daughters, are . . . extreme. I have seen balls . . . where the splendor of the rooms, and the variety and richness of the dresses, did not suffer in comparison with Europe."[15]

HOUSING FOR THE POOR

The domestic entertainments of the rich certainly did not compare with those of the urban poor, whose cramped and overcrowded houses made it difficult to entertain inside their homes. Instead, their poverty forced them into the streets, parks, or taverns that served their kind. Greed and callousness among the urban aristocrats, along with local governments run by equally wealthy officials who gave top priority to the needs of the city's well-to-do, largely explain the stark contrast in living conditions between rich and poor. The urban gentry were able to build grand mansions because of their exploitation of slaves, indentured servants, and poor white laborers in construction. Meanwhile, local governments failed to adequately expand city limits to meet exploding populations, leading to massive overcrowding. By 1760 the approximately 15,000 residents in Philadelphia were crowded into 0.6 square miles while the 22,000 New Yorkers in 1776 were crammed into a triangle 4,000 feet wide and 6,000 feet from its base to its apex. Even Newport lost its rural feel as early as 1726 when some residents complained that "the Compact Body of the Town is so fil[l]ed that it is difficult to find conveneant Space to erect a Small Cotage."[16]

Exacerbating the housing problem were rich speculators who monopolized much of the urban real estate. In late colonial Philadelphia, for example, just 10 percent of the wealthiest residents held 70 percent of the real estate in the city and collected 90 percent of the rents. One local real estate mogul had 90 rental properties at the time of his death in 1756. This extreme inequality in property holdings meant that approximately 80 percent of the city's heads of household did not own the dwelling in which they lived. Their meager wages simply prevented them from buying their own home. Well-to-do property owners took advantage of this situation to further augment their wealth by subdividing their rental properties and then charging high rents to poor people who, because of their low wages, had no choice but to share their already cramped living quarters with either boarders or sometimes even entire families. This capitalist-driven housing market forced the poorest to live in the streets. When the poor in New York City squatted on city property, callous officials ordered local constables to "Cause their Hutts to be demolished . . . as public Nusances."[17]

Urban officials responded also to the housing shortage by dividing and further subdividing streets to make room for homes that builders crammed onto the narrow roads and alleys. This led to the construction of rowhouses that shared "party walls," allowing residents to easily hear the conversations and activities of neighbors living next to them. One visitor to Charles Town observed in a particularly congested part of the city "a low Set of Wood Tenements, with Walls little thicker than a Sheet of Brown paper, pent up on all Sides by Wooden Structures." Homes for the poor in Philadelphia were perhaps worse, often described as "huts," "sheds," or "mean low box[es] of wood." These makeshift "sheds" were also small, averaging only 512 square feet in size. In this cramped spaced crowded an average of seven to nine people.[18]

Such crowded conditions created some unusual sleeping arrangements—at least by modern standards of privacy. Practical necessity often required several children of both sexes to crowd into a single bed, or children to sleep with parents, or servants and slaves to share beds in unheated lofts and garrets. Children were sometimes present in the same room with a copulating couple. One four-year-old girl reported to a servant that she saw a man "lay on the bed with her mamma," and heard him tell the mother to "lay up higher." Cramped quarters sometimes required strangers to share beds, as revealed when Anne James of Boston testified in 1767 that while living with her brother she shared a bed with two adult sisters. Some poor couples even allowed another woman into their bed because of a lack of sleeping space in their small homes. Such scenarios reveal that many early Americans had no great concern for privacy, even in sexual matters. Those who did took to barns, sheds, root cellars, outhouses, fields, and the woods for their most intimate moments. Still, they were not always successful in finding solitude, as one surprised Boston couple discovered in 1702 when they were caught and convicted of "unlawful Copulation and fornication" in the common training field.[19]

With little living space and less money, the urban poor owned few home furnishings and hardly any conveniences or luxuries. Dr. Benjamin Rush noted that in his visits to the "huts" of Philadelphia's poor, "often I have ascended the upper story of these huts by a ladder, and many hundred times have been obliged to rest my weary limbs upon the bedside of the sick (from the want of chairs)." Even Jacob Barr, one of the wealthiest laborers in the city, lived with his wife and four children in a single room containing two beds, a chest and table both made of cheap pine, and two old chairs. Jacob and his wife Margaret slept in one bed, while their four girls all shared the other one. The parents most likely sat in the two chairs while the children either sat on the chest or the floor. Margaret cooked with a cheap earthen pot, a sauce pan, a skillet, a tea kettle, a spit, and a "flesh iron." The family ate their food out of one pewter plate and six pitchers. They did not own any cutlery, so they must have eaten mostly stews and soups from the pitchers and used their hands to tear apart bread and meat, which they took directly from the saucepan and skillet. The few luxuries they owned included a table cloth, "course sheets" for the beds, two rugs, and a "looking glass" (mirror). Their home lacked candles, which suggests that the family spent their evenings in the dark. The Barrs did not even own a chamber pot (the proverbial "pot to pee in") and so were forced to trudge to the privy located in the backyard every time nature called. If this was the material condition of a successful laborer and his family, one can only imagine the living standards of the urban masses who were not so "prosperous."[20]

Such cramped and crowded living conditions bred filth and disease. The physician Benjamin Rush, when visiting homes of Philadelphia's poor, feared the risk of "not only taking their disease but being infected with vermin." New York's poorer wards had "neusous stenches," according to one visitor, while a Bostonian found the back alleys and lanes of his home town intolerable. "How could I live in such a place as this," he asked rhetorically, "where the comfort of a refreshing breeze can never come, how can these miserable people bear this stench and filth." The urban poor had to endure these putrid and unhealthy living conditions because the governing elite refused to provide poorer neighborhoods with the same street-cleaning efforts as were received in the more well-to-do parts of town. Typical in this regard was Philadelphia, where Tom Trudge, a self-proclaimed "poor fellow," charged that regular cleaning occurred only on those streets "honoured with the residence of the gentry." With putrefying dead animals and piles of trash strewn throughout the streets, ponds of stagnating water emitting "noxious effluvia," and impure air swarming with flies, it is no wonder that contemporaries described poor neighborhoods as "the *wrong* end of the city." For living in the wrong part of town, the poor paid a heavy price with higher disease and lower life expectancies than their rich counterparts who lived in the right part of town.[21]

Neighborhoods and Suburbs

This bifurcated urban landscape is seen in the development of neighborhoods differentiated according to wealth and occupational structure. By the late colonial period the demography of the cities was like a series of concentric zones, with merchants and professionals living in the core of the city, surrounded by prosperous craftsmen, who in turn were surrounded by a belt of the laboring poor. Of course, the compactness of these "walking cities" made a well-defined segregation impossible. Some of the urban genteel still shared space with such common folk as laborers, watchman, and even goatkeepers who lived in the alleys and lanes behind grand houses in the center of the cities. During the course of the eighteenth century, however, the local aristocracy increasingly strove to monopolize the better parts of town to the exclusion of their social inferiors. Others sought to completely escape the congestion, noise, and noxious odors by retreating to new suburbs developing just outside of towns. One exception to this settlement pattern is Charles Town, where rich planters "desired nothing so much as to escape the lonely, rural, fever-infested Low Country for a taste of the man-made town." Still, the planter-merchant elite segregated themselves from their social inferiors by building their urban palaces together in the same neighborhoods along King and Meeting Streets and along the Battery (the walk along the seaside). The Battery would eventually become the city's leading attraction and the main stage for the public display of the planters' wealth and power.[22]

Privies and Outbuildings

For all the distinction in homes between rich and poor, one common structure that was egalitarian in both design and use was the privy. When nature called, colonists had to trudge outdoors, day or night, through rain and snow, to the outdoor privy (or "necessary") that was usually situated behind the house close enough to be reached quickly in an emergency. This preindustrial toilet was nothing more than a deep hole in the ground around which was a square or rectangular wooden structure for privacy. Sometimes the hole was lined with boards or stones, but most were left bare. Seating involved a wide board with a hole in the middle. A basket, box, or bag held the corncobs, leaves, and after the 1720s, newspapers used for personal sanitation. Of course, these wiping supplies left the user anything but clean. Nor did colonists wash their hands afterwards as washbasins were absent in outhouses. Not surprisingly, colonists suffered from roundworm, whipworm, and other parasites that caused them considerable intestinal turmoil and hurried trips to the privy. While taking care of personal business, users had to contend with scurrying rats that were attracted to the putrid environment of privies and, perhaps worse, with mischievous kids who got their kicks overturning occupied outhouses.[23]

Privies were just one of many types of structures that crowded the home lots of city dwellers. Behind the main house were various support buildings that included kitchens, wash houses, workshops, and housing for servants, slaves, and apprentices who were forced to live near the stench of waste dumps, privies, and agricultural service buildings like cow-houses, barns, and stables. Further blurring the rural with the urban were pigs, goats, geese, and other animals that were sometimes penned in backyards with cows and horses.

GARDENS

The rural aspect of urban lots is further exemplified by the planting of gardens both for practical and ornamental use. An Englishmen visiting the small village of Charles Town in 1682 observed that "their Gardens begin to be supplied with such European Plants and Herbs as are necessary for the Kitchen, viz: Potatoes, Lettuce, Colewarts, Parsnip, Turnip, Carrot and radish; Their gardens also began to be beautified and adorned with such herbs and Flowers which to the Smell or Eye are pleasing and agreeable, viz: the Rose, Tulip, Carnation and Lilly, Etc . . ." The Dutch in New Amsterdam were just as avid gardeners. Even the "meanest dwelling" had a little back garden, if only a few yards square, with a few rows of vegetables and herbs and a couple of flower beds with a bench on which to sit and relax. A visitor to Philadelphia in the late eighteenth century observed that behind each house in the city "is a little court or garden." Meanwhile, to "live and keep house in [colonial] Boston," explains one modern scholar, "was to grow a garden" with vegetables, herbs, salads, and berries.[24]

While the mass of city folk cultivated small backyard gardens mostly for practical purposes, the urban elite attached to their grand Georgian mansions equally spacious and spectacular gardens that included geometric plantings, gravel and sand paths, terraces, and architectural features like statues, gazebos and fish ponds—all enclosed with a decorative brick wall or wooden fence. The urban elite devoted so much attention to their ornate and refined formal gardens because they were considered an extension of the parlor, another stage for genteel performances. To put on a grand performance, the local aristocrats gathered plants from the ends of the Earth, imported marble statues, purchased benches and stools, and hired professional gardeners to lay it all out in a pleasant design that they hoped would stimulate conversation while they took their guests for walks through their gardens. As a reflection of its owner, the garden was itself on stage for guests. If not done right, a garden could cause its owner as much embarrassment among his peers as awkward dancing at an assembly.[25]

URBAN FIRES

No matter if one lived in a crude and cramped shed or a spacious palatial mansion, both were susceptible to fires that all too frequently swept through the five seaports. Poorly maintained chimneys, lightning, arson, and especially human carelessness were the main causes of urban fires. In 1676 a tailor's apprentice in Boston allowed a candle to fall over and ignite his master's home. Over the next four hours the fire quickly spread throughout the neighborhood to consume more than 50 homes, a church, and several warehouses before it was finally extinguished by a timely downpour of rain. Thirty years later Boston suffered an even more destructive fire when an old, drunk woman unwisely placed some highly combustible oakum too close to an open flame in her house. Charles Town, too, was the victim of carelessness in 1740 by a saddler who allowed a flame to get out of control. A "most dreadful fire" quickly spread throughout the trading district, destroying over 330 homes and many storehouses. A year later a New York City repairman carelessly left hot coals on the roof of the governor's mansion, which caught fire and spread to the buildings in nearby Fort George. The fact that an open flame was an everyday part of life for colonists, who used fire as their main source of heat and light as well as in cooking, baking, and numerous manufacturing enterprises, explains how easily and frequently such accidents could occur.

Early Fire-Prevention Measures

City officials implemented fire-prevention measures and acquired fire-fighting equipment usually *after* experiencing a destructive fire. Boston's first destructive fire in 1653 finally motivated town selectmen to enact the city's first fire-fighting measures by ordering every home owner to have a ladder that reached the roof and a 12-foot pole with a "good large swab at the end of it." After several fires threatened to destroy New Amsterdam, Director Peter Stuyvesant finally initiated a number of fire codes in 1647 that included forbidding the construction of wooden chimneys and thatched roofs; ordering citizens to regularly clean their chimneys; purchasing at public expense fire ladders, fire hooks, and 250 fire buckets; and appointing eight unpaid volunteers to form a "rattle watch" to patrol the city streets at night looking for potential arsonists and waking up the town with their wooden rattles in the event of a fire. Charles Town would have benefitted from such measures in its early years. Instead, the city suffered three "great fires" between 1698 and 1700 before the provincial assembly finally passed a series of fire codes that required citizens to replace wooden chimneys with ones built of brick or stone, forbid them from erecting wooden homes and keeping hay or straw in kitchens, and empowered fire commissioners to destroy any structure considered a "common nuisance." Both Boston and Philadelphia went so far as to ban the smoking of tobacco outside because "fires have been so often occasioned by smoking tobacco" out of doors, while Newport denied its residents the dangerous pleasure of "throwing squibs of powder & lighted fire-works on the streets."[26]

Fire-Fighting Equipment

Despite all precaution, fires inevitably broke out in the cities. In trying to extinguish them, residents were armed with crude equipment and dangerous methods that were often no match for large infernos. Most basic were fire ladders, water buckets, long poles with swabs at the end to extinguish embers on rooftops, and hooks and chains to pull down buildings to create a fire break. When hooks and chains were unavailable, firemen used gunpowder to blow up buildings in the path of an inferno. Early fire engines proved nearly worthless in both putting out fires and reducing the danger to firemen. America's first fire "ingin," built in Boston in 1653, was a 3-foot-long metal syringe that would have had difficulty extinguishing a grease fire in a housewife's cooking pan. Little better in extinguishing flames or making fire-fighting less dangerous was an English fire pump first used in Boston in 1676 that was essentially a wooden box about the size of a modern bathtub that shot water in short, erratic streams. The introduction of state-of-the-art fire engines imported from London in the early 1730s and capable of pumping 200 gallons of water a minute up to a distance of 150 feet made fighting fires less dangerous but more exhausting as it required up to 18 men to operate the machine.[27]

Fire Companies and Clubs

The enormous amount of manpower and skill necessary to operate fire engines, as well as to coordinate all fire-fighting efforts, brought about the establishment of fire clubs and "engine companies." Boston, plagued by six infernos between 1653 and 1760, paved the way by creating America's first fire company in 1679 when the General Court hired 12 men to care for and manage the city's first fire engine at public expense. Boston established another fire-fighting first in 1718 when leading citizens there created the nation's first private fire company, in which members pledged to assist one another "in case it should please Almighty God to permit the breaking out of fire in Boston." Soon thereafter residents in the other cities formed their own mutual aid clubs, some of which were organized by trade, like Philadelphia's Cordwainers Fire Company, or by wealth, like the silk-stocking Hand-in-Hand Fire Company. However, because these private clubs offered protection only to other members (identified as such with plaques on their homes), city governments by the 1730s formed public engine companies to better protect the lives and property of all their citizens.[28]

Fighting Fires

Despite the creation of public and private fire companies, fire-fighting was a communal effort that bore no attachment to the concept of rugged individualism. When an individual's property caught fire, officials rang church bells that brought all able-bodied residents to the fire armed with buckets, ladders, hooks, chains, and scavenger bags. Citizen "bucket brigades" formed a double line from a water source (a public pump, well, river, or ocean), and filled buckets were passed up the line to the fire, where the contents were thrown at the burning building. The empty buckets would be quickly passed back, via a second line, to be refilled. Directing these bucket brigades were the more well-to-do members of private fire clubs, who generally kept a safe distance from fires. Rather than actually fighting fires up close, they instead patrolled the streets protecting the property of their fellow club men from looters. The difficult and dangerous job of actually extinguishing infernos was left to less affluent men. This was especially true in Charles Town, where poor whites and slaves were required to answer the cry of "Fire!" upon pain of a £5 fine if a white man, or 39 lashes if a slave. In fighting blazes, these brave men frequently felt the lash of flickering flames as they entered burning buildings with their engines. If a fireman escaped the dangers of the inferno, he might lose his life to either exploding gunpowder, common in homes, or collapsing roofs.[29]

While firemen were bravely risking their lives fighting the inferno, hundreds of residents throughout town rushed to the scene of the blaze, sometimes running into other terrified people scrambling to escape the fire's path. "The distressed inhabitants of those

Print of Firefighting in 1733. Despite its simplicity, this wood engraving of "Firemen at Work in 1733" illustrates the dangerous, laborious, and frenzied nature of firefighting in the colonial cities. Men in the "bucket brigade" work frantically to fill the fire engine, which is operated by several men who laboriously work the pump that feeds the hose. Conspicuously missing from this quaint illustration would be men blowing up buildings to create a firebreak, a crowd of onlookers that would gather to watch the conflagration, along with people rushing in and out of homes to remove their valuables. (Library of Congress, Prints and Photographs Division, Reproduction # LC-DIG-ppmsca-01574)

buildings wrapped in fire scarce knew where to take refuge," wrote one eyewitness to Boston's 1760 inferno, "numbers were confined to beds of sickness, as well as the aged and infant, when removed from house to house, and even the dying were obliged to take one remove before their final time." Authorities in Boston partially blamed the lack of success in extinguishing the 1711 fire that burned much of the city on the "great Cloud of Confusion that often falls out at a Fire; where No Body governs, NoBody Obeys, very few will work, and a great many Lookers on . . . only incumber the ground." The town selectmen were particularly upset with the "pernicious Practice" of women attending fires and doing nothing but causing a "great Interruption" in efforts to extinguish the infernos. Some thieves took advantage of the chaos during a fire to "rob, plunder, embezzle, convey away and conceal the goods and effects" of their distressed neighbors.[30]

Private Insurance and Public Relief

These destructive fires often left hundreds of people destitute and homeless. The numerous infernos in Charles Town prompted entrepreneurs there in 1736 to establish the country's first insurance company against fire. Calling itself the "Friendly Society," the company promised to insure "our Respective Messuages and Tenements in Charles Town from Losses by Fire." The insurance company prospered with a fund of approximately £100,000 until 1740, when a disastrous fire forced the Friendly Society into bankruptcy. More successful was Benjamin Franklin's "Philadelphia's Contributionship for the Insurance of Houses from Loss of Fire," founded in 1752. The company quickly signed up more than 140 subscribers and was able to pay its first loss, amounting to £154, the following year. Today, the Contribution remains the oldest mutual fire insurance company in America.[31]

Not only did the devastating 1740 fire in Charles Town bankrupt the nation's first fire insurance company, but its aftermath provides an excellent example of how officials and residents at the time responded to assist those suffering from such calamities. With little public resources, families left homeless following a fire crammed themselves into surviving homes belonging to generous relatives and friends, while others without this option were forced to live on the streets begging for relief. Scores of the most destitute lined up at the door of St. Philip's Church, the local Anglican church that was responsible for poor relief in the capital. The numerous people seeking aid quickly overwhelmed the resources of St. Philip's. Private citizens raised £471, but these funds were quickly exhausted. The provincial assembly responded by coughing up a niggardly £188 and beseeching officials in the northern colonies, the West Indies, and even Parliament for assistance. Within a month bread, flour, and money began arriving from Philadelphia, Boston, and Barbados. The House of Commons, wanting to keep one of its most lucrative colonies in good graces, provided an unprecedented £20,000 to beleaguered citizens of the city. Perhaps not surprisingly, the wealthy merchants who lost their property in the fire received 70 percent of the financial aid, leaving the numerous homeless poor with crumbs. As historian Matthew Mulcahy explains, this disaster relief was intended largely to stabilize the floundering city by "supporting the elites."[32]

"Wrath of God"

This elitist distribution of public relief is ironic considering that the Reverend Josiah Smith of Charles Town put much of the blame on the well-to-do for bringing down this "Terrible Wrath of God." This "severe piece of divine Conduct," Smith exclaimed, was the result of a sinful people who "have forsaken the Covenant of the Lord of God." After blasting residents for engaging in sodomy, miscegenation, prostitution, and blasphemy, the Harvard-trained minister directed special condemnation toward his front-row parishioners, especially for their "haughty Scorn" toward the poor and their "abundance of Idleness" spent shopping for expensive clothing, gambling on cards and dice, and attending extravagant balls and assemblies. Such sinful behavior, Smith warned, "cannot escape the just Judgment of GOD!"[33]

Evidently residents of Charles Town did not stop their sinful ways, for nearly 12 years later, in September 1752, a hurricane slammed into the Carolina capital with such ferocity that it blew ashore all vessels in the harbor. As boats were hurled against homes and storefronts, poor people from the White Point neighborhood climbed onto their roof-tops and watched in fright as the water rose higher and higher. Some were swept away as the storm drove their shacks off their foundations. Many other terrified residents, like the Bedon family, tried running to higher ground to escape the storm surge rapidly flooding their homes. Like so many, Mrs. Bedon and her three children were sucked under the rushing, swirling, debris-laden torrent and drowned. In a matter of hours, the hurricane demolished 500 homes and numerous stores, warehouses, and wharves and killed approximately 95 people. When the water finally receded, the streets were littered with tons of debris and the decaying bodies of dead people and animals. After removing the debris and bodies, city officials crammed the homeless poor into the city workhouse and bound out the children of the poorest families. While affluent officials ripped apart destitute families, well-to-do vulture capitalists reaped a fortune by purchasing for shillings on the pound the now empty lots in White Point once occupied by the city's poor and reselling them to the urban gentry, who built exquisite summer mansions on them.[34]

STREET LIFE

Roads

Urban residents could also not escape the poor condition of roads in the cities. For much of the colonial period, the lack of public funds prevented officials from paving or draining the dirt roads that became near-useless mud pits in wet weather. Those who did dare to traverse the mire were rewarded with mud-soaked shoes and mud-splattered clothing from horses and carts flinging wet dirt behind them. Even in dry weather the unpaved roads were so bumpy that people riding, or rather rattling, in carts, wagons, and carriages were left physically sore. The poor condition of unpaved roads also hindered traffic and endangered public health. Tragically, one child playing in the middle of a Newport street in 1734 was drowned when he fell into a water-filled hollow log used for watering cattle.

To ameliorate these problems, city officials by the early eighteenth century began to devote considerable attention and money toward paving and draining their main thoroughfares. Boston led the way in this regard during the 1720s by devoting the large sum of £3,275 a year towards paving its public ways with gravel and paving stones and banning from the roads wagons carrying loads of more than a ton. Newport used its duties from the lucrative slave trade, property taxes, and subscriptions from lotteries to give its residents well-paved roads. On the other hand, the lack of a city government in Charles Town virtually ensured that residents there would traverse on unpaved and rutted roads during much of the colonial period. Some civic-minded residents raised funds to pave the main thoroughfares of Broad and Queen Streets, but the anemic support for internal improvements from the Commons House forced Charlestonians to walk mostly on unpaved roads. The city corporation that ran New York City was nearly as negligent on this issue by simply requiring residents to pave in front of their houses with pebblestone and to keep their streets in good repair. Not until the late 1750s did officials in New York embark on an ambitious program of street paving "with all conventional Speed." Meanwhile, improvements in Philadelphia's roads were more the result of private initiative as indolent and indecisive public leaders rarely troubled themselves with the city's growing pains. This forced exasperated residents to voluntarily pave the portions of street and sidewalks before their homes and businesses. The result was an irregular patchwork of paved roads. One visitor to the Quaker City in 1748 observed of the town thoroughfares that "Some are paved, others are not."[35]

Lighting

Daily life for residents of the five cities did not stop when the sun set. The close proximity to friends and neighbors, along with many taverns, parks, markets, and other places for congregation that included city streets, offered an active night life not found in rural settlements. However, this night life came with a certain amount of danger. As one writer to the Boston *Newsletter* explained, more people frequently went out at night on "calls of friendship, humanity, business or pleasure" and needed protection from insults and theft as well as from "scenes of lewdness and debauchery which are so frequently committed with impunity at present." Despite such nocturnal dangers, urban officials ignored the issue of street lighting for most of the colonial period, leaving it to private residents to "light the way" by hanging lights from windows of their houses. Some public-spirited citizens of Philadelphia, fed up with the wretched conditions of the city's unlighted ways, created a plan in 1749 to put lamps at their front doors and hiring a lamplighter to tend them. This voluntarism primarily benefitted the more affluent neighborhoods, prompting Philadelphia's lower sort to demand a law for "enlightening the streets, land, and alleys" at public expense. Similarly, residents in Newport, Boston, and New York erected glass lamps at their own expense outside of homes and businesses. City officials did little to support these private efforts besides enacting and enforcing laws against destroying lamps, which were an alluring and irresistible target to nocturnal vandals who enjoyed throwing stones, oyster shells, and apples at the glowing beacons. Despite such vandalism, urban residents by the end of the colonial period could walk the main streets at night under the glow of flickering lights that provided both illumination and some safety.[36]

Animals

Residents were forced to share the streets both day and night with numerous cows, goats, sheep, hogs, dogs, cats, and rats that turned the cities into gigantic barnyards. Always a nuisance and sometimes a terror, these animals always left behind filth and stench in the streets that was impossible to avoid. Also impossible to avoid were the packs of dogs that roamed the streets chasing pedestrians and any moving vehicle, attacking livestock, and barking and howling day and night, to the maddening frustration of the townspeople. The "multitudes of dogs" that ran amok in the streets of Philadelphia causing "great loss of sleepe and other damages" prompted local authorities in 1712 to prohibit the keeping of "great Dogs" within the city limits and permitting citizens to kill on sight any dog causing "mischief." Meanwhile, the many "Mischevious Mastiffs, Bull Doggs, and other Useless Dogs" in New York City forced the local government to require all owners of "great Bitches" to pay a fee for the privilege of ownership and to keep their pets chained in their yards upon pain of a large fine. Nearly as great a nuisance were pigs. So many porkers ran loose in Newport in the early 1700s that small children were "in danger of being destroyed by them." By 1745 town officials impounded all stray animals and awarded peregrinating pigs to the "seizors." Officials in Charles Town sought to solve two growing problems—stray animals and poverty—by passing a law in 1746 that allowed pigs and sheep at large to be killed and given to the poor. The filth of urban streets also attracted countless rats, which practically took over Boston in 1741, compelling the General Court to offer a bounty for each rodent killed. Many boys had fun sport that year catching and killing more than 8,400 rats.[37]

Street Cleaning

The thousands of horses, cows, pigs, goats, and dogs that wandered the cities deposited tons of animal excrement and rivers of urine onto the streets. Humans also used the streets as "necessaries," urinating and even sometimes defecating in back alleys. Careless pedestrians frequently stepped in piles of manure. More fortunate ones walked away with soiled shoes and clothing; the less fortunate slipped and fell onto the soiled street, a folly that undoubtedly caused laughter among bystanders, especially children. Contributing to the stench and danger were outside privies that sometimes overflowed into the streets and townsmen throwing out into the streets their garbage, rotten produce, and the butchered carcasses and entrails of chickens, pigs, and goats that they had consumed. Sarah Eve of Philadelphia complained that the city stank of "shad and other smells as disagreeable." Still, as late as 1750 Philadelphia's mayor condemned the populace for "heaping great Piles of Dirt and Filth" in the streets so that it clogged the drains and allowed "an intollerable Stench" to pervade throughout the city "whereby Distempers will in all probability be Occasioned."[38]

Motivated by a belief that there was a relationship between filth and disease, city officials hired public "scavengers" to remove the filth from the streets. Newport even employed one man whose sole duty was to "bury all the Dead Doggs and other carrion that Lye in ye Streets of this Town." Virtually all of these colonial garbage men came from the lowest rung of society. Many were black, and all were rewarded with salaries so meager that they sometimes went on strike. It is both ironic and tragic that these poor scavengers rarely worked in their own neighborhoods. Instead, wealthy town officials instructed them to devote most of their efforts toward cleaning the streets in the merchant district and more well-to-do parts of town, making these public cartmen the personal garbage men of the urban elites.[39]

Beautification

This street cleaning was part of a larger campaign by townspeople to beautify their cities. Beginning in the early 1700s, town officials ordered residents to plant shady trees before their homes to protect pedestrians from the "violence of the sun in the heat of the summer and thereby be rendered more healthy." Mulberry, water poplars, elms locusts, and lime trees lined Philadelphia's main streets, while New York's Broadway contained assorted trees that provided "an agreeable shade" and "a pretty effect" for pedestrians. Not to be outdone, residents of Charles Town lined their main thoroughfares with cypress, cedar, and pine. Broadway was so "delightful a Road and walk of great breadth, so pleasantly green," according to Governor John Archdale in 1696, "that . . . no Prince[s] in Europe, by all their Art, can make so pleasant a sight for the Whole Year." Residents further enhanced the appearance of their towns by clearing vacant lots of rubbish and "stinking weeds" and replacing it with English grass.[40]

Traffic Congestion

These beautification efforts could not hide the congestion that plagued urban streets. Cluttering the lanes were wandering pigs, goats, and dogs; townsmen on foot or horseback; artisans carrying heavy loads, pushing wheelbarrows, or rolling barrels; draymen driving wagons; packhorsemen pulling horses; logmen hauling firewood; children playing games; and above it all, genteel ladies and gentlemen riding high in their fancy coaches. Further clogging the thoroughfares were piles of stones, dirt, firewood, lumber, and other debris that workmen and homeowners frequently dumped at the edges of streets. Those who dared to walk or ride in the congested and cluttered streets sometimes found themselves "Entangled amongst Waggons, Dreys, Market Folks, and Dust." An Englishmen visiting New York City at the end of the colonial period found the waterfront area "jammed up with carts, drays, and wheelbarrows; horses and men were huddled promiscuously together, leaving little or no room for passengers to pass...Everything was in motion; all was life, bustle, and activity."[41]

Contributing to this chaos was a lack of laws regulating street traffic. As late as 1765 Boston became the first city to publish rules for riding and driving, namely, "Always to keep on the Right-Hand Side of the Way." This laissez-faire approach toward street traffic inevitably led to frequent accidents. Elizabeth Drinker of Philadelphia had so many frights on the road in 1767, including the overturning of her carriage with her baby inside, "that I can not bear to think of riding with any satisfaction," she wrote to a friend. Like today, speeding was the leading cause of road accidents as riders raced their horses, carts, and carriages through the crowded streets "to the great endangering [of] the bodies and lives of many persons, especially children, who are ordinarily abroad in the streets, & not of age or discretion suddenly to escape such danger." City newspapers too frequently contained sad news like the following item found in a 1733 issue of the *Boston News Letter*: "Stephen Lamb, A Child of about Five Years old, at the South End of the Town, was run over by a cart, and died immediately thereafter." Street-side property was also at risk from reckless drivers, who crashed into homes and businesses so frequently that townsmen installed wooden posts in front of their property to protect it from "Damage by Carts."[42]

Noise Pollution

All this street life made cities extremely noisy places, even by modern standards, and residents had an impossible time finding quiet. Horses clogging loudly on cobblestone streets, wagons rumbling along on metal-rimmed wheels, hawkers standing on street corners shouting out items for sale, construction workers and blacksmiths hammering, sawyers sawing, draymen cracking whips and cursing, merchants and ships' captains shouting orders to underlings, auctioneers exclaiming in their stentorian voices "Once, twice, another cent," and numerous snorting pigs, barking dogs, and baying goats—all created a noisy din that left a constant buzzing in the ears of city folk. Loud street traffic on King Street in Boston so disrupted debates of the General Court that in 1747 it blocked the street with chains during its proceedings. A young

View of New York City, 1797. This 1910 print of New York City at the corner of Wall and Water Streets about 1797 provides a rather accurate depiction of street life in the largest cities. The major thoroughfares were crowded with pedestrians, carriages, workers, dogs, horses, barrels, boards, and other obstructions that made traversing the streets a difficult and dangerous task. (Library of Congress, Prints and Photographs Division, reproduction # LC-USZ62-98020)

and serious John Adams, recently removed from the quiet of Braintree, eloquently described the dissonance of city life:

Who can study in Boston Streets? I am unable to observe the various objects that I meet, with sufficient precision. My eyes are so diverted with chimney-sweepers, sawyers of wood, merchants, ladies, priests, carts, horses, oven, coaches, market-men and women, soldiers, sailors; and my ears, with the rattle-gabble of them all, that I cannot think long enough in the street, upon any one thing, to start and pursue a thought, I cannot raise my mind above this crowd of men, women, beasts, and carriages, to think steadily. My attention is solicited every moment by some new object of sight, or some new sound. A coach, cart, a lady, or priest, may at any time, by breaking a couplet, disconnect a whole page of excellent thoughts.[43]

Just as noisy was Philadelphia, where one college student wrote home that from his window on Second Street he could see the "thundering of coaches, Chariots, Chaises, Waggons, Drays, and the whole Fraternity of Noise almost continuously assail our ears." Sarah Pemberton found herself so "heartily tir'd of the Noise &

hurry of this town" that she could not wait to escape to her family's country estate.[44]

Gardens and Commons

Townspeople could find a temporary escape from the noise and congestion in the parks, gardens, and commons that dotted the urban landscape. William Penn had the foresight to include five public parks for residents of the Quaker city, while Newport and Boston both set aside large, tree-lined common areas as permanent parks for their residents to enjoy. One English traveler visiting the Puritan capital observed that "Every afternoon, after drinking tea, the gentlemen and ladies walk the Mall and from thence adjourn to one another's houses to spend the evening.... What they call the Mall is a [1,400 foot] walk on a fine green common ... with two rows of young trees planted opposite to each other, with a fine footway between, in imitation of St. James Park." New Yorkers wanting to escape the noise and congestion of city streets could go to several public parks to either take leisurely walks or play assorted field games. The city's aristocracy, on the other hand, raised their noses at public parks and the common folk who frequented them. Instead, they preferred the private pleasure gardens like Vauxhall Garden overlooking the Hudson River, where, for a price, they could indulge in sumptuous dinners, bowl on the greens, stroll down the shaded garden paths, and attend special attractions like wax figures, magicians, musical concerts, and firework displays. [45]

CONCLUSION

Over the course of the eighteenth century, colonial cities evolved from relatively small, medieval-like villages with a few thousand residents living in mostly simple wooden homes and walking on dirt roads filled with all sorts of animals to large, modern metropolises with brick houses, fire protection, paved and tree-lined streets, and public parks. The wealthy elites who governed the cities welcomed and advanced some of this modernity, particularly in providing public services that made urban life safer and more convenient. At the same time, they fought to preserve certain traditions, particularly their self-proclaimed right to govern. To that end, the genteel built impressive mansions with well-manicured gardens that, at least to them, demonstrated those positive qualities necessary for responsible leadership. They used their political power to

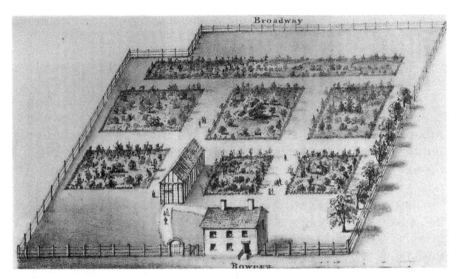

Illustration of Vauxhall Gardens, New York City. The Vauxhall Gardens of New York City, named for the Vauxhall Gardens of London, included a pleasure garden and theater that catered to the well-to-do. Opened in 1767 and originally located on Greenwich Street near the Hudson River, it was a square garden divided by four gravel paths adorned with shrubs, trees, busts, and statues. A large house on site provided accommodations for dining, musical concerts, and special events. (Library of Congress, Prints and Photographs Division, Reproduction # LC USZ62-115483)

ensure that the neighborhoods in which they lived had relatively clean, well-paved streets that further distanced themselves from the lower sort. Meanwhile, the urban grandees who controlled the government and owned most property remained indifferent to the needs of the lower- and many middle-class folk who lived in cramped and overcrowded housing in filthy, disease-ridden neighborhoods that indicated their inferiority and inability to lead.

NOTES

1. Alice Morse Earle, *Home Life in Colonial Days* (New York: Grosset & Dunlap, 1898), 2; Stephanie Grauman Wolf, *As Various as Their Land: The Everyday Lives of Eighteenth-Century Americans* (New York: Harper Perennial, 1994), 54–55.

2. Hugh Morrison, *Early American Architecture: From the First Colonial Settlements to the National Period* (New York: Oxford University Press, 1952), 9.

3. Earle, *Home Life*, 3; Morrison, *Early American Architecture*, 9; Leland Roth, *American Architecture: A History* (Boulder, CO: Westview Press, 2001), 50.

4. Richard Bushman quoted in David Freeman Hawke, *Everyday Life in Early America* (New York: Harper & Row, 1988), 50.

5. Hawke, *Everyday Life*, 53–56.

6. Donald Graves, "Bedding, Beds, and Bedsteads," *Early American Life* 18 (1987): 72 (quote); Keith Krawczynski, *William Henry Drayton: South Carolina Revolutionary Patriot* (Baton Rouge: Louisiana State University Press, 2001), 173 (quote).

7. John C. Miller, *The First Frontier: Life in Colonial America* (New York: Dell, 1966), 175; Claudia D. Johnson, *Daily Life in Colonial New England* (Westport, CT: Greenwood Press, 2002), 80; Hawke, *Everyday Life*, 53; Morrison, *Early American Architecture*, 46.

8. David H. Flaherty, *Privacy in Colonial New England* (Charlottesville: University Press of Virginia, 1972), 43 (quote), 36–39, 44–53, 69–71, 74–75; Charles Hammond, "The Dilemmas of Domestic Service in New England, 1750–1850," in *House and Home*, ed. Peter Benes (Boston: Boston University Press, 1988), 61–62.

9. Esther Singleton, *Dutch New York* (New York: Dodd, Mead & Co., 1909), 54–55.

10. Walter J. Fraser, *Patriots, Pistols, and Petticoats: "Poor Sinful Charles Town" during the American Revolution* (Columbia: University of South Carolina Press, 1993), 17 (quote); Richard Waterhouse, "The Development of Elite Culture in the Colonial American South: A Study of Charles Town, 1670–1770," *Australian Journal of Politics and History* 28 (1982): 397–99; Peter Coclanis, "The Sociology of Architecture in Colonial Charleston: Pattern and Process in an Eighteenth-Century Southern City," *Journal of Social History* 18 (1985): 612–13; Robert G. Miner, *Colonial Homes in the Southern States* (New York: Arno Press, 1977), 153.

11. Morrison, *Early American Architecture*, 513 (quote); Stuart Blumin, *The Emergence of the Middle Class: Social Experience in the American City, 1760–1900* (Cambridge, MA: Harvard University Press, 1989), 22, 44–45; Billy G. Smith, *The "Lower Sort": Philadelphia's Laboring People, 1750–1800* (Ithaca, NY: Cornell University Press, 1990), 159–60.

12. Blumin, *Emergence of the Middle Class*, 53–58.

13. Roth, *American Architecture*, 69–70; Susan Mackiewicz, "Philadelphia's Flourishing: The Material World of Philadelphians, 1682–1760," Ph.D. dissertation, University of Pennsylvania, 1988, 242–44.

14. Robert A. Leath, " 'After the Chinese Taste': Chinese Export Porcelain and Chinoiserie Design in Eighteen-Century Charleston," *Historical Archaeology* 33 (1999): 48–58; Sheila Skemp, "A Social and Cultural History of Newport, Rhode Island, 1720–1765," Ph.D. dissertation, University of Iowa, 1974, 19, 223.

15. David L. Barquist, " 'The Honours of a Court' or 'The Severity of Virtue': Household Furnishings and Cultural Aspirations in Philadelphia," in *Shaping a National Culture: The Philadelphia Experience, 1750–1800*, ed. Catherine Hutchins (Winterthur, DE: Winterthur Museum, 1994), 327 (quote); Blumin, *Emergence of the Middle Class*, 39 (quote); Sarah Fatherly, *Gentlewomen and Learned Ladies: Women and Elite Formation in Eighteenth-Century Philadelphia* (Bethlehem, PA: Lehigh University Press, 2008), 65.

16. Carole Shammas, "The Space Problem in Early United States Cities," *William and Mary Quarterly* 57 (2000): 509–10; Bridenbaugh, *Cities in the Wilderness*, 148–50; Skemp, "A Social and Cultural History of Newport," 13 (quote).

17. Sharon Salinger and Charles Wetherell, "Wealth and Renting in Pre-Revolutionary Philadelphia," *Journal of American History* 71 (1985): 828, 831–37; Sharon Salinger, "Spaces, Inside and Outside, in Eighteenth-Century Philadelphia," *Journal of Interdisciplinary History* 26 (1995): 5; Bridenbaugh, *Cities in the Wilderness*, 307 (quote); Bridenbaugh, *Cities in Revolt*, 226 (quote); Flaherty, *Privacy in Colonial New England*, 51; Smith, *The Lower Sort*, 104.

18. Bridenbaugh, *Cities in Revolt*, 228 (quote); John K. Alexander, *Render Them Submissive: Responses to Poverty in Philadelphia, 1760–1800* (Amherst: University of Massachusetts Press, 1980), 22 (quote); Blumin, *The Emergence of the Middle Class*, 45; Salinger, "Spaces, Inside and Out," 19, 22; Shammas, "The Space Problem," 512.

19. John D'Emilio and Estelle Freedman, *Intimate Matters: A History of Sexuality in America* (Chicago: University of Chicago Press, 1998), 17 (quote); Flaherty, *Privacy in Colonial New England*, 82 (quote).

20. Smith, *The Lower Sort*, 162.

21. Shammas, "The Space Problem," 524 (quote); Bridenbaugh, *Cities in the Wilderness*, 16–18, 165–66, 321–22; Bridenbaugh, *Cities in Revolt*, 31, 240–41; Alexander, *Render Them Submissive*, 21–22 (quotes); Carl Abbott, "The Neighborhoods of New York, 1760–1775," *New York History* 55 (1974): 50 (quote).

22. Abbott, "The Neighborhoods of New York," 35–36; Sam B. Warner Jr., *The Private City: Philadelphia in Three Periods of Its Growth* (Philadelphia: University of Pennsylvania Press, 1968), 11–14; Smith, *The Lower Sort*, 164–65; Blumin, *The Emergence of the Middle Class*, 47; Bridenbaugh, *Cities in the Wilderness*, 306; Flaherty, *Privacy in Colonial New England*, 33; Bridenbaugh, *Cities in Revolt*, 25 (quote); Skemp, "A Social and Cultural History of Newport," 13; Enrico Dal Lago, "The City as Social Display: Landed Elites and Urban Images of Charleston and Palermo," *Journal of Historical Sociology* 14 (December 2001): 385–86.

23. Amos Long, "Outdoor Privies in the Dutch Country," *Pennsylvania Folklife* 13 (1963): 33–38; Charles L. Fisher, Karl Reinhard, Matthew Kirk,

and Justin DiVirgilio, "Privies and Parasites: The Archaeology of Health Conditions in Albany, New York," *Historical Archaeology* 41 (2007): 173–89.

24. James R. Cothran, *Charleston's Horticultural Heritage* (Columbia: University of South Carolina Press, 1995), 22 (quote); George C. Rogers Jr., "Gardens and Landscapes in Eighteenth-Century South Carolina," in *British and American Gardens in the Eighteenth Century*, ed. Robert P. MacCubbin and Peter Martin (Williamsburg, VA: Colonial Williamsburg Foundation, 1984), 148; Singleton, *Dutch New York*, 29–30; Elizabeth McLean, "Town and Country in Eighteenth-Century Philadelphia," *Eighteenth Century Life* 8 (1983), 136 (quote); Peter Benes, "Horticultural Importers and Nurserymen in Boston, 1719–1770," *Horticultural Importers and Nurserymen* 20 (1995), 39–40 (quote).

25. Richard Bushman, *The Refinement of America: Persons, Houses, Cities* (New York: Vintage Books, 1992), 39, 130–32; Cothran, *Charleston's Horticultural Heritage*, 30–31; Lucinda Brockway, "The Historic Designed Landscapes of Newport County," *Newport History* 64 (1991): 65; McLean, "Town and Country," 140.

26. Dennis Smith, *Dennis Smith's History of Firefighting in America: 300 Years of Courage* (New York: Dial Press, 1978), 4–6; John V. Morris, *Fires and Firefighters* (Boston: Little, Brown & Co., 1955), 10–20, 37–39; Stephanie Schorow, *Boston on Fire: A History of Fires and Firefighters in Boston* (Beverly, MA: Commonwealth Editions, 2003), 5–6; Bridenbaugh, *Cities in the Wilderness*, 207–8, 209 (quotes), 308; Donald J. Cannon, ed., *Heritage of Flames: The Illustrated History of Early American Firefighting* (Garden City, NY: Doubleday & Co., 1977), 60–63, 75–77.

27. Smith, *Smith's History of Firefighting*, 6; Schorow, *Boston on Fire*, 5; Morris, *Fire and Firefighting*, 11–16, 32–33; Bridenbaugh, *Cities in the Wilderness*, 208–9.

28. Schorow, *Boston on Fire*, 9 (quote); Benjamin Carp, "Fire of Liberty: Firefighters, Urban Voluntary Culture, and the Revolutionary Movement," *William and Mary Quarterly* 58 (2001): 785–87, 791–92; Bridenbaugh, *Cities in the Wilderness*, 211, 369–70; Cannon, *Heritage of Flames*, 125, 133; Morris, *Fires and Firefighting*, 27–28.

29. Bridenbaugh, *Cities in Revolt*, 105; Smith, *Smith's History of Firefighting*, 9; Carp, "Fire of Liberty," 784–85.

30. Smith, *Smith's History of Firefighting*, 20 (quote); Morris, *Fires and Firefighting*, 24–25 (quotes).

31. Smith, *Smith's History of Firefighting*, 13; Bridenbaugh, *Cities in the Wilderness*, 372.

32. Kenneth Scott, "Sufferers in the Charleston Fire of 1740," *South Carolina Historical Magazine* 64 (1963): 203–6; Walter J. Fraser Jr., *Charleston! Charleston!: The History of a Southern City* (Columbia: University of South Carolina Press, 1989), 67–69; Matthew Mulcahy, "The 'Great Fire' of 1740 and the Politics of Disaster Relief in Colonial

Charleston," *South Carolina Historical Magazine* 99 (1998): 137–57 (quote on page 137).

33. Josiah Smith, "The Burning of Sodom, with Its Moral Causes Improv'd in a Sermon" (Charlestown: D. Fowler, 1741), 3–15. For similar sermons, see Increase Mather, "Burnings Bewailed in a Sermon Occasioned by the Lamentable Fire which Was in Boston, October 2, 1711 (Boston: Timothy Green, 1711); and Jonathan Mayhew, "Sermon Occasioned by the Great Fire in Boston, March 20, 1760."

34. Bridenbaugh, *Cities in Revolt*, 19, 227; Fraser, *Charleston! Charleston!* 84–85; *South Carolina Gazette*, September 19, 1752.

35. Bridenbaugh, *Cities in the Wilderness*, 155–58, 317 (quote); Bridenbaugh, *Cities in Revolt*, 28, 30 (quote), 158, 239.

36. Bridenbaugh, *Cities in the Wilderness*, 169 (quote); Bridenbaugh, *Cities in Revolt*, 33–34, 242.

37. Bridenbaugh, *Cities in the Wilderness*, 19, 167 (quotes), 323, 398; Bridenbaugh, *Cities in Revolt*, 32–33.

38. Billy G. Smith, "Walking Moraley's Streets: Philadelphia," *Common-Place* 3 (July 2003): 8; Fatherly, *Gentlewomen and Learned Ladies*, 119 (quote); Bridenbaugh, *Cities in Revolt*, 31 (quote).

39. Bridenbaugh, *Cities in the Wilderness*, 16–18, 165–66, 321–22; Bridenbaugh, *Cities in Revolt*, 31, 24–44.

40. Bridenbaugh, *Cities in the Wilderness*, 169–70.

41. Bridenbaugh, *Cities in the Wilderness*, 164–68, 324; Bridenbaugh, *Cities in Revolt*, 34–35; Blumin, *The Emergence of the Middle Class*, 20 (quotes).

42. Bridenbaugh, *Cities in Revolt*, 341 (quote), 35 (quote); Bridenbaugh, *Cities in the Wilderness*, 21 (quote), 323–24 (quote), 168 (quote).

43. Bridenbaugh, *Cities in Revolt*, 35–36.

44. Ibid., 243 (quote); Fatherly, *Gentlewomen and Learned Ladies*, 119 (quote).

45. Bridenbaugh, *Cities in the Wilderness*, 170, 325 (quote); Thomas Garrett, "A History of Pleasure Gardens in New York City, 1700–1865," Ph.D. dissertation, New York University, 1978, 67–69, 79–86.

10

Food and Dining

INTRODUCTION

Because the five major cities in colonial America were, in varying degrees, cultural melting pots of peoples from many different places, races, and faiths, it is only natural that this diversity showed in the complex culinary traditions of those who inhabited these cosmopolitan urban centers. "At no time in modern history," explains historian James McWilliams, "have so many cultures with so many culinary possibilities at their disposal found themselves vying for space in the same geographical region as they were in colonial British America."[1] This culinary melting pot originated with the first arrival of Europeans to the New World, a meeting that sparked an exchange in foodstuffs that revolutionized the diets, eating habits, and health of the American colonists. The settlers' diets were enriched with such native foods as turkey, maize, beans, pumpkins, squash, chocolate, and green and red peppers. The New World vegetable crops in particular were more nutritious and produced higher yields than the cereal crops of Europe, like wheat and rye. Early settlers also had access to forests filled with an abundance of wild game, berries, and nuts, and rivers and coastal waters teeming with aquatic life. At the same time, European colonists brought Old World foods and domestic animals to America: wheat, rye, peaches, apples, turnips, beets, cabbage, lentils, carrots, honeybees, pigs, chickens, cattle, sheep, and goats. Rice, yams, and black-eyed peas, brought over from Africa by slavers and traders, further enriched the American diet. Enhancing the ingredients of this culinary cooking pot is the fact that each ethnic group and race brought its own recipes and cooking techniques to America, which were adapted and modified to meet the prevailing conditions and foods available in the New World. Over time, colonists integrated these diverse foods, recipes, and cooking techniques into a richly unique diet that helped make eighteenth-century Americans the tallest and healthiest people in the world.

This complex culinary process occurred over a long period. The first decades of settlement in the five cities were lean years of survival and colony building. Early settlers learned from Native Americans what was edible and recognized similarities between the North American plants, animals, fish, or birds and those they knew in Europe. To supplement their general scarcity of domesticated livestock, the first generation of residents exploited wild game and fish like deer, raccoons, opossums, turtles, seafood, and various birds. John Lawson of South Carolina remarked of possum that it "tasted between young Pork & Veal, their Fat being as white as any I ever saw," while the Dutchman Adriaen Van der Donck of New Amsterdam reported of raccoons: "When their meat is roasted, it is delicious food, but when it is stewed, it is too luscious, on account of its fatness."[2]

However, as towns grew in size and wealth, and as trade ascended in importance across the Atlantic economy, the cities' inhabitants developed a richer diet that was as diverse as the people themselves. The cities, with their multiethnic populations, markets, and specialty shops, offered a greater variety of food and recipes than were available elsewhere. Unfortunately, not everyone could afford the rich bounty available in the cities, which, over time, developed a relatively large underclass. Consequently, distinctions in diets and dining customs between the social classes became more pronounced during the eighteenth century. The upper class used their superior diet and more refined eating habits to further justify their hegemony over their alleged inferiors, who ate "gross food" in a crude manner. Culinary distinctions also emerged in the different geographical regions along the Atlantic coast. The New England, Middle, and Southern colonies, with their different climates, soils, and populations, created diets unique to each region. Thus an examination of the diets and eating customs in the five principal colonial cities offers an excellent opportunity to understand better the genesis of America's culinary melting pot.

KITCHEN

At the center of this culinary kaleidoscope was the kitchen, which in most early American homes was not a separate room but part of the larger "common room." However, kitchen arrangements varied according to region and social class. City folk residing in homes on small pieces of land often placed kitchens in the basements of their homes. In cold-weather colonies, settlers preferred having a kitchen in the common room of the house to radiate heat into other rooms. The persistent heat of Charles Town encouraged home owners there to move the kitchen apart from the main house. Many homes belonging to the upper class also had outside kitchens, which often doubled as the dwelling structure for the cook and her family.

No matter the location of the kitchen, the housewife cooked her family's meals in a cavernous stone or brick fireplace, often 4 to 10 feet across and 5 feet high. Assisting the cook was an assortment of tools. Most important was a lug pole of green wood or iron with attached pothooks that allowed cooks to hang pots and kettles by their handles. To move a kettle on or off the fire, a cook had to step into the hearth opening near the fire. This danger was mitigated with the introduction in the mid-1700s of iron cranes with a swing arm that enabled the cook to take pots and kettles off the hooks without having to step into the fireplace. Cooks managed fires by moving hot coals with tongs and shovels. In preparing a meal, the colonial housewife relied on a variety of cooking implements—iron kettles, skillets, frying pans, griddles, roasting spits, toasting ovens, tongs, mortars and pestles, skewers, knives, bowls and bellows. Many of these items sat on the side of the hearth or hung overhead on beams or from pegs or hooks in the walls. Sacks and bags also hung from beams to hold dry foodstuffs, while herbs were often placed on the mantle for the cook's convenience. Further cluttering the kitchen were a water pail and wash bench; barrels for salt meat and fish, corn meal and flour, molasses, cider, and beer; and kegs to store gunpowder and rum. However, only the wealthiest families possessed all of this cooking equipment; most lower-class housewives were forced to make do with just a large iron kettle, which considerably limited her cooking methods.[3]

In addition to limited cooking equipment, colonial cooks labored within tight confines with little work surface. Housewives worked

Colonial Fireplace. This 1902 photograph of a colonial-era fireplace includes many period pieces that a housewife would use to cook the family meal. Note the crane inside the oven that allowed the cook to move the cooking pot toward her away from the fire. The oven is located on the left side of the fireplace. (Library of Congress, Prints and Photographs Division, Reproduction # LC USZ62-113458)

on top of barrels, chests, dressers, and dining tables—if the family was fortunate enough to have one. Even the homes of many gentry lacked kitchens with work surfaces, forcing their housemaids to prepare food by holding bowls or cutting boards on their lap, perching on a stool, or even kneeling on the floor or hearth. Easing the burden of preparing and cooking food for urban housewives were the numerous commercial food businesses in the main cities. Millers, bakers, confectioners, butchers, and brewers allowed a busy housewife with the money to reduce her time in the kitchen by purchasing bread, butter, cheese, pastries, candies, beer, and even cured, salted, and smoked meat. Still, cooking in colonial America was a labor-intensive and time-consuming enterprise.[4]

COOKING

For cooks with a fully equipped kitchen, five cooking methods were available: boiling, roasting, broiling, frying, and baking. Of these, boiling was the most common method as it allowed a busy housewife to throw meats, vegetables, and grains into a large kettle and simmer them for hours while she attended to other chores. Poaching was a popular method for cooking fish. Less common was roasting on a spit, which required careful attention to the heat of the coals, the turning of the spit, and proper basting. Turning the spit was frequently the work of a servant or slave in well-to-do-households and a young boy in lower-class homes. A few ingenious cooks, though, used dogs trotting on a treadmill to turn the spit or used a device attached to chains that fitted over cogged wheels similar to clockworks. These methods were made obsolete with the invention of the roasting oven, a tin box that reflected heat back onto the side of the roast facing away from the fire. Broiling meat, on the other hand, was done on rectangular or circular iron grids mounted on short legs and moved by a long handle. Frying became a relatively popular method of cooking in early America partly because almost everyone owned a skillet and partly because colonists consumed prodigious amounts of pork, the high fat content of which made it perfect for frying. Not all housewives, however, enjoyed an oven in their kitchen, an unfortunate circumstance that forced them to bake food by placing it directly on the hot hearth, inverting a pot over it, and piling coals onto and around the pot. More fortunate were those cooks who owned a Dutch oven, an iron pot with a depressed lid allowing coals to be placed on top. Those women who could afford it simply took their bread and pastries to a baker's shop, where they rented oven space, or bought bread and pastries from the many bakers in town. Experienced cooks were able simultaneously to utilize all these cooking methods—hanging pots and kettles over the fire, baking in reflecting devices at the sides, roasting in front of the fire, making sauces on small piles of coals, and baking bread in a kettle surrounded by coals.[5]

The colonial cook began her day by starting a fire, either kindling it with coals or lighting the wood with a tinder box. Often she had multiple fires going at once: a large fire for boiling, a medium fire for roasting, and a group of embers for frying. Having no thermometer, the cook measured the heat by placing her hand over the fire.

Recipe for Roasted Rabbit

Baste them with good butter, and dredge them with a little flour. Half an hour will do them at a very quick clear fire; and, if they are very small, twenty minutes will do them. Take the livers with a little bunch of parsley and boil them, and then chop them very fine together. Melt some good butter, put half the liver and parsley into the butter; pour it into the dish, and garnish the dish with the other half. Let your rabbit be done of a fine light brown.

Susannah Carter, *The Frugal Colonial Housewife*, 1772.

Practice taught her how hot the fire was by how long she could hold her hand above the flames. She then reduced the fire with water or increased it with bellows as needed. Most colonial kitchens also lacked clocks, forcing cooks to calculate cooking time by the progression of the sun. Not surprisingly, food prepared on cloudy days could be as distasteful as the weather. Of greater inconvenience for housewives was the lack of running water in their homes. Some urban homes belonging to the well-to-do had private wells in their backyards or courts, but most homes did not, requiring housewives to tote heavy pails of water from a distant public pump.

With fire and water at hand, the cook next carried out the laborious task of preparing the food for cooking: plucking the feathers from birds and fowl, chopping and trimming meat, cutting vegetables, cleaning fish, making dough, and filling pies, among countless other preparations. In preparing her meals, the colonial housewife relied on recipes handed down orally from previous generations. Because most women at this time could not read or write, few recipe books were printed in America, and none before 1742.

The colonial housewife did not need a cookbook to tell her that cooking food was difficult, hot, and often dangerous work. Managing the large iron kettle, which often weighed as much as 40 pounds, was no easy task. Neither was moving heavy skillets with handles sometimes three feet long. Both tasks required the cook to work close to the fire, which invited accidents. To prevent such an unwanted event, wise cooks hitched up their skirts, petticoats, and aprons. Many others worked in a "state of undress" for both safety and comfort. Still, cooks were frequently burned and scalded for their efforts; some even died from their injuries. This partly explains why upper-class women often employed domestic servants or exploited female slaves to cook for their families.[6]

URBAN FOODWAYS

Adding to the rich diet of urban settlers is that housewives living in the five major port cities in North America had a much greater variety of foodstuffs available to them with which to cook than did their rural counterparts. These cities were the focus of a growing trade that exported and imported goods from their hinterlands, other colonies, and other countries. This was a critical step toward the convergence of a unique style of American food. For example, Boston imported flour from New York and Pennsylvania in exchange for salt fish. New York City received beef, pork, and fruits from Virginia and fish, cider apples, and biscuits from New England. Charles Town imported corn and salt fish from New England in exchange for rice. Philadelphia traded wheat flour and fruits with Charles Town in exchange for rice. These cities also imported foods and luxuries from abroad. From the West Indies they received sweet potatoes, oranges, pimientos, chocolate, molasses, coconuts, sugar, ginger, and herbs. From France, Spain, and the Canary Islands came citrus fruits, olive oil, spices, and wines. Closer to home, these commercial centers received perishable produce, livestock, and wild game from nearby farmers and hunters.[7]

Urban Markets

City dwellers usually purchased these and other goods in public markets, where numerous vendors sold a variety of meats, fish, fruits, nuts, vegetables, and nonfood items. Public markets were a necessity early on in the port cities. Boston, for example, had outgrown its own food resources by 1640 and could no longer support itself agriculturally. To ensure that urban residents had a regular supply of food, officials in the five cities established markets and designated their operating hours. To protect consumers from hucksters and cheats, city officials also passed ordinances prohibiting forestalling and requiring market clerks to check the accuracy of weights and measures and to examine the quality of bread and meat from bakers and butchers. Still, "scandalous frauds in weights and measures" by numerous vendors and butchers selling meat "blown up or winded" were all too common. Savvy women brought their knives and skepticism to markets, where they sliced and peered into joints, poked into butter, and tasted and smelled to check on the quality of goods. When purchasing goods, women often engaged in sharp negotiations for the lowest price, sometimes lying about competitors' prices in order to win a discount. Mary Pinckney of Charles Town admitted to a friend that "I went to several shops, & then beat down, which I am sorry to say is generally obliged here."[8]

Despite the presence of hucksters and cheats, urban markets still provided residents with a dizzying array of food and manufactured goods. Philadelphia's market house, which extended a quarter of a mile and housed over 250 vendors who sold an extraordinary store of provisions, was perhaps the most admired and impressive in the 13 British North American colonies. Philadelphia's market was also famous for its cleanliness and its strict enforcement against forestalling and the selling of adulterated food. Even smoking was prohibited in the market house. New York City had five public markets, prompting one resident to boast that "No part of America is supplied with markets abounding with greater plenty and variety. We have beef, pork, mutton, poultry, butter, wild fowl, venison, fish, roots, and herbs, of all kinds in their seasons." Charles Town had a "fine market" at Broad and Meeting Streets that sold all varieties of meat and produce. Likewise, Newport's market supplied "all kinds of provisions," according to one observer. "Fish are plenty and rather cheaper than at New York. Fruits are plenty, tho' not in such abundance as to the South; they have also great plenty of cucumbers, melons, squashes, etc., growing in the fields." All urban markets were affected by the seasonality of foodstuffs. "After the season for fowls," one traveler to Philadelphia noted, "comes the fisheries of the spring," while "in the beginning and middle of summer it is difficult to procure fresh provisions of any kind."[9]

As popular public venues, market houses attracted people of all classes, races, and nationalities, creating a spectacle for the eyes and a cacophony for the ears. Like many people today who go to large shopping malls, some found entertainment in simply watching the human zoo that characterized urban markets. Many men in particular received "no small Satisfaction in seeing the pretty Creatures, the young Ladies, traversing the place from Stall to Stall," observed a visitor to Philadelphia's public market in 1724.[10] Others went to the markets to see the public floggings, to taunt criminals held in stocks, or to watch African slaves examined and sold like livestock.

Food Shops and Vendors

The market house was not the only place where urban residents could buy foodstuffs. The increasing size and wealth of the cities in the eighteenth century encouraged the development of retail shops selling specialty goods to well-to-do clients. Some retail stores sold a wide variety of imported luxury items, from sugar, tea, spices, and coffee to wines, dried fruits, chocolate, and lemons. Other retail shops specialized in single items, such as tobacco, sweets, and baked goods. The cities also contained many small food shops, often managed by women, who catered to the lower classes. For those without ovens, the cities provided many food service shops where women could take their "prepared victuals" to be roasted or baked. An even more prominent part of urban life was the numerous peddlers hawking oysters, milk, butter, cheese, fruits, and vegetables either on street corners or door to door.

Taverns

For professional men and travelers, the many taverns in eighteenth-century cities offered a smorgasbord of dishes. The Tontine House in New York City, for example, served from 12 to 16 dishes each day, including bear steak, venison, turkey, duck, lobster, terrapin, oysters, and pigeon. Boston, too, had some outstanding places to eat. A foreign traveler described a meal at a Boston tavern in the mid-1700s as follows: "At two o'clock dinner was announced, and we were shown into a room where we found a long table covered with dishes, and plates for twenty persons. We were served with salmon, veal, beef, mutton, fowl, ham, roots, puddings, etc., etc. Each man had his pint of Madeira before him."[11]

DIET

Meat

The diet of early town-dwelling Americans was characterized by an imbalance of too much meat, fat, and starchy foods and too few fruits and vegetables. In a land abundant with wild game and oceans filled with sea creatures, it is no wonder that the diets of early Americans revolved around meat. In the early years of settlement, game was not only the main meat of the colonists but often the main food. Nearly any type of animal that could be caught found its way to the settlers' table. An incomplete list includes bears, foxes, panthers, otters, beavers, muskrats, porcupines, skunks, opossum, turtles (and their eggs), frogs, geese, ducks, eagles, swans, cranes, and herons. The numerous passenger pigeons, which were sold in urban markets for as little as six for a penny, were a popular food source for the poor, as were oysters, which were also bountiful and cheap. As they lived near rivers and the ocean, fish and shellfish were also an important part of the settlers' diet.

Of course, hunting and fishing are difficult and not always successful. So from the beginning colonists wisely imported domesticated animals such as chickens, cattle, sheep, goats, and pigs for a more reliable source of meat. Because cattle could fend for themselves, beef animals were branded and allowed to forage wherever they could find food. South Carolina, Rhode Island, and Connecticut were renowned for their flourishing cattle industries. Goats, which lived off the land and which provided colonists with both milk and meat, were also an important source of protein. Even more important to the diet of Americans were chickens, which were plentiful, cheap, and an excellent source of both meat and eggs. But the king of meats to most early Americans was pork. This was not because it was necessarily the tastiest flesh but because the lowly pig multiplied prodigiously, required minimal upkeep as it fed off garbage thrown in the street, and supplied fat that was rendered into lard, and because nearly every part of the pig (except the proverbial squeal) was useful for eating or making household items. Overall, urban residents consumed a wide variety of animals from land, sea, and air. Archaeological excavations of faunal assemblages from eighteenth-century Boston trash pits provide some insight into this rich smorgasbord as a percentage of the colonists' overall meat diet: sheep/goats (17%), cattle (14%), fish (13%), pigs (12%), chicken (9%), geese (8%), pigeons (7%), turkeys (6%), ducks (5%), and miscellaneous (9%).[12]

Indian Triad

Next to meat, the Indian triad of corn, beans, and squash provided the most important staples of the early American diet. Of these three, Indian corn, which flourished on nearly all soils along the Atlantic coast, was most important. European settlers quickly adopted corn into their diet for its ease in planting, harvesting, and storing; its high yields per acre; its versatility in cooking; and its use as food for both humans and livestock. Consequently, people of all classes and of all regions ate a prodigious amount of corn, but rarely as a vegetable. Instead, most corn was ground into meal and boiled to make porridges and baked to make bread and cakes.

Boiled bag puddings made from corn and sweetened with molasses were a popular dish prepared by housewives because they could be left unattended for long periods and hung inside a pot that was being used to cook other foods at the same time.

Colonists also readily adopted the America bean into their diet, partly because it looked much like the European broad bean. A cheap source of protein, beans were usually not eaten alone but were mixed with corn and other vegetables, and sometimes meat, to make succotash or other dishes. Bostonians preferred either to bake their beans or to make bean porridge as part of their standard Saturday night fare. On the other hand, black-eyed peas, brought over from Africa, were more popular among Charles Town residents, who mixed them with onions, salt, pepper, rice, and pork. The third member of the Indian triad, squash, also became an important ingredient in many recipes. Squashes were usually stewed with meats or candied with fresh fruits. Pumpkin, a winter squash, was another favorite food among early Americans, who turned it more into a dessert by serving it with sugared water or molasses and baking it as pies, puddings, and sometimes bread.[13]

Vegetables

Vegetables (excluding corn and squash) were not a popular food item among most early Americans in the seventeenth century, a carry-over from England where vegetables were viewed as more fit for hogs than humans. Credit is often given to German and Dutch immigrants for more varied and careful vegetable cultivation than was typical of the English, who were often described as being careless of their gardens. By selling their superior produce to nearby urban markets like those in Philadelphia and New York City, the Germans and Dutch cultivated a growing taste for vegetables and roots among other colonists. Over time, some middle- and upper-class urban residents cultivated their own produce gardens, where they grew turnips, carrots, beets, peas, cabbage, okra, Jerusalem artichokes, onions, and asparagus, among others. Wild greens like pigweed, cress, milkweed, leeks, and swamp cabbage were usually eaten raw. Most other vegetables were boiled, which depleted them of valuable nutrients. Still, vegetables could be enjoyed year round by either preserving them in fat crocks or storing them in dry cellars. One important exception to this pattern of consumption was the urban poor, who had no space to grow vegetables and little money to buy them.[14]

Bread

Bread, which was eaten at all meals, was an essential part of the diet of all social classes. The poor tended to rely more on it for their daily sustenance than did others because it was plentiful and relatively inexpensive. Bread was so important to most people, in fact, that city officials regulated both the quality and the price of bread to ensure that it was unadulterated and affordable. In making their bread, colonists relied primarily on such popular European grains as wheat, barley, and rye. To add an extra boost of flavor and sweetness, Americans often mixed molasses in with the bread dough. And when bread went stale, the frugal housewife would use it as an ingredient in other dishes such as bread fritters and French toast.[15]

Fruits and Nuts

American colonists were not satisfied with eating just staple foods. They also added fruits, nuts, and berries to their diets. Fruits were popular among the colonists not just for their taste but also for their versatility. Apples, in particular, were manipulated into a variety of products, from apple cider and apple sauce to apple butter and apple pies and dumplings. Peaches were also popular throughout the colonies. In Charles Town, residents soaked them in corn whiskey before eating them, while in Pennsylvania peaches were so numerous that they were fed to the hogs, which some people believed gave a superior flavor to the pork there. Equally as versatile as fruit were berries, which settlers picked from the forest during the spring and early summer. Huckleberries, whortleberries, cranberries, gooseberries, raspberries, blackberries, blueberries, and strawberries were all either eaten raw with cream and sugar, baked into pies, or pounded into a hard paste, cut into squares, and chewed like candy. Housewives also preserved these fruits and reconstituted them later for pie filling or tarts. They also boiled them with sugar to make marmalade and jellies. Finally, colonists picked from trees a wide variety of nuts to complement their diet. Chestnuts, filberts, walnuts, and hickory nuts were all eaten in abundance, either pickled, in stuffing, as a catsup to flavor their meat and vegetables, or simply raw as a snack.[16]

Herbs and Spices

European immigrants brought over herbs and spices that they used to doctor their food. The English enjoyed sweet marjoram, summer savory, parsley, and sweet thyme, while the Dutch used a group of savory and sweet herbs, along with lovage, oregano, and horseradish. In 1709 John Lawson of Carolina observed in local gardens fennel, parsley, borage, clary, marigolds, marjoram, savory, dill, and seeds such as caraway, coriander, cumin, and anise. The upper class used expensive spices with a heavy hand not just to flavor their food but also to demonstrate their wealth and status. Salt and pepper were the most widely available seasonings for most classes, followed by nutmeg, mace, cloves, ginger, and allspice. Colonial cooks flavored many dishes, both meats and vegetables, with an abundance of butter or lard. They also used fat from pork to flavor baked beans, chowder, porridge, vegetables, and even puddings and pies. Much healthier was the use of currants and raisins to enhance the taste of puddings, porridges, and mushes.[17]

Desserts

The copious quantities of fruit and the abundance of inexpensive sugar and molasses from the West Indies encouraged among early Americans an addiction to desserts. Of the two sweeteners, molasses was more popular, especially among the poor, because it was far less expensive than sugar. Some urban residents kept beehives from which they acquired honey. With such an abundance of sweeteners available to the colonists, virtually no food on the American table escaped a sweetener of some kind. Sugar, molasses, and honey were used to sweeten puddings (both the fruit and vegetable kind), milk dishes, vegetables, breads, and meats, particularly pork. Of course, sweeteners were the star ingredient in desserts like custards, fruit creams, cookies, cakes, tarts, pies, and cobblers. Americans also sugared their nuts and fruits; some even used sugar to make candied lemon peels, a favorite snack among children. The temptation for sweets was greatest for residents of the five cities, which had many bakers, confectionaries, and housewives selling desserts of all kinds. The well-to-do who could afford the more expensive processed sugar paid dearly for their sweet tooth with rotten teeth and unattractive smiles.[18]

PRESERVING FOOD

In an era without refrigeration, much of the colonial housewife's labor was directed not toward cooking food but preserving it. Preservation methods included salting, drying, smoking, pickling

Recipe for Boiled Rice Pudding

Take a quarter of a pound of rice, and half a pound of raisins stoned. Tie them in a cloth, so as to give the rice room to swell. Boil it two hours. And serve it up with melted butter, sugar, and grated nutmeg thrown over it.

Susannah Carter, *The Frugal Colonial Housewife*, 1772.

in vinegar, fermenting, and preserving with sugar or alcohol. Salt was essential to preserving meat and fish as it drew the moisture out of the meat and created an environment hostile to most bacteria. Well-cured salted meats and fish required soaking and boiling to prepare them for consumption, both to rehydrate them and to remove excess saltiness. Smoking extended the life of meat or fish even longer than salting as it created mildly toxic compounds within the meat that both inhibited the growth of bacteria and enhanced the flavor of the meat. "Jerky," which settlers learned how to make from the Native Americans, was beef meat cut into very thin strips and held over a slow fire that dried it out. Pickling with vinegar was the usual way to preserve vegetables, particularly cucumbers, cabbage, asparagus, and green beans that could not be dried. Housewives sometimes pickled oysters, mussels, and clams. Fermenting cabbage into sauerkraut was a favorite preservation method among the German. Colonists often preserved fruit by drying it in the sun, immersing it in alcohol, or simply making it into alcoholic beverages like apple cider and peach brandy.[19]

DRINK

To wash down their food, Americans relied on a variety of beverages. Alcohol of many varieties was the drink of choice among all colonists, both young and old, male and female. Not only did colonists consume alcohol at nearly every meal, but they also used just about every possible occasion as an excuse to imbibe: weddings, funerals, trials, elections, auctions, town meetings, royal birthdays, holidays, dances, balls, concerts, christenings, church communions, childbirth, ministerial ordinations, business deals, and even while working. Even small children consumed diluted beer, cider, wine, and liquors. By the American Revolution an average American over 15 years old drank just under six gallons of absolute alcohol each

Recipe for Pickled Asparagus

Gather your asparagus, and lay them in an earthen pot; make a brine of water and salt strong enough to bear an egg, pour it hot on them, and keep it close covered. When you use them hot, lay them in cold water two hours, then boil and butter them for table. If you can use them as a pickle, boil them and lay them in vinegar.

Susannah Carter, *The Frugal Colonial Housewife*, 1772.

year, which is two-and-a-half times more than the modern average of alcohol consumption. Foreign travelers were shocked at the amount of alcohol colonists consumed. A Swedish visitor reported a "general addiction to hard drinking," while a visitor from England noted that intoxication "pervaded all social classes." It is no wonder therefore that colonists had more than 230 slang terms for inebriation. Some of the more colorful of these include: "casting up his accounts," "kissed black Betty," "drunk as a wheelbarrow," "seen the devil," "cherry-merry," "cock-eyed," "moon-eyed," "pigeon-eyed," "as dizzy as a goose," "had a kick in the guts," "sees two moons," "lost his rudder," "glazed," "stewed," "soaked," and "got the Indian vapors." Urban residents consumed large amounts of alcohol partly out of necessity, as they tended to pollute their water resources with refuse, and partly because they believed alcohol held medicinal qualities against a variety of diseases and ailments, from cholera, malaria, fevers, and lethargy to snakebites, frosted toes, broken legs, and depression. Many settlers also turned to alcohol, finally, to ease the burden of carving out a civilization in the unforgiving American wilderness.[20]

No matter their reasons for drinking, Americans created and imported a variety of alcoholic beverages to quench their thirst. Hard cider, made from fermented apples, was a popular drink among all classes, especially in New England. Beer was an even more popular beverage, so much so that settlers established breweries shortly after their arrival to America. To make the bitter product from crude breweries more palatable, Americans frequently sweetened their beer with molasses or sugar, while others spiked it with some spirit, usually rum. Americans also made home-made wines and cordials from cherries, blackberries, persimmons, currants, and mulberries. The well-to-do, however, preferred heavy, sweet wines imported from Spain and Portugal, along with punch

Recipe for Elder Wine

When the elder-berries are ripe, pick them, and put them into a stone jar; set them in boiling water, or in a slack oven, 'till the jar is as warm as you can well bear to touch it with your hand; then strain the fruit through a course cloth, squeezing them hard, and our the liquid into a kettle. Put it on the fire, and let it boil, and to every quart of liquor add a pound of Lisbon sugar, and scum it often. Then let it settle, and pour it off into a jar, and cover it close.

Susannah Carter, *The Frugal Colonial Housewife*, 1772.

and brandy made from distilled corn, peaches, cherries, grapes, and wild plums. Financial constraints steered the poorer folk to less expensive alcoholic beverages like cider, beer, and especially rum, which had a relatively high alcohol content. Satiating much of the lower classes' desire for rum was Boston, whose numerous rum distilleries were producing over a million gallons of the dark, potent beverage by 1730. Much of this rum, along with other alcoholic beverages, was sold in the dozens of taverns that dotted the urban landscape.[21]

Colonists also consumed a wide variety of nonalcoholic beverages. Many people, especially the poor, bravely drank water, which was often mixed with cider, ginger, or molasses to make it more potable. Milk was an important foodstuff in all of the cities. Tea, coffee, and chocolate were imported to America by the 1690s from Asia, the Near East, and Central America, respectively. Of these, tea was most popular among all social classes. To differentiate themselves from their inferiors in consuming tea, the urban gentry mimicked their European counterparts in creating a complex, expensive, and time-consuming ritual surrounding their "tea time" that included an artistic performance in brewing and serving tea, the proper placement of napkins and spoons, the correct manner of holding a tea cup, the use of silent signals to request or deny more tea, and the serving of assorted pastries and sometimes sweetmeats—all served in or on silver tea pots, sugar bowls, trays, and porcelain cups and plates.[22]

FOOD, CLASS, AND POWER

As this elitist tea ritual shows, food and dining in early America had important implications for defining class distinctions and access to power. On the surface, this may seem odd as there was little difference in physical stature between lower- and upper-class Americans, which indicates that even the poor were reasonably well nourished compared with the rich. Yet such information relating diet and height can be misleading, especially as it applies to the laboring poor in the cities. A modern study of colonial Philadelphia, for example, reveals that the diet for the city's poor was "minimal in both quality and cost." In all, Philadelphia's lower-class adult men consumed daily approximately 3,179 calories (nearly 2,000 calories came from grains; 528 from meat, mostly beef and veal; and 572 from milk, butter, and molasses), an amount that provided insufficient calories for the more than approximately 4,000 calories needed for the arduous labor they performed. This suggests that the laboring poor worked less productively and effi-ciently than they would have if they had access to an adequate diet. The laboring poor's poverty-level wages, coupled with the high cost of food in the Quaker city, explains their meager diet. Making it difficult for the poor to supplement their diet during hard times is that the crowded alleys where most of them lived made garden-ing impractical and owning a cow even less feasible. More often, poor folk survived by reducing their food costs and eating larger quantities of flour, cornmeal, and rice—foods with the highest caloric yield for the money but a bland, nonnutritious diet that left people susceptible to dietary deficiency ailments like pellagra and the numerous diseases that plagued the city.[23]

The primary dietary difference between rich and poor was the quality of food, not the quantity. The poor ate simple, unsophisti-cated meals of beans, corn meal, root vegetables, and occasionally meat, all of which was usually boiled together into a stew, porridge, or gruel. Bread was often used to spoon up their liquid meal. Fruits and garden vegetables rarely made it into the mouths of the poor. Meat, too, was often too expensive for the lower class to purchase. When the poor were fortunate enough to eat meat, it was often the old, tough, stringy flesh of animals past their prime. During hard economic times, cats, dogs, and even rodents made their appear-ance in poor folks' cooking pots. And when dogs and rats became scarce food items in the cities, the poor took matters into their own hands, as 200 Bostonians did in 1713 by rioting through the streets searching for food. Thereafter Boston selectmen stored surplus corn to sell to the needy during the winter months.[24]

The well-to-do, on the other hand, rarely suffered from such privation. They had a more complicated and nutritious diet than the poor that included higher quality, greater variety, and larger amounts of meats, vegetables, breads, fruits, and desserts flavored by an assortment of spices and herbs. Specialty meats, cheeses, desserts, and beverages, often imported or commercially produced, were enjoyed exclusively by the upper classes.

To the upper class, the better food they consumed was a means to further justify their alleged superiority and therefore their exclusive right to rule. Early British Americans brought with them from England a philosophy of food that helped them define social status, virtue, personal health, appearance, behavior, and ability. According to this ideology, each food had distinctive traits, either good or bad, that were transferred to the eater. "A plentiful and varied diet of high quality fine foods created refined, virtuous, and talented people," author Trudy Eden explains. "A more restricted diet composed of poor quality coarse foods made the people who ate them coarse, even beastly." This "you are what you eat" philosophy had important political and social implications. Because the wealthy consumed a better-quality diet, a diet that allegedly made them more virtuous, talented, and food-secure, they were most fit to rule. The common folk, by contrast, were unfit to rule because they ate "gross foods" that left them bereft of virtue. Of course, this was a self-serving ideology created by the gentry. Nevertheless, their perception of food, at least in part, supported the hierarchical social structure and reaffirmed their entitlement to power. This was both a philosophy and circumstance manufactured by the upper class, who paid their employees low wages and provided servants and slaves with a crude diet that prevented them from acquiring the quality of food that would help enable them to claim rights to power. Meanwhile, the considerable income the rich received from exploiting the poor and enslaved allowed them to achieve the "golden mean" of food security that contributed to a sense of emotional well-being and superiority. Although this was probably not a conscious conspiracy on the part of the elites, it nevertheless served their larger goal of ensuring that the lower sort never had these cultural tools necessary to claim power and prestige.[25]

REGIONAL DISTINCTIONS

Distinctions in diet were not limited to class but also extended to the three general geographic regions along the Atlantic coast: the New England, Middle, and Southern colonies. Each had its own unique soil, climate, natural resources, and mix of races and nationalities that gave food in each region its own distinctive flavor.

Because the five cities under study are found in all three regions, with Boston and Newport residing in New England, New York and Philadelphia in the Middle Colonies, and Charles Town in the lower South, an examination of people's diets in these port cities provides a revealing reflection of the regional differences in eating habits among early Americans.

New England

Residents of Boston and Newport had a relatively simple diet, as the short growing season in New England and the marginal fertility of its soil allowed only limited varieties of fruits and vegetables. A typical daily diet for most middle-class Boston families was a breakfast of bread and milk; a dinner consisting of corn pudding or pea and bean porridge, followed by bread, meat, roots, pickles, and cheese; and a supper that was made from leftovers from breakfast. Even the gentry might eat modestly in the morning, although they could afford to eat meat and fish at all meals, along with vegetables, puddings, and desserts like tarts. The less well-off, on the other hand, ate a simple boiled dinner of corn and bean porridges flavored with salt pork and root vegetables. Boston brown bread, made with rye flour and sweetened with molasses, was a favorite among all residents. The versatile pumpkin was widely utilized by New Englanders, who roasted, mashed, broiled, and baked the winter squash into a variety of dishes.

New Englanders supplemented this relatively banal diet with an assortment of seafood, which was sometimes broiled and fried but more often was turned into rich chowders, cakes, pies, stews, and hash. Residents of Boston and Newport would often celebrate the bounty of the sea with a "turtle frolic," a grand social event centered around the ceremonial cooking of a huge sea turtle. For those who could afford dessert, there were custards, puddings, applesauce, trifles, tartlets, fruit pies, raisin-filled puddings, and baked apple and raisin balls. Boston tea, buttered rum, port wine punch, or hot mulled cider helped to cleanse diners' palates after eating. In developing their cuisine, New Englanders stayed more loyal to traditional English cooking habits than any other region in British America.[26]

Middle Colonies

The better soil and warmer climate of the Middle Colonies, along with the region's more diversified population, allowed residents of New York City and Philadelphia to enjoy a varied diet that was

English-oriented but flavored with strong contributions from Dutch and German immigrants. The Dutch introduced to America waffles, crullers, doughnuts, pancakes, coleslaw, cookies, cottage cheese, and headcheese. Other common Dutch dishes included cabbage with sausage, split-pea soup, stewed dishes of meat and fish, and fried raisin yeast bread, apple turnovers, and assorted salads of cooked and uncooked cold vegetables with dressings of oil and vinegar. German immigrants to the region, meanwhile, worked hard to recreate and eat a steady and familiar diet of pot roast, dried apples and ham, dumplings, sweet yeast bread, pickled cabbage, apple cake, and fried flour soup. Popular dishes include *dummus* (omelet made with potatoes and fish), *schales* (a casserole made with egg, milk, potatoes, and fish), *griewesupp* (soup made with chicken and pork), *schnits un knepp* (a German apple-and-ham dish), *fastnachts* (German doughnuts), *torte* (flat and round cake or bread), and assorted fruit pies and puddings.

Despite the culinary diversity of the region, many residents of the Middle Colonies ate a monotonous diet. The Swedish botanist Peter Kalm spent a week with a New York Dutch family in 1748 and described "the same perpetual evening meal of porridge made of corn meal." Breakfast was equally austere: "they drank tea in customary way by putting brown sugar into the cup of tea. With tea they ate bread and butter and radishes" and occasionally cheese placed on buttered bread. Part of this frugal dining was cultural, especially among the Quakers and Dutch who practiced an "eat to live" rather than a "live to eat" philosophy. One visitor among the Dutch in New York City was impressed that "they never served more than was consumed before they left the table" and were "careful not to load up the table with food as the English are accustomed to do."[27]

Lower South

Of all the colonists, Carolinians developed the most tolerant approach to food that made their cuisine the most unique in North America. Mirroring its racial and ethnic makeup, the recipes in colonial Charles Town were greatly influenced by African, Caribbean, French, and English cooking techniques. African slave women ruled in many Charles Town kitchens, bringing their native recipes, cooking techniques, and penchant for spicy foods into their masters' homes. The African slave ships brought over *benne* (sesame) seeds, which were used in stews, brittles, cookies, and other pastries. Rice, another African import, was (and still is) a very popular food among Charles Town residents, who used it in a variety of dishes from breads, croquettes, and stews to fritters, pilaus, and griddle cakes. Sweet potatoes, cultivated by slaves, were also popular in Charles Town, and were made into pies, pones, and puddings. Slaves also grew okra, black-eyed peas, eggplants, and various greens, which they sold in the Charles Town market. Like most early Americans, South Carolinians also ate corn in its traditional forms. A variety of meats were also available, especially beef. South Carolinians imported slaves from West African cattle-grazing regions for the express purpose of raising large herds of cattle. Charles Town aristocrats, in fact, often entertained by barbecuing whole steers. Poorer folk had to settle for the less expensive pork.[28]

It was seafood dishes, however, that put Charles Town on the culinary map. Trout, catfish, mullet, whiting, blackfish, oyster, crab, shrimp, and turtle were some of the favorite seafood consumed by Carolinians. French colonists in Charles Town brought recipes that brought a more refined and sophisticated element to many of these seafood dishes. Cream of crab soup, oyster soup and stew, deviled clams and crab, clam fritters, shrimp and rice croquettes, green corn pie with shrimp, and shrimp with hominy were some of the more favorite seafood dishes served in the southern capital. Okra was sometimes used to both flavor and thicken some of these dishes. Coconut tarts, sweet potato pies, and sweet pickled watermelon were common desserts, which were sometimes washed down with "plantation toddy," spiced tea, "planter's punch," and flip, a potent alcoholic beverage.[29]

DINING HABITS

Dining equipage and etiquette in colonial America varied over time and across class lines. During the difficult colony-building years of the seventeenth century, eating was more a matter of crude survival than a sophisticated custom. Most food consisted of simple stews, mushes, and porridges. Eating utensils, drinking cups, chairs, and tables were scarce. Moreover, early Americans were still more medieval than modern in their dining habits. Meals were communal, with people sharing utensils, cups, and plates as much out of custom as out of necessity. Often families shared one wood or pewter noggin, which passed from mouth to mouth for all to drink. Most families also shared a trencher, a 10-inch to 12-inch rectangular block of wood as thick as 3 or 4 inches with a bowl carved into it to make a dish. After the main course, the trencher (plate) was turned over and dessert was served on the clean side.

In consuming their meals, most seventeenth-century Americans ate with spoons made from either horn, wood, gourd, or shells, as forks were uncommon before the American Revolution. Some families dispensed with trenchers and spoons altogether and instead served "spoon meat" on thick slices of bread. Knives were a popular eating utensil among early Americans, even for children. One colonial woman reminiscing about her childhood commented, "When I was a child, I ate with my knife, and the great lesson was, to teach me to put it in my mouth with the edge from the lips." Colonists used knives less to cut chunks of meat than to anchor the meat down while dirty hands tore off smaller pieces and shoved them into mouths. Obviously, eating was a messy act in early America. The poor wiped their greasy hands onto their breeches or dresses, while upper-class diners ate with a large napkin to protect their valuable clothing. Adding to the messiness of the early American meal was the lack of chairs and tables. Few families had enough chairs for all family members to sit while eating. Children traditionally ate their meals while standing or, if they were lucky, sitting on chests and kegs. When the meal was over, food scraps scattered across the table and floor. Cleaning up was a quick affair, with the housewife hastily sweeping up the crumbs and wiping off the trenchers with a wet (and probably dirty) cloth before putting them away.[30]

During the eighteenth century the colonists' dining became more refined as wealth increased and mass-produced dining equipage became more available and affordable. One aspect of refinement was the appearance of individual place settings. Tables and chairs became more available, and knives, forks, spoons, and plates were placed before each diner. The simple fork significantly refined table manners as hands no longer had to touch food and greasy fingers no longer had to be wiped on table cloths or clothes. Meanwhile, fewer middle- and upper-class folk ate from a common serving bowl or platter. Wooden trenchers were replaced with pewter plates in middle-class homes, while the well-to-do dined on china. Benjamin Franklin, for one, could mark his rise from an apprentice printer to a wealthy owner of printing presses, real estate, and other property by noting how his table improved from crude implements to pewter to silverware and china. "[M]y breakfast was a long time bread and milk (no tea)," Franklin noted, "and I ate it out of a twopenny earthen porridger, with a pewter spoon. But mark how

Dining Room of the Nichols-Wanton-Hunter House, Newport, Rhode Island. As wealth increased in the urban cities, dining habits grew more sophisticated and genteel among the affluent who could afford a separate dining room in their home with a mahogany dining table and chairs, porcelain plates, silver cutlery and serving sets, and crystal drinking glasses, as exemplified in the Nichols-Wanton-Hunter House in Newport, Rhode Island. (Library of Congress, Prints and Photographs Division, HABS RI, 3-NEWP, 11-26)

luxury will enter families, and make a progress, in spite of principle: being call'd one morning to breakfast [by my wife], I found it in a China bowl, with a spoon of silver!"[31]

The genteel, in seeking to further separate themselves from the vulgar masses and demonstrate their cultural superiority, enthusiastically embraced more refined dining habits. They often had a separate dining room dedicated to eating and entertaining that included a cloth-covered dining table with matching chairs, and ornate furniture pieces for displaying silver and ceramics for food service. Equally ostentatious were elaborate table settings that included a silver fork, knife, and spoon for each diner and numerous beautiful platters and bowls that held a generous variety of things to eat.

Meals among the urban elite became an elaborate procession of courses that were guided by books detailing symmetrical placement of serving pieces. Many adopted the French order of the meal, which began with soups and appetizers, followed by roasted meats, side dishes, and a dessert of fruits and sweet meats. As explained by historian Edward Pearson, "the dinner party functioned as a significant moment in the construction of an elite sensibility. From the ornamentation of the dining room itself, to the elegance of the table decorations and the quality of the courses consumed, to the artistry of the toasts and the wit of the conversation, power and authority were embedded in the words spoken and the food consumed." This culture of power is illustrated in a dinner party thrown by Charles Town merchant and slave trader Miles Brewton of Charles Town in 1773. Attending was Josiah Quincy of Boston, who noted in his diary that he was greeted by his host in "the grandest hall" decorated with "azure blue satin window curtains, rich blue paper … elegant pictures, excessive grand and costly looking glasses, etc." The elegant mahogany table was set with "very magnificent plate [and] large exquisitely wrought Goblet." During the multicourse dinner, "a very fine bird (presumably a parrot) flew about the room picking up the crumbs … and perching on the windows and chairs."[32]

Just as important to genteel dining were table manners. To that end, many followed Eleazor Moody's 1715 *School of Good Manners*, which instructed its readers to never "Come to the table without having your hands and face washed, and your head combed." To keep grease off hands and face, this early etiquette book told children not to "gnaw [on] bones at the table but clean them with thy knife (unless they be very small) and hold them not with a whole hand but with two fingers." A washbasin near the table could be found in many upper-class homes so a second washing could remove the grease not left on the napkin. Cleanliness at the dining table was therefore a sign of gentility and good breeding. So was the act of eating, which the genteel demonstrated by the refined manner in which they held their eating utensils, their upright posture, their chewing of food with a closed mouth, and the leisured pace with which they consumed their multicourse meals. While dining, George Washington followed these two maxims: "Put not another bit into your mouth 'til the former be swallowed;" and "Cleanse not your teeth with the Table Cloth, Napkin, Fork or Knife."[33]

In short, dining etiquette became an important means by which the upper class, who dined on elaborately prepared meals at a table with erect posture and with fine cutlery, separated themselves from the lower class, who continued to eat simply prepared meals with fingers and a hunched back. The Maryland aristocrat Dr. Alexander Hamilton was so disgusted by the eating habits of a Pennsylvania ferryman and his family that he declined their offer to dine with them on a homely dish of fish. "They desired me to eat, but I told them I had no stomach. They had no cloth upon the table, and their mess was in a dirty, deep, wooden dish which they evacuated with their hands, cramming down skins, scales, and all. They used neither knife, fork, spoon, plate, or napkin because, I suppose, they had none to use." This crude dining display paled in comparison to table manners in a Philadelphia tavern, "which exceeded every thing I had seen for nastiness, impudence, and rusticity," according to Hamilton. "He [a man named McGraw] told us he was troubled with the open piles [hemorrhoids] and with that, from his breeches, pulled out a linnen handkercheff all stained with blood and showed it to the company just after we had eat dinner." Disgusted diners quickly left the table. Indeed, the middle and lower classes did not have time for long, multiple-course meals followed by cracking nuts, eating fruit, and drinking toasts like the wealthy, leisured class. One Englishman visiting a Boston tavern observed that people wolfed down their food while talking with their mouths full, and when they finished eating they immediately left to attend business, "for," he said, "the Americans know the value of time too well to waste it at the table."[34]

CONCLUSION

Cooking and dining in the five colonial cities was, curiously enough, both medieval and revolutionary. Throughout the colonial period food preparation and cooking techniques changed little from the primitive, labor-intensive, and often dangerous methods people had used for hundreds of years. The modern kitchen with its many labor-saving devices and grocery stores with their commercial abundance were at least 150 years away. Unlike most Americans today who get their food inspected, washed, and neatly prepackaged (often frozen), our colonial forebears intimately knew their food. They killed their own game, butchered their own livestock, caught their own fish, brewed their own beer, churned their own butter, grew their own vegetables, and chopped down and burned their own fuel—all things that most modern Americans would find either too burdensome or gruesome.[35] Equally distasteful to modern Americans would be the crude and communal nature of dining in early America, with family members and guests all dipping their spoon bread into a common pot, pulling off chunks of meat with dirty hands, sharing drinking cups, chewing with mouths full of food, cleaning teeth with knives, and wiping greasy hands on clothes. Only during the latter part of the colonial period did a small minority of well-to-do urban folk develop a more modern culinary fare and dining habits.

Despite the medieval nature of early American cooking and dining, the five colonial cities were at the center of a revolution in diet that ultimately led to the creation of a uniquely American foodway characterized by the culinary contributions of the numerous ethnic and racial groups who resided in the cities. Regional variations existed but were considerably blurred during the eighteenth century by growing trade between the five main ports. Urban residents therefore enjoyed a greater variety of food and dishes than anyone in the Western world, a smorgasbord that greatly enriched their daily lives and their health. This culinary melting pot, which first began in the colonial cities, would eventually spread with the expanding nation to become the American standard. However, not all city folk enjoyed this American bounty. The numerous urban poor continued to eat a monotonous and bland diet of one-pot meals, often gruels and porridges served on wooden plates and quickly wolfed down with the aid of spoon bread. Meanwhile, urban aristocrats used their growing wealth to cultivate a more enriched diet and refined dining habits as a means to further demonstrate their superiority and therefore their singular right to rule. Food and dining, like so much else of colonial society, helped to define class and power.

NOTES

1. James McWilliams, *A Revolution in Eating: How the Quest for Food Shaped America* (New York: Columbia University Press, 2005), 9.

2. Sandra Oliver, *Food in Colonial and Federal America* (Westport, CT: Greenwood Press, 2005), 48.

3. Helen Newberry Burke, *Foods from the Founding Fathers: Recipes from the Colonial Seaports* (Hicksville, NY: Exposition Press, 1978), 14; Susannah Carter, *The Frugal Colonial Housewife* (Garden City, NY: Dolphin Books, 1976), iii; Richard J. Hooker, *Food and Drink in America: A History* (Indianapolis, IN: Bobbs-Merrill, 1981), 26; Sally Smith Booth, *Hung, Strung and Potted: A History of Eating in Colonial America* (New York:

Clarkson N. Potter, 1971), 23; Oliver, *Food in Colonial and Federal America*, 90–92, 101.

4. Oliver, *Food in Colonial and Federal America*, 103, 124.

5. Gerry Schremp, *Celebrations of American Food: Four Centuries in the Melting Pot* (Golden, CO: Fulcrum Pub., 1996), 7; Joyce Carlo, *Trammels, Trenchers, and Tartlets* (Saybrook, CT: Peregrin Press, 1982), 18–19; Booth, *Hung, Strung and Potted*, 11, 17; Hooker, *Food and Drink in America*, 26–27; Carter, *Frugal Colonial Housewife*, iv–v; Oliver, *Food in Colonial and Federal America*, 107.

6. Waverly Root and Richard de Rochemont, *Eating in America: A History* (New York: William Morrow & Co, 1976), 75–78; Stephanie Grauman Wolf, *As Various as Their Land: The Everyday Lives of Eighteenth-Century Americans* (New York: Harper Perennial, 1994), 93; Hooker, *Food and Drink in America*, 25–26; Booth, *Hung, Strung and Potted*, 15; Carlo, *Trammels, Trencher, and Tartlets*, 20; Carter, *Frugal Colonial Housewife*, vii.

7. Karen J. Friedman, "Victualling Colonial Boston," *Agricultural History* 47 (1973): 190; Hooker, *Food and Drink in America*, 34–35.

8. Carl Bridenbaugh, *Cities in the Wilderness: Urban Life in America, 1625–1742* (New York: Ronald Press, 1938), 351; Ellen Hartigan O'Connor, "The Measure of the Market: Women's Economic Lives in Charleston SC and Newport, RI, 1750–1820," Ph.D. dissertation, University of Michigan, 2003, 236, 258 (quote); Friedman, "Victualling Colonial Boston," 196.

9. Billy G. Smith, *The "Lower Sort": Philadelphia's Laboring People, 1750–1800* (Ithaca, NY: Cornell University Press, 1990), 34; Carl Bridenbaugh, *Cities in Revolt: Urban Life in America, 1743–1776* (New York: Ronald Press, 1955), 81 (quote); Burke, *Foods and the Founding Fathers*, 102 (quote); Bridenbaugh, *Cities in the Wilderness*, 352; Friedman, "Victualling Colonial Boston," 202–3; Billy G. Smith, "Walking Moraley's Streets: Philadelphia," *Common-Place* 3 (2003): 5 (quote).

10. Bridenbaugh, *Cities in the Wilderness*, 350.

11. Friedman, "Victualling Colonial Boston," 199–200; Bridenbaugh, *Cities in the Wilderness*, 341–44; Bridenbaugh, *Cities in Revolt*, 276–79; Hooker, *Food and Drink in America*, 73–74; Carlo, *Trammels, Trenchers, and Tartlets*, 40 (quote).

12. Wolf, *As Various as Their Land*, 91–92; Root and Rochemont, *Eating in America*, 68–69; Booth, *Hung, Strung and Potted*, 69, 73, 91–98; Hooker, *Food and Drink in America*, 27–29, 54–55; Friedman, "Victualling Colonial Boston," 195; Keith Stavely and Kathleen Fitzgerald, *America's Founding Food: The Story of New England Cooking* (Chapel Hill: University of North Carolina Press, 2003), 102; David B. Landon, "Interpreting Urban Food Supply and Distribution Systems from Faunal Assemblages: An Example from Colonial Massachusetts," *International Journal of Osteoarchaeology* 7 (1997): 55.

13. Hooker, *Food and Drink in America*, 31–32, 49; Booth, *Hung, Strung and Potted*, 125–36; Friedman, "Victualling Colonial Boston," 195.

14. Oliver, *Food in Colonial and Federal America*, 56; Hooker, *Food and Drink in America*, 4, 29–30, 51; Booth, *Hung, Strung and Potted*, 139–40.

15. Hooker, *Food and Drink in America*, 31–32; Meta P. Fayden, "Indian Corn and Dutch Pots: Seventeenth Century Foodways," Ph.D. dissertation, Cornell University, 1993, 172; Friedman, "Victualling Colonial Boston," 195; Booth, *Hung, Strung and Potted*, 169–82.

16. Booth, *Hung, Strung and Potted*, 157–61; Hooker, *Food and Drink in America*, 30–31, 59.

17. Burke, *Foods from the Founding Fathers*, 15; Schremp, *Celebrations of American Food*, 6; Hooker, *Food and Drink in America*, 34; Oliver, *Food in Colonial and Federal America*, 72–74.

18. Hooker, *Food and Drink in America*, 33–34; Booth, *Hung, Strung and Potted*, 183–89.

19. William E. Burns, *Science and Technology in Colonial America* (Westport, CT: Greenwood Press, 2005), 52–55; Oliver, *Food in Colonial and Federal America*, 116–21.

20. William J. Rorabaugh, *The Alcoholic Republic: An American Tradition* (New York: Oxford University Press, 1979), 6 (quote); Eric Burns, *The Spirits of America: A Social History of Alcohol* (Philadelphia: Temple University Press, 2004), 8–31; Booth, *Hung, Strung and Potted*, 199–214; Benjamin Franklin, "The Drinker's Dictionary," January 13, 1737, *Pennsylvania Gazette*.

21. Schremp, *Celebrations of American Food*, 4; Hooker, *Food and Drink in America*, 35–38.

22. Hooker, *Food and Drink in America*, 35–38; Booth, *Hung, Strung and Potted*, 199–214; Oliver, *Food in Colonial and Federal America*, 83; Rodris Roth, "Tea-Drinking in Eighteenth-Century America: Its Etiquette and Equipage," in *Material Life in America: 1600–1860*, ed. Robert St. George (Boston: Northeastern University Press, 1988), 439–58.

23. John Komlos, "On the Biological Standard of Living of Eighteenth-Century Americans: Taller, Richer, Healthier," *Munich Economics* (2003): 2–15; Richard H. Steckel, "Nutritional Status in the Colonial American Economy," *William and Mary Quarterly* 56 (1999): 31–52; Smith, *The Lower Sort*, 95–104 (quote from p. 97); Oliver, *Food in Colonial and Federal America*, 202.

24. Hooker, *Food and Drink in America*; 64–65; Bridenbaugh, *Cities in the Wilderness*, 196–97; Wolf, *As Various as Their Land*, 91.

25. Trudy Eden, *The Early American Table: Food and Society in the New World* (De Kalb: Northern Illinois University Press, 2008), 10–98, 20 (quote).

26. Burke, *Foods from the Founding Fathers*, 27–71, 104–43; Hooker, *Food and Drink in America*, 40, 48, 67; Schremp, *Celebrations of American Food*, 10; Carlo, *Trammels, Trenchers, and Tartlets*, 41; McWilliams, *A Revolution in Eating*, 10–11, 60–62, 81.

27. Burke, *Foods from the Founding Fathers*, 166–68, 174–202, 280–319; Hooker, *Food and Drink in America*, 40–41, 69; Fayden, "Indian Corn and Dutch Pots," 137, 158, 163–64; McWilliams, *A Revolution in Eating*, (quotes from pp. 172 and 184).

28. Burke, *Foods from the Founding Fathers*, 27–71, 104–43; Hooker, *Food and Drink in America*, 40, 48, 67; Schremp, *Celebrations of American Food*, 10; Carlo, *Trammels, Trenchers, and Tartlets*, 41; McWilliams, *A Revolution in Eating*, 10–11, 60–62, 81.

29. Burke, *Foods from the Founding Fathers*, 213–50; Hooker, *Food and Drink in America*, 41–42; Schremp, *Celebrations of American Food*, 12–13; Booth, *Hung, Strung and Potted*, 28–29.

30. Claudia L. Bushman and Richard L. Bushman, *The Early History of Cleanliness in America* (Newark: University of Delaware Press, 1983), 18 (quote); Richard L. Bushman, *The Refinement of America: Persons, Houses, Cities* (New York: Vintage Books, 1992), 74–75; Root and Rochemont, *Eating in America*, 74; Schremp, *Celebrations of American Food*, 5–8; Burke, *Foods from the Founding Fathers*, 16; Hooker, *Food and Drink in America*, 27, 66–67; Booth, *Hung, Strung and Potted*, 35–38; Carlo, *Trammels, Trenchers, and Tartlets*, 35, 45–46; Wolf, *As Various as Their Land*, 94.

31. Timothy Breen, *The Marketplace of Revolution: How Consumer Politics Shaped American Independence* (New York: Oxford University Press, 2004), 154.

32. Edward Pearson, " 'Planters Full of Money': The Self-Fashioning of the Eighteenth-Century South Carolina Elite," in *Money, Trade, and Power: The Evolution of Colonial South Carolina's Plantation Society*, ed. Jack P. Greene, Rosemary Brana-Shute, and Randy J. Sparks (Columbia: University of South Carolina Press, 2001), 307–8.

33. Bushman and Bushman, *The Early History of Cleanliness*, 7 (quote); Arthur Schlesinger, *Learning How to Behave; A Historical Study of American Etiquette Books* (New York: Macmillan, 1947), 5 (quote); Richard L. Bushman, *The Refinement of America*, 75–78; Booth, *Hung, Strung and Potted*, 41; Schremp, *Celebrations of American Food*; 8; Carlo, *Trammels, Trenchers, and Tartlets*, 54.

34. McWilliams, *A Revolution in Eating*, 216; Bushman and Bushman, *The Early History of Cleanliness*, 12 (quote); Lorinda B. R. Goodwin, *An Archaeology of Manners: The Polite World of the Merchant Elite of Colonial Massachusetts* (New York: Kluwer Academic, 1999), 36 (quote); Oliver, *Food in Colonial and Federal America*, 27 (quote).

35. McWilliams, *A Revolution in Eating*, 4–5.

11

Clothing and Cleanliness

INTRODUCTION

A common misconception that many Americans today have about early America is that the New World frontier encouraged and fostered an egalitarian spirit among the European settlers and their descendants—that from the beginning of American colonization settlers took advantage of the "virgin wilderness" to create a new society based on freedom, tolerance, and equality as a model for the rest of the world. This Pollyannaish perspective of the American past is grossly incorrect. European settlers, particularly the elites, brought to the New World their long-held belief that human beings were unequal, an inequality that was sanctified by law, religion, custom, and tradition. A strict social hierarchy existed in Europe in the late sixteenth century where gender, wealth, inherited position, and political power affected everyone's status. European colonizers did their best to recreate in America the customary class system of their homeland. Generally, they were quite successful.

CLOTHING AND CLASS

This inequality and class distinction in early America is perhaps most conspicuously observed in the colonists' clothing. Early

American elites, like their European counterparts, were very class conscious and were determined to ensure that everyone understood their place in society. Clothing helped to define this social order, and in such a simple and nonverbal way that everyone could understand it. This was important because custom dictated how people of different classes should interact with one another. The upper class, for example, wore fine clothing made by local master tailors that visibly demonstrated their social preeminence and privilege so that, at least in part, the lower orders would give them the deference and respect they expected. It was customary in New England for the lower sorts to curtsy or bow before their superiors and to address them as either Master and Mistress, Gentleman and Gentlelady, or at the very least, Mister and Misses. The ordinary clothing worn by the lower classes, in contrast, allowed the gentry easily to identify those people below them so that they could interact with them in accordance with their lowly social position. Joseph Wanton of Newport, a "proud foppish fellow" who wore "ruffles and laced clothes," refused to "take notice of or speak to a poor man," according to neighbors. A more violent disdain for the lower sort is found in Governor William Cosby of New York, who while wearing his English high-style finery and riding in his gilded coach ordered his coachmen to whip a farmer driving his rickety wagon on the same road because the man wearing coarse homespun "did not drive so quickly out of his way as he expected."[1]

To prevent men and women of "meane condition, education and callings" from wearing the "garbe of Gentlemen," well-to-do leaders in some colonies passed sumptuary laws. In 1654 the Massachusetts General Court rebuked the excesses of the poor for wearing clothing "to the dishonor of God" and "altogether unsuitable to their poverty." Specifically, only gentlemen were permitted to wear gold or silver lace, "great boots," and "new fashions," while women of similar rank were permitted to wear silk and tiffany hoods and wide sleeves with lace. Despite such prohibitions, many common folk flouted sumptuary laws. This was not difficult to do. Female servants sometimes received a silk scarf from a sympathetic mistress, and more than one beau flattered his sweetheart with jewelry or a piece of finery. Some poorer women knew how to make lace, which they sewed into their clothing. Thus, ordinary women sauntered around town wearing feather boas, silk hoods, coral necklaces, rings, and gloves. As late as the mid-1670s authorities in Boston continued to deride and haul before the court lower-class women for wearing "vain, new strange fashions ... with naked breasts and arms, addition of superfluous ribbons, both on hair and apparel." Meanwhile, ordinary yeomen sported doublets (close-fitting body garments), jackets, breeches, hats, gloves, and other fancy accessories.[2]

Sumptuary laws became a dead letter by the early eighteenth century as Britain flooded the five commercial centers with cheap manufactured goods, including clothes and fabrics, that allowed the middling group, and even some of the lower sort, to acquire those external evidences of wealth. This democratization of fashion allowed almost anyone of moderate means to publicly present himself or herself as a gentleman or lady, with the respect and privileges generally accorded that class. A gentleman writing in the *Boston Gazette* complained in 1765 that "We run into . . . Extremes as to Dress; so that there is scarce any Distinction between persons of great Fortune, and People of ordinary Rank." This egalitarian trend in fashion prompted urban elites to publish hyperbolic, fear-mongering screeds against this threat to both their social hegemony and to the elitist social hierarchy. This "ridiculous Mimickry" by the "poorest, meanest" people, opined one New Englander, represented social anarchy that would eventually lead to the "whole nation fall[ing] to ruin," while a Philadelphia grandee compared the "quick advancement of fashion" in "this young city" to a "pernicious distemper . . . infecting those of an inferior class." The "pernicious distemper" this gentleman referred to was "insubordination" among the lower sort. Others of his class agreed. "I have been in Company with Men when they have been meanly dressed," complained one Southern gentleman, "and they have been as still and humble as a Bee, and at other Times have seen them with their Sunday or Holyday Clothes on, and they have been as impudent and bold as a Lion." The "wanton disregard for the symbolic rules of apparel," explains historian Timothy Breen, "threatened to subvert the reflexive displays of public deference that the members of each class were expected to show to superiors as well as to inferiors." By doing so, ordinary folk were participating in a quiet yet threatening bid for respect and power.[3]

To counter this threat from below, upper-class men created a new genteel dress code that was more complex and more difficult to imitate by the working class. Instead of wearing flamboyant costumes adorned with lace, ruffles, brooches, silk roses, and chains and carrying canes and swords in gloved hands, colonial gentlemen adopted a more conservative fashion that was less colorful and garish but one that still relied on fine fabrics like satin and silk and an aristocratic cut and pattern. For special occasions like balls and assembly meetings, gentlemen donned waistcoats that were delicately embroidered in silk, gold, or silver thread with floral or geometric designs. Accessories were mostly functional: silver knee, shoe, and stock buckles; a watch; a tricorn hat; and perhaps a ring, an intricately tied cravat, and a powdered wig. More unusual but equally as functional were corsets and false pads, which some men wore to either diminish overdeveloped bellies or to enhance underdeveloped calves and buttocks.

SLAVES

As some urban elites feared, this "contagion" for fancy clothing spread even to their slaves. As early as 1735 South Carolina leaders complained that black people wore clothes "much above the condition of slaves," complete with watches, powdered wigs, and silver buckles. A decade later the Charles Town grand jury complained that black women in the city dressed "in Apparel quite gay and beyond their Condition." This sartorial display among slaves was greatest in the urban areas, where they had more opportunities to earn money to purchase clothing, to steal it, or to acquire it from masters who often gave their cast-off clothing to bondsmen. No matter how slaves acquired such finery, it instilled in those bondsmen who wore it an egalitarian spirit that threatened the racial class system. One white man believed that blacks had an almost insatiable desire to "raise Money to buy fine Cloaths" that only encouraged them to be "so bold and impudent that they insult every poor white person they meet." One South Carolinian in 1772 observed "a great Difference in Appearance and Behavior, between *the Negroes* of the Country, and *those* in Charles Town." Although the former were "generally clad *suitable* to their Condition," the latter were "the very *Reverse*—abandonedly *rude, unmannerly, insolent* and *shameless*." He further lamented that "many of the *Female* Slaves [are] by far more *elegantly* dressed than the Generality of *White Women* below Affluence," a state of affairs which he attributed to "scandalous *Intimacy*" between the *Sexes of different Colours*."[4]

Despite such complaints, this slave challenge to the sartorial status quo was more the exception than the rule. In return for a lifetime of servitude and labor, most urban slaves were either given readymade clothes or used coarse "negro cloth" to make trousers, petticoats, and shirts. Charles Town merchant Robert Pringle instructed his London factors to send "white, Blue, and green pla[i]ns for

Negro clothing," as well as coarse linens, stockings, and leather shoes. Not only was their everyday clothing ill-fitting and uncomfortable, it was often drab and tattered. Advertisements for runaway slaves in Charles Town newspapers describe the best garments they possessed: "a negro cloth jacket with blue lapels, and a large negro cloth wrapper . . . an Osnabrugs shirt and breeches and red waistcoat with a narrow Slip of osnabrugs down the back . . . a white negro cloth jacket and breeches, a pretty good felt hat and an old wig." Still, many urban bondsmen were able to create their own unique wardrobe by cobbling together cast-off clothing from their masters and materials from their own purchases. One New England runaway became a conspicuous target for slave catchers by taking with him a new coat and claret-colored vest (worn with mixed red, white, and yellow buttons), a worn grey coat with a red-and-white striped vest, a pair of deerskin breeches, a pair of checked long trousers, a striped shirt, and one checked shirt. Slave women could be just as colorful in their clothing, mixing yellow gowns with red petticoats, accented with such accessories as African-style kerchief turbans, ribbons, multicolored beads, necklaces, bracelets, and hoop earrings. Clothing was therefore both a symbol of autonomy for the slaves and a form of resistance to white authority.[5]

Some male slaves further subverted white authority by either wearing white powdered wigs or styling their hair to resemble fashionable wigs. Others demonstrated their individuality and ties with their African past with elaborate hair designs reflecting tribal affiliation, status, sex, age, and occupation. To that end, some slaves wore their hair long and bushy on top; others cut it short or even shaved their heads completely. A slave's hair might be closely cropped on the crown but left long elsewhere, tied behind in a queue, combed high from the forehead, plaited, curled on each side of the face, knotted on top of the head, or left bushy and long below the ears. Combing hair over into "a large roll" was a common style among black women, as was wearing a "head rag" to either hide sores caused by ringworm, a common ailment, or to cover a healthy head of hair and keep it that way. Other slaves covered their hair because of frequent ridicule from whites, who referred to black people's hair as "wool," an association with animals that was hardly accidental.[6]

UNIFORMITY AND DISTINCTIONS

Although there were significant class and racial distinctions in clothing, there was little regional distinction in early American costumes. American elites in the five cities sought to ape the life-style, manners, and dress of the English gentry. Additionally, the main ports imported from Britain and India the same fabric and patterns. The growing commerce between the American coastal towns during the eighteenth century further helped to unify ideas of dress and fashion. Governor William Tryon of New York observed in the early 1770s that "more than Eleven Twelfths of the Inhabitants of this Province both in the necessary and ornamental parts of their Dress are cloathed in British Manufacturers, except [for] Linen from Ireland and hats and Shoes manufactured here." Perhaps most mimetic in following English fashion were the aristocrats of Charles Town, where storekeepers advertised "English grey hairs," "super fine broad Cloths . . . of the Colours most in fashion when he left London," and "Stays . . . which are very much worn by young Ladies in England."[7]

Still, the American environment, regional culture, and religious values contributed to unique distinctions in colonial apparel. The hot and humid summers of Charles Town, for example, often forced residents to wear less and lighter clothing than those residing in the North. Genteel women not expecting visitors would wear negligee-style undergarments covered with a striped cotton robe. During summer months, merchants and lawyers went about the southern capital in linen shirts and breeches or in unlined Chinese silk "ban-yan" robes that were worn over light silk waistcoats and satin breeches. Upper-class women eschewed wigs in favor of light caps, while men exchanged their powdered wigs for turbans. Meanwhile, the Dutch in New York City could be distinguished by their more colorful materials, their use of fur in underlying and trimming their gowns and cloaks, the use of hair ornaments among women, and the wearing of a "chatelaine" of gold or silver at the waist, from which hung keys, thimble, scissors, and various scent boxes and trinkets. The Quakers, who believed that "all excess is evil," adopted a plain and sober style of dress that lacked what they considered useless or superfluous decoration: "gaudy, flowered or striped stuffs," ornate buttons, ribbons, gold ornaments, silver shoe buckles, plumes, laces, "gaudy stomachers," bonnets with "gaudy colours," or perriwigs "unless necessitated." An exception was the affluent "Quaker grandees" who paraded around Philadelphia and Newport in clothing just as fashionable as other urban aristocrats. In 1749 the Philadelphia Quaker Quarterly Meeting complained that "it is obvious that Pride and Superfluity too much Prevails both in apparel and Furniture amongst many of our

Puritan Woman's Costume. This typical Puritan woman's costume shows a short Dutch waistline with the bodice made to fit above a loose-fitting skirt. A broad falling collar of linen drapes the shoulders and front. Plain linen cuffs were turned back from the wrist. The Puritan woman dressed her hair plainly, often brushed back and twisted into a knot and covered with a hood. Blunt-toed shoes with wooden heels were usually covered by the long skirt. (Elisabeth McClellan, *Historic Dress in America, 1607–1800* [Philadelphia: George Jacobs, 1904])

Puritan Man's Costume. Strength, durability, and stoutness characterized the Puritan man's costume to meet the rigors of pioneer life. In this illustration, the man is wearing a long-waisted doublet buttoned down the front and muted in color. His great coat is three-quarters long, and his breeches are of the knicker-bocker type and button down the side. A simple band of linen tied with cords is worn around his neck. Heavy woolen stockings fastened under the breeches just above the knee. Puritan men wore their hair cropped close to the head, which was topped with a broad-brimmed hat with a high crown. (Elisabeth McClellan, *Historic Dress in America, 1607–1800* [Philadelphia: George Jacobs, 1904])

Profession." A similar sartorial transformation occurred among well-to-do New England Puritans, who like the Quakers reacted only to excess in dress and extremes in fashion. Contrary to popular belief, the Puritans did not wear plain clothing marked by "sad" colors of gray and black. The liberty of the New World compelled some to express their desire for fine and colorful clothes by imitating the latest fashions in clothing that included a veritable rainbow of colors—russets, browns, scarlets, Bristol reds, Kendall greens, watchet blues, purples, and oranges.[8]

UPPER-CLASS WOMEN

Styles in clothing changed considerably during the protracted colonial period, most notably in upper-class attire. Ordinary people could not afford the luxury of following the latest fashions from London as their meager incomes forced them to hand down a suit of clothes from one generation to the next until it finally became too threadbare to wear. The one group most acutely aware of changes in fashion consisted of genteel ladies who practically made a business out of changing their clothing and hairstyles according to the latest fashion. One wag in the mid-1700s lampooned the constant succession of changes in female attire in the following lines:

> Now dress'd in a cap, now naked in none;
> Now loose in a *mob*, now close in a *Joan*;
> Without handkerchief now, and now buried in ruff;
> Now plain as a Quaker, now all in a puff;
> Now a shape in neat stays, now a slattern in *jumps*;
> Now high in French heels, now low in your pumps;
> Now monstrous in hoops, now trapish, and walking
> With your petticoats clung to your heels like a maulkin;
> Like the cock on the tower that shows you the weather,
> You are hardly the same for two days together.[9]

Although this satirist greatly exaggerated the rate of change in women's fashions, clothing styles among the genteel did undergo a few major alterations during the colonial period. During much of the seventeenth century, upper-class women wore a bodice that was low-waisted, tightly laced, and fell to a point in the front. The neckline was high and often topped with a ruffled collar, while sleeves reached the wrist and ended in a laced cuff. Skirts were long and cone-shaped—narrow at the waist and large at the bottom. Hidden beneath the long skirt were shoes that closely fitted the foot

Quaker Costumes. Although not a distinctive type of dress, the attire worn by Quakers was noted for its neatness, plainness, and simplicity. (Elisabeth McClellan, *Historic Dress in America, 1607–1800* [Philadelphia: George Jacobs, 1904])

and ended in a square toe and that were decorated at the instep with a ribbon rose. Unlike their shoes, women at this time showed off their hair, which was often kept high over the forehead and decorated with feathers. When women did don hats, they resembled those worn by men, with a truncated crown and wide brim. Like their hair, women often feminized their hats with feathers or ribbon. During cold weather, women covered themselves with shawls or capes. Accessories were relatively few: gloves, feathered fans, paint, powder, patches, and small vanity mirrors that hung from their waist.[10]

As Western society became more liberal in the eighteenth century, so did aristocratic women's fashions. This is graphically seen in the very low-cut bodice, revealing an eye-catching décolletage. Some bold women drew further attention to their nearly naked chests by placing either real or artificial flowers in their cleavage. Encouraging this titillating fashion were local shopkeepers who sold "Italian Breast Flowers" and "bosom bottles" to place them in. The new fashion also allowed for the bodice to hang off the shoulders and sleeves to end at the elbow instead of the wrist, both styles that revealed more skin. Ruffles and lace adorning the bodice around the neckline and at the end of sleeves drew further attention to these new physical revelations. As a further decorative element, some women included on the front of their bodice a stomacher, a long piece of cloth shaped in the form of an inverted triangle and often containing a colored pattern in contrast to the bodice.[11]

The most distinguishing feature of upper-class women's dress during the eighteenth century was the hoop, which was a large, bell-shaped petticoat or skirt that was stiffened underneath by whalebone. The size of the hoop increased or decreased depending on how informal or formal the occasion was. The larger the hoop size, the grander the entrance made by its wearer. With its rich flowered brocade, silk, satin, and velvet cloth, the outlandishly sized hoops were designed to garner as much attention as the ladies' décolletage. The broad hoop was also intended to make a woman's waist appear smaller. To further facilitate this, all women, no matter their shape, squeezed themselves into a stay or corset. Fashion dictated that women wear stays nearly all the time, often during sleep, a practice that weakened back muscles and thereby forced women to wear corsets for back support. Corsets also restricted mobility, which led to the genteel courtesy (curtsy) among females known as the sink. Men at the time must have been pleased by the effects of corsets, which not only narrowed a woman's waist but also forced her breasts so high that it was often necessary for women to insert a kerchief or ruffle to hide their nipples. Because the hoop petticoat left women "almost naked," it met with some criticism among the fashionably conservative who argued that ladies wearing them "proved themselves whores." The character of those who wore petticoat hoops aside, such an outfit would not be complete without accessories. Silk or goatskin gloves, silk purses, tortoiseshell pocket books, and fans were most popular among upper-class women when they went out on the town. The five cities also had jewelers who offered rings, earrings, pearl necklaces, solitaires, lockets, diamonds, rubies, emeralds, sapphires, and crystal "bosom buttons" to those who could afford them.[12]

WOMEN'S HAIR STYLES

Although women in the eighteenth century lowered their necklines, they did not do the same with their hair. Exposing one's cleavage was fashionable, but letting one's hair down was considered risqué. Instead, after 1700 it became popular for women to dress their hair in a simple style, usually drawn loosely back from the forehead with a bun of various styles on top. Younger women might arrange curls round the face or allow stray locks to fall casually about the temples. To look younger, older women sometimes dyed their greying hair by washing it in a mixture of rhubarb shavings and white wine and afterwards drying it in the sun. Despite the considerable preparation in styling and dying their hair, women frequently covered it with small round caps (called "heads") of various styles that were often trimmed in lace, ribbons, and flowers, or by donning stylish hats, often made of straw, over their caps.[13]

Near the end of the colonial period, some genteel ladies followed French and English hairstyles by dressing their hair ridiculously high in towering, wire-framed headdresses that invited stares, ridicule, and sometimes embarrassment to those who followed this absurd and impractical fashion. After witnessing 11 women with towered hair walking through New York City, one young woman lampooned to a friend that these ladies had among them on their head "an acre and a half of shrubbery, besides grass-plots, tulip beds, kitchen gardens, peonies, etc." One Boston socialite in 1771 had the embarrassing misfortune of being thrown from her carriage and into the street, tearing off her "great headdress" in the process. Onlookers had a good laugh as she desperately picked up the tow, yarn, horse hair, curled human hair (often from corpses), and hay that had spilled out of her headdress. A peeved Sarah Eve of Philadelphia protested the "social kissing" practiced by local gentlemen because it "disorders one's high Roll." Her complaint is understandable considering that even without such "disorders," fashionable women had to take their "high roll" headdresses to local wig makers every few weeks to have them taken apart and rebuilt. Between visits to wig makers, women set mouse and louse traps in their hairpieces at night to keep them clean of vermin and doused them heavily with scented powders and perfumes in a losing battle to hide the overpowering stench, which contributed to an itchiness that could only be satisfied with ivory head-scratchers. This form of suffering for beauty did not last long as the high roll fell out of fashion during the American Revolution when it became un-American to display extravagant attire, especially that associated with the Old World.[14]

WOMEN'S SHOES

Because hoop skirts generally did not reach the floor, women paid closer attention to their shoes, which were frequently embroidered with flowers on silk or satin and ornamented with a diamond or silver buckle. Women also put up with high heels for a time during the early 1700s, but the difficulty of walking and dancing in high heels, as well as the great possibility of embarrassing oneself by tripping and falling in them, led to their demise by the 1730s in favor of short-heeled shoes. To protect their expensive footwear from the rain and mud, upper-class women wore "pattens" or "clogs" over their lightly soled shoes.[15]

COSMETICS

Aristocratic ladies did more than don fine clothing, flashy jewelry, and fancy shoes to improve their appearance. They also used a variety of cosmetics on their faces to deceive men of their true appearance and to try and give themselves what nature denied. Clever shopkeepers played to female vanity by claiming that their "princely beautifying lotions" and cold creams rendered the skin "as soft as velvet" and "beautif[y] the face, neck, and hands to the utmost perfection." Various "waters" and "whiteners" promised to remove all spots, pimples, and freckles from the face and hands. Well-to-do ladies sought to look as white as possible to differentiate themselves from lower-class women, who had tanned skin from working in the sun. Thus, the whiteness of skin was an indicator of class among women and conspicuously distinguished the leisured from the laborer. This explains why genteel women paraded around town carrying umbrellas and wearing bonnets and gloves to preserve their skin from the damaging sun. Smell was also a defining characteristic of class. To avoid reeking like an unwashed, sweaty maidservant, upper-class ladies used an assortment of expensive perfumes on their bodies and clothes and wore finely crafted pomanders filled with perfumes that hung on a chain from the neck or from a girdle in front of a dress. Aiding a woman's quest for gentility and beauty was her "dressing box" that contained a dizzying array of items: a looking glass (mirror); tortoiseshell and ivory combs and brushes; decorative fans; China patch-boxes; ivory bodkins; velvet masks; an assortment of necklaces and ear-rings; Italian breast flowers; crystal bosom buttons; feathers; tweez-ers; curling irons; cold creams; wash balls; bleaches; scented powders; hair dyes; false hair; hair pins; eye shadow; lotions; beau-tifying oils; tooth pickers; cinnamon, mint, and peppermint waters; and various spoons, dishes, and bowls for mixing the various com-pounds considered necessary to improve the skin, eyebrows, lips, hands, and hair.[16]

Rather than enhancing their beauty, some upper-class ladies actually ruined both their looks and their health to achieve this ideal by using beauty lotions and waters containing such toxic and poi-sonous elements as lead, sublimate of mercury, mercuric sulphide, verdigris, and arsenic. Over time, regular use of such toxic elements ravaged the skin and caused both hair and teeth to fall out, leaving devotees a rotting wreck by the age of 30. Less affluent ladies saved money, their looks, and sometimes their lives by applying home-made beauty aids often made from household items. Some women went to bed with a mask of bacon strips on their face, which was supposed to keep the skin soft, create rosy cheeks, and prevent wrinkles. More disgusting to modern tastes was the use of puppy-water (the urine from a young dog) in cosmetics. Almost edible was a crude cosmetic base powder to enamel face and hands made from either flour or corn starch and scented with toilet water. To red-den lips, some women applied a red rouge made from crushed cochineal beetles, while others sucked lemons or applied a "Scarlet Lip Salve" made from hog fat cooked in crushed roses. To define eyebrows and highlight lashes, women used lampblack (carbon). For the finishing touches ladies strategically placed small black beauty patches on their faces, which were originally created to hide the sores from venereal disease but which later became de rigueur among the fashion conscious.[17]

As women got older, no amount of beauty cream and cosmetics could hide their deteriorating appearances. Instead of accentua-ting their looks as they had during their youth, older women increasingly did their best to hide the physical effects of aging. Many still wore makeup, although less of it, and they dressed more conservatively. Mature women wore large caps tied underneath the chin to hide their graying and thinning hair and perhaps to lift a sagging chin. They also strategically placed kerchiefs above the neckline of their dress and donned long-armed gloves to cover skin that was wrinkled and speckled with liver spots. Even the dresses worn by mature women—with their solid, dark colors and few trimmings—reflected the deteriorating beauty of older women. In short, colonial women were expected to dress their age.[18]

PREGNANCY AND CLOTHING

Pregnancy was a frequent condition for nearly all women of childbearing years. As a woman's body changed during each pregnancy, so did her clothing. Instead of buying or making separate maternity outfits, pregnant women in early America simply modified their usual clothing as their waists expanded. Short gowns, which were relatively unfitted, required little alteration and were therefore well-suited and popular attire during pregnancy. Petticoats, which pregnant women adapted by loosening the ties, completed this two-piece outfit. Some women in the "family way" wore a long apron over their clothing to cover their expanding abdomen. However, pregnancy did not keep middle- and upper-class women from wearing stylish bodices. They simply removed the triangular stomacher and replaced it with a wider one to allow waist expansion. Some women, on the other hand, put off such alterations for as long as possible by wearing heavy stays during much of their pregnancy. One can only imagine how much this practice contributed to the numerous miscarriages and stillbirths at the time.[19]

LOWER-CLASS WOMEN'S CLOTHING

Although upper-class women's fashion changed styles during the colonial period, the same cannot be said for clothing worn by lower-class women. The laborious lifestyle of lower-class women dictated that her clothing be simple, sturdy, and functional. A cheap linen shift served as the first layer of clothing, over which was worn a jacket (made from cheap textile or sometimes leather) similar to a vest that was fastened down the front with laces or hooks and that might have some boning in it to provide support. However, excessive boning was rare in ordinary women's clothing because it hindered their ability to work. Accompanying the jacket was a skirt, often striped or checkered, made from such coarse materials as calico and linsey-woolsey. Although skirts were impractical in many ways to working women, they did allow for easy expansion during pregnancy and hid bulky menstrual rags and ties. Some lower-class women wore short gowns over petticoats, while others pinned a short apron or pinafore to the gown or bodice to protect the outfit. Many women belonging to the lower sort, perhaps more out of necessity than design, created their own unique fashion by wearing mismatched yet colorful outfits. One runaway Irish maidservant was described by her master as wearing "a calicoe short gown stamped with red and white linens running through the same, one pea green quilted petticoat [and] one flannel ditto" along with "stockings, black shoes, a check apron, and two handkerchiefs. . . ." Thick stockings, stout country-made shoes, and a kerchief wrapped around the neck completed the outfit. Except for straw hats, linen caps, and shawls, accessories were a luxury for most lower-class women.[20]

MEN'S CLOTHING

Unlike the clothes worn by lower-class women, working-class men's clothing more closely followed the fashionable ideal. The main distinction between lower- and upper-class men's clothing was not in style but in basic silhouette, textiles, and accessories. Until about 1680 the average man's costume consisted of a tight-sleeved shirt, doublet (a vest-like garment often made of leather), full-cut knee breeches, and a cloak for cold weather. Upper-class men distinguished themselves by adding ruffs around their necks and turn-backed cuffs at the end of sleeves (often ruffed), by donning jewelry (watches, rings, and silver and gold knee, shoe, and stock buckles) and fringed gloves, and by carrying swords or canes. The clothing worn by the genteel was made of finer, softer, and more expensive material than that worn by their social inferiors, all of which demonstrated that they were above performing manual labor. Wide-brimmed wool hats with a high crown and often turned up on one side with feathers stuck in for decoration were the most popular headgear among men.[21]

Near the end of the seventeenth century, the doublet worn by men gave way to the coat and waistcoat (vest). Knee breeches and a shirt remained part of the basic male costume, however. As with lower-class women, the clothing of most laboring men had to be durable, plain, and practical to fit their vigorous lifestyle. Plain shirts and coats worn by working-class men were made from strong fabrics of linen, wool, or cotton. As armor against the dirt of daily labor, a leather waistcoat was worn over the shirt. Leather aprons, the most identifiable article of clothing among laborers and craftsmen, gave added protection to clothing and body. Urban workers eschewed the stylish close-fitting knee breeches, silk stockings, and long coats worn by the wealthy for more practical loose-fitting woolen knee breeches or trousers, linen or wool shirts, coarse woolen stockings, and heavy coats of gray corduroy that came either with or without sleeves. Buckled shoes and a cocked hat completed the working man's outfit. It is important to note that this general description does not encompass the distinctions in clothing worn by the variety of urban workers. More successful craftsmen, for example, sometimes wore simpler and less costly versions of higher-class clothing. At the other end of working-class spectrum were sailors and day laborers, who could be easily identified by their canvas or heavy linen "petticoat trousers."[22]

MEN'S HAIRSTYLES

The one item that drew the greatest attention in upper-class men's fashion—and one that the lower classes could not afford to imitate— was the wig. Beginning in the early 1700s, well-to-do men in America began shaving their heads and covering them with expensive powdered wigs that were difficult and time-consuming to maintain and even more difficult to wear with any grace. Wearing a wig required straight and upright posture and slow and careful movements of the head and body, otherwise the wearer risked "flipping his wig," a most embarrassing event. Despite this risk, urban gentlemen kept wigmakers very busy. The Newport wigmaker John Tipson had so much business that he was forced to buy an indentured servant to aid him in his work. On the other hand, powdered wigs were impractical for working-class men, who generally wore their hair long, either flowing naturally to the shoulders or sometimes tied in the back pony-tail style.[23]

MEN'S GROOMING

Upper-class men in early American proved that vanity was not limited to the ladies. Colonial gentlemen devoted just as much time,

Gentleman's and Lady's Costume, ca. 1770s. Being a gentleman or a lady in eighteenth-century America was a physically uncomfortable experience, as the clothing shown here suggests. Once in the privacy of his home, the gentleman removed his heavy coat, wig (if wearing one), and tight-fitting vest and exchanged them for a more comfortable garment. The gentle lady experienced the further suffering of wearing a tight corset that, over time, could alter her skeletal structure and the position of her organs. (Elisabeth McClellan, *Historic Dress in America, 1607–1800* [Philadelphia: George Jacobs, 1904])

attention, and expense to their grooming and self-adornment as did their wives. A gentleman's finely crafted dressing table was cluttered with razor cases and shaving equipment, scissors, combs, pen knives, curling irons, nail clippers, tweezers, oil bottles, powder puffs, brushes, soap, wig ribbons, and cravats. His daily ritual in making himself presentable involved lathering and shaving, removing all traces of soap with a lotion, and applying rouge, followed by a foundation of fine powder to tone down the harshness of the coloring. Some men also applied black patches of gummed silk to conceal facial blemishes, while the more fashion-conscious wore them for no other reason than to identify their social status. Just as status-oriented was a gentleman's wig, which could be made up in a multitude of styles by local barbers. With names like the "pigeon's wing," the "comet," the "cauliflower," the "staircase," the "wild boar's back," the "rhinoceros," the "corded wolf's paw," the "she-dragon," the "snail back," and the "artichoke," upper-class colonial men's hair styles almost make modern-day punk hairdos banal by comparison. After dressing his hair and sprinkling it with grey or blue powder and perfume, the gentleman next tied his muslin cravat, scented his silk handkerchief, and filled his snuff-box before finally donning his gold-trimmed beaver or felt hat and taking his gold- or ivory-headed walking cane to sally forth to a local ball, political assembly, or concert.[24]

CHILDREN

Like aristocratic adult fashion, clothing worn by children also underwent changes during the eighteenth century. For most of the colonial period, parents tightly wrapped their partly clothed infants in layers of narrow bands of fabric, called swaddling, under the misguided belief that it would speed up the development of straight limbs. Aside from the obligatory cloth diaper, other articles of clothing worn by babies included caps, shirts with long sleeves for home wear, and frocks (fitted dresses) for public wear. As if swaddling was not restrictive enough, upper-class children as young as one year old were required to wear stiffened stays in the hope that it would encourage good posture and form a fine figure. Girls had to suffer stays into adulthood; some even had to endure the additionally painful indignity of having to hold their head upright at all times or else have their chin pricked by a pin that was fastened in the front of their dress. Boys, on the other hand, could shed their corsets when they graduated to trousers, which usually occurred by the age of six or seven. Before then, boys' and girls' clothing was nearly indistinguishable from one another. Because young boys were not yet competent to join their fathers in the field or shop, they were considered in the "woman's domain," a dependent status that required them to wear long-skirted dresses and caps similar to those worn by their sisters and mothers. Boys even had long hair dressed like the girls. Still, there were gender differences in clothing that were obvious to people at the time. For example, boys wore cap cockades while girls wore cap ribbons. The upper part of a boy's dress, additionally, was cut to suggest a doublet while sleeves ended in cuffs, a man's style. Nevertheless, young boys must have anxiously awaited the day when they could discard their petticoats and put on their first dress suit, which was an important rite of passage from the dependent female domain to the dominant male one. Young boys were not yet considered adults, though. To reflect this intermediate stage in their lives, they wore a short jacket and long trousers, much like those worn by lower-class sailors and soldiers, instead of the breeches and long coats worn by gentlemen.[25]

The tight bodices, the stiffened stays, and the multiple layers of clothing made it impossible for middle- and upper-class children who wore such costumes to exhibit the natural exuberance of youth. In fact, such adult-style clothing was designed to enforce a sense of decorum in children that encouraged them to behave like adults. This philosophy guided middle- and upper-class parenting until about the mid-eighteenth century when child-rearing authorities gradually came to accept and to promote the idea that childhood was a separate stage in life and that parents should encourage their children to engage in the natural play of youth. To that end, parents discarded stays and dressed their children in clothes that were more comfortable and more suitable for play. With this new daily wear, boys and girls could now do what comes naturally to children: run and tumble, climb and jump, and throw and catch.[26]

ETIQUETTE

Just as important as clothing to status was comportment, manners, and mastery of one's body. Developing courtly manners became increasingly important to urban elites during the eighteenth century with increasing challenges to their authority from below. In defending the traditional hierarchy, urban aristocrats responded by following an elaborate etiquette borrowed from the European courtly class. Mastering the rules of courtly conduct became essential to indicate good breeding and claims to privilege and power. Luckily for those aspiring to gentility, numerous etiquette manuals were available. Most were English imports like Henry Peachman's *The Compleat Gentleman* (1622), Richard Brathwaite's *The English Gentleman* (1630), and Richard Allestree's *The Whole Duty of Man* (1660). For the ladies, there was Lord Halifax's *The Lady's New Year's Gift* (1688), the anonymous *Ladies Library* (1714), and William Kendrick's *The Whole Duty of Woman* (1761). It is worth emphasizing that these conduct books provided only a guide for proper social conduct among those aspiring to gentility. They do not necessarily describe actual behavior.[27]

Etiquette books, when treating behavior in company, instructed the socially ambitious to avoid tooth-picking, belching, spitting, passing wind, licking fingers, and peering into a handkerchief after blowing one's nose "as if pearls or rubies might have descended from your brain." Courtesy books also warned the genteel against all sorts of "*odde ridiculous* gestures" like fidgeting, twisting in one's seat, drumming finger's on tables, rubbing one's hands, pulling one's ears, and biting fingernails. This obsession with self-control included avoiding all "rude" noises such as coughing, sneezing, sighing, yawning, humming, whispering, and even breathing too loudly. Women, in particular, were to avoid all expressions of anger and to speak in a soft and courteous tone. Nor was it considered "*comely* to *run* along the *streets*, or to make so much haste that you *pant*, and *blow*, and *sweat*," explains one author, "for that belongs to the *foot-man*, not to *Gentile* persons." Men and women therefore revealed their class by the way they walked. For a price, local dance masters were willing to instruct the well-to-do in achieving this grace and bearing. Women wearing restrictive corsets had no choice but to carry themselves in a graceful and elegant manner because the fashion forced upon wearers an upright posture, restrained gestures, and a slow gait.[28]

In acquiring courtly manners and grace, the urban grandees manufactured an air of superiority over others to further legitimize their social dominance. Critical to this hegemony was deferential treatment from the lower sorts. Ministers, schoolmasters, and courtesy-book authors all published a flood of tracts that emphasized rituals associated with deference to superiors. One Puritan minister, for example, instructed children to put "suitable marks of civil respect and honours on others, especially on superiors or those in authority." School master Samuel Moody advised youngsters to be "humble, submissive, and obedient to those whose Authority by nature or providence has a just claim to your subjection . . . Be always obsequious and respectful, never bold, insolent, saucy, either in words or Gestures" to those in authority. One courtesy book even emphasized to common folk that social distinction and deference were part of God's plan: "In regard to these degrees and Distinctions of men are, By God's Wise providence, disposed for the better ordering of the world, there is such a *civil respect* due to those whom God hath dispensed them, . . . therefore, all inferiors are to *order themselves lowly and reverently to all their betters.*" The implication here is that "inferior" folk who failed to show reverence to their "betters" were opposing God's will. To discourage such blasphemy, elitist writers gave numerous instructions on how inferiors were to conduct themselves around their betters. This included, among other things, to always walk behind a social superior, not to look one in the eye when addressing him or her, to wait for a superior to initiate conversation, to address superiors with reverent titles, to refrain from interrupting or contradicting them, and not to discuss issues that were "above" one.[29]

MIDDLE-CLASS REVOLUTION

By the mid-eighteenth century, however, the emergence of a middle class that made up perhaps 20 percent of the urban population broke down the exclusivity of good manners and rituals of deference by appropriating and emulating the social characteristics of the genteel. Facilitating this attack on deference and upper-class hegemony over proper public behavior was a new variety of advice manuals from Britain written by members of the middle class who focused on relations between equals. They warned their middling readers against servility and instead counseled them to demonstrate pride by showing respect to superiors "in an easy unembarrassed and graceful manner." Like courtesy books for the gentry, those for the middle class emphasized bodily self-control, but in a more detailed manner. This was critical for many urban professionals, who could easily lose customers, clients, or patients by displaying roughness or irascibility. In the highly competitive yet often economically unstable urban economy, it was simply a question of "polish or perish." Middle-class courtesy books therefore gave elaborate advice against "distortions of the face": sticking out one's tongue, making "wry" or "ridiculous" faces, ogling or winking, squinting or yawning, primming the lips, or lifting the eyebrows.

They also detailed specific rules for body carriage: not to walk with "monstrous strides" or with arms "projected or tossed backwards and forwards like a plowman sowing corn." Only advice books for the middling class advised readers not to handle their own bodies in public, thrust their hands inside their clothing, or groom themselves before company and instructed them to avoid all rude, indecent, and improper actions before equals. Even children belonging to the middle class were given instructions for proper conduct, often in charming verse: "I must not sit in others places; Nor sneeze, nor cough in people's faces. Nor with my finger pick my nose, Nor wipe my hands upon my clothes."[30]

This advice helped the middle class to enter a new role, one that promoted greater social equality if not an outright opposition against the upper sort, who were clearly anxious about this threat to their social and cultural hegemony. One gentleman from Philadelphia calling himself "Blackmore" viciously mocked this "half-gentry" of petty merchants and other middling sort who seek to become "Gentlefolk" simply upon "find[ing] themselves in circumstances a little more easy." But it was "no easy thing," he argued, "for a Clown or a Labourer, on a sudden to hit in all respects, [to acquire] the natural and easy Manner of those who have been genteely educated." Those not content with their station were doomed to humiliation, according to "Blackmore," because

Without Experience of Men or Knowledge of book, or even common Wit, the vain Fool thrusts himself into Conversation with People of the best sense and the most polite. All his absurdities, which were scarcely taken notice of among us, stand evident among them, and afford them continual Matter of Diversion. At the same time, [those] below cannot help considering him as a Monkey that climbs a Tree, the higher he goes, the more he shows his Arse.[31]

CLEANLINESS

Contributing to this patrician-plebeian divide during the eighteenth century was a new emphasis on cleanliness by the urban gentry who sought to demonstrate their superiority over the unwashed urban masses with clothes and bodies that both looked and smelled clean. By the early 1700s wearing clean clothes and smelling nice was becoming a sign of gentility and civilization. This was a stark departure from the previous century, when it was common for people of all classes to wear the same clothes for weeks, sometimes months, between cleaning.

Underneath the unwashed clothing worn by early Americans were dirty bodies that went unwashed year after year. Both medical and religious authorities at the time advanced theories against regular bathing. Doctors still held to the medieval belief that a crust of dirt on the body served as protection against dangerous foreign bodies, insects, and the like and against the spread of plague. Meanwhile, ministers discouraged cleanliness by branding frequent bathing as narcissistic self-indulgence that they claimed was offensive to God. John Wesley's famous epigram "Cleanliness is, indeed, next to godliness" referred to "neatness of apparel," not to cleansing the body. On a more practical level, bathing was a time-consuming and laborious task that entailed filling a bucket with water from a distant pump and carrying the heavy water-laden bucket from the pump to the house just to fill the makeshift bathtub that few colonists even had. If one wanted a hot bath, a fire had to be built and the water heated. Even the well-to-do, with all their servants and slaves to make them a bath, rarely bathed. Typical is the experience of the wealthy Quaker Elizabeth Drinker, who in 1798, at the age of 65, bathed in a shower box that her husband set up in the backyard of their house in Philadelphia. "I bore it better than I expected," she confided in her diary, "not having been wett all at once, for 28 years past." With many colonists bathing only once a generation, early Americans lived in close connection with each other's dirt, excrement, and body odor. This was especially so in the more densely populated urban centers.[32]

For everyday cleanliness colonists relied on a basin of water and a towel. Yet even the simple practice of splashing one's face with water was not important enough to warrant separate washbasins. A search of all estate inventories for Essex County, Massachusetts (including Boston) from 1636 to 1763, for example, turned up not a single example of a washbasin. This explains why the Annapolis physician Alexander Hamilton, while staying at a home in Boston in 1744, noticed the man of the house using the same basin to shave in, wash hands and face, clean cabbage, drink his soup out of, and finally use as a punch bowl. For those without shame, there were nearby rivers, ponds, and ocean to disrobe and dip in. Although most of this swimming was more for recreational purposes than a desire for cleanliness, some upper-class men did follow a growing trend in Britain of bathing outdoors. Tragically, a few discovered that this pursuit of cleanliness could be harmful to one's health, like Dr. James Halkerston of Boston, who drowned in 1721 after going "to the Foot of the Common to wash himself in Swimming."

A Philadelphia lawyer met a similar fate in 1725; when washing himself in the Schuylkill River, he "went beyond his Depth and was unfortunately drowned." The dangers of outdoor bathing aside, such public display of immodesty offended local prudes, at least in Boston, where in 1757 some residents made a "great complaint" of "many persons Washing themselves in Publick . . . to the Great Reproach of Modesty and good Manners." The town meeting responded by ordering that no person above the age of 12 years swim nude before sunset nor "swim to such parts of the Town, as to be plainly within Sight of any Dwelling House."[33]

This trend in bathing reflected a new attitude toward cleanliness in the eighteenth century, particularly among the gentry, who increasingly equated cleanliness with such cultural values as "civil" and "polite." Those who remained dirty, on the other hand, were excluded from polite society and branded by clean folk as "uncivilized" and "rude." The Virginia aristocrat General George Washington thought the lower-class men who made up the Continental Army under his command were "an exceeding dirty and nasty people." To avoid such undesirable classification, etiquette books of the time admonished the well-bred to "be always neat and cleanly," which among other things meant washing hands and face before eating and keeping nails and teeth clean, and "to be extremely clean in your person" so "not to be offensive to other people." These instructions on cleanliness, however, did not necessarily imply that one should take a bath. Instead, the urban elite relied on a "dry cleaning" method whereby an individual simply wore a linen shirt (or chemise for women) under the outer garments. The upper class believed that the rubbing action of cloth touching the skin would not only remove dirt but would also protect outer clothing from perspiration and unseemly odors. Exchanging dirty linens with clean ones was in effect to wash. To further distance themselves from the unwashed masses, the well-to-do also turned to perfume, powder, and sachets (perfumed bags) worn on the body to surround it with good smell. Because only the affluent could indulge in this new practice of bodily purity with the purchase of expensive perfumes and linens that required frequent washing, an olfactory boundary emerged between the rich and the poor. One could literally smell class in eighteenth-century America.[34]

However, the increasing availability of relatively inexpensive British linens flooding the commercially oriented urban centers after 1740 allowed a growing number of people from middling means to acquire this mark of gentility and cleanliness. Local merchants and shopkeepers widely advertised in local newspapers that they had in their shops printed "Linens, Callicoes, Silks, & c in good Figures, very lively and durable Colours," noting that they were "without the offensive smell which commonly attends the Linens printed here." The upper class responded to this middle class assault on their exclusive claim to cleanliness by wearing high-end, bleached holland linens that were often laced and visible in the collars and cuff. The genteel expected the linens they wore to be snow white and freshly laundered, a conspicuous mark that helped the genteel to identify their peers both by sight and smell. Enabling the urban aristocracy to meet this higher standard of cleanliness and gentility were personal servants, slaves, and poor laundress women who washed the fine clothes belonging to the affluent. Ironically, the sweat-inducing work laboring people performed for the rich compromised their ability to remain clean in their own persons and therefore doomed them to be looked upon as an inferior and "exceeding dirty and nasty" people in the eyes of George Washington and others of his class.[35]

DENTAL CARE

The upper class also distinguish themselves from their social inferiors by displaying whiter teeth and fresher breath. This was important in a society in which so much business, socializing, and politics took place face to face. In an attempt to keep a pearly smile and fresh breath, the well-to-do purchased from shopkeepers and apothecaries abrasive toothpowder made from either ground bones, pumice stone, cuttlefish, red coral, salt, or chalk that was sweetened with honey, sugar, and fruit peelings. An advertisement for one such toothpowder promised that it "cleanses the teeth and gums from all foulness, preserves them sound and free of pain, prevents those decaying from growing worse, renders them clean and white as ivory, and the breath perfectly sweet and agreeable." Missing from this ad was a warning that these abrasives, if used often, would wear away the enamel on teeth and encourage staining. To apply the abrasive toothpowder, some colonists used a damp cloth made of coarse linen, often wrapped around a stick, while others made toothbrushes from fibrous and woody roots whose ends were frayed to create crude bristles. To freshen one's breath, early Americans used mouthwashes made from sweet wines, honey, mint, cinnamon, and cloves. The lower sort who could not afford toothpowders and mouthwashes cleaned their teeth after meals with either their fingernails or a knife, a crude display that only reaffirmed their lowly status in the eyes of the elite. This lack of dental hygiene gave lower-class folk a foul breath that further disgusted the upper classes who came into contact with them. The Maryland physician Alexander Hamilton, for one, complained in disgust one morning that "my barber came to shave me and almost made me sick with his . . . stinking breath."[36]

No matter if one was rich or poor, few colonists who reached middle age could smile without displaying one or two gaps in their teeth. Keeping all of one's teeth was difficult to achieve among a people who often consumed too little vitamin C and too much white sugar, both of which contributed to rotting gums and tooth loss. The eventual loss of a tooth often began with a toothache, which early Americans remedied with various herbs like chamomile or opium prescribed by some urban doctors. Some desperate sufferers relied on folk magic, like the one cure for toothache that instructed the patient to apply the thighbone of a toad to the aching tooth. If the pain persisted, the tooth had to be pulled, which meant a trip to a low-class chirurgeon barber who used unsanitary instruments that were a cross between items found in a medieval torture chamber and a modern-day toolbox. To numb the pain during tooth extraction, barbers used either alcohol or laudanum, an opiate. Barbers commonly tried to reimplant the original tooth after cleaning and filling it with either gold or lead, a procedure that met with mixed results. In doing so, some barbers sadistically cauterized diseased gums with a hot iron and screwed in posts in empty sockets (to the jawbone) as a receptacle for the tooth. If enough teeth were removed, it left the cheeks hollow. To avoid the appearance of advanced age resulting from hollow cheeks, colonists inserted into their mouths cork pads or had made wooden dentures bound with spiral springs onto which bone or ivory shapes were fixed. Because bone and ivory lacked enamel coating, they were prone to decay and contributed to bad breath. For this reason human teeth were preferred, most often procured from corpses, especially those of young battlefield victims.[37]

MENSTRUATION

A circumstance of hygiene unique to women is menstruation, which early Americans equated with bodily pollution as they believed menstrual blood was filled with toxins that could harm the health of sexual partners and increase the chance of producing monstrous offspring. Some physicians even discouraged women from preparing food during their menstrual period. While early modern people considered menstrual blood toxic, they believed menstrual odor to be seductive and an appeal for fertilization. Whether toxic or seductive, the bloody discharge could not be ignored. Women in colonial America dealt with "Eve's curse" by wearing a cumbersome and uncomfortable diaper of bird's-eye or outing flannel that often caused soreness and rashes. Other women used homemade vaginal suppositories made from old rags, thus giving birth to the crude phrase "on the rag" to describe a woman who is in her menstrual period. Scant evidence suggests that some lower-class women may have simply bled into their undergarments.[38]

CONCLUSION

Far from reflecting an equalitarian society, daily life in the five colonial cities was marked by stark social inequalities between a small, privileged upper class and the masses below them who were required by custom to show proper respect and deference to their superiors. The urban aristocrats used genteel forms of clothing, comportment, and cleanliness in an attempt to solidify these class distinctions and their exclusive right to rule. This inequality contributed to an intensifying class war during the eighteenth century as those from the middling group, and even some poor folk, tried to enter the exclusive aristocratic society by softening traditional forms of deference and emulating their superiors in dress, etiquette, and cleanliness. Urban grandees resisted this threat to their hegemony from below by altering those cultural characteristics they deemed necessary for upward social mobility, traits that normally required considerable money and leisure, to ensure that the privileged elite came only from the respectable moneyed class.

NOTES

1. Sheila Skemp, "A Social and Cultural History of Newport, Rhode Island, 1720–1765," Ph.D. dissertation, University of Iowa, 1974, 224 (quote); Alan Tully, *Forming American Politics: Ideals, Interests, and Institutions in Colonial New York and Pennsylvania* (Baltimore, MD: Johns Hopkins University Press, 1994), 372.

2. Karin Calvert, "The Function of Fashion in Eighteenth-Century America," in *Of Consuming Interests: The Style of Life in the Eighteenth Century*, ed. Cary Carson, Ronald Hoffman, and Peter Albert (Charlottesville: University Press of Virginia, 1994), 252–56, 258 (quote); Patricia Trautman,

"Dress in Seventeenth-Century Cambridge, Massachusetts: An Inventory-Based Reconstruction," in *Early American Probate Inventories*, ed. Peter Benes (Boston: Boston University Press, 1987), 52–63 (quote from page 52); Patricia Trautman, "When Gentlemen Wore Lace: Sumptuary Legislation and Dress in 17th-Century New England," *Journal of Regional Cultures* 3 (1983): 17 (quote).

3. Timothy Breen, *The Marketplace of Revolution: How Consumer Politics Shaped American Independence* (New York: Oxford University Press, 2004), quotes from pp. 156–58, 165; Jonathan Prude, "To Look upon the 'Lower Sort': Runaway Ads and the Appearance of Unfree Laborers in America, 1750–1800," *Journal of American History* 78 (1991): 125, 155–56.

4. Shane White and Graham White, "Slave Clothing and African-American Culture in the Eighteenth and Nineteenth Centuries," *Past and Present* 148 (1995): 160–61 (quotes); Breen, *The Marketplace of Revolution*, 165 (quote).

5. Kathleen Brown, *Foul Bodies: Cleanliness in Early America* (New Haven, CT: Yale University Press, 2009), 108 (quote); Gail Gipson, "Costume and Fashion in Charleston, 1769–1782," *South Carolina Historical Magazine* 82 (1981): 233 (quote); William D. Piersen, *Black Yankees: The Development of an Afro-American Subculture in Eighteenth–Century New England* (Amherst: University of Massachusetts Press, 1988), 101.

6. Shane White and Graham White, "Slave Hair and African American Culture in the Eighteenth and Nineteenth Centuries," *Journal of Southern History* 61 (1995): 50–63; Willie Morrow, *400 Years without a Comb* (New York: Milady, 1984), 3–25.

7. Breen, *The Marketplace of Revolution*, 37 (quote); Richard Waterhouse, *A New World Gentry: The Making of a Merchant and Planter Class in South Carolina, 1670–1770* (New York: Garland Press, 1989), 97 (quote).

8. Gipson, "Costume and Fashion in Charleston," 234; Edward Warwick, Henry C. Pitz, and Alexander Wyckoff, *Early American Dress: The Colonial and Revolutionary Periods* (New York: Bonanza Books, 1965), 109–10, 128–31, 172, 202–6; J. William Frost, *The Quaker Family in Colonial America: A Portrait of the Society of Friends* (New York: St. Martin's Press, 1973), 190–95 (quotes from p. 194); Sarah Fatherly, *Gentlewomen and Learned Ladies: Women and Elite Formation in Eighteenth-Century Philadelphia* (Bethlehem, PA: Lehigh University Press, 2008), 64–65 (quote).

9. Esther Singleton, *Social New York under the Georges, 1714–1776* (New York: D. Appleton & Co., 1902), 244.

10. Warwick, Pitz, and Wyckoff, *Early American Dress*, 68–70.

11. Warwick, Pitz, and Wyckoff, *Early American Dress*, 173–174, 193; Gipson, "Costume and Fashion in Charleston," 228.

12. Singleton, *Social New York*, 225, 252; Stephanie Grauman Wolf, *As Various as Their Land: The Everyday Lives of Eighteenth-Century Americans* (New York: Harper Perennial, 1993), 269; Bruce C. Daniels, *Puritans at*

Play: Leisure and Recreation in Colonial New England (New York: St. Martin's Press, 1995), 196 (quote).

13. Georgine de Courtais, *Women's Hats, Headdresses and Hairstyles: Medieval to Modern* (Mineola, NY: Dover, 1973), 76–86.

14. Kate Haulman, "A Short History of the High Roll," *Common-Place* 2 (October 2001): n. p. (quote); Warwick, Pitz, and Wyckoff, *Early American Dress*, 184, 187; Singleton, *Social New York*, 211–12 (quote).

15. Warwick, Pitz, and Wyckoff, *Early American Dress*, 192; Singleton, *Social New York*, 222; Gipson, "Costume and Fashion in Charleston," 236.

16. Brown, *Foul Bodies*, 132; Gilbert M. Vail, *A History of Cosmetics in America* (unknown binding, 1947), 77; Singleton, *Social New York*, 224.

17. Maggie Angeloglou, *A History of Make-Up* (Durrington, UK: Littlehampton Books, 1970), 48–56; Vail, *A History of Cosmetics*, 46–8, 78; Sally Pointer, *The Artifice of Beauty: A History and Practical Guide to Perfume and Cosmetics* (Stroud, UK: The History Press, 2005), 92–96; Gipson, "Costume and Fashion in Charleston," 236.

18. Linda Baumgarten, *What Clothes Reveal: The Language of Clothing in Colonial and Federal America* (New Haven, CT: Yale University Press, 2002), 176.

19. Ibid., 146–56.

20. Diana de Marly, *Dress in North America: The New World, 1492–1800* (New York: Holmes & Meier, 1990), 54; Calvert, "The Function of Fashion," 259–60; Baumgarten, *What Clothes Reveal*, 15–20, 118 (quote).

21. Baumgarten, *What Clothes Reveal*, 122; Warwick, Pitz, and Wyckoff, *Early American Dress*, 60–64.

22. Peter F. Copeland, *Working Dress in Colonial and Revolutionary America* (Westport, CT: Greenwood Press, 1977), 5–9, 56, 159–63; de Marly, *Dress in North America*, 52–53; Baumgarten, *What Clothes Reveal*, 122–27; Gipson, "Costume and Fashion in Charleston," 239–40.

23. Richard Bushman, *The Refinement of America: Persons, Houses, Cities* (New York: Vintage Books, 1992), 70–74; Calvert, "The Function of Fashion," 260–70; Wolfe, *As Various as Their Land*, 269–70; Warwick, Pitz, and Wyckoff, *Early American Dress*, 149–52; Singleton, *Social New York*, 181–95; Baumgarten, *What Clothes Reveal*, 108–12; Skemp, "A Social and Cultural History of Newport," 17.

24. Vail, *History of Cosmetics*, 37–41; Singleton, *Social New York*, 174–79.

25. Wolf, *As Various as Their Land*, 112–13; Singleton, *Social New York*, 227; Calvert, "The Function of Fashion," 279; Baumgarten, *What Clothes Reveal*, 158–66; Warwick, Pitz, and Wyckoff, *Early American Dress*, 238.

26. Calvert, "The Function of Fashion," 279; Baumgarten, *What Clothes Reveal*, 166–71.

27. Arthur Schlesinger, *Learning How to Behave: A Historical Study of American Etiquette Books* (New York: Macmillan, 1947), 6–9.

28. Brown, *Foul Bodies*, 35 (quote); C. Dallett Hemphill, *Bowing to Necessities: A History of Manners in America, 1620–1860* (New York: Oxford University Press, 1999), 26 (quotes).

29. Hemphill, *Bowing to Necessities*, 20, 22.

30. Ibid., 20–24, 74.

31. Fatherly, *Gentlewomen and Learned Ladies*, 30.

32. Richard L. Bushman and Claudia L. Bushman, "The Early History of Cleanliness in America," *Journal of American History* 74 (1988): 1217, 1214.

33. Bushman and Bushman, "The Early History of Cleanliness," 1227; Brown, *Foul Bodies*, 135 (quote); David Flaherty, *Privacy in Colonial New England* (Charlottesville: University Press of Virginia, 1972), 82 (quote).

34. Bushman and Bushman, "The Early History of Cleanliness," 1220 (quotes); Brown, *Foul Bodies*, 26–33.

35. Brown, *Foul Bodies*, 105 (quote), 148.

36. Brown, *Foul Bodies*, 136–37 (quotes); Angeloglou, *A History of Make-Up*, 50; Pointer, *The Artifice of Beauty*, 131.

37. Walter Hoffman-Axthelm, *History of Dentistry* (Berlin: Quintessenz, 1990), 218; Pointer, *The Artifice of Beauty*, 130–31; Angeloglou, *A History of Make-Up*, 72; Rebecca Tannenbaum, *Health and Wellness in Colonial America* (Westport, CT: Greenwood Press, 2012), 31.

38. Brown, *Foul Bodies*, 36; Janice Delaney, Mary Jane Lupton, and Emily Toth, *The Curse: A Cultural History of Menstruation* (Urbana-Champaign: University of Illinois Press, 1988), 138; http://www.mum .org/pastgerm.htm. I would like to thank Karen Williams, librarian at Auburn Montgomery, for notifying me of this web site.

12

Health and Medicine

INTRODUCTION

Sickness, disease, and death were a routine part of everyday life in colonial America. This was particularly true for residents of the five principal cities. The maritime character of their economy, their position as entry points for immigrants, and their relatively crowded and unsanitary living conditions all contributed to making the port cities some of the unhealthiest places in which to live during the eighteenth century. Residents of these cities were continually plagued by, and frequently died from, smallpox, diphtheria, yellow fever, measles, malaria, dysentery, typhus, and various respiratory diseases. When major outbreaks of these diseases occurred, local officials responded with standard practices of the day: quarantining the sick, improving sanitary conditions within the city, and inoculating the healthy, at least in the case of smallpox. These diseases, especially when they reached epidemic proportions, took a tremendous toll not just on people but also on the local economy and government. At times epidemics brought life in the cities to a virtual standstill. Coping with the death and disruptions caused by frequent outbreaks of fatal illnesses was a harsh aspect of everyday urban life.

Overall, though, urbanites had much greater access to medical care than their rural counterparts, largely because the high rate of illness in these five cities attracted the greatest number of trained physicians, surgeons, amateur medical practitioners, apothecaries, and sellers of patent medicines in North America. With such a variety of medical providers available to them, early Americans did not practice a rugged individualism in treating their illnesses and injuries. Rather than bleed their own veins, suture their own wounds, inoculate themselves against smallpox, pull their own rotten teeth, reduce their own dislocated joints, set their own broken limbs, remove their own kidney stones, cut cancer form their own breasts, and amputate their own limbs, colonists eagerly sought out experienced medical practitioners in hopes of making them well again. But given the crude state of medicine at the time, it is debatable whether this greater access to medical care was a benefit or a curse to the inhabitants of these cities. The lack of knowledge concerning illnesses and diseases, along with a laissez-faire approach toward medicine, allowed medical quackery to thrive in the disease-ridden cities. No matter if one turned to a university-trained physician or an ignorant quack, the sick were often victims twice over because many "cures" did more harm than good to the patient. Most victimized were the poor, who lacked a decent diet, resided in overcrowded housing and filthy neighborhoods, and had little access to any medical care. Both the local governments and private charity provided few resources to assist the sick poor, who suffered from worse health conditions and shorter lives than the more affluent in a largely free-market capitalist health care "system." Therefore, wealth often determined who received medical treatment and who did not, who got well and who remained sick, and who lived and who died.

The five seaports under study were the unhealthiest places for human habitation in North America during the eighteenth century. Worst of all was Charles Town. Its tropical climate made it such an unhealthy place that the southern capital earned the unenviable reputation as "a great charnal house."[1] Adding to the unhealthiness of Charles Town and the other cities were the many migrant ships disembarking diseased passengers and the overcrowded living conditions, which, in turn, facilitated the spread of deadly diseases. Despite ordinances against doing so, residents dumped their garbage in the streets, which only attracted loose animals that freely roamed the streets, dumping tons of manure and rivers of urine throughout the cities every day. Additionally, privies frequently overran into the streets, and inadequate sewage disposal resulted in contaminated public water supplies. Although officials understood the relationship between cleanliness and disease prevention, they made half-hearted attempts to keep the streets clean and to provide residents with fresh drinking water. For all these reasons, the urban centers were seedbeds for a variety of deadly diseases. (See Table 12.1.)

SMALLPOX

Those diseases that most ravaged urban residents and filled them with paroxysms of fear were smallpox, yellow fever, dysentery, and respiratory illnesses. Perhaps the deadliest and most terrifying of these diseases was smallpox. One terrifying aspect of smallpox were its symptoms—pustules that could cover the entire body and even inside the mouth and throat where they might erupt and therefore make swallowing difficult and sometimes impossible, or affect the eyes and lead to blindness, or blend into one another, causing layers of skin to peel off completely. Not surprisingly, many victims of smallpox succumbed to the disease. Not only did smallpox kill in large numbers, those lucky enough to survive suffered debilitation and a disfigured face. Usually the disease was imported by sea from major port cities in the Caribbean and Great Britain, but occasionally it was brought by infected soldiers returning home from war. Outbreaks of smallpox reached epidemic proportions with frightening regularity. Boston suffered a severe outbreak in 1721 when over half of the 10,600 residents contracted smallpox, 900 of whom died. The disease attacked "all sorts of people," according to one eyewitness, even "children in the bellies of Mothers." One visitor to New York City during an outbreak of smallpox in 1679 found in the homes many "children sick with the smallpox ... We went into one house," he wrote, "where there were two children lying dead and unburied, and three others sick, and where one had died the week before." Smallpox epidemics swept through Charles Town on a regular basis. The worst occurred in 1760 when over two-thirds of the city's 8,000 residents were struck by the malady, which was brought in by soldiers returning from fighting the Cherokee in the backcountry. As many as 730 succumbed to the disease, a death toll that "almost puts a stop to all business," lamented a survivor. The governor declared a fast day on April 25 to pray for the afflicted city. The prayers went unanswered, at least until November, when officials declared the epidemic officially over.[2]

Table 12.1. Epidemics in the Cities

Boston

Year	Disease	Death Toll	Year	Disease	Death Toll
1657	Measles	?	1730	Smallpox	500+
1667	Smallpox	180	1735	Scarlet Fever	100+
1669	Dysentery	?	1740	Typhoid Fever	?
1678	Smallpox	800+	1748	Measles	?
1689	Smallpox	320	1748	Diphtheria	?
1699	Influenza	?	1749	Pleurisy	?
1702	Smallpox	300	1751	Smallpox	569
1713	Measles	150+	1764	Smallpox	170
1721	Smallpox	899	1769	Dysentery	180

Charles Town

Year	Disease	Death Toll	Year	Disease	Death Toll
1698	Smallpox	300+	1738	Whooping Cough	?
1699	Yellow Fever	300+	1739	Yellow Fever	?
1706	Yellow Fever	?	1745	Yellow Fever	?
1710	Dysentery	?	1747	Measles	?
1711	Smallpox	?	1748	Yellow Fever	?
1711	Pleurisy	?	1749	Pleurisy	?
1714	Yellow Fever	?	1759	Whooping Cough	?
1724	Diphtheria	?	1759	Measles	?
1728	Yellow Fever	?	1760	Smallpox	730
1732	Yellow Fever	130+	1763	Smallpox	?
1734	Typhoid Fever	?	1765	Whooping Cough	?
1738	Smallpox	295	1772	Measles	900+

New York

Year	Disease	Death Toll	Year	Disease	Death Toll
1702	Yellow Fever	570	1740	Typhoid Fever	?
1714	Measles	?	1743	Yellow Fever	217
1729	Measles	?	1745	Smallpox	?
1731	Dysentery	?	1749	Pleurisy	?
1731	Smallpox	?	1752	Smallpox	?
1732	Yellow Fever	?	1758	Smallpox	?
1738	Smallpox	?			

Philadelphia					
Year	Disease	Death Toll	Year	Disease	Death Toll
1699	Yellow Fever	220	1757	Dysentery	?
1730	Smallpox	100+	1755	Smallpox	?
1732	Smallpox	?	1759	Typhoid Fever	?
1736	Smallpox	?	1759	Measles	?
1741	Yellow Fever	200+	1762	Yellow Fever	?
1748	Measles	?	1763	Diphtheria	?
1749	Yellow Fever	?	1773	Smallpox	300+
1749	Pleurisy	?			

INOCULATION

While many people turned to prayers to control smallpox, others turned to science, specifically inoculation. This simple but dangerous technique involved taking a small amount of pus from the lesion of an infected person and placing it under the skin of a well person. The resulting infection was usually mild and chances for survival far greater than in cases of infection through ordinary contact. The practice originated in China and was brought to the Western world in the early eighteenth century. Dr. Zabdiel Boylston of Boston became the first physician in North America to utilize this technique in 1721 when he inoculated nearly 300 people during a smallpox epidemic that swept through the city. Of these, only six died, or a case fatality rate of about 2 percent. By contrast, nearly 15 percent of those infected by natural means succumbed to the disease. News of the success of smallpox inoculation in Boston spread rapidly throughout the colonies. Newspapers in the five cities advertised the sale of inoculation pamphlets, and physicians, church leaders, and laymen began praising this new medical breakthrough. The "Eruptions are few, the Symptoms light, the Danger next to none, the Recovery easy," extolled a proinoculation editorial in the *Pennsylvania Gazette*, "and the patient is equally secured from this Distemper for the future, as he would be by having gone thro' it in the natural Way." The realities of inoculation were much different, at least according to Solomon Drowne, a Rhode Island college student who, not long after undergoing the procedure in 1772, wrote that he felt "sick as a Dog ... my joints are stiff & ache, a Pain in my Back & Head, from which the Dr. concludes the Small Pox will break out upon me tomorrow." The next day he noticed that "the Pock begin to make their appearance upon the Skin, very much resembling Flea Bites." Three days later he had "about fifty [pocks] in my Face and upwards of forty on my left Hand and fifty on my right." When the smallpox had run its course, he washed himself "with Rum all over."[3]

Despite the success of smallpox inoculation, some colonists opposed it because they saw it as tampering with God's plan. One inoculation opponent went so far as to throw a gunpowder grenade through a window of the home of Cotton Mather, an early proponent of inoculation, with this note attached: "Cotton Mather you dog, damn you, I'll inoculate you with this, with a pox to you." Others viewed inoculation quite differently, especially ministers who urged their reluctant parishioners to utilize this heavenly remedy from God. "We ought to be thankful for God for the Discovery of a medicine so efficacious in antidoting and subduing the Malignancy of this infectious and formidable Distemper," wrote one New England minister. Indeed, many colonists residing in the major port cities had much to be thankful for regarding smallpox inoculation, for it was the major factor in reducing fatalities from this highly contagious and deadly disease. (See Table 12.2). This may explain why residents often turned inoculation into a social event, with entire families and groups of friends undergoing the procedure together.[4]

YELLOW FEVER

Nearly as deadly and terrifying to residents of the five cities as smallpox was yellow fever, a tropical infectious disease that primarily targeted the major seaports with their commercial ties to tropical areas. The large pools of stagnant water that often appeared around the city's waterfronts also attracted the disease-carrying *Aedes aegypti* mosquito. Because this deadly mosquito feeds only when the temperature is above 60 degrees, those cities with warmer climates bore the brunt of the disease. Boston and Newport, for example, were little affected by yellow fever. New York City suffered occasionally from yellow fever, especially in those areas that had been "built upon a swamp," explained the local physician Cadwallader Colden, and in the vicinity of the docks where much of the "nastiness of the town is thrown." The worst outbreak there occurred in the summer of 1702 when 570 people perished from the disease. Residents of Charles Town, a city residing in a semi-tropical environment and surrounded by mosquito-breeding rice

Table 12.2. Smallpox Inoculation

Date	Number Inoculated	Deaths	Proportion
1721	247	6	1 in 42
1730	400	12	1 in 33
1752	2,109	31	1 in 170
1764	4,977	46	1 in 108
1776	4,988	28	1 in 178

Duffy, *Epidemics in Colonial America*, 36.

fields, had the dismal ignominy of suffering the most yellow fever outbreaks—a total of seven between 1699 and 1762. (See Table 12.1.) What made yellow fever especially horrifying to sufferers was its telling symptoms—jaundice that gives its victims yellow skin and eyes, and the vomiting of partially digested, dark colored blood. For this reason contemporaries often referred to yellow fever as "black vomit."[5]

DISRUPTIONS TO DAILY LIFE

Outbreaks of both smallpox and yellow fever could paralyze a city. New York City's 1702 yellow fever epidemic either killed, sickened, or forced so many local politicians to flee into the countryside that local government came to a halt. Similarly, the 1699 yellow fever outbreak in Charles Town took half the provincial legislators, the chief justice, the receiver-general, and the provost marshal. The "destroying Angel slaughtered so furiously with his revenging Sword of Pestilence," wrote one lucky survivor, "that the dead were carried in carts, being heaped up one upon another Worse by far than the great Plague of London . . . Shops shut up for 5 weeks; nothing but carrying Medicines, digging graves, [and] carting the dead." That same year yellow fever ravaged Philadelphia so badly that one Quaker publicly offered himself as a sacrifice for the people in hopes that his self-immolation would bring an end to the plague. During the 1731 smallpox epidemic that took 549 lives in New York City, an eyewitness reported, "Here is little or no News in this Place, nothing but the melancholy Scene of little Business, and less Money. The Markets begin to grow very thin; the small-Pox raging very violently in Town, which in a great measure hinders the Country People from supplying this Place with Provisions." When the contagion later spread to Charles Town, so many residents fled into the back-country that "there were not a sufficient number of persons in health to attend the sick," noted a shocked observer, "and many persons perished from neglect and want." Indeed, at times fear so gripped urban residents during an epidemic that they refused to assist the sick, leaving them to die alone in their homes or even in the streets, where they sometimes laid for days before taken to the city graveyard.[6]

MISCELLANEOUS DISEASES AND AILMENTS

Although epidemics of smallpox and yellow fever struck enormous fear and grief into residents of the five great cities, they were not the leading causes of death during the colonial period. This ignoble honor went to dysentery and various respiratory diseases that flourished in the crowded and unsanitary conditions of the colonial cities. The cooler climates of Boston and Newport contributed to the outbreak of various respiratory illnesses that sometimes reached epidemic proportions. A severe "epidemical cold" (probably pneumonia) ravaged residents of Boston in 1699. "No man living [can] remember such a time as was hereby brought upon us," lamented a local minister. A generation later the Puritan city was hit by another severe "Cold & Cough" that proved particularly mortal to many of the "most ancient founders" of the city.[7] Even the southern city of Charles Town suffered occasional outbreaks of respiratory illnesses, as in 1711 when pleurisy "carried off abundance of our inhabitants," according to one local minister, who added that the capital "looks miserably thin and disconsolate, and there is not one House in Twenty I speak modestly that has not Considerably suffered and still labours under this general Calamity."[8]

Many urbanites also "considerably suffered" from dysentery, or the "bloody flux" as contemporaries called it. An infectious disease characterized by bloody diarrhea, a high fever, and severe stomach cramps, dysentery was often brought by sick immigrants disembarking from disease-ridden ships. Crude methods of waste disposal, lack of refrigeration, and poor standards of hygiene in the cities allowed dysentery to regularly and quickly spread throughout much of the community. At times perhaps half of all residents would contract the illness; of these, perhaps 15 percent would die, mostly infants and children. Yet many adults also succumbed to the symptoms, which were quite painful and chronic and sometimes lingered for months before the disease either departed or killed its victim. One unfortunate Charles Town missionary afflicted with the disorder described the painful and annoying symptoms as an "Obstinate Diarrhea that will yield to no Medicine or Skill of the Physician." He added that he had "not one day or one Night's ease or rest" for the past four months and that "no less than fifteen times a night I am oblig'd to get up, and that accompanied by the Most excruciating pains in my Bowels, my back, [and] my loins." The painful, persistent, and sometimes fatal nature of dysentery compelled some desperate people to try distasteful and bizarre remedies that only added to their discomfort. Some suggested pills made of black pepper, turpentine, and flour; others recommended butter mixed with beer and molasses. For the truly desperate, there was this remedy: "Take an Egge and Boyle it very hard, then pull off the Shell, and put it as hot as you can well endure, into the fundament [anus] of the patient Grieved and when it is much abated of the heat, put in another Egge in the same manner."[9]

What made dysentery so deadly was that it severely weakened its victims, thereby making them susceptible to other maladies, particularly diphtheria, scarlet fever, measles, whooping cough, and mumps. Because of their youth and undeveloped immune system, children were most susceptible to these contagious diseases. In 1735 over 100 children in Boston, already weakened by the diphtheria and smallpox that swept through the city the previous year, succumbed to scarlet fever. Few children reached puberty without an attack of measles, which could reach epidemic proportions and prove fatal to the young. In 1713 over 150 children in Boston died from the infection, which quickly traveled to New York City and Philadelphia, where it proved so "very mortal" to youngsters that local ministers refused to visit and baptize dying children. Whooping cough, another childhood disease, became a problem in the major urban centers by the mid-1700s. Charles Town, for example, suffered three major epidemics of whooping cough between 1738 and 1765. In all three cases it was imported into the city by ship and "did not spare anyone who had not passed through it before."[10]

A disease more specific to adults was syphilis, or the "King's Evil" as colonists called it, which thrived in the port cities with their large number of sailors, soldiers, and prostitutes. Local authorities recognized the health problems related to prostitution and at times tried to eradicate the injurious and illegal practice. Their efforts were rarely successful, which allowed "young venereal hussies" like Sarah Evans of Philadelphia to "innoculate" others. Although rarely fatal, the disease did injure the health of many people of both sexes. By the 1760s there was a considerable increase in newspaper advertisements of pills and potions to cure venereal disorders, which suggests that there was a corresponding rise in venereal complaints. Most popular were imported cures from abroad like "Dr. Sanxay's Imperial Golden drops," and "Keyer's famous pills." One alleged cure for syphilis was an ointment made from "hogs fat and deer dung." Although this "recipe" failed to cure one afflicted with syphilis, its application likely prevented the sufferer from spreading the disease to others. More popular in the suppression of syphilis were mercury pills that only created worse medical problems for the sufferer.[11]

Further debilitating the health of early Americans was heavy metal poisoning, particularly with lead. Not only was much of their cider, wine, rum, and other spirituous liquors contaminated with traces of lead from the manufacturing process, but they repeatedly took in small amounts from lead-containing pewter earthenware, cooking and serving utensils, water cisterns, household paints, cosmetics, and even medications. Over time, chronic lead poisoning contributed to multiple health problems that included abdominal pain, severe headaches, confusion, loss of coordination, slurred speech, kidney failure, and sometimes seizures.[12]

Less harmful but still irritating were the parasitic intestinal worms that inhabited every city dweller at one time or another. Crowded and unclean living conditions in the cities were a breeding ground for these parasites. Remedies to rid the body of worms ranged from pink root and calomel to rectified oil of tar and exotic mixtures of herbs, minerals, fruit juices, and liquors. One German folk remedy for intestinal worms was both dangerous and cannibalistic: "Take the bone of a man and make scrapings and mix it with a quantity of white lead and a little oil. If this does not bring relief, take a little alum afterwards."[13] If not suffering from intestinal turmoil caused by worms, colonists experienced severe itching caused by another parasite—the itch mite. A neglect of skin hygiene and cleanliness served as a breeding ground for these "scabies," as colonists called them. The great frequency of advertisements of nostrums for "the itch" in city newspapers attests to the ubiquity of scabies.

GOVERNMENT RESPONSE TO DISEASES AND ILLNESSES

To combat these epidemics and illnesses, city governments enacted numerous measures: quarantining the infected, regulating certain "noxious" trades, and paving and cleaning streets. The first line of defense made by urban officials in containing the spread of contagious diseases was the creation of quarantine hospitals, commonly referred to as pesthouses. Usually located on a nearby island, pesthouses held diseased sailors, ships' passengers, and local inhabitants who were required to stay until a physician declared them well. These pesthouses did little to help those infected with contagious diseases. A concerned resident of Charles Town lamented that if only the pesthouse on Sullivan's Island "was made tight, warm and comfortable ... and ... some person was appointed constantly to reside on the Island ... who would say we wanted common humanity." The primary purpose of pesthouses was not to treat the infected but to simply isolate them to protect the larger community.[14]

Although the germ theory of disease was yet unknown, people at the time generally believed that "noxious air" caused by unsanitary conditions posed a danger to public health. The New York City Common Council recognized this risk and so in 1744 passed a sanitation code, arguing that "the health of the Inhabitants of any City Does in a Great Measure Depend upon the Purity of the Air of that City and that when the Air of a City is by Noisome Smells Corrupted Distempers of many Kinds are thereby Occasioned." To reduce the risk of "corrupted distempers," urban authorities passed numerous ad hoc ordinances to clean up the city streets. This included removing slaughtering houses and tanneries outside of town, fining anyone caught throwing "any intralls of beast or fowles or garbidge or Carion or dead dogs or Catts or any other dead beast or stinkeing thing, in any hieway or dich or Common," hiring cartmen to carry away dung and garbage from the streets, and paving main thoroughfares. All these measures were costly, but when Philadelphia went on a street-paving campaign in the mid-1760s, Dr. Thomas Bond was certain that "the whole Expense of Paving will be repair'd in ten years, by the lessening of Physic bills alone."[15]

FAITH AND MEDICINE

As with most else in society, early Americans believed that health and healing were in God's hand. The clergy in particular interpreted illness—both on an individual and community level—as brought by God as punishment for sinful behavior and incentive to reform. One clergyman made a list of misconduct he believed had brought on a smallpox epidemic: "pride, covetnousse, animositys, personal neglecte of gospelizing our youth, and of gospelizing of the Indians ... drinking houses multiplied." When God inflicted his wrath on a city by bringing an epidemic, the prime defense was prayer and appeals for reformation. Collective guilt required collective repentance. When diphtheria swept through Boston in 1735 and 1736, for example, Massachusetts Governor Jonathan Belcher proclaimed January 8 to be a "Day of solemn Prayer and Humiliation with Fasting" in hopes of appeasing "the holy Anger of Almighty God ... in sending us a mortal Sickness." If the therapy worked "it was a gift of God's beneficence," explains historian Michael Flannery, "if it failed the family, the cleric, and the physician would take solace in the deceased's salvation."[16]

THE PRACTICE OF EARLY AMERICAN MEDICINE

Considering that contemporaries believed that spiritual and physical therapy went hand in hand, it is no surprise that some of the earliest physicians in colonial America were ministers, who were often the most educated men in a community. The Puritan divine Cotton Mather referred to this union between the two professions as an "angelic conjunction." But as the urban centers expanded, these part-time medical "angels" were supplanted by a wide variety of medical practitioners, from those carrying a medical degree earned from a European university to quacks who appropriated the title "doctor." Of the approximately 3,500 men who practiced medicine in America before 1776, only 11 percent held a medical degree. For those who could not afford to attend a European university for medical training, there was the apprenticeship system, whereby a local physician, for a fee, would train a young apprentice in the art of healing for about three to five years. According to one critic of medical apprenticeship, "The mechanic, to acquire the lowest Trade, serves a much longer time than most of the students of Physic do to learn ... to be DOCTORS." Further limiting the quality of medical apprenticeship is that the physician often treated his apprentice more like an indentured servant. Much of the work performed by medical apprentices—grooming horses, cleaning equipment, and collecting fees, among other drudgery—was of dubious value in learning medicine. In between serving as a personal servant and groomsman to his medical master, the apprentice tended to the doctor's shop, mixed prescriptions, read books in his preceptor's library, and accompanied him on calls where the apprentice might get the opportunity to bleed, cup, and apply poultices.[17]

Competing with local physicians were ships' surgeons, who often plied their trade while their ships were in port. Lancing boils, setting fractures, and dressing wounds were their specialties. Itinerant physicians and healers also set up shop in the major urban centers where they could attract quite a following with clever salesmanship and lofty promises. Doctor Anthony Yardell, a mountebank who traveled from city to city, attracted customers by setting up a stage in the middle of town on which two boys "entertained spectators by walking on their hands & by various feats of activity," reported one eyewitness. "The Doctor harangues on what he can do, the terms on which he doth anything, the way he goes on in. He harangues on the virtues of certain Medicines he hath to sell."[18] These "certain medicines" were undoubtedly cure-all elixirs that contained opiates and mercury that brought relief to the patient in the short run but only encouraged addiction and ruined health over the long term. The cities also abounded with untrained medical quacks who preyed on the desperate and poor who could not afford the services of more professional care.

Contributing to the dubious quality of medical care in the cities was the limited understanding at the time of disease and medicine, which had not advanced far beyond the ancient Greek theory of humoralism that viewed health as a natural balance of the body's humors (yellow bile, blood, phlegm, and black bile) and their respective elements or qualities (hot and dry, hot and moist, cold and moist, and cold and dry). Humoral imbalance was caused by too much or too little of one or more elements or qualities. To restore humoral balance, and therefore one's health, physicians of the day prescribed depletory remedies: bleeding, purging, vomiting, sweating, and blistering. A satirical poem of the day summed up medical therapies in 10 words: "*Piss, Spew,* and *Spit/Perspiration* and *Sweat/ Purge, Bleed,* and *Blister/Issues* and *Clyster.*" Not so funny was the procedure for bloodletting, which involved either applying leeches or using a scarificator, an instrument with a number of tiny blades released by a spring. After making the wound, the physician exhausted the air from a cupping glass by burning in it a piece of brandy-soaked paper and then applied the cup over the wound to draw out the blood. Afterwards, he removed the glass and applied a mild ointment on the wound. To make a blister-issue, the physician applied a powder of Spanish flies to promote a discharge of matter. To draw out larger quantities, the physician made an incision on the nape of the neck and threaded a silk cord through the wound, leaving several inches of cord hanging out at each end. After he removed the needle, the physician treated the cord with an irritating ointment and pulled it back and forth through the skin each day to encourage a discharge of purulent matter.[19]

As we know today, these "remedies" severely weakened the infected by robbing the patient of vital fluids needed to combat illnesses. Countless people died from these treatments, which some contemporaries, recognizing their harmful nature, equated with murder. One Boston physician commented that the routine medical practice included "bleeding, vomiting, blistering, [and] purging." If the illness continued, he sarcastically added, there was "repetendi, and finally murderandi." It was not uncommon for a doctor to take 20 to 40 ounces of blood from a patient, who often lost consciousness and who sometimes died from the massive loss. Others died from being administered massive amounts of purgatives. One New York City physician administered 32 drugs in the course of one woman's illness, nearly two-thirds of which were purgatives that caused her to vomit incessantly until she finally died two days later.[20]

If purging and bleeding did not kill a patient or make him or her sicker, then the medicines—and the haphazard way in which doctors prescribed them—sometimes did. Physicians prescribed drugs to fine-tune each patient's special internal equilibrium. The most used drugs included mercury (cathartic), opium (narcotic), ipecac (emetic), camphor (narcotic), snakeroot (tonic), Jesuit's bark (tonic), rhubarb (cathartic), and castor oil (cathartic). Not only did practitioners administer drugs in unbelievable quantities, but they also compounded them into prescriptions with no guidelines and measured them out without any degree of accuracy. Perhaps less harmful but certainly more nauseating was the use of dung and urine in prescriptions for many illnesses. Cotton Mather, a Boston minister and part-time physician, claimed in his medical treatise that human excreta was a "remedy for Human Bodies that is hardly to be paralleled," while urine, he added, had "virtues far beyond all the waters of medicinal springs." One remedy for diphtheria, for example, called for the afflicted to gargle every morning with "the fluid from the stool of a cow." Almost as revolting was one particular cure for a toothache, which involved placing "fresh cow manure" on the side of the sufferer's face to "draw out" the pain. In the end, the physician and historian J. Worth Estes estimates that up to 95 percent of adult patients survived these disgusting and sometimes dangerous remedies. This is perhaps a testament more to the healing powers of nature than those of colonial physicians, who had a reputation among some as "licensed assassins," "pests of society," and "butchers of human kind."[21]

SURGERY

Far more harmful to patients than nauseating remedies was the lack of concern for hygiene during medical operations. This was particularly true in the case of surgeons, who were not university-trained physicians but members of a little-respected manual trade associated with barbering and bonesetting. For many, surgery was a side-job practiced by ferrymen, shipmasters, lawyers, tailors, tavern keepers, cordwainers, and other tradesmen. Their work was limited to cutting ulcers and boils, treating open wounds, setting bones, and performing amputations. It was an unfortunate individual who had to seek the services of a surgeon, who often worked without anesthetic and who had no understanding of the value of cleanliness. One medical historian estimated that the unhygienic conditions under which surgeons operated caused death in 70 percent of cases of compound fractures and 50 percent of all amputations. If infection did not kill the patient, the shock from the surgery sometimes did. When a limb was amputated the surgeon placed it across two vertical boards, fractured the bone with a blow from a narrow sledge, sawed off the limb as fast as he could, cauterized the stump with either a hot iron or boiling oil, bandaged the wound, and sent the patient home. The only painkillers available to the patient were opium, Indian hemp, alcohol, water hemlock, and tourniquets applied tightly to numb the nerves. It was the fortunate patient who fainted during amputations.[22]

The reputation of surgeons and physicians was apparently so poor that when they did successfully perform a surgery it sometimes became part of local folklore. Cotton Mather felt compelled to include in his book *Remarkable Providences* (1684) the surgery of a young girl who suffered a serious head injury when a hinge from a cart pierced her skull, leaving "some of the brains . . . and other bits scattered on her forehead." Two local surgeons "gently drove the soft matter of the bunch into the wound," placed a silver plate over the exposed brain matter "to defend it from any touch or injury," and then plastered over the entire wound. Miraculously, the child lived to be a mother of two children and suffered no after-effects other than the tendency of her brain to "swell and swage" according to the tides. Similarly, when Zabdiel Boylston of Boston successfully removed a kidney stone "of considerable bigness" from a young boy in 1710 without killing him, the editor of the *Boston Newsletter* felt he "could not fail to make [it] Publick." Ten years later the *Boston Gazette* reported another "miracle cure" performed by Boylston, who treated a woman suffering from breast cancer by "Cut[ting] her whole Breast off."[23]

FOLK REMEDIES

Except for such extreme emergencies, early Americans "seem to have come into this world and left it without any burning need for regular medical interventions," notes historian G. B. Warden. Most health care took place in the home and was usually administered by a family member or a neighbor who depended on home-made medicines and salves and on traditional healing practices. Ingredients for these home remedies included herbs and plants that were often grown in backyard gardens or obtained from local apothecary shops. Early settlers also utilized nontraditional remedies borrowed from Native Americans for wounds, sores, and burns based on the healing properties of native plants like sassafras and Seneca snakeroot. For most other cures, however, colonists turned to printed sources like John Tennent's *Every Man His Own Doctor* (1727), an almanac, or remnants based on folk tradition. One such folk tradition was the doctrine of signatures, a belief that plant characteristics such as shape, size, and color helped reveal what illnesses that plant was useful in treating. For example, heart-shaped plants were thought to be good for the heart, walnuts for the brain, and the like.[24]

People today will find some of these folk cures and remedies sickening, laughable, or simply unbelievable. One folk practitioner claimed to cure fevers by inscribing letters on pieces of bread and having the patient eat one piece a day until the afflicted recovered. One cure for arthritis, letting "honeybees sting you," certainly took a sufferer's mind off of the pain caused by his or her affliction. Only the most desperate sufferer of scabies would apply a remedy consisting of crushed worms, hog lard, turpentine, and brandy all stewed together. Laying a muskrat pelt upon one's chest was supposed to "make breathing easier" for the asthma sufferer. One cure for shingles advised desperate sufferers to apply an ointment made from a mixture of cat's blood, cream, and moss from inside a well. To get rid of a cold, some colonists applied a mixture of onions and butter to the throat and chest or stuffed orange rinds up their nostrils. A common recipe for cough syrup consisted of boiled goldenrod mixed with sugar and peppermint for flavoring. Those suffering from earaches had several remedies to choose from— pouring onion juice into the ear canal, stuffing into the ear a wad of cotton dipped in molasses, and for babies, eating bone marrow from a hog. Even less palatable was one cure for reducing a fever—swallowing a spider mixed in syrup. Drinking millipedes with the "heads off, stampt in white wine or beer" was used by some women experiencing sore breasts following childbirth. African American folk practitioners made a tea out of cockroaches as a remedy for lockjaw and a potion comprised of vinegar and red ants as a cure for rheumatism. Sniffing powdered moss was supposed to ease a headache, while "sniffing your fingers after you have picked the stinking sweat that is between your toes" was supposedly a cure for menstrual cramps. Ridding a head of lice involved washing the head with alcohol and sand. "The lice will get drunk," the remedy goes, "and thinking they are on sand, will fight each other to the death." Just as laughable was wrapping smoked bacon around one's neck as a remedy for a sore throat. Similarly, some slaves wore asafetida, better known as "devil's dung," around their necks to ward off asthma, measles, whooping cough, mumps, smallpox, and diphtheria. This plant has little medicinal value, but its terrible odor tended to keep people with colds at a distance and, hence, kept harmful germs away. Less offensive but equally ineffective were necklace charms made by slave conjurers that might contain anything from graveyard dirt, reptile parts, and insects to pins, hair, herbs, and nail clippings. For obvious reasons many slaves turned to the alleged healing power of whiskey, sometimes mixing it with lemons or garlic to cure a variety of ailments from colds and fevers to worms and measles.[25]

Because medicine was not a closed profession at this time, women administered much of this "natural healing." Indeed, playing "Dr. Mom" was as much a part of a woman's role as cooking. Most women learned basic medicinal remedies for common ailments through oral tradition from their mothers and other matriarchs. Women grew medicinal plants in their kitchen gardens alongside vegetables and culinary herbs. Because women were the "weaker vessel," according to Cotton Mather, the kinds of medicines they administered should be "harmless," ones of the mild garden-herb variety. Illustrative is a "Mrs. Fields" who sold a green ointment made from common herbs that she claimed "cureth all spraines and Aches Cramps and Scaldings and cutts healeth all wounds . . . it will heale old Rotten sores and bites of Venemous Beasts." Some civic-minded upper class housewives stored a supply of remedies that she would give to less fortunate and less knowledgeable neighbors. Cotton Mather noted with "extreme satisfaction" that his wife "attained unto a considerable skill in physick and chyrurgery, which enabled her to dispense many safe, good, and useful medicines unto the poor that had occasion for them." Women also went over to each other's homes to watch over and help nurse sick family members. Such altruism reminds us that medical care in early America was a cooperative effort.[26]

ASTROLOGY AND MEDICINE

Whereas some colonists looked to the earth for healing remedies, others looked to the sky. Many people at the time closely linked medicine to astrology, a belief that the planets and stars played a critical role in determining a person's health or illness. Even some physicians consulted the heavens to determine the appropriate times to let blood, perform surgery, and administer medicines. Giving credence to the connection between health and astrology was the theory advanced by astrologists that each body part or organ had shared characteristics with signs of the zodiac. Leo presided over the heart because the strength of the lion was located in its heart, it was claimed, and Scorpio presided over the genitals because a scorpion's strength was located in its tail. Understanding this relationship was important in determining the proper times for administering medicines, letting blood, gathering herbs, and performing surgical procedures.[27]

Reflecting the popularity of astrology were the numerous colonial almanacs that regularly dispensed advice on the best times to let blood, purge, dispense medicine, and even to bath and cut one's hair. Typical is the following passage found in a 1694 Boston almanac:

> With Electuaries, the Moon in *Cancer.*
> With Pills, the Moon in *Pisces* . . .
> Good to take Vomit, the Moon being in Taurus.
> To purge the Head by sneezing, the Moon being in
> *Cancer, Leo,* or *Virgo.*
> To make Clysters, the Moon being in *Aries,*
> *Cancer,* or *Virgo.*
> To stop Fluxes and Rheums, the Moon being in
> *Taurus, Virgo,* or *Capricorn.*

> To Bath when the Moon is in *Cancer, Libra,*
> *Aquarius,* or *Pisces.*
> To cut the Hair of the Head or Beard, when the Moon is in *Libra,*
> *Sagitarius, Aquarius,* or *Pisces.*[28]

Some almanac makers like Nathaniel Ames even used astrology to warn readers in 1745 of potential dangers to one's health in the year ahead, predicting the coming of "peripneumonick and plueritick Fevers, Coughs, Asthmas, and Disorders of the Lungs" in January, and "nervous slow fevers" and "stagnation of the Blood" in April.[29]

Much more practical and useful was the pithy advice on a healthy lifestyle contained in almanacs. Nathaniel Ames's 1755 *Almanack*, for instance, championed the benefits of physical work, particularly for growing "strong Nerves," preventing "Rheumatic Pains or coughs from Eastern Blasts," and promoting the "Balmy Dew of Sleep." The "inactive Sluggard," the almanac warned, is condemned to insomnia because "his flacid Nerves are unstrung, his nature stinks, his meals oppress, his Sleep is frantic with pale Spectres, coin'd in his delirious Brains; and monstrous Paintings shock his Soul all Night." Many almanacs also preached against intemperance, "the very fruitful Mother of innumerable Distempers, Ailments and Pains." The *New England Almanack* asserted that the "three doctors, Diet, Quiet, and Temperence, are the best physicians." Finally, *Poor Richard's* "Rules of Health and Long Life" advised readers, among other things, to "eat for Necessity, not Pleasure" because a "sober Diet ... preserves the Memory, helps understanding, [and] allays the Heat of Lust."[30]

MEDICAL QUACKS

The laissez-faire circumstances of medicine in early America and the poor reputations of some physicians allowed medical quacks to flourish in the cities. "Quacks abound like Locusts in Egypt," complained one New York City resident in 1757. Without medical societies or licensing laws until the late colonial period, virtually any smooth-talking person, no matter how uneducated, could open a medical practice and claim to have the ability to cure every disease and illness known to man. One Rhode Islander opined that "any ignorant plow-boy may live six months or a year with some old Quack, who perhaps started up in the first place from an obscure cow-doctor, and if he can talk glib and has a good stock of impudence, will gain reputation and practice as soon as the best Physician." As an example, one New York City medical self-starter

The Anatomy of Man's Body as govern'd
by the Twelve Conftellations.

Here I fit naked, like fome Fairy Elf,
My Seat a Pumpkin; I grudge no Man's Pelf;
Though I've no Bread, nor Cheefe upon my Shelf;
I'll tell thee gratis, when it fafe is,
To purge, to bleed, or cut, thy Cattle, or —— thy felf.

♈ *The Head and Face.*

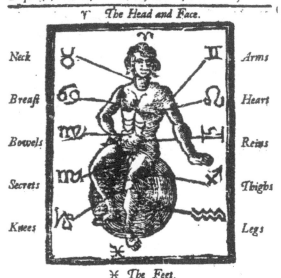

Neck	Arms
Breaft	Heart
Bowels	Reins
Secrets	Thighs
Knees	Legs

♓ *The Feet.*
To know where the Sign is.

Firft find the Day of the Month, and againft the Day you have the Sign or Place of the Moon in the 5th Column. Then finding the Sign here, it fhews the part of the Body it governs.

The Names and Characters of the Seven Planets.
♄ Saturn, ♃ Jupiter, ♂ Mars, ☉ Sol, ♀ Venus,
☿ Mercury, ☽ Luna, ☊ Dragons Head and ☋ Tail.

The Five Afpects. ♂ Conjunction, ✳ Sextile,
☍ Oppofition, △ Trine, ☐ Quartile.

Common Notes for the Year 1734.
Golden Number   6 ⎰ Cycle of the Sun   7
Epact   6 ⎱ Dominical Letter   F

"The Anatomy of Man's Body as Govern'd by the Twelve Constellations." Many early Americans followed the ancient medical system that regarded various parts of the body, diseases, and drugs as under the influence of the sun, moon, and planets, along with the 12 astrological signs. This illustration from the 1734 issue of *Poor Richard's Almanack* shows "Zodiak Man" with the signs of the zodiac linked with various parts of the anatomy. (Charles Evans, *Early American Imprints*, Series 1, no. 3657) worked as a shoemaker until he happened to cure an old woman of a "pestilent mortal disease." Word spread of his miracle cure, and soon people from all quarters sought his treatments. Realizing he was on to something, the shoemaker quit cobbling shoes and instead fell to the "cobbling of human bodies." Even more shocking, literally, was the use of electricity on patients suffering from tooth-aches, headaches, deafness, sprains, and nervous disorders. How-ever, the "Emperor of Quacks" was the London mountebank James Graham, who traveled to the American cities promoting his "Grand Celestial Bed," which he assured childless couples that copulating on would bring immediate conception.[31]

MIRACLE CURES AND PATENT MEDICINES

These medical quacks were equally notorious for selling miracle cures made from roots, leaves, and horns that provided little medicinal value. One Massachusetts medicine man advertised that he had a cure for rattlesnake bite, inflammation of the blood, and "any breeding sore whatsoever." Samuel Hawkes of Boston adver-tised his "celebrated Fever-Powder," which promised to "remove the most obstinate fever whatever when they have yielded to noth-ing else." Another Boston medicine man peddled a "white powder of a sweetish taste" as a cure for gout. Not a few of these quacks were women. The "Dutch ladies" of Charles Town, for example, advertised their own inherited "secret remedies" for dysentery and other ailments. One Mary Ann Davis offered a "sovereign rem-edy" for hemorrhoids. Perhaps the most successful medical con was pulled off by the Charles Town slave "Negro Caesar," who received his freedom and an annual allowance of £100 from the provincial assembly for his remedies against poison and rattlesnake bite.[32]

Competing with these American home-made miracle cures were more than 75 different British patent medicines imported into the colonies and sold in large quantities by medical quacks, dry-goods merchants, and apothecaries. These elixirs were popular among the gullible masses who could not afford the high cost of visiting a physician for medical treatment. Instead, for a few pence one could purchase a cure-all that contained a concoction of "mysterious ingredients." "Buyer beware" certainly applied in this era of medi-cal laissez faire as manufacturers of patent medicines were not required to either list the ingredients of their product or make accu-rate claims as to its efficacy. Without government restraint, claims made by these medical charlatans exploited the most desperate

LOKIER's Pills, Bateman's Drops, fine Lan-
cets, Surgeons Pocket Inftruments, Drugs and Medicines. Juft im
ported, and to be fold by William Mercer, *in* Hanover Square, *in*
the Houfe where Doctor Nicoll *formerly lived.*

FEMALE CORDIAL.
An agreeable, pleafant and fafe Medicine, peculiarly adapted to
the delicate nervous Texture of the Female Sex, and gives immediate and lafting Relief, Price 4s. 6d,
     ALso: Artificial Slate Memorandum Books, Mufick Books,
New Mufic, &c.

Advertisement for Medicines. Colonial newspapers are replete with
advertisements like these for medicines and elixirs sold in urban shops
and apothecary stores. Some clever medicine men increased their income
by concocting special potions for the "delicate nervous Texture of the
Female Sex."

and naïve. Daffy's Elixir, a "Health-Bringing Drink," was claimed to
cure gout, kidney stones, colic, scurvy, dropsy, rickets, consumption, and "languishing and melancholly." Royal Honey Water was
sold as "an Excellent Perfume" and as "good against Deafness,
and to Make Hair grow." Godfrey's Cordial claimed to remedy
"all manner of pains in the bowels, fluxes, fevers, small pox, measles, rheumatism, coughs, cold and restlessness in men, women
and children and particularly for several ailments incident to
child-bearing women and relief of young children breeding their
teeth." Robert Turlington's "Balsam of Life" promised to provide
"a remedy for Every Malady . . . it strengthens and corroborates
when weak and declining, vivifies and enlivens the Spirits, mixes
with Juices and Fluids of the Body and gently infuses its kindly
Influence into those Parts that are most in Disorder." That many of
these "magic potions" contained opium or alcohol explain much
of their popularity. Mothers even administered small amounts to
restless infants as a "sleeping poppy" that, sadly, put some into an
eternal sleep. Less addictive but equally as harmful was the mercury chloride found in many patent medicines that ruined the
health and shortened the lives of those who drank them.[33]

REGULATION OF MEDICAL PRACTICE

Although many sick urban residents turned to quacks for medical
attention, others recognized the harm they caused to the community.

One Bostonian critical of the medical parasites that abounded in the Puritan city sarcastically remarked that these "pretended doctors have slain their thousands; but happily for them the ground covers their miscarriages." The numerous medical charlatans in New York City were "plagues extraordinary," according to one resident, who he claimed annually stole £20,000 from the purses of the public under the "specious pretense" of "acting the physician." In 1760 the New York legislature, believing that "many ignorant and unskillful persons in Physic and Surgery [are] endangering the lives and limbs of their patients," passed a law requiring anyone wanting to practice "physick and surgery" in the provincial capital to pass an examination before a local medical board. In the end this law failed to prevent "quacks and pretenders" from wreaking their "dismal havoc" as the law exempted anyone already practicing in the city and officials refused to convict violators of the provision.[34]

PROFESSIONALIZATION OF MEDICAL PRACTICE

The push for medical regulation in the mid-eighteenth century came from university-trained physicians who sought to eliminate some of their competitors while at the same time professionalizing the practice of medicine. To that end, physicians in the five cities formed medical organizations to exchange ideas and to advance the understanding of diseases and their causes. As early as 1735 physicians in Boston formed the Physical Club, the country's first medical society. The group met regularly in a local tavern where they "drank punch, smoked tobacco, and talked of sundry physical matters." Physicians in New York City were meeting regularly in a medical society by the early 1760s. Doctors in Philadelphia formed their own medical society in 1765, which met weekly to listen to papers and to take part in discussions. In other cities medical practitioners called one another into consultation and generally did their best to raise the standards of their profession. One way in which they did this was through public lectures in anatomy, sometimes making demonstrations on a cadaver. Dr. John Jeffries of Boston had his public lecture on anatomy ended prematurely when a mob made off with his cadaver.[35]

Some urban doctors raised the standard of their professions by publishing scientific descriptions of local diseases and offering treatments. The Boston physician Thomas Thacher published the colonies' first medical treatise, *A Brief Guide to the Common People of New England How to Order Themselves and Theirs in the Small-Pocks or Measles* (1667) that provided some "simple and sensible rules" for treating these diseases. In 1743 Dr. Cadwallader Colden of New York City published his "observation" of the yellow fever epidemic that swept through the capital in 1741 and 1742. Yellow fever also caused many deaths in Charles Town, where Dr. John Lining wrote an accurate description of the plague in 1753 that was later published in the *Edinburgh Medical Journal*. Smallpox, too, received considerable attention from urban doctors, who published their studies to the great benefit of many. One of the most important of these was Dr. Adam Thomson's *Discourse on the Preparation of the Body for the Small-Pox*, published in 1751. In his discourse the Philadelphia physician argued that inoculating a patient in the leg was safer because it was further from the brain and other vital organs in the event of a "serious reaction." Thomson's method proved so effective during the Boston epidemic of 1752 that physicians throughout Europe adopted this "American Method" for smallpox inoculation. However, not all physicians focused their studies on major epidemic diseases. Others devoted their attention to such maladies as lead poisoning, pleurisy, and diphtheria, to name just a few. In all, physicians in the five seaports published more than 23 medical studies between 1743 and 1760.[36]

MEDICAL COLLEGES

The professionalization of medicine is also reflected in the establishment of formal medical colleges in the major urban centers. With the population in the American colonies doubling every generation, there was an increasing need for professionally trained physicians in both the town and countryside. However, only a very small percentage of American families could afford to send a son away to Europe to earn a medical degree. With so few university-trained physicians in America, many communities in the country were left entirely "destitute of all the aids of Medical science," according to one Philadelphia physician. Even in larger towns doctors had no opportunities for medical education, which left them in a "pitiful state of ignorance." To help rectify this egregious problem, two Philadelphia physicians educated at the University of Edinburgh, Drs. William Shippen and John Morgan, established the first medical school in America at the College of Philadelphia in 1765. Two years later New York City established a medical school at King's College, now Columbia University. The two schools offered courses in anatomy, surgery, physiology, pathology, chemistry, and midwifery.

Instructors used cadavers to demonstrate amputations, castrations, trephinings, tonsillectomies, lithotomies, the removal of tumors, and the surgical treatment of hernias, emphysema, and hydrocele. Because the schools did not provide students with cadavers, some resorted to robbing graves to fill this need. Instruction therefore left much to be desired, at least according to one graduate of King's College who claimed that lectures were presented in an "insipid dry & harsh manner." A student at the College of Philadelphia claimed that he "left the university as ignorant as he came there." One graduate was so upset with a particular faculty member that he angrily wrote, "The Devil take him, he got more from me than I ever got from him." Still, within a few years both medical schools were conferring degrees on young men who helped to fill a growing need in America for professional medical care.[37]

MEDICAL CARE FOR THE POOR

Most in need of professional medical care were the urban poor, who suffered most from illnesses, disease, and injuries. Residing in crowded neighborhoods filled with pools of stagnating water, putrid garbage, and dead animals; eating an inadequate diet; sleeping in shacks that provided little protection from the elements; and performing hard and dangerous physical labor—all made the poor more susceptible to illness and injury. In seeking medical remedies for their many maladies, the poor had few options. Relatives and friends were sometimes unable to provide assistance as they were often just as destitute. Many sick poor living in the cities were transients with no relatives and few friends. Most others were the aged, widows, single mothers, and the mentally ill whose poverty prevented them from seeing a physician, most of whom had little concern or charity for those who could not pay their bills. One Philadelphia physician, whenever asked to attend the poor, would drive away the messenger with angry curses. Another doctor, called to attend a poor man who was dying, replied, "then I can do him no service. Let him die, and be damned." Neither could most urban poor grow their own herbs to concoct folk remedies as they generally lived in overcrowded areas that lacked backyards necessary to cultivate a garden. Those who could scrape up a few spare pence might purchase one of the many advertised home-made miracle cures and patent medicines that did more harm than good. The fortunate few were who received medical charity from private groups that opened up those "hospitals" for blacks, sick sailors, and transients.[38]

Supplementing private medical charity were local governments that at times paid a physician a few pounds a year to care for the poor, a paltry sum that did not encourage quality medical care. City governments also auctioned off the sick poor to the lowest bidder, a practice that encouraged miserly care for the patient. Providing little better medical care for the indigent were the hospitals city governments established during the eighteenth century to meet the growing needs of the cities' poor. These early medical facilities were really glorified infirmaries that consisted of a few rooms in the local house of correction. Only Philadelphia built a separate hospital to treat its sick poor. Records from the Pennsylvania Hospital in the mid-1750s show that ulcers were by far the most common ailment among patients (30%), followed by lunacy (12%), dropsy (11%), rheumatism and flux (both 6%), and assorted medical maladies ranging from aneurysm, diseased eyes, fistula, and palsy to vertigo, fracture, uterine disorder, and harelip.[39]

The quality of medical care provided at these infirmaries was generally poor. The warden at Charles Town's public hospital, for example, so badly mistreated the patients that they chose to "beg about the Streets [rather] than to take relief there." Further driving the sick to the streets was the diet given to patients in the Charles Town hospital, which was so inadequate that there were periodic outbreaks of scurvy among the residents. Meanwhile, the hospital in New York City had no regular medical attendant, which may explain why bed linens were seldom washed, bodies were stowed in beds "as thick as they could lie," wrote one eyewitness, and the stench of unwashed bodies caused visitors to vomit. It was simply a "public receptacle for poor Invalids," wrote one physician, "undeserving of the name of an Hospital." As for the medical treatment provided there, the disgruntled doctor added that it was doubtful whether it "be a reproach to the Community or a Benefit to the Patient." Equally reproachable was Philadelphia's public hospital, which so mistreated its patients that city officials complained that "many individuals forewent assistance for long periods rather than endure the prisonlike atmosphere" of the hospital. The only time local governments became aggressive in treating the sick poor was during an outbreak of smallpox, but this concern was more for the welfare of the larger community than the individual poor.[40]

In the end, the negligible medical care received by the poor from both stingy local elites and pinch-penny urban governments did little to alleviate their many life-shortening health problems. The working poor in Philadelphia, for example, were four times more likely than the upper class to die of yellow fever, three times more likely to die in childbirth, and two times more likely to die from tuberculosis. Those who suffered most from inadequate health care were indentured servants whose wealthy masters simply wanted to extract as much labor out of them as possible with a minimum of cost. Treating humans simply in terms of a cost-benefit ratio had tragic results for these unfree peoples, whose life expectancy in Philadelphia was nearly 20 years less than that of their free white counterparts.[41]

CONCLUSION

The conditions that allowed for such stark differences in the health and life expectancies between the rich and poor and the free and unfree were not accidental. They resulted from a practice among political leaders to take a largely laissez-faire approach toward public health. Yet private charity proved inadequate in confronting the growing number of sick poor in the urban centers during the eighteenth century as the well-to-do tended to take a callous view of the indigent, whom they increasingly associated with criminal elements of society. Local governments responded to this failure in charity by providing only token assistance to the sick poor. They also did nothing to stop medical quackery or prohibit the sale of cure-all elixirs that were known by some to be harmful to those who consumed them. Because of their poverty, the urban poor had little alternative but to use the services of medical charlatans and consume poisonous patent medicines that only further ruined their health and shortened their lives. The urban poor therefore learned the hard way that a free-market capitalist approach to medical care, the economy, and the workplace can be hazardous to one's health.

NOTES

1. Peter A. Coclanis, "Death in Early Charleston: An Estimate of the Crude Death Rate for the White Population of Charleston, 1722–1732," *South Carolina Historical Magazine* 85 (1984): 289–91.

2. John Duffy, *Epidemics in Colonial America* (Baton Rouge: Louisiana State University Press, 1953), 48 (quote); John Duffy, *A History of Public Health in New York City, 1625–1866* (New York: Russell Sage Foundation, 1968), 34–35 (quote); Suzanne Krebsback, "The Great Charlestown Smallpox Epidemic of 1760," *South Carolina Historical Magazine* 97 (1996): 35 (quote); Rebecca Tannenbaum, *Health and Wellness in Colonial America* (Westport, CT: Greenwood Press, 2012), 86.

3. Duffy, *Epidemics in Colonial America*, 32; David A. Copeland, *Colonial American Newspapers: Character and Content* (Newark: University of Delaware Press, 1997), 180 (quote); Joyce Goodfriend, "New York City in 1772: The Journal of Solomon Drowne Jr.," *New York History* 82 (2001): 43–44 (quote).

4. Tannenbaum, *Health and Wellness in Colonial America*, 95 (quote); Barbara M. Ward, "Medicine and Disease in the Diary of Benjamin Walker, Shopkeeper of Boston," in *Medicine and Healing*, ed. Peter Benes (Boston: Boston University Press, 1990), 51–53; Copeland, *Colonial American Newspapers*, 182 (quote).

5. Gerald Grob, *The Deadly Truth: A History of Disease in America* (Cambridge, MA: Harvard University Press, 2002), 75–76; Duffy, *Epidemics in Colonial America*, 138–39; Duffy, *History of Public Health in New York City*, 43 (quote).

6. John Duffy, "Yellow Fever in Colonial Charleston," *South Carolina Historical Magazine* 52 (1951): 190–91 (quote); Duffy, *History of Public Health in New York City*, 35 (quote); Grob, *The Deadly Truth*, 76; Joseph P. Waring, *A History of Medicine in South Carolina, 1670–1825* (Columbia: South Carolina Medical Society, 1964), 37 (quote); Robert V. Wells, "A Tale of Two Cities: Epidemics and Rituals of Death in Eighteenth-Century Boston and Philadelphia," in *Mortal Remains: Death in Early America*, ed. Nancy Isenberg and Andrew Burstein (Philadelphia: University of Pennsylvania Press, 2003), 65–66.

7. Duffy, *Epidemics in Colonial America*, 188, 192.

8. Waring, *History of Medicine in South Carolina*, 24.

9. Grob, *The Deadly Truth*, 84–86, 90–91; Duffy, *Epidemics in Colonial America*, 185–88, 214–15, 217 (quote), 221 (quote); Tannenbaum, *Health and Wellness in Colonial America*, 98.

10. Duffy, *Epidemics in Colonial America*, 181 (quote); Ernest Caulfield, "Early Measles Epidemics in America," *Yale Journal of Biology and Medicine* 15 (1943): 534–45; Ernest Caulfield, "Some Common Diseases of Colonial Children," *Publications of the Colonial Society of Massachusetts* 35 (1942): 24–53.

11. Carl Bridenbaugh, *Cities in Revolt: Urban Life in America, 1743–1776* (New York: Capricorn Press, 1955), 317; Duffy, *Epidemics in Colonial America*, 235.

12. Roslyn S. Wolman, "Some Aspects of Community Health in Colonial Philadelphia," Ph.D. dissertation, University of Pennsylvania, 1974), 283–93.

13. Ibid., 332.

14. William Williams, "Independence and Early American Hospitals," *Journal of the American Medical Association* 236 (July 5, 1976): 35 (quote); John Blake, "The Medical Profession and Public Health in Colonial Boston," *Bulletin of the History of Medicine* 26 (1952): 219; Claude E.

Heaton, "Medicine in New York During the English Colonial Period," *Bulletin of the History of Medicine* 17 (1945): 22 (quote).

15. Duffy, *History of Public Health in New York City,* 45 (quote); John Blake, *Public Health in the Town of Boston, 1630–1822* (Cambridge, MA: Harvard University Press, 1959), 15 (quote); Wolman, "Some Aspects of Community Health in Colonial Philadelphia," 256 (quote); John Duffy, *The Sanitarians: A History of American Public Health* (Urbana: University of Illinois Press, 1990), 11–33.

16. Tannenbaum, *Health and Wellness in Colonial America*, 36 (quote); Michael Flannery, "Healers at the Pool of Bethesda: Christian Faith in Anglo-American Medicine," *Fides et Historia* 36 (2004): 39 (quote); Ernest Caulfield, "A History of the Terrible Epidemic, Vulgarly Called the Throat Distemper, as It Occurred in His Majesty's New England Colonies between 1735 and 1740," *Yale Journal of Biology and Medicine* 11 (1939): 252 (quote).

17. David Humphrey, "The King's College Medical School and the Professionalization of Medicine in Pre-Revolutionary New York," *Bulletin of the History of Medicine* 49 (1975): 219 (quote); Genevieve Miller, "Medical Education in the American Colonies," *Journal of Medical Education* 31 (1956): 85; Jane B. Donegan, *Women and Men Midwives: Medicine, Morality, and Misogyny in Early America* (Westport, CT: Greenwood Press, 1978), 95–96; William D. Postell, "Medical Education and Medical Schools in Colonial America," *International Record of Medicine* 171 (1958): 365–66; Martin Kaufman, *American Medical Education: The Formative Years, 1765–1910* (Westport, CT: Greenwood Press, 1976), 6–9.

18. Peter Benes, "Itinerant Physicians, Healers, and Surgeon-Dentists in New England and New York, 1720–1825," in *Medicine and Healing*, ed. Peter Benes (Boston: Boston University Press, 1990), 97.

19. Martha K. Robinson, "New Worlds, New Medicines: Indian Remedies and English Medicine in Early America," *Early American Studies* 3 (2005): 103 (quote); Genevieve Miller, "A Physician in 1776," *Journal of the American Medical Association* 236 (July 5, 1976): 29.

20. Duffy, *Epidemics in Colonial America*, 8 (quote); Duffy, *History of Public Health in New York City,* 63.

21. Duffy, *Epidemics in Colonial America*, 8 (quote); Margaret Coffin, *Death in Early America: The History and Folklore and Superstitions of Early Medicine, Funerals, Burials and Mourning* (New York: Thomas Nelson, 1976), 220; J. Worth Estes, "Patterns of Drug Usage in Colonial America," in *Early American Medicine: A Symposium*, ed. Robert Goler and Pascal Imperato (New York: Fraunces Tavern Museum, 1987), 36, 33; David Cowen, "The Foundations of Pharmacy in the United States," *Journal of the American Medical Association* 236 (July 5, 1976): 83–86; George Gifford Jr., "Botanic Remedies in Colonial Massachusetts, 1620–1820," in *Medicine in Colonial Massachusetts, 1620–1820*, ed. Frederick Allis (Boston: The

Colonial Society of Massachusetts, 1980), 265–68, 275; Robert Goler, "A Household and Its Doctor: A Case Study of Medical Account Books in Colonial America," in *Medicine and Healing*, ed. Peter Benes (Boston: Boston University Press, 1990), 77–80; Kaufman, *American Medical Education*, 11.

22. William Wigglesworth, "Surgery in Massachusetts, 1620–1800," in *Medicine in Colonial Massachusetts, 1620–1820*, ed. Frederick Allis (Boston: Colonial Society of Massachusetts, 1980), 218–24; Duffy, *Epidemics in Colonial America*, 6–7.

23. A. Scott Earle, *Surgery in America* (New York: Praeger, 1983), 2–8.

24. G. B. Warden, "The Medical Profession in Colonial Boston," in *Medicine in Colonial Massachusetts, 1620–1820*, 153 (quote); Robinson, "New Worlds, New Medicines," 97–107; John Blake, "Early American Literature," *Journal of the American Medical Association* 236 (July 5, 1976): 41–45.

25. Tannebaum, *Health and Wellness in Colonial America*, 38 (quote), 43; Patricia Watson, "The 'Hidden Ones': Women and Healing in Colonial New England," in *Medicine and Healing*, 29 (quote); George Dow, *Every Day Life in the Massachusetts Bay Colony* (Boston: Society for the Preservation of New England Antiquities, 1935), 178, 187 (quotes); Coffin, *Death in Early America*, 219–22 (quotes); Herbert C. Covey, *African American Slave Medicine: Herbal and Non-Herbal Treatments* (New York: Rowman & Littlefield, 2007), 23–146.

26. Watson, "The 'Hidden Ones,' " 25–26, 32 (quotes); Tannenbaum, *Health and Wellness in Colonial America*, 160–61; James Volo and Dorothy Volo, *Family Life in 17th and 18th Century America* (Westport, CT: Greenwood Press, 2006), 216.

27. Thomas Horrocks, *Popular Print and Popular Medicine: Almanacs and Health Advice in Early America* (Amherst: University of Massachusetts Press, 2008), 17–19.

28. Ibid., 23.

29. Ibid., 29.

30. Ibid., 82–83, 69–71.

31. Copeland, *Colonial American Newspapers*, 192 (quote); Whitfield Bell Jr., *The Colonial Physician and Other Essays* (New York: Science History Publications, 1975), 14 (quote); Humphrey, "King's College Medical School," 215.

32. Blake, *Public Health in the Town of Boston*, 42 and 43 (quotes); Blake, "Medical Profession in Colonial Boston," 224 (quote); Copeland, *Colonial American Newspapers*, 192 (quote).

33. George Griffenhagen, "Old English Patent Medicines in America," *Pharmacy in History* 34 (1992): 205, 207, and 203 (quotes), 218–19; Wolman, "Some Aspects of Community Health Care in Colonial Philadelphia," 102 (quote); Copeland, *Colonial American Newspapers*, 187–88; Tannenbaum, *Health and Wellness in Colonial America*, 162–63.

34. Kaufman, *American Medical Education*, 11 (quote); Duffy, *History of Public Health in New York City*, 65–66.

35. Blake, *Public Health in the Town of Boston*, 45 (quote); Philip Cash, "The Professionalization of Boston Medicine, 1760–1803," in *Medicine in Colonial Massachusetts, 1620–1820*, 77.

36. Blake, "Diseases and Medical Practice," 360; Bridenbaugh, *Cities in Revolt*, 200–201.

37. Carl and Jessica Bridenbaugh, *Rebels and Gentlemen: Philadelphia in the Age of Franklin* (New York: Oxford University Press, 1965), 287; Postel, "Medical Education in Colonial America," 368–69; Kaufman, *American Medical Education*, 28 (quote); Humphrey, "King's College Medical School," 232.

38. Douglas L. Jones, "Charity, Medical Charity, and Dependency in Eighteenth-Century Essex County, Massachusetts," in *Medicine in Colonial Massachusetts, 1620–1820*, 202–4; Bell, *The Colonial Physician*, 22 (quote); Joseph Waring, "Medicine in Charleston at the Time of the Revolution," *Journal of the American Medical Association* 236 (July 5, 1976): 32.

39. Thomas Purvis, *Colonial America to 1763* (New York: Facts on File, 1999), 177.

40. Waring, *A History of Medicine in South Carolina*, 49 (quote); Tannenbaum, *Health and Medicine in Colonial America*, 195 (quote); Heaton, "Medicine in New York," 15 (quote); Williams, "Independence and Early American Hospitals," 36–37; Jones, "Charity, Medical Charity, and Dependency," 206–11.

41. Billy G. Smith, *The Lower Sort: Philadelphia's Laboring People, 1750–1800* (Ithaca, NY: Cornell University Press, 1990), 55.

13

Recreation

INTRODUCTION

Americans today are spoiled with a nearly endless variety of recreational diversions and considerable leisure time to participate in them. Television, radio, computers, video games, bicycles, automobiles, amusement parks, movie theaters, vacation resorts, museums, novels, and organized sports—all are part of a vast culture of entertainment that consumes much of modern Americans' time, money, and energy. In stark contrast, few people living in colonial cities had the time, money, and energy to cultivate and indulge in many extracurricular activities. A 70-hour workweek, a lack of equipment for games, and clerical disapproval of pointless play kept most urban residents from devoting much time to fun and games. This was particularly true in the early years of colony building when residents spent their limited leisure time toward honing certain survival skills such hunting, fishing, and marksmanship. An occasional recreational holiday and festival interrupted their busy quest for survival.

However, as life in the cities became more settled, secure, and prosperous, residents found more disposable time and money for leisure and created more opportunities for recreation. Additionally, a decline in religious asceticism during the early 1700s contributed to a more positive attitude toward leisure. Instead of viewing idle amusements as "deviltry," a growing number of colonists, including Puritanical Boston ministers, viewed "innocent and moderate recreational pleasures" as both "useful and necessary to soul and body."[1] Together, these new opportunities for and attitudes toward recreation allowed for the development of a leisure revolution in the major cities that by the mid-1700s organized, commercialized, and governed many forms of entertainment. This new "leisure ethic" found expression in a variety of activities, from horse racing, tavern going, musical concerts, theatrical plays, blood sports, and social clubs to billiards, dancing, cricket, bowling, and card playing. All of these recreational activities required multiple participants, thus demonstrating that early Americans were anything but rugged individualists when pursuing pleasure.

This pursuit of pleasure by urban residents differed markedly from that of their country counterparts, whose isolation made it difficult to find companions in play and whose unending toil forced them to mix pleasure with purpose. Farm dwellers occasionally interrupted their daily grind with such dual-purpose relaxations as hunting, fishing, trapping, corn husking, barn raising, and chopping bees. Freed from having to combine work with play, city folk, on the other hand, were allowed to develop a taste for pleasure for its own sake. Urban dwellers also benefitted from living in a culturally diverse setting that introduced a rich array of recreational diversions derived from throughout Europe and Africa. Still, the striking feature of leisure and recreational activities in the colonial cities after 1720 is their similarity. As each city became more Anglicized and grew more prosperous (at least for some) during the course of the eighteenth century, they "all began a parallel effort to imitate the cultural life of the mother country," explains historian Ronald Davis. "As they came more closely to approach their ideal, life in urban colonial America became more cosmopolitan on the one hand, more alike on the other."[2]

However, within the increasingly urbane and unified forms of leisure were important distinctions between classes and genders, distinctions that sometimes added tension and distance between differing groups of people. The urban elite, in particular, cultivated a genteel form of leisure distinct from that of the lower sort, at least in part as a means to demonstrate their alleged superiority and therefore their exclusive right to rule. This attempt by the elites to use recreation partly as a tool for hegemony did not always sit well with some lower-class folk, who sometimes contested their "superiors" over use of particular places for entertainment. Elitism and class warfare therefore exemplified some of the recreation in the colonial cities.

CHILDREN

Recreation and play are most often associated with childhood, a carefree time of life with relatively few responsibilities and considerable idle time. This view may be true for modern-day children but does not apply to colonial-era youth, most of whom did not have carefree, play-filled childhoods. Religious asceticism, the need for a family economy, and a belief that childhood was simply preparation for adulthood limited the ability of children to play. Yet such self-imposed restrictions could not curb children's natural proclivity for play. The major urban centers, in particular, offered many unique opportunities for children to have fun. The numerous doorways, alleys, and hideaways in the cities made hide-and-seek a popular game among urban boys and girls. Other popular amusements enjoyed by both sexes included blind man's bluff, prisoner's base, red rover, hop-scotch, thread the needle, cat's cradles, jump ropes, tag, "I spy," marbles, spin the top, blowing soap bubbles, flying kites, and leap frog. Less familiar to today's children were games such as "button, button," "honey pot," "break the Pope's neck," "pitch and hussel," and "chuck farthing."[3]

The few books written specifically for children beginning in the mid-1700s focused on heavy-handed moral lessons, specifically exhorting their readers to be good, virtuous, and obedient to parents and God or else face eternal damnation in hell. Even if they behaved virtuously, children were taught that they were innately evil. In *The Fairchild Family*, for example, young readers were instructed to memorize the following prayer: "My heart is so exceedingly wicked, so vile, so full of sin, that even when I appear to be tolerably good, even then I am sinning. When I am praying, or reading the Bible, or hearing other people read the Bible, even then I sin. When I speak, I sin; when I am silent, I sin." In this way, children's literature, in a psychologically damaging manner, served less to entertain than to indoctrinate.

By the age of six or seven, recreation for boys and girls became segregated by gender. Much of the recreation for girls centered in the home playing with dolls or in parlor games, activities that were supposed to help prepare them for their later roles as mothers and wives. On the other hand, boys were encouraged to engage in rigorous outdoor play that would help develop the physical strength needed as adults. Accordingly, boys disturbed pedestrians by playing football, stoolball (a forerunner of croquet), and ball and bat and by rolling hoops and rims in the city streets. In the winter both boys and girls in northern cities raced their home-made sleds through town and had snowball fights. Both young and old enjoyed ice skating, a recreational activity brought over by the Dutch. Sadly, some skaters learned the hard way the dangers of "skating on thin ice." Hotter months brought city children to the ocean or nearby rivers and ponds where they swam and took boat rides. More daring boys shinnied up the topmasts of ships anchored in the harbor striving to be the first to place a cap on the tip. From there some thrill-seeking daredevils jumped into the water.[4]

As children grew older and more independent, their amusements sometimes became more lascivious and rebellious. Courting couples walked the city streets in the evenings, while others escaped the watchful eyes of their parents by absconding into the country where they might enjoy a picnic, pick berries, and engage in illicit sex. In 1674 John Loring of Boston was prosecuted for "making Love to & engaging the affections of Mary Willis . . . without her parents consent & after his being forewarned by them." Sometimes leading up to such carnal behavior were "kissing games" that were popular among teenagers. More brazen teenagers openly frolicked and drank in the city streets. As early as the mid-1600s Boston authorities complained of youths who took the liberty to "walke & sport themselves in the streets or fields" where they "disturbed the religious preparations of others, and . . . too frequently repaire to publique houses of entertainment & there sitt drincking." More mischievous youngsters threw snowballs, mud clods, and rocks at horses and their riders. Other pranksters got equal enjoyment by tying fire-crackers to horses' tails or throwing them into houses, knocking on doors and immediately running away, greasing doorknobs, placing manure and greased feathers on door-steps, ringing church bells and crying "fire" late at night, lacing a neighbor's cook pot with tobacco and other nauseating ingredients, and loitering on the streets harassing and frightening pedestrians.[5]

WOMEN

Whereas children enjoyed the greatest opportunities for recreation, women enjoyed the least. An endless variety of labor-intensive tasks consumed nearly all of a woman's waking hours. Further circumscribing women's opportunities for social diversions was an etiquette that considered it inappropriate for respectable women to patronize taverns and other masculine arenas or to engage in sports and most physical recreations. Consequently, women, particularly of the poorer classes, did much of their socializing at home with other women. Here they combined domestic work with pleasure by organizing sewing circles, spinning contests, quilting parties, and candle dippings while exchanging neighborhood gossip. Second to the home in affording women the opportunity for associating with friends was church. Here, before and after the services, women exchanged gossip, discussed scriptures and sermons, met new acquaintances, renewed old ones, and exchanged invitations.

More so than her gender, a woman's wealth and class determined how much time she could devote to pursuits of pleasure. With servants or slaves to perform most of the housewifely duties, colonial gentlewomen had considerable time to socialize and gossip with women who were similarly fortunate. George Bisset of Newport believed the favorite pastime of most local gentlewomen was engaging in "the fashionable topics of slander and defamation." When not gossiping, upper-class women in Newport were also fond of horseback riding. In the spring and summer they often rode out to Hog's Hole, a freshwater pool situated on an ocean cliff, where they drank tea and enjoyed the view. When not visiting or vacationing, many affluent women could be found in the numerous retail shops perusing and purchasing their contents. Shopkeepers tempted women with eye-catching displays of the latest fashions, accessories, and beauty aids. Further tempting urban ladies into shopping was the socializing with other women that often accompanied it, thereby turning a necessary drudgery into a pleasurable pastime. Mary Drinker of Philadelphia went to "sundry shops" with female friends, combining these trips with visits to drink tea and outings to see sights like the "burnt Buildings on Society Hill." Anne Deas of Charles Town confided that on a fine day "I would like very much to go & walk about the town & procure a few things that I want at the shops, & visit my friends." Bringing children along on shopping excursions could be risky business, however, as Margaret Manigault of Charles Town discovered when in a toy shop her young son grabbed hold of a bell and wheedled "Do Mama, buy it for me—Oh do Mama, Do Mama."[6]

Even more tempting to upper-class ladies were the numerous private balls held in the cities, where "the Musick played so sweetly," wrote Eliza Wilkinson of Charles Town, "that I could not keep my feet still." Many women of the patrician class also busied their feet to theatrical performances, plays, and concerts that emerged in the five cities beginning in the early to mid-1700s. The life of an urban lady was so leisured as to cause some women to complain that they spent their lives dealing with "trifles" to become "frivolous creatures" who thought of nothing but "Dress, receiving and returning Visits, tea drinking and Cardplaying" so that a woman's "Time [lay] heavily on hr Hands at Home except there be company to direct her, and her chief delight [was] gadding abroad."[7]

Women of all classes enjoyed walking through the town common with each other or their favorite beau or husband. Cards, chess, backgammon, and billiards were games women shared with men. Women also joined men in sailing and fishing and accompanied them to horse races, resorts, and exhibitions. However, women rarely participated in these public spectacles in the same manner as men as custom relegated them to roles as spectators and cheerleaders. When recreating in mixed company, moreover, all proper young women were urged to "speak little and only where there is a necessity for it," and above all, to speak "with a proper deference, and not to talk on subjects which may be supposed to be out of the reach of ... [their] understanding." Any broadening of women's social lives during the colonial period "came in large measure," according to historian Sheila Skemp, "from their role as ornaments and enhancements to the festivities of men." Still, some women flouted this chauvinism by racing their carriages through city streets and in the winter riding sleighs and skating on frozen ponds.[8]

HOLIDAYS

Early Americans observed fewer holidays than Europeans, largely due to their Protestant beliefs that equated holiday festivals with paganism and sin. This was particularly true concerning the Catholic Church's liturgical cycle of saints' and feast days. Included in this ban were Christmas, Easter, and other religious holidays, which Protestants believed were too "Popish." As a result, early colonists transplanted to America only a fraction of Europe's many folk festivals and seasonal customs. Nevertheless, residents of colonial cities still had numerous opportunities during the year to attend an assortment of public, and largely secular, festivities.[9]

New Year's Day

New Year's Day was a particularly festive celebration for residents in the five major cities when wagonloads of people rode about town in almost a mob-like manner, visiting the homes of acquaintances of everyone in the group. Contributing to the festive atmosphere were the many toasts made as an excuse to consume vast quantities of alcohol. Some of the more intoxicated revelers accentuated their cheers by firing guns into the air.[10]

Election Days

The annual election day was a holiday urban residents enjoyed. Although its purpose was to choose members for public office, and although local ministers began the public holiday with a sermon, the day eventually took on a nonpolitical and unreligious tone that involved drunken revelry that would "dishonor God with great bravery," lamented one Boston minister. Even slaves in Boston and Newport celebrated this day by holding elections of their own "kings" that included a formal inauguration ceremony and parade complete with horses and carriages, the playing of African games, and singing and dancing to music played in a distinctly West African style. One white observer in Newport watching the festivities in 1756 commented: "Every voice in its highest key in all the various languages of Africa mixed with broken and ludicrous English filled the air, accompanied with the music of the fiddle, tambourine, banjo and drum."[11]

Training Day

From four to six times a year the local militia was called together for drills that included going through the manual of arms, marching up and down the town common, and firing their muskets a time or two at targets. Although training day had an important practical purpose, it quickly devolved to become "little other than Drinking Dayes," according to Cotton Mather. After perfunctorily going through their "training," the militia members and spectators let loose with a day-long celebration that often turned into a raucous, drunken affair with men engaging in contests of marksmanship, mock battles, wrestling matches, foot races, jumping contests, and fighting while women sat on the sidelines "watching the boys display their prowess." Afterwards, women and men joined together for a "training day dance" that often developed into more lascivious conduct among some revelers.[12]

Shrove Tuesday

Laborers in Boston celebrated Shrove Tuesday, the day before Ash Wednesday and Lent, by "cock-shailing" in the city streets. This old

English tradition involved a man leading a cock with a bell around its neck down a street followed by several blindfolded men trying to hit the chicken with sticks, stones, and whips with the intention of killing the hapless bird. With the dead chicken in hand, the participants would march off in triumph to celebrate at the nearest tavern. Likewise, the Dutch in New Amsterdam/New York City celebrated Shrove Tuesday not as a religious feast but as an evening of wild extravagance. While adults drank and ate to excess, children walked through the city streets wearing masks and a "devil's suit of clothes" while rattling a pot and singing the following verse:

> I've run so long with the rumbling pot
> And have as yet no money to buy bread,
> Herring-packery, herring-packery,
> Give me a penny and I'll go by![13]

Guy Fawkes Day

A holiday to which all Protestants in all colonial cities looked forward every year was Guy Fawkes Day. This celebration originated with the November 5, 1606, attempt by a Catholic terrorist named Guy Fawkes to blow up Parliament with barrels of gunpowder. However, the discovery of the "gunpowder plot" in the nick of time gave Protestants in England and America a reason to commemorate the failed "Catholic conspiracy" every year with rowdy celebrations that included the firing of cannon, dancing and marching through the city streets, and singing and chanting anti-Catholic slurs while parading effigies of Guy Fawkes, the Pope, and the Devil. Some rougher elements of Boston took the festivities one step further by blackening their faces and arming themselves with sticks and clubs before going to people's houses and demanding money from the residents. Equally unruly mobs from the north and south end of the Puritan capital competed to capture and destroy the other side's straw effigies of the Pope. On one particularly horrific occasion, a group filled their effigy with cats so that when it burned onlookers could be treated to what sounded like "the Pope hissing in agony." Celebrants were witness to a much more tragic event during the 1764 Guy Fawkes Day celebration when a cart carrying the north-end Pope crushed and killed a young boy.[14]

Pinkster Day

A holiday more unique to the colonies was Pinkster Day, an annual celebration held in New York City that merged Dutch and African traditions. Deriving from the Dutch word for Pentecost, Pinkster Day began with religious services on Pentecost Monday followed by a Tuesday holiday of feasting, drinking, and dancing. Local blacks, both free and enslaved, took full advantage of the opportunity to hold a boisterous celebration by dressing in elaborate costumes and dancing to African music in the streets. One white observer noted that the dancing among the couples began slowly but grew gradually more "rapid and furious" so that eventually perspiration flowed "in frequent streams from brow to heel." At times the festivities of the celebrants grew so loud that "they might be heard half a league off," complained one white New Yorker.[15]

Royal Events

Royal anniversaries, the king's birthday, British military victories, and the arrival of new governors were all occasions for residents of the capital cities to celebrate with fireworks, the firing of cannons, the displaying of colors, the illuminating of the town with bonfires and candles, militia units marching through the street to the sounds of drums and trumpets, and other "public demonstrations of joy." Such celebrations were capped by private balls for the gentry and civic banquets for the masses. Here revelers danced, feasted, imbibed countless toasts, and listened to laudatory speeches by public figures. Eventually the festivities spilled from the mansions and taverns back into the streets where the festivities originally began.

Fairs

In the early years of settlement residents of the five cities held annual fairs that drew numerous people from the surrounding region. Most came to enjoy such traditional fair activities as singing, dancing, and music; foot races; boxing and wrestling matches; grinning and whistling contests; watching jugglers, jesters, strong men, dancing bears, fortune tellers, and puppet shows; rope walking; and greased pig contests. All this activity made people hungry, which attracted many food vendors selling such delicacies as waffles, oil fritters, cakes, pastries, cheese, and assorted meat products. Meanwhile, merchants and Native Americans satisfied people's hunger for material goods by selling hand-made trinkets. Younger participants had a hunger of a different type, which they satisfied in part by participating in lascivious "Indian dances" that authorities condemned as "very prejudicial to the adjacent inhabitants."[16]

Carnival Entertainment

As the cities grew in size and wealth, they attracted a growing number of itinerant showmen from abroad who offered a wide variety of carnival-like entertainment. For a small fee, people could gaze at slack-wire performers, contortionists, acrobats, tumblers, jugglers, and magicians. In 1757 many Bostonians left their work to witness the daredevil performances of John Childs, who flew around local church steeples from a long rope attached to the top of the churches. Less thrilling were waxworks of European royalty that made the rounds in the port cities, along with exhibits of exotic animals such as lions, tigers, leopards, electrical fish, porcupines, camels, polar bears, buffalo, ostriches, and monkeys that performed an assortment of tricks. Meanwhile, the more intellectually inclined attended scientific displays that included optical machines, musical clocks, planetariums, microscopes magnifying an assortment of living and dead objects, and depictions of "electrical fluid." In 1764 William Johnson of Newport fascinated the curious with his electrical experiments, one of the more suggestive of which he called "The Salute repulsed, or Fire darting from a Lady's Lips or Cheek, so that she may defy any Gentleman to Salute her."[17]

SADISTIC ENTERTAINMENT

The early modern period proved that one person's suffering was another's entertainment. Moralists, magistrates, and ministers all agreed that criminal behavior was best deterred if all punishments—from public humiliation and whippings to the more gruesome mutilations and executions—occurred in full view of all members of the community, including children. Some city folk relieved their boredom, while perhaps satisfying a sadistic streak, by hurling invectives, rotten vegetables, eggs, and manure at defenseless criminals held in stocks. More bloodthirsty spectators got their kicks watching the convicted get an ear cut off or receive bloody floggings to their bare backs.

The exposed breasts of female flogging victims only added to the excitement of the event for many voyeurs. Even more exciting to some was watching a person condemned to execution kicking and twitching violently at the end of a rope as he or she slowly strangled to death, or in some extreme cases, burned alive at the stake.

Some men quenched their thirst for blood by attending cock-fighting and bull-baiting contests in taverns and back alleys where men bet on which animal would survive in these "death matches." Although some ministers like Increase Mather of Boston condemned these blood sports as counter to God's instructions for men to be "Merciful to his Beast," few colonists questioned the morality of forcing two animals to fight to the death. Neither did colonists see anything immoral with the game "pulling the goose," which involved a rider, while going at a full gallop, trying to pull the head off a greased goose hanging upside down from a tree limb. Equally cruel yet fun to some teenaged boys was "clubbing the cat," a sport in which participants threw clubs at a loosely cooped barrel that contained a cat inside. When the barrel eventually split apart, the "pitchers" chased the dazed cat, throwing stones at the frightened feline until it finally succumbed to the blows.[18]

HUNTING AND FISHING

Living in an urban setting did not stop men in the cities from participating in outdoor sports such as hunting and fishing. Like their rural counterparts, urban men hunted with enthusiasm in the surrounding countryside, shooting at just about anything that moved. Lower-class men used these firearms to hunt for subsistence, while well-fed gentlemen killed deer, bear, turkeys, and other fowl for the sport. Some of the gentry even kept game preserves and deer parks for their uses. By the early eighteenth century, elite men in all the major cities turned hunting into a social outlet by organizing exclusive, all-male hunting clubs and holding fox hunts in an attempt to emulate the English aristocracy. To improve their hunting skills, men held shooting matches in the city commons or even in the streets, where they sometimes fatally shot innocent bystanders. At times even Native Americans demonstrated their marksmanship by staging archery exhibits in the cities in which they shot their arrows at half-pennies put on top of posts. They "hit it so often & shot so true & with such force," remarked one amazed Philadelphian, "as was very surprising."[19]

Goose Pulling, Dutch Style. Some early Americans enjoyed a variety of blood sports involving the torment, torture, and eventual death of assorted animals. One favorite blood sport was pulling the goose, which had different variations to it. In this illustration, some Dutch men try to wring the neck of an upside-down goose tied to a wire while standing in a boat. This version added extra tension and excitement to onlookers as the goose puller risked falling into the water. (Esther Singleton, *Dutch New York* [New York: Dodd, Mead & Co., 1909])

FIELD GAMES

Even though everyday life in the preindustrial era involved considerable physical exertion, urban residents still had the energy to participate in a wide variety of field games played on the town common and other open spaces in the cities. Golf was popular among the gentry, who were the only ones who could afford the expensive equipment imported from Europe. Young men of all classes enjoyed playing field hockey, soccer, cricket, stoolball (a form of croquet), and rounders (similar to modern-day baseball). Much more violent was the ritualized combat of football, in which any number of players lined up against each other and tried to push a ball through their opponents and then past some defined goal line. Equally dangerous to pedestrians was the game "long bullets," whereby contestants slung for distance an artillery object weighing anywhere from one to two pounds up a street or alley. Less harmful to bystanders was pitching quoits, which were iron or wooden rings that the players would attempt to toss on posts. Bowling was a very popular pastime among both the Dutch and English who brought the sport to America in the seventeenth century. A similar game played on special greens or in gardens was "bowls," a game whereby players rolled a wooden bowl (ball) toward a smaller ball (jack) at the opposite end of the green so that the bowl came as close as possible to the jack.[20]

CLASS WAR IN THE STREETS AND COMMONS

As implied above, much recreation took place in the city streets and commons. This was particularly true for lower-class folk, whose homes were either too small or dismal to entertain in. Slaves, servants, and sailors who owned no homes simply sought to remove themselves from the ever-watchful eyes of their masters. For both these groups, the streets and commons became a temporary escape, a place where they could gather to play assorted games, throw dice, race horses, dance, frolic, and occasionally fight. In short, they claimed the streets and commons as their own.

However, this lower-class street life, which could turn raucous as participants often lubricated their recreation with a good deal of alcohol, upset the refined sensibilities of the local aristocracy who sought more peaceful forms of public entertainment. Their attempts at a quiet stroll through town or a staid game of bowls in the commons were often rudely interrupted by the lower sort who competed for the same recreational space. In response, local elites took their complaints to city officials, who issued ordinance after ordinance prohibiting the playing of games in streets. Authorities especially targeted servants and slaves by passing laws preventing them from assembling in large numbers and placing curfews on them. To further reclaim the streets from the lower sort, city governments hired constables to arrest those violating these laws. Such action only drove some street people to the public commons, where they upset their betters with rowdy recreation. In the end, threats of fines and corporal punishment failed to drive the underclass entirely from the streets and commons, forcing the urban elites to eventually concede defeat by pursuing their high-style leisure in exclusive gardens and coffee houses that catered to the well-to-do seeking to further separate themselves from their social inferiors.

GAMBLING

One popular diversion that cut across class, racial, and gender lines was gambling, which added excitement, risk, competition, and the "dream of gain" to many recreational activities. Wagering was the primary point in cock fights, bull baits, and other blood sports. Betting large sums of money on thoroughbred races was a means by which genteel men demonstrated wealth. In taverns men of all classes bet on backgammon, billiards, shuffleboard, dice, and cards. Pitching pennies against a wall was a popular activity among sailors in the cities. Women, too, wagered on both horses and cards. Still, it was men who monopolized gambling in colonial America. For many men, gambling and the socializing associated with it became an addiction that harmed both their finances and their marriages. One disgruntled Charles Town woman married to a gambling addict exclaimed in the local press that such men as her husband "throw away Hundreds, nay Thousands of Pounds, in one evening without the least Remorse, [though] their helpless Infants may suffer for the future by their present Imprudencies." For this reason, among others, church leaders frequently preached against gambling and government authorities sought to restrict gaming and ban certain sporting events that contributed to it. In the end, neither fear of damnation nor threats of fines could curtail gambling, which remained an everyday fixture of colonial life.[21]

WATER SPORTS

Some residents of the port cities took advantage of the nearby ocean, bays, rivers, and ponds to participate in water sports. Boating was popular among all classes, the only distinction being the size of the vessel. The wealthiest enjoyed naval excursions on roomy pleasure boats, while the less affluent plied the waters in crowded canoes, rafts, and rowboats. For those with the ability, swimming was a popular way to spend away a warm afternoon, although respectable women rarely went swimming as contemporaries considered it a tomboyish activity. Much more respectable were the private bathing houses where gentlemen and ladies could swim in safety with cork jackets and afterwards feast on fish, crabs, and lobster.[22]

READING

A recreational activity enjoyed more indoors that outdoors was reading. Although not exclusively an upper-class recreational activity, reading did require the ability to read, some wealth to purchase books, and leisure time to read them—all qualities held most by the well-to-do. The subject matter of books read by the urban gentry was overwhelmingly utilitarian in nature. Of 874 titles in a Boston bookseller's invoice of 1685, 391 were schoolbooks, 311 religious works, 50 books on navigation, and 36 works on law, with the remaining 21 equally distributed among medicine, history, and military science. Of these, the Bible was the most read, but published sermons against temptations, sin, and assorted evils were also popular reading material among the literate, who were attracted to the often lurid and titillating material of their contents. Masturbation, for example, was the subject of many published sermons. One diatribe against "onanism" sold over 15,000 copies in New England alone, a bestseller for the day. Seventeenth-century New Englanders also enjoyed reading handbooks on how to die, funeral sermons, and elegies for important leaders. Courting young men and women, who often held reading parties, preferred salacious, bawdy books; Indian captivity tales with details of sexuality and torture; and confessions of notorious criminals that gave lurid accounts of horrible deeds intended to lead readers to a more pious path. This was the theme of popular books like Lewis Bayly's *Practice and Piety,* John Bunyan's *Pilgrim's Progress,* and John Foxe's *Book of Martyrs,* where readers could find edifying lessons in ethics and good morality. Equally edifying and almost as popular were historical works, both classical and modern. From Greek and Roman historians like Herodotus, Tacitus, and Polybius, colonists drew lessons of statecraft. Likewise, Sir Walter Raleigh's *History of the World,* Bishop Gilbert Burnet's *History of the Reformation in England,* and many other histories were popular among the learned for their instructive value. Other practical works that colonists bought and treasured were courtesy manuals for aspiring ladies and gentlemen, medical books offering the latest remedies, legal handbooks, military manuals, and guides on navigation and surveying.

Trends in reading shifted away from the pious during the eighteenth century as society in general, particularly in the major urban centers, grew more secular. Some of the most popular and influential writers in the early 1700s were Joseph Addison and Richard Steele, producers of the *Tatler* and *Spectator* magazines. These English organs contained moral and social lessons penned in a plain yet entertaining style that found numerous imitators among colonial writers, including Benjamin Franklin. The plays of William Shakespeare; the poetical works of George Herbert, Francis Quarles, and Abraham

BOOKS,

SOLD by B. FRANKLIN, at the Post-Office in Philadelphia.

BAILEY's ⎱
Dyche's ⎰ Dictionaries.
Cole's
English ⎱
Latin & ⎰ Grammars.
Greek
Ruddiman's Rudiments,
Stirling's Cato,
English Bibles of all sorts,
French & Welsh Bibles,
Psalters,
Primers,
Tatlers,
Guardians,
Independant Whig,
Persian Tales,
Chinese Tales,
Don Quixot,
Æsop's Fables,
Shaftbury's Characteristics,
Herodotus in English,
History of Tamerlain,
------of Genghizzcan,
Herrera's History of America,
Vertot's Revolutions of Rome
   Sweden and Portugal,
Lahontan's Voyages,
Boyle's Philosophy abridged by
   Dr. Shaw, 3 Vols. Quarto,
Boyle's theological Works in
   3 Vols. Octavo,
Gravesande's Philosophy,
Ward's Mathematics,
Wingate's Arithmetic,
Mott's mechanic Powers,
Builders Dictionary,
Langley's Architecture,

Switzer's Water-works,
Love's Surveying,
Whole Body of Arts 2 Vols.
   Octavo.
Rollin's Belles Letters,
Woodward on Fossils,
Fuller's Medicina gymnastica
Keil's Animal Oeconomy,
Clarendon's History,
Monteth's Memoirs,
Ray on the Creation,
Newton's Chronology on large
   Paper,
Cato's Letters,
Young Man's Companion,
Fisher's best Ditto,
Religion of Nature delineated,
Hutcheson of Beauty & Virtue,
Campbel on moral Virtue,
Lucas's Enquiry after Happi-
   nefs,
Epictetus's Morals,
Sherlock on Judgment,
Ditton on the Refurrection,
Fofter's, ⎱
Tillotfon s ⎰ Sermons.
Whitefield's

   Where may be also had,
great Variety of other Books
of Ethics, Natural Philofo-
phy, Mathematics ; and Claf-
fics, with Delphin and Vario-
rum Notes, very reafonably.
   Alfo Stationary Ware of all
Sorts.
   And POCKET
ALMANACKS, for 1743.

Advertisement for a List of Books sold in B. Franklin's Print Shop. This advertisement for books sold by Benjamin Franklin in his Philadelphia print shop shows the enormous variety of reading material available to residents of the five cities, at least for those with the ability, leisure, and money to purchase and read books.

Cowley; and classics by John Milton, Thomas More, Francis Bacon, Edmund Spencer, Jonathan Swift, and Laurence Stern were read by colonists with an advanced literary taste. Nonfiction works by Michel Montaigne, René Descartes, John Locke, and others also predominated among the urban intelligentsia.

Less refined readers like servants, sailors, and rebellious young people, on the other hand, found escape in numerous lurid, exotic, mysterious, and sensational books and pamphlets imported from Europe during the eighteenth century. Booksellers in the major cities sold a whole range of classical and modern homoerotic texts; prostitution adventure narratives; trial reports containing salacious details of murder, seduction, and sexual assault; travel accounts of strange lands; accounts of death experiences; and the latest medical quackery like *A Treatise Proving that Most of the Disorders Incident to the Fair Sex Are Owing to Flatuancies Not Seasonably Vented*. Even more popular among common folk were almanacs, first published in the colonies in 1639, which contained original poetry, moral precepts, humorous essays, pithy proverbs, tall tales, sexually suggestive jokes, and adventure narratives often involving Native Americans. More serious but less popular were American magazines, first produced in Philadelphia in 1741, that were modeled on London magazines. They included poetry and satirical pieces and essays on history and science, along with subjects of local interest such as government, agriculture, trade, religious controversies, manufacturing, and money. Finally, colonial newspapers, most of which were published in the five principal cities, contained material that found appeal among both the urban grandees and literate lower sort—governors' proclamations and excerpts from legislative journals, local news (including weddings, deaths, and assorted tragedies), unusual incidents reported from other colonies, poems, satirical pieces, serious essays on a variety of subjects, and advertisements for runaway servants and wives, slave sales, lotteries, sporting events, cultural announcements, lists of imported goods for sale, and services offered by school teachers, dancing and music masters, and various tradesmen.[23]

ELITE RECREATION

As implied in the introduction to this chapter, urban elites enjoyed distinctive forms of recreation from their social inferiors. This was intentional as the urban aristocracy sought to distance themselves from their social inferiors during their leisure hours, or if joining the lower ranks in recreation, to display a cultural superiority to them. To help support their claims to the highest social status, the urban gentry nurtured a specific code of manners and cultivated skills that required considerable time and money only available to the moneyed class. To that end, ladies and gentlemen learned to dance, ride, and play musical instruments from experts who taught these skills for a fee. The most cultivated gentlemen also learned to fence. The upper class considered these skills the epitome of culture and refinement. Conversely, those lacking these traits belonged to the vulgar masses. Not wanting to rub elbows with their uncultured inferiors, the urban aristocracy restricted participation in their recreational activities to members of their own class. These exclusive social activities helped to both bind members of the upper class together and protect their social hegemony from unwanted encroachments by the lower sort.

Winter Season

Like their British counterparts, the colonial urban aristocracy organized an exclusive social world around two "seasons": the winter season featuring recreational activities in the city and a summer season spent in the country at estates and spas. During the winter months the urban upper crust attended exclusive musical concerts (elaborated below) intended not just to entertain but also to construct more rigid social ranks. At least this was the belief of one "Tom Trueman," who wrote in the Philadelphia press that concert subscribers were people who "publickly stile themselves, exclusive of all others, the BETTER SORT of People" who "look on the Rest of their Fellow Subjects . . . as Mob and Rabble."[24]

Equally elitist and exclusive were formal dancing assemblies established by the well-to-do, who paid a yearly fee to help subsidize the cost of refreshments and rental of an appropriate room where they danced, played cards, and gossiped. Cultivating this elitism were dance schools like the one run by Mary Cowley of Newport, who welcomed only "Gentlemen and Ladies of Family Character." Further restricting membership were assembly directors who tightly controlled the guest list, which read like a social register of political and economic leaders and their families. The exclusivity of the balls made them the highlight of the winter season and highly popular among the local aristocracy. One male subscriber to the Philadelphia Dancing Assembly reported in 1749 that the group held "a very handsome assembly once a fortnight . . . It consists of eighty Ladies & as many Gentlemen." The event, he added, was "extremely sociable chearful & good natur'd." Less good natured was the intense judging of dress and dancing skills that accompanied this arena of social display and performance. In their public performance, both men and women attending balls were seeking to solidify their own personal claims to elite status while enjoying the close physical company of the opposite sex. To encourage proper decorum on the dance floor, some dance clubs admonished men against taking "indecent Liberty or Familiarity" with the ladies.[25]

Another recreational arena of public performance among the urban elite was the theater, discussed in greater detail below. More edifying than entertaining were public lectures conducted by learned men. For a fee, one could listen to talks on history and philosophy or see displays of electricity and medicine. Some of the city's more scientifically inclined even formed scientific groups, whose well-educated members gathered and discussed information in a leisured and social atmosphere of dining and drinking. The educated elite also formed exclusive library companies, whose members were limited to subscribers who paid a yearly fee and passed a vetting process conducted by the company's directors. The rooms of these private libraries were as much places for socializing as learning, for they "served as a convenient place for the city's prominent people to read and socialize," explains historian Sarah Fatherly, "to see and be seen."[26]

Summer Season

When winter eventually gave way to summer, the urban aristocracy fled the city to their genteel country estates that dotted the surrounding hinterland. Encouraging them to escape to their rural mansions was the increasing hustle and bustle of city life as commerce hit its peak season and as the rising temperatures intensified the noxious odors wafting through the streets. Disease, too, seemed to flourish more during the summer. The urban upper crust therefore built rustic retreats complete with ha-has, meadows, and open gardens that provided an ideal pastoral setting for devoting long periods of time in intellectual work. Elizabeth Hudson of Philadelphia believed that because reading was "very Ingrossing both of our time & thoughts," it needed to be done in a place of "retirement," that is, a "country estate." Men and women of fortune also devoted numerous hours writing poetry and prose or simply

Photograph of the Redwood Library, Newport. Established in 1747 by
Newport native Abraham Redwood, the Redwood Library is the oldest
lending library in the United States and the oldest library building in continuous use in the country. Newport architect Peter Harrison designed the
library in the Georgian-Palladian style. It is considered the first classical
public building in America and a work of architectural beauty. Both in its
classical architecture and the original collection of 751 titles it housed, the
Redwood Library reflected the growing culture and desire for knowledge
among the city's middling and upper classes. The library was a self-
supporting enterprise and was therefore reserved for the enjoyment
of the more affluent residents. The library lent only to subscribers, who had
to pay an annual fee to retain their membership. (Library of Congress,
Prints and Photographs Division, HABS RI, 3-NEWP, 15-3)

penning long letters to friends and relatives. When not reading or
writing, the upper ranks organized festive traveling parties that visited the growing number of country estates outside the cities.
Hannah Callender of Philadelphia, for one, enjoyed the "mirth on
the road" while traveling to the Hamilton family's Bush Hill estate,
while Edward Burd got "much pleasure" from the "company of so
many young People" on a trip to a "young Gentleman's Country
Seat" outside the Pennsylvania capital. Once at their destination,

visitors immediately began the main reason for their visit—to critique the quality of the home, its furnishings, and the surrounding grounds. Hannah Callender was impressed with one country home for its fine paintings, bronze statues, and hallways tastefully "adorned with instruments of music, coat of arms, crests and other ornaments." Far from considering these visits an intrusion, the owners of these country estates welcomed them as a means to publicly display their wealth and taste and thereby enhance their claims to elite status. Some hosts were so eager to show off their silver dining and tea settings that they broke social etiquette by serving dinner at an inappropriate time and tea in an inappropriate setting, behavior that displayed a "shallow elegance."[27]

When not touring and critiquing country estates, the urban leisured class participated in a growing spa culture. During the eighteenth century savvy entrepreneurs used natural springs to spur a fad for water spas among the well-to-do who summered in the country. Typical was the Yellow Springs spa near Philadelphia, where well-to-do guests took in the "special waters," relaxed in heated baths, walked through peaceful meadows and woods, and danced and dined in an opulent hall. Some families spent their entire summers bathing, socializing, and relaxing at these water resorts. Whether they stayed just a few days or a few months, vacationers met and socialized with fellow elites from far and wide. While at the Bristol Bath north of Philadelphia, Elizabeth Drinker socialized with fellow Philadelphians; visitors from nearby New York, New Jersey, and Maryland; and some travelers as far away as North Carolina and Jamaica. Such extensive recreating encouraged a growing class consciousness and unity among America's aristocracy.[28]

Horse Racing

Falling between the winter and summer recreational seasons was the racing of thoroughbred horses, the "sport of kings." Whereas ordinary men (and some women) enjoyed racing their nags in the city streets, the elites promoted a highly formal, regulated, and public form of horse racing intended to distance themselves further from the lower classes while presenting themselves as members of an American aristocracy. This was especially true in New York and South Carolina, where horse racing became an obsession among the ruling elite who wagered enormous sums on the speed of their thoroughbreds. These race meets were some of the most important social events of the year as they included considerable high social drama, particularly for the gentry who sought to use the highly visible special occasions to help solidify their social dominance. This dominance is illustrated in elevated and exclusive seating that allowed the elites to literally stand above the unwashed masses. The gentry also reminded the lower sort of their inferior status by limiting thoroughbred contests to the upper class. After all, one gained respect and honor only by victories over one's equals, never by competing against inferiors. In promoting these great public displays, the local aristocrats "helped convince subordinate groups that the gentry culture was something to be esteemed," explains historian Timothy Breen. "By conceding the superiority of gentry culture, the common people were more likely to acquiesce in the gentry's control of the political and economic life of the colonies." For the elites, recreation was part of a larger culture of power intended to solidify their hegemony.[29]

Clubs

Upper-class men also promoted elitism in their leisure by forming exclusive social organizations. The names of some of the clubs— the Smoking Club, the Laughing Club, the Convivial Club, the Philosophical Club, the Marine Society, the Ugly Club, the Knights Terrible, the Mount Regal Fishing Club, the Physical Club, the Hunting Club, the Dancing Assembly, the Flying Club, and the Jockey Club—reveal the interests and activities of their members. Despite the differences in name, these clubs and their members shared some commonalities that included meeting regularly in a local tavern or coffee house catering to the wealthy to talk business, play cards, throw dice, and especially drink. One group of New York City free blacks and slaves subverted class order by forming their own club that mocked the rituals and drunken debauchery of genteel club meetings. For this disrespectful behavior toward their "betters," members of the all-black Geneva Club were brought before the New York Supreme Court and chastised for their "impudence." Less offensive to urban elites were the many artisan groups who formed their own private clubs. Charles Town craftsmen, for instance, organized the Carpenters Society, the Master Tailors' Society, and the Barbers' Society, all of which sought to promote the welfare of their members and the advancement of more popular participation in government.[30]

THEATER

Another popular form of entertainment in the principal cities, and one that further hardened class lines, was the theater. As a formal form of entertainment, the theater developed late in the colonial period due in part to northern religious leaders who believed that the "wanton gestures, amorous kisses, lascivious whorish actions ... and witty obscenities" in modern plays posed a threat to morals, and partly due to the reputation of traveling actors as immoral vagabonds and debtors. As a result, urban residents were almost totally dependent on "alien plays and players" from England. Genteel Americans, additionally, believed in the superiority of English culture in all its forms and did their best to emulate it. Two exceptions were in Boston and Newport, whose leaders banned the theater because they believed plays "sucked out of the Devil's teats to nourish us in idolatrie, heathenrie, and sinne." The theater met with greater acceptance in Philadelphia—despite some opposition from local Quakers who viewed the theater as "synagogues of Satan"—and in New York and Charles Town, both of which lacked a tradition of religious asceticism. Beginning in the 1740s London theatrical groups regularly toured these cities performing such popular plays as "The Provok'd Wife," "The Suspicious Husband," "The Fair Penitent," "Hamlet," "The Gamester," "Romeo and Juliet," "The Mourning Bride," and "A Wonder! A Woman Keeps a Secret!" Interspersed between the acts were various side-show entertainments: acrobatics, magic shows, firework displays, Indian war dances, slack-wire dancing, "Punch and Judy" puppet shows, and muscular feats. [31]

The theater, like most else in colonial society, was segregated by class. The well-to-do sat in expensive and exclusive box seats in the front of the theater while working-class folk were relegated to the cheap seats in the balcony, where they often created a noise "not unlike Noah's ark in their imitation of the whistles and yells of every kind of animal." These "ruffians in the gallery" also did not hesitate to hurl rotten produce and invectives at the manager and actors if they refused shouted requests for plebeian ballad operas, which contained "street tunes" and "strong doses of theatrical vulgarity." Meanwhile, the genteel could be just as annoying with their habit of wandering on stage with the actors in order to "better display their fine clothing." Disruptions to performances sometimes became so frequent that stage managers hired constables to apprehend and eject troublesome offenders. However, these disturbances were mild compared to the violence against the stage in

New York City in 1766 when a plebeian mob, upset over the performance of extravagant plays at a time when "great numbers of poor
people can scarce find a means of subsistence," stormed the play-
house and dismantled it piece by piece before burning it in a huge
bonfire. In destroying this symbol of perceived elitism, these not-
so-deferential common folk were giving their social superiors a
powerful lesson in morality.[32]

Middle–Class Opposition

As the above anecdote illustrates, many common folk were disgusted by the urban elite's hedonistic and luxurious lifestyle. This
was particularly true among the emerging middling sort who lived
by a different set of cultural values that emphasized hard work,
frugality, and altruism. In Charles Town, for example, middle-class
tradesmen, shopkeepers, and ministers showed little deference
toward their superiors by publicly railing against the overindulgence
of rich planter-merchants in their urbane pleasures and their vanity
and fashion that they believed undermined the health of the entire
body politic. Most vocal and persistent in their discontent were dissenting ministers like Josiah Smith, who largely blamed the local
elite's dissolute lifestyle for the 1740 fire that destroyed much of
Charles Town. According to Smith, the Charles Town aristocracy were
an overly proud and vain class who were addicted to the "Vices of the
Age"—costly clothing, furniture, china, paintings, jewelry, and other
"tinkling ornaments"—and an "abundance of idleness" that included
billiard tables, cards, dice, balls, and night-time assemblies that were
"an abomination to God." Such moral indictments fell on deaf ears
as Charles Town's privileged class continued to engage in a whirlwind of hedonistic self-indulgence. More than 30 years later the
Baptist minister Oliver Hart, a transplanted Pennsylvanian from
humble origins, published a sermon viciously attacking the local elite
for devoting so much of their time and money to attending balls,
assemblies, concerts, and the theater, a profligate lifestyle that he
believed brought on "the destruction of soul and body."[33]

MUSIC

Residents of the five cities enjoyed listening to a wide variety of
music in their daily lives. In the streets, homes, and workplaces
one could hear people singing, in a variety of foreign tongues,
bawdy Elizabethan ballads; Scottish, Swedish, and German folk

Table 13.1. From Scripture to Psalm

King James Version	Bay Psalm Book
The Lord is my shepherd;	The Lord to me a shepherd is
I shall not want;	Want Therefore shall not I.
he maketh me to lie down	He in the folds of tender grass
in green pastures;	Doth make me down to lie.

songs; and African music with its unique antiphonal (call-and-response) interaction. Contrasting with this vernacular music was the high-styled music of the European masters, whom the urban genteel classes, in their attempt to cultivate an air of sophistication and superiority, viewed as the only tunes "appropriate for their public amusements." While in church, people of all classes sang psalms and hymns, which were accompanied by a variety of musical instruments by the eighteenth century. This rich diversity of music in the cities contributed to what historian Cynthia Hoover has described as a "split musical personality."[34]

Church Music

An important part of each city's "musical personality" was church music. Singing in church was a part of nearly all religious services, except for those of the Quakers, who preferred to worship unhindered by hymns and instrumental music. Even New England Puritans appreciated good music and enjoyed singing psalms in church, which they believed were the "noblest form of musical expression."[35] To that end, residents of Boston and Newport utilized the 150 religious psalms included in the *Bay Psalm Book*, published in 1640 in Cambridge, Massachusetts. The psalms were essentially Biblical texts set to verse, set in four-line stanzas and cast in common meter. Table 13.1 compares a text of the Bible (King James Version) with its equivalent in the *Bay Psalm Book*.[36]

However, because the *Bay Psalm Book* contained no music and many could not read either music or printed English, deacons would "line out the psalms" by singing the psalm line by line, pausing for the congregation to repeat the line they had just sung. Not only did this back-and-forth process slow the pace of singing, it left songs "to the mercy of every unskillful throat to chop and alter, to twist and change," opined one critic, which resulted in music "miserably tortured and twisted and quavered . . . into a medley of confused and disorderly voices."[37]

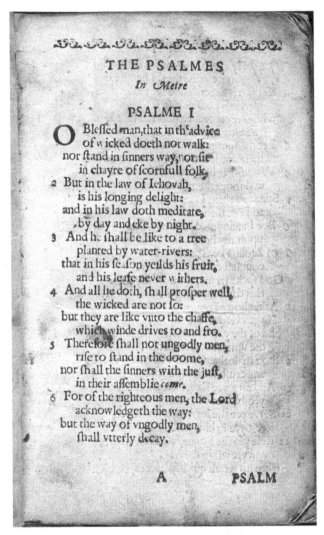

THE PSALMES

In Metre

PSALME I

O Blessed man, that in th'advice
of wicked doeth not walk:
nor stand in sinners way, nor sit
in chayre of scornfull folk.
2 But in the law of Iehovah,
is his longing delight:
and in his law doth meditate,
by day and eke by night.
3 And he shall be like to a tree
planted by water-rivers:
that in his seafon yeilds his fruit,
and his leafe never withers.
4 And all he doth, shall prosper well,
the wicked are not fo:
but they are like vnto the chaffe,
which winde drives to and fro.
5 Therefore shall not ungodly men,
rise to stand in the doome,
nor shall the sinners with the just,
in their assemblie come.
6 For of the righteous men, the Lord
acknowledgeth the way:
but the way of vngodly men,
shall vtterly decay.

A   PSALM

Page from *The Whole Book of Psalmes Faithfully Translated into English Metre* **(1640).** The first book still in existence published in British North America is The Whole Book of Psalmes Faithfully Translated into English Metre, published in Cambridge, Massachusetts, in 1640. The principle author and translator was Richard Mather, who received assistance from 30 other New England ministers. The psalms themselves are metrical translations contorted into vernacular poetry meant to be sung as hymns during religious services. In fact, *The Whole Book of Psalmes* included a lengthy treatise on the lawfulness and necessity of singing psalms in church. (Library of Congress, Rare Book and Special Collections Division, Online Catalog)

This tortured singing eventually inspired Puritans in Boston to reform the "Old Style" of singing in church with a "Regular Way" that
emphasized the uniformity of notated music. By the 1720s itinerant
music masters, many from England, established singing schools in
Boston and Newport to teach the faithful how to read music and
sing in key. These singing schools injected much energy and excitement into the social life in the two northern cities. "I have no inclination for anything," wrote one young Boston man, "for I am almost
sick of the world and were it not for the hope of going to singing-
meeting tonight and indulging myself in some of the carnal delights
of the flesh, such as kissing, squeezing, etc., I should surely leave it
now." Evidently more went on in singing schools than simply training voices. Still, the improvement in singing led to the emergence of
choirs whose members sometimes sought to monopolize singing in
church. A critic in 1764 referred to one choir group in Boston as "a
set of Geniuses who stick themselves up in a Gallery" and who
"seem to think that they have a Privilege of engrossing all the singing to themselves . . . by singing such Tunes, as is impossible for
the Congregation to join in." Accompanying the elitist-minded
choirs were a variety of musical instruments, from tuning forks,
flutes, and fiddles to oboes, clarinets, and bassoons. However, one
musical instrument Puritans absolutely refused to allow in church
was the organ, which they believed symbolized the hated musical
traditions of the Roman Catholic Church.[38]

Residents of the other cities, which lacked a tradition of Puritan
asceticism, did not experience the struggle over music in church as
did their neighbors to the north. Anglicans, who followed a liturgical
cycle closely resembling that of the Catholics, had few reservations
over musical expressions in church so long as they were "dignified
and in good taste." Similarly, the Moravians adored music in all its
forms and took church singing as an art form. Equally enthusiastic
about music in their worship were the Germans and Swedes, who
sang hymns from the mother country accompanied by church organs
they brought from Europe. One Swedish pastor in Philadelphia took
church singing so seriously that he imposed a fine of six shillings on
members of his congregation for "untimely singing."[39]

Secular Music

Refinement in church music was soon followed by a growing
elegance in secular music. This was particularly true among the
urban elite, who considered the ability to sing and play a musical

instrument as an essential social grace and an important mark of social distinction. To help them achieve this social distinction, professional musicians, many from Europe, established musical schools in the cities that catered to the local aristocracy. These urban music schools, in turn, encouraged the production of public musical concerts performed by groups of amateur and professional musicians. Many of the earliest musical performances were "benefit concerts," one-time happenings performed by a local organists, itinerant musicians, or newly arrived singers who arranged the events for personal profit. Other concerts were charity benefits given to raise money for worthy causes. Only in the late colonial period did upper-class music lovers create musical societies comprised of dues-paying members who sought to promote the art. The first of these was the St. Cecilia Society, formed in Charles Town in 1762. It supported an orchestra of paid musicians who gave regular fortnightly concerts in European classical music for the well-to-do members, who attended the events "dressed with richness and elegance." The elegant dress of music lovers did not necessarily match their behavior, at least according to one disgruntled New York City concertgoer who complained that instead of hearing "a modest and becoming silence" at a recent concert, "nothing is heard during the whole performance but laughing and talking very loud, squawling, overturning the benches . . . behavior more suited to a broglio than a musical entertainment." Despite the lack of decorum at these events, music was a means by which the elite promoted an aristocratic social image; as such, it was the "special ornament of the wealthy," explains music scholar Ronald Davis, "who hovered over it and smothered it like the dilettantes they were."[40]

While the upper class supported European classical music, the remaining city folk preferred humming and singing folk songs and ballads brought over from the Old World. Even the Puritans of Boston had a sizable store of "neat and spruce ayres." Throughout the cities one could hear numerous craftsmen, servants, and slaves singing and whistling a variety of tunes while they went about their work, sailors singing their risqué chanties along the waterfront, urban youth singing sentimental and bawdy ballads in the streets, mothers humming lullabies to their children in their homes, and drummers tapping out military music during militia marches. But perhaps the real center of popular music in the cities was the tavern, a natural gathering place where drunkenness and rowdiness were tolerated, if not outright encouraged. Part of the rowdiness in these "dens for the idle" was boisterous and out-of-tune singing of earthy ballads like "Kiss Me Quick, My Mother's Coming," "Our Polly Is a Sad Slut," "Bonny Lass under a Blanket," and "Sweetest When She's Naked." It was partly for this reason that ministers frequently warned their congregations against taverns, which they claimed were havens for "bad Company" who had a "greater relish . . . for filthy Songs and Ballads than for the Holy Scriptures."[41]

DANCING (NON-ELITE)

Because of its tendency to promote intimacy between the sexes, Puritan ministers and Quaker leaders also warned others against dancing. Such warnings went increasingly unheeded as colonists used just about every kind of social activity—from weddings and turtle frolics to holidays and royal celebrations—as an excuse to dance. Sailors, inebriated with alcohol, performed "dueling jigs" in low-end taverns. Young men and women, in particular, were notorious for secretly gathering in private to participate in more salacious "gynecandrical dancing." Even African slaves in Charles Town held informal dances on weekend nights. A local newspaper in 1772 described such a "Country Dance" among blacks that consisted of about 60 people "provided with Music, cards, Dice, &c." Part of the entertainment included men and women satirizing the dancing styles of their masters and mistresses. By burlesquing white manners and pretensions, Charles Town slaves were able to, in the words of historian Richard Crawford, "claim a cultural power that white hegemony could neither control nor eradicate."[42]

DRINKING CULTURE AND TAVERN LIFE

As the above narrative suggests, many recreational activities among adults included the consumption of alcohol. No celebration, festival, holiday, sporting event, business transaction, political campaign, or social gathering would be complete without vast quantities of liquor. This circumstance compelled the Boston minister Benjamin Wadsworth in 1730 to ask the rhetorical question: why was it that all who "[enter into] a bargain, make up accounts, pay or receive a little money, but that they must need to go to a tavern, and solemnize the matter as it were by swallowing strong drink?" Part of such complaints from ministers derived from the concern that taverns had a much stronger attraction than churches. The fact that taverns greatly outnumbered churches in the major urban centers gave legitimacy to such concerns. Even Puritan Boston in 1737 had one licensed tavern for every 25 adult males![43]

Not to be confused with the modern bar where people go to drink and socialize, taverns served a multitude of purposes: as eating and sleeping establishments, places where a weary traveler could find a meal and a bed far from home; as places of entertainment where people could play billiards, cards, backgammon, shuffleboard, attend concerts and balls, bet on a cock fight, watch sideshow curiosities like tightrope walkers, acrobats, magicians, and animal tricks, or simply read a newspaper; as meeting places for exclusive gentlemen's clubs, whose members mixed altruism with alcohol; as places of business, where merchants, ships' captains, and planters transacted much of their business; as auction houses, where people could bid on slaves, horses, furniture, boats, and sundry other items; as classrooms, where teachers and dance masters sometimes taught their pupils; as political meeting places, where candidates politicked among the "rabble" and local politicians sometimes held their meetings; and even as courthouses, where local judges and juries determined the fate of accused criminals, undoubtedly at times under the fog of inebriation.

As the center of business, government, and social life of the cities, taverns attracted a diverse clientele. A visitor to Philadelphia in 1744 found in a local tavern a very mixed company of different nations and religions. There were

Scots, English, Dutch, Germans, and Irish; there were Roman Catholics, Church Men, Presbyterians, Quakers, Newlight men, Methodists, Seventh Day men, Moravians, Anabaptists, and one Jew. The whole company consisted of twenty-five planted round an oblong table in a great hall well stocked with flies. The company divided into committees in conversation; the prevailing topic was politics and conjectures of a French war. A knot of Quakers there talked only about selling of flour and the low price it bore. They touched a little upon religion, and high words arose among some of the sectaries, but their blood was not hot enough to quarrel...[44]

This mixed company also extended to sleeping accommodations, in which strangers shared the same room and often the same bed, a practice commonly referred to as "pigging together." Even female travelers expected to share their rooms, and sometimes their beds, with strange men. Such arrangements made for some rather "strange bedfellows," to say the least. One traveler staying overnight in a Boston tavern complained that he was "disturbed by some privateers who brought theyr girles thither to make merry and were so till 2 in the morning in the same room where I was in bed." And because bathing was not a common practice and sheets were laundered infrequently, patrons also had to share their dirty and foul-smelling beds with bed bugs, lice, and other six-legged vermin that left bloody bites all over their bodies. One traveler staying in a New York City tavern noted that it was "as vile a house as I would ever wish to be in," and added that his horse had the "better end of the bargain."[45]

Of course, the main attraction at any tavern was alcohol. To slake their thirst, taverngoers consumed large quantities of cheap rum and beer, or if they could afford it, the more expensive wines and spirits. Heavy drinking was a requirement of the tavern experience, encouraged by the ritual of toasting to health, fortune, or anything else drunken revelers could think of to justify taking another swig of alcohol. In New Amsterdam men drank the "clover leaf," consuming three drinks in quick succession, as the saying was that all good things came in threes. Male taverngoers, already filled with too much drink, sometimes made deadly bets with each other to see who could down the most alcohol. Excessive alcohol consumption undoubtedly encouraged the numerous and assorted hi-jinks inflicted on unsuspecting and inebriated customers. A group of heavy drinkers in a Philadelphia tavern "got to making Sport" with one of their drunken companions by tripping his heels and throwing him down on the floor repeatedly, abuse that led to the poor man's death. Heavy drinking, especially in working-class and sailors' taverns, often led to drunken brawls that could prove just as fatal. More salacious were inebriated female taverngoers who sometimes allowed men to take turns gleefully measuring a portion of their anatomy with their hands to see who could come closest to the exact measurements, a game appropriately called "grading the beef." One female participant from Boston noted that "Ladies were normally permitted to keep on their stocking," but added that "when my turn came about, and I was last, decided since I was so lit up by the drink to remove my stockings and have myself measured about the thighs—which broke up the roister and sent us all home in a merry mood." Other tavern revelers were not so merry after closing time and continued their riotous and destructive behavior when they stumbled into the streets and proceeded to break windows and lamps, enter people's homes to demand drink, and assault constables attempting to quell the violence. [46]

Recognizing the vast number of "tippling houses" in the cities as "nurseries of vice and debauchery," local officials sought to regulate them. This was particularly true of the dram houses found on the

The Pink House, at 17 Chalmers Street in Charles Town. The Pink House, at 17 Chalmers Street in Charles Town, served as a tavern where sailors drank grog and prostitutes plied their trade in what was then the city's red-light district called Mulatto Alley. Built in the 1690s with West Indian coral stone that had a natural pink cast, the building was known as the Pink House from the beginning. It is reputedly the oldest standing tavern in the South and the oldest building in Charleston. It currently serves as an art gallery. (Library of Congress, Prints and Photographs Division, Reproduction # LC-G612-T01-23780)

waterfront and in the laboring-class sections of cities, which upper-class authorities singled out for "special treatment." Philadelphia officials limited residents to a one-hour stay in taverns unless they were involved in "conducting business." Authorities in Massachusetts, additionally, printed the name of "problem drinkers" in handbills and posted them over tavern doors. Officials in other cities sought to curb alcohol abuse by placing limits on the amount of alcohol a tavern keeper could serve a patron and limiting their hours of operation. When authorities bothered to enforce these laws, they almost always targeted the most vulnerable members of society—servants, slaves, sailors, and common laborers—while leaving alone elite white men engaged in heavy drinking and "late-night frolicking."[47]

This elitism is also seen in the drinking accouterments and rituals that upper-class men used in an attempt to prove they were of the "better sort" and thus justify excluding the lesser sort from their company. The fine china punch bowls, silver spoons and ladles, crystal glasses, and imported liquor used by well-to-do taverngoers were all conspicuous displays of gentility. Gentlemen also distinguished themselves with their toasting rituals that were intended to display breeding, knowledge, and wit. To further demonstrate their breeding, upper-crust taverngoers discussed topics such as English poets, foreign writers, political philosophers, and ancient history that one could only acquire through reading and education. Many commoners were unimpressed by such supercilious displays. Laborers filled with "liquid courage" often refused to defer to their "social superiors" in tavern encounters, much to the aggravation of upper-class patrons who expected such deferential treatment. For this reason, among others, well-to-do taverngoers in the five cities segregated themselves in separate rooms and booths set aside for gentlemen. Still others founded their own taverns and coffee houses so that they could have a place to socialize and do business away from the common folk's barroom conversations. In Newport, for example, the Flying Horse was a mecca for ships' captains who had just come into port full of tales and the adventures they had experienced on their latest voyage, while Jacob Hassey's coffee house was a popular gathering place for the city's commercial elite.[48]

CONCLUSION

The major colonial cities were the centers of culture and recreation in North America and offered the greatest opportunities for their residents to participate in a diverse array of leisurely pursuits, many of which, in one form or another, are still practiced today. As such, the colonial seaports can be seen as modern in that they set the future direction of leisure in the United States. Further reflecting the modern aspect of early American urban recreation was its stark class quality, with the upper and lower classes often having distinctive and separate forms of leisure. The urban aristocracy, in particular, cultivated a culture of power by manufacturing exclusive recreational activities. Some of this exclusivity was a response from the lower sort who sought to democratize leisure by competing with their superiors over similar spaces for recreation. Since then ordinary Americans have made considerable progress democratizing recreation. In response, today's upper class, like their colonial counterparts who did not deign to associate with those they considered below them, continues a modern form of recreational elitism with Shakespearean theaters, symphony orchestras, city ballets, country clubs, and exclusive "box seats" at major sporting arenas—all of which are intentionally priced so high that the lower classes will never have access to them, except as hired help. In its own way, recreation demonstrates that American society has always been sharply divided along class lines.

NOTES

1. Thomas R. Davis, "Sport and Exercise in the Lives of Selected Colonial Americans: Massachusetts and Virginia," Ph.D. dissertation, University of Maryland, 1970, 95.

2. Ronald L. Davis, *A History of Music in American Life: The Formative Years, 1620–1865* (Malabar, FL: Kreiger, 1982), 38 (quote); Nancy L. Struna, "Sport and the Awareness of Leisure," in *Of Consuming Interests: The Style of Life in the 18th Century*, ed. Cary Carson, Ronald Hoffman, and Peter Albert (Charlottesville: University Press of Virginia, 1994), 441–44.

3. Alice M. Earle, *Child Life in Colonial Days* (New York: Macmillan, 1899), 347–49.

4. L. Douglas Good, "Colonials at Play: Leisure in Newport, 1723," *Rhode Island History* 33 (1974): 16; Esther Singleton, *Dutch New York* (New York: Dodd, Mead & Co., 1909), 312–13; Earle, *Child Life*, 342–74.

5. Carl Bridenbaugh, *Cities in the Wilderness: The First Century of Urban Life in America, 1625–1742* (New York: Capricorn Books, 1938), 117 (quote); Singleton, *Dutch New York*, 311 (quote); Nancy Struna, "Puritans and Sport: The Irretrievable Tide of Change," in *The American Sporting Experience: A Historical Anthology of Sport in America*, ed. Steven A. Reiss (New York: Leisure Press, 1984), 20 (quote); Good, "Colonials at Play," 13 (quote);

Stephanie Grauman Wolf, *As Various as Their Land: The Everyday Lives of Eighteenth-Century Americans* (New York: Harper Perennial, 1994), 132–34; William Pencak, "Play as Prelude to Revolution: Boston, 1765–1776," in *Riot and Revelry in Early America*, ed. William Pencak, Matthew Dennis, and Simon P. Newman (University Park: Pennsylvania State University Press, 2002), 129–33.

6. Bridenbaugh, *Cities in the Wilderness*, 41; Julia Cherry Spruill, *Women's Life and Work in the Southern Colonies* (Chapel Hill: University of North Carolina Press, 1938), 85, 110, 282; Sheila Skemp, "A Social and Cultural History of Newport, Rhode Island, 1720–1765," Ph.D. dissertation, University of Iowa, 1974, 240–41 (quote); Patricia Cleary, " 'She Will Be in the Shop': Woman's Sphere of Trade in Eighteenth-Century Philadelphia and New York," *Pennsylvania Magazine of History and Biography* 119 (1995): 191–92; Ellen Hartigan O'Connor, "The Measure of the Market: Women's Economic Lives in Charleston, SC and Newport, RI, 1750–1820," Ph.D. dissertation, University of Michigan, 2003, quotes from pp. 229, 239, 277–79; Richard L. Bushman, "Shopping and Advertising in Colonial America," in *Of Consuming Interests*, 236–37; Terrence H. Witkowski, "The Early Development of Purchasing Roles in the American Household, 1750–1840," *Journal of Macromarketing* 19 (1999): 107–10.

7. Walter J. Fraser Jr., *Patriots, Pistols and Petticoats: "Poor Sinful Charles Town" during the American Revolution* (Columbia: University of South Carolina Press, 1976), 21 (quote); Bruce C. Daniels, *Puritans at Play: Leisure and Recreation in Colonial New England* (New York: St. Martin's Press, 1995), 194–98; Struna, "Sport and the Awareness of Leisure," 425–26; Nancy L. Struna, "Gender and Sporting Practice in Early America, 1750–1810," in *Sport in America: From Wicked Amusements to National Obsession*, ed. David K. Wiggins (Champagne, IL: Human Kinetics, 1995), 24–25; Skemp, "A Social and Cultural History of Newport," 24 (quote).

8. Skemp, "A Social and Cultural History of Newport," 238–39 (quotes).

9. Thomas L. Purvis, *Colonial America to 1763* (New York: Facts on File, 1999), 284–85; Elliott Gorn and Warren Goldstein, *A Brief History of American Sports* (New York: Hill and Wang, 1993), 33.

10. Good, "Colonials at Play," 13–14.

11. Louis B. Wright, *Life in Colonial America* (New York: Capricorn Books, 1965), 207 (quote); Richard Crawford, *A History of America's Musical Life* (New York: W. W. Norton & Co., 2001), 111 (quote); William D. Pierson, *Black Yankees: The Development of an Afro-American Subculture in Eighteenth-Century New England* (Amherst: University of Massachusetts Press, 1988), 118–28; Donald R. Wright, *African Americans in the Colonial Era: From African Origins through the American Revolution* (Wheeling, IL: Harlan Davidson, 1990), 115; Lorenzo J. Greene, *The Negro in Colonial New England* (New York: Columbia University Press, 1948), 249–52.

12. Harry M. Ward, *Colonial America, 1607–1763* (Englewood Cliffs, NJ: Prentice Hall, 1991), 172 (quote); Purvis, *Colonial America to 1763*, 303; George Francis Dow, *Every Day Life in the Massachusetts Bay Colony* (Boston: Society for the Preservation of New England Antiquities, 1935), 114; Davis, "Sport and Exercise," 89–90; Wright, *Life in Colonial America*, 207–8; Daniels, *Puritans at Play*, 99.

13. Nancy L. Struna, *People of Prowess: Sport, Leisure, and Labor in Early Anglo-America* (Urbana: University of Illinois Press, 1996), 92–93; Singleton, *Dutch New York*, 303–4 (quote).

14. Dow, *Everyday Life*, 116; Struna, *People of Prowess*, 133–34; Struna, "Sport and the Awareness of Leisure," 437; Daniels, *Puritans at Play*, 103; Purvis, *Colonial America to 1763*, 286 (quote).

15. Crawford, *History of America's Musical Life*, 111–12 (quote); Clayborne Carson, Emma J. Lapsansky-Werner, and Gary B. Nash, *African American Lives: The Struggle for Freedom* (New York: Pearson Education 2005), 97 (quote).

16. Singleton, *Dutch New York*, 315–20; Bridenbaugh, *Cities in the Wilderness*, 119; Good, "Colonials at Play," 14 (quote).

17. Arthur Schlesinger, *The Birth of the Nation: A Portrait of the American People on the Eve of Independence* (New York: Knopf, 1969), 220; Dow, *Everyday Life*, 117; Louis B. Wright, *The Cultural Life of the American Colonies* (New York: Harper & Row, 1957), 187; Esther Singleton, *Social New York under the Georges, 1714–1776* (New York: D. Appleton & Co., 1902), 316–26; Skemp, "A Social and Cultural History of Newport," 231 (quote).

18. Thomas L. Altherr, ed., *Sport in North America: A Documentary History*, vol. 1 (Gulf Breeze, FL: Academic International Press, 1992), 73 (quote); Wright, *Life in Colonial America*, 197; Singleton, *Dutch New York*, 292–93; Dow, *Everyday Life*, 112–14.

19. Altherr, *Sport in North America*, 41 (quote), 47–51, 212, 409, 429, 435; Singleton, *Dutch New York*, 296; Singleton, *Social New York*, 265; Davis, "Sport and Exercise," 100.

20. Purvis, *Colonial America to 1763*, 303; Wright, *Life in Colonial America*, 202; Altherr, *Sport in North America*, 161, 76–83.

21. Keith Krawczynski, *William Henry Drayton: South Carolina Revolutionary Patriot* (Baton Rouge: Louisiana State University Press, 2001), 35 (quote); Gary S. Cross, *A Social History of Leisure since 1600* (State College, PA: Venture Pub., 1990), 53–55; Wright, *Life in Colonial America*, 202–3; Edgar J. McManus, *Law and Liberty in Early New England: Criminal Justice and Due Process, 1620–1692* (Amherst: University of Massachusetts Press, 1993), 52–53; Purvis, *Colonial America to 1763*, 302; Daniels, *Puritans at Play*, 176; Schlesinger, *The Birth of the Nation*, 216.

22. Altherr, *Sport in North America*, 20–33; Daniels, *Puritans at Play*, 174–75; Singleton, *Social New York*, 266.

23. Bridenbaugh, *Cities in the Wilderness*, 129–39; Robert E. Spiller et. al., *Literary History of the United States* (New York: Macmillan, 1948), 18–19; Clare

Lyons, "Mapping an Atlantic Sexual Culture: Homoeroticism in Eighteenth-Century Philadelphia," *William and Mary Quarterly* 60 (January 2003): 144–46; Purvis, *Colonial America to 1763*, 246–59; Louis B. Wright, *The Cultural Life of the American Colonies, 1607–1763* (New York: Harper & Row, 1957), 145–65; Russel B. Nye, *American Literary History: 1707–1830* (New York: Alfred Knopf, 1970), 114–15; William P. Trent, ed., *The Cambridge History of American Literature* (New York: MacMillan Co., 1917), 121–22.

24. Sarah Fatherly, *Gentlewomen and Learned Ladies: Women and Elite Formation in Eighteenth-Century Philadelphia* (Bethlehem, PA: Lehigh University Press, 2008), 97–98.

25. Skemp, "A Social and Cultural History of Newport," 234–25 (quote); Fatherly, *Gentlewomen and Learned Ladies*, 99 (quote).

26. Fatherly, *Gentlewomen and Learned Ladies*, 108.

27. Ibid., 123, 127, 129.

28. Carl Bridenbaugh, *Cities in Revolt: Urban Life in America, 1743–1776* (New York: Capricorn Books, 1955), 166, 367–68; Barbara Carson, "Early American Tourists and the Commercialization of Leisure," in *Of Consuming Interests*, 374, 384, 390–92, 401–2; Fatherly, *Gentlewomen and Learned Ladies*, 124–25.

29. Timothy Breen quoted in Benjamin Rader, *American Sports: From the Age of Folk Games to the Age of Spectators* (Englewood, NJ: Prentice Hall, 1983), 21 (quote); Altherr, *Sport in North America*, 233; Wright, *Life in Colonial America*, 197; Dow, *Everyday Life*, 112–13; Singleton, *Dutch New York*, 296; Struna, "Puritans and Sport," 22.

30. Sharon Salinger, *Taverns and Drinking in Early America* (Baltimore, MD: Johns Hopkins University Press, 2002), 79–82; Good, "Colonials at Play," 11; Samuel Lilly, "The Culture of Revolutionary Charleston," Ph.D. dissertation, Miami University, 1971, 94.

31. Daniels, *Puritans at Play*, 66–67 (quotes); Constance D. Sherman, "The Theater in Rhode Island before the Revolution," *Rhode Island History* 17 (1958): 12; Hugh F. Rankin, *The Theater in Colonial America* (Chapel Hill: University of North Carolina Press, 1960), 24, 32, 62, 92–94, 124-27, 131; Thomas J. Wertenbaker, *The Golden Age of Colonial Culture* (Ithaca, NY: Cornell University Press, 1949), 34; Wright, *Cultural Life of the American Colonies*, 184; Schlesinger, *The Birth of the Nation*, 222.

32. Cynthia Adams Hoover, "Music and Theater in the Lives of Eighteenth-Century Americans," in *Of Consuming Interests*, 336 (quote); Rankin, *Theater in Colonial America*, 27, 64, 71, 97, 99 (quote), 110, 171, 176; Davis, *A History of Music*, 38 (quote); Frederick P. Bowes, *The Culture of Early Charleston* (Chapel Hill: University of North Carolina Press, 1942), 101–4; Mary J. Curtis, "The Early Charleston Stage: 1703–1798," Ph.D. dissertation, Indiana University, 1968, 58–108; Wertenbaker, *Golden Age*, 52–54; Singleton, *Social New York*, 280–81.

33. Josiah Smith, "The Burning of Sodom, with Its Moral Causes" (Charles Town: 1741), 12–16; Emma Hart, *Building Charleston: Town and*

Society in the Eighteenth-Century British Atlantic World (Charlottesville: University of Virginia Press, 2010), 151–55.

34. Davis, *A History of Music,* 57 (quote); Hoover, "Music and Theater," 308 (quote).

35. Davis, *A History of Music,* 6.

36. Crawford, *History of America's Musical Life,* 24.

37. Daniels, *Puritans at Play,* 54.

38. Daniels, *Puritans at Play,* 52–60, 62 (quote); Crawford, *History of America's Musical Life,* 26, 35 (quote); John T. Howard, *Our American Music: A Comprehensive History from 1620 to the Present* (New York: Thomas Crowell, 1929), 4, 11–15; Hoover, "Music and Theater," 320–21; Davis, *A History of Music,* 14–15.

39. Davis, *A History of Music,* 42; Crawford, *History of America's Musical Life,* 49–50; Howard, *Our American Music,* 25.

40. Howard, *Our American Music,* 30 (quote), 33–34 (quote); Davis, *A History of Music,* 50.

41. Davis, *A History of Music,* 19 (quote); Daniels, *Puritans at Play,* 65.

42. Davis, *A History of Music,* 20; Crawford, *History of America's Musical Life,* 73, 105 (quote).

43. Salinger, *Taverns and Drinking,*138 (quote), 185, 205; Daniels, *Puritans at Play,* 144–45; Richard P. Gildrie, *The Profane, The Civil, & the Godly: The Reformation of Manners in Orthodox New England, 1679–1749* (University Park: Pennsylvania State University Press, 1994), 63–83.

44. Peter Thompson, *Rum Punch & Revolution: Taverngoing & Public Life in Eighteenth Century Philadelphia* (Philadelphia: University of Pennsylvania Press, 1999), 83.

45. Kym Rice, *Early American Taverns: For the Entertainment of Friends and Strangers* (Chicago: Regnery Gateway, 1983), 102 (quote), 103–5; Salinger, *Taverns and Drinking,* 211 (quote), 214.

46. Salinger, *Taverns and Drinking,* 69–73, quote on p. 70; Davis, "Sport and Exercise," 91 (quote); Gildrie, *The Profane,* 75–77; Singleton, *Dutch New York,* 269, 289; Thompson, *Rum, Punch & Revolution,* 101–2; Daniels, *Puritans at Play,* 144–59; Rice, *Early American Taverns,* 34–36; Ann Pinson, "The New England Rum Era: Drinking Styles and Social Change in Newport, R.I., 1720–1770," *Working Papers on Alcohol and Human Behavior* 8 (1980): 18–20.

47. Salinger, *Taverns and Drinking,* 89–145.

48. Peter Thompson, " 'The Friendly Glass': Drink and Gentility in Colonial Philadelphia," *Pennsylvania Magazine of History and Biography* 113 (1989): 550–59; Gildrie, *The Profane,* 75; Rice, *Early American Taverns,* 38–39; Thompson, *Rum, Punch, and Revolution,* 106–10; Skemp, "A Social and Cultural History of Newport," 20–21.

14

Arts and Sciences

INTRODUCTION

As a frontier people battling for a living at the far edges of the British empire, Americans during much of the colonial period devoted little time and energy toward scientific and artistic pursuits. Clearing fields, establishing settlements, building trade, and fighting Native Americans and the French or Spanish, as the case was, consumed the lives of the early settlers. Such a strong survival mode encouraged a practical-mindedness among early Americans that concomitantly discouraged nonessential thought and activity. Most settlers would have agreed with the New England author that "The Plow-man that raiseth Grain is more serviceable to mankind than the painter who draws only to please the Eye."[1] It was not until the eighteenth century that the critical ingredients for the flowering of the arts and sciences—wealth, education, leisure, social agencies, and aspirations to elegance—were in adequate supply. These ingredients were in greatest abundance in the five principal cities, which, as major seaports and commercial centers, were also best situated to receive from Europe the latest intellectual and cultural currents of the age. It is therefore in these seaports that nearly all of the intellectual and artistic advances in the colonies took place, and each city quickly became the intellectual and cultural center of its region.

However, the major cities served as more than just receptacles for imported ideas and culture; they also served as funnels for its distribution into the interior of America. Hawkers and peddlers, their carts loaded with newspapers and books originating from urban printing and book shops, carried many of the new ideas to country towns. Meanwhile, more educated frontier folk picked it up when they went into the city on business, and young city-trained men carried it with them when they traveled westward in search of better opportunities.

The urban-centered nature of colonial arts and sciences gave them much of their direction and character. The city's close connections with Europe, coupled with America's relative primitiveness, ensured that early American culture would borrow heavily from that of the Old World. Still, the derivative quality of early American society was tempered by the colonists' utilitarian outlook toward most things and their less deeply rooted traditions. This allowed the colonists to import enlightened ideas and foreign culture while shaping them to suit their own unique needs. Because such intellectual and cultural pursuits required wealth and some leisure, colonial arts and sciences was supported almost exclusively by a small number of enlightened and sophisticated aristocrats. It is important to emphasize, however, that with only a few exceptions early American artists, writers, and scientists were amateurs in their fields. These dilettantes did not lead cloistered lives but instead earned their living through some trade or profession such as physician, lawyer, minister, printer, limner, teacher, artisan, merchant, politician, or a combination of these occupations. Pursuing the arts and sciences was a part-time passion for them.

SCIENCE

One area in which American culture flourished was in science. This was partly due to the fortunes of timing, as the colonies were settled during the scientific revolution of the late sixteenth and seventeenth centuries, and partly due to America's unique natural environment and geographical location. The scientific revolution, with its emphasis on identifying the laws governing nature through carefully organized experiments and systematic observations, brought about a new and practical way of viewing the universe. Through this scientific method, great European scientists like Nicolaus Copernicus, Johannes Kepler, Galileo Galilei, and especially Isaac Newton challenged and eventually overthrew the traditional Aristotelian natural philosophy and created new theories in fundamental disciplines like astronomy, physics, chemistry, and natural history. Through such new knowledge, it was hoped that men could not only know the world but that they might also control it for the benefit of mankind. The English philosopher Francis Bacon, for one, strongly encouraged scientists to place a more practical use to their knowledge by creating devices that would benefit industry, agriculture, and trade.

This new and practical way of viewing the world had an enormous appeal for Americans, a new and practical people. As such, Americans, more than any other group of people, adopted the idea that through reason people could discover and comprehend the natural laws that governed every phase of life. In turn, this new scientific approach toward the world tended to make the American mind "more secular, more this-worldly, more rationalistic, and more ingenious," in the words of historian Max Savelle. At the same time, it tended to widen divisions in society between the educated elites and the uneducated masses. The new science, with its strong emphasis on higher mathematics, mechanical explanation, induction, empiricism, and rationalism, was not intended for the shallow minds of the common people, many of whom continued to hold more of a magical and supernatural explanation for the natural world. This made science part of America's high culture that only served to further distance itself from the vernacular culture of the lower-classes.[2]

Not all colonial American cities made an equal contribution in the sciences. Boston, with a large concentration of learned clergymen and nearby Harvard College, was the center of scientific inquiry in North America from the seventeenth century until the mid-1700s, when Philadelphia stole this honor with its founding of the American Philosophical Society and America's first medical school and with its numerous internationally recognized scientists. This fact appears counterintuitive at first glance because of Boston's strong theological culture, but the Puritans saw no conflict between science and religion. "Philosophy [science] is no Enemy, but a mighty and wondrous incentive to Religion," explained the Puritan divine Cotton Mather. Armed with the new scientific principles of the age, Puritan scientists and ministers used it to confirm the accuracy of the Bible, not to challenge it.[3] Taking a more secular approach toward science were progressive-minded Philadelphians who strongly believed in the pursuit and advancement of knowledge in all its forms, a philosophy they put into practical effect with the creation in the early 1760s of the University of Pennsylvania and the American

Philosophical Society. With a few notable exceptions, most educated and wealthy residents of both New York City and Charles Town were too concerned with materialistic and hedonistic pursuits to devote much attention to scientific inquiry. Likewise, Newport contributed little to the advancement of science in America, mainly because of its relatively small and rural environment and the dominance of nearby Boston. Its merchant elite did create a Society for the Promotion of Knowledge during the 1720s to discuss and debate questions of religion, morality, philosophy, and history, but their discussions frequently turned instead to talk of privateering and shipping. Nevertheless, America's amateur scientists made important contributions in astronomy and botany—the former because of Americans' unique position to observe celestial bodies from a perspective different from that of Europeans, and the latter because of America's distinctive, diverse, and largely unclassified plant and animal life.

Astronomy

Some of the greatest achievements of the scientific revolution occurred in astronomy. The discoveries of Tycho Brahe, Copernicus, and Galileo all revolutionized the understanding of the solar system. Although no colonial scientist of the period came near to matching the contributions of any one of these great minds, Americans were in a unique situation to add to this growing body of knowledge. The distance of America from Europe meant that the colonists were able to observe many celestial phenomena that Europeans could not, particularly eclipses of the sun and moon, transits of the planets across the sun, observations of meteors and comets, and occurrences of the aurora borealis. These early astronomical observations were conducted almost exclusively by educated Bostonians, who benefitted greatly from the faculty of nearby Harvard College.

America's first amateur astronomer was John Winthrop Jr., an Irish-educated (Trinity) lawyer, who in the 1660s turned his telescope to the largest planet in the solar system and discovered a fifth satellite of Jupiter. Thomas Brattle, a Boston almanac writer and graduate of Harvard, achieved international acclaim in 1680 with his careful and accurate tracking of a comet, the findings of which he published in his almanac the next year and sent to England's prestigious Royal Society. His work provided an important key in correcting one of the most common misconceptions of astronomy when Isaac Newton used it to substantiate his argument that orbiting satellites followed an elliptical rather than a circular path. Thomas Robie, a Bostonian who taught mathematics and astronomy at his alma mater of Harvard from 1712 to 1722, published papers at the Royal Society on the aurora borealis, measurements of the halo surrounding the solar eclipse of 1722, and a transit of Mercury over the Sun the following year. Perhaps just as importantly, Robie helped to popularize astronomy in New England by publishing his research in local newspapers and in his own almanac.[4]

Standing on the scientific shoulders of these men was John Winthrop IV, a great-grandson of John Winthrop Jr., a celebrated instructor at Harvard and one of the most outstanding American scientists of the eighteenth century. He published investigations of sunspots observed with his naked eye in 1739; the transit of Mercury over the sun in 1740, 1743, and 1769; and a scientific expedition to St. John's, Newfoundland, to observe the transit of Venus across the sun on June 6, 1761. The latter was a rare event, and one that astronomers hoped to use to determine the distance from the Earth to the sun. Although his estimated distance of 94,030,000 miles from the Earth to the sun is a distance greater than is now accepted, Winthrop's were the only American figures made available to the world of science. Winthrop added to his reputation for his theory that an earthquake was caused by a wavelike undulation of the Earth's crust. In his study of the 1755 earthquake that shook New England, Winthrop reported that "our buildings were rocked with the kind of angular motion, like that of a cradle; the upper parts of them moving swifter, or thro' greater spaces in the motion of the earth." However, Winthrop's published observations did little to quiet the many New England ministers who explained in their sermons that the earthquake was a sign of God's wrath. More impressed was London's Royal Society, which published at least nine of Winthrop's papers and elected him as a member in 1766.[5]

The only early American astronomer of note residing outside of Massachusetts was David Rittenhouse, a self-taught Pennsylvania prodigy who possessed great facility in mathematics and mechanical invention. A clockmaker and surveyor by trade, Rittenhouse used his genius to build an orrery in 1767, a mechanical planetarium that depicted the relative positions of the planets for any time over a 5,000-year period. His creation caused quite a stir among the press, which lauded its builder as a man of "singular Genius." Rittenhouse also constructed an astronomical observatory outside of Philadelphia and greatly improved telescope techniques by placing spider lines at the focus. Rittenhouse put all this to good use in

Apparent Time.	Diff. Long. Sun & Venus.	Venus Lat. South.
4^h 21^m 27^s	9^m 2^s	10^m 47^s
23 2	9 4	10 50
27 25	9 25	10 52
35 17	9 56	10 55
37 45	10 8	11 00

THUS in the short interval of Time that was permitted, I determin'd five positions of the Planet on the Sun; and by laying off the differences of Longitude and the Latitudes, the Planet's path over the Sun may be drawn, and its situation determin'd in respect of the ecliptic,

or

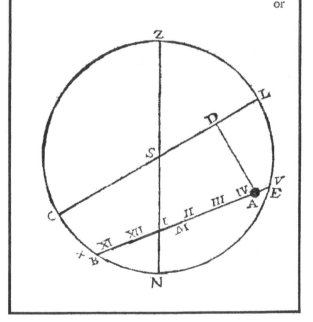

Page from John Winthrop's *Relation of a Voyage.* The transit of Venus is among the rarest predictable astronomical phenomena and is often separated by gaps of over 100 years. Thus the transit of Venus on June 6, 1761, which was visible in North America only in Canada and the Spanish West, was a significant astronomical event. The only American scientist who made the trek to observe it (in Newfoundland) was Harvard professor John Winthrop, who sought to find the parallax of the sun, knowledge of which would better enable scientists to determine the distance of the sun and of all the planets. He published his calculations and the path Venus took across the sun, shown here, in his *Relations of a Voyage from Boston to Newfoundland, for the Observation of the Transit of Venus.* (Charles Evans, *Early American Imprints*, Series 1, no. 9040)

1769 in observing the transit of Venus. His results were the best obtained, and his computed parallax of the sun the most accurate then known. He later passed down his skills and knowledge to the next generation of scholars as a teacher at the College of Philadelphia and promoted the sciences in the young nation as president of the American Philosophical Society from 1791 until his death in 1796.[6]

Natural History

As significant as the advances and contributions made by early Americans to astronomy, the quintessential colonial science was natural history. Here colonial scientists took advantage of their "peripheral position" to undertake investigations that were impossible across the Atlantic—the study of America's abundant and largely unexplored natural environment. One of the first to do so in a scientific manner was James Logan of Philadelphia. A wealthy Irish-born Quaker who served as William Penn's personal secretary, Logan used his fortune to build an experimental garden where he carried out a series of carefully controlled experiments of sex in plants that demonstrated the function of the various organs, particularly what he called the "male seed" in the propagation of Indian corn. In 1734 Logan detailed his findings in the Royal Society's *Transactions* and distributed it to the leading European botanists. The famed Swedish botanist Carl Linnaeus was so impressed by Logan's work that he named a genus for him.[7]

Linnaeus bestowed a similar honor on Dr. Alexander Garden of Charles Town by naming the familiar gardenia after him. This honor was well deserved, especially considering that the transplanted Scotsman worked in a near intellectual vacuum. According to Garden, South Carolina was a "horrid country," a place where "eating, drinking, lolling, smoking, and sleeping" constituted the essence of people's "life and existence." Most galling to the physician was that "there is not a living soul [here] who knows the least iota of Natural History."[8] To help satisfy his need for intellectual camaraderie, Garden corresponded with all the leading American and European naturalists of the mid-eighteenth century and forwarded to them large collections of dried plants and seeds, which he classified himself using Linnaeus's system of binomial nomenclature. Garden also discovered many new genera of South Carolina plant life, which were assimilated in Linnaeus's *Systema Naturae*. Also finding their way into *Systema Naturae* were Garden's descriptions and specimens of numerous varieties of fish, reptiles, and insects from South Carolina, a relatively rare excursion into zoology by an American botanist. But Garden's greatest claim to fame was his study of *Corals and Corallines*, which showed that coral organisms are animals.[9]

The greatest colonial botanist was John Bartram, a Pennsylvania Quaker whose greatest contribution resulted from his extensive travels throughout the colonies scouring the forests with a missionary's zeal gathering new plants and seeds for his large botanical garden located on the banks of the Schuylkill just outside of Philadelphia. In his travels Bartram also collected insects, birds, and fossils and made keen observations of the habits of Native Americans he met, which he described in his *Observations* (1751). He further demonstrated his status as an amateur zoologist by publishing papers in the Royal Society's *Philosophical Transactions* on insects, snake teeth, and mollusks. Linnaeus called him "the greatest contemporary natural botanist in the world." King George III even appointed Bartram the official royal botanist for the American colonies. Although Bartram was more of a "noble nurseryman" than a "systematic botanist," he did more to advance the knowledge of American plant and animal life than any of the more learned botanists in his country.[10]

AMERICAN RENAISSANCE MEN

Bartram's close friend Benjamin Franklin exceeded all previous American scientists in his breadth of research, inventiveness, and personification of the enlightened belief that through reason men can better understand and improve themselves and the world in which they live. Franklin's success as a Philadelphia printer allowed him to retire in 1748 and pursue full time his growing interest in "philosophical studies and amusements." In his studies Franklin employed pure research with a utilitarian purpose, to make science a useful servant to man. This didactic method led to his invention of such practical items as the Franklin stove (from his studies of heat and ventilation), the bifocal lens (from his studies of optics), and the lightning rod (from his studies of electricity). Franklin's discoveries in electricity, principally that lightning was an electrical phenomenon and the single fluid concept of positive and negative charges, brought him international fame as a scientist of the first magnitude and election to England's Royal Society in 1756 and to the French Academy of Sciences in 1772. Less well known are Franklin's studies of the habits of ants, the organisms in sea water, wind currents, eclipses, the origins of storms, and measurements of the Gulf Stream, among many other interests.[11]

Much less well known but certainly deserving recognition as one of early America's most versatile scientists is Cadwallader Colden, a Scotsman who immigrated to America in 1710 after earning a masters degree from the University of Edinburgh and medical training in London. Revenues from several political offices gave Colden the time and leisure to pursue his varied scientific interests, which included researching and writing on such subjects as cancer, diphtheria, light, color, mathematics, history, and anthropology. But Colden's most important scientific contributions were made in botany, particularly his description of more than 300 new plants from around his home in New York City. In gratitude, Linnaeus named the plant genus *Coldenia* after him.[12]

VISUAL ARTS

The nurturing and growth of the visual arts in early America was a protracted process. During much of the seventeenth century, settlers were too concerned with simple survival to devote much attention to aesthetics. Once conquering the American wilderness and amassing some wealth, well-to-do colonists developed a taste for the refinements of life. In particular, this culturally self-conscious American nouveau riche sought to have their likenesses put to canvas to illustrate their wealth for both their contemporaries and their descendants. Artists therefore showed their wealthy subjects dressed in the finest clothing, surrounded by ornate furnishings and sometimes even with a coat of arms in the background to give them the appearance of courtly aristocrats. Art in early America was therefore an elitist pursuit and one partly intended by the upper class to distinguish themselves from the lower sort. Motives aside, this ever-increasing market for portraits among the urban gentry attracted many second-rate painters from Europe to the major American cities and encouraged aspiring urban artisans to try their hand at the visual arts. Further encouraging the development of artistic talent in the major metropolitan centers was the increasing availability there of painters' supplies, prints, books, and lessons. Benjamin West and John Singleton Copley are two examples of young American artists who benefitted from growing up in one of the principal cities.[13]

Portraiture

Portraiture in seventeenth-century America was a part-time craft performed by limners who got their start painting houses, carriages, and signs. These untutored amateurs (nearly all lost to history) had little knowledge of technique and perspective but a strong interest in realistic detail that resulted in excessively flat paintings of "hard-bitten men, of sturdy women and of children," writes Oliver Larkin, "who looked like miniature men and women." Dutch realism in New Amsterdam is illustrated in a portrait of Peter Stuyvesant by an unknown limner that revealed the aging governor "in all of his strength and ugliness." Early portraits of Puritan grandees from Boston were just as unflattering in the face as artists put most of the their efforts in painting the stylish and colorful clothing, lace, silk gloves, gold necklaces, pearl earrings, jeweled rings, and other emblems of prosperity worn by their subjects that, at least to them, proved that they enjoyed God's pleasure.[14]

American painting received an infusion of artistry and skill during the early eighteenth century when trained painters from abroad—lured by the increasing prosperity of the colonies—arrived in growing numbers to paint with varying competence portraits in a modest version of the aristocratic court style of England. One of the earliest of these overseas artists was Henrietta Johnston, an Irish woman who arrived in Charles Town in 1708 with her husband, the Reverend Gideon Johnston. Despite her limited artistic training, Johnston helped support her large family of 11 children by painting graceful portraits in pastel crayons (a rarely used medium) of personal friends and local dignitaries. Johnston's style reflected the aristocratic court style fashionable in England at the time—the use of elegant poses, grandiose settings, rich attire, and animated faces. This style served her well in Charles Town, where the rising planters and merchants there sought to communicate refinement and cultural sophistication. Seven years after Johnston's death in 1728, the Swiss Jeremiah Theus established a practice in the southern capital where for 40 years he painted in the "school of flattery" by making his female subjects prettier than they really were and augmenting the egos of his male sitters by making them appear dignified and superior.[15]

In stark contrast to the flattering and decorative style of portraiture in Charles Town, the Scottish painter John Smibert, who settled in Boston in 1730, had to paint more simple and honest likenesses of his Puritanical patrons, who wanted to be shown as

Portrait of Sir William Pepperell by John Smibert, 1746. The figure in this painting, William Pepperrell, earned a baronetcy from King George II for his success as a commander of a colonial militia against the French at Louisbourg in 1745 during King George's War (1740–1748). The "hero of Louisbourg" commissioned Boston-based artist John Smibert to paint a portrait of him standing in full military uniform. Behind him in the distance the battle is represented with cannon balls arching down upon a French fort among gunfire and smoke. (Library of Congress, Prints and Photographs Division, Reproduction # LC USZ62-75604)

"sober, intelligent and respectable citizens of distinction." One exception to this frank realism was middle-aged female sitters who insisted that Smibert portray them as ever youthful, without wrinkles, blemishes, or gray hair. Meanwhile, Smibert depicted his male subjects with an "intense aliveness," writes one modern art scholar, and an "almost arrogant forcefulness." In this way, Boston's mercantile class kept Smibert very busy over the next 20 years, during which time he painted over 250 portraits of New England's leading families.[16]

Competing with Smibert for customers were native-born artists Robert Feke, Joseph Badger, and John Greenwood. Of these, the self-taught Feke was the most skilled and successful. His lack of training steered him toward an honest style bereft of studied posing and decoration, a style that meshed with the taste and values of his New England subjects. Perhaps most reflective of Feke's style and skill is the large group portrait of Isaac Royall Jr. and his family made in Boston in 1741. Four years after Feke's death in 1750, the English-trained drapery painter Joseph Blackburn arrived in Boston, where over the next nine years he painted over 150 portraits of New England's leading citizens in the new Georgian Rococo style that emphasized high-fashion attire imbued with lace, embroidery, flowers, and fruit. Blackburn returned to England in 1763, a departure perhaps hastened by the rapid emergence of the painting prodigy John Singleton Copley. Young Copley's natural artistic talents benefitted from working with his father-in-law Peter Pelham, Boston's leading engraver of mezzotint portraits, and exposure to Smibert's tiny gallery and the scores of European prints sold in the city's bookshops. Unlike his predecessors, Copley painted realistic portraits that, even among his female sitters, revealed their facial flaws such as moles, sagging skin, and wrinkles. This is detailed in his portrait of Mrs. Thomas Boylston (1766), whose face was "excruciatingly plain," but under Copley's hand, explains art critic Wayne Craven, that "plainness is made a virtue and imbued with gentility." The growing political tensions in Boston in the early 1770s, coupled with his desire to make his mark painting grand historical themes in the bigger artistic world of London, compelled the ambitious Copley to quit his country in 1774.[17]

One of the first foreign painters attracted to the growing wealth and cultural sophistication of Philadelphia was the professionally trained Swede Gustavus Hesselius, who arrived in the Quaker capital in 1712. For more than three decades Hesselius flourished as Philadelphia's favorite artist. To meet the demand of his more plain Quaker clients, he moved away from the aristocratic ideal of elegance and flattery toward a plainer, uncompromising realism. His realistic approach toward painting "generally does Justice to his men," remarked one contemporary critic, but not so much "to ye fair sex, and therefore few care to sitt to him." Although Hesselius's realism was not a hit with the ladies of Philadelphia, it did serve him well in his 1735 portraits of two Lenni-Lenape Indians (Lapowinsa and Tishcohan), which are considered by art critics as his best and most important work. The vacuum filled by Hesselius's retirement in the early 1750s was filled by the talented artist Benjamin West, the "Raphael of America," who did likenesses of Pennsylvania grandees until his departure in 1760 for Europe, where he became internationally famous for his epic portraits of historical events and royal figures.[18]

The common element throughout American painting in the eighteenth century was its "directness, realism, honesty, and relative simplicity," explains historian Max Savelle, traits that most reflected the early American character.[19] As such, it was this realism in American painting that made it distinct from that found in Europe. Yet alongside this distinctiveness in form is a similarity in purpose. The American aristocracy, in commissioning costly portraits, sought to emulate their European counterparts by portraying themselves—both to contemporaries and family descendants—as a superior people who rightly deserved their wealth and power. Early American portraiture was therefore both a self-gratifying indulgence by the elites and an expensive exercise in egotism.

Sculpture

Sculpture as an independent art form did not exist in America until after the American Revolution. Prior to this epochal event, carving in either stone or wood was an auxiliary craft practiced by artisans as an aside to their main practice—furniture or architectural decoration, ship's carvings, or gravestones. Practical-minded colonists did not design their homes, public buildings, or common squares to hold statuary. Moreover, the Puritans looked upon sculpture with suspicion because of its association with idolatry and the Catholic Church, which encouraged the placement of statues of religious figures in its houses of worship. Ironically, then, it was the Puritans who around the 1670s initiated an American sculpture tradition with gravestone carvers using well-established designs and standard motifs that visually illustrated the Puritan concepts of and preoccupation with death.[20]

Gravestone of William French. This photo is of the gravestone of William French, reputedly the first man killed in the Revolutionary War. The inscription reads, in part, "In memory of William French . . . who was shot at Westminster, March ye 13, 1775 by the hands of the Cruel Ministerial tools of George ye 3rd . . . in the 22d year of his Age." Note the inscribed artwork on the side and the carved angel at the top flying heavenward. (Library of Congress, Prints and Photographs Division, Reproduction # LC-D4-70096)

The primary motif of gravestone sculpture was the winged skull, a double symbol emphasizing the certainty of death but also the transmigration of the soul from earthly to eternal life. More rare were those headstones with winged cherubs carrying away a coffin that also signified resurrection. Often near the winged skull was an hourglass accompanied by the Latin messages "Fugit Hora" (Time Is Fleeting) and "Memento Mori" (Remember You Will Die) reminding the living that death is always drawing nearer. More richly carved headstones were often crowded with other symbols of death: crossed bones, skeletons, scythes, snuffed candles, coffins, and grim reapers. Further illustrating the dual messages of gravestone iconography was the placement of stylized plants and flowers representing regeneration and the "hoped for life in paradise." Amid these symbols of life and death were coats of arms and crude portraits of the deceased carved on the gravestones of the wealthy by the early 1700s. Conspicuously absent from the headstones are religious motifs—the cross, Christ, Mary, or God—a reflection of the secular nature of Puritan funerals. To the Puritans, carved headstones, no matter how richly decorated, were not considered a form of art but a utilitarian device to convey specific messages to the living.[21]

One of these messages was elitism, a desire among the upper class to conspicuously advertise their material success and lofty status from the grave to contemporaries and subsequent generations. By the 1670s the rising merchant and professional class in Boston had the disposable income to commission larger and more decorative gravestones that stood out from the sea of small, simple, and primitively carved headstones adorning the graves of their less affluent but equally dead neighbors. This elitist and egotistical trend among the affluent was not isolated to Boston but developed elsewhere throughout the colonies with the increasing disparity in wealth between the rich and everyone else. The poorest members of society, in fact, were unceremoniously dumped in unmarked paupers' graves. Derided and demonized while alive, the poor were unworthy of remembrance in death. Thus, by the eighteenth century the varied landscape of headstones in cemeteries showed that even in death there was no equality in early America.

Woodcarving

Like stone cutting, wood carving was an auxiliary to other utilitarian crafts such as architecture, furniture making, and ship building. Like the society it reflected, the few examples of American-made wood carving that have survived from the seventeenth century contain simple, low-relief surface decoration of geometric or stylized floral designs applied to Bible boxes, chests, and chairs. Likewise, carved architectural decorations were virtually nonexistent before 1700, with the exception of pendants beneath an overhang or turned banisters on a stairway. Not until around the 1720s with the growth in the major urban ports of a wealthy genteel class aspiring to conspicuously display their success did a high-style sculptural art develop, one that replaced the primitive medieval folk-art motifs with classical motifs (egg-and-dart designs, dentils, pilasters) found in English design books containing engraved illustrations of architecture and furniture. To meet this demand, professional carvers set up shop along or near the wharf sections of the burgeoning cities of the seaboard from Boston to Savannah. In addition to providing ornate classical decorations on furniture and the interiors of homes, these professional wood carvers produced a variety of objects, from mantels and rocking horses to ships' figureheads and shop signs.[22]

Silver

A sculptor who worked with an entirely different material was the silversmith. Like a sculptor, the silversmith had to know how to shape his materials with artistic talent, taste, and design to transform humble silver into artistic communion cups, plates, punch and sugar bowls, tea and coffee pots, sauceboats, chafing dishes, tankards, candlesticks, and snuffboxes that, for all their beauty, were used for ordinary functions in homes and churches. Perhaps the most artistic pieces of silver, and certainly the most heavily decorated, were produced during the late seventeenth and early eighteenth centuries by Boston and New York silversmiths. This ornate and heavily embossed style began to fall out of fashion not long after England passed a law in 1697 that raised the content of pure silver, which made the metal softer and less suitable for ornate forms. Thereafter, silversmiths created pieces with the smooth surfaces and graceful curves emblematic of the Queen Anne style of furniture of the period. Others found inspiration from Oriental rice bowls in designing teapots and silver bowls. By mid-century the embossed and heavily ornate style in silverware once again became popular among the genteel. The conspicuous style certainly mirrored the decorative interiors of the Georgian mansions where the upper class displayed their silverware.

LITERATURE

Much like art, literature during the colonial period reflected the time, place, and especially the mind of the people that produced it. For much of the seventeenth century this meant the viewpoint of conservative, pragmatic, moralistic, and industrious middle-class Englishmen who were most concerned with promoting their material welfare and saving their souls in a new land that first needed subduing and settling. When these early colonists did put quill and ink to paper, they did so with a practical purpose, and that purpose was for the most part not to entertain either their contemporaries or their descendants. This was especially true with the New England writers who dominated the production of American literature during the first century. Southerners wrote little during this period, and little of importance. New England Calvinists, on the other hand, felt that they were part of a great religious experiment that needed to be both promoted and preserved. The importance of the message even affected the writing style, which eschewed Elizabethan circumlocution and decorations and instead tended to be plain and pithy. Much of the plain prose produced in New England during this early period was by men residing outside of Boston because every township had a learned minister. Over time, though, the best minds gravitated to the Puritan capital so that by the end of the century the bay town far surpassed other New England towns in literary achievement.[23]

This process played out in urban communities along the Atlantic seaboard during the eighteenth century. Polite literature flourishes best not in a wilderness but in towns with men and women who possess some leisure and who have access to the intellectual infrastructure of urbane life—schools, libraries, booksellers, printing presses, and discussion clubs. Despite these advantages, the literary men and women living in the provincial cities were still forced to focus their attention on the affairs of life. No American at this time earned his bread by his pen alone. Still, eighteenth-century Americans produced a great deal of writing. Most of it included histories, biographies, and journals or diaries. Examples of drama, fiction, and imaginative poetry are rare for this period, and what the colonists did produce failed to match the quality of Europe's best. Yet the provincial nature of colonial prose should not obscure the important fact that by the mid- 1700s colonial writers were creating a distinctive American literature, one that reflected unique American ideals, experiences, and history. Less unique was the growing secularization of American literature during the second half of the colonial period, a trend that mirrored the growing secularization of both European and American society brought on by the scientific revolution and Enlightenment thinking. Between 1730 and 1775 the percentage of all religious titles published in the colonies dropped from 48 percent down to a mere 16 percent.

No matter its form, quality, or uniqueness, American literature throughout the colonial period was inherently elitist in nature. Imaginative writing requires some leisure and education, two things that belonged exclusively to the wealthy and educated few who dominated the cultural, economic, and political scene. To better control society, these learned elites spilled a considerable amount of ink promoting conformity in thought and behavior among the masses. This is particularly true in sermons, biographies, and autobiographies. Granted, colonial writing contained considerable contention, especially in religious and political circles, but this contention was largely between members of the upper class. Much of the rest of early American writing had the self-serving purpose of glorifying the achievements of upper-class leaders while ignoring the contributions of the common people. The mass of poorly educated and overworked Americans had little time and ability to write and publish their experiences and opinions. The educated elites therefore used even literature as a tool to help maintain their hegemony.

Religious Writing

Religious texts dominated the early American writing scene for nearly a century. This was largely because the majority of writing in seventeenth-century America was done by New England Puritans, who were not only the most literate group of early settlers but who were divinely inspired to write about their attempt at building God's kingdom in the American wilderness. Because ministers were the official spokesmen of New England, and because the church stood as the center of community intellectual life, Puritan writing manifested itself most commonly in sermons, which accounted for 40 percent of all items published in America between 1639 and 1730. Ministers in Boston, in particular, were some of the most influential public figures in New England and took an active involvement in the most important religious and social topics of the day. Some of the issues that prompted them to put their thoughts to paper included the rise of dissident opinions, the

defense of congregational church polity, and the question of toleration. The prolific yet dogmatic John Cotton presented an unapolo-
getic aristocratic conservatism and religious authoritarianism that
challenged any threat to the political, social, and religious status
quo. When Roger Williams criticized Massachusetts's theocratic
leadership and advocated religious toleration and democracy,
Cotton lashed back: "Democracy, I do not conceyve that ever God
did ordeyne as a fit government eyther for church or commonwealth." Later, the father-son team of Increase and Cotton Mather,
teachers of the Second Church of Boston (1664–1728), together
wrote more than 600 books, many of them sermons denouncing
the growing licentiousness and degeneracy they perceived. Because
many of the Mathers' sermons (and those of other Puritan divines)
warned against temptations, sins, and assorted evils, much of what
they wrote contained material that both titillated and horrified their
readers. Explicit sermons on masturbation, apparitions, earthquakes,
witches, demons, blaring trumpets, sudden storms, destructive fires,
two-headed cows, voices in the night, and "things preternatural"—
often delivered in colorful and riveting prose—had significant entertainment value.[24]

Religious Histories

The writing of history for the American colonists was an exercise in
celebration, one that had significant importance for a people acutely
aware of their unique role in building a new, and hopefully better,
society in the American wilderness. This sense of destiny was
expressed by nearly all colonial historians, but especially so during
the seventeenth century among New England Puritans who believed
they were carrying out God's plan to build a new Jerusalem. This is
typified in the work of Edward Johnson, a Boston jurist whose
History of New England (1654) defended the Puritan settlers as soldiers
of the Lord in a pagan wilderness. Throughout his work he compares
the experiences of the American Puritans with those of the Old
Testament Israelites. Johnson's intent was, in part, to prove that the
events of Massachusetts history were part of God's grand providential design. When the Puritans were hungry, explains Johnson,
"Christ caused an abundance of very good Fish to come to their nets
and Hookes," and when hostile Indians threatened their settlements,
a smallpox epidemic decimated them like "a wondrous worke of the
Great Jehovah."[25]

Treatment of Native Americans

Out of the bloody conflicts between Indians and settlers arose the first authentically native American literature—Indian captivity and deliverance narratives. The more than 500 captivity narratives followed a formulaic script and purpose: to describe the "struggle waged between the red servants of Satan and the captive Christian for his soul; it was a story of trial and victory," explains scholar Russel Nye, "of suffering and martyrdom, and came complete with sentimentality, moralizing, psychological probings, and exciting narrative." And exciting narrative it was. Readers were riveted to their graphic and detailed descriptions of raids, death of family members, forced marches, bizarre social practices, sexual depravity, torture, assimilation, adoption, and eventual rescue and repatriation—in religious terms, redemption.[26]

Some of the most popular historical works graphically described the many violent contests between Indians and settlers. In two separate historical accounts of King Philip's War, *A Brief History of the Warr with the Indians* (1676) and *A Relation of the Troubles which Have Hapned in New England, by Reason of the Indians There* (1677), Increase Mather interpreted the bloody conflicts between New Englanders and Native Americans as battles between Christianity and the devil. To Mather the Indians were "Savage and wild beasts" richly deserving annihilation. In his *Narrative of the Troubles with the Indians* (1677), Mather's fellow Boston clergyman William Hubbard attributed the Indian-settler conflict to natural and human factors. Like Mather, however, Hubbard described the Algonquian as a "bloody and deceitful monster, very stupid and blockish," a "Murderer from the beginning" and a "Cannibal."[27] Bostonian Daniel Gookin, on the other hand, described the Native Americans in his *Historical Account of the Doings and Sufferings of the Christian Indians of New England* (1677) as "children of light instead of children of the devil." More a work of anthropology than history is Cadwallader Colden's *History of the Five Indian Nations* (1727), which devotes considerable attention toward describing the character, personalities, and lifestyle of Native Americans (Iroquois) without the supercilious and racist language of earlier generations. Thirty years later Charles Thomson, a teacher in the Quaker school in Philadelphia, wrote an *Inquiry into the Causes of the Alienation of the Delaware and Shawanee Indians* (1759) to vindicate the Friends' policy of respect and friendship toward local Indians. Like no other American writer before, Thomson detailed the many unscrupulous tactics used by whites to cheat the Indians out of their land, most notably the infamous Walking Purchase of 1737, and their pernicious consequences on Indian-white relations.[28]

Provincial Histories

The writing of history took an important turn in the eighteenth century with the appearance of several histories of the colonies. These histories differed from earlier ones in that they were more secular in tone but, like earlier works, expressed a strong belief in America's importance in the world. This sense of American destiny is reflected in the *Chronological History of New England in the Form of Annals* (1736) by Thomas Prince, a Boston clergyman. He describes events in New England as under providential direction, but in doing so he was driven as much by patriotism as religion. In this way Prince's history is important for expressing a growing self-consciousness among Americans of their country as both distinctive and superior. A budding love of country and provincial pride also motivated William Smith, a lawyer and New York City official, to write a *History of the Province of New-York* (1757). In lawyer-like language Smith provided a comprehensive chronicle of New York under British rule, focusing on such themes as trade, religion, and especially the colony's faction-ridden political scene. Without even pretending to be objective, Smith used his book to justify the New York Assembly in its struggle against the royal prerogative and to attack his political enemies. Equally biased yet more vitriolic is the work of another William Smith, provost of the College of Philadelphia, who used cold statistics, gruesome atrocity stories, and scurrilous name-calling in his two histories of Pennsylvania (1755 and 1757) to characterize the Quaker-dominated Assembly as a group of peace-loving republicans who were more concerned with using tax money to build hospitals and libraries in the capital instead of forts out west to protect settlers from Indian attacks.[29]

Less political and polemical is John Callender's *Historical Discourse on the Civil and Religious Affairs of the Colony of Rhode Island* (1739), one of the best historical treatises produced in the English colonies for its "catholicity of treatment, accuracy, and straightforward literary style." It was surpassed in quality of scholarship by Massachusetts governor Thomas Hutchinson's three-volume *History of the Province of Massachusetts* (1764–1778), which argued for the greatness of the American people, the distinctive nature of America, and its novelty in the history of the world. More objective than most earlier historians in his approach, Hutchinson treated the Native Americans and religious dissenters with unusual sympathy. The Scotsman and Boston physician Dr. William Douglass had less patience than Hutchinson in providing historical accuracy and objectivity in his *A Summary, Historical and Political, of the British Settlements in North America* (1747–1752). Still, Douglass's multivolume history is a significant literary work, if for nothing else because it set out to chronicle all of the colonies as a whole. By doing so, Douglass expressed the realization that, in the words of historian Max Savelle, "an American entity, rather than thirteen disconnected colonies, was already in existence."[30]

Further south, Robert Beverly of Virginia produced one of the earliest literary works that was self-consciously American with his 1705 *The History and Present State of Virginia*. Unlike New England historians who portrayed their region as a religious model watched over by a Protestant Jehovah, Beverly approached Virginia in a largely secular manner. In a plain style, he showed particular pride in the colony and his desire to maintain its distinctiveness and independence by strongly and sometimes sarcastically rebuking his fellow Virginians for depending too much—economically, socially, and culturally—upon the mother country. Hugh Jones's *The Present State of Virginia* (1724) is a short and readable history that took a less critical approach toward his fellow Virginians, partly because he sought to use his history to promote support in England for Virginian enterprises. This may also explain why he gave an extraordinarily favorable view of slavery and an equally friendly account of Indians and their way of life. Less favorable towards the lifestyle of backcountry folk in North Carolina is the work of gentlemen chronicler William Byrd II of Virginia, whose *History of the Dividing Line* (1724) satirizes in condescending language the crudity of frontier life. More a work of true history is Alexander Hewat's *An Historical Account of . . . South Carolina* (1779), which chronicles the early settlement of the province; wars with Indians, the Spanish, and pirates; the ravages of smallpox and yellow fever on inhabitants; the condition of slaves; and the customs of local Indians.

Natural History

The unmapped and undocumented American wilderness inspired many early American explorers to write informative and entertaining narratives of the unique American landscape and the flora, fauna, and natives that inhabited it. Of the many such narratives, the best ones come from writers based in Philadelphia. Philadelphia mapmaker Lewis Evans, in his *Geographical, Historical, Political, Philosophical and Mechanical Essays* (1755–1756), eloquently describes the landscape west of the Ohio River Valley: "To look from these Hills into the lower Lands is but, as it were, into an Ocean of Woods, swell'd and deprest here and there by little Inequalities not to be distinguished, one Part from another, any more than the Waves of the real Ocean." Less vivid in his descriptions of the American landscape was the botanist John Bartram, a friend and sometimes traveling companion of Evans. In describing the Susquehanna Valley, for instance, Bartram had this to say: "the land hereabouts is middling white oak and huckleberry land . . . we went up a vale of middling soil, covered with high oak Timber, nearly west to the top of the hill . . . from whence we had a fair prospect of the river Susquehanah." Fortunately for later scholars, Bartram's laconic writing style was not inherited by his son William, who spent the years from 1773 to 1778 botanizing in the Floridas, Georgia, and the Carolinas. Using a rich and colored vocabulary, the younger Bartram wrote with a "conscious artistry" in his descriptions of the region's flora and fauna. Of equal value were his observations of the Creek, Seminole, and Cherokee Indians, whom he characterized in the more benevolent stereotype of noble savage.[31]

Biography

Colonists wrote biography and autobiography for the same reasons they wrote history—to demonstrate the unique purpose of their colonies and their equally unique people. New England Puritans produced more biographies and autobiographies than any other group in colonial America. This is largely because they felt that their providential mission to establish a "city upon a hill" in the New World was so important that it deserved to be recorded in painstaking detail for the instruction of future generations. Not surprisingly, hagiographic biographies of Puritan leaders abounded. This genre is best represented in Cotton Mather's *Magnalia Christi Americana* (1702), a massive book containing more than 60 biographies of lay and religious leaders. Mather's purpose in writing this largely ecclesiastical history of New England was to check the rising forces of secularism and worldliness by "arousing New England's pride in its past," writes scholar Russell Nye, "and by

guiding the next generation to an equally glorious Puritan future."
Mather therefore compared the experiences of Puritan spiritual
leaders with those of Biblical leaders to convince others that New
England was still part of God's special purpose in the world. In
doing so, he was copying a formula already established by his
father Increase, who in 1670 wrote a biography of *his* father, founder
of the Mather dynasty and patriarch of the Massachusetts Bay
colony. Increase further promoted the Mather dynasty, and the
New England way, by writing his own autobiography.[32]

Equally didactic was another genre of self-writing: the confession
of infamous criminals. Between 1700 and 1740, 27 such confession-
als were published in Boston alone. To illustrate the dangers of
immoral behavior, authorities throughout the colonies encouraged
criminals facing execution to describe their life history with the purpose of explaining the type of "bad behavior" that eventually led
them to the gallows. Authorities hastily published these brief biographies as moral instruction, particularly for the young. However,
because material in them was inherently salacious, containing lurid
accounts of murder, rape, incest, infanticide, and other heinous acts,
these "gallows confessions" were a very popular form of literature
for both urban and rural folk.[33]

Personal Diaries and Autobiographies

Many other colonists also expressed their thoughts in diaries and
autobiographies, some of which also had an edifying purpose.
Although not fully published until the nineteenth century, best
known of these is Benjamin Franklin's *Autobiography*, or memoir as
he called it, in which the successful printer selected important
moments in his life to tell a story explaining the factors contributing
to his rise form "rags to riches," along with the mistakes he made
along the way. In this sense, Franklin's work is a moral tale. But it
is much more because Franklin, more than any other previous
writer, managed to incorporate himself into the spirit of his time
and place: eighteenth-century Boston and Philadelphia. Franklin's
worldly success is a reflection of America's success. The characteristics Franklin emphasized in his book—tolerance, good will, intelligent skepticism, common sense, belief in man's rationality, hope
for betterment, faith in his progress, and even self-deprecating
humor—reflect the values and attitudes of America during his lifetime; his work also contains colorful descriptions of urban religious
revivals, public improvements, social life, and building institutions

such as a library, schools, an orphanage, and printing establishments. For this reason, Franklin's *Autobiography,* more than any other work, contains the essence of what life was like in eighteenth-century urban America.[34]

Much more private and introspective were numerous "spiritual autobiographies" of New England Puritans concerned with grace and personal salvation. The most revealing and influential of these is the diary of Samuel Sewall, a Boston jurist. Sewall's introspective diary, which covers the years 1673 through 1729, provides valuable insight into the Puritan mind at a time of enormous social, religious, and political upheaval in Massachusetts. His garrulous detail of every sort of minutiae of Boston life is also a valuable source for historians.

Poetry and Humor

Poetry in colonial America was varied both in style and manner. It was largely derivative and imitative, especially of the Bible and the Greek and Roman classics, but also of contemporary English literary masters such as Michael Drayton, George Herbert, Samuel Butler, and Alexander Pope. In New England, seventeenth-century Puritans were influenced more by the Bible when putting words to verse. In penning verse, early Puritans writers often stressed a utilitarian purpose above poetic values, resulting in forced and difficult-to-read rhyme. This is perhaps best illustrated in the popular *Bay Psalm Book* (1640), which translated and rendered the Hebrew text of the psalms into English meter. Illustrative is the Twenty-Third Psalm:

> The Lord to me a shepherd is
> want therefore shall not I.
> He in the folds of tender grass
> doth cause me down to lie.[35]

Whereas the *Bay Psalm Book,* despite its rough and graceless form, held popular appeal and went through numerous editions, most of the poetry written by the colonists was never printed. This is partly because poetry, as perhaps the most personal and emotional form of the belles lettres, was (and still is) often committed to the pages of diaries and never intended for others to read.

One writer who presented his poems to the public was Nathaniel Gardner, Boston's premier poet during the mid-eighteenth century. His popularity lies with his ability to appeal to all people, with erudite poems referencing classical and Biblical allusions for the more learned and more common and witty compositions for the masses. The following verse about a mutt "dogging" a funeral procession with loud barking and howling no doubt made many readers chuckle:

> What Dogg so fine or Ear cou'd boast
> But sacred song still touch'd him most
> Amidst the solemn public Train
> Chanting in holy David's Strain
> He felt the musick warm his Breast
> And rais'd his Notes above the rest.[36]

The poems of Anne Bradstreet, America's first published poet, were anything but witty and humorous. Instead, the English-born (1612) and privately tutored Bradstreet wrote somber poems reflecting on her personal experiences living in early Massachusetts—pregnancy, illness, and tragedy—and sappy sonnets expressing love for her father, husband, and children. The latter style is exemplified in her poem "To My Dear and Loving Husband," which reads in part:

> If ever two were one, then surely we.
> If ever man were lov'd by wife, then thee.
> If ever wife was happy in a man.
> Compare with me ye women if you can.

Evoking emotions of another kind was the terrifying poetry of the Reverend Michael Wigglesworth, particularly his 224-stanza "Day of Doom" (1662), which includes fierce denunciation of sinners and graphic images of damnation. The following stanza describing the torment of hell awaiting sinners helps explain why the poem became America's first bestseller and was used to instruct children and adults in the Puritan faith well into the eighteenth century:

> For day and night, in their despight, their torments smoak ascendeth.
> Their pain and grief have no relief, their anguish never endeth.
> There must they ly, and never dy, though dying every day:
> There must they dying ever ly, and not consume away.

For those seeking literary recognition, aspiring writers could turn to colonial newspapers, magazines, and almanacs that frequently published poems and puns. The *American Magazine*, published in Boston from 1743 to 1745, peppered its contents with light-hearted humor, sometimes in verse. The following is a sample:

> A Riddle for the Ladies,
> To you fair maidens, I address;
> Sent to adorn your Life:
> And show who first my name can guess,
> Shall first be made a wife . . .[37]

Likewise, Philadelphia's *American Magazine* contained humorous efforts by local wits such as "Timothy Timbertoe," who satirized the city's "ladies" for wearing less and less clothing, particularly on their chest:

And tho' some people are malicious enough to insinuate, that this is done to cool their own and inflame the breasts of others, yet I am far from entertaining any such injurious opinion of my fair countrywoman . . .

As this seems a fair challenge to the other sex, I expect every day to see the gentlemen begin to strip; and doubt not but the spirit of emulation will at least bring us to the primitive happiness of innocense, and a Fig-leaf . . .[38]

Indeed, racy articles became so acceptable by 1764 that the *Universal American Almanack* used sex as the theme for each of its monthly poems atop each month's calendar. The one for July reads:

> This Month the thirsty Traveller will try,
> And southern Maids in Bed half naked lie;
> On Hay tricks play the country-Lass and Clown,
> While Lords and Ladies kiss on Beds of Down.[39]

Almanacs printed in the cities also included humorous verse for the common people, who enjoyed reading satirical attacks on some of the more reviled people in colonial society. One small verse found in Nathaniel Ames's *Astronomical Diary* pokes fun at spinsters:

> Now freezing cold,
> which makes old Maids to fret and scold.

Another one lampooned assorted leaders:

> Politicians, Projectors, Directors
> Dictators and Detractors,
> How many there be?
> But how fruitless are most,
> You may easily see.[40]

The most popular and widely read humorist in eighteenth-century America was Philadelphia's Benjamin Franklin, who peppered his *Poor Richard's Almanack* and the *Pennsylvania Gazette* with a broad range of humor that included verse, stories, fables, moral essays, tall tales, and dialogues. The latter style is illustrated with the following fictitious exchange in the form of a letter to the editor:

I am about courting a girl I have had but little acquaintance with. How shall I come to a knowledge of her faults, and whether she has the virtues I imagine she has?
     Answer. Commend her among her female acquaintances.[41]

At times Franklin's humor could verge on the risqué, as in the story of the man in Bucks County who had pewter buttons melted off his trousers by lightning, to which Franklin added the editorial comment that "Tis well nothing else thereabouts was made of pewter."[42]

CONCLUSION

By the end of the colonial period, the state of the American mind, as illustrated in its arts and sciences, was distinct from that of Europe. Granted, when settlers first arrived in the New World, they slavishly tried to maintain the culture of their mother country. But the unique frontier situation provided by the New World required the colonists to put a premium on pragmatism. This is seen in the colonists' view toward the sciences, which focused on the practical achievement of scientific research instead of the advancement of scientific theory. This strong pragmatism, forced upon the colonists in their struggle to survive in the American frontier, helped to make Americans the most inventive people in the world. This pragmatism is also reflected in much of early colonial writing, which had a didactic purpose to it. For sure, aspiring colonial writers emulated the style of the European masters, but more distinctive were the subjects they wrote about. Their singular experiences and history in building a new civilization in the American wilderness provided the material for the creation of a unique form of American literature. Nor did colonial painting, which the urban elite commissioned more for economic and social purposes than as expressions of aesthetic creativity, escape this American pragmatism.

Although the New World environment shaped the development of American arts and sciences, it never would have flourished without the wealth, leisure, educational institutions, social organizations, libraries, and printing presses necessary to cultivate the arts and sciences found in the five principal cities. Much of this cultural fertilizer was provided by the urban elite, who from the beginning made a conscious effort to set the tone and standard of American culture. They did this not so much to impose a cultural hegemony on all colonists but more to create a cultural chasm between themselves and their social inferiors. As a result, the aristocrats of Boston, New York, Philadelphia, Newport, and Charles Town had more in common intellectually and culturally with each other than they did with other classes in their own cities. In this regard, colonial culture served to both unify and divide Americans. It also helped to solidify class distinctions and the idea, at least among the upper class, that not all Americans were equal.

NOTES

1. Clinton Rossiter, *The First American Revolution: The American Colonies on the Eve of Independence* (New York: Harcourt, Brace and Co., 1953), 199.

2. Max Savelle, *Seeds of Liberty: The Genesis of the American Mind* (Seattle: University of Washington Press, 1948), 85 (quote); William E. Burns, *Science and Technology in Colonial America* (Westport, CT: Greenwood Press, 2005), 148, 127–29.

3. Savelle, *Seeds of Liberty,* 90 (quote); Burns, *Science and Technology,* 126; Rossiter, *The First American Revolution,* 207.

4. Thomas L. Purvis, *Colonial America to 1763* (New York: Facts of File, 1999), 266–67; Brooke Hindle, *The Pursuit of Science in Revolutionary America, 1735–1789* (Chapel Hill: University of North Carolina Press, 1956), 87.

5. Savelle, *Seeds of Liberty,* 94 (quote); Hindle, *The Pursuit of Science,* 98–100.

6. Hindle, *The Pursuit of Science,* 171, 134 (quotes), 169–75.

7. Ibid., 22.

8. Ibid., 50–51 (quote), 53.

9. Ibid., 50–57.

10. Hindle, *The Pursuit of Science,* 20–26; Savelle, *Seeds of Liberty,* 109, 117.

11. Hindle, *The Pursuit of Science,* 76–79.

12. Ibid., 46 (quote), 38–48.

13. Edgar P. Richardson, *Painting in America: From 1502 to the Present* (New York: Thomas Crowell, 1956), 71; Margaretta M. Lovell, "Painters and Their Customers: Aspects of Art and Money in Eighteenth-Century America," in *Of Consuming Interests: The Style of Life in the Eighteenth Century,* ed. Cary Carson, Ronald Hoffman, and Peter Albert (Charlottesville: University Press of Virginia, 1994), 287; Ellen G. Miles, "The Portrait in America, 1750–1776," in *American Colonial Portraits: 1700–1776,* ed. Richard H. Saunders and Ellen G. Miles (Washington, DC: Smithsonian Institution Press, 1987), 37–38; Wayne Craven, *American Art: History and Culture* (Boston: McGraw Hill, 1994), 95; Richard H. Saunders, "The Portrait in

America, 1700–1750," in *American Colonial Portraits*, 24; Anna Wells Rutledge, "Artists in the Life of Charleston: Through Colony and State, from Restoration to Reconstruction," in *American Philosophical Society Transactions* 39 (1949): 114.

14. Oliver W. Larkin, *Art and Life in America* (New York: Rhinehart & Co., 1949), 19 (quote); Craven, *American Art*, 42–45; Savelle, *Seeds of Liberty*, 433; Louis B. Wright, *The Cultural Life of the American Colonies, 1607–1763* (New York: Harper & Row, 1957), 298.

15. Savelle, *Seeds of Liberty*, 434; Louis B. Wright, "From Wilderness to Republic, 1607–1787," in *The Arts in America: The Colonial Period*, ed. Louis B. Wright et al. (New York: Charles Scribner's Sons, 1966), 160; Elisabeth L. Roarke, *Artists of Colonial America* (Westport, CT: Greenwood Press, 2003), 102; Richardson, *Painting in America*, 38–39; Carolyn J. Weekley, "The Early Years, 1564–1790," in *Painting in the South, 1564–1980*, ed. Ella-Prince Knox (Richmond: Virginia Museum of Fine Arts, 1983), 10–12.

16. Richard H. Saunders, *John Smibert: Colonial America's First Portrait Painter* (New Haven, CT: Yale University Press, 1995), 76 (quote); Larkin, *Art and Life*, 47 (quote).

17. Craven, *American Art*, 73, 99 (quote); Savelle, *Seeds of Liberty*, 442–43; Roarke, *Artists of Colonial America*, 155.

18. Roarke, *Artists of Colonial America*, 119 (quote); Richardson, *Painting in America*, 35.

19. Savelle, *Seeds of Liberty*, 443.

20. Craven, *American Art*, 50; Roarke, *Artists of Colonial America*, 54–57; Wayne Craven, *Sculpture in America* (New York: Thomas Crowell, 1968), 5.

21. Craven, *American Art*, 51; Roarke, *Artists of Colonial America*, 62.

22. Craven, *Sculpture in America*, 8.

23. Russel B. Nye, *American Literary History: 1607–1830* (New York: Alfred Knopf, 1970), 17; Purvis, *Colonial America to 1763*, 252–55.

24. William P. Trent, *The Cambridge History of American Literature* (New York: Macmillan, 1917), 37 (quote), 65–66; Bruce C. Daniels, *Puritans at Play: Leisure and Recreation in Colonial New England* (New York: St. Martin's Press, 1995), 21–22, 27; Emory Elliott, ed., *Columbia Literary History of the United States* (New York: Columbia University Press, 1988), 56–57; Nye, *American Literary History*, 21, 25–30; Robert Spiller et. al., *Literary History of the United States* (New York: Macmillan, 1948), 35.

25. Nye, *American Literary History*, 30; Spiller, *Literary History of the United States*, 35 (quote).

26. Nye, *American Literary History*, 53 (quote); Daniels, *Puritans at Play*, 40–41.

27. Elliott, *Columbia Literary History of the United States*, 51–52; Harry Ward, *Colonial America, 1607–1763* (Englewood Cliffs, NJ: Prentice–Hall, 1991), 312 (quote).

28. Wright, *Cultural Life*, 161 (quote); Spiller, *Literary History of the United States*, 90.

29. Savelle, *Seeds of Liberty*, 376–77, 381, 385; Spiller, *Literary History of the United States*, 89–90.

30. Savelle, *Seeds of Liberty*, 379, 383 (quote).

31. Spiller, *Literary History of the United States*, 91.

32. Nye, *American Literary History*, 77 (quote); Savelle, *Seeds of Liberty*, 377; Elliott, *Columbia Literary History of the United States*, 67–71.

33. Daniels, *Puritans at Play*, 41–42.

34. Elliott, *Columbia Literary History of the United States*, 74, 80–81; Nye, *American Literary History*, 170–173.

35. Elliott, *Columbia Literary History of the United States*, 84.

36. David S. Shields, "Nathaniel Gardner, Jr., and the Literary Culture of Boston in the 1750s," *Early American Literature* 24 (1989): 203.

37. Savelle, *Seeds of Liberty*, 391.

38. Ibid., 391.

39. Clare Lyons, *Sex among the Rabble: An Intimate History of Gender and Power in the Age of Revolution, Philadelphia, 1730–1830* (Chapel Hill: University of North Carolina Press, 2006), 121.

40. Savelle, *Seeds of Liberty*, 392.

41. Ibid., 393.

42. Ibid., 393.

15

Cities in Rebellion

Traditionally, historians of early America have treated the colonial period as an inevitable prelude to the American Revolution. I do not adhere to this interpretation and have deliberately made no such connection between the colonial and revolutionary periods. Nevertheless, I do believe that the major urban centers played the critical role in mobilizing Americans—both in the cities and the hinterland—toward independence from Great Britain. I would go so far as to argue that without the five main urban centers there would have been no successful American Revolution and therefore no independent United States of America.

Much of the reason for this lies with the fact that the urban commercial centers were hit first and hardest by imperial policies, and their residents were therefore more likely to rebel against the mother country. This was especially true for city merchants whose livelihood suffered from a contraction of hard currency following Parliament's passage of the Currency Act of 1764, which prohibited the colonies from printing their own money, and the issuance of writs of assistance, or general search warrants, used by British customs agents to catch American merchants who had a long-standing tradition of smuggling illegal goods. Such policies forced a growing number of merchants to call in their loans, which still did not save many from bankruptcy. The economic downturn of merchants trickled down to artisans, who now had to settle their accounts with these merchants. Meanwhile, an economic depression following the Seven Years War, three boycotts of British goods between 1765 and 1775, and increasing food prices only intensified the hardship of the urban masses. Artisans and laborers had the added frustration of having to compete with the growing number of slave and immigrant laborers, as well with British soldiers sent to the urban centers to maintain order but who often took jobs on the side. Thus, the timing of Parliament's attempt to tax the colonists with the Stamp Act in 1765 and the Townshend duties in 1767 was inopportune at best, and it convinced many urban folk that British imperial policies were a coordinated attack against their "lives, liberties, and property." Just as upsetting to the colonial ruling elite was the Crown's attempt to challenge the power of the provincial assemblies and to replace native-born Americans on the colonial councils with British "placemen."[1]

Given these circumstances, it is not surprising that urban residents "drew upon their turbulent history of charged political action" and "civic-consciousness," explains historian Benjamin Carp, to become "the first to voice their discontent."[2] Helping to organize and mobilize this discontent was the city's built-in infrastructure for protest—printing presses, political institutions, fraternal and civic organizations, churches belonging to dissident faiths, waterfronts that attracted sailors with a history of protesting affronts to their rights (impressment), and numerous taverns where leaders regularly gathered to plot political action. Residents of the cities used these public arenas to spread their discontent in a number of ways: merchants meeting to plan countermeasures, printers publishing patriot propaganda, ministers preaching the gospel of revolution from the pulpit, patriot propagandists traveling into the hinterlands to convince wavering frontiersmen, and rebel politicians plotting to create shadow governments. The common element in all these activities is their attempt to either mobilize support for the patriot cause or to silence opposition to it. By doing so, the five cities played the critical role in advancing and achieving the cause for American independence.

Critical to the success of the patriot cause in the five cities was the action of committees made up of common folk, popularly known as Sons of Liberty, who rebel leaders used to enforce nonimportation measures and intimidate local crown officers and their loyalist supporters. More appropriately called "Sons of Terrorism," these urban enforcement committees used acts of terror against opponents to the American cause that included hanging loyalists in effigy, vandalizing their homes and shops, carting them through the streets, beating them, and even tarring and feathering them. One unfortunate man in Charles Town who unwisely denounced patriot measures was given a "new suit of Cloaths" made of tar and feathers by the local enforcement committee. Afterwards a mob of 500 people carted the bloodied and burned man throughout the capital before finally pumping him full of water and tossing him off a wharf into the harbor.[3] Such acts of sadistic terrorism ordered by patriot leaders and carried out by their enforcement committees occurred numerous times in the five cities. By giving the urban masses a semblance of authority and power—albeit in the streets only—patriot leaders nevertheless created a political Frankenstein's monster that did not always behave as they would like. Instead, the "people" increasingly pushed for measures to advance their own interests, sometimes using "street politics" to pressure leaders to give in to their demands. In 1775 Lieutenant Governor William Bull of South Carolina was pleased to inform the Earl of Dartmouth, the secretary of state for the colonies, that: "The Men of property begin at length to see that the many headed power of the People, who have hitherto been obediently made use of by their members and occasional riots to support the claims set up in America, have discovered their own strength and importance, and are not now so easily governed by their former leaders."[4]

As a result of such popular political awakenings, well-to-do patriot leaders, who saw the five principal cities as vital for mobilizing popular resistance to British measures before 1776, afterwards saw these same urban centers and their uncontrollable masses as threatening to the established plutocracy. Thomas Jefferson was not alone among American leaders in expressing the idea that "the mobs of the great cities" were "sores" on the body politic. Authorities in nearly all of the new states therefore removed their capitals from larger coastal cities to much more sparsely populated villages in the interior. Only Boston remained the center of government in its respective state. Nor did national leaders want to contend with the unruly urban rabble. In 1791 President George Washington publicly proclaimed that the "tumultuous populace of large cities are ever to be dreaded." Perhaps not coincidentally, that same year Congress located the country's capital in a tiny village along the Potomac River far away from New York City and Philadelphia, previous locations of the nation's political epicenter.[5]

Bostonians Paying the Excise Man. This 1774 British propaganda piece depicts the tarring and feathering of the highly unpopular Boston commissioner of customs John Malcolm for allegedly assaulting a shoemaker. American patriots commonly used this painful and humiliating form of punishment against British officials and outspoken American loyalists to either make them reform their behavior or leave town. This sadistic act had the desired effect. Malcolm soon moved to England, where he ran unsuccessfully for Parliament. (Library of Congress, Prints and Photographs Division, Reproduction # LC-USZ62-1308)

This geographical gamesmanship suggests that during the American Revolution the upper-class patriot leaders exploited the urban masses for their own self-serving reasons. Once the British were out of the United States and American leaders had exclusive control of the government, city leaders quickly discarded the urban rabble as a political threat to their hegemony by removing the seats of power far from the big cities. Common folk in the major cities therefore could no longer influence the political process as before. This allowed the established elites to control public policies without having to worry much about the concerns of the "tumultuous populace of large cities" that Washington and his class so "dreaded." The motives of the nation's Founding Fathers in gaining independence from Great Britain were therefore not to advance democracy but instead to preserve their political dominance and their "liberty" from any perceived threats either from above or below. The five cities were at the heart of this contest over both "home rule" and "who shall rule at home."

NOTES

1. Gary Nash, *The Urban Crucible: The Northern Seaports and the Origins of the American Revolution*, abridged ed. (Cambridge, MA: Harvard University Press, 1986), 200–22.

2. Benjamin Carp, *Rebels Rising: Cities and the American Revolution* (New York: Oxford University Press, 2007), 5. The following analysis benefits enormously from Carp's seminal study of the role played by the five cities in the American Revolution.

3. Keith Krawczynski, *William Henry Drayton: South Carolina Revolutionary Patriot* (Baton Rouge: Louisiana State University Press, 2001), 196.

4. Keith Krawczynski, "William Henry Drayton: South Carolina Revolutionary Patriot," Ph.D. dissertation, University of South Carolina, 1998, 252.

5. Carp, *Rebels Rising*, 220.

Selected Bibliography

Ahlstrom, Sydney. *A Religious History of the American People*. New Haven, CT: Yale University Press, 1972.

Alexander, John K. *Render Them Submissive: Responses to Poverty in Philadelphia, 1760–1800*. Amherst: University of Massachusetts Press, 1980.

Archdeacon, Thomas. *New York City, 1664–1710: Conquest and Change*. Ithaca, NY: Cornell University Press, 1976.

Baumgarten, Linda. *What Clothes Reveal: The Language of Clothing in Colonial and Federal America*. New Haven, CT: Yale University Press, 2002.

Beeman, Richard R. *The Varieties of Political Experience in Eighteenth-Century America*. Philadelphia: University of Pennsylvania Press, 2004.

Blumin, Stuart. *The Emergence of the Middle Class: Social Experience in the American City, 1760–1900*. Cambridge, UK: Cambridge University Press, 1989.

Bolton, S. Charles. *Southern Anglicanism: The Church of England in Colonial South Carolina*. Westport, CT: Greenwood Press, 1982.

Bonomi, Patricia. *A Factious People: Politics and Society in Colonial New York*. New York: Columbia University Press, 1971.

Booth, Sally Smith. *Hung, Strung and Potted: A History of Eating in Colonial America*. New York: Clarkson N. Potter, 1971.

Bowes, Frederick P. *The Culture of Early Charleston*. Chapel Hill: University of North Carolina Press, 1942.

Boydston, Jeanne. *Home and Work: Housework, Wages, and the Ideology of Labor in the Early Republic.* New York: Oxford University Press, 1990.

Breen, Timothy. *The Marketplace of Revolution: How Consumer Politics Shaped American Independence.* New York: Oxford University Press, 2004.

Bridenbaugh, Carl. *Cities in Revolt: Urban Life in America, 1743–1776.* New York: Ronald Press, 1955.

Bridenbaugh, Carl. *Cities in the Wilderness: Urban Life in America, 1625–1742.* New York: Capricorn Books, 1938.

Brown, Kathleen. *Foul Bodies: Cleanliness in Early America.* New Haven, CT: Yale University Press, 2009.

Burns, William E. *Science and Technology in Colonial America.* Westport, CT: Greenwood Press, 2005.

Bushman, Richard. *The Refinement of America: Persons, Houses, Cities.* New York: Vintage Books, 1992.

Butler, Jon. *New World Faiths: Religion in Colonial America.* Oxford, UK: Oxford University Press, 2008.

Carp, Benjamin. *Rebels Rising: Cities and the American Revolution.* New York: Oxford University Press, 2007.

Cogliano, Francis. *No King, No Popery: Anti-Catholicism in Revolutionary New England.* Westport, CT: Greenwood Press, 1995.

Coffin, Margaret M. *Death in Early America.* New York: Thomas Nelson, 1976.

Cohen, Sheldon S. *A History of Colonial Education, 1607–1776.* New York: John Wiley & Sons, 1974.

Copeland, Peter F. *Working Dress in Colonial and Revolutionary America.* Westport, CT: Greenwood Press, 1977.

Craven, Wayne. *American Art: History and Culture.* Boston: McGraw Hill, 1994.

Cremin, Lawrence. *American Education: The Colonial Experience, 1607–1783.* New York: Harper & Row, 1970.

Daniels, Bruce. *Puritans at Play: Leisure and Recreation in Colonial New England.* New York: St. Martin's Press, 1995.

Davis, Ronald L. *A History of Music in American Life: The Formative Years, 1620–1865.* Malabar, FL: Kreiger, 1982.

Dinkin, Robert J. *Voting in Provincial America: A Study of Elections in the Thirteen Colonies, 1689–1776.* Westport, CT: Greenwood Press, 1977.

Dow, George. *Every Day Life in the Massachusetts Bay Colony.* Boston: Society for the Preservation of New England Antiquities, 1935.

Duffy, John. *Epidemics in Colonial America.* Baton Rouge: Louisiana State University Press, 1953.

Earle, Alice M. *Child Life in Colonial Days.* New York: MacMillan, 1899.

Earle, Alice M. *Home Life in Colonial Days.* New York: Grosset & Dunlap, 1898.

Eden, Trudy. *The Early American Table: Food and Society in the New World.* DeKalb: Northern Illinois University Press, 2008.

Ellis, John T. *Catholics in Colonial America*. Baltimore, MD: Helicon, 1965.

Fatherly, Sarah. *Gentlewomen and Learned Ladies: Women and Elite Formation in Eighteenth-Century Philadelphia*. Bethlehem, PA: Lehigh University Press, 2008.

Flaherty, David H. *Privacy in Colonial New England*. Charlottesville: University Press of Virginia, 1972.

Fraser, Walter J. Jr. *Patriots, Pistols and Petticoats: "Poor Sinful Charles Town" during the American Revolution*. Columbia: University of South Carolina Press, 1976.

Friedman, Lawrence M. *Crime and Punishment in American History*. New York: Basic Books, 1993.

Frost, J. William. *The Quaker Family in Colonial America: A Portrait of the Society of Friends*. New York: St. Martin's Press, 1973.

Gilje, Paul A. *Liberty on the Waterfront: American Maritime Culture in the Age of Revolution*. Philadelphia: University of Pennsylvania Press, 2004.

Gilje, Richard P. *The Profane, the Civil, & the Godly: The Reformation of Manners in Orthodox New England, 1679–1749*. University Park: Pennsylvania State University Press, 1994.

Glover, Lorri. *All Our Relations: Blood Ties and Emotional Bonds among the Early South Carolina Gentry*. Baltimore, MD: Johns Hopkins University Press, 2000.

Godbeer, Richard. *Sexual Revolution in Early America*. Baltimore, MD: Johns Hopkins University Press, 2002.

Goodfriend, Joyce D. *Before the Melting Pot: Society and Culture in Colonial New York City, 1664–1730*. Princeton, NJ: Princeton University Press, 1992.

Greenberg, Douglas. *Crime and Law Enforcement in the Colony of New York, 1691–1776*. Ithaca, NY: Cornell University Press, 1974.

Greene, Lorenzo J. *The Negro in Colonial New England*. New York: Columbia University Press, 1942.

Griffith, Ernest S. *History of American City Government: The Colonial Period*. New York: Oxford University Press, 1938.

Grob, Gerald. *The Deadly Truth: A History of Disease in America*. Cambridge, MA: Harvard University Press, 2002.

Harris, Leslie. *In the Shadow of Slavery: African Americans in New York City, 1626–1863*. Chicago: University of Chicago Press, 2003.

Hart, Emma. *Building Charles Town: Town and Society in the Eighteenth-Century British Atlantic World*. Charlottesville: University of Virginia Press, 2010.

Herndon, Ruth Wallis. *Unwelcome Americans: Living on the Margin in Early New England*. Philadelphia: University of Pennsylvania Press, 2001.

Hindle, Brooke. *The Pursuit of Science in Revolutionary America, 1735–1789*. Chapel Hill: University of North Carolina Press, 1956.

Hooker, Richard J. *Food and Drink in America: A History*. Indianapolis, IN: Bobbs-Merrill, 1981.

Horrocks, Thomas. *Popular Print and Popular Medicine: Almanacs and Health Advice in Early America*. Amherst: University of Massachusetts Press, 2008.

Hull, N. E. H. *Female Felons: Women and Serious Crime in Colonial Massachusetts*. Urbana: University of Illinois Press, 1987.

Krawczynski, Keith. *William Henry Drayton: South Carolina Revolutionary Patriot*. Baton Rouge: Louisiana State University Press, 2001.

Lombard, Anne S. *Making Manhood: Growing Up Male in Colonial New England*. Cambridge, MA: Harvard University Press, 2003.

Lyons, Clare. *Sex among the Rabble: An Intimate History of Gender and Power in the Age of Revolution, Philadelphia, 1730–1830*. Chapel Hill: University of North Carolina Press, 2006.

Main, Jackson Turner. *The Social Structure of Revolutionary America*. Princeton, NJ: Princeton University Press, 1965.

Marietta, Jack D., and Rowe, G. S. *Troubled Experiment: Crime and Justice in Pennsylvania, 1682–1800*. Philadelphia: University of Pennsylvania Press, 2006.

McKee, Samuel. *Labor in Colonial New York, 1664–1776*. New York: Columbia University Press, 1935.

McManus, Edgar J. *Black Bondage in the North*. Syracuse, NY: Syracuse University Press, 1973.

McManus, Edgar J. *Law and Liberty in Early New England: Criminal Justice and Due Process, 1620–1692*. Amherst: University of Massachusetts Press, 1993.

McWilliams, James. *A Revolution in Eating: How the Quest for Food Shaped America*. New York: Columbia University Press, 2005.

Morris, John V. *Fires and Firefighters*. Boston: Little, Brown & Co., 1955.

Morris, Richard B. *Government and Labor in Early America*. New York: Harper & Row, 1946.

Morrison, Hugh. *Early American Architecture: From the First Colonial Settlements to the National Period*. New York: Oxford University Press, 1952.

Newcomb, Benjamin H. *Political Partisanship in the American Middle Colonies, 1700–1776*. Baton Rouge: Louisiana State University Press, 1995.

Nye, Russel B. *American Literary History: 1607–1830*. New York: Alfred Knopf, 1970.

Olwell, Robert. *Masters, Slaves, and Subjects: The Culture of Power in the South Carolina Low Country, 1740–1790*. Ithaca, NY: Cornell University Press, 1998.

Pencak, William. *Jews and Gentiles in Early America, 1654–1800*. Ann Arbor: University of Michigan Press, 2005.

Perkins, Edwin J. *The Economy of Colonial America*. New York: Columbia University Press, 1988.

Piersen, William D. *Black Yankees: The Development of an Afro-American Subculture in Eighteenth-Century New England*. Amherst: University of Massachusetts Press, 1988.

Pointer, Richard. *Protestant Pluralism and the New York Experience: A Study of Eighteenth-Century Religious Diversity*. Bloomington: Indiana University Press, 1988.

Purvis, Thomas. *Colonial America to 1763*. New York: Facts on File, 1999.

Quimby, Ian. *Apprenticeship in Colonial Philadelphia*. New York: Garland Press, 1985.

Rankin, Hugh F. *The Theater in Colonial America*. Chapel Hill: University of North Carolina Press, 1960.

Ray, Sister Mary Augustina. *American Opinion of Roman Catholicism in the Eighteenth Century*. New York: Columbia University Press, 1936.

Reps, John W. *The Making of Urban America: A History of City Planning in the United States*. Princeton, NJ: Princeton University Press, 1965.

Richardson, Edgar P. *Painting in America: From 1502 to the Present*. New York: Thomas Crowell, 1956.

Roarke, Elizabeth. *Artists of Colonial America*. Westport, CT: Greenwood Press, 2003.

Rossiter, Clinton. *The First American Revolution: The American Colonies on the Eve of Independence*. New York: Harcourt, Brace and Co., 1953.

Roth, Leland. *American Architecture: A History*. Boulder, CO: Westview Press, 2001.

Salinger, Sharon. *Taverns and Drinking in Early America*. Baltimore, MD: Johns Hopkins University Press, 2002.

Salinger, Sharon. *"To Serve Well and Faithfully": Labor and Indentured Servants in Pennsylvania, 1682–1800*. Cambridge, UK: Cambridge University Press, 1987.

Savelle, Max. *Seeds of Liberty: The Genesis of the American Mind*. Seattle: University of Washington Press, 1948.

Schlesinger, Arthur. *The Birth of the Nation: A Portrait of the American People on the Eve of Independence*. New York: Knopf, 1969.

Schwartz, Sally. *"A Mixed Multitude": The Struggle for Toleration in Colonial Pennsylvania*. New York: New York University Press, 1987.

Singleton, Esther. *Dutch New York*. New York: Dodd, Mead, & Co., 1909.

Singleton, Esther. *Social New York under the Georges, 1714–1776*. New York: D. Appleton & Co., 1902.

Smith, Billy G. *The "Lower Sort": Philadelphia's Laboring People, 1750–1800*. Ithaca, NY: Cornell University Press, 1990.

Smith, Merril D. *Breaking the Bonds: Marital Discord in Pennsylvania, 1730–1830*. New York: New York University Press, 1991.

Spruill, Julia C. *Women's Life and Work in the Southern Colonies*. Chapel Hill: University of North Carolina Press, 1938.

Stavely, Keith, and Fitzgerald, Kathleen. *America's Founding Food: The Story of New England Cooking*. Chapel Hill: University of North Carolina Press, 2003.

Struna, Nancy L. *People of Prowess: Sport, Leisure, and Labor in Early Anglo-America*. Urbana: University of Illinois Press, 1996.

Sweet, William W. *Religion in Colonial America*. New York: Cooper Square, 1965.

Teaford, Jon C. *The Municipal Revolution in America: Origins of Modern Urban Government, 1650–1825*. Chicago: University of Chicago Press, 1975.

Thompson, Peter. *Rum Punch & Revolution: Taverngoing & Public Life in Eighteenth Century Philadelphia*. Philadelphia: University of Pennsylvania Press, 1999.

Wall, Helena M. *Fierce Communion: Family and Community in Early America*. Cambridge, MA: Harvard University Press, 1990.

Warwick, Edward, Pitz, Henry C., and Wyckoff, Alexander. *Early American Dress: The Colonial and Revolutionary Periods*. New York: Bonanza Books, 1965.

Wilson, Lisa. *Ye Heart of a Man: The Domestic Life of Men in Colonial New England*. New Haven, CT: Yale University Press, 1999.

Wolf, Stephanie G. *As Various as Their Land: The Everyday Lives of Eighteenth-Century Americans*. New York: Harper Perennial, 1993.

Wright, Louis B. *The Cultural Life of the American Colonies, 1607–1763*. New York: Harper & Row, 1957.

Wulf, Karin. *Not All Wives: Women of Colonial Philadelphia*. Ithaca, NY: Cornell University Press, 2000.

Index

About the Author

A native of San Antonio, KEITH KRAWCZYNSKI is professor of history at Auburn Montgomery in Montgomery, Alabama. He holds degrees in history from the University of Texas at San Antonio, Baylor University, and the University of South Carolina. He is the author of *William Henry Drayton: South Carolina Revolutionary Patriot*, editor and coauthor of *History in Dispute: The American Revolution*, coauthor of *A Historic Context for the African American Military Experience*, and author of numerous articles and book chapters on early American and African American history. When not teaching or writing, he enjoys harassing his wife, playing with his two sons and four dogs, banging his drums to heavy metal, collecting and reading classic science fiction magazines, visiting old cemeteries, rescuing Boston Terriers, giving speeches to historic and civic groups, bowling, and weight lifting.